A HISTORY OF
AMERICAN ECONOMIC LIFE

Edward C. Kirkland

A HISTORY OF
AMERICAN ECONOMIC LIFE

fourth edition

Appleton-Century-Crofts
EDUCATIONAL DIVISION
Meredith Corporation   New York

To R. B. K.

PREFACE

Many years ago, when this volume first came out, Dixon Ryan Fox placed it in the tradition of "the systematic history of work." I have often and wryly reflected upon this characterization. Perhaps that first printing in the early thirties was a sort of guide for an up-to-date Swiss Family Robinson seeking to learn how to recreate a modern economy in an unknown continent. In any case since the twenties and thirties the hospitable nature of economic history has welcomed many new approaches. Without a precise or inclusive enumeration, I can recall offhand business-cycle theory, the rejuvenation of political economy, entrepreneurship, the problems of growth, and, most recently, "the new economic history," with its emphasis upon quantification, economic theory, and upon what didn't happen. Though each of these approaches has made its contribution, they cannot be said to be of equal merit.

As I have written before, those who would like to know how the present version of this book differs from its predecessors must examine it. Since I have had the opportunity completely to revise and rewrite a text whose last edition came out fifteen years ago, my present intentions are naturally somewhat different. First, I hope I have caught and corrected the errors of detail to which all scholarly effort seems susceptible. In matters of structure and interpretation I have sought to embody the findings of more up-to-date investigation and research. Some of this has been in the tradition of historical and narrative writing; some of it has not. Of the newcomers among approaches I have found the increasing attention to the interrelationships between government and economic activity the most congenial. This may be a matter of personal temperament and training. Also, historical occurrences since World War II seem to reinforce the value of this approach. The capitalism, to use an abstraction, of today is so far removed from the capitalism of the early twentieth century that I have organized my last three chapters in a manner somewhat different from the earlier ones. In spite of all this tampering, I have retained my conviction that men and individuals are the center of history. They are the creators and actors; theirs are the aspirations, the responses, the decisions, and the calculations.

No textbook writer can please everybody. In the eyes of some to have written a text at all is an offense. Conceivably, the book may not even be long enough to explain the author's methodology. But every discipline must have some material core. As one of the more thoughtful of the robber barons once put it, "I thought they taught me Latin and Greek because there was something there to teach." Originally I wrote this volume so teachers would have something there to teach. And the process of teaching can make room for dissent as well as agreement. This does not impress me as an unworthy or unobtainable objective.

Thetford, Vermont   E. C. K.

CONTENTS

A HISTORY OF
AMERICAN ECONOMIC LIFE

Founding the British Colonies

A National Program

Over a period of three centuries, from the middle of the fifteenth to the middle of the eighteenth, English writers from time to time
published their thoughts on the sources of national prosperity. Their different statements do not add up to a consistent doctrine; the period was
too long and too varied, and the authors, to a large extent business or
other practical men, were addressing themselves to concrete situations
and short-run considerations. Nevertheless, since certain persistent threads
ran through all their arguments, others have christened the resulting
theory *mercantilism*. Nor were Englishmen the only formulators of this
creed.

Mercantilism asserted the powerful state was obligated to adopt policies that would further the economic welfare of the nation. In its simplest,
or crudest, form economic well-being required keeping within the country enough gold and silver to facilitate commerce, and, less certainly,
enough to lead to a gradual rise in prices and thus to the stimulation of
the economy. Here the contemporary example of the Spanish Empire,
with its silver in Mexico, its gold and precious stones in South America,
and its "bullion fleets" annually transporting these treasures to the
mother country, was very convincing. But a country which did not have
such "mines in its own bowels" had to obtain treasure in other ways:
"The ordinary means therefor to increase the wealth and treasure is by
Foreign Trade, wherein we must ever observe this rule: to sell more to
strangers yearly than we can consume of theirs in value." A favorable
balance of trade was thus the central objective of mercantile policy, and
to obtain this balance any nation had to adopt, if the logic held, an
extensive and complicated series of measures. The government must
stimulate, by bounties and other means, domestic production of goods
which could be exported; manufactured goods, since they required the
most labor, best met this criterion. The government must restrict imports
by protective tariffs and embargoes; and it must even determine the

1

trends of domestic consumption. Far too many Englishmen, one pamphlet of 1664 asserted had been "of late years besotting themselves in a beastly manner, sucking smoak and drinking healths." (Scratch a zealot for thoroughgoing regulation of business and you usually scratch a bluenose.)

Because of their emphasis upon calculation and their use of a method of presentation which often appeared to prefer arithmetic to prose, it is easy to think the mercantilists had purely economic motives that were directed solely to material gain for the nation of which they were citizens. Such an inference is exaggerated. The sense of national destiny and of sharing in its realization did not in Elizabethan England, for example, spring solely from the pocketbook or the exchequer. National greatness and national power were, in themselves, exciting satisfactions.

Since mercantilist writers were often government officials as well as businessmen, they had perforce a concern with policy. Mercantilism involved a colonial as well as a domestic policy. As a source of commodities colonies could substitute for foreign countries and additionally furnish products which the mother country could reexport to maintain the advantage of its favorable balance of trade. The colonies might also provide a market for home manufacture, and one pamphleteer thought each white colonist in the sugar islands "occasions the consumption of more of our native commodities and manufactures, than ten at home do." According to mercantile tenets, if the colony lay overseas, the government should monopolize the carrying trade for its subjects so that "the carriage will be earned by our people," and the numbers of seamen and strength of the fleet would both be increased. Generally, colonies should be and remain dependent on the mother country.

Mercantilism had its side effects. When the government did so much, it tended to expand its own power and grow careless about authoritarianism. By preferring to sell to and buy from people it knew and whose area it ruled, the government chose the interests of its "household" as against those of "strangers." The result of power and exclusiveness was war or a peace hardly distinguishable from war. Piracy, for example, under governmental auspices was not a vice but a virtue, winning for its practitioners, a Drake or a Hawkins, preferment and titles.

The Company as an Instrument of Colonization

On an April Sunday in 1607, three small vessels, four hard months out of London, entered Chesapeake Bay, and those on board, after looking around for a few days, chose a place which they christened Jamestown for what proved to be the first enduring English settlement on the North American continent. Short-run considerations—fresh water and ease of mooring vessels—were probably the chief ones in their decision. Whether those landing knew it or not, Jamestown also had strategic advantages, for it was near the mouth of Chesapeake Bay, one of the great water indentations along the Atlantic coast, and from the Bay deep rivers led inland to the West and North. Jamestown lay roughly midway between the Spanish Empire, which had been developing for over a century in South and Central America, in the islands of the Caribbean, and in Florida; and the French Empire, which contemporaneously with Virginia was catching hold along the St. Lawrence.

A mixture of motives led to these overseas outthrusts from the countries of northern and western Europe. Occurring as colonization did toward the end of the Middle Ages, the zeal to spread Christianity, of the preferred variety, was one of its motives. While the attempts of the Spanish sovereigns to Catholicize the Indians left their mark in the missions of California and Texas, and French efforts provided the heroic record of the Jesuits along the St. Lawrence and the Great Lakes, Protestant nations like England professed the aim of spreading the "Gospel" rather than the "Faith." The promoters of the Virginia enterprise, for instance, sought and obtained the backing of the clergy, "the most articulate and vocal members of society."

But as the times turned increasingly toward secular concerns, the material advantages of overseas enterprises came to the surface. Colonization was a means to individual and national wealth. The Spaniards had found treasure in Mexico and Peru; and the importation of gold and silver from the Spanish Main had enriched the Spanish sovereigns, made Spain a great power, and, running through the channels of European trade, had occasioned an inflation which disturbed and transformed the economies of western Europe. The planners of the Virginia enterprise could not escape the contagion of the successful Spanish application of mercantilism. The planners' estimates of the gains from the new country, however, based upon the patterns of colonies located in the tropics and possessing deposits of precious metals, were unfortunately misleading in Virginia.

Nonetheless, the Virginia colonists had at once to clear the land in order to have space for homes and self-supporting agriculture. In the process they either burned the trees and derived from the ashes chemical products useful in English industry, or hewed the trees into clapboards for the London market. Since there were grapes, there should be wine; since there was sand, there should be glass; since mulberry trees could grow in Virginia, there should be silk; and since there was ore, there should be iron. Better that England should draw these products from Virginia than from, say, France. Consequently, workmen skilled in these trades were sent to Virginia. As it turned out, none of these enterprises either enriched the mother country or contributed to the welfare of the colony.

Failure to realize these objectives of production bid fair to be fatal. The colony had not come into being through a government appropriation or a grant from a foundation; nor could the inhabitants or planners resort to either for succor. If they had been a part of the Spanish or, less certainly, of the French Empire, they might have expected assistance from the sovereign. But the English kings, however intensely interested in colonization, had started out by conferring this function through a charter upon a group of investors or speculators. In 1600 they had thus chartered the East India Company and assigned to it the eastern hemisphere from Africa to the Straits of Magellan. Many of the merchants and noblemen who had invested in the East India Company invested as well in what became known as "The Treasurer and Company of Adventurers and Planters of the City of London for the First Colony in Virginia."

Virginia was an estate owned by the company. The money which the "adventurers," as the investors were called, supplied was used to buy goods for the colony, to recruit colonists, and to provide vessels for transporting "planters" and goods to America. When the commodities or "supply," arrived in Virginia, they were placed in the "magazine," from which they were issued to the "planters," most of whom were under indenture to the company and thus essentially its employees. The products which the planters raised were on their side placed in the magazine, transported to England, and sold there to provide a return to the adventurers. The company riveted all these arrangements upon the colony by reserving to itself a monopoly of its trade. In short the Virginia plantation was a collective shaped by the need for protecting and promoting a profitable colony.

On these scores it was a disappointment. The Virginia enterprise dissipated the original investment and the later contributions raised from its cajoled and harried investors and other sources. The want of returns created factions within the company which quarreled with each other and with the planters; starvation, disease, and Indians were responsible for a mortality of nearly 70 percent in the colony's population. The original planters in 1607 had numbered perhaps 144; by 1622 the Virginia population was 1,240. A quarrel with the king over the marketing of tobacco—the one crop the colonists found profitable to produce and sell —crowned the misadventure; and in 1624 the king withdrew its charter and transformed Virginia into the first royal colony.

Georgia and the settlements of the Pilgrims at Plymouth and of the Puritans at Massachusetts Bay were other British colonies established under the auspices of the company system. They were not pure instances of commercial enterprise. Georgia was chartered in 1732, and its trustees were less animated by the acquisitive instinct than they were by the religious and charitable movements of the Age of Walpole. The Massachusetts colonies, settled over a century earlier, soon deviated from the mercantile or plantation type. They were located in the northern territory which James I, when he was partitioning his American claims in 1606, assigned to the Plymouth Company. In 1621, the survivors of that organization, together with many interested in the Virginia Company, secured incorporation from the king under the title of "The Council established at Plymouth in the County of Devon, for the Planting, Ruling and Governing of New England in America." This concern secured rights to fish, trade, and colonize in the domain between the fortieth and forty-eighth parallels and extending from the Atlantic to the Pacific Ocean. Within this territory the Pilgrims settled at Plymouth, but in order to get there they had to enter into an agreement with a group of London merchants. Each emigrant to America was counted as owning one share in this enterprise, and so was each contributor of £10. For seven years the colonists were to be provided with supplies purchased by these funds; for seven years all the products of the colonists were to be contributed to a common fund. The agricultural products would keep the colonists alive, the fish and fur would be marketed in England for a profit. By 1624 some seventy London capitalists had invested £7,000 in the enterprise. Here were all the aspects of a plantation of the Virginia variety. For a shorter time the same generalization was true of the settlers around Massachusetts Bay. They had come thither under the auspices of individuals who had secured a grant of land from the New England Council, and in 1629 a charter from the king established them as the "Company of Massachusetts Bay in New England." Externally Massachusetts Bay's forms corresponded to those of the first Virginia Company, which had introduced this method of colonization some twenty years before. But in practice the later company never adopted any of the plantation measures of its predecessors.

The company plantations in America brought no financial rewards to the investor in their stock. By 1621, three years before Virginia lost its charter, the Company of Adventurers had risked nearly £200,000, a staggering sum for that time, without any return of interest or principal. Nor was the investor in the Pilgrim community happier. After the Plymouth plantation had struggled for a few years without returning dividends, the merchants in despair offered to cancel their claims, and in 1627 an agreement with some of the leading colonists resulted in the discharge of these obligations for £1,800. Considering their original investment, the London capitalists were heavy losers. It is impossible to draw up a balance account for the Massachusetts Bay Company.

If these colonies were to have made their mother country rich and self-sufficient and their investors wealthy, they should have been established at other spots than those on the North American coasts where they operated. Though optimists espied "mountains of gold," these proved frauds or delusions. No populous ancient civilization was at hand to exchange rare and exotic goods they had raised or collected—tea, silk, or spices—for European commodities. The trading post worked in the hemisphere of the East India Company and farther north in the western hemisphere, as the Hudson's Bay Company was to demonstrate. In the British colonies on the North American mainland, however, settlers had to hew out a foothold in the wilderness, placate the native inhabitants or destroy them, raise food for themselves, and discover through trial and error the occupation which could provide a surplus for export and thus make profitable the heavy investment originally required and justify a further flow of capital, of goods, and of settlers. As a form of colonization, the company proved inadequate to this task; absentee direction joined local ineptitude in paralyzing leadership and enterprise.

The colonial companies for one reason or another had gradually abandoned their system of collective enterprise. At Plymouth it was observed that unmarried men disliked growing supplies for men with wives and children; and the energetic hated to contribute to the feeding of the lazy. Accordingly in 1623 the settlers were given individual holdings.

In Virginia, while the company continued its own plantation, at least on paper, it began from time to time to distribute particular plantations to individuals, singly or in groups. These planters, who had come on their own and stuck it out, might receive as much as one hundred acres for their enterprise; adventurers, who had stayed at home, received the same amount, apparently as a dividend on their investment, for each £12 10s. they had contributed. Associated groups of adventurers, sometimes called "hundreds," might petition for larger contiguous grants of land for private plantations. Some of these grants carried a nominal quitrent, a shilling or two. As "divisions" of land succeeded each other over time, the arrangements grew more generous; eventually every member of an immigrant family or those who had sent or transported immigrants received headrights of fifty acres. After 1620 when the Virginia Company abandoned its trade monopoly, these plantations could buy and sell through channels of their own choosing. The pursuit of such "private endeavors" apparently promised greater success than did operation for the "public ends" for which the company had originally been established.

The Proprietorships

Until the establishment of Georgia, no more company plantations were made in British North America. Colonization was now undertaken under the proprietary system, by which land was assigned by the

Crown not to a corporation but to an individual or a group of individuals known as proprietors. The rights and obligations of both grantor and grantee were modeled upon English precedents, particularly those existent in the County Palatine of Durham, which is mentioned in many of these American grants and which was in the Middle Ages a creation for the frontier of England. The grantee was given practically complete possession of his province. It is a little startling to consider that William Penn could sell, mortgage, lease, devise, or convey in trust the whole of Pennsylvania, but it was true. The proprietor in his turn owed a quitrent for his holding to the king. In the cases of Pennsylvania and Maryland the fee was merely nominal—Indian arrows or beaver skins; in the case of the Carolinas, there were to be some financial payments. These landlords should be regarded as investors in large estates from which they hoped to receive some income, usually through the transfer of their land to actual settlers. The purchase price, if one was set, would constitute one return, and then there were the quitrents which the settlers owed to the proprietor just as the latter had owed them to the king.

The first successful application of the proprietary system to an American colony was Maryland. Among the motives which influenced Sir George Calvert, later Lord Baltimore, to found that province, worldly ones played the more important part. Calvert was an inveterate colonizer. He had been the recipient of various Irish plantations; he was a shareholder in the Virginia Company, a member of the Council of New England, and had attempted to establish a colony in Newfoundland. After a charter for Maryland had been secured from the Crown in 1632, Calvert's descendants ran the province in a fashion designed to increase the family income. Most of the proprietorships, however, were associated with nobles or gentlemen of the English Restoration days. Carolina was the first. In 1663 Lord Ashley, enlisting seven fellow politicians into a group of proprietors, obtained from the king a grant of the territory southward of Virginia. At the same time two of the participants in this transaction, Sir George Carteret and Lord Berkeley, engaged the favor of James, Duke of York, who had just received New York from his royal brother Charles as a feudal holding, and emerged as proprietors of the territory at present comprising the state of New Jersey. Their claims to this region underwent bewildering metamorphoses, and the territory eventually passed into the hands of two groups of associates, among whom was William Penn. Some years later, in 1680, Penn petitioned the king for a more "plantable" land in America in consideration of "the debts due to him and his father from the Crown"; and in the same year he received the land which became known as Pennsylvania. This recital of the colonies actually established under the proprietary system does not do justice to the interest displayed by Englishmen of position in American land. A whole array of unfulfilled grants and projects increase the evidence that many noblemen and others in England looked to the New World as a means of recouping their fortunes or increasing their income through the creation and exploitation of great estates in land.

The returns to proprietors from their holdings were usually as feeble as the earnings of the colonizing companies. This was true of the quit-rents in the Carolinas and in New Jersey. In Pennsylvania and Maryland a real effort was made to make the quitrent a source of revenue. Although the Penns were never consistently successful, they collected between 1700 and 1779 £63,679 8s. 3½d. and were fortunate at the time of the Revolution, when the assembly abolished the proprietary rights, in receiving a gift from that body of £130,000. In Maryland the most efficient system in the colonies was devised, and the Calverts drew a considerable income from its operations. By the middle of the eighteenth century they were receiving over £4,000 annually and by 1774, on the eve of the Revolution, the return was £8,518 6s. 2d.

During the Revolution the feudal exactions in every colony were gleefully abolished by the colonial legislatures or allowed in some more quiet fashion to lapse. While final confiscation distressed proprietors or their successors, they had all along found it difficult to draw up a rent roll, create a tax-collecting organization, and stem the popular desire to possess land free and clear. In the Jerseys this popular hostility was fed by immigrants from New England who were accustomed to an unencumbered freehold. In the course of an effort to collect quitrents in 1745, a pamphlet of the anti-proprietary party declared: "No man is naturally entitled to a greater proportion of the earth than another; but tho' it was made for the equal use of all, it may nevertheless be appropriated by every individual." The ownership and management of land became the chief magnet which attracted the attention of wealthy or influential men to the British colonies and led humbler individuals to cross the ocean and build homes in the New World.

A Spectrum of Land Systems

In the New England colonies of Massachusetts, Connecticut, and Rhode Island, the land was transferred from the colony to private owners through the successive establishment of new towns by town proprietors. A group of individuals proposing settlement would petition the general court, or legislature, for a grant; a committee of that body would lay off the grant—often a township six miles square—and this land would then be conveyed to the petitioners or proprietors. In the early period there were no quitrents or financial payments to the colony, for the colony did not regard the land as a source of revenue. The Puritans, moreover, were determined to be "the supreme lords of their own lands" and disliked the distinction between landlord and tenant. The first obligation of the proprietors was to lay out the town with its common, its burying ground, its school and church lots, and the town plots of the proprietors. Then they divided the arable land and made such arrangements for the joint use of the woodlands and pasture as were necessary. Upon the proprietors devolved the necessity of constructing roads, securing the erection of a gristmill and sawmills either through financial aid or through grants of land, arranging for the defense of the town if it were on the frontier, and providing for the construction of a meetinghouse and the employment of a permanent minister. This system of community settlement was favored by the religious and social organization of the Puritans, and it also stimulated immigration into New England.

In the eighteenth century a secular breeze lessened the religious atmosphere of New England, and consequently in the laying out of new towns there was a breakdown of the old social-religious-economic system. In Massachusetts the first breach occurred when townships were laid out to be granted to soldiers who had served in the Indian wars. By 1762 Massachusetts was actually auctioning her western townships to the highest bidder. The old oversights had broken down. The same tendency operated in Connecticut and in New Hampshire. These new grants were not occupied by actual proprietors. They were purchased by colonial speculators and land jobbers who hoped to make money from the appreciation of land values. The anomalous spectacle now appeared of a town proprietor owning shares in many townships. Salesmen peddled proprietors' rights through New England and neighboring colonies and occasionally carried them to England. As the century wore on, speculation became a fever infecting the whole community, from merchant to minister. One of the greatest plungers was John Nelson, a wealthy West Indies trader of Portsmouth, who owned proprietorships in forty-six townships in Vermont and New Hampshire. For the moment these land boomers overreached themselves. The proprietors had no notion of becoming settlers, and they had difficulty in stocking their land with others, in spite of the bonuses which they offered for settlement. Since the conditions of the grants could not be fulfilled, petitions poured in for a postponement of requirements, and where this was not granted the townships returned to the original grantor, the colony.

In the southern colonies an entirely different land system had appeared. Indeed, under the regime of the Virginia Company, all the future methods of landholding had already originated. Of them all, the headright became the most important. The process of interpretation and of fraud made more generous even this liberal device. No matter how often an inhabitant of Virginia crossed the ocean, each voyage counted for fifty acres, captains on vessels received fifty acres for each passenger and seaman, each member of the crew swore out fifty acres for himself as an immigrant. One man would serve as an excuse for repeated grants. Thus an indentured servant would provide fifty acres to the captain whose vessel carried him, fifty acres to the merchant who purchased him, and fifty acres to the planter who purchased him from the merchant. Finally the granting of lands was made more simple, if not more honest, when the clerks in the office of the secretary of the colony simply made out headrights from lists of names and sold them for one to five shillings apiece. Since no other method of acquiring public land existed until the direct purchase by money or tobacco was authorized in 1705, liberal interpretation of the headright system was necessary in order to contrive a flexible and adaptable land system. His headright secured, the owner would locate his acres on the unoccupied land of the colony, apply for a survey at the surveyor's office, and finally register his grant with the secretary. The settler then had two reguirements to discharge. He must seat his grant and must pay an annual quitrent. The former requirement was easily discharged by building a ramshackle cabin on the plot, by allowing the cattle to browse through the woods, and by planting an acre of tobacco or corn, which might in later years be choked by weeds.

The headright system of land acquisition was adopted in the other southern colonies. Lord Baltimore used it in Maryland, and so did the more numerous proprietors of the Carolinas and the philanthropic promoters of Georgia. Everywhere these grants were subject to quitrents which were designed to yield revenue. In the proprietary colonies the proprietors usually reserved areas for themselves which they intended to dispose of to others or to operate as their own manors. Most manorial estates, however, remained paper proposals.

This southern system had many contrasts with that of the New England colonies. The southern settlement was individualistic rather than cooperative. Its method of "indiscriminate location" led to a greater confusion of boundaries and to a more scattered and dispersed settlement than that of the New England township. The size of holding was larger in the South than in New England. This last characteristic was, however, due as much to the agricultural methods and crops of the South as it was to the land system.

The land systems of the middle colonies blended those of their northern and southern neighbors. When New York became an English colony it was required by the peace treaty to preserve the property rights of the Dutch settlers, whether in patroonships or in smaller allotments. The former arrangement apparently appealed to the English officials, for they proceeded to create large manors which rivaled their Dutch predecessors; nine were successful, each having privileges like those of the manor in England. The township system in New York was both Dutch and English, for the New England township had been transported by Yankee emigrants to Long Island and Westchester County. The same emigration had carried the town to the Jerseys, where headrights and proprietary reservations were already in existence. The Pennsylvania land system was one of the most interesting and important in the colonies, and one of the most chaotic. It was in a continual state of alteration and development. In his first scheme, issued in 1681, Penn reserved for himself one-tenth of every 100,000 acres, the "proprietary tenth." The remainder was disposed of on varying conditions. He offered for sale at the price of £100 and a small quitrent large estates of 5,000 acres, and then he granted for a quitrent smaller estates of not more than 200 acres, with 50 acres for each servant brought in and 50 acres to the servant when he became free. A township system whose area and division differed from those of New England was later developed and partially applied in the central and western portions of the colony.

In the eighteenth century a distinctly new method of land acquisition appeared. Pennsylvania attracted a great flood of immigration, and these immigrants, Scotch-Irish and German, were ignorant of the local customs and without money. Pressing to the newer regions, they settled upon the unoccupied lands on the frontier or reserved lands and exhibited an obstinate indifference to regular land laws. The Scotch-Irish were apt to appeal to Natural and Divine Law to justify their doings. Invading one of the proprietary manors, they alleged "it was against the laws of God and Nature that so much land should be idle while so many Christians wanted it to labor on and to raise their bread." Of course force could be used to dispossess trespassers, but there was an obvious injustice in such action unless recompense was made for the settlers' improvements. By the middle of the century the Pennsylvania land office recognized these squatters' rights by providing that the colonist who settled upon unappropriated land, built a cabin, cleared away the forest, and grew crops was entitled when the land was surveyed to his holding upon payment of the regular purchase money. This custom of preemption was carried by the stream of population which left Pennsylvania for new lands to the south and west. It is significant that during the Revolution Virginia and North Carolina enacted preemption laws which applied to the land claimed by these states west of the Appalachians.

Though the designation of certain events as critically significant is a dangerous practice, the settlement of Pennsylvania and of Philadelphia, one senses, marked a turning point in the course of North American settlement. When, in a little less than two decades after 1680, Philadelphia accumulated a population of 5,000, while it had taken New York City seventy years to become a place of the same size, settlers and managers had mastered the art of colonization. By the end of the seventeenth century the population of the English colonies had filled in the American coast from the Kennebec to Albemarle Sound and had settled the region around Charleston. The frontier had been pushed inland to the fall lines of rivers from the Hudson to the James. In the eighteenth century before the American Revolution, the population had occupied the interior of Connecticut and Massachusetts, and the frontier had encroached upon southern New Hampshire and Vermont. In the South, Georgia was founded and gradually peopled, and from the coastline of the Carolinas settlement slowly spread up the river valleys until it was halted by the belt of pine barrens which cut off the western area. In Virginia the settlers crossed the Piedmont and penetrated the Blue Ridge into the Great Valley, a remarkable geologic trough extending southwest from New Jersey and Pennsylvania into Georgia and Alabama. This Great Valley, in reality a series of parallel valleys and small ridges, is rich in limestone soils and is one of the most fertile regions in the United States. The Virginians were anticipated by settlers from Pennsylvania. In that colony, Germans, Scotch-Irish, and native Americans pressed westward through the easy water gaps, came into the Valley, and then marched southward along its course through Maryland and Virginia. When they approached its southern terminus, they spilled eastward into the Piedmont, or foothill region, of the Carolinas and then began the penetration of the trans-Appalachian country. By 1775 there were scattered frontier stations in Kentucky and Tennessee.

Abreast with the pioneer in his advance toward the frontier, came the speculator in western lands. By the middle of the eighteenth century such speculation had become a mania, and companies were formed or projected to undertake this supposedly profitable way of making money. In 1753 Connecticut investors formed the Susquehanna Company to exploit the territory, claimed under the "sea-to-sea" charter of their colony, in the Wyoming Valley of northern Pennsylvania. Stock was issued, and soon over eight hundred "wholesome persons," including politicians and their relatives, had purchased shares in the undertaking. Actual settlement, however, was delayed by English opposition, Indian irritation, and a long conflict with the State of Pennsylvania. In the mountain region of North Carolina, Judge Richard Henderson gathered together a group of well-to-do acquaintances and relatives, storekeepers, lawyers, and the like, into first the Louisa Company and then the Transylvania Company. Henderson entered into an arrangement with Daniel Boone, hunter, trapper, and explorer of romantic fame, by which the judge furnished legal advice to Boone, who was encumbered by debts, while the frontire hero engaged on his part to locate the best lands west of the mountain ranges. He was at his task as early as 1764, but it was not until 1775 that the group of proprietors purchased from the Cherokees 20 million acres of land, the larger part of which lay between the Kentucky and the Cumberland River, for £10,000 in goods and money. They then hired Boone and others to trace out the Wilderness Road which led through the "high swung gateway" of the Cumberland Gap and then north into Kentucky, where the grant lay.

The projects of speculators in the middle colonies were legion. From Virginia came the Ohio Company of 1747, which included prominent Virginians and important financiers of Great Britain who petitioned for a grant of 500,000 acres on the upper Ohio and guaranteed to settle it with five hundred families within fourteen years. In 1763 several prominent Marylanders and Virginians formed the Mississippi Company and petitioned for the modest area of 2.5 million acres of land to lie on both sides of the Ohio River and about the eastern bank of the Mississippi. In return they proposed to settle two hundred families. The roll of the Virginia shareholders included the first names of that colony, the Fitzhughs, the Lees, and George Washington. Indeed Washington must be counted among the greatest of the colonial land plungers. He purchased claims to western lands which had been granted by the Virginian or English government as bounties to soldiers in colonial wars; he participated in land companies; he advertised his lands in the papers of Great Britain and Ireland; and at the time of his death he valued his largest holdings of western lands about the Ohio and the Great Kanawha at approximately $300,000. The possession of these western lands goes far to explain Washington's extraordinary interest in the improvement of means of communication with this region. Or one might say that his faith in the destiny of the West accounted for both.

The activities of the Virginians had aroused meanwhile fears in Pennsylvania, where it was almost a proverb that "every great fortune made here within these fifty years has been by land." Especially interested were the fur-trading companies that had carried on their business across the mountains. After various manipulations, there emerged in 1769 the Grand Ohio Company. This was a grandiose but significant organization. It proposed to purchase from the king for £ 10,460 7s. 3d. and a small quitrent after twenty years an area estimated to contain 20 million acres south of the Ohio River and adjoining the western boundaries of Virginia, Maryland, and Pennsylvania. Handsome profits were anticipated. The organizing genius of this company was Samuel Wharton, partner in the famous Philadelphia fur-trading house of Boynton, Wharton, and Morgan. Wharton was an excellent example of the eighteenth-century promoter—ambitious, skillful, and not too scrupulous. The colonial shareholders in this organization included the Whartons, George Croghan, representative of the Lancaster fur traders, Sir William Johnson, superintendent of Indian affairs, and Benjamin Franklin. To these were added the English investors. Many were included because of their political influence; other Englishmen were interested from the financial viewpoint. In fact the English were "new-land mad" and noblemen and commoners alike were all eager to make their fortunes from the lands of the New World. While these schemes were in process, the stream of settlement had already directed itself toward these western regions.

It is tempting to infer that this enlargement of the populated area was due to the pressure of population and the rise in the price of land. In the eighteenth century both Penn and the Calverts raised their schedule of prices, and in New England the land near the coast rose in value. During the 1700's there seems to have been a slight but steady rise in land prices. Perhaps all the "good" land and that favorably situated had been taken and later comers had to push beyond the settlements. While the situation varied between colonies and from time to time land policies and price schedules probably did not prevent settlers from getting land. The lament in the colonies was not a lack of land but a lack of people. The want of their presence, energy, and skill held back prosperity, not the want of acres.

Population: Sources, Status, Distribution

Immigration into the English colonies came in spurts. The first spurt occurred largely before 1650. It was an English and Puritan migration, and the desire to found an ideal Biblical community was a strong motive for it. Ten or a dozen ships a month discharged their human cargoes in Massachusetts; and in 1645 the population of Massachusetts Bay was over 16,000, more than that of all the rest of British America. The Puritan wave died away after 1660. In the next century immigrants began to arrive in considerable numbers from Germany, Scotland, and Northern Ireland. The last, Ulstermen, were Scotch-Irish. They or their ancestors had been pioneers before their arrival in America, for they had swarmed from Scotland to the Ulster plantations, which were contemporaneous with England's colonial efforts in this hemisphere. In Ulster they fought the native Irishman very much as their offspring later fought the American Indian. Toward the close of the seventeenth century the economic life of the Irish plantations was, however, hampered by English restrictions prohibiting the export of many vital agricultural products. After 1717 when the leases came due, the landlords doubled or trebled rates. As a result the Scotch-Irish emigrated in droves to the New World. At the same time the emigration from Germany began to assume important proportions. The German immigrants to the colonies came largely from the southern states about the Rhine, the Palatinate, Württemberg, Baden, and the German portions of Switzerland. These regions had been devastated by the armies of Louis XIV because they were a granary for his foes, and the backward conditions of German feudalism were no inducement to peasants to remain tied to lands which were periodically ravaged.

The colonizers and proprietors of lands in America sought to induce emigration from these discontented areas. The greatest promoter of them all was William Penn. Agents were sent out to stimulate German migration; and a flood of propaganda was unloosed in various pamphlets which were translated into German, Dutch, and French, and spread widely over the Continent. His *Further Account of the Province of Pennsylvania,* dated 1685, is an admirable example of this promotion literature. It dealt first with the "Produce of the Earth"—grass, vegetables, peaches, "Muskmellon, and Water Mellons," and even the "Weeds of our Woods" upon which cattle could be grazed—then with the "Products of Our Waters," which ranged from "Mighty Whales" to oysters; and finally with the low price and abundance of "Produce in General." The activities of proprietors and land agents were supplemented by shipowners who employed representatives and paid commissions for every passenger to be shipped across the Atlantic. This type of solicitor, the "Newlander," flourished in Germany. In 1749 there were one hundred and forty-three engaged in the business and they received a commission equivalent to seven dollars per head. The presence and promises of the Newlander anticipated the oil promoter of a later generation. He wore a gold watch chain, jingled the coins in his pocket, and exuded an air of prosperity. The New World, under his imagination, was the means by which "the maid has become a lady, the peasant a nobleman, the artisan a baron." So devastating were the effects of his solicitation and so tainted with fraud were his performances that some German states attempted to prevent his activities.

After 1770 these new strains united with a quickened stream of English migrants to American shores. The peace of 1763 had quieted the imperial struggle between England and France—war always upsets migration—and the long prosperity of England gave way to hard times. Crops were poor and the enclosure of small farms for a more profitable form of agriculture on large units raised rents and dispossessed small farmers. In the years before the Revolution immigration increased markedly. By 1775 the total population of the colonies was 2.5 million. Virginia was probably the most populous colony; Pennsylvania, the second, and Massachusetts, the third.

In nurture and, perhaps, education these immigrants represented a capital investment. It cost money to get to the New World and the impoverished and hard-up, precisely the classes moved to migrate, did not have passage money. Instead they had time and strength or skill to sell. So they discounted their future by becoming indentured servants, by apprenticing themselves to a master bound for the colonies or to an agent, in this country or abroad, who provided masters with servants. These indentures usually ran for seven years and the master or agent provided passage money and some other expenses varying betwen £10 and £12. Redemptioners were immigrants with a little money who turned it over to some shipper and then attempted when they arrived in the New World to collect enough from friends or relatives to discharge the remainder of their indebtedness or sold themselves and the members of their families into a sufficient tenure of service. In particular the German and the Irish employed the device of redemption, which was more commonly used in the eighteenth than in the seventeenth century. The servant business gave vessels a back-cargo, American importers a headright to land, and the colonists a labor force. From time to time in different colonies—usually southern—one white person in ten was under indenture. To the colonies—with the exception of the Puritan ones—not less than one-half nor more than two-thirds of all white immigrants had come as indentured servants, redemptioners, or convicts, who also were usually put under indenture.

With a few exceptions, all these immigrants came voluntarily. After the completion of their indenture, servants entered the ranks of freemen, took land, and began to work for themselves. Their differences from others became then of concern chiefly to statisticians and genealogists. Such was not the case with the immigrant who came here under duress— the Negro slave. His presence was not the result of accident or human depravity. Like the indentured white, he was brought in to supply the needed labor force. His journey was a long one. Over narrow jungle paths coffles of slaves were brought from the interior of Africa, sometimes for a distance of 1,000 miles, to the Guinea coast. Nations who controlled the west African coast sought to formalize the slave business by placing it under the *asiento,* a pawn of war or diplomacy granted to the victor in either. Since this monopoly bred interlopers, Negro chiefs bartered their captives to European or American sea captains. Thus the first slaves were introduced into the English continental colonies in 1619, when a Dutch privateer sold in Virginia some slaves captured from an enemy slaver. Until the turn of the century slavery did not thrive, but after 1700 the increase in the traffic was rapid.

The ocean voyage to this country has often been described in horrible pictures. But Henry Laurens of South Carolina wrote in 1768:

Yet I never saw an instance of cruelty in ten or twelve years' experience in this branch [the slave trade] equal to the cruelty exercised upon those poor Irish. . . . Self interest prompted the baptized heathen to take some care of the wretched slaves for a market, but no other care was taken of those poor Protestant Christians from Ireland but to deliver as many as possible alive on shoar upon the cheapest terms, no matter how they fared upon the voyage nor in what condition they were landed.

Though slavery was scattered as far north as New Hampshire, the heaviest concentration outside the Caribbean was in the southern colonies. The first national census in 1790 stated there were nearly 700,000 slaves in the new nation.

But not all Americans were immigrants; people were born here. Shortly before the American Revolution Benjamin Franklin brought his curiosity to bear upon the native birthrate. This was larger than in Europe, for America's ample lands encouraged Americans to marry earlier than Europeans and to have more children. The future was reassuring. Franklin concluded, "Our people must be doubled every twenty years." Actually these figures were too sanguine. After 1660 population doubled every twenty to twenty-five years.

Land may have been important, but natives and foreign-born were not dispersed evenly over its area. For instance many concentrated in cities and towns. Figures for the total nonagricultural population are not available for the colonies as a whole, but estimates in 1775 for the five leading port cities—New York, Philadelphia, Boston, Charleston, and Newport—placed their combined populations at approximately 104,000. Too much can be made of this urban phenomenon. An agricultural, even a scattered community with commerce and communication can produce a high culture as the estates of Virginia planters and the Concord shack of Henry D. Thoreau demonstrate. By bringing people together, however, urbanization facilitates the division of labor, the technical advance of industry, the provision of facilities like banks and schools, and stimulates the necessary extension and improvement of the means of transportation.

Through good fortune and their ability to adapt to it the English had built a substantial outpost of empire in North America. Their triumph was signalized by the Peace of Paris in 1763, when, having defeated France, the victors practically rearranged the world as they chose. On this continent they elected to acquire Canada as an addition to the old thirteen colonies. To an immeasurable extent these achievements were a result of national and colonial policies as well as of the efforts of individuals. The increase of population was a proof that colonial growth had bettered the condition of men and raised their level of expectations. Whether the balance of interests between colonies and mother country which had begun the colonization movement could continue was another question.

Subsistence, Staples, and Statutes

In contrast to the industrial and commercial maturity of European nations, the colonies in America were in their economic youth. They were a new country. Extensive manufacturing, therefore, was out of the question. They lacked laborers skilled in industrial technique, the capital for creating a complicated industrial structure, and a populous market. Consequently they turned for their livelihood to such of their natural resources as could be exploited by comparatively unskilled labor without a heavy investment of funds and as could be exchanged in some overseas market for the commodities which they could not produce themselves. On every side there was opportunity. The New World encouraged the fur and timber trades by its forest resources, the fisheries through the proximity of inshore grounds and offshore banks, and agriculture through the untaxed fertility of its soils. That these extractive occupations of the colonies were in approximate harmony with the mercantilist ideas of the day, which regarded colonies as a source of needed raw materials, was indeed a happy coincidence.

An industrial colony, which many of the Virginia adventurers planned for, was, as we have seen, out of the question. Their immense distance from the mother country, the irregularity in the dispatch and arrival of supplies, and the cost of transporting heavy goods a long distance compelled the colonists to provide their own subsistence. The forests furnished building material and fuel; the fertile land promised crops. But there were agricultural disappointments, for the planting of small grains like wheat did not originally prosper, and the few domestic animals did not always thrive in the New World, where they were subject to loss and depredation from wild animals and Indians. The simplest way for the colonist to survive was to purchase or seize the food supplies of these seminomadic Indians, shoot game or catch fish, and, for the rest, hope or pray for the arrival of the next ship from home.

Subsistence Farming

Though the Indians lacked domestic animals, they did grow Indian corn, or maize. Since corn was planted in hills rather than rows, its cultivation did not require careful preliminary clearing of the land; hoe cultivation sufficed for its culture. Corn was easier to harvest than wheat and husking easier than threshing. Finally, corn yielded a larger crop, and it did not require a mill to convert its kernels into cornmeal. In short corn was a less demanding crop. By the mid-thirties the Virginia colonists had apparently solved their food problems enough to have "a very great plentie" of meat, dairy products, and corn.

In all the colonies, as time passed, an agriculture of self-subsistence prevailed. The family built its own house and barns, manufactured its own fabrics, shoes, and clothes, made its gadgets and equipment of wood, and lived on its own produce. Nearly every farm museum in the nation has assembled the evidence of this simplicity, independence, and ingenuity. Some subsistence farmers boasted they could get along with the expenditure of ten dollars of cash a year. Though their operators might thus approximate the dream of a self-reliant Arcadia, such farms generally did not endure long; in the older colonies subsistence farmers retreated to areas away from river and road; and on the frontier along the western edge of the colonies they pressed ahead into the wilderness until the arrival of the country store or the itinerant peddler soon shattered their isolation.

As farmers began to sell or barter commodities—salted or smoked meats, cheese, and heavily salted butter, all of which did not spoil and could pay the cost of transportation—subsistence farming began to crumble around the edges. The small rural trades might suffice to finance some limited purchases of West Indian goods, for example, sugar, coffee and rum, or European goods, like superior fabrics and metalwork; but they were not the way to wealth. Commercial farming required something more: the discovery and development of a "staple," as the phrase of the day put it. Prerequisites for the production of staples were relative ease of transportation, cultivation of larger land units, a more considerable labor force, the assistance of capital, and a wide market demand. Since these conditions were not always or immediately present in North America, the colonists in their search for staples turned to natural resources which were easily available or whose acquisition or growth might be interlocked with other activities.

The Fur Trade

Of these extractive natural industries, both the Virginia and the Plymouth colonies turned for a brief time to the fur trade. The European demand for fur was insatiable. The fine peltries were a badge of distinction, worn by royalty and nobility, by university officials, and by the rising merchant classes; and the coarser skins were part of the clothing of the lower classes. To satisfy the European demand the fur-bearing animals had already been hunted and trapped in the great northern regions of Russia and Siberia, and so rapid had been the exhaustion of that supply that by the late eighteenth century the Russian traders had crossed the Bering Strait and pushed down the northwestern coast of North America. Meanwhile the French, along the St. Lawrence and Great Lakes, and the Dutch, and later the English, along the Hudson, had commenced their inroads from the Atlantic coastline, and with such success that the supply of furs from the eastern half of America had shifted the fur markets of Europe from the East to the West. Vienna, Danzig, and Lübeck gave way to London, Amsterdam, and Paris.

As a staple the fur trade had the disadvantage of soon exhausting the natural resource upon which it was based, especially in quality skins. But it overcame the requirement of a large labor force, for it was one occupation which relied upon Indian laborers or traders. So the tide soon moved into the interior of the continent. As early as 1716 the Indians were fetching from the Great Lakes the peltries they exchanged in the East. Eventually a chain of many links bound these red men to the aristocrats who purchased their beaver in western Europe.

In the English trade of the mid-eighteenth century, for instance, a London merchant would dispatch on credit to some Philadelphia trading house a supply of Indian goods: guns, gunpowder, strouds—an Indian blanketing, preferably in gay colors, like "Deep Blue or Lively Red"—linen and calicoes "of the brightest and flourishing collours," lace, thread, ribbons, women's stockings, "red, yellow, and green," kettles, traps, Jews'-harps, metal tools, bells, whistles, knives, rings, jewelry, and looking glasses. After the all-important item of rum had been added at Philadelphia, the goods were carted inland to the storehouse of the firm at Lancaster. From these supplies the trader to the West would secure upon credit the goods which he needed, and packhorse trains of twenty horses, belled and saddled with loads of one hundred and fifty pounds, would carry them over the trails from the Susquehanna to the forks of the Ohio. At strategic points in the West there were minor storehouses at which the Indians could trade, or from which the goods could be moved to the Indian villages or councils. This relationship, running from London to the Falls of the Ohio, could be duplicated with a change of western terminus many times over in Pennsylvania and New York, or in the Carolinas and Georgia.

The fur trade, thus moving westward, became the property of the colonies which had the best access to the interior of the continent, as did the French. Toward the close of the seventeenth century, however, the French trade was enfiladed by English competitors. The threat from the north was the "Governor and Company of Adventurers of England Trading into Hudson's Bay." This Hudson's Bay Company secured a charter from the king in 1670, sent vessels to that remote region, and waged a thirty years' war with its French rival, the Compagnie du Nord, until the Treaty of Utrecht set the seal on English success. The menace from the south was the New York and Pennsylvania fur trade. In New York the English were the heirs to the strategic position which the Dutch had occupied on the Hudson and Mohawk rivers, which formed, with the exception of the St. Lawrence valley, the best approach to the interior of the continent. The Dutch frontier post, Fort Orange, became the great English fur center, Albany. Like the Dutch, the English were allied with the Iroquois, who, since the furs of their own region were soon exhausted, acted as middlemen in transferring the furs of the "Far Indians" to the English traders. To maintain this role it was more advantageous for the Iroquois to seek alliance with the English than with the French, and it was also necessary to keep the former from a direct trade into the West. New York traders, therefore, did not penetrate into the remote western regions. Fort Oswego, constructed in 1722 at the southeastern corner of Lake Ontario, was their farthest post. Even its establishment alarmed the Iroquois, for it opened up a direct trade with the western Indians. The Pennsylvania traders, however, had invaded the Ohio valley. At first the French had abandoned to them the area east of the Maumee-Wabash route, but by the middle of the eighteenth century the French sought to make the whole Ohio basin French by fortifying the French-Allegheny line. The value of the annual fur business in the northern district, roughly north of the Potomac and Ohio rivers, was estimated in the 1760's at £180,000.

In the South, the traders of the Carolinas and later of Georgia found access to the West around the tip of the Alleghenies. They spread with great rapidity. Within thirty years after the founding of the Carolinas one trader penetrated to the mouth of the Arkansas, and later traders reached the Ohio and planned to invade the upper Mississippi. Charleston, South Carolina, remained the center of the trade, but in the eighteenth century Augusta, Georgia, became its western entrepôt. From that place in 1740 2,000 packhorses made the journey into the interior, and five vessels carried cargoes worth between £20,000 and £30,000 down to Charleston. Annual exports of more than 200,000 deerskins were common from that port by 1730. It was a leather rather than a fur trade. On this southern frontier, the English met the competition of the French from New Orleans and Mobile, and forged an alliance with the Cherokees to keep their Gallic rivals in check, just as they had utilized the Iroquois in the North against the same enemy.

In this international competition both parties had advantages in dealing with the Indians. The French were able to arouse them against the English because the English trader was the forerunner of settlement. Forewarned by the experience of the tribes east of the Appalachians, the western Indian perceived that settlement was the beginning of the end for his race. On the other hand, the English had everywhere the advantage of offering the Indian better goods at lower prices. In the seventeenth century the Indians paid at Montreal five beavers for a musket, at Albany two; at Montreal two beavers for six pairs of stockings; at Albany one. In every product but powder the English had a great superiority. Even their rivals admitted it, as a clandestine export of English goods from New York to Montreal showed. The superiority and cheapness of English goods were due to many reasons. The French restrictions on trade to New France and the difficulties of transporting goods from Europe, particularly during wartime when the French lacked the control of the sea, raised their prices. English goods, moreover, were manufactured more cheaply.

British supremacy in the fur trade was assured in 1763 when France surrendered her Canadian possessions by the Treaty of Paris. English and Scotch companies and merchants now clutched at the traffic in furs carried on from Quebec, but the Scotch were more successful. From their ranks emerged the great fur barons who were to rule the trade in the future. The Illinois country, however, remained the preserve of Spanish and French traders from New Orleans and St. Louis, for it was impossible to transport goods as cheaply overland to that region as it was to pole them up the Mississippi. Spain, unfortunately for England, had been allowed to retain the west bank of the Mississippi and New Orleans, the natural outlet for the great river basin.

The fur trade colored the whole of colonial life. It elevated the Indian in a twinkling from the Stone Age to the Age of Metals; and with his civilization thus disrupted, his dependence upon the trade was almost pathetic. Kettles, metal tools, and above all guns and gunpowder had become unbelievably vital. From this trade, moreover, the Indian unfortunately derived his notions of the white race. Very few responsible men of high character undertook its dangers and uncertainties. Governor Dinwiddie of Virginia characterized the traders "as the most abandon'd Wretches in the World." The exchange of furs was accompanied by a "frolic" induced by rum and lasting for days. The participants in these fracases were occasionally killed and frequently injured. Under such circumstances the barter of goods for furs was characterized by every imaginable form of low cunning and fraud. The Indians, dizzy with liquor and drugs, were imposed upon by false scales and crooked dealing. For such abuses the Indian, armed with the weapons he had obtained in the fur trade, took his revenge by an attack upon some innocent settlement.

Because of the fur trade's abuses and its international importance the separate colonies attempted to impose regulatory measures. Licenses for the trade were required and some check upon the use of rum was attempted. Massachusetts established and operated fur "factories" to assure

Indians fair dealing, and Pennsylvania used this device for a longer
period. The intercolonial rivalry in the fur trade prevented the success
of this "states' rights" policy. After the Seven Years' War the English
government attempted a policy of imperial regulation, which sought to
draw a dividing line, located at different times along the Appalachian
Mountains, to separate settlement from Indian territory. This line was
not to be permanent, but was to be moved westward as the expansion of
settlement necessitated. Beyond this line no one could carry on the Indian trade without a license and without giving bonds. Rules regulated
the amount of credit given to the Indian and the price of goods. The
sale of rum and guns with rifled barrels was forbidden. All this effort
proved futile. At the time of the Revolution no satisfactory scheme for
regulating the Indian trade had been found.

Forests and Policy

Timber, like furs, came from the wilderness of the new country, and the timber resources seemed inexhaustible. The "Appalachian
ranges and the shore regions had the finest forest that has existed in the
historical period outside of the tropics," wrote a later American geogra-
pher. In the North the white and red oak were the most valuable hardwoods; but "the noble white pine tree" of the lumberman's song was the
king not only of the conifers but of the forest. Growing to astounding
size, often with a thickness at the butt of four or five feet, its tall sym-
metrical trunk towered upward to a crown of branches, and its wood,
straight-grained, free from knotholes, was easily worked. The resources
of the South were at first comparatively neglected, but eventually the excellent qualities of its yellow pine and live oak were recognized.

The commercial value of this remarkable forest area, however, bore
no proportion to its abundance. In fact the forest was often a hindrance.
It had to be cleared away before the ground could be cultivated, and
usually these fallen trees were destroyed in the easiest fashion. Yet from
the burning of the hardwoods, the settler could extract potash or its
derivative pearl ash. These substances were used in making soap, in treating cloth, and in other processes, such as glassmaking. Since the manufacture of potash and pearl ash required no equipment more elaborate
than a large iron pot and a small kiln, the making of "sop" ashes was
the occasional occupation of hundreds of households from Maine to
Georgia. The importance of both by-products was evident only when
the totals for all the colonies were amassed.

The commercial lumber industry followed the fall line of the rivers
in the middle and northern colonies, for here water power was available
to transform the timber resources into merchantable shapes. From the

James River to the District of Maine, oak trees were fashioned into timbers, sawed into planks, or made into cooperage—barrel staves, heads, and hoops. In New Hampshire and Maine the white pine forests touched the sea, and the fall line, near the coast, was easily reached by water transportation. Here the lumber industry reached its apogee. In 1720 the Piscataqua, a tiny New Hampshire stream, was lined with seventy sawmills turning out 6 million feet a year of planks, boards, shingles, and staves. So wasteful was the exploitation of the forest that the industry early in the eighteenth century began its eastward migration along the coast of Maine. Portsmouth, New Hampshire, had a new lumber-port rival in Falmouth, the present Portland. In 1762 a great forest fire, sweeping from New Hampshire into Maine for a distance of fifty miles, drove the lumber industry even farther east. Meanwhile in North Carolina a lumber industry had grown up along the Cape Fear River.

The forests of the English colonies were also an untapped resource of those timbers and naval products which were required for a war navy or a mercantile marine in the days of the sailing ship. The white-pine region could furnish masts, yards, and spars; the oak forests could provide the pieces for the frame or skeleton; and from pines, South and North, could be bled the pitch, tar, and resin, the "naval stores" so essential in shipbuilding. The melted pitch filled in the calked seams of the vessel, tar preserved the cordage, and a mixture of pitch and resin was used to protect the underwater parts of wooden vessels before the days of coppering. Not only were these products indispensable for a maritime nation but around them hung the mercantilist aroma.

Nonetheless, it was touch and go whether the colonists would supply the British market with naval stores. England drew her supplies from the forests of the "East Country" or of the "Northern Crowns," terms applied to the Baltic countries or to others akin to them, like Norway. Though the trade to the Baltic was often interrupted by war or ice, the ports of the East Country were nearer England than those in North America, voyages were shorter, and transportation costs less. Furthermore, the inhabitants had acquired skill in the manufacture of naval stores and made a somewhat superior product. Even the prospects of a certain return from contracts to supply the royal navy could not assure that naval stores would become a colonial staple—without government assistance or direction. In the eighteenth century Great Britain attempted to supply the needed aid and the guidance. A system of bounties on tar, pitch, resin, and turpentine sought to equalize the cost of transportation from America with that from the East Country. As for masts the government instituted the device of the "King's Woods" reserving for the Crown all trees over twenty-four inches in diameter on public land; these were marked with the king's arrow. These regulations, favorable or otherwise, were designed particularly for the northern colonies of

New England and New York. In spite of much effort and official activity, they failed to work there and ironically succeeded better in Virginia and the Carolinas. North Carolina in particular took the lead. It had the forest resources, and the work of tapping the trees and collecting the liquid was carried on mainly by small farmers, who sometimes invaded the Crown lands and sometimes hired slaves to carry on what had become a woodland rather than a plantation industry.

The American Fisheries

The natural resources of the land were supplemented by those of the sea. Stretching in a long arc from the tip of Long Island to the eastern edge of the Great Bank of Newfoundland, lay one of the finest fishing grounds in the world. The area is a shallow one, for the continental shelf underlies it and forms the famous fishing "banks"; and the cool Arctic current, flowing over it from the north, makes it an ideal home for all varieties of fish, of which the cod was the most important in colonial times. The catches of this area found a ready market in the West Indies and in European countries. There fish was a common diet for the lower classes and a delicacy for the aristocrat. The retainers of the Earl of Northumberland in the sixteenth century lived on a monotonous diet in which fish was served for three-quarters of the year; and the lord and lady of the establishment on one occasion sat down to a breakfast of "a quart of beer, as much wine, two pieces of salt fish, six red herrings, four white ones, and a dish of sprats." The dietetic restrictions of the numerous Catholic fast days increased the consumption of a generally basic foodstuff.

Holland with its herring industry had been the chief purveyor to the European market, and its success had aroused the envy of its neighbors. Now the American grounds offered a chance of breaking the Dutch predominance, and England found mercantilist arguments enough to justify activity in this new arena of international competition. First, there was the home market. Threatened by the Protestant Reformation, which might have weakened the religious reasons for fish eating, the market was preserved by legislation. In 1563 Parliament passed an act levying heavy fines upon flesh eating on Wednesday and Saturday, and, among other reasons for the measure, the promotion of the fisheries was listed. A foreign market was also eagerly desired, for through the export of fish to the Catholic countries the coveted balance of trade could be increased. Finally, the fisheries were seen to have a direct connection with sea power. The fisheries required vessels, and they "have ever beene the Chiefest Seminarie and Nurserie" of seamen for the royal navy. Every consideration, therefore, dictated their wholesale national support by bounties, rebates, protection, and national favoritism.

In American waters England had to compete not only with her European rivals but with her own colonies. In this respect the southern colonies were not offensive, for, although they had access to rich fishing grounds, they preferred to make money from their fertile agricultural land. In New England, on the other hand, granite and the glacier had formed nearly everywhere a rocky land. But it had the sea. The bays and harbors of its indented coastline, the blue water at the end of every village street beckoned seaward. To trade and to fisheries, therefore, New Englanders turned from the beginning. At first they were content to tap the inshore resources of the gulf of Maine. Descriptions make the mouth water. The Reverend Francis Higginson, first minister to Salem, wrote of the codfish and "such abundance of mackerels, that it would astonish one to behold," of the bass, "a most sweet and wholesome fish," and lobsters, some weighing sixteen pounds, of which he was "soon cloyed," "they were so great and fat, and luscious." Long before the settlement of Massachusetts Bay in 1630 the shore of that region had been dotted by fishing stations for the vessels which repaired thither from the west counties of England; and Sir Ferdinando Gorges had planted stations along the Maine coast or encouraged others to do so. When the colonists came over, these stations, often attracting English fishermen, became fishing settlements. A Marblehead fisherman said truly of the town's ancestors who came from Cornwall and the Channel Islands, they "came not here for religion. Their main end was to catch fish."

The fishing activities of New Englanders were first confined to the "inshore grounds." But by the middle of the seventeenth century they were sending vessels to the "offshore banks," a veritable cockpit of international competition. The New Englanders soon demonstrated their advantages even over the fleets and fishermen hailing from the west coast of England. After all, the New England ports were nearer to the scene of activity than Devon. The small specialized vessels from Marblehead or Gloucester could make several voyages a year and return easily to port for reprovisioning, repairs, and recreation. The arrangements for drying and curing fish at New England places were also superior to those along the inhospitable coast of Newfoundland. In 1700 New Englanders exported over 10 million pounds of fish and surpassed Great Britain both in quality and in quantity. Though such an outcome was not to the taste of some mercantilist thinkers in the mother country, the American fisheries persisted in growing. In the decade 1765–1775, 665 vessels were engaged in the New England codfishery, 4,405 men were employed as their crews, and the total value of the catch was estimated at $1.3 million. In truth the fisheries were the "New England Silver Mine."

The sight of "mighty whales spewing up water like smoke from a chimney" was a common one off the New England coast, and whales washed ashore were cut up and tried out for the oil, which furnished a superior illuminant in candle or in lamp. On Long Island such accidental whaling methods gave way to a system. In 1644 Southampton was divided into four wards to furnish watchers on the beach. When a whale was sighted crews were sent out to harpoon him and drag him inshore, where others reduced the blubber to marketable products. Nantucket undertook this offshore whaling from the first. Masts were set up on the south shore of the island and permanent watchers were maintained. Gradually whaling on the deep took the place of these amphibious methods, and in the eighteenth century American whaling vessels had hunted their quarry throughout the Atlantic. Leaving the right whale to the English, French, and Dutch whalers, they sought particularly the sperm whale, which was fiercer but yielded an oil three or four times as valuable. By the Revolution the ports which were to become famous in the nineteenth century had entered upon their historic career. Sag Harbor had surpassed the earlier of the Long Island whaling ports; New Bedford had begun in a small way; but Nantucket was the real overlord of the Atlantic whaling grounds. Chiefly to these ports the whaling fleet of 360 vessels brought back its annual tribute of 45,000 barrels of sperm and 75,000 pounds of bone. But these figures are futile to convey the sweep of an industry which, as Edmund Burke put it, "vexed" the seas from Hudson Bay to the Falkland Islands, from Africa to Brazil.

The fisheries colored colonial life, as the fur trade had done. They spurred on the struggle between France and England for territorial acquisition, for land afforded a base of operations and in a day when international law was more nebulous than at present the possession of a coast justified a claim to an exclusive but indefinite jurisdiction of the adjacent waters. Hence the tenacity with which France held on to a portion of Newfoundland, to the islands of the St. Lawrence, to Cape Breton, and to Acadia, and hence the intensity with which these districts were coveted by New England fishermen. The difficulty of arousing the colonies to military ardor vanished when these regions were the object of acquisition, and their ire was all the greater when English statesmen recurrently damaged colonial interests by the return of these fishing bases to France. The Peace of Paris at last broke the fishing supremacy which the French had enjoyed until the middle of the eighteenth century. Under the terms of that treaty, they retained only the small islands of St. Pierre and Miquelon, and the right to dry fish upon certain shores of Newfoundland.

Agricultural Staples

Since land was abundant, the discovery of an agricultural staple would obviously serve more purposes profitably than exploitation

—and in some instances destruction—of the natural resources of forest and sea. Even the management of the Virginia Company had attempted to realize their visions of silk and wine production. Unchanged by these experiments, the southern colonists instead found in New World agriculture an answer to their quest: tobacco.

Three days after his discovery of America, Columbus referred in his *Journal* to the use of tobacco, and in a little over a century Europe, Africa, and Asia were using it. Consequently, the arrival of tobacco in England long antedated the Virginia colony. Sailors introduced its use. Sir Walter Raleigh, the world's most famous smoker, popularized it as a pastime of the best people, and in the seventeenth century its use was extended from smoking to chewing and to snuff. In England, as elsewhere, the arrival of this novel plant was the occasion of a lively discussion. The most distinguished opponent of tobacco was King James. In 1604 appeared his *A Counterblaste to Tobacco*. Although it added little to the argument, its phraseology and its thought were peculiarly characteristic of the Stuarts. He asserted that tobacco's smell was a proof of its poisonous nature, and requested that his people should not imitate "the barbarous and beastly manners of the wild, godless, and slavish Indians, especially in so vile and stinking a custom." Other writers rushed to the defense of the new practice on the ground that tobacco had medicinal properties and its consumption was a pleasant pastime and a social amenity. This strange controversy can be appreciated only when the seriousness of its protagonists is understood. In the seventeenth century the use of tobacco presented the moral equivalent of the present opium problem. But the dictates of morality, whether they were voiced by the English Stuarts or the Persian Khan, did nothing to stay the use of this American product. The demand for it seemed insatiable.

Since tobacco for English consumption was at first supplied from the Spanish colonies, the moralists who argued against tobacco were joined by the mercantilists who were aghast at the resulting export of bullion. By 1615 England was losing £200,000 in payment for these imports. But already a beginning had been made to quiet the fears of these alarmists. The cultivation of tobacco had begun in the Caribbean islands, and in 1612 John Rolfe, the famous husband of the famous Pocahontas, undertook the cultivation of tobacco in Virginia for his own use as a smoker and for sale as a cash crop in England. At once there was a revolution in the prospects of the colony. The staple for which the colony had yearned was now discovered. Virginia proved to be well suited to the production of the new crop. The rich fertile soil of the river valleys was an ideal medium for its growth; the deep and numerous rivers—Virginia was the Netherlands of the New World—allowed ocean vessels to penetrate far inland to plantation wharfs to put tobacco on board; and there was infinite land for expansion. The crop needed an extensive area. Although

less ground was required for tobacco than for wheat, and the clearing of
the forest could therefore be accomplished piecemeal, the planters continually moved cultivation to new areas in search of a soil which would
give the right taste to the leaf and furnish ample fertility to grow large
plants when measures to ration the number of plants set out put a
premium on their size. The European demand spurred the use of these
resources. Prices were at first so high that a man could make six times as
much in tobacco as he could in wheat. No wonder that Virginia became
infatuated with the Indian weed. The streets and marketplaces of Jamestown were planted with it. Artisans and clergymen had their tobacco
patches. It drove out the cultivation of other products, particularly wheat,
and threatened to reduce the colony to the starvation of the early days.
Local authorities had to pass regulations requiring each planter to raise
enough grain for the support of the persons dependent upon him.

The Stuarts might deplore a colony "built upon smoke," and attempt
to direct its energies to other lines for moral and mercantilist reasons.
It was in vain. The tobacco area was continually expanding. At first it
had been confined to the banks of the James and a small district on the
eastern shore of Chesapeake Bay. Eventually, however, it spread northward to new river valleys, the York, the Rappahannock, and the Potomac,
and then westward along their courses. The boundary of Maryland offered no real barrier, for the settlers of Lord Baltimore's province found
their soil adapted to tobacco and the value of the staple equally enticing.
Tobacco plantations arched the head of Chesapeake Bay and followed
down its eastern shore until they joined with the earlier Virginia plantations in that district. Southward tobacco pushed its frontiers into the
Albemarle Sound country of the Carolinas, and the settlers in this region, bred in the tobacco tradition of the Old Dominion, began its cultivation in the third tobacco colony, North Carolina. But North Carolina
never rivaled its northern neighbors in Colonial times. Her tobacco development was to come later. The total of American production mounted
dizzily. In 1617 Virginia exported 20,000 pounds; in 1770 the amount
exported from America was over 100,000 pounds.

In the early years the quality of the tobacco was frequently injured
by the methods of handling it. The original colonists knew nothing of its
proper culture and the new arrivals who rushed into its cultivation were
equally uninformed. Under these circumstances it was difficult to build
up a body of technical knowledge. The most glaring losses occurred, however, in the treatment of the crop after it was gathered from the fields.
Here carelessness and ignorance deprived the tobacco of over half its
value. Until 1620 it had been cured simply by heaping it upon the
ground, and it had been shipped in rolls to foreign markets. The manipulation necessary in the formation of these rolls injured the leaf, and the
greed of the planters who stuffed the wrappings with inferior tobacco did

not improve matters. Well through the seventeenth century Spanish tobacco was deemed greatly superior, and English smokers gladly paid the
higher prices which it brought. To improve the quality Virginia eventually passed inspection laws. All tobacco was to be brought to public
warehouses for appraisal, and for each hogshead properly inspected and
labeled tobacco notes or "warehouse receipts," were issued. They were
negotiable instruments and were made legal tender for debts within a
limited region. Eventually the notes fell into the hands of an importer
who demanded delivery of the commodity. Thus tobacco became a
medium of exchange and of deferred payments.

In the fields and curing sheds the cultivation of tobacco was an exacting occupation. But the problems of tobacco transcended agricultural
methods. The momentum its cultivation acquired prevented deviation
from the single-crop system. The result was overproduction and a fall in
price. In 1617 it had been 5s. 3d. a pound; by 1666 it had fallen to a half-
penny. The decline over a series of years was general; but it was frequently interrupted by the most disheartening variations. The tobacco
colonies vacillated from plenty to poverty. The crop of 1666 was so
enormous that even a large fleet could not carry it away, and it was asserted that Virginia grew enough in two years to supply the British trade
for three years. Some method of reducing the supply had to be discovered. In 1630 the number of plants was limited to 2,000 for every individual in a family, and the number of leaves to be gathered for each
plant was limited to nine. A few years later this ration was reduced to
1,500, and planters were forbidden to transfer their allotments to each
other.

By the sixties, however, it was apparent that the individual province could not curtail production. If Virginia limited her supply, her
self-denial would be undone by an enlarged production in Maryland or
North Carolina. Restraint upon such competition required intercolonial
action. First, the possibility of royal interference was investigated. The
king, however, proved to be uninterested. A large tobacco crop yielded
large import duties to the treasury, and this royal self-interest was reenforced by that of English merchants, who enjoyed the privilege of
purchasing tobacco at low prices in a glutted market. Attempts were then
made at some form of intercolonial agreement. Treaties were indeed
drawn up either limiting planting before a certain date or suggesting a
planting recess for a year. But some party usually found it advantageous
to withdraw from these agreements before their restrictions went into
effect. Convinced of the futility of this procedure, the people took things
into their own hands. In 1682 mobs attacked plantations and destroyed
tobacco in the hills. Each planter, his own supply gone, was then eager
to help out the good work by devastating the field of his neighbor.
Eventually the militia had to be called out to put an end to this out-

break and some of the plant cutters were executed. Such hardships might be expected to lead to some permanent and suitable method of curtailment. But the next year prices were higher, planters basked in renewed prosperity, and the formulation of a policy was discarded. Such performances certainly justified the rather cynical judgment of Nicholas Spencer. "By my observation," he wrote, "I cannot persuade myself that either a cessation or a stint in the number of plants will effect what is intended. The work must do itself; the crop must grow to such vast quantities that no one will come to fetch it, and then the law of necessity will force them to new industries." This iron law of supply and demand was probably not as powerful a force as soil exhaustion in bringing about a change in the agricultural patterns of Virginia and Maryland. In the eighteenth century the plantations turned so extensively to corn and wheat that by 1770 the export of these products was many times that of Pennsylvania, commonly esteemed the provision colony par excellence. A Virginia commentator called "ye article of wheat" a "kind of second staple" and predicted that in time it would be the equal of tobacco.

Livestock raising furnished another variant to staple production not only in Virginia but in all the southern colonies. The forested land which gave small comfort to grazing animals was in places interrupted with unused Indian fields or "savannahs," small prairies with natural grasses. Since these were not originally owned by anyone and were not in cultivation there was an open range for cattle and for hogs. Most southern colonies enacted regulations allowing cattle, sheep, and hogs to roam at large and unmolested. The burden of protecting crops was not upon the owner of the animals but upon the grower of the crops. All areas unprotected by the rambling, lazy, wasteful, worm fences were a common grazing ground. The care of livestock was simpler in these southern colonies than in the North. For the southern winter was not so rigorous, and shelter was unnecessary; so the animals ran wild.

As cultivated crops spread, the droving industry tended to move toward the unfenced West. Cowboys, long whips, and cow pens were the visible features of this occupation. They may have been introduced from the West Indies where droving in the Spanish islands resembled that in Spain. Be that as it may, at intervals droves of cattle and hogs were collected and driven down to the seacoast markets at Norfolk, Charleston, Baltimore, and Philadelphia. Sometimes feeders fattened up the animals before they were slaughtered and shipped out in the export trade.

Although tobacco remained the staple year in and year out of Virginia and Maryland, its cultivation did not spread to the other southern colonies, nor did the growth of sugarcane, the staple of the Caribbean islands, find lodgment there. At first the proprietors of the Carolinas cherished visions of their property as a sort of Garden of Eden of exotic products. An experimental garden, established in the mainland colony, demonstrated that "Wine, Oyle, Silk, Indicoe, Tobacco, Hemp, Flax, and some say ginger would grow there." This catalogue proved delusive. But in 1696 rice was introduced from Madagascar, and by the turn of the century that crop had fulfilled its promise of success. Thereafter its spread was rapid.

In the culture of rice the fields do not necessarily have to be flooded, but they gain from that process. The water keeps down the weeds, fertilizes the fields, and keeps the stand from breaking in storms. Consequently, the rice fields were laid out in the inland swamps which could be flooded from reservoirs and streams. This method of irrigation was uncertain, and it did not make available the great swamps bordering the rivers of the coastal plain. By the time of the Revolution, however, rice growing had migrated to these latter regions, which a new system of tide flooding had made it possible to cultivate. The river banks were diked, and as the tide pushed back the fresh water, gates were opened and the flood let in and retained until the proper period of inundation was over. Naturally, great care had to be taken to prevent any saltwater from seeping in, and frequent samples were taken.

Somewhat later rice culture was dovetailed with the culture of indigo. If the former sought the lowlands, the latter, no "marsh crop," grew best in the sandy soils which were back from the rivers. And the rhythm of cultivation in indigo was so different from that of rice that the two could furnish continual employment. The introduction of indigo was the work of a great woman experimenter, Eliza Lucas. Her father, a West Indian governor, acquired plantations near Charleston, and upon them his daughter attempted the cultivation of cotton, ginger, alfalfa, and indigo. In 1743 she succeeded in domesticating indigo; others introduced improvements and refinements; and indigo became almost immediately a staple. So overjoyed was the British government that in 1748 Parliament voted a bounty of sixpence a pound. The production of the dye was a combination of agriculture and manufacturing. Both were ticklish businesses. The plant generally yielded two harvests, one in June or July and the other in August or September. The fields had to be carefully tended, and in cutting and in carrying the leaves great pains had to be taken to prevent the bluish tinge from being rubbed off. The gathered leaves were then placed in vats for fermentation; at the end of twelve hours the dye had soaked out and the water was drawn off into other vats and agitated under paddles; samples were then taken frequently, and at the crucial moment the lime water was poured in to precipitate the brewing. Finally the water was drawn off, the residuum was collected, pressed, dried, and prepared for shipment.

The production of these staples was not confined to South Carolina. They spread across the boundary of North Carolina and extended the "Rice Coast" from the southeastern corner of that colony. In Georgia, where conditions were otherwise favorable, rice and indigo aroused the opposition of the philanthropic trustees, who hoped to grow other exotic products and who insisted upon small holdings and the prohibition of the slave trade. The prosperity of the colony was retarded but not permanently prevented by their policy. Inroads had been made upon their schemes before the charter was surrendered in 1752. After that year Georgia was allowed to develop without their direction, and its coastal region soon imitated that of South Carolina.

The Plantation

Before it was quite clear what their colony could do, the managers of Virginia had tried to run their enterprise as a large estate, producing articles with a labor force of servants. The managers had been absentees. This initiatory enterprise had been a plantation. As a result of inexperience and the assumption of too wide a range of functions and responsibilities, the undertaking had broken down and private plantations had taken its place. The prerequisites for their success were an owner-manager on the grounds, the acquisition of a considerable area of land, and the provision of a labor force. To a varied degree each of these items required the investment of capital.

To distinguish the descendants of families who came to Virginia before the start of tobacco culture from those who came thereafter is probably a task beyond documentation and certainly beyond the abilities or means of any individual, no matter how inspired with genealogical zeal. But it is clear that as time passed and the realization grew that men could not only survive in Virginia but could also acquire wealth there, the stream of immigration quickened and deepened. Younger sons who could not look forward to an inheritance moved to Virginia from the English gentry, from trade and the professions, and from the ranks of servants of the Crown.

Often such younger sons had or could obtain enough money to pay their passage. An indenture could provide for those without means. Meanwhile the earlier servants of the Virginia Company had graduated to freedom and had taken up land and perhaps acquired a small competence. When the first William Byrd, destined to become a great name in Virginia, came to the colony in the second half of the seventeenth century, he was the eldest son of a well-to-do London goldsmith, and he had an uncle in the colony of whom he was fortunately an heir. The acquisition of land was not an expensive process; headrights were as easily come by as the premium covers to soap or cereal boxes in a later generation. Laxness in administration and corruption of officials made it possible to assemble easily a plantation large enough for profitable

production. At the end of the seventeenth century members of the planter
class held on the average at least 5,000 acres. In the colony's total population one in every four families owned from 500 to 20,000 acres. The
remaining families, who owned less than 500 acres apiece, constituted
the farming, or yeoman, class. Of the staple crops, whose cultivation required additional preliminary investment, rice was the most exacting.
Dikes, levees, ditches, and gates were expensive. The great Carolina
plantations along the Ashley and Cooper rivers wore a more stately air
than the farms and plantations, many of the latter only partly cultivated,
along the James and the Potomac.

As for the labor force, the owner of a southern farm and members
of his family provided it. If he wished to enlarge his scale of operations
and get ahead, the farmer bought an indentured servant or two. Through
the first part of the seventeenth century, indentured white servants furnished the work force for farm and plantation. Servants had advantages
because they had mastered to some degree the skills and methods of
European agriculture or industry. The cost of importing a servant in
the seventeenth century was probably £10 to £12. But the employment of servants had disadvantages. Like apprentices everywhere they
were "unruly," and if they skipped the job the master had trouble finding them. Furthermore, their term of service was limited; after seven
years they ceased being employees. In the last quarter of the century,
the plantation colonies on the mainland followed the example of the
Caribbean islands and turned toward Negro slavery.

Specific instances, as in the Carolinas where four of the colonies'
proprietors were also proprietors in the Royal African Company to
which Britain had assigned the trade, helped explain the preference for
Negroes. But there were deeper reasons. It was thought that the Negroes'
experience in Africa or in Barbados or Jamaica, from both of which
islands many were resold, had better fitted them to work in hot and
damp places. The period of "seasoning" was not so great a hazard. This
advantage was debatable. Though ignorant of European agricultural
methods, slaves could soon master the tasks of simple and routine operations in growing American staples. Their term of service was not for
seven years but for life and so was that of their children after colonial
legislation had been altered to sanction such arrangements. Negro women
could work in the fields or in the home. Slaves did not cost quite as
much to maintain as did white servants, although their original price
was higher. At the end of the seventeenth century the price for a newly
imported Negro averaged roughly £20; just before the Revolution the
average was £40 to £50, while prime field hands were £50 to £80.

The large plantation which produced staples for a profit had a
greater appeal to those with money to lend than did operations with
more commonplace methods of production. And credit was necessary for

buying supplies in advance, growing a crop and transporting it overseas, and purchasing a labor force. English merchant houses provided these funds in return for the consignment of the crop by the planter. These credits were for long terms—twelve or eighteen months—and they were often renewed in case the value of the consignment did not meet them. The system of consignment worked well enough in Virginia and Maryland as long as broad navigable rivers enabled the units of the "tobacco fleet" to float up to the very wharves of the plantations for discharge and loading. In the Carolinas, staple trade tended to center in the small ports and in Charleston.

The credit system for its success depended upon a shrewd knowledge of personalities. So while the principals of the mercantile houses resided in Great Britain, they sent out junior partners, frequently relatives, as agents or factors to Virginia. It was said one of the stipulations between the principals of these houses and the young men they sent to Virginia as clerks was they were not to marry there. These clerks came with the prospect of being admitted as partners in some branch of the central establishment, and "it might weaken the sordid attachment to their patrons if they formed an attachment of a purer tenderer nature to the fair daughters of their customers." Like most prohibitions, this was inoperable. In any case a river of credit flowed across the Atlantic to the Caribbean and to the mainland colonies from Georgia to Virginia. Migrants, bent upon establishing a career as merchants, came from England to the colonies. They not only opened shops and counting offices but they established families and became colonials. By the mid-eighteenth century, for instance, Scots, the Chinese merchants of the eighteenth century, had come to Virginia, penetrated inland, and established a structure of commercial relationships which undermined the consignment system. The stores these newcomers established bought tobacco from the planters or farmers with cash or with imported goods and slaves, and in turn secured from their English connections the long credits the trade required.

The Provision Colonies

The inherent geographical and climatic conditions of the colonies were so varied and their acquired social or cultural characteristics so different that agricultural distinctions between them were bound to emerges.

In New England agriculture became at certain times and in certain places a commercial enterprise. But self-sufficiency and a market limited to the locality were its chief characteristics. Nearly every farmhouse had its small garden of vegetables and an orchard of ramshackle fruit trees.

Farmers grew small fields of cereals. Farms were generally stocked with a few cattle, a pair of work oxen, some sheep, and a number of swine. Generally, the domestic animals were expected to live off the land. In the cultivation of crops there was little rotation to preserve the soil's fertility, and few undertook the care and labor of spreading manure over the land in tillage. As John Adams summarized the situation: "You will never get . . . wheat to grow in New-England in quantities to constitute a steady staple, without an expensive cultivation and that expense will never be repaid while wheat, rye, and corn have such a formidable rival in commerce." Before 1700 the cultivation of wheat had moved into the Connecticut valley where there was level land, rich from the decomposition of soft rocks and river deposits. Even in this Eden, the "blast" now known as the black stem rust ravaged the crop as it had in older settled areas. Although it was nearly two hundred years before European scientists described the life of the parasite that caused this destructive scourge and discovered that barberry bushes played the part of an intermediate host, the observation of colonial farmers demonstrated the connection between such bushes and the rust and some towns and states passed legislation for the barberry's destruction. Such preventive measures were inadequate then, and by the time of the Revolution wheat had taken flight to western Massachusetts and Connecticut and to northern Vermont. Corn was left as the mainstay of New England.

By the eighteenth century some regional specialization in livestock production had also developed within New England. Droves of cattle were driven to Boston from Vermont and New Hampshire, and in the Connecticut valley around Springfield, Massachusetts, they were fattened for market. New England, moreover, presented unusual advantages for sheep raising, since the large islands off the coast—Martha's Vineyard, Nantucket—the islands of Narragansett Bay and the Narragansett country afforded protection against the forays of wild animals and dogs. The Narragansett country, indeed, is an exotic in New England history. Situated within the angle formed by the junction of Long Island Sound and Narragansett Bay, it had a climate of unusual mildness for New England. Salt lagoons and marshes piercing the shoreline made it easy to fence in natural reservations. The herbage was suitable for sheep and cattle grazing. Here were large plantations, some of them running into thousands of acres, cultivated by slave labor. Several hundred sheep were often pastured upon one of these plantations, and animals were exported to the herders of other colonies. In general, however, the domestic animals imported into New England from Europe had been poor in quality, and since there was no definite knowledge of breeding in the colonies, nothing stayed the degeneration brought about by colonial conditions. Poor as her livestock types were, New England salted and barreled her pork, made some salty butter, and manufactured some cheese.

The role of New England, however, was not to be agricultural. Like her fur trade, the importance of her agriculture was evanescent. To be sure, in the seventeenth century she became self-sufficing, and throughout the eighteenth century miscellaneous agricultural products were shipped from her ports in the coasting and export trades. But she grew increasingly dependent upon outside sources for her grain supplies. Boston in 1700 was already importing grain from the Connecticut region; by midcentury these supplies were so uncertain that she imported from New York, Philadelphia, and Baltimore; by 1800 even the former grain-growing area in the Connecticut valley was importing its flour.

In the middle colonies the soil was more hospitable to agriculture than in New England. The coastal plain, with a sandy soil which could be cultivated for grass and grain crops only with a knowledge of modern agricultural methods, was of importance in New Jersey and nowhere else. As late as the Revolution a large area in the southeastern part of that colony was still uninhabited. But the Piedmont, running through the northwestern part of the colony and broadening into a wider area in Pennsylvania, had clay soils which were generally of good fertility. Then there were the central valleys of New York and Pennsylvania. In the former colony the Mohawk and in the latter the broad diagonal of the Great Valley had layers of underlying limestone whose decomposition had formed some of the richest agricultural land in the country.

The same crops, with the trifling exception of some tobacco grown in Pennsylvania, were raised in the middle colonies as in New England. But not in the same proportions. Wheat usurped the place occupied by Indian corn. From the first wheat was successfully acclimatized. Before 1645 the Dutch settlers had raised it on a commercial scale in New Netherland, and in Pennsylvania it was at once at home. As the country developed, the area sown to wheat increased, for the soil was suited to it and pests were not destructive. The latter, too, were combated by the use of winter wheat, which was sown in August and was strong enough in the following year to resist the blast. Long Island and the fertile limestone areas of the Mohawk valley were the producing areas in New York; New Jersey was an important producing state by 1750; and in Pennsylvania it had become before the Revolution "the grand article" of production. The middle colonies were the granary of North and South.

The condition of animal husbandry resembled that in the New England colonies. Stock raising was a frontier occupation. By the eighteenth century western Pennsylvania and the uplands of Virginia and North Carolina had developed the western cattle business of the colonial days. Ranchers of these regions built up herds of more than 1,000 head and pastured them on the open range of the western regions. These were the predecessors of the cattle barons and cowboys of the Great Plains. Select animals cut out from their herds were driven northward through the

Great Valley. New animals were added from place to place. Finally the droves were driven down to Philadelphia to join others which had come from New York and from the country near at hand. Often the cattle after their long drive were turned over to be fattened by farmers near Philadelphia or its satellite towns.

In general, agricultural methods in the middle colonies were more advanced than in the Puritan colonies of New England. In the growing of grains they followed a more careful tillage, clearing the soil more thoroughly of sticks and roots, and plowing it more carefully. The natural meadows for growing grass were on occasion carefully irrigated by turning aside a stream and letting its waters penetrate the soil. And greater use was made of fertilizers. By 1750 animal manuring had been supplemented by experiments with amendments, such as lime and gypsum, which restored essential elements to the soil. In 1730 the interest of public men and agricultural amateurs led to the establishment in Philadelphia of a botanical garden. John Bartram, Quaker botanist, was its directing genius. Bartram also established a farm on which he tried out advanced methods. He had both drained and irrigated meadows; he used red clover in rotations; he spread his fields with mud, lime, ashes, manure; he raised heavy crops per acre; and his cows, "deep-bellied, short-legged, having udders ready to burst," were a sharp contrast to the wiry animals so commonly seen elsewhere.

The general superiority of the middle colonies as an agricultural region was due to many factors. Their endowment of soil and climate fitted them for agriculture. The fairly densely settled regions around Philadelphia, Baltimore, and New York increased the value of land and provided markets. A somewhat more careful agriculture was made profitable in these restricted districts. A final reason for their agricultural supremacy was their settlement by races whose agricultural practices were more advanced and deep-rooted than those of the English. In this classification fall the Dutch settlers of New Netherland. At the time they migrated from Holland, their native country was pursuing an intensive agriculture, features of which were later to be embodied in that remarkable transformation known as the English agricultural revolution. In the New World the Dutch introduced superior grades of livestock, and their tillage methods were more thorough and careful than those of the English.

In Pennsylvania the German immigration was decisive. Conservative, they refused to abandon their traditional European practices in favor of the expediencies of frontier agriculture. Searching out the limestone areas and the heavily wooded regions which seemed to promise fertility, they undertook a permanent rather than a transitory agriculture. Instead of girdling the trees, as did the Scotch-Irish and English, they felled them and then grubbed out the roots and bushes. Their care of animals was equally prudent and skillful. The cattle were housed in the winter because it kept them sleek and they required less food than when exposed to the rigors of the outdoors. And they developed a famous breed of colonial horses, the Conestoga, named from a small creek in Lancaster County. These animals were draft horses, and several pair hauled to market the Conestoga wagon, the predecessor of the prairie schooner. From the pioneer log cabin the German farmer graduated to a substantial stone farmhouse. Nearby was the two-story Swisser barn, with the animals' stalls on the first floor. Teams could be driven into the second floor, since the barn was generally built near a slope or bank for that purpose. The second floor served for threshing, and the hay and other grasses were stowed in great mows at the side of the room. A roof "having deep sides or pitch" gave the necessary height to the second story. These solid structures became a characteristic feature of the Pennsylvania landscape.

Northern agriculture did not generally require the employment of a large disciplined labor force. In New England the farmer and his sons were adequate for the majority of the seasonal tasks, and when there was a job beyond the family's capacity—the raising of a house or a barn—the neighbors turned to and made it a community enterprise. In the middle colonies the Germans did not hesitate to utilize their women in the fields —a vestige of European peasantry which struck New England observers as strange and of doubtful propriety. Under a regime of self-sufficing farming such measures were adequate. However, when commercial agriculture or specialization began, an additional hand or two was often required. To employ labor meant to pay high wages because of labor scarcity. These necessities—or opportunities—encouraged some form of bonded labor.

The immigration of indentured servants into New England was always small and after 1645 it was negligible. In the northern colonies Pennsylvania was the indentured servants' most important destination. Indeed, from 1750 to 1775 the number of indentured servants and redemptioners coming thither was at least twice that to Maryland or Virginia. Nearly two-thirds were from Ireland; somewhat less than a third were Germans. Some arrived already indentured; others, who arrived without papers, were generally indentured according to the custom of the country. Details of this contract were carefully regulated by legislation. The servant guaranteed to furnish industrious labor and to avoid the vices which might interfere with the proper discharge of his duties. The master on his side promised fair treatment, food and lodging, and, on the completion of the indenture period, certain rewards. Pennsylvania legislation of 1700 declared that each servant on discharge was entitled to "two compleat suits of apparel," one new ax, one "Grubing Hoe" and one "Weeding Hoe." At the same time, under the regulations of Penn, he was entitled to fifty acres of land. The Pennsylvania servant was thus able to start out as a freeman under excellent conditions. In fact, there were immigrants with sufficient means for an independent estate who indentured themselves in order to learn the methods of the new country.

Negro slavery was not of importance in the northern colonies. This contrast to the South must not be ascribed to the superiority of northern principles. The Puritans of New England owned slaves, and even Roger Williams, whose liberality and broad-mindedness irritated authorities in Massachusetts and elsewhere, saw no objection to the traffic in Indian slaves. In Pennsylvania and the affected portions of New Jersey, Quaker principles tended to be hostile to the idea of enslavement, but William Penn, the founder, was apparently not influenced by those scruples. He owned slaves. Principles aside, nothern conditions did not operate against the limited application of Negro slavery. The Narragansett country had a slave population of Indians and Negroes which varied at times from a third to a half of the free white population; and in New York, the northern colony with the largest slave population, nearly one out of every nine inhabitants was a Negro. In Narragansett the proximity of Newport, the American center of the slave trade, was the explanation. The slave ships brought back and sold the Negroes whom they could not dispose of in the more exacting southern markets. In the case of New York slavery was an urban phenomenon as much as an agricultural one.

Skill and Power

In the colonies beginning industry or manufacturing faced many handicaps: a lack of wealth for investment; a shortage of trained workers, poor transportation, and the consequent limitation of the market. The first occupational adjustment had been made in agriculture. Until staples and transport and commercial relationships developed, agriculture was self-sufficing. So, in a sense, was manufacturing. An observer just after the Revolution wrote of the "union of manufactures and farming." In this union a household industry made goods for its own consumption and in its spare moments for a localized or neighborhood market. First, the farm manufactured food products. The head of the family slaughtered his own cattle and hogs and pickled his pork. Beef, hams, fish, and eels were cured in the smokehouse. Grain was made into meal at home. If the corn was soft, it was laboriously put through a grater, and if it had hardened, it was churned into meal by the hominy block, a pit burned in the large block of wood into which a large pestle, often suspended from a bending sapling, was pounded.

Besides meat, the slaughtered livestock provided fats and hides. The former, along with the wax of bayberries, was made into candles, which were dipped repeatedly into the hot tallow and then hung up to cool. These crude dip candles required little apparatus. A candle mold turned out a better product. The skins of domestic and wild animals were cleaned of their hair by a solution of lye ashes burned from the farmer's own trees, tanned in a brew made from the bark of the farmer's own hemlocks or oaks, and greased into pliability by the farmer's own hands. The family then made this leather into clothing and rough shoes or moccasins. The only instrument needed was an awl to punch the holes through which the leather thread or thongs were carried.

The textiles made by the family for its own use were of the coarser sort. The fibers came from various sources. The colonial sheep industry by the time of the Revolution supplied an adequate quantity of inferior wool. Small flax patches furnished the linen fibers, and imports of cotton from the West Indies supplied this "vegetable wool." These various fibers were made into plain yarns and woven either into plain cloths or into mixed goods whose names, if not use, have come down as a traditional inheritance. Linsey-woolsey was a combination of flax and wool popular in the northern colonies and on the western frontier. Jean, of cotton and wool, was a pioneer cloth. Fustian, a blend of cotton and flax, predominated in the south. Or, if sex distinctions are more important than geographical ones, linsey-woolsey entered the clothes of women and girls, while jean was masculine.

Of the preparatory processes in textile manufacturing, that of flax was easily the most burdensome. After the stalks had been rotted in the fields, the woody portion surrounding the fibers was mashed by a flax brake, a modified flail, and then finally removed with the swingling knife. Both operations were so laborious that they were performed by the men or boys. Then the matted fibers were handed to the women, who combed them with the hatchel, a wicked-looking instrument bristling with rows of spikes. The preparation of wool was somewhat less laborious. After a thorough washing, the tufts of wool were drawn over a card, a block studded with wire teeth, and then a second card was passed over the first to straighten out the fibers. Sometimes a combing process intervened before spinning.

Although the size of the spinning wheel varied for flax and woolen and for the nature of the yarn to be produced, the operation was identical in all cases. Upon a horizontal spindle, kept in rapid rotation by a cord or band from the large wheel, the fiber was fed from the hand of the spinner, the hand continually advancing and retreating to pull out and twist the fibers and give them some tensile strength. In its essence weaving is a simple process which the modern child learns in the kindergarten rather than in the home. At the end of a handloom upon which threads of stout yarn had been set up as the warp, the long way of the cloth, stood the weaver. Bending over, he cast from one side to the other between the parallel strands of the warp a shuttle which carried the threads of the woof (the modern term "filler" is an excellent definition), and then shoved these threads firmly into the warp with his hands. The upper threads of the warp were then changed to the lower position and the process was repeated.

The finishing of the cloth put requisitions upon strength, skill, and care. Linen had to be bleached to bring it to the required degree of whiteness; sometimes thirty or forty bleachings were necessary. Woolens were fulled and dyed. By the former process the loose and irregular product of the handloom was given an even and firmer texture by shrinking in warm water, in which soap of fuller's earth was dissolved, and by pounding with sticks or mallets. Dyeing, before the days of synthetic products, utilized colors from barks and plants, berries and nuts. These native dyes were often displaced by more exotic stuffs, of which the greatest was indigo, the blue dye. Purchased from the local store or an indigo peddler, it was mixed with urine and poured into the dye pot, which occupied a favored place by the kitchen fire. In the use of indigo domestic dyers became most expert. Applied to checks and stripes, it was woven into shirts, spreads, aprons, bedticks, and other patterns which became conventionally blue and white.

The household could manufacture its food and its textiles. The abundant forests furnished material which the family could shape to its other needs by the use of a few tools and the exercise of moderate strength and dexterity. The crude homemade furniture of the log cabin—tables and stools and beds—has become traditional through the repetition of the Lincoln story. Rakes and other farm tools, platters, bowls, and trenchers, a whole array of "dish furniture," was burnt or whittled from wood. Brooms, buckets, and baskets were manufactured at the fireside. Fortunately it was a wooden age. The working of that material was a less stubborn and skillful task than the manipulation of the metals. Even there the household was occasionally competent.

With the increase of settlement and the improvement of the means of communication, the processes of production which required more specialized skill or the use of simple machinery were transferred to other agencies. First came the artisans who had mastered some particular craft or calling. Often these men were itinerants. A wandering life avoided responsibilities; a young journeyman might thus seek an attractive village in which to locate; but most important of all, it was simpler in a region of dispersed homesteads to carry the skill to the product than to transport the product to the skill. The chandler arrived with his nests of candle molds; the wandering butcher came to slaughter the cattle as effectually as the wandering woodcutter the forest. Itinerant tailors brought to the making of suits a greater degree of fit and finish than the housewife. Of particular importance were the cobbler and the weaver.

Shoemaking and weaving were both tasks which required great skill, and the transition to artisan labor in these occupations was hastened by their difficulty. Whatever his occupation, the visit of a wandering artisan broke the monotony of household life and brought to its hearth a load of gossip and a touch of the outside world.

Certain processes of manufacture required trained skill as well as heavy labor. To grind grain and saw boards was hard work. Sawmills and gristmills appeared in the farming regions almost contemporaneously with their settlement. The simplicity of such mill apparatus assisted this extraordinary mobility. Since the rotary saw had not been invented, the sawmill utilized the long sash saw of the hand sawyers. Instead of two men, one in a pit below the log to pull down and another standing above it to pull up, a waterwheel was substituted for the one and a pole for the other. Such a saw was extremely ineffective. Often it could not plow through thick trees, and hardwoods presented such a problem that resort frequently had to be made to pit sawing. Still, such mills with a labor force of two could turn out 1,000 feet of pine lumber a day and do the work of twenty hand sawyers. Perchance the sawmill or its workers could manufacture the staves, headings, and hoops that were put together in barrels or hogsheads in which everything from whale oil to tobacco was marketed. The gristmill was on the same small scale. Its series of stones, at first imported from England, might turn out ten to twenty barrels of flour a week. Both sawing and milling were sometimes combined in one establishment and usually one or the other added fulling by waterpower. This laborious task adapted itself nicely to the simple arrangement of hammers driven from a waterwheel.

The small colonial mills were housed in a structure which cost little more than the owner's dwelling. They were erected usually on the smaller streams, since the construction of large dams was an engineering and financial burden not to be lightly assumed. Sometimes an undershot waterwheel was simply placed in the flow of a stream. A labor force of two or three men, or of a father and son, could perform any of the tasks of such establishments. Over these old mills hangs the leisurely air of another day. If the stream went dry in summer or froze in winter the mill owners ceased operations and cultivated their corn or sat by the fire of the country store. For them manufacturing was incidental to farming or storekeeping. For their customers, taking grain to the mill or hauling in a few logs was a social occurrence long to be anticipated. Into the contented neighborliness of such an arrangement it is a pity that government had to intrude. But since waterpower was generally esteemed a public property disposed upon private individuals, the right of regulation was not questioned. Sawmills and gristmills both charged tolls for their services (generally a proportion of the grain ground in the case of gristmills), and these were fixed by the state.

The primary iron industry which smelted and shaped the iron ore for the use of reproductive manufacturers was sometimes organized in a fashion similar to the gristmills and sawmills. The iron ore was handled by a bloomery, in which an open fire, driven by a bellows, melted the ore together with the charcoal fuel, which absorbed the oxygen elements in the ore. Then a hammer, powered by a waterwheel, worked the resulting "bloom" into a bar in which the metal was cleansed of carbon and other impurities. This wrought iron from a bloomery forge furnished a satisfactory metal for the tools and equipment required by a farming community. Such small-scale establishments were widely dispersed because they fed upon the iron ores easily available in the ponds and swamps of the coastal plain in Massachusetts, Long Island, and New Jersey. From the abundant forests the iron masters obtained the charcoal fuel essential for their operation.

In the manufacturing arts during the colonial centuries—in Europe as well as in America—production depended not only upon the brawn of the worker but upon his knowledge of and skill in a particular craft. Such artisans were a numerous element in the stream of migrants across the Atlantic. As the tumultuous and unsettling adjustments to conditions in the New World eased by the end of the seventeenth century, these arrivals no longer found it necessary to turn at once to farming or turn into itinerants. The growth of cities, the multiplication of towns, and some expansion and improvement of communication and transport, gave a market which the craftsmen could serve by settling down. As always the variety of tastes, associated with the appearance of social classes and status, aided the specialization of crafts. In 1697 Philadelphia had fifty-one manufacturing handicrafts and on the eve of the Revolution between a third and a half of its gainfully employed people were artisans. Some, such as wigmakers, catered to the fripperies and follies of fashion; others were fundamentalists, making clothes and shoes or kitchenware. Most of these shops worked on a dual basis. Their customers might bring their own material to be manufactured into finished articles; or they might order an article made from the supplies which the craftsman had obtained by purchase or exchange. In either case, the product was "bespoke work." When the artisan and his apprentices were not busy on an order the shop might turn to manufacturing "store goods" to be sold or exchanged for raw materials, peddled about the vicinity, or marketed in intercolonial trade.

Often through chance, and sometimes by plan, colonial communities specialized in artisan production of certain commodities. The fur trade furnished the raw material for the manufacture of beaver hats, and hatters congregated in New York, Charleston, Philadelphia, and lesser centers. In 1732 Parliament was informed that Massachusetts and New York made 10,000 hats annually. In 1750 a Welsh cordwainer arrived in

Lynn, Massachusetts. He began making high-quality women's shoes which "exceed those usually imported, in strength and beauty, *but not* in price." His output in 1767 was estimated at 80,000 pairs. In Germantown, near Philadelphia, shops on a long two-mile street specialized in making stockings. Their estimated output in 1768 was 6,000 dozen pairs.

Artisan-made furniture underwent a similar development. Bars, taverns, and public buildings required simple, sturdy, and inexpensive chairs. Boston for a time supplied them but by the mid-eighteenth century, Philadelphia was shipping Windsor chairs in an intercolonial traffic. The colonials lit their way with lamps or candles. They first used whale oil, itself a product tried out in one of the colonial boiling industries; a superior candle was made from a pasty substance found in the head of the sperm whale. By the middle of the eighteenth century, artisans and merchants had domiciled spermaceti candle factories in Boston, Philadelphia, and in Newport and Providence, Rhode Island. In the last city the leading merchants, the Browns, tried to bring about an agreement to fix prices for the raw material and, less frequently, for the finished product.

The new conditions which enabled artisans and their allies to organize and extend their production had an impact upon the mill industries. Along the coast from New England to Virginia, where streams or their estuaries furnished a water power to put machinery in motion and a mooring where sailing vessels could be loaded, and where there was a hinterland in which grains were cultivated, merchant mills appeared to grind grain. Their owners didn't do "bespoke" grinding for a statutory toll; they bought the grain, ground and stored it, and then shipped it to relatively distant markets. At Philadelphia, and at Wilmington, Delaware, this development was most impressively demonstrated. Both cities had access to wheat fields and water transportation; and two tiny streams, the Wissahickon of Philadelphia and the Brandywine of Wilmington, furnished power for scores of gristmills. At the end of the Revolution these mills as well as those at Baltimore were transformed by the inventions of Oliver Evans. It was in 1782 that he conceived "the great design of applying the power that drives the millstones to perform all the operations which were hitherto effected by manual labour, viz.—from receiving the grain from the wagon or ship until manufactured into superfine flour, ready to be packed into barrels." By exceedingly ingenious mechanical contrivances the grain was carried to the top of the mill and on its first descent was cleaned and ground. Then it was again raised by a series of elevators on its second descent, cooled, sifted, and barreled.

Luckily along the Atlantic coast lumber, as well as power sites, lay at the edge of navigable waters. As in the case of grain, sawmills appeared at commercially strategic posts from the Cape Fear River in North Carolina to the counties in Maine adjacent to New Hampshire. Indeed between Maine and New Hampshire lay the remarkable estuary of the Piscataqua River. Into a saltwater anchorage, twenty or so miles long, poured an army of little streams with waterpower; at every hand lay an impressive forest of oak and white pine. In 1705 there were seventy Piscataqua sawmills; by midcentury these and other mills had dumped enough sawdust from "the pine which is believed to be very ungrateful to the Fish when Mixed with the Water," to ruin the salmon industry. Along the Piscataqua the mills fashioned their boards and planks into rafts which were floated downriver for loading onto larger vessels. On the Merrimack, whose lower reaches in Massachusetts were not navigable, those who made staves and shingles fastened them in bundles and tossed them into the stream. When they reached Newburyport, they were "pickt out again by people that attend on purpose about the town and delivered to the Owners thereof"—a sort of honor system of transportation and delivery. The technical level of these commercial sawmills can only be inferred. It is safe to say it was more advanced than in merely local establishments busy on "cheap and light work," equipped with one saw, and run by a labor force of a man and a boy.

Obviously the colonies had a great superiority over England in the building of ships. The use of wood over the years, including charcoal in the metal trades, was depleting English forests, while American forests were untouched. The crafts required were not too exacting. Fishermen, acquainted with a ship and its parts, could and did turn to their construction, and a carpenter who could build a house supposedly could build a vessel. The adventurers who financed the fishing stations and the plantations along the New England coast usually sent over shipwrights to give instruction in shipbuilding. These enterprises usually turned first to the construction of small undecked sailing vessels for the fisheries or for short journeys along rivers or near the shore. Later the shipyards turned out decked vessels with a larger tonnage, capable of overseas commerce with Europe and the islands of the Caribbean. By 1760 the different colonies were building from three hundred to four hundred vessels a year, exclusive of fishing boats. There were shipyards in Charleston, Baltimore, Philadelphia, and along the Delaware. From New York City through New England their number thickened. No place seemed too tiny to build ships. Scituate, a small town on a small river south of Boston, became practically a shipbuilding annex to the latter city. Ships were built north of Boston at Salem, Cape Ann, and along the Merrimack river. The Piscataqua, however, was the thriving center of this enterprise. One Portsmouth builder, a certain Captain Boyd, had seven ships on the stocks at once and was so driven building ten ships a year that "For forty days I have been out of bed so early that I did not know which was the right side to my Breeches or Stockings. I scarce have time to eat or sleep." In 1769 the Piscataqua district produced one-third as many vessels as all Massachusetts. Shipbuilding brought in its train the growing of hemp and the building of ropewalks, the production of tar and pitch, and the manufacture of duck and ironware. Since many of these American-built ships were sold overseas, a West Indian observer could write of Boston in 1750 with something of a sneer: "I do not see Any thing they can call a Staple among them save Ship Building and Something of the fishing trade."

Probably the largest industrial establishments in the colonies were ironworks. In technology and business organization the commercial ironworks moved away from a simple bloomery and forge and from a partnership of artisans. In the mid-seventeenth century certain leaders of the Massachusetts Bay Colony determined to use the deposits of iron ore in the colony to supply an iron-refining establishment. They secured the incorporation of the "Company of Undertakers for the Iron Works," collected £1,000 from "eleven English Gentlemen," and enlisted some skilled workers from abroad. After vicissitudes those in charge chose to locate their works near the deposits of iron ore in certain low-lying meadows and swamps along the Saugus, a stream north of Boston. The place had woods for charcoal and a stream for waterpower and navigation. The Saugus or Hammersmith works smelted the ore in a furnace in which a water-driven bellows blew a blast through the furnace's charge. When the molten mass was tapped, the iron, cleansed of its oxides, ran into molds which shaped hollow and cast ware—pots, skillets, kettles, and the like—or into trenches where it cooled into a sow and pigs. The brittleness of the product made little difference in castware, but pig iron required further manipulation at a forge to make a wrought iron strong enough for other uses. There were repeated heatings, stirrings, and hammerings before the bar iron was fit to be shipped out and sold to blacksmiths who shaped it into tools and other equipment. Hammersmith also had a rolling and slitting mill which took bar, flattened it through rollers into plate and slit it into rods, which farmers or artisans cut into nails required by America's wooden buildings. The Saugus establishment produced a wrought iron by the "indirect process" as contrasted to the "direct process" of the bloomery.

Throughout the seventeenth century Massachusetts was the chief iron producer of the colonies. In the next century the industry moved to New Jersey, Maryland, Virginia, and Pennsylvania. In general these establishments used ores harder than the bog ores which lay in or near the surface of the earth and which mining simply scooped up. A term often attached to these new operations was "iron plantation." In addition to the ironworks, these plantations included a sawmill and a gristmill, an ironmaster's store, cottages for the workers, a manor house for the ironmasters, thousands of acres of woodland to provide charcoal, and

smaller areas for growing supplies for the workers. One of these plantations was that of Peter Hasenclever, a Prussian immigrant to Great
Britain where he became naturalized and established a mercantile firm
in London and organized the "American Iron Company." He purchased
more than 50,000 acres of land, built furnaces, forges, and subsidiary
equipment in northern New Jersey, and transported 535 workers and
their families from Germany and England. One of the most large-scale
industrial enterprises in the American colonies, Hasenclever's business
went bankrupt. Despite this particular failure, the manufacture of iron
in America, early dreamed of in Virginia, constituted in 1775 nearly a
seventh of world production.

Governmental direction and control of the processes of production
and distribution were unquestioned and embraced as many aspects as
the colonies could legally exercise power over. Sometimes the sheer necessity of survival justified these decisions and actions. But as soon as the
art of colonization could be taken for granted, promotional motives predominated. Here and there, land grants were conditioned upon the
grantees "settling" population upon them; "proprietors" of towns were
directed to establish grist and saw mills. The state voted bounties on the
production of linen, woolen, and cotton cloth; prohibited the export of
certain products or aided that of others by arranging for their inspection,
as with tobacco and wheat, or by establishing standards of quality or
determining the proper size of containers. Few facts of economic life
escaped governmental attention.

As for labor, legislation regulated the terms of indenture, granted
exemptions from certain civic duties—for instance, service in the militia
—to the practitioners of certain crafts, and at least in one instance specified the ratio of slaves to indentured servants in an employer's labor
force. In the case of the Saugus Ironworks, the Massachusetts General
Court gave it a land grant and the right to take ore and charcoal from
public lands; and finally granted it a monopoly of twenty-one years on
the manufacture of iron and an exclusive right to all iron mines, discovered or undiscovered, within the limits of the colony. The enterprisers had to meet a deadline in production and could not sell their
iron for more than £20 a ton, a very generous price. The historian of
the concern concludes, "It is doubtful if any single private enterprise in
New England, in the whole colonial period, was so well favored by the
government."

As is usually the case, the government relied upon education, either
in its public welfare or anti-poverty aspects, to initiate and develop industry. About the middle of the eighteenth century, individuals with
philanthropic or profit-seeking motives established societies to encourage
manufacturing. These societies were located in the eastern seaport cities
and they had some of the aspects of a manufacturing corporation, for

example, subscribers had limited liability for the debts of the enterprise, and they elected their directors. In Boston the "Society for Encouraging Industry and Employing the Poor" built a "Manufacturing House" and leased it to various tenants. One tenant opened a spinning school with nearly four hundred spinning wheels, worked by women and children; he sold the yarn or had it woven on the premises by handlooms. With the advent of the Revolution and in the years of adjustment thereafter, Americans widely copied these innovations, which prefigured the textile corporation and factory developments of a later day.

Trade, Traders, and the Laws

The age of discovery had demonstrated that man could use space to conquer space; navigators, equipped with astrolabe and sextant, determined their longitude and latitude by drawing a line upon the stars and calculating their own position. Gradually the accumulation of voyages and the studies of thoughtful men introduced a new age of cartography. Voyages across the Atlantic still took time and abounded with dangers. The safe transport of settlers to the New World, however, continued; and the products they found or produced were staples wanted by a market in the homeland. A main concern of imperial maritime policy was the facilitation and protection of this commerce.

Intercolonial Commerce

Meanwhile, the same sea connected the colonies with each other. The advantages it furnished for the carriage of goods were unevenly distributed. The islands of the Caribbean—after 1650 the "Sugar Islands"—had usable ports and were near the mainland. The southern colonies from Virginia to Georgia had long lazy rivers winding inland, and every large plantation had its wharf, where vessels from England tied up to receive their cargoes. Where these rivers were lacking or too shallow, cities like Charleston, South Carolina, or Norfolk, Virginia, served as entrepôts for the exchange of goods. While the rivers north of the "Tobacco Coast" often appeared magnificent, for instance, the Susquehanna or the Connecticut, they were, with the exception of the Hudson, not navigable very far inland except by rafts or at times of high water. The transport of goods inland consequently had to take to the land. On very few products could producers or forwarders afford to pay the excessive charges which such journeys involved. Such handicaps were peculiarly severe in frontier regions of dispersed settlement and long distances. To cover the costs of transportation the Philadelphia fur traders, for instance, added 20 to 30 percent to the prices of the goods which they shipped over the mountains. Even when roads were cut through to the Ohio during the French and Indian wars, and the dispatch of pack trains from the East to Pittsburgh became a considerable business, only a few goods could be carried profitably. Iron products and salt were shipped westward; furs and whisky, valuable articles of small bulk, were brought back on the return journey.

Nearer the coast the situation altered. Here there was a relative density of population. Boston, Newport, Providence, New York, Philadelphia, Charleston, and Baltimore furnished considerable markets and impressed observers with their settled air. Around Boston there grew a considerable land transportation, particularly in the winter when the snow remedied and concealed the deficiencies of the highways. But water transportation remained cheaper. In shipping wheat from the Connecticut valley to Boston, for instance, it cost a shilling to cart a bushel from Northampton, Massachusetts, to Windsor, Connecticut; from Windsor the rate by the river to Hartford was only twopence, and by river and sea from Hartford sixpence more. Thus the total freight from the farm was 1s. 8d., of which far the larger part was for the short land cartage.

In the middle colonies New York had the Hudson. By 1770 well over a hundred vessels were engaged in the trade between Albany and New York. The latter city stood also at the northern end of a regular wagon traffic started in 1732 with Philadelphia, the only land barrier being the narrow one across Jersey between the Delaware and the Raritan. Around Philadelphia improved highways made possible the transportation of grain for some fifty or sixty miles, and the Conestoga wagon, rounded at the bottom to prevent the contents from shifting, covered with a linen top, and crammed with a diverse cargo, drove down to the urban market. Philadelphia combined the trade following the Delaware and that following the Schuylkill and drew overland by transshipment a part of the Susquehanna traffic which flowed down to Baltimore. Between all these port cities there developed a very considerable coastal trade. At Boston, New York, and Philadelphia coastal commerce by 1768-1772, judged by entrances and clearances, surpassed commerce to Great Britain. The American shipbuilding industry provided the small vessels, particularly the sloop, which the navigation of narrow or shallow waters required, and the taking of small risks made prudent.

Traders and Their Troubles

Transportation was not enough. Trade demanded as well the presence of institutions and individuals whose function was to collect and pay for the product and arrange for its carriage and final distribution among actual sellers in a market. These middlemen, it was commonly believed, performed no function. The history of the colonies demonstrates the fallacy of this assumption. Only when a chain of communication, confidence, command, and credit had been forged between producer and ultimate consumer was the interchange of colonial products possible. The history and qualities of that connection varied with geography and commodity.

Almost from the beginning of the tobacco trade the impulse for development came from abroad. An English merchant, generally from London, sent his vessels to the James or the Potomac to purchase the new crop. The ship took along a supply of manufactured and other articles needed in these agricultural colonies. As the system became better established, the planter consigned his crop to the merchant who marketed it overseas for a commission, generally 2.25 percent of the sale price. These returns the consignment merchant placed on his books and drew down as he made purchases and shipments on the planter's order. Since planters were generally optimistic, they customarily overestimated the market value of their crops and fell into the habit, in spite of resolute intentions, of going into debt to their merchant consignees. Such debts accumulated over the years and were sometimes bequeathed to descendants. As this arrangement suggests, a planter-merchant relationship might endure over several generations. If the planter were free to exercise options, he might shop around among consignment merchants. In any case, credit advanced by merchants abroad kept the system going.

In the eighteenth century a new way of marketing tobacco somewhat altered these traditional patterns. The overseas merchant saw the advantages of having a resident representative in the colonies. He usually sent out a younger member of his family or at least some promising youngster of his own social class, or group. These "factors," as they were called, were tied by kinship or status to their employers, and this identity of interest seemed to guarantee their honesty, responsibility, and competitive hustle. Factors could assemble a crop before the arrival of the tobacco fleet, and thus lessen the turn-around costs of shipping. They also ran a store, or "factory," where they sold plantation supplies. They could appraise the worth and energy of individual planters and press for the payment of slow debts. The factors assembled the tobacco at their store and wharf and purchased the crop for cash or for a running credit at their store.

Many Americans who owned large plantations along navigable rivers performed the same functions as the factor in much the same way. The Byrds, Carters, Carrolls, and Washingtons thus became merchant planters. Eventually the collected cargoes shipped by consignment or other methods were sent to English merchants. There as the eighteenth century wore on, the tobacco trade began shifting from London to the "outports," of which Glasgow was the most important. In 1707 the Act of Union between England and Scotland had struck away the legal disabilities upon Scottish trade; and the banks and scarlet-cloaked "Virginia dons" of Glasgow took advantage of the opportunity. Since the staples in the other mainland plantation colonies, indigo and rice, for instance, were marketed through a port, a merchant class developed there in a slightly different way.

Merchants and shopkeepers of varied degree had been an element in the great migration to Massachusetts and New England in the thirties. Many of them had liquidated considerable estates before their departure, and they were consequently provided with some capital to finance commerce until the region discovered staples of its own to even the balance. It was a tight squeeze, but it succeeded.

Apparently the colonies were capable of generating and training their own merchant class. Roughly by the end of the seventeenth century a roll call of Philadelphia Quaker merchants disclosed that the wealthiest and most powerful did not come directly from England but from other English colonies in the Caribbean or on the mainland. In Boston, for instance, Thomas Hancock started his business career as an apprentice to a bookseller and built the House of Hancock, more famous for his successor and son, John Hancock; and in the Providence plantations, the Browns widened a family trading enterprise until four brothers about midcentury constituted a powerful mercantile quartet with interests in manufacturing as well as in trade. The fact that the colonies could produce their own merchant class did not mean they were cut off from the British mercantile community. As late as the Revolution many businesses were in reality Anglo-American family concerns. London merchants sent their brothers or other relatives to America and Americans themselves moved to London to enter or continue along the paths of commerce.

The functions of the merchants gave them a sense of craft identity; they became a pivotal group in the colonies and in imperial relationships. If they shipped in the coasting trade, they had correspondents or agents in the ports to which they specialized in trading; in foreign trade they had associates at London or the English outports, such as Bristol. In America they sought friendly relations with the English governors and the bureaucracy of colonial administrators. These could award government contracts, for example, to supply troops, and could tip the balance for other favors. In London the merchants sought to influence and advise ministers and Parliament. But for all their importance and success, the merchants faced deep difficulties.

The severest was a lack of money or coin. Complaints about currency were often no doubt a catchall excuse for incompetence, but there was a genuine need for a medium of exchange or standard of value bearing some relation in its amount to the extent of business in the community. The English colonies had no mines of the precious metals and to obtain gold and silver through trade was so time-consuming that development loitered and meanwhile demanded a regime of sacrifices. A community blessed with resources and promises of plenty could not look with composure upon this situation. As a consequence the colonies reverted to arrangements described even today in rural areas as "swapping time" or "swapping goods." Although these transactions were clothed on the books in a money terminology, goods or labor were exchanged not for coin, but for each other.

At the simplest level the shopkeeper credited his customers with the products—cider, eggs, cheese, yarn, flax, and the like—that they brought in and deducted from these products' value the goods which he sold them. College bills were paid with a variety of articles, and one Harvard student in the seventeenth century discharged his academic obligations with an old cow. This swapping system was early modified by the use of articles other than gold or silver as media of exchange. Indian wampum (highly polished beads, manufactured from shells and then strung together) served as currency. Where a widely cultivated staple existed with an assured market, the commodity itself was made currency. Thus the Carolinas used tar and rice; and in eighteenth-century Virginia the certificates of deposit issued by warehouses where tobacco had been appraised and stored formed the currency. One serious difficulty with these book-barter currencies was that the market value of commodities fluctuated in spite of statutes, and the currency therefore lacked stability. Another difficulty arose, of course, because these currencies were not of universal jurisdiction. Massachusetts had different values for tobacco than Virginia, and foreign nations preferred the metals which were "precious" because of their inherent value.

In the absence of cash, commerce was based, as far as feasible, upon long credits. At one end of the credit chain the English merchant exporting manufactures to the colonies expected a credit of ninety days from the manufacturers. To his American purchaser the English supplier extended a year's credit. This seemed a customary period, but exceptions altered cases. Hard times forced Thomas Hancock to ask a longer credit, since he in turn was "obliged to Give one two & more years Credit for the best Goods wee Sell to our Country Chaps." Clearly those who bought at retail with "country pay" not only expected to pay in barter but demanded a long time to settle. No matter how long the shopkeeper proved willing to "carry" his customers, there always came a "payday." Often it seemed as if at every step along the credit chain, there was a continuous conspiracy to postpone settlements and keep the ball of credit rolling. Perhaps this was least true in England for there the merchant was advised "to have some estate, stock, or portion of his own, sufficient to enable him to carry on the traffic he is engaged in." This capital "wise traders" should not jeopardize in a single transaction of buying and selling for credit. Accidents and disappointments were particularly apt to happen to "young beginners, whose chiefest, or perhaps, only stock might be the opinion of their capacity, industry, and honesty." Whatever the ultimate security, English credits and English financial institutions, merchants and bankers, were the chief support of colonial commerce.

Meanwhile in a less developed America, trade brought in a small supply of metallic currency, which came chiefly from the Spanish and Portuguese colonies; the Spanish dollar and its "bits" were the most important coins. The equivalent of the Spanish dollar in English money varied from place to place. In 1704 Newton assayed it at the English mint as worth 4s. 6d. So avid were the colonies for such coins that legislative enactments overvalued them in the hope of getting and keeping them within the colony. As a result of this shady intercolonial rivalry the Spanish dollar had different values from colony to colony and even from time to time. Massachusetts raised it to 5s. and then to 6s.; South Carolina put it at 4s. 8d., while North Carolina pegged it at 8s.; the middle colonies favored 7s. 6d. Some colonies forbade the export of gold and silver coins to other colonies, and the chests of departing travelers were subjected to harrowing scrutiny lest they smuggle away metallic contraband.

Sophisticated thinkers on the subject of currency were speculating meanwhile upon the possibility of multiplying the usefulness of coin by the issue of paper money at a ratio more favorable to coin than one of exact equivalence, or perhaps by substituting some other backing—perhaps goods—or making the paper legal tender in payment of public and private debts or both. Foreign commerce seemed to provide a promising precedent for these schemes. In good measure such commerce was being financed by bills of exchange drawn against the balances accumulated in the hands of British merchants from previous shipments from America or elsewhere. The merchants were bankers, and the bill of exchange, representing an existing business transaction, was in essence a check.

In the eyes of colonists chafing at the handicaps an insufficiency of means placed upon their development, paper currency had merit. To meet their own financial difficulties colonial governments turned to "bills of credit" to be redeemed when taxes were collected. Massachusetts was the pioneer in the issuance of these bills, but at least eight other colonies had followed her example by 1775. The real value of such currency as measured in terms of gold and silver depended upon the confidence of the public in their redemption, which in turn depended upon the size of the issue, the nearness of the date of redemption, and the community's willingness or ability to pay taxes.

Of more general importance were the issues of colonial "loan bills." They were sometimes issued by associations of individuals who contributed land or other property as a basis for bills which they hoped to keep afloat by their own credit, by an agreement to accept them as payment in all transactions, or by a promise of redemption at some future date. Generally the colonial governments were suspicious of such private enterprises and preferred to supply such credit facilities on their own account. In Massachusetts these loan bills were simply issued by the state on real estate or other security, and their repayment with interest by the borrowers was provided for over a series of years. Extravagant issues were made repeatedly after the first issue in 1711. In Pennsylvania the device was handled with greater skill. In 1722 the colony established a public loan bank. Among the agitators for this institution was Benjamin Franklin, whose *A Modest Inquiry into the Nature and Necessity of a Paper Currency* anticipated modern thinking in its argument that the currency of a nation must bear some relation to the value of its trade and the number of its business transactions and advocated the use of paper money as a flexible instrument of adjustment. The security taken by the Pennsylvania bank for its loans was land, double in value the amount of money loaned, and a bond and attachment upon the borrower's whole property. The debt was to be repaid in twelve annual installments with interest at 5 percent. Not more than £200 could be loaned to any one person. Every colony except Virginia issued loan bills.

The experience of the colonies with these currency experiments was not uniform. From New York to Maryland the fluctuations in the value of paper emissions were not great enough to impair their utility. In Massachusetts, Connecticut, Rhode Island, and the Carolinas the value in terms of English sterling sank sharply. Part of Rhode Island's paper money finally sank as low as 23-to-1. Such depreciation profoundly affected the welfare of different classes of the community. Debtors were benefited. Inflation brought higher prices for the products which they sold, and they were therefore more easily enabled to earn the money to discharge the obligations they had previously assumed. On the other hand, persons who received a fixed income from mortgages in land, investments in securities, or payments on insurance found no increase in their incomes to match the increase in living expenses. But persons receiving fixed income were not numerous in the colonies. Overseas the English merchants did not relish receiving the discharge of their American debts in other than sterling.

The British government had for decades followed a somewhat permissive policy toward colonial paper currency. But in the mid-eighteenth century depreciation had gone so far that in 1751 Parliament clamped down on New England, where existing bills were to be retired in accordance with their acts of authorization; and paper money issued thereafter could not be legal tender in payment of private debts. To meet their obligations colonial governments could emit bills of credit, provided taxes were committed to their redemption within two years. In 1764 Parliament forbade legal tender laws throughout the colonies and provided that such existing issues be sunk at their expiration date. To rivet things down Parliament in 1773 defined the previous two regulatory acts by denying to colonial paper currency the quality of legal tender in the payment of private debts.

Acts of Trade and Navigation

Differences in geography, climate, and commodities which could be advantageously produced underlay the colonies' foreign commerce; but the decisions and methods of private persons operated its mechanisms, and the mercantilist policy of the mother country consciously mapped the channels for this commerce and dictated the nationality of the vessels that could follow them. Legislation of this sort had been passed as early as the end of the fourteenth century. Orders-in-Council of a mercantilist cast had been issued during the reigns of the first Stuarts, but the great period of mercantilist legislation was the second half of the seventeenth century. The first Navigation Acts of 1650 and 1651 came during the Puritan supremacy of Oliver Cromwell; a whole series of acts, 1660, 1662, 1663, 1673, was passed by the Parliament of the restored Stuarts; and this maze of regulation was clarified and summarized by the Act of 1696 in the reign of William and Mary. At first glance it is surprising that a continuity of policy should persist through the alternations of sovereigns supporting such different religious and political programs. But underofficials influential in shaping this policy were adroit enough to hold office under rulers or kings of different stripes; the economic classes benefited by this legislation were always vocal; and mercantilism was the unquestioned formula for national power. Mercantilism was, besides, a response to concrete political situations rather than theoretical abstractions. Sovereigns needed revenue and customs duties provided them. In the first half of the seventeenth century, the Dutch merchant marine and trading systems had a headstart over Great Britain's, and the Dutch navy was so powerful in war that its fleet sailed into the Thames and burned English vessels. After the Dutch threat was ended France became the enemy.

While the provisions of these mercantile acts from 1650 to 1696 were a tangle of complexities and constantly required definition and redefinition, their purposes were comparatively simple. The first aim was to create a national merchant marine which in peace would furnish business for shipbuilders, employment for seamen, and profits for shipowners; and in war auxiliaries for the navy and a pool of seamen to be impressed into the latter. Legislation from Richard II to Elizabeth I had aimed at these targets. Now since the American colonies had been planted, there was a larger field from which foreigners could be excluded. At first there was no settled policy. The colonizing companies more or less enforced their monopoly against foreigners and other Englishmen; colonial governors occasionally put the clamps upon trade in foreign vessels; and the king issued orders and instructions. In 1624, for instance, James I forbade the importation of tobacco into England in "forrayne bottoms," and since a previous order had required all tobacco, whether destined for foreign markets or not, to be brought to England, this later royal pronouncement in theory prevented foreign vessels from handling the most important export of the North American colonies. Other scattered instructions attempted to exclude foreign carriers in a similar fashion from the import trade. The years of domestic confusion in England attendant upon the struggle between king and Parliament tore loopholes through such tentative measures, and the Dutch began to invade the English colonial routes.

In 1650 Parliament abruptly intervened. An act forbade all foreign ships "to come to, or Trade in, or Traffique with" any of the English colonies in America without a license. This policy of exclusion was soon inserted in the more formidable Navigation Act of 1651. In its regulations for the carrying trade, that act provided that European goods might be imported into England, Ireland, and the colonies only in English vessels or in vessels belonging to the place of production or to the port from which such goods were usually shipped. All goods from or produced in Asia, Africa, and America might be imported into the mother country or into the colonies only in ships which belonged to "the people of this Commonwealth or the Plantations thereof, and whereof the masters and mariners are also for the most part of them of the people of this Commonwealth." Although the main object of this act was the transfer of the carrying trades from Dutch to English hands, its precise effect upon colonial shipping was uncertain. Were the people of the colonies included in "the people of this Commonwealth"? The Navigation Act of 1660, the Magna Charta of the English sea trade, brought greater clarification. It declared all exports from and imports to the English colonies in Asia, Africa, and America must be carried in English vessels or those which had been built in and belonged to the colonies. The master and at least three-quarters of the crew of these ships had to be English. Two years later an act gave final definition to the nationality of the crew. The term "English" was to include "His Majesties subjects of England, Ireland, and his plantations."

These acts definitely admitted colonial shipping to the privileges and monopolies, including the trade between Europe and England, accorded to the English merchant marine. There were a few exceptions, but the generalization holds true. Such an inclusion was naturally of the greatest benefit to the colonies. For the metropolis it was likewise advantageous. The plantation trade was a great stimulus to the English merchant marine, for the transatlantic journey was a long one and colonial cargoes were bulky. A larger number of vessels was therefore required for this commerce than for shorter hauls of more valuable commodities. The Commissioners of the Customs in 1678 wrote with enthusiasm that "the Plantacon trade is one of the greatest Nurseries of the Shipping and Seamen of this Kingdome, and one of the greatest branches of its Trade."

A second purpose of these statutes was to make sure that the colonial products desired by the English metropolis should be delivered to her or her satellite settlements and not elsewhere. The charters of the early trading companies to Europe had contained the germ of this principle, and in America it was first applied in the laboratory of the tobacco trade. By 1621 the tobacco crop was far too large for absorption by the English market, and the Virginia Company meditated dumping its surplus in various Continental ports. This procedure was abruptly terminated by an order of the Privy Council declaring that Virginia tobacco must first be shipped to England. Other acts followed. The Stuarts were all the more eager for this form of regulation, since these imported products paid duties upon their arrival in England and thus helped to alleviate the financial perplexities in which these sovereigns were continually involved.

With the Restoration this early policy was placed upon a firmer basis by enumerating in the various Acts of Trade of Navigation the products which must be shipped only to England, Ireland, Wales, Berwick-upon-Tweed (whose location on the Scottish frontier had given it an unusual political status), or the other colonial plantations. The Act of 1660 designated as enumerated articles, sugar, tobacco, cotton, ginger, indigo, and various other dyes. Of these products only tobacco was of importance at the time to the American continental colonies. Their other products might go wherever they wanted—in the proper shipping. Later acts extended the enumerated list. Naval stores and rice were added in 1704. The latter article, however, might go directly to any European port south of Cape Finisterre, an exception which permitted direct colonial trade to the Iberian peninsula and the Mediterranean. In 1722 beaver and other skins were placed on the enumerated list, and after the Seven Years' War most products from the tropical and temperate colonies joined them. In the enumerated category were hides and skins, potash and pearl ashes, iron and lumber. This was such a considerable list that exceptions were soon allowed. Iron and lumber might be shipped to any place in America, Africa, or Asia; and in 1765 direct exports of colonial lumber were allowed to Europe south of Cape Finisterre. In the previous year the American rice colonies had even been permitted to ship their product to any part of America to the southward and to the Caribbean.

One explanation for this policy of enumeration was the requirements of the English market. The crying insistence of her merchant marine and royal navy amply explain the enumeration of naval stores and ship timbers. The expansion of the English textile manufacture placed a premium on dyestuffs and sop ashes. A more varied, generous, comfortable standard of living, at once cause and effect, required the importation of tobacco, foodstuffs, and other commodities from the colonies. But enumeration was designed for broader purposes than satisfying domestic needs. Beaver skins, hides, naval stores, sugar, rice, tobacco—all were reexported. Even if they left England in their crude state, they often redressed an unfavorable balance of trade. But the mercantilist planned that these colonial products whose original cost was small should be transformed by the artisans and manufacturers of the metropolis into articles whose value for reexport was much greater than that of the imported raw material. Everyone benefited by this arrangement. English employers were given profits, and English workers employment. English merchants had the business of forwarding the products, and English shipowners had more numerous voyages. Finally, the government would collect customs which would have been lost if the products had been carried directly to the European markets. The full amount of these customs did not always accrue to the government. In order to encourage the reexport trade, drawbacks on the import duties were paid when the goods again left England. These varied. In general, tariff acts remitted half the duties as a drawback, but on the most important enumerated products (tobacco and sugar) all import duties were eventually repaid. Nevertheless so dearly was this form of revenue cherished that when the carriage of rice to Europe south of Cape Finisterre was permitted, the commodity, even though it did not pass through Great Britain, paid the English import duties less the drawback.

The tobacco trade, of all the commerce from North America, best illustrated the influence and implications of this policy of enumeration. Tobacco exports to Great Britain increased enormously. As early as 1685, the revenue derived by the Crown in duties was between £ 100,000 and £ 130,000. The ocean carriage gave employment in the same year to "200 sail of ships." In England hundreds were engaged in manufacturing pipe tobacco or snuff; and tobacco merchants, shippers, colonial planters, and English statesmen cooperated to enlarge the European markets for the product. By the end of the seventeenth century three-quarters of the tobacco imports into England were reexported. Holland consumed 8,-220,000 pounds, a quantity larger than that used by English smokers. Ireland and Germany were other important markets. Even Spain, whose colonies produced the best tobacco in the world, imported the English product. The considerable exports to Sweden were regarded with special favor as a redress to England's customary threatening balance of trade with the Baltic regions. Particular attention was paid to Russia, where a large population had a "passionate love of tobacco." The privilege of entering these markets was eventually won from the czar, only to be lost again. In spite of such reversals, the Continental markets grew. In the years before the American Revolution only one-fifth of the exports shipped from Virginia and Maryland was consumed in England.

The third aim of the Acts of Navigation and the Laws of Trade reversed the enumeration process. Goods destined for the colonies must be shipped from England. This was obvious in the case of English products, but such European and Asiatic goods as the American colonies insisted upon consuming were in general to be transported to the colonies only by way of the metropolis. The first act which formulated this principle was that of 1663. It provided that all European goods for the colonies must be shipped from England, Wales, or Berwick-upon-Tweed in vessels legal under the Navigation Act. The purposes of this Staple Act were manifold. Designed to give the English rather than the European merchant the profitable business of supplying the colonies with the goods which they needed, it hoped to stimulate "the further imployment and increase of English shipping and seamen" by establishing two voyages, one from Europe to England and a second from England to America, rather than a single direct voyage. The act would increase the customs revenue through the payment of duties; and it would increase "the vent of English woolen and other manufactures and commodities" at the expense of their European competitors.

The exceptions to this general legislation prove even more precisely the sway of mercantilist motives. The direct importation of certain European articles was allowed by the Act of 1663. Salt, obtained largely from southern Europe, could be brought directly to the colonies in order that their fisheries might not be hampered in the rivalry with the French and the Dutch. Some consideration was also shown to Portugal, which was gracefully included for many purposes within the English system because of its economic dependence. Wines from the Portuguese islands, the Madeiras and Azores, were allowed the privilege of a direct voyage. After 1763 the English ministry sought to make this commerce conform to the general pattern. A heavy duty was placed upon wines imported directly into the colonies, a low one on wines imported via England. In view of this arrangement it was hoped that the Portuguese beverages would in the future flow to the colonies by way of the metropolis. Some of the disadvantages of using England as a supplier of certain staples were eased by the drawbacks paid upon imported European goods which were reexported from England to the colonies. On some foreign commodities—manufactured iron and steel, cordage and sailcloth—these drawbacks were not given. Here apparently the English government was determined to give even greater favors to its own industries.

Similar in purpose to this legislation was that which prohibited the colonies' manufacture of products that ought to be produced in the mother country. The colonies must not become competitiors. Since England always regarded the woolen industry as a mainstay of her economy and had favored it by legislation, Parliament in 1699 acted directly to provide that no woolen yarn or woolen manufactures, being the products or manufacture of any of the English plantations in America, could be exported from the colonies or transported from one colony to another. Alarmed by the fact that American hatters could get their raw material more cheaply than Britishers could, Parliament in 1732 placed a similar ban on hats. Because of its manifold forms, iron was such a puzzle that Parliament did not act until 1750. Then it encouraged the production of pig iron and bar iron in the colonies by allowing their duty-free importation into England. The act, however, forbade the erection in the colonies of any mill for slitting or rolling iron, or of any plating forge, or any furnace for making steel. In other words, the colonies were to get their finished products from England.

Legislation so extensive and detailed as this would certainly benefit some interests; it was certain also to cost others something. It is a temptation to believe the beneficiaries were always British and those who paid always colonial. For instance, under the provisions of the Acts of Trade and Navigation goods were not bought in the cheapest or sold in the dearest market. But the statutes forbade this halcyon form of exchange for the citizens not only of the colonies but also of the metropolis. Take the matter of enumeration. By sending his product to Europe via England, where it was burdened with customs duties and extra freight rates and commissions for handling, the colonist received less for it than he could have received by sending it directly to its destination. The balance of this simple statement, however, is at once upset by a number of compensations. Certain products, such as indigo, which had to be shipped to England, could not have been produced in the colonies without the bounty which was paid upon their arrival in England, Wales, or Berwick-upon-Tweed. In the case of these enumerated products the burden was upon the English consumer and taxpayer rather than upon the colonist. Other articles from the colonies were admitted into the metropolis duty-free or at low rates, while competing products from other nations were charged heavily. Finally, certain colonial commodities were given a virtual monopoly of the English market. The English consumer was literally compelled to use colonial tar, colonial sugar, and colonial tobacco.

In the case of tobacco the colonial producers received even further consideration. Tobacco growing in England was forbidden because James I felt the soil of England should be put to some nobler purpose. In 1652 Parliament prohibited the planting of tobacco in England on the ground that it tended "to the decay of Husbandry and Tillage, the prejudice and hindrance of the English plantations abroad, and of the Trading, Commerce, Navigation and Shipping of the Nation . . ." and authorized any person to enter the tobacco fields and destroy the plants. Tariffs on imports were more easily collected than excises on English farmers. Despite these prohibitions the cultivation of the plant continued and became a profitable business in the southwestern counties of Gloucester and Worcester. The planters threatened violence to anyone who attempted to destroy their crops, and issued a defiance against the county justices who had been commanded to carry out the governmental policy. But the central government was obdurate in its devotion to the interest of colonial planters and the importers who flourished on that trade. During the Restoration such vigorous measures were taken that by the end of the century the English tobacco-growing industry had been extirpated. Fifty years later an English writer thought that the prohibitions upon iron manufacturing in the colonies "will not be a greater hardship upon them than the Prohibition of the Planting of Tobacco in Great Britain is to us."

On the surface the colonists were likewise penalized by the Staple Act of 1663 and other acts compelling them to obtain most of their European goods from England rather than directly from Europe. Such legislation normally would have extorted higher prices from the colonists than those paid by the English consumer. On the other hand, the colonial consumer was often favored as compared with the English purchaser. Certain products, notably calicoes, which could not be legally imported into England for sale there could be shipped to the colonies. Certain British products, moreover, when shipped abroad received bounties in order to encourage their manufacture. These bounties not only were paid from the British treasury and hence were a tax upon the English people, but they enabled the manufacturers to sell these articles in the colonies at a price below that charged in the metropolis. British and Irish linens benefited by this arrangement.

Still another item confuses the question of whether the colonies or the mother country were more constrained by this legislation. The preamble of the Staple Act stated that one of its purposes was to make navigation to and from England and the colonies "more safe." This was not a pious platitude. Ocean trade was subject to all sorts of dangers. The frequent wars of the period let loose a flood of privateers and warships to prey upon commerce. Protection had to be accorded to national vessels by proper convoys. Then there were swarms of pirates. One group of buccaneers infested the West Indies and on occasion used the continent, especially North Carolina, as a base of operations. In Algeria, Tunis, and Tripoli was a second nest of more professional pirates—the Barbary corsairs. Refusing to confine their operations to the Mediterranean, they penetrated on occasion to the English Channel and interfered with the tobacco ships sailing from Virginia. Intermittent punitive expeditions were dispatched against them and naval vessels had to be stationed in the Mediterranean to enforce such agreements as the corsairs could be compelled to sign. The concentration of trade routes sought by the English Acts of Navigation and Trade made easier the protection of commerce. And the cost of that protection, which was enjoyed by the colonists as well as by the English, was assumed solely by the latter.

The contention has often been advanced that these English acts caused little trouble to colonial trade because they were evaded. Paeans have been sung to "Yankee smartness" and smuggling has been condoned on the ground that everything is fair in love, war—and commerce. In spite of evasions at certain times and for certain commodities, it seems more likely that the Acts of Trade and Navigation so far discussed were not extensively violated. The reason was simple. In the main the regulations expressed in the acts coincided with the natural conditions of trade. The colonies benefited by their inclusion within the world of British shipping; they were protected in the English market; and as for European goods, they would have had them from England anyway. England manufactured most articles as cheaply as any nation in Europe, and Americans would have imported their woolens and their hardware from her whatever the legislation. Even the goods not produced advantageously in England and drawn by the colonies from Europe would probably have gone through the former in transit. England served as a great warehouse into which commodities from all parts of the world flowed. A vessel could obtain at London or other ports a diversified cargo; it was spared the expense and trouble of collecting it from all quarters of the world.

The Flow of Foreign Commerce

More than the conscious policy of the Acts of Trade and Navigation, economic conditions in North America and in extracolonial markets fashioned the commerce of the colonies. Colonial needs determined the character of colonial imports; the variety and abundance of colonial production set the nature of colonial exports. In the mirror of foreign trade economic conditions, not legislation, were reflected. This generalization (like most) requires an immediate exception. The existence of the East India Company and its privileges excluded colonial commerce from the eastern hemisphere. Conceivably, the Acts of Trade and Navigation worked less directly to the same end in northern and western Europe. Colonial "world" trade was with only part of the world.

On the North American continent there were differences between northern and southern colonies. South of Pennsylvania lay the great staple-producing colonies. The Carolinas had indigo and rice; Virginia and Maryland tobacco. These tropical or semitropical products inevitably found their most extensive market in Europe, and their inclusion in the enumerated commodities reflected this situation. The amount shipped elsewhere was infinitesimal. By 1770 the exports from the British colonies of tobacco, of which Maryland and Virginia were the chief producers, were valued at approximately £906,000. This sum was well over a quarter of total colonial exports. Practically all the tobacco was shipped to Great Britain. Rice, the next southern staple of importance, had a more diffused destination. Under the exceptions allowed by the Acts of Trade, half of the crop, whose total value in 1770 was £340,692, went directly to southern Europe and the West Indies. Practically all of the indigo, valued at £131,552, went to Great Britain. In return for these products, the southern colonies imported from England the manufactured and exotic products which they needed. By any test these southern colonies were peculiarly dependent upon commerce. Toward the end of the Colonial period five of them, Maryland, Virginia, the Carolinas, and Georgia, shipped more than half the exports and received more than half the imports of colonial commerce. And this commerce was carried on predominantly with the English metropolis. In this trade, however, the values of the exports and the imports did not balance. So great was the deluge of staple crops poured across the Atlantic that their value usually far exceeded that of the imports. How then could the debts of Virginia planters have become "hereditary," as Jefferson put it?

The answer probably was the extravagance and ostentation of plantation life, which was an early example of "conspicuous consumption." Another answer was the failure of export and import statistics to include a multitude of charges, from freight charges—tobacco ships were built in England and owned by English merchants—to commissions for selling tobacco on consignment and for bringing furniture and equipment as a return shipment.

Foreign trade in the colonies north of Maryland was a less simple matter. This was not because these colonies lacked staples. Although no northern commodity compared with tobacco, the exports of wheat and bread and flour, valued in 1770 at £636,000, were the second largest item in the colonial export trade. More important than rice in export columns was fish, the typical New England staple. In 1770 the total export value of dried fish was over £375,000, and fish pickled in barrels brought the sum near £400,000. If the values of the various lumber products from naval stores to knockdown houses, from ship timbers to sop ashes had been added together, they would easily have equaled that of exported indigo; and whale products—candles, oil, and fins—nearly approached the importance of this exotic dye. Furs, peltries, livestock, all ran into impressive figures.

It was the nature of these staples that complicated northern commerce. Great Britain regarded most of these northern products either with indifference or with actual hostility. The depressing stricture which an English writer applied in 1690 to New England, "By Tillage, Pasture, Fishing, Manufactures and Trade, they to all Intents and Purposes imitate Old England," was true in greater or less degree of all the northern colonies. The fish caught by New England fishermen and cured in New England ports competed in the West Indies and in Europe with the catches of the English fishermen; the wheat and flour of the middle colonies supplied southern Europe and the West Indies at the expense of British farmers; New England manufacturers provisioned the English fleets in North American waters and supplied them with nets, lines, and other equipment more cheaply than the English outfitters who should have had the business. Unwelcome as all this was, without exports of their own the northern colonies could not pay for the commodities which they must and should have from Great Britain. The most obvious mercantilist policy was to stimulate the production of some staple. As we have seen, the bounties on the production of naval stores were meant to be one step in providing the northern colonies with exports with which to pay for their imports.

Forbearance in passing legislation or in pushing it to extremes was also a parliamentary policy. In spite of the grumbling of shipbuilders along the Thames, colonial vessels were included in the favoritism of the Navigation Acts and were sold to British purchasers. And although fisherfolk in the west of England disliked the competition of New Englanders on the Grand Banks, Parliament did nothing to check this development. While colonial trade with northern and western Europe was nonexistent, that to southern Europe grew and was even permitted by exceptions to statutory prohibitions. Colonial vessels sailed directly to Portugal and Spain or, penetrating the Strait, stood off for Marseilles and Leghorn, the distributing ports of the Mediterranean and the centers of its numerous trade routes. Lumber and various food products were the chief items in this commerce. In the former category were naval timbers. These were sent frequently to southern Europe during the seventeenth century, and their shipment continued even after they were enumerated in 1704. Josiah Gee, English mercantilist, defended this illicit commerce. The Spanish had plenty of oaks and pines, he wrote, "but their indolent temper is such that if they can purchase what they want with money, they care not to stretch out a hand to help themselves (and I should be sorry that we should stir them up to become industrious)." More important was oak cooperage, which in 1770 constituted over half the value of the total timber exports. Oak staves, headings, and hoops were sent to Portugal, Madeira, and the Azores to be assembled into the barrels for their famous beverages. So important was this trade that less than a year after lumber had been placed upon the enumerated list, Parliament permitted exceptions for direct shipments to Europe south of Cape Finisterre.

Wheat and flour were the chief exports from the northern colonies to Europe. By 1770 New Jersey, Pennsylvania, and New York were producing agricultural supplies for export. In that year 588,000 bushels of wheat and 18,000 tons of bread and flour were sent to southern Europe. By all odds this market was the most important one in the world for the American grain trade. It was the chief one also for the products of the fisheries. To these Catholic countries with their numerous fast days New England catered with a fine distinction. The "Spring fare," large and thick fish, were selected for this exacting market and then cured very carefully on flakes and housed in case of bad weather. When the flesh was completely dried, the fish were kept alternately above and below ground until they "became so mellow as to be denominated dun fish." The flavor of these dunfish appealed to the sensitive palate of the Latin consumer, and the thorough process of curing enabled long transportation of the fish without decay. In 1770 two-thirds of the export of dried fish went to southern Europe.

Nearer home were the islands of the Caribbean. Fortunately their preoccupation with sugar cultivation by a slave system—a preoccupation which deepened in the last quarter of the seventeenth century—made them complementary to the mainland colonies. The Caribbean market needed lumber in many forms and in large quantities. Thither the colonies from New Hampshire to Virginia exported planks, boards, and shingles for houses, slave quarters and sugar mills; they also shipped knock-down houses, cut out by North American sawyers, to be set up on arrival. Sugar, rum, molasses, demanded containers. Heads, hoops, staves, were dispatched separately or in the form of hogsheads, casks, or barrels. On some vessels a cooper went along and assembled the materials into finished products during the voyage. Shortly before the Revolution the islands took annually over 11 million staves and headings and nearly 36 million feet of boards.

Although it was perfectly possible for the "Sugar Islands" to grow their own food supplies and planters did produce a considerable amount of food truck, more money was to be made from sugar specialization. According to one writer's calculations, an acre planted to sugar would yield sufficient to purchase five acres of Indian corn. So the West Indies drew their supplies from the food areas of the mainland colonies. Indian corn obtained a West Indian outlet, and bread and flour found here their greatest market. Dried and pickled meats were sent from practically all the colonies. And then there were the fisheries. Although planters were fussy about the quality of their own fish, the New Englanders found it possible to ship an inferior quality known as West Indian, or Jamaica, fish for the slaves. In the eighteenth century the deep-sea mackerel joined the cod as an article of export. The products of America's freshwater fisheries, shad, alewives, and other pickled fish, likewise rolled down to St. Kitts or Barbados. These mainstays of the export army were followed. by a host of camp followers; bushels of peas and beans and barrels of beef and pork from the lower James, ropes of onions from New London, spermaceti candles from Rhode Island, leather and rice from Charleston, were crowded into small vessels with live sheep and hogs, oxen for use in the fields, and horses to turn the sugar mills and "to carry the customs officers out of the way when smugglers landed their goods." In 1770 the total value of exports shipped to the West Indies was £844,000. In the same year the exports to Great Britain were valued at £1,686,000. Exports from the colonies to the West Indies were subordinate only to those to Great Britain.

Indeed all these trades interlocked. The West Indies trade lubricated them all, for it was the great source of bills of exchange on London and thus helped northern merchants pay for their imports from the mother country. The sugar-plantation owners generally had a credit balance at their London factors or consignees, which they could draw upon to pay for their imports from the Piscataqua to Norfolk. So much for their direct influence. To the North American mainland the West Indies planters also returned sugar and molasses as a back cargo. In the eighteenth century Rhode Island, Massachusetts, and Connecticut built enough works to distill molasses to justify being designated the "Rum Coast." The coasting trade carried this native rum to the southern colonies, where slaves consumed it, and to the fisheries, where it washed down the diet of salt pork and ship bread. From both these destinations traders could bring back bills of exchange on London. Rum formed part of the cargo sent in slave traders to western Africa; the slaves were bartered in the West Indies for bills of exchange on London or Bristol. Whatever their meanderings, the vessels in the West Indian trade were predominantly American-built and American-owned; their freight earnings were an item in balancing a hard-pressed trade.

This West Indian commerce perplexed thinkers speculating about a nationalistic organization of trade and those who had to enact legislation. A simple interchange of goods for goods across the Atlantic between metropolis and colonies raised conflicts between interests which were hard enough to adjust and reconcile; an imperial structure of complementary colonies might become one of contradictory colonies. Sugar planters in the British islands in the Caribbean, like their competitors elsewhere, faced the necessity of disposing of two products—molasses and sugar. Refining methods of that day turned these out at the ratio of 2-to-1. Consequently the British producers successfully turned to the distillation of rum from molasses. If Jamaica, Barbados, and other British isles had existed in an empty sea perhaps all might have been well; instead they were scattered among other islands flying the Spanish, the Danish, the Dutch, or the French flag. Neither the Dutch nor French followed the innovation of the English islands; the French, for instance, disliked molasses in its raw state and they had no intention of encouraging its distillation into a beverage which might compete with their own favored brandy industry. Consequently, since vessels from the mainland colonies could buy molasses much more cheaply in these non-British colonies, they did so. About half the molasses imports were used in cooking, medicine, and brewing molasses beer; the other half, the colonies, particularly Massachusetts and Rhode Island, distilled and sold for about half the price of imported rum. Nagging factors such as these disturbed advocates of a self-sufficing empire in which the colonies were to complement each other.

As the British sugar planters reflected upon their inferior economic position, they concluded they must erase the advantage consumers on the mainland had in buying molasses in a cheaper foreign market. This West Indian sugar interest was influential, for many of the "sugar nabobs" had drawn wealth from their plantations and returned to Britain. If they were not members of Parliament, they at least had the ear of those who were. These influences prevailed to pass the Molasses Act of 1733. It did not prohibit trade with the foreign sugar islands, but it levied the following duties upon all sugars, rum, and molasses imported from them into the colonies: ninepence on each gallon of rum, sixpence on each gallon of molasses, and five shillings on each hundredweight of sugar. Those who violated the provisions of this act were punished by the forfeiture of the suspected goods, a portion of which was set aside as a reward to informers and prosecutors. Although the Molasses Act ostensibly compromised the controversy between the mainland and the British West Indies, it actually decided in favor of the latter by simply laying a 100 percent duty upon molasses from anywhere except the English West Indies. Consequently, there *was* one aspect of commercial regulation which the mainland colonies disobeyed. They imported sugar, molasses, and rum in the most brazen fashion, and the New Englanders even dispensed with the unique talents for evasion which Colonel William Byrd of Virginia once ascribed to them: "They have a great dexterity at palliating a perjury so well as to leave no taste of it in their mouth, nor can any people like them slip through a penal Statute." The act was so generally disregarded that the price of rum in Massachusetts declined rather than increased after the imposition of these duties, and only £800 was collected annually under the act's provisions.

The imperial authorities ignored this disobedience because the West Indian sugar planters suddenly came to the conclusion that the real cause of their misfortune was the provision of the English Acts of Trade which compelled them to ship their sugars to Great Britain, and which consequently handicapped these sugars in the European market. Parliament attempted to redress this disadvantage. In 1764 the Sugar Act regulated the West Indian trade. Although this bill, like the Molasses Act, sought to hamper the French sugar islands and benefit the British, a new motive for it was the necessity of raising money for the support of the imperial establishment in the American colonies. The importation of rum from foreign colonies into the American colonies was prohibited, and the sugar rates were left at the level of the Molasses Act. As for molasses, after a prolonged debate Parliament placed a duty of threepence a gallon upon the foreign product in the hope that this duty would be low enough to encourage legitimate importations and so raise a revenue. Two years later the tariff was reduced to one penny and applied to both foreign and British molasses.

Legislation aside, the foreign trade between the colonies and Great Britain slowly mounted in value. Edmund Burke, in his famous oration "Conciliation with America," stated that British exports to North America and the West Indies had risen from £483,265 in 1704 to £4,791,734 in 1772. Toward the close of the Colonial period Americans secured nearly 60 percent of their imports from Great Britain and sent her 55 percent of their exports. The North American colonial trade had become the largest single item in Britain's entire foreign commerce. By and large these interchanges represented a mutual advantage. One recent calculation estimates that the Acts of Trade and Navigation in 1773 cost Americans between $2,560,000 and $7,038,000 net. Though these figures seem to afford a wide margin of error, another estimate objects to their underlying hypothesis and to their failure to include all items. Still another calculation estimates the cost of being an American rather than an Englishman on a per capita basis in 1770; for the colonists, the net loss was 42 cents a person. If the colonists knew this, to risk a revolution because of the Acts of Trade and Navigation was irrational indeed. But there is little evidence that the colonists had this information, and there is a great deal of evidence that economic exploitation was not the primary cause of the Revolution.

Whatever its risks and trials, the welfare of America in Colonial times depended to a degree never since equaled upon foreign commerce. Without it, the thin fringe of settlement along the Atlantic coast could have existed—but only on a primitive and simple economic scale. A higher degree of comfort and material development would have arrived only after a longer period of self-sufficing agriculture and manufacturing. With foreign trade, on the other hand, specialization by the colonies in the products most suited to their circumstances was possible. Their natural resources could be rapidly exploited and shipped abroad in a crude or semimanufactured form in exchange for the products which were more advantageously produced in other countries. Wherever there was an abundance of material prosperity, there was foreign trade. The export of tobacco built the mansions of the Virginia tidewater, equipped them with pictures, furniture, and plate, and supported their courtly social life. Rice and indigo performed the same legerdemain farther south. In New England the merchant and the shipbuilder owed their higher standard of life to overseas trade. And the cities of Boston, New York, Philadelphia, Baltimore, and Charleston were built upon foreign commerce. Everywhere the exchange of goods across the water quickened and enriched colonial economic life.

Naturally the merchant class, or at least those affluent enough to be designated "merchant princes," constituted with the planters—many of whom also performed mercantile functions—a colonial elite. Estimates of wealth and numbers are difficult to secure. In 1676 there were, according to the penetrating Edward Randolph, thirty merchants in Boston worth between £10,000 and £20,000. Thomas Amory died with a fortune of over £20,000; Peter Faneuil had investments of £14,800 in Bank of London stock and in other securities; Thomas Boylston was worth $400,000 before the Revolution; Henry Laurens of South Carolina was on the way to getting rich when he left business; in Pennsylvania the Quaker merchants left accumulated fortunes. The well-being of this merchant class was reflected in its standard of living. The Massachusetts merchant had houses in town and country estates at Cambridge, Milton, or Harvard. The merchant of Burlington built his house on the high ground which sloped back from the Delaware. The Philadelphia businessman had his estate in West Jersey or along the highways which radiated from the metropolis where he made money. Their standard of life can be traced in the comforts and luxuries of life they ordered from their correspondents for personal use. Among other items Faneuil imported for his bachelor regime in Boston tripe, bacon, citron water, games such as backgammon and chess, an English gardener, a chariot, four horses "right good or none," and a coachman "the Noted's man in England." The existence of this class of conservative wealthy men colored colonial history, political and social as well as economic.

Merchants and Conflict

As a class which had succeeded and prospered, the merchants were instinctively against riots and tumults and lesser disturbances fracturing colonial relationships with the mother country. But in the quarter century between 1750 and 1775, events and policies weakened their allegiance to a British-imposed system of commerce and navigation. For one thing, the balance of trade drifted against them. Before 1750 the trade of the American colonies had enjoyed a favorable balance with the English metropolis. Although the northern colonies had imported a greater value of commodities from Great Britain than they had been able to meet by exports, the overseas movement of the staples from the southern colonies had more than redressed this deficiency. But after 1750 this balance of trade swung heavily against the colonies as a whole. Great Britain's industry, already quickened by the Industrial Revolution, was producing a surplus; the great manufacturing towns, London, Bristol, Hull, Liverpool, Glasgow, Manchester, Birmingham, Sheffield, Leeds, were pushing their products into the colonial field. This "American trade" now constituted from one-sixth to one-third of the total trade of Great Britain. The colonies could not pay for these imports with specie, although they squeezed every possible remittance from the indirect trades with the West Indies, Spain, Portugal, and the wine islands. The only alternative was an expansion of credit, and this the British merchants, yielding to temptation, were eager to supply. Borrowing capital in England and Scotland, they extended long-term credits to America "beyond the bounds of prudence." Whereas in 1755 colonial imports from Great Britain were beginning to exceed colonial exports thither, in 1770 the balance of trade in favor of Great Britain was nearly £3 million.

While the American merchants were straining every nerve to meet this growing tide of indebtedness, the cessation of war with France in 1763 cut down Great Britain's export of specie to the colonies for payments to troops and for supplies. The postwar effort of Parliament to devise a system of colonial taxation incidentally required the payment of duties in gold, silver, or bills of exchange and thus operated as a further drain upon American specie reserves at a time when the payment for imports was difficult enough. Particularly upsetting to mercantile composure in this period of tumult was the Tea Act of 1773. This unfortunate statute, designed to rescue the East India Company from the bankruptcy threatened by its accumulation of a huge surplus stock of tea, allowed the company to ship tea in its own vessels to selected consignees. This arrangement undermined the existing array of middlemen, shippers, and importers and allowed the company by direct methods to undersell American competitors. The colonial merchants as well as the English merchants dealing in tea were aghast. Both were faced with the loss of their profits in tea. The Americans were alarmed by the principle of the act. Other companies might receive favors for other goods—silk, drugs, spices. "America," as one merchant wrote, "would be prostrate before a monster that may be able to destroy every branch of our commerce, drain us of all our property, and wantonly leave us to perish by thousands." The merchant class did not react as a unit. Henry Laurens of South Carolina wept when he first heard of the Declaration of Independence and aligned himself with the revolutionaries. But when the British troops vacated Boston in 1775, they were accompanied by more than two hundred merchants.

So weak and tangential were colonial grievances on the matter of trade that the Declaration of Independence which exhaustively listed every cause for rebellion failed to mention the Acts of Trade and Navigation even in part. Yet in the very same year Adam Smith, whose *Wealth of Nations* undermined the structure of mercantilism, wrote, "To prohibit a great people from making all that they can of every part of their own produce, or from employing their stock and their industry in the way they judge most advantageous to themselves, is a manifest violation of the most sacred rights of mankind." While this emphasis upon individual rights might appeal to American patterns of thought, it did not prevent the Constitution's makers from granting to the new Republic the power "To regulate Commerce with Foreign Nations, and among the several States." Only by 1787 they were granting this power to their own government rather than conceding it to an alien one.

A New Start:
Agricultural Expansion
and Agricultural Methods

The Revolution: Governments and Their Purposes

Since the Revolution was fought without the benefits of the internal combustion engine, high explosives, and electronic systems, the damage directly caused by warfare was relatively slight by modern standards. The rural regions in the South and the slave force suffered great hardships. The British or the Americans put to the torch port communities like Norfolk and New London; and the British troops who occupied Philadelphia and New York left behind run-down and partially ruined cities; the population of American cities declined 50 percent in the first year of the war. Certain callings disappeared. The historian of the fisheries wrote a brief epitaph: "The American fisheries were annihilated during the revolutionary war." But agriculture, the occupation of most Americans, was too resilient to meet such a fate. If material things did not suffer overmuch, relationships, organizations, and institutions did. Thus, after the war when the thirteen colonies sought independently by measures largely impromptu and desperate to better their economic condition, they discovered the necessity of radical readjustments in public and private finance, foreign trade, and the management of public lands.

During the eighties the states which had not already done so established a variety of state governments and in this way climbed out of the "state of nature" that pamphleteers and others were always detecting or discussing. Americans were meanwhile groping toward "a more perfect union." According to historical and popular opinion, they attained it with the formation and adoption of the Federal Constitution in 1787–1789. In April of the latter year the nation inaugurated Washington as its first President and set sail on its course. The government, a federal one, attempted to divide government powers between the sovereignties of the states and the Federal government. This classic confrontation has been a theme of American history. In terms of policy the division meant, often enough a debate over which agency possessed the legal power to seek an objective, and it has thrown over that debate a veil of constitutionality, or its opposite, when often there was a wide measure of agreement over the merit of the proposed aim. Constitutionality was a practical matter and not an abstraction or rationalization, though on occasion it could be either or both.

When the United States was formed, its population, according to the census of 1790, was 3,929,000; and its landed area was 864,746 square miles. By the time the Treaty of Peace ended the Revolution, the nation extended from the Atlantic to the Mississippi; and its northern and southern boundaries were so blurred that it took decades of diplomacy and conflict to make them precise. Originally the Republic did not extend at one extreme to the Gulf of Mexico, for the Florida peninsula and a narrow appendage running westward to a terminus on some disputed river were given to Spain; at the northern edge in the West geographical ignorance and national rivalries obscured the boundary running from Lake Superior to the Mississippi River. Various rights—for instance, of navigation—were associated with these disputed areas. Of course the population was not dispersed evenly throughout the area. According to the census of 1790, the population in the western states and territories was 109,000, settled almost exclusively in Kentucky and Tennessee. Virginia was the most populous state, Pennsylvania the second, and Massachusetts the third. At the same date there were six cities, each with 8,000 or more inhabitants, in the United States; the urban population, thus defined, constituted 3.4 percent of the nation's total.

The American Dreams

Since the United States was a new nation with the political freedom to make a new start, it was natural to speculate on the use to be made of its resources, including land, and on the most advantageous employments for its human resources. Ordinarily such speculations are the province of visionaries with tongue and pen. But the generation of the Revolution and the following years had devoted much thought and effort to justifying a revolution and forming a constitution. In that generation's activities the mind was not at a discount, and its members had demonstrated thought and learning could arrive at workable conclusions. It would be silly to assume that accomplishments of this quality and magnitude were confined to a handful and that all fell in behind the leadership of a few. Nonetheless, the fact that thinkers had attained positions of influence and direct political power has given a simplicity and a peculiar staying power to the political and economic designs of Alexander Hamilton and Thomas Jefferson and the associates of each.

It is exceptional for a cabinet officer to write position papers that have become memorable over the ages. Alexander Hamilton was Secretary of the Treasury when he composed his Report on Manufactures in 1791. Hamilton thought human labor devoted to manufacture was superior to that devoted to agriculture; it was "constant" not "seasonal," "uniform" not "careless," and "more ingenious." It was therefore "more productive." On an earlier occasion he had stated:

> The prosperity of commerce is now perceived and acknowledged by all enlightened statesmen to be the most productive source of national wealth. It stimulates and gratifies consumption and by promoting the introduction and circulation of the precious metals, those darling objects of human avarice and enterprise, it serves to vivify and invigorate the channels of industry.

As an administrator facing a concrete problem, Hamilton believed that policy should seek an admixture of manufacturing with agriculture. For his program as a whole the means he sought were a protective tariff and bounties for infant industries, the establishment of a "national bank to increase public and private credit," and, somewhat less explicitly, government aid to improvements in transportation. If all this sounded like the old mercantilism—and it certainly did—the rest of the world was to blame: "If a system of perfect liberty to industry and commerce were the prevailing system of nations, the arguments which dissuade a country, in the predicament of the United States, from the zealous pursuit of manufactures, would doubtless have great force."

Not all Americans agreed with Hamilton's diagnosis of the national situation nor with the policy he advocated to handle it. Jefferson had a different vision of the desirable American. He preferred the farmer. One of his arguments was utilitarian—agriculture, depending on nature's bounty, was a "more productive" occupation than manufacturing. For the husbandman "one grain of wheat . . . renders twenty, thirty, or even fifty fold. . . . Pounds of flax, in his [the manufacturer's] hands, yield, . . . but pennyweights of lace." Beyond this consideration lay ideological ones: "Those who labor in the earth are the chosen people of God if ever He had a chosen people. . . . They are the most vigorous, the most virtuous, and they are tied to their country and wedded to its liberty and its interests by the most lasting bonds." Cities were corrupt and the artisans who lived there, since they were dependent upon employers, were not free; suitors and subjects, they were "panders of vice." Foreign trade and manufacturing, Jefferson would consign to foreign hands, just as the Chinese did with the Europeans. Or if you disapprove of the eloquence you can say Jefferson looked upon "rurality as a superior way of life."

Regional and partisan interests, the personal ambition of rulers and of those aspiring to office, were sure to spoil the extreme purity of both Hamilton's program and Jefferson's. Still, their original polarity of thought about national policies for American development kept working up like the grain of the wood through the overlays of paint the passing generations applied to it.

In his administration in the mid-twenties President John Quincy Adams recapitulated in his first address to Congress a Hamiltonian program. The nation was to use its then abundant revenues for welfare and prosperity "by laws promoting the improvement of agriculture, commerce, and manufactures, the cultivation and encouragement of the mechanic and of the elegant arts, the advancement of literature, and the progress of the sciences, ornamental and profound." More specifically the President approved Federal financial aid to roads and canals, to "seminaries of learning," and to "lighthouses of the sky," by which he meant observatories. His warning that the worldwide "spirit of improvement" might be "palsied by the will of our constituents" showed he did not expect all his fellow Americans to agree with him.

Thirty years later, on the other hand, President Franklin Pierce vetoed a grant of 10 million acres of land to the states for the support and care of the indigent insane.

All the pursuits of industry, everything which promotes the material or intellectual well-being of the race, every ear of corn or boll of cotton which grows, is national . . . for each one of these things goes to swell the aggregate of national prosperity and happiness of the United States; but it confounds all meaning of language to say these are "national," as equivalent to "Federal," so as to come within any of the classes of appropriation for which Congress is authorized by the Constitution to legislate.

On these premises, some other jurisdiction, that of "the individual States, would be competent" to legislate. Here was an authoritative echo of the Jeffersonian preferences.

Of course the changes over time would have been enough to explain continuances, reversals, and modifications in the Hamiltonian or Jeffersonian programs. I don't refer to separate events, but to an alteration in the contour of the problems the government and its officials confronted. By 1860 the population—31,443,321—of the nation had multiplied eight times since the first census; the landed area—2,969,640 square miles—had grown between three and four times since 1790. Responsible for the last increase were diplomacy and war; responsible for the first figure was a high native birthrate. Any statistical exactness on the numbers of natives and aliens is difficult for the census did not provide figures for the foreign born and for those of foreign parentage until 1850 and 1870 respectively. Figures of a sort, however, have been compiled for immigration, the second source of additions to the population. In 1820 the United States admitted 8,000 immigrants; the figure rose to a peak of 419,000 in 1854 and then declined. These ebbs and flows in arrivals corresponded to changes in economic conditions in the United States and to expulsive factors—sometimes almost too disastrous to be designated as economic—abroad. For instance, the immense outpouring from Ireland in the later forties and early fifties was a flight from famine brought on by the potato rot of 1846 and its aftermath. By and large, Ireland, Germany, and England were the big three sources of American immigration.

Meanwhile internal migration had regrouped the American people. Figures for this movement, like those for race and parentage, are lacking before 1850. Certain crude aggregates give an idea of the movement. By 1860 New York was the largest state and Pennsylvania the second. Virginia, which in 1790 had led, was in 1860 surpassed by Ohio, Indiana, Illinois, and Missouri, none of which in 1790 had been states or contributors to the census columns. In 1790 Kentucky and Tennessee, then the populated West, together had a little more than 100,000 inhabitants; in 1860 each had over a million. Of such was the western movement. At the same time Americans were moving into cities. If one defines a city as a community of 8,000 or over, there were in 1860 141 cities instead of 6. The urban population in 1860, 5,072,000, constituted 16.1 percent of the nation's total. Since the nation's birth the urban trend had been noticeable everywhere. Thirty years before the Civil War, as Pittsburgh, Cincinnati, Louisville, and St. Louis showed, cities had "sprung up in the forest." The unexpected materialization of these urban places filled the traveler with surprise and awe. If Jefferson had still been alive, these trends might have overturned his sanguine belief that America should and would continue to be agricultural "as long as we remain virtuous; and I think we shall be so, as long as agriculture is our principal object, which shall be the case while there remain vacant lands in any part of America." But how long is long? Jefferson guessed that the "immensity of land" would last for a thousand years. He foresaw neither the rapidity of exploitation of natural resources nor the swiftness with which agriculture spread.

Trapper and Lumberman: Forerunners of Agriculture

After the Revolution as Americans advanced the frontier into comparatively unsettled territory, they recapitulated colonial history in their reliance upon pioneer extractive industries—the fur trade, the lumber trade, and agriculture.

The fur trade, as before, sought the finer furs of the mink, the otter, the fox, the lynx, and the beaver and conducted a more utilitarian trade in deerskins and buffalo hides. Cutthroat competition prevailed, and every greedy trader rushed in to make money while it was possible. Under the impact of their attack the fur centers of the continent were rapidly pushed to geographical or national limits. The trade for a while lingered east of the Mississippi. But after years of hunting and trapping by French, English, and Americans the yield in this area began to decline; the decade of the thirties marked the beginning of the end; and the forties witnessed the final catastrophe. Meanwhile the fur empire had moved westward into the trans-Mississippi region. In colonial times this area had been penetrated by traders, but its intensive and wholesale exploitation awaited the nineteenth century. The fur capital of this new region was St. Louis. In this city, controlling the rivers that drained the fur areas, outfits were collected for dispatch to distant posts; hunting expeditions made preparations; and all the great fur companies had their resident representatives. To it came the furs to be baled and shipped down the Mississippi to New Orleans or eastward by waterways and land carriage to New York or Canada. It was the Montreal of the West. Although in this area trade was kept alive by the buffalo until after the Civil War, the catch of fine furs was diminishing by 1840.

The international character of the trade—it involved conflicts with Great Britain, for instance, from Detroit to the Columbia—and the relations which it created with the Indians inevitably involved national regulations for its conduct. The character of the trappers and the methods of the trade both suggested the possibility of improvement. At first the government contented itself with issuing traders licenses which could be secured only by presenting a certificate of moral character and by furnishing a bond to obey the Indian regulations. This method, however, was so ineffective that at the suggestion of President Washington Congress embarked upon the Indian trade itself. Posts were to be built by the government in the Indian country, and at these government factories officials were to give the Indian a fair price for his furs and conduct the business without the liquor and deceit which generally accompanied it. But after a history of alternating success and failure the national government abandoned this form of regulation in 1823. One reason for this abandonment was the inability of the government to compete with the private trader. The government factories, for instance, could not use liquor or advance credit to the Indian. A second explanation lay in the niggardly support given to the system by Congress. The factors which influenced Congress, then, were of importance. The most telling attacks were made by Thomas Hart Benton, master of language, English, classical, and profane, and Senator from Missouri, where the fur traders came from. When his campaign of vilification was successful, he received congratulations from the representatives of the American Fur Company for freeing the country from "so gross and unholy an imposition." In reality the St. Louis gang rather than the country was free.

In the nineteenth century the fur traders sought to correct the instability of their trade through the formation of fur-trading companies which carried on large-scale operations. The American Fur Company gradually gained, however, a predominant position. The nearest American equivalent to the great trading organizations of an earlier day—the company's opponents knew it as "a sort of bastard East India Company" on a small scale—it was the creation of John Jacob Astor, one-time German immigrant and later the builder of the first great American fortune. At first he invaded the Old Northwest and gained a virtual monopoly of the Great Lakes fur trade. Then, shrewdly recognizing the potentialities of the trans-Mississippi region, he attempted to develop the trade of the Columbia valley, but when this enterprise met with misadventure he undertook the successful exploitation of the Missouri region. During its heyday the American Fur Company was certainly a remarkable organization. Its posts extended from Mackinac to Fort Benton on the upper Missouri. On the Great Lakes it had vessels for the carriage of furs and for a subsidiary industry, lake fishing. On the Missouri, first keel boats and later a steam vessel transported Indian goods to the posts and brought back the annual catch. The ramifications of the company even extended overseas, for it purchased its supplies in England, France, Venice, and Trieste, and sold its furs from Canton to London. Through the latter the furs found their way to the Leipzig fairs, which at Easter and Michaelmas were the world's greatest fur markets. Even so powerful and profitable an enterprise could not withstand the exhaustion of resources and changes in the market. By the mid-thirties the great promoter of the trade, John Jacob Astor, had sensed its decline. In 1834 he visited England and wrote, "It appears that they make hats of silk in place of beaver." Astor returned to this country and sold out his interests in the American Fur Company. His successors and the big St. Louis traders hung on for a few years more, and then they too withdrew.

In colonial times the foreign market in England, in southern Europe, in the wine islands, and in the West Indies had stimulated a commerce in lumber and had created lumbering centers which were not mere adjuncts to farming or means of satisfying a merely local demand. Between the Revolution and the Civil War a more important domestic market appeared. The urban industrial regions of the northern states no longer had forest resources immediately at hand; and when agricultural settlement began to overflow the treeless prairies stretching from Indiana across the Mississippi, even the farmers became purchasers rather than hewers of timber. The construction of railroads, with their demands for ties and for wooden bridges, furnished another market. An industry sprang up to meet these requirements.

Since the United States had at hand a virgin forest, apparently in-

exhaustible, the lumberman could pick and choose his timbers for size
and for species. Except for special uses he ignored the hardwoods because
they could not stand water transportation in drives or rafts, and relied
upon softwoods—hemlock, spruce, and, above all, the white pine. In the
utilization of these natural resources before 1860 Pennsylvania, New
York, and Maine were the most important states. Naturally the industry
clustered about waterways. They furnished the power for the sawmills
and the avenue of transportation for raw material and finished product.
In Maine, the Pine Tree State, the Penobscot, whose outstretched
branches tapped territories from Moosehead Lake to the New Brunswick
line, became the dominant river. Log drives of pine and spruce followed
these turbulent waterways to the battery of sawmills on the lower river,
and at Bangor the finished lumber was loaded upon ocean-going vessels.
In New York the Erie Canal gave a cross-state artery and made Albany
a great lumber center, while Lake Champlain, the Hudson River, and a
connecting canal gave a north-and-south highway which brought down
to the sawmills of Glens Falls, as to Bangor, an army of logs, still in the
early fifties at least twelve inches thick at the butt. In Pennsylvania the
sawmills followed the forest inland, and down the Allegheny, Delaware,
and Susquehanna came huge ungainly rafts of planking or hewn timber
to be sold in Pittsburgh, Philadelphia, or Baltimore.

The lumber industry, like the fur trade, moved westward. In the
Northwest canny lumbermen saw a lumber El Dorado. The Great Lakes
furnished an admirable means of transportation, Chicago was a growing
city, the prairie markets were easily reached, and in Wisconsin and the
upper peninsula of Michigan were beautiful pine trees, reminiscent of
the virgin forests back east and growing upon the public domain, which
could be purchased from a beneficent government with good luck at a
minimum price of $1.25 an acre. The migration of the lumber trade com-
menced. It included the more enterprising lumber kings and the more
ambitious young men; and likewise the teamsters, axmen, foremen,
French Canadians, Scotch, and Irish, who joined the Germans and the
Scandinavians in the new lumber camps. Even the myths of the industry
were preserved. The Shanty Boy Ballads, the lumberman's folk song,
placed in a western setting the disasters of the log drive and the sorrows
of unrequited love; and Paul Bunyan and Babe, his big blue ox, the
legendary heroes of the lumber camp, performed in Wisconsin and Michigan new feats rivaling those once done in New Brunswick and New York.

Down the rivers which flow into Lake Michigan and Green Bay the
log drives came at the freshet season to be gathered safely within the
booms on the lower reaches where waterpower dictated a mill site. The
timbers were sawed and then floated in scows or rafts to lake schooners
which carried them to the lake markets. The Menominee, flowing into
Green Bay, became the greatest lumber-producing center in the world.

Its annual production reached 6 or 7 million feet, its drives turned miles of river into a solid mass of logs, and twenty-three mills poured "out lumber in an unending stream," wrote Stephenson, an emigrant from Maine, presenting "a pageant not unlike that which I had contemplated along the Penobscot from Oldtown to Bangor." Although Buffalo and Milwaukee were important markets, the great timber port of the Lake region was Chicago. Piles of lumber bordered its waterfront for miles. By 1860 neither Albany nor Bangor could rival it.

Land Policies in State and Nation

So strong and so untamed was the American impatience to possess land that the novel situations introduced by national independence almost immediately gave a chance to originate a new land system or to liberalize the old. The Revolution, for instance, provided an opportunity for destroying the feudal incidents to which property had been subjected in the Colonial era. The payment of quitrents was erased by legislation or was allowed to lapse. This movement against irritating feudal vestiges was directed at the same time against two other features of colonial land tenure which seemed unpleasant to the radical temper of the Revolution: the customs of entail and primogeniture. These were legal devices by which property was kept in the hands of the same family for generation after generation. Entail forbade the alienation of land, and primogeniture provided that the eldest son alone should inherit the entire real estate in case his father died intestate. On this side of the Atlantic, seven colonies, mostly southern ones, mirrored to a minor extent these two features of the English land system. During the Revolution the repeal of entails and primogenitures began, and within ten years of the Declaration of Independence entails disappeared in all but two states, where they were unimportant; within twenty-five years primogeniture had everywhere followed suit. The ease with which these changes took place suggests the abolition dealt with symbolic vestiges rather than actual legal burdens.

At the same time the Loyalists, who had been so unfortunate as to embrace the losing side in the Revolution, suffered a miserable and universal proscription which did not ignore the practical advantage of confiscating their real estate. In New York confiscated royalist land probably brought 3,150,000 Spanish dollars into the state treasury; returns from the sale of such land in Maryland were more than £450,000. The seizures and sale of this land resulted in the creation of small holdings rather than large estates. New York endeavored to discourage the sale of lots of more than 500 acres, and records of some of her great estates reveal that they were sold to many purchasers. The redistribution of land brought about by the American Revolution cannot, of course, be compared with that in

France during the French Revolution either in extent or in importance, and neither then nor later did large land holdings disappear in the United States. In the South great plantations still existed and landed grandees along the Hudson or in upper New York State owned manors sometimes of over 100,000 acres, and cultivated by leaseholders or tenants, at least until the anti-rent wars of the 1840's and resulting legislation modified the system.

Long since, in the 1780's, the new nation had laid the groundwork of a national land policy. The ordinances then enacted and subsequent measures, modifying and elaborating them, were to apply to the national domain which came into being as a result of land cessions by the states to the central government. Seven states possessed or imagined they possessed under their original charters claims to the areas west of the Appalachian Mountains. These were Massachusetts, Connecticut, New York, Virginia, North and South Carolina, and Georgia. The jealousies of the small towards the large states, the intermingling of the boundaries, the vagaries of title, and some degree of self-sacrifice combined to compel these states to surrender their western territories to the United States. The cession began in 1781, when New York took action; it ended in 1802, when Georgia, tired out with her efforts at state administration, completed the process. The domain thus created "to be disposed of for the common benefit of the United States" has been constantly enlarged. The Louisiana Purchase, the Florida acquisition, the fruits of the war with Mexico, the Oregon territory, the Gadsden Purchase have all been additions to this original nucleus. The lands of Texas alone never became a part of the national domain; they were retained by the state. The amount of land owned by individuals in these areas at the time of the acquisition was, in comparison with the total, trivial. At the present time, when private ownership in land predominates throughout the nation, it is difficult to conceive that the Federal government at one time or another has been the owner of an estate of 1.3 billion acres.

The sheer immensity of these Federal figures is apt to dwarf the importance of other land operations in the transitional period after the Revolution. As a matter of fact, in the West of the early nineteenth century there were extensive areas never included in the public domain, and probably only a quarter of the immigrants to the western lands before 1820 were affected by the national land policy. Some of the states sold their western holdings, as did New York and Georgia; others used them to compensate their citizens for their sacrifices during the Revolution, as did Connecticut and Virginia in Ohio. Many of the sales were to purchasers of large holdings, some of whom were foreigners. Perhaps the prince of speculators was an American, Robert Morris, Philadelphia merchant and famous financier of the Revolution. By 1795 his North American Land Company had assets of 6 million acres from Georgia to

Pennsylvania; he speculated in real estate in Washington, the new capital, and owned lands on the St. Lawrence. Before bankruptcy engulfed him, he had made resales to Americans and to Dutch and English, for foreigners were as "new-land mad" as they had been before the Revolution.

However ephemeral may have been the fortunes of these "proprietors" of the new Republic, these men were the medium by which the lands were placed in the settlers' hands. Generally the first step was the survey. In the northern areas it usually laid out townships which were sometimes sold whole to single speculators or to groups of settlers, who worked to establish a community life. In addition other aspects of colonization were attempted. The first agent dispatched by the English purchasers to their holdings in western New York laid out towns; surveyed and constructed roads; advanced seeds, provisions, farming tools, and livestock to occasional settlers; built log cabins, sawmills, and gristmills; and sold land. The New Englander penetrating westward into New York and northern Ohio thus found in these developments arrangements suggestive of the communal townships of his colonial inheritance. Only here the large capitalist rather than the town proprietors furnished the directing power and eased the course of settlement.

As the advance of settlers occupied the more accessible tracts and raised their prices, the policy which the national government had adopted for the public land became of supreme importance. The fundamental principles of that policy had been determined by the ordinances of 1785 and 1787. The latter, embodying an earlier ordinance, established the political principles under which American colonization was to proceed. The settled land of the public domain was not to remain in permanent subjection to the mother country, but, after passing through various stages of territorial organization, was to be organized into new states which were to be admitted to the Union upon terms of equality with the older ones. Thus, the American settlers on the national domain were not to occupy a permanent colonial status, but were, as far as democracy permitted, to shape the policy of their government.

The Ordinance of 1785 defined the land policy for the national domain. In view of the colonial dislike for quitrents and the democratic temper of the American Revolution, it naturally rejected the possibility of transferring the land to private hands under some arrangement of lease or rent. Rather the title was to pass, unencumbered with feudal fees, to the freeholder. A decision as to the methods of transfer was more complicated, for colonial practices in the northern and southern colonies had differed. Northern precedents, however, left the greater impress upon the national system. Indiscriminate location was rejected for a rectangular system of survey in advance of settlement. The land was laid out in townships, six miles square: the township was subdivided into sections

a mile square—640 acres. The sixteenth in each township was reserved
for the support of schools. These geometric details gave each piece of
property accurate bounds and a definite situation. Thus it was easy to
locate a purchase in the wilderness and to avoid boundary disputes. Both
these advantages facilitated actual settlement and gave a spur to speculation. Land could be transferred from buyer to seller with almost the ease
of a bushel of wheat or corn. Under the provisions of this ordinance half
of the townships were to be sold entire to purchasers, the other half were
to be sold in sections. The land was to be sold at auction, but no price
lower than a dollar an acre was to be accepted.

The Liberalization of National Policy

The Ordinance of 1785 instituted a land policy whose further
development was conditioned by a quarrel between different schools of
political thought, different sections, and different economic groups. On
the one hand were those who urged that the government should dispose
of its land prudently under somewhat severe terms, and on the other
were those who insisted upon a generous land policy. The controversy
between the two raged over such points as the size of the minimum allotment offered for sale, the price per acre, the terms of payment, or such
larger questions as preemption, graduation, or homestead.

By 1820 the liberal policy had won a great victory on the first cluster
of questions. The minimum purchase area had been steadily reduced
from 640 acres in 1796 to 80 acres in 1820, a reduction carried still further
in 1832 to 40 acres; and the minimum price had fallen from $2.00, which
had been set by an act in 1796, to $1.25 per acre. The only reversal in this
development was the repeal in 1820 of the credit arrangements granted
by the Act of 1800, which had postponed one-quarter of the payment for
two years and a final quarter for four years. But the fact that speculators
and purchasers were in arrears to the government for a sum of $21 million
was an unanswerable demonstration of the imprudence of credit
advances.[1]

[1] THE DEVELOPMENT OF GOVERNMENT LAND POLICY

Act	Minimum Purchase Acres	Minimum Auction Price per Acre	Conditions of Sale
1796	640	$2.00	{ ½ cash (cash deposit, rest 30 da.) { ½ credit (1 yr.)
1800	320	$2.00	{ ¼ cash, ¼ credit (40 da.)
1804	160	$2.00	{ ¼ credit (2 yr.) { ¼ credit (4 yr.)
1820	80	$1.25	Cash
1832	40	$1.25	Cash

The words "graduation" and "preemption" have at present the dull sound which attaches to dead political and economic issues. Before 1860 they aroused the enthusiasm of a crusade. Both causes were created by the rapidity with which the West was settled. The frontiersman, farmer, or speculator, confronted by the inexhaustible public domain, pushed forward, selecting the better lands. Behind in the surveyed areas he left islands of poorer land which found no purchasers, and those who desired a lowering in the price of sale saw here an opportunity for their argument. In 1854 Congress finally passed a graduation act which reduced the minimum price to $1.00 per acre after the land had been for sale ten years and made further reductions to 12.5 cents for land thirty years unpurchased.

Entirely different conditions were responsible for the preemption policy. In this case the settlers, outrunning the course of surveys, had settled upon the public domain. Actually this was indiscriminate location. In theory these squatters were criminals, for they trespassed upon land before it was open for sale. When the first townships were laid out in Ohio the military forces which accompanied the surveyors held off the Indians on the one hand and drove away the squatters on the other. Since the practice was too profitable and too deep-seated to be exterminated, Congress fell into the habit of legalizing these squatter invasions in special instances. Finally in 1841 it passed a general preemption law by which heads of families, men over twenty-one, and widows were allowed to settle on 160 acres of unsurveyed public land with the right of purchase at the minimum price when the land was placed on sale. The acts of 1841 and 1854 were but preludes to the complete victory of the liberal land party in the Homestead Act of 1862. This statute gave 160 acres in the public domain to "any person who is the head of a family, or who has arrived at the age of twenty-one years, and is a citizen of the United States, or who shall have filed his declaration of intention to become such." The only conditions which the government as donor exacted from the beneficiary were that he pay certain very small fees, and that he live upon his homestead or cultivate it for a period of five years. Thus the act was the ideological fulfillment of a long agitation and trend in American history. In practice other methods—sale, preemption, gifts to railroads, states, and veterans—long remained the chief avenues of land disposal.

John Quincy Adams, as well as anyone, expressed the statesmanship of those opposed to this successful liberal land policy. To his mind the public land was a great national resource from the careful administration of which funds would flow, to be devoted to the well-being, happiness, and education of all the people. Like Jefferson, Adams had a streak of the visionary. Easterners who dreaded the growing political power of the newer states in the West, and eastern landowners who saw the value of their real estate impaired by competition from the cheaper and more fertile lands of the West formed a broader base of opposition to the liberal land policy. Such dissenters were by no means confined to the Atlantic seaboard. In 1832 Henry Clay, Kentuckian, opposing a reduction in the price of public land, asserted that such a proposal would lessen the value of real estate in Ohio, Kentucky, and Tennessee and "impair the value of the property of the Yeomanry of the country." So quickly had settlement made even the West east.

As we have seen, Jefferson's words had provided the ideology for the liberal land policy. Land sold on liberal terms or given away to actual settlers promoted a true democracy. Every man had an equal opportunity to own land and the assurance of freedom from dictation by employer or landlord. Later such sentiments found a vivid spokesman in Thomas Hart Benton, Senator from Missouri. In words reminiscent of the Scotch-Irish squatters in Pennsylvania and of the New Jersey quitrent rioters, he said, "I speak to Senators, who know this to be a Republic, not a Monarchy, who know that the public lands belong to the People and not to the Federal government." The choice lies between the freeholder and the tenant. "Tenantry is unfavorable to freedom. It lays the foundation for separate orders in society, annihilates the love of country, and weakens the spirit of independence." At the same moment in the East the National Reform Association, an organization advocating land donations to actual settlers, was distributing a pamphlet, *Vote Yourself a Farm:*

If a man have a house and a home of his own, though it be a thousand miles off, he is well received in other people's houses; while the homeless wretch is turned away. The bare right to a farm, though you should never go near it, would save you from many an insult.

Beneath the rotund balderdash of the politician and the exaggeration of the pamphleteer was the thought that only in an equality of economic power lay the possibility of genuine freedom and democracy.

It was ostensibly the purpose of the government land policy to transfer the public domain to persons who would live upon it and cultivate it. It was not designed to enrich speculators. The enthusiasm for the Pre-emption and Homestead Acts was in part attributable to the hope that these democratic measures would outwit the speculators. Yet in 1862 an English observer wrote:

There are no statistics which show how many Yankees went out West to buy a piece of land and make a farm and home, and live and settle, and die there. I think that not more than one-half per cent of the migration from the East started with that idea; and not even half of these carried out the idea.

This thought was not another half-baked generalization by a glib foreign observer. In a sense every American pioneer farmer was a speculator. He hoped that the price of his land would be increased by that "great western staple, the Progress of the Country," and he often bought more land than he could cultivate with the design of selling this surplus for higher prices. A characteristic distinguishing the American farmer from the European peasant has been the former's willingness to gamble on land prices and recoup his losses on crops through appreciation of land values. In addition to the farmer, merchants, physicians, politicians, the small-town fry of the western movement, were speculators on a small scale in agricultural land. These phenomena were too accepted and universal a part of American life to arouse disfavor. It was the large absentee speculator who became the foe of the people. They "produce more poverty than potatoes and consume more midnight oil in playing poker than of God's sunshine in the game of raising wheat and corn." Here was the land monster.

Large-scale speculation runs back, of course, to the colonial era. It began in the public domain as soon as the Revolution was over, for during the period of the Confederation the land system had not been crystallized and the Confederation government, frantic for funds, saw an opportunity for obtaining money through the sale of government land in large chunks. Individual purchasers were eager to oblige. While some like Morris were purchasing state lands, others bought heavily in the Federal domain. In 1788 John Cleves Symmes, a wealthy New Jerseyite, petitioned for a million acres between the Great and Little Miami rivers in Ohio and paid no more than a dollar an acre. In the same year the Ohio Company, composed of former officers in the Revolutionary Army, proposed to purchase over a million acres in southeastern Ohio at a dollar an acre or less in depreciated Continental currency. In order to win Congressional assent, they had to unite their project with the more dubious scheme of the Scioto Associates, a group of aggressive speculators who bought to resell to Dutch and French purchasers. The calculations of Symmes and the Scioto Associates went awry, but the Ohio Company in its purchase laid out towns, gave grants of land to sawmills and gristmills, supported soldiers, undertook the construction of forts, granted loans, built houses for actual settlers, and in short performed in the Ohio wilderness the functions which chartered companies or proprietors had carried on in colonial Virginia and Massachusetts. The records of the company are too vague to show whether these operations were profitable.

These three enterprises were the only large sales of land authorized by Congress. Later speculative enterprises had to conform to the pattern of the national land laws. Large holdings could be acquired, of course, through large purchases at the auctions of the public land. The speculative gentry were also on a continuous search to find ways of purchasing land more cheaply. The Graduation Act was one loophole, and the generous provisions of this statute were consistently evaded. Congress showered a second bonanza upon the speculators in 1847, when it began giving soldiers who had served in American wars a warrant for 160 acres of the public domain and five years later made these warrants assignable. Speculators purchased such script from the recipients for from 50 cents to $1.15 an acre. In Iowa the one hundred and forty largest purchases of land by military script averaged 9,860 acres apiece; one purchase exceeded 250,000 acres. Individuals or companies built up large holdings. One of the latter, the Northwest Land Company, had for sale in the fifties 450,000 acres in the western states. These speculators did not always deserve popular obloquy. Some made improvements upon their holdings; others gave credit to purchasers; their resales were usually made at small profits. Taxes remorselessly ate up their possible gains. On the other hand, speculators corrupted land offices and legislatures and, by holding land off the market, dispersed settlement and angered the pioneer. Occasionally these large landholders sought to cultivate rather than sell their holdings. They developed tenancy, perhaps to cope with the problem of squatters, or farmed with hired labor.

Whatever the merits or demerits of the national land system, the public domain was settled with bewildering rapidity. The spectacular figures for the population increases in the western states have been given earlier in this chapter. These accretions to the population of the western states came from the same sources as those of the colonial West: immigrants from Europe and native Americans from the regions "back East." Although most of the immigrants upon their arrival stayed in the East, thousands of English, Germans, and Irish moved westward. In Iowa in 1860, for instance, one out of every seven or eight inhabitants was foreign-born. To be a "lord of the soil" was the ambition which moved native and alien to go West.

A Belgian investigator, pooh-poohing the political organization of the government as the cause of emigration, wrote in 1846, "Land which is cheap, of an almost unlimited extent, fertile enough to make capital unnecessary for its exploitation, is a powerful attraction for the agricultural populations of Europe. During the nineteenth century this attraction has been more powerful than any institution made by men." The same call moved the westward migration of native Americans. The London *Spectator* shrewdly observed the American West was to the State of Massachusetts or New York what North America as a whole was to Great Britain and Ireland. In other words, the European migration was but a feature and a fraction of the larger migration which was taking place continually within the states of the Federal Union. The whole East felt the drain. Certainly the states mentioned by the *Spectator* compensated their losses by the growth of commerce and industry and a population swelled by urban migration and European arrivals. On the other hand, the agricultural states of the East, like contemporary European countries, feared they were being "embowelled" of their human resources.

The price which those who went West actually paid for land is not so simple as the statute books would suggest with their minimum price of $1.25 at auction. And the price of land was fundamental, for it was the basic capital investment of agriculture. Eventually only a small proportion of the acreage sold by the Federal government in the 1850's went at or above the minimum price. Through the operation of graduated prices a large portion sold for less than $1.25 an acre. The government meanwhile was granting a still larger acreage under military warrants. If the original grantee used them, the cost of land to him was nothing; if assignees used warrants, they could buy land for less than $1.25 an acre. The government also granted lands to states and to private corporations, such as railroads. The prices at which the states resold to actual farmers varied; private corporations like the Illinois Central might charge $10 an acre on resale, but the railroad granted six years to pay, while the government had abandoned credit sales years before. In addition the settler had to meet the costs of clearing forested lands or breaking prairie sod, of buying seed and tools, of fencing his fields, of building his house and stables. Omitting land payments, it is estimated a settler in the 1850's needed $1,000 as minimum capital to start western prairie farming. But the sum depended upon individual circumstances, upon the location and scale of the farm, and upon the willingness of the pioneer to forego comfort and conveniences.

Agricultural Pioneering

Although there were many common features to this movement into the Mississippi basin, the agricultural aspect of that vast interior was not uniform from the Great Lakes to the Gulf of Mexico. Differences in physiography or in climate or in soil combined to mark across the West broad zones of different agricultural development. In a way the economic differentiation which had occurred east of the mountains in the thirteen colonies was extended to the larger area of the new nation. In the North the production of wheat, corn, and livestock preempted the area north of the Ohio and the Missouri rivers; the growth of other agricultural staples, of which the newest and the greatest was cotton, colored the expansion westward into the gulf states. Between these contrasts lay a mediating region which continued west of the Alleghenies the functions which northern Virginia, Maryland, and southern Pennsylvania had performed in colonial times. The Border states were not only Border states politically. Behind the party preferences and political performances of Kentucky, Tennessee, and Missouri lay an economic background which intermingled the characteristics of northern and southern agriculture.

The western domain which northern agriculture was to occupy before 1860 stretched from the Appalachian Mountains to a western limit following in an irregular fashion the hundredth meridian. The Great Lakes were its northern boundary; on the south it filtered into the Border states. It is a region drained by three great river systems, the Ohio, the upper Mississippi, and the Missouri. With the exception of the Allegheny plateau, which tilts northwestward from the Appalachian regions and disappears soon after it crosses the Ohio River, the region is one of lake plains, clustering about the Great Lakes, or prairie plains, sweeping westward until they reach the area of diminishing rainfall. This western domain's characteristics require superlatives. Most of it is comparatively level and extremely fertile. North of the Ohio and the Missouri the cause of this happy condition was the comparatively recent covering of the area by the glacial ice cap; its action pulverized rocks whose chemical constitutents are exceedingly valuable for plant life, and it laid down this material in a thick layer whose fertility was great and not easily exhausted. Because of the nature of the land over which it spread, the glacier deposited fewer of those areas of sand and of rock which did so much to hamper New England agriculture. In the nonglaciated land of Tennessee and Kentucky the value of the soil ranges from the infertile shale soils in the east to the rich alluvial bottoms of the rivers. In places a substratum of lime approaches the surface and creates spots of almost startling fertility. In Kentucky these limestone areas were distinguished by the riotous growth of the bluegrass. These limestone areas have an almost inexhaustible fertility, for deep subsoil plowing continually brings to the surface elements valuable for plant life. Throughout the whole region the rainfall is sufficient for agriculture and is generally well distributed; the time between frosts is long enough for the growing season; there is an abundance of sunshine. There is hardly an area in the world better suited for agricultural pursuits.

The first farmers crossing into this region found the conditions of pioneering were the same as those of the first one hundred and fifty years of American settlement. They were penetrating a heavily wooded region. For the settlers this primeval forest at once eased and hindered existence. The fallen timber furnished material for the inevitable log cabin, for the fences which were a necessity when a mixed agriculture of livestock and grain growing was to be pursued, and for fuel. Timber was adapted in the West "for purposes more anomalous, where wooden pins are substituted for nails, and wells are curbed with hollow logs, where the cabin door swinging on wooden hinges, is fastened with a wooden latch, and the smoke escapes through a wooden chimney. . . . Well may ours be called a *wooden country*."

On the other hand the ground had to be cleared in order to be cultivated and the American pioneer farmer became such an expert in the methods and instruments of destruction that guidebooks published for European immigrants advised them to purchase a farm already cleared, since the Yankee was three times as efficient a woodsman as the newcomer. The ax was developed to a point of efficiency equaled by few other tools. With this instrument smaller trees were notched and then brought down in a mass of entangled branches when a larger neighbor was chopped through. The whole pile was burned to add its ashes to the already fertile topsoil of the forest. Or the Indian-colonial method of girdling trees might be utilized and the crop planted below the leafless branches. An area thus rudely cleared might not be improved for several years. The stumps remained to plague the plow or the dead trees stood until they fell through decay or fire.

As the farmer pushed westward he was eventually confronted by a changed and challenging environment. The forested regions surrendered to the open prairie. There were, however, transition areas. In northern Ohio and Indiana small prairies were interspersed with the timber lands, and in southern Michigan and Wisconsin there were oak openings. These were beautiful parklike areas in which a few magnificent trees were spaced and the tangle of the forest gave way to prairie grass or low shrubbery. As western Indiana was reached the prairies became larger and finally in northern and east-central Illinois began the real prairie, which swept westward mostly treeless except for the heavy stands in river valleys and fringes along smaller watercourses. The reason for the appearance of these prairies is now believed to be a rainfall which permitted the growth of vegetation but was not sufficient to protect forests against recurrent fires. The pioneer did not have the advantage of this speculation. Bred to a forest farming, he believed that trees were a symptom of a "strong" soil and their absence on the prairie was a presumption of soil sterility. More vital was the upset which the prairie gave to forest technique. Material for cabins, fences, fuel was lacking. Well digging was frequently difficult, for the water lay under a lime substratum which only improved drilling processes pierced. Then there was the prairie grass. Its deep-thrust roots and closely matted surface spread a sod which was an impervious mass to the ordinary plow and was with difficulty planted to crops. All these disadvantages were heightened by the apprehension which these wide spaces with their limitless horizon inspired. They were open in winter to the unchecked winds, and it was said that the scorching rays of the summer sun maddened and destroyed the brain. As contrasted with the woods, the prairies gained an undeserved reputation for unhealthiness.

Population, however, edged out into these regions. The smaller prairies and the oak openings were first utilized. Then settlement skirted the edge of the large prairies. The ever running tide of settlers, however, gradually forced those who wished land onto the open prairie. The extension of railroads made timber supplies available. Wire fencing was introduced to enclose the fields, sod houses and barns were the temporary substitutes for the log cabin. And for breaking the soil, a heavy plow was designed to turn up a very shallow but broad furrow; it was pulled by three or four pair of oxen. In this way the grass and roots were most effectually exposed for decay. Although there were no rocks, the soil was so tough that the plowshare had to be sharpened every mile. Then the farmer planted his seed in the upturned furrow by picking a hole in it with an ax or mattock and dropping in his "sod" corn. This task would be done in the spring. The summer was devoted to building his house and fences and breaking more prairie for a sowing of wheat in the autumn. As compared to forest farming the start of a prairie farm was probably less expensive, although still barrier enough for the needy pioneer. The breaking task required such an investment in tools and such skill that it was generally turned over to professionals. The cost of preparing an acre—approximately $1.50—was more by a few cents than the cost of the land purchased from the government. And there were the other costs of timber for fence posts, for barns, and for the farm house. But once the initial handicaps were surmounted the prairie farm was superior. The soil was richer with the accumulated decay of roots and grasses, and with its absence of stumps and trees it was cultivated with greater ease and less vexation.

Under these pioneer conditions agriculture was self-sufficing until the improvement or construction of means of transportation hitched the farm to a local market of some western town or city or to some other section of the country or perhaps even to abroad. Meanwhile corn and wheat provided the chief cereals and the flour. Pumpkins and beans were grown in the cornfields, other vegetables came from the small vegetable patch tended by the woman of the family. Large herds of pigs foraged a living and after a few weeks of stuffing with corn were slaughtered for mess pork, bacon, and hams. A cow or two grew fat on the wild rye or buffalo grass, furnished milk, and on demise provided a fresh roast or smoked beef. The oxen, whose slow prodigious strength made them superior to horses for prairie work, eventually suffered the same fate. A few nondescript sheep provided mutton and fleeces for manufacture into pioneer clothing. The labor force was the family, and a high birthrate and large families were the rule. To hire outsiders as additional help to one's sons and daughters cost money. Everyone wanted to be a landowner rather than an agricultural laborer.

Aside from a small class of professional pioneers who enjoyed the loneliness and freedom of self-sufficing agriculture, most farmers desired to be on the make. To do this, however, they had to escape from the circle of self-sufficiency and raise an agricultural surplus which could be sold off the farm. The development of commercial agriculture, with its attendant problems, was just as pressing for the Iowa pioneer in the nineteenth century as it had been for the English emigrant to colonial Virginia in the seventeenth.

The farmer, therefore, devoted himself to those agricultural staples of the North which could form the basis of a commercial agriculture. They were Indian corn and wheat. The first of these could be grown almost everywhere in the Middle West; its yields were large, and its cultivation was easy. Although corn was taken to market, it more commonly furnished the basis for less bulky products which were more readily transportable. It might be distilled into whisky, or it might be used as a fattening crop for hogs and for beef steers, which could be driven easily to market. Livestock raising was one of the fundamental occupations of western farming. Wheat, however, was the cash crop par excellence, though it could not be grown as widely as corn and a year's cultivation of corn was often necessary as a preparation of the soil. Wheat did not require an interval of feeding to stock; it was more valuable than corn in proportion to its bulk, and it stood the costs of transportation better. Unlike corn it had a world market.

The shift from self-sufficing to commercial agriculture was made at various times. It cannot be dated precisely. For one thing, the transition was piecemeal; even on a single farm some operations might be commercially orientated, while others like butchering remained self-sufficing. For another thing, the date of the change varied from region to region as wider markets became available. In the decade or so following 1835 the growing urban areas along the Atlantic reached via the Erie Canal, the Great Lakes, and Ohio canals furnished a market for the interior agricultural counties of Ohio; the shipments of wheat and flour eastward from Cleveland and Toledo shot upward. Ohio agriculture had shifted to the new base of commercial agriculture. In the fifties the same transformation moved farther west. In two decades within these western states, north-and-south roads like the Illinois Central multiplied; railroads from Cincinnati and Chicago, probing west, reached the Mississippi River, and railroads from the East broke through the Appalachian mountains and sped across the flatter lands to Chicago and St. Louis. At the Pittsburgh or Wheeling gateways, commodities from the West could continue eastward by the Pennsylvania Railroad or the Baltimore and Ohio. In the fifties railroad transportation had a limited impact upon Ohio, as the state was fairly well settled and economically mature; but their penetration of the newer states was explosive. Illinois, Indiana, and Wisconsin in 1859 led the states in wheat production and deserved

the contemporary sobriquet, "the feeding power" of the nation. Their
peak year was 1859. At no time after the Civil War was the grain trade
of the Old Northwest as important to other sections as in the late fifties.

The history of corn was somewhat different. It could be grown almost
everywhere and under ordinarily careful tillage its yield per acre did not
decline as rapidly as that of wheat. It was comparatively immune to
agricultural pests. Pioneers almost immediately planted it. For years a
great deal of what was planted went to waste for lack of a market. The
South, as it happened, was a corn consumer. Corn was the staff of life
for slaves—on the average each slave annually consumed from 12 to 15
bushels and from 150 to 200 pounds of pork and bacon—the equivalent
of a dressed hog. Nor was corn segregated food; southern whites consumed
almost as much. But since production in the South from 1839 to 1859
was not large enough to equal demand, the region turned northward.
The Ohio River basin became corn's particular province. On the north
side were the rich bottomlands along the Scioto and Miami where fields
of one thousand acres laid down to corn aroused the admiration of
observers; on the southern side were the limestone areas of Kentucky and
Tennessee. The Ohio River with its tributary streams constituted a
natural system of transportation, down which farmers or others could
ship their corn and provisions on flatboats to New Orleans and ports
above it along the Mississippi. In 1839 the leading states in corn production were Tennessee, Kentucky, and Virginia. By 1859 Illinois, Ohio,
and Missouri had seized supremacy; Illinois raised twice as much as
Tennessee.

The rhythm and direction of change took a somewhat different
course in the case of livestock. The problem of markets was easier,
for animals could be driven to market. This the colonial period had
demonstrated. When farmers moved into the trans-Appalachian West
there was for the moment a question whether the animals could stand
the long drive. As early as 1810, however, some 40,000 swine were driven
from Ohio to the East. The western hog was rugged. Roaming the
forests or prairies, he lived on berries, roots, and grasses, and then in
the autumn grew fat on the mast of nuts and acorns. From the way
he fed and eluded wild animals, he acquired a rangy quality. Large-
boned, long-legged, fleet, he deserved his colloquial appellation of "wind-
splitter" or "razorback." Somewhat earlier, in 1802, cattle raisers in Ohio
and Kentucky were driving their stock to eastern centers and thus dis-
pelling the fear that these creatures would lose too much weight to
make the operation profitable. Long drives from the West to the
South or East had developed. A class of professional drovers undertook
these operations; their herds stirred up great clouds of dust, and the
drovers put up overnight at "drove stands," equipped with the necessities
of barroom for the men and pens and fodder for the animals. Canals and

steamboats had relatively little direct effect upon the drovers' business. But water transportation had an indirect effect upon the hog trade. These animals could be pickled as pork or cured as ham and bacon and their flesh was still palatable. Merchants and capitalists from the East started packing enterprises at Ohio River towns around 1818: Cincinnati became the packing center of the West. These packing localities exported to the South along the riverways, and they were located in the midst of the Corn Belt, where half of the crop in 1860 was used to fatten hogs and cattle and to make whisky.

As the railroads spread to and through the West, they brought about a shift in livestock production. It was not as pronounced as with grains. By the mid-fifties, however, farmers were aware it was both cheaper and more convenient to ship live hogs by rail than to drive them to market. With beef cattle the response to changed conditions was more complicated. By 1860 Texas with its open range and favorable climate had become the breeding and raising center for steers. Drives of these animals started northward and eastward to the midwestern packing centers or to more remote markets; they usually halted their animals for an interval of fattening with corn in eastern Iowa and Illinois—Kentucky had once performed this function—and they proceeded by rail to their final destination. Since the refrigerator car had not yet been invented, this was a live animal traffic. Though some railroads could not have made both ends meet without the revenue from this traffic, the cattle car became a traffic problem for them. Such cars had to return empty on the westward journey.

The change to commercial agriculture once made in the West, the aspect of the countryside altered. Observers as they moved back from the line of frontier settlement noticed that the ugly exploitation of land was mingled with symbols of a new urbanity and prosperity. The log cabin had been replaced by a frame or brick house or had been converted into a stable. The fields were cleared of stumps and better fenced. A more permanent class of cultivators had purchased the soil from its earlier possessors. The rural community altered. The French traveler Ampère thus described the "embryogeny" of Ogdensburg, New York:

Imagine big streets and black mud; sidewalks made of planks, here and there replaced with magnificent flag-stones; clumps of trees which belonged but now to the primeval forest; roughly enclosed ground—lots which appear to be abandoned—they belong to some one, but are not yet cultivated—and beside these abandoned lots imagine attractive gardens, elegant "cottages," the most modern civilization establishing itself on land cleared only yesterday; comfort along side the rude and the unpolished; cows grazing not far from a dry-goods store in the windows of which one may see styles from the Fashion Magazines and the pictures of the members of the provincial government; bales of merchandize in the street among overturned tree-trunks; a mixture of disappearing wildness and incoming industry, a combination of the Iroquois and the Chinese.

Meanwhile the agriculture of the East reacted to the competition from the more fertile and more easily cultivated land of the West. As early as the 1830's Massachusetts and Maine were driven to offering bounties on the production of wheat. Three decades later a New Englander was bemoaning the decline of the cattle trade in his area. He wrote:

It was admitted all around that owing to the great facilities for bringing cattle from the far west at a low price,—cattle which had roamed on the prairies, costing the government price, $1.25 per acre, and fattened upon corn worth 10 cents per bushel—we here could not compete on pastures worth $30 per acre and corn worth 75 cents.

For the East the loss of manpower through westward migration was also a prodigious drain. Its extent can only be surmised. But in 1850 there were approximately 1.5 million natives of New England in New York and the north-central states; and from New York and Pennsylvania over 1.3 million citizens had migrated, and these states received no reimbursement for the unproductive years of childhood and adolescence these persons spent within state borders. The same considerations applied to the migrants' children, a future labor force. Furthermore, many of the immigrants carried with them funds and movable property. If the farms which they left went out of cultivation entirely there was a loss of a part of the original investment for clearing and improving them. If these farms were sold in the open market their price was lowered through competition with other abandoned areas. The advertisements of land for sale ran into hundreds of thousands of acres, and some of it found no purchasers at any price. All in all, the temporary loss to certain areas in the East through westward migration is incalculable.

The Improvement of Agriculture

It is unjust to stigmatize the agricultural practices of the American farmer in the light of modern agricultural science, but only a knowledge of that subject makes it possible to evaluate the short-term or long-term results of his methods. Although many of the conclusions reached by scientific agriculture about soil fertility and soil exhaustion seem to the layman exceedingly tentative in character, there is a general agreement that phosphorus, potash, nitrogen, lime, and sulphur are necessary for healthy plant life. Some of these elements are withdrawn very slowly from the soil by growing plants; others are rapidly depleted. They can be restored by animal manure, soil amendments, artificial fertilizers, or by certain rotations. For instance, plants which are nitrogen fixers—beans, peas, clover, alfalfa—replace the nitrogen which is so rapidly consumed by certain crops; the same end can be attained by allowing the field to grow up to vegetation whose slow decay increases the nitrogenous content of the soil. More important than the amount of these elements in the soil is their availability to the roots of the plants. Their degree of decay or solubility, the presence of parasites, diseases, and weed toxins in the soil which hamper plant growth, and the activity of favoring influences such as some bacteria—all these are vital. So rotations of crops are necessary not only to restore fertility, but to rid the soil of parasites, weeds, and even of insect pests, whose life cycle is often closely interlocked with that of a single crop. Lime and manure are applied not only because they are plant foods, but because the former counteracts the toxins created by plant growth and bacteria and the latter improves the mechanical composition of the soil.

After all these precautions there still remain two menaces to a wise and permanent agriculture, leaching and erosion. Rain is responsible for both. In leaching rain washes from the soil the materials in solution before they are absorbed by the plants; in erosion it carries away into rivers or into the sea the surface soil itself, which contains the life-giving elements. In the days before agricultural cultivation the matted roots of trees and grasses prevented these losses, but plowing, harrowing, and pulverizing the soil for crops has destroyed this protection. The losses through erosion are staggering. According to one estimate, a tenth of the tillable land in Kentucky has been destroyed through this process, while according to another, farmland equal to the total cultivated area of England has already been abandoned in this country because of soil erosion.

American farmers did use rotations to some extent, but they were not always intelligent rotations. To interrupt the planting of the same crop year after year with an interlude of corn shaded out the weeds, but it restored no nitrogen; to throw a field into summer fallow invited losses through erosion. Nor was the resort to manuring customary. From grazing the livestock over the fields a haphazard fertilization resulted. But fields were rarely planted to grass, and the livestock usually ranged at large in the woods or in pastures where their manure went to waste. Occasionally, after a crop had been cut they were turned in to graze on the stubble, but this period was short. The accumulation of manure in stables and yards was felt to be a burden rather than an advantage to the farmer. Many barns were built over streams or banks so that the manure would not accumulate, and was often dumped into swamps or marshes where it could not offend the eyes or nostrils of the cultivator.

American farmers have consequently been censured as reckless exploiters, mining the soil of those elements of fertility which should have been conserved for posterity. This reproach is exaggerated. Losses through erosion and leaching are, of course, irreplaceable. On the other hand, sulphur and phosphorus were not withdrawn from the earth in dangerous amounts, and the slow process of nature restores the nitrogenous content of the soil. Although American methods momentarily exhausted the soil for the particular crops which were raised, that condition has not been permanent. The whole debate was, however, largely academic. The nation had turned over its agricultural development to the competition of individual farmers. They were likely, therefore, to adopt the easiest way of making money. Under the American conditions of a scarcity of capital and labor and an abundance of cheap land, the farmer inevitably chose to use the soil for all it was worth and then move elsewhere to repeat the process on new acres. It did not pay to farm well. The patriotic defense advanced by the census of 1860 had an economic basis:

> Our land is not so thoroughly under-drained, manured, and cultivated as that of England, Scotland, or Belgium; but we can, and do now, produce a bushel of wheat at much less cost than the most scientific farmer of England can by the best approved method of cultivation, even if he paid nothing for the use of his land.

But although it may have done less permanent injury than some critics assert, this exploitation of the soil's resources handicapped agricultural development. It established a pattern of agricultural practices which were difficult to alter when changed circumstances and new knowledge put a premium upon adaptation and improvement. Wasteful habits stood firm. In Wisconsin during the fifties, even when the wheat crop was unprofitable, the farmers continued to raise wheat through sheer momentum. The Scandinavian immigrants to that state, originally acquainted with dairy farming, swung over to wheat growing, cultivated that cereal year-in and year-out, and eventually found it difficult to readjust themselves to their original occupation, dairying, when the decline of wheat growing made such a change necessary. Carelessness bore the seal of success. Different practices were viewed with an air of contempt or superiority. A popular book on agriculture in 1860 stated: "Scientific agriculture stands today with phrenology and biology and magnetism. No farmer ever yet received any benefit from an analysis of the soil and it is doubtful if any one ever will."

The Agricultural Revolution: Abroad and at Home

The prerequisites to agricultural change were human ingenuity, courage to make experiments, money to initiate new methods and to endure the strain of their failure, and patience. All these qualities

were more apt to exist in an older agriculture than in one as rapidly
expanding and as highly mobile as was America's. Thus it happened
that a group of gifted amateurs in England were effecting in the
eighteenth century a revolution in agricultural knowledge and practice.
One of the first of these amateurs was Jethro Tull. He published in
1733 a remarkable classic, *The Horse Hoing Husbandry,* in which he
advocated the sowing of seeds not broadcast, but in drills or rows, and
emphasized the importance of the cultivation of the fields while the crop
was growing. Charles, second Viscount Townshend, at the same time
was experimenting with rotations, including the artificial grasses and
turnips, to restore the fertility of his soil and to produce abundant food
for a greater number of livestock, whose manure could be returned to
the fields. Later Robert Bakewell, though he had little more scientific
knowledge about breeding than his predecessors, for like them he bred
like-to-like and best-to-best, was quick to realize the new qualities desired
in livestock—meat rather than draught power, for instance—used in-
breeding somewhat more audaciously to stabilize desired traits, and,
perhaps most important of all, fed his animals generously. Finally at
the end of the eighteenth century the new knowledge and the new
methods of agriculture were disseminated by able popularizers, of whom
Arthur Young was deservedly the most famous, and put into practice
by farmers possessing intelligence and capital.

Then in the nineteenth century scientific knowledge began the more
accurate explanation of existing empirical methods and initiated the
adoption of novel practices. The development of chemistry was primarily
responsible for the change, and its pioneers all made contributions.
Progress was so rapid that by 1840 the German investigator Justus von
Liebig was able to issue in German and English his *Organic Chemistry
in its Relations to Agriculture and Physiology,* the basis even today of
scientific agriculture. Through analysis Liebig had become convinced
of the importance of the elements nitrogen, phosphorus, and potassium
to plant life and insisted upon their restoration to the soil in amounts
proportioned to their presence in the plant's ash. Although his fundamental contributions were sound, he went astray with the belief that
sufficient nitrogen was replaced by precipitation from the atmosphere
and that ash analysis was the proper determinant for fertilizer application. Later investigators corrected or amplified these theories. J. B. J. D.
Boussingault demonstrated the value of additional applications of
nitrogen and showed that legumes, in a fashion then unexplained, fixed
nitrogen from the air. In England J. B. Lawes and J. H. Gilbert, the latter
a pupil of Liebig, began at the laboratories and farm of Rothamstead,
"the oldest agricultural research station in the world," founded in 1843,
the half-century of experiments that were to fashion modern scientific
agriculture. They reinforced Boussingault's emphasis upon nitrates and

proved that some plants could profitably use greater amounts of minerals than Liebig had recommended. Thus the first steps toward soil analysis and the more scientific preparation and use of fertilizers had been taken.

The features of this agricultural revolution were adopted slowly in America. One explanation of this tardiness was the human preference for what is tried and therefore "true." A second explanation was peculiarly American. With an abundance of fertile land at low prices, "it was," in Jefferson's words, "cheaper to clear a new acre than to manure an old one." A third was the highly tentative character of agricultural knowledge itself. An American in 1860 could say with truth,

> Every question of the science and practice of Agriculture, such as plowing, draining, drilling, quantity of seed per acre, time of harvesting, cutting hay, feeding, manuring, and so on through every labor of the farm to sowing the seed again, is in doubt and uncertainty, and on almost any of these various questions two parties could be arrayed nearly equal in numbers.

But if agriculture were to survive in the eastern states it would have to find in new practices an escape from the invincible competition of the West. The handicaps of the East were discouraging. For one reason or another, its soil endowment was inferior to that of the western areas, where the new kingdoms of wheat, corn, livestock, and cotton were being established. In New England the soil was difficult to cultivate, and although it held its fertility after years of tillage, its natural richness did not equal that of the western prairies. In the South the surface fertility of the soil had been exhausted by cotton and tobacco crops, and the soil itself, lighter than in the northern states, had been a fearful victim of erosion. Nor was the West, with all its advantages, indifferent to the benefits of change. Improvements conceivably might reduce labor and other costs, or increase the yield per acre or the value of livestock. Farmers could increase their gains. Still, the situation was more critical in the eastern states.

When farmers turned toward change, they found at the beginning no institutions in the United States for diffusing a knowledge of the new methods of European agriculture or for conducting research and experimentation of their own. As in England, the improvement of American agriculture was, until the Civil War, largely the work of inspired individuals who had usually inherited wealth or acquired a competence from occupations other than agriculture or who, while in the midst of their agricultural innovations, still drew a steady income from other pursuits. For this type George Washington set the illustrious pattern. He made with his own hand a careful analysis of such English books as Tull's *The Horse Hoing Husbandry*, corresponded with progressive agriculturists abroad, including Arthur Young, with an almost pathetic humility, experimented with manure, soil amendments, and rotation, tried to breed up his domestic animals, and fought erosion as an enemy. Later men, similarly proud to bear the title "agriculturist," did even more. Some created an agricultural press more reliable than the granny's lore of the almanac and more regular than the occasional articles in country newspapers. Between 1819 and 1860 approximately two hundred and fifty agricultural magazines were started; most died, but at least one survived to attain a circulation of 100,000 in 1864. Still it was estimated that in the half-century before 1870, agricultural periodicals reached only one in ten among Illinois farmers. Nor did the metropolitan press ignore the subject. Both the *New York Times* and the *New York Tribune* had agricultural departments, and the weekly edition of the latter carried the zeal of Greeley and the information of Solon Robinson, one of the great agricultural writers of the era, into thousands of homesteads. Others turned their farms into training schools or demonstration projects for the neighborhood.

These agricultural leaders soon formed societies whose rosters in the eighteenth century read like a list of the signers of the Declaration of Independence or the Constitution. The lead was significantly taken by the eastern states. In 1785 the Philadelphia Society for Promoting Agriculture and the South Carolina Agricultural Society were formed. The example was followed in cities, towns, and states as far north as Maine. The membership of such organizations was catholic, for doctors, lawyers, ministers, statesmen, politicians, and businessmen were all admitted on the ground that, as the Philadelphia Society announced, "The interests of Commerce, Arts, and Manufacturers, form with Agriculture, an indissoluble union." Practical farmers justly asserted that these societies tended to reflect the "literary" or "philosophical" interests of "gentlemen" or "book" farmers and that too much time was devoted to papers celebrating, with a wealth of classical allusion, the worth of farming as an ennobling occupation. But Elkanah Watson, one-time merchant and speculator, later a large landowner near Pittsfield, Massachusetts, was the originator of a more popular and effective organization. At his suggestion, a few neighbors, following a practice which had grown up in England and France, held in 1810 an agricultural fair on the village green and exhibited their improved livestock. So successful was this innovation that the Berkshire Agricultural Society was established to perpetuate the custom. The idea now enlarged in Watson's mind. He would establish elsewhere similar county organizations of practical farmers to hold county fairs. These annual celebrations were to be social in character, with church services of "animated pastoral prayers and appropriate odes," parades in which officers and members marched, and an agricultural ball in the evening; but their main purpose was the award of premiums for the best exhibits. The movement for a time met with great success, declined for fifteen years after 1825, and then revived, particularly in the western areas of the United States. A list of "boards and societies" in 1858 enumerated over nine hundred organizations in the country.

These societies became the chief organized agencies for agricultural improvement in the nation. Their fairs varied the dull routine of rural life, and, more important, the exhibition of livestock and the demonstrations of farm machinery and implements exerted a tangible educational influence. But these societies were more than fairs; they operated throughout the year. Some possessed experimental farms, others imported improved cattle and tested agricultural machinery, and nearly all had meetings, sometimes as often as once a month, which discussed agricultural problems and listened to papers. These proceedings were published in the local press or, if the society was affluent, in separate volumes, many of which remain a valuable source of agricultural knowledge of the day. Little by little these groups took on a public character. The state gave them financial assistance for premiums or other projects and occasionally coalesced representatives of the different county associations into a state board of agriculture. The national government was slow in giving financial aid, but in 1839 it appropriated $1,000 to be spent under the direction of the Patent Office for the benefit of agriculture. From year to year the sums were increased, and in 1862 agriculture became a distinct government department.

Agitators for increased governmental assistance always placed in the forefront of their objectives the creation of an institution for teaching and promoting the industrial or agricultural arts. A start had been made early in the century as some college professors of natural history gave incidental attention to its bearing upon agriculture, and in the lower schools the interest in vocational studies aroused in this country by pedagogical experiments in Europe, particularly in Switzerland, often stimulated a very considerable instruction in practical agriculture. But by the Civil War there were few institutions that had the means or the men for agricultural research and instruction in scientific agriculture. Michigan had just established the first state-supported agricultural college, the Michigan Agricultural College. It had an experimental farm and offered a "wide range of instruction in English Literature, in Mathematics, and in Natural Science. Special attention will be given to the Theory and Practice of Agriculture in all its departments and minutiae." In Pennsylvania Evan Pugh, who had studied in Germany and at Rothamstead and demonstrated his abilities as a research man in agriculture, was heroically trying, as president, to get the Agricultural College of Pennsylvania under way. Meanwhile Yale had secured a head-start and preeminence. In the forties she had established a School of Applied Chemistry in the Department of Philosophy and the Arts.

J. P. Norton, who had studied in the laboratory of the Agricultural Chemical Association in Edinburgh, was its first professor of agricultural chemistry. His book, *Elements of Scientific Agriculture* (1850), although only a text, was the most important American volume in its field since the *Essays* of Jared Eliot. In the fifties S. W. Johnson, who had studied under Norton and under Liebig at Munich, secured an appointment to the school, became chemist for the Connecticut State Agricultural Society, and began a scientific analysis of fertilizers. He was to become the most influential agricultural scholar in his generation. Both Norton and Johnson came from American farms; both epitomized the transit of agricultural knowledge across the Atlantic.

It was a common observation in England that the improvements in livestock inspired a quicker imitation than those in tillage or cultivation. A Bakewell sheep was obviously so superior to the common animal that seeing was believing. The same generalization was true in this country, for improved livestock were introduced with comparative rapidity. In the large, the history of this movement again demonstrated the dependence of American changes upon European innovations, for Americans identified improvement with importations of better animals from abroad. Undoubtedly these foreign superiorities were often more advertised than real, and in America factors like generous feeding were responsible for American accomplishments.

Only in the case of hogs were importations of better breeds comparatively unimportant. This was not because the American breeds were an excellent base for experimentation, but because the rapid maturity and large litters of the animal made improvement easy. So, although boars of various breeds were imported from Europe and Asia, the native stock generally furnished the sows. Of the European breeds the Berkshire had the greatest vogue, but breeds produced in this country were equally favored, and the Poland China came to occupy a position equivalent to that of the shorthorn among cattle. Perhaps as important as the new blood was the care given to hogs. Except in the frontier regions, they were no longer turned out to be companions of the forest animals. They were often sheltered, curbed in pens for the whole or part of their lives, and fed more generously with corn. The typical American hog under these benign circumstances became a small-boned animal, his body a barrel of fat set solidly upon four short legs, his head and ears small, his tail short. The change, however, was not solely esthetic. His sides and quarters were loaded with pork fat.

American native cattle, a mixture of everything and "not very celebrated for anything," were "small, short-bodied, thin and coarse-haired, steep rumped, slab sided, having little aptitude to fatten, or to lay the fat on the right place." Importation of English breeds, not exactly identified, began immediately after the Revolution. Their effect was negligible. After the second war with Great Britain, American fanciers imported the shorthorn. They were not primarily dairy animals: instead their rapid maturity, their great weight, and their beautifully marbled flesh made them prime beef cattle. These attractive characteristics suited them for the trans-Appalachian area where the rich pastures and corn-fields in the Ohio and upper Mississippi valley provided their feeding requirements. Animals were imported directly into Kentucky or sold westward from eastern herds into that state and Ohio. Finally in 1834, a group of individuals formed the Ohio Society for Importing English Cattle. Funds were raised through the sale of shares of stock at $100 a share, a cattle dealer, was sent abroad to obtain the finest shorthorns irrespective of price, and nineteen animals were brought back. These were kept with later importations until 1836, when a sale dispersed the improved cattle through the Middle West and immediately realized a dividend for the subscribers. The importation of shorthorn cattle was the outstanding importation of cattle before the Civil War.

The enthusiasm for improved breeds was often so intense and so fleeting that their importation and subsequent domestication has been lumped under the heading of "manias" or "crazes." This classification was especially pertinent in the case of sheep. Before any profitable reason for improving the American breed of "natives" existed, amateurs and wealthy farmers had begun the importation of the Spanish merino, a sheep with a very fine and soft wool. These sheep were so much prized that Spain had placed an embargo on their export, and breeders in England, Germany, and France had gone to considerable expense and danger to obtain animals for their herds. In 1802 there were two very important shipments of merinos to the United States. Robert R. Living-ston, an American diplomat and a landed grandee of New York, sent to his large estates two pair of merinos selected from the French flocks; and Colonel David Humphreys, returning from his position as minister to Spain, was graciously allowed to evade the embargo and bring directly to America a flock of merinos to form the nucleus of the herds on his large estate in Connecticut. Here the matter bade fair to stop.

But in 1808 the wool manufacturing of the country entered upon seven years of hothouse stimulation, during which international con-fusions of one sort or another practically cut off the importation of English woolens and made woolen manufacture in this country profitable. The demand for fine wool far exceeded the supply, and prices for pure merino wool ran up to the dizzy sum of two dollars a pound. A merino craze swept over the country. Everyone wished to own such valuable animals. Livingston sold purebred ewes at $1,000, and Humphreys sold two rams and two ewes for $1,500 apiece. Meanwhile, in Spain, as a result of the Peninsular War, the embargo on exports had been raised, and owners of merinos were eager to convert their flocks into cash before they were slaughtered or dispersed. With that providential coincidence which seemed to have placed sheep fanciers in Peninsular diplomatic posts, William Jarvis of Vermont was consul at Lisbon. At once he undertook shipments which were the first in a positive stampede. Within sixteen months more than 19,000 merinos were sent to the United States. Although these extensive importations brought a reduction in the price of individual animals, the high price of wool still made sheep growing very profitable, and the common farmer, responding to the speculative excitement, purchased representatives for his herds. In many places along the Atlantic coast sheep raising became a major enterprise. Then came the inevitable deflation. After the war the competition of European woolens depressed wool prices and blighted the royal anticipations of the American speculators. Expensive animals were worth but a part of the former value. Disappointed farmers either sold their merino flocks to the butcher or neglected them.

In the 1830's the wool industry enjoyed a brief second blooming. The number of sheep increased 60 percent during the decade, and the quality was improved. Renewed concentration was placed upon the American merino. Native breeders, particularly those in Vermont, had developed a merino with fleece still fine but slightly heavier and longer. These became world famous. As these facts suggest, the East still retained the major share of the industry. New York's herds were in the western and central portions of the state—a broad zone paralleling the Erie Canal. Pennsylvania's holdings were more scattered. In New England a definite sheep district had grown up in the Berkshire Hills and in Vermont. This state was unique in the country. In the five years after 1832 its sheep increased over a million in number; it had more sheep per acre than any state in the Union; it was the home of the greatest breeders; and sheep there were a major industry. But the whole East was so touched by this episodic prosperity that an editor even foresaw the time when the wool of the North would rival King Cotton as a staple.

As it turned out, this was but the fancy of the moment. Between 1840 and 1860 sheep husbandry, quantitatively considered, remained at a standstill in the nation. But there were shattering displacements within its boundaries. The industry rushed westward. Ohio snatched the golden fleece from New York. The simple explanation for this dramatic overturn was the comparative cheapness of raising sheep in the West. The land in the East was a considerable expense—sheepwalks in Vermont were valued at thirty dollars an acre—but that in the West was cheap or might be grazed over for nothing. In the East there was the necessity of sheltering and feeding the sheep during the winter months; this was unnecessary in the western regions. The reason that western competition had not been damaging previously can be stated in one word—transportation. Not until after 1840 when the Erie Canal and the cross-state canals in the

Middle West had been opened, was it possible to transport wool profitably in great quantities from the West. Then once again the East faced adjustment. While some of the more famous Vermont breeders continued to produce selected stock for western purchasers, most eastern sheep-owners discarded the merino for the long-wool mutton types. Their coarser and longer fleece could be used in textile manufacturing, and their carcasses supplied the growing demand for mutton. Although importations of Southdowns and of improved Leicesters furnished a start for the new specialization, the extensive sheep industry of the East was not restored.

Observers in the Berkshires and central New York pointed out that the sheep craze had interrupted the development in dairying already taking place in these regions. After 1840 cold mathematical calculation sent the farmer back to this occupation. It was said that the annual return at prices current in 1850 from eight sheep, which consumed the same amount of feed as a cow, was about fourteen dollars; but the receipts from the cow ranged from thirty to sixty dollars. There were other advantages in dairying. Hogs were raised to hog down the food neglected by the cattle and to consume the waste milk; the prices of butter and cheese did not fluctuate as widely as those of wool, and a new market for these dairy products was opened in the export trade; the labor of the whole family could be utilized in dairying, but not in sheep growing. Finally, the dairy business enabled the eastern farmer to compete with the western prairies. The fresh milk sold in the eastern urban centers before the days of refrigeration had to be produced near at hand; the manufacture of butter and cheese required care, skill, and labor—pains which the western farmer did not find it necessary to take. With the decline of sheep raising, therefore, dairying came in with a rush.

At first the dairying area was confined to the western counties of Connecticut and Massachusetts, to the districts along the lower Hudson, particularly Orange and Duchess counties, and to the region around Philadelphia. By 1860 it had spread into Vermont, which was the first New England dairying state; it had supplanted the declining wheat yields of the Mohawk valley and invaded the Genesee country, creating in central New York a dairying rival to Orange County; it had moved westward to the Western Reserve of Ohio, where the production of cereals had never been as promising as the opportunities for grazing; and it had enlarged its area in Pennsylvania. In spite of the growing production of Ohio, the industry remained predominantly an eastern one. In 1860 New York State alone produced nearly half the cheese made in the country and nearly a quarter of the butter. Her supremacy was not only quantitative but qualitative. "Orange County" butter, although by no means confined in its manufacture to that district, provided a standard and was purchased by the United States Navy because it best withstood the heat of the tropics. Its superiority seems to have been due to the carefulness of and the exactness in its preparation.

The spread of dairying in the East worked a revolution in the treatment and breeding of milch cows. These animals were no longer left to shift in the open through the winter, but were better housed and fed. The improvement in milk breeds was effected through specialization. Cattle no longer were bred at the same time for beef and milk. After 1840 they were selected for their dairy qualities. Native animals who were good milkers were retained in the herds; the others were culled out and sold. There were scattered importations of Jerseys, Guernseys, and Ayrshires. The average yield of milk per cow was increased. According to statistics compiled by the Massachusetts Society for Promoting Agriculture, between 70 and 100 pounds of butter was a fair annual return from a cow in 1800; by 1840 the amount had increased to 166 pounds. The evolution of the cow into a milk machine had begun.

Scientific Tillage

No comparable achievement attended the introduction or breeding of plants. The first duty was pursued, to be sure, with organized zeal. Naval and consular officials, at the direction of the government, sent back seeds and plants from abroad; travelers with agricultural interests returned laden with vegetable booty; and the Patent Office distributed seeds of novelties to American farmers and grew tea plants and pomegranate cuttings in its "propagating houses" in Washington. Perhaps the most important immigrant arrived in 1819 without official fanfare: Mediterranean wheat, a semihard red winter wheat, whose greater hardiness and early maturity enabled it to challenge the attacks of rust and Hessian fly. But the period as a whole lay between the great importations of colonial times and the more systematic introductions of a later date. Nor did ordinary farmers and their leaders possess a knowledge of the techniques required for plant breeding. They could do no more than select from the accidental mutants and hybrids in their fields the seeds of specimens that seemed unusually productive and otherwise desirable. Although this method was not scientific, it gave new varieties of wheat, corn, and cotton.

Farmers with a bent for improvement were more concerned with the question of rotations and fertilizers. The Agricultural Revolution in England had early emphasized these matters, and now Americans worked out rotations for their own conditions. Although often advised to follow the British pattern, they discarded the turnip. In our northern zones this root would not winter in the ground, and it required a great deal of labor. Indian corn served just as well, for its cultivation killed the weeds and demanded less labor; its leaves and ears furnished fodder. Increased attention was given to artificial grasses, for in the eastern states the native grasses, generally speaking, were unsuitable for livestock. Natural meadows were occasionally reseeded; the grass sequence in rotations was prolonged, and the uplands were sown with the European grasses introduced in the Colonial era. Thus eastern farms grew hay for the markets of eastern cities and forage for their greater herds and flocks. In 1860 New England and the Middle Atlantic states produced 76 percent of the hay in the United States.

Clearly the question of fertilizers and rotations were interlocked. But it took years of experimentation and research to determine what crops and what soils required what fertilizers and in what amounts. The old distaste for animal manure passed away. Reformers from Maine to Georgia emphasized its importance, and popular opinion approved the saying, "The size of the manure pile is the measure of success in agriculture." But the management of livestock to produce the greatest offal, the protection of manure from leaching in the rain, and the time and manner of its application were matters of excited debate. Others directed their attention to the mineral manures, gypsum and marl. The former added calcium and sulphur directly to the soil, and by stimulating the growth of legumes it returned nitrogen to the fields. Early in the nineteenth century a rage for "gypsum and clover" swept the East; it yielded results—on the right soils. Marl, usually rich in calcium carbonate and lime, sweetened an acid soil and prepared it for animal manures. A scientific appraisal of its value waited upon the work of Edmund Ruffin, a Virginia planter without formal scientific training, whose book *Essay on Calcareous Manures* (1832) was declared at the end of the nineteenth century to be the "most thorough piece of work on a special agricultural subject ever published in the English language." In lower Virginia, where this fertilizer was used, the worn-out soils spurted forward under its application and the whole of agriculture was revived. Then in the forties Americans learned the miraculous value of guano, the dried droppings of birds on the islands off the coast of Peru. One writer in 1844 declared, "In effect, this article *Guano,* will transfer the Western lands to the Atlantic." Finally in the next decade a New Jersey agriculturist, J. J. Mapes, patented a nitrogenized superphosphate, the first complete artificial fertilizer in the United States.

These innovations not only aided general farming but assisted specialized agricultural production where favored districts facilitated such development. The urban markets made possible intensive agriculture in truck farming. Near the large cities, Baltimore, Washington, Philadelphia, New York, Boston, the land rose in value, and it was ditched, drained, and highly fertilized. Often immigrants trained abroad in market gardening leased and finally purchased the land. These same markets made possible a better fruit culture. Previously apples and peaches had been prized preeminently for their beverage possibilities, but overproduction and a temperance movement had destroyed the value of this market. Orchards were neglected and the fruit fed to animals. After 1840, however, the city markets called for fresh fruit, and comparatively rapid transit carried the product toward the demand. New York State developed apple orchards, New Jersey and Delaware and Maryland grew peaches, and the Ohio and Missouri valleys began grape cultivation.

With the increased rotation of crops and the use of fertilizers went a change in the methods of cultivation. In the South the great problem was that of erosion. Deeper plowing, advocated as a means of lessening this evil, gave plant roots greater freedom for growth and produced a layer of earth which absorbed the rains and prevented gullying. On the hills the old method of plowing up and down and thus constructing perfect channels for erosion was succeeded by the practice of horizontal plowing. Here and there in the East the old methods of broadcasting seed gave way to the drill, and the cultivation of the fields grew more frequent.

Agricultural Machinery

America's most original contribution to the agricultural revolution was the invention of agricultural machinery. It would be pleasant to presume this preeminence was due to the superior inventive capacity of the American mind, but, as a matter of fact, the conditions of American agriculture accounted for American prowess. American farmers made profits most easily when they expanded their production by opening and cultivating new lands. The absence or primitiveness of farm tools and implements limited the area utilized or made cultivation so burdensome as to be intolerable. A labor force, other than the family, was hard to come by. A modern machine would multiply the effectiveness and speed the operations of the farmer and his sons.

The variety of appliances which were invented or improved—hay tedders, mowing machines, hayrakes, cultivators, drills—is a challenge to description, but the more fundamental improvements were made in plowing and reaping instruments. The plow, in spite of its comparatively simple appearance, is the result of many inventions and a rather complicated evolution. The colonial plow was a clumsy instrument. It required several horses or oxen to pull it, and two or three men to guide it and keep it in the ground, and it turned up an edged rather than a flattened furrow. Each plow was unique, for the local blacksmith, using his own designs, made it of wood with perhaps the wearing edges clumsily protected by iron strips. The first improvements in this imperfect tool were made by theorists. Thomas Jefferson, speculating on the proper lines for the moldboard, worked out mathematical formulae which, with little revision, have stood the test of experience. With less effort the furrow slice was now evenly cut, gradually raised and turned over, flattened, and broken. The friction was so reduced that the team was halved and one man was able to do the plowing.

These theoretical contributions, important as they were, would have failed unless embodied in an instrument more carefully and more permanently constructed than the old plow. Although at the close of the eighteenth century a patent for a cast-iron plow had been granted, its disadvantages hampered its introduction. Cast iron was easily broken, and the cutting parts were dulled. Jethro Wood, a New York Quaker, in 1819 overcame these initial difficulties. The share, the moldboard, and the landslide were all separately cast and then fastened together into the whole instrument. If any piece needed to be replaced, an interchangeable part could be inserted by the farmer without the aid of a skilled plowright. The moldboard of the Wood plow utilized in part the Jeffersonian formulae. As long as hoe and ax were the tools relied upon for planting and growing corn, it took, according to estimates, in about 1800, 344 man-hours to produce one hundred bushels of corn and 185 to harvest an acre of cotton. By about 1840 these estimates were 276 and 135 manhours respectively.

When settlement spread to the prairies, the cast-iron plow was unable to break their heavy soils. The moldboard scoured poorly, and the plow plunged about in the turf. An Illinois smith, John Deere, then built a very light plow of high-grade rolled steel which cleaned beautifully. The widespread use of this improved machine was for a time retarded by the difficulty of securing metals, but by 1847, when he began the manufacture at Moline, American steel of the desired quality was available. As Deere's experience suggests, plow making had been placed on a factory basis. As early as 1830 two factories in Pittsburgh were manufacturing 34,000 plows a year, and by 1858 Deere's annual output at Moline was 13,000. Cheaply turned out by large-scale production, expertly designed, constructed of proper materials, and equipped with interchangeable parts, the American plows became the standard of the world. They were exported to Europe, and at the great London Exhibition of 1851 they won the commendation of the judges for their "extraordinary cheapness and lightness of draught."

The improvements in this fundamental instrument were, however, less startling than those which revolutionized the cutting of grain. By the end of the Colonial era farmers were commonly using the cradle, a scythe with a rack of long fingers above it, to harvest small grain. The rack caught and kept the cut stalks in such good order that they could be bound and stacked with comparative ease. Since it could cut and gather half an acre of grain a day, the cradle made possible a larger harvest than the scythe or sickle. But when the harvest season lasted only a week to ten days, the cradle's accomplishment was still insufficient for grain growing on a very large scale. A farmer must be able to reap as much as he could sow.

But the difficulties of a mechanical reaper were bafflingly numerous. It had to run over uneven ground, cut the stalks and deliver them in an orderly arrangement, and somehow furnish the power for such operations. The natural source of power was the rotation of the wheels of the reaper over the field, but how draft animals were to pull any such contrivance through standing grain without trampling the grain down was so perplexing that the early experimenters put the animals behind their inventions and had these contraptions pushed over the fields. Eventually, however, the idea of placing the horses to one side of the cutting edge was adopted. After heartbreaking trials with various devices a cutting edge consisting of a serrated knife moving back and forth between stationary fingers, which gathered up the grain in tufts, was invented. Other improvements were a divider, which separated the grain to be cut from that left standing; a reel, a device with a sort of windmill effect, which in its revolutions pushed the grain against the reciprocating knife and then laid the stalks evenly upon the grain platform behind the cutting edge; and a seat on the machine for the driver and worker who raked the stalks off the platform. All of these arrangements, with the exception of the divider, had been devised by various inventors and were combined in 1822 by an English schoolteacher, Henry Ogle, into a single machine.

What relation these earlier English experiments and the early American experiments had with the two American creators of the reaper is a matter of conjecture. At least the thing was in the air. The struggle between the two American inventors, Obed Hussey and Cyrus Hall McCormick, is one of the vivid tales of American invention. Hussey, a Nantucket sailor, dreamy and rather impractical, patented his machine in 1833. McCormick, a farmer mechanic from the western valley of Virginia, was a hard-headed inventor and businessman. His first patent was secured in 1834, but three years earlier his first reaper had cut a very small stand of grain. The great superiority of these solely American reapers over their predecessors was in the cutting edge. The projecting fingers were grooved, and the reciprocating knife was jagged with teeth which worked in and out of these grooves. The grain brought back by the reel was thus clipped or sawed most effectively. The angle of the teeth and the shape of the groove were the subject of experimentation over a period of years, so that finally the grain never clogged in the apparatus and the reaper could mow without racing the horses. In the course of these improvements the machines of McCormick and Hussey began to resemble one another. The actual contribution of each inventor thus became a matter of controversy which dragged through lawsuit after lawsuit.

In spite of their early invention, the difficulties of manufacturing reapers and securing their adoption prevented their widespread usefulness. It was not until the decade of the fifties that they spread rapidly to the grain-growing western prairies for which they were particularly suited. With the plow the American reaper made the journey to the London Exhibition of 1851, where it eventually won the approbation of the London *Times,* at first merely amused by its curious appearance. But the American reaper's greatest triumph was at the Paris Exhibition of 1855, where it was entered in a contest with English and Algerian reapers. The Algerian reaped nearly an acre of oats in seventy-one minutes, the English in seventy-six, and the American in twenty-two. Whoever may have been the inventive genius which created this American product, McCormick rather than Hussey reaped the material rewards and was the better businessman. In 1848 he moved his factory to Chicago to be at the door of the rising wheat empire of the West; he was constantly on the alert for improvements; and in his competition with others he employed an efficient ruthlessness. His advice to one of his lieutenants in a lawsuit in Maryland was, "Meet Hussey in Maryland and put him down." In the second half of the fifties, McCormick was producing, though not always selling, over four thousand reapers a year. Aside from particular illustrations of individual machines and their inventors, American agriculture in 1845–1855 invested an average of $11 million a year (1910–1914) in implements and farm machinery: in the next decade the average was $25 million.

Undoubtedly, machines quickened and eased agricultural operations. The horse hayrake, often driven by a boy, performed the work of seven men with hand rakes; the mowing machine did as much as a crew of ten men equipped with the old scythes; the reaper which cut fifteen acres a day kept a crew of only nine men busy binding compared to a gang of fourteen using cradles; the corn cultivator made it possible for a man to cover three acres for one with the old plow; Pitt's mechanical thresher —American improvements grafted upon a Scottish invention—"which literally devoured the sheaves of wheat," could thresh over twelve times as much in an hour as six men equipped with the old hand flails. While the man-hours per acre decreased, the further influence of machinery upon yield is uncertain. Too many factors are involved for isolation and quantification. Indeed, it might be argued that machinery reinforced the tendencies toward wasteful and extravagant methods. For with the improved machinery it was possible for a man to farm extensively thirty, forty, or sixty acres rather than ten or fifteen.

Southern Agriculture

New Staples for Old

By their Revolution, Americans cut themselves out of the Acts of Trade and Navigation. This excision had repercussions upon southern agriculture. The British bounties which had made possible the growth and processing of indigo in the South were withdrawn; and as Britain turned to alternative sources of supply, the American industry was practically extinguished. British legislation no longer enumerated tobacco as a commodity which must be shipped to British ports; and the English market, once assured to the American producer, was from time to time practically closed by duties which sometimes mounted to 900 percent ad valorem. European nations had their own commercial systems also; and since customs upon tobacco were easily levied and collected, the Europeans began erecting tariff walls to stimulate domestic production or to favor their colonies in the East and West Indies or producers in Latin America. The price of tobacco fell so low that only exceptionally favored areas in the United States could afford to continue growing it. The third colonial staple, rice, constituted the fourth most valuable agricultural export, and it also had the good fortune to experience a growth in the domestic market.

Nonetheless the South assured its specialization in staple production by the discovery of new staples, one of which was sugar. In 1860 the value of sugar shipments abroad was not impressive: brown sugar, valued at approximately $103,000, was sent primarily to Canada; and refined sugar, valued at approximately $30,000, was exported to Latin American markets, principally in Chile. On the other hand exports of cotton mounted repeatedly to spectacular levels. In 1784 when an American ship attempted to unload eight bales of cotton at Liverpool, the customs officers seized them on the grounds that so much cotton could not have been raised in the United States. In 1860 the United States exported 3,774,000 bales, of which 2,669,000 bales went to Great Britain. Of its own production the United States consumed 978,000 bales.

The achievements with both these staples depended to an exceptional degree upon the invention of machinery or the correct use of manufacturing methods. Both successes occurred long before the 1850's, the decade when mechanical methods generally took hold in American agriculture. Sugarcane had been introduced from Santo Domingo into Louisiana during the eighteenth century by the French in the frantic effort to give their colony at the mouth of the Mississippi some profitable pursuit. The refining of the syrup, however, was so crude that the product never found a foreign market. The first planter to produce sugar on a successful and conspicuous scale was a Creole, Étienne de Boré. In 1794 he planted a crop of the native cane, erected a grinding and boiling mill, and employed an expert sugarmaker. In the following year the critical test occurred. A large crowd gathered to watch the concentration of the juice, and when the crystallization of the fluid successfully took place "the wonderful tidings flowed from mouth to mouth and went dying in the distance as if a hundred glad echoes were telling it to one another." Boré was acclaimed as the "Saviour of Louisiana." He presumably derived more satisfaction from the $12,000 which he secured by the sale of his first crop.

Cultivation of sugarcane was confined to a small area. Aside from a few plantations in Georgia and Florida and an insignificant offshoot to the Brazos River in Texas, the industry always clustered along the bayous, watercourses, and rivers of southeastern Louisiana. In this sugar district, extending only as far north as the junction of the Mississippi and Red rivers, the soil was rich and the growing season ordinarily long enough to allow the crop to mature before the arrival of the first autumn frosts. The plantations bordered the rivers whose banks built by rich deposits of silt, alone furnished land sufficiently dry for cultivation. Since even these strips were occasionally inundated by floods, the construction of levees had to be undertaken. It was not as difficult a task as today, for the open valley above Vicksburg impounded the waters, distributed their flow more evenly, and lowered the level of the Mississippi freshets along the lower river. In spite of these advantages the waters would occasionally break through and destroy a portion of the crop. The natural disasters of temperature and flood, changes in cotton prices, which from time to time were so high as to persuade planters to abandon one staple for the other, and the changes in tariff duties—all occasioned extreme fluctuations in the industry's history. Sugar production, nevertheless, marched forward. In the first decade of the century French immigrants, rushing in terror to Louisiana from the Negro insurrections in Santo Domingo, pushed the cultivation of sugar, their favorite staple, northward from New Orleans. Anglo-Americans filtered in from the East and copied their methods. The crop of 1853 produced a total of 450,000 hogsheads—over 220,000 long tons—a figure not reached again until the close of the nineteenth century.

The Cotton Kingdom

The traveler through the southern states might be impressed by rice and sugar; he was certain to be stunned by cotton. From Charleston, where the wharves were piled high "with mountains of Cotton, and all your stores, ships, steam and canal boats [were] crammed with and groaning under the weight of Cotton," to Tennessee, where they thought poorly of Kentucky because cotton would not grow there, the crop was a veritable "plague." Only when the traveler reached the Ohio River did he find a boat which "had not a bale of cotton on board, nor did I hear it named more than twice in 36 hours."

This "plague" had been made possible by the curious history of cotton. Cotton cloths had first been introduced into Europe from the Orient; by 1700 the cotton industry was established in Great Britain, and later it was revolutionized by new machinery, run by water or steam power, and grouped in factories. The new rapidity and cheapness of production stimulated the market for cotton cloths, but consumer and manufacturer alike faced the shortage of cotton fibers.

Production in the United States erased this deficiency. Here in the Colonial era cotton fibers had been utilized in textile production and the supply had been in part imported from the West Indies and in part grown in small patches in some of the colonies. Its extensive cultivation was checked by the difficulty of separating the lint from the seed. It took nearly a day to clean a pound of the material. A remedy might be discovered in either of two fashions. Some different variety of cotton might be discovered whose seed was less tightly wrapped in the fiber than in the green-seed, short-staple cotton, or else machinery might be invented to perform the process of separation effectively. In point of time the former alternative came first. Several planters began experimenting after 1786 with a variety introduced from the Bahamas, a "sea island cotton." Its two-inch fiber was longer and silkier, and the seeds could be popped out by passing it between the rollers of the roller gin, a machine which the cotton producers of India had utilized. Sea island cotton, however, was not the salvation of the South. Although it was grown, often on a large scale, until the Civil War it remained a cotton crop de luxe. The plant was exceedingly sensitive to frost; its cultivation required great care; and the district in which it could be grown was confined to a narrow strip on the coast and offshore islands of Georgia and South Carolina.

The area for green-seed, short-staple cotton was not so limited. The invention of a cotton gin which could separate the seed from the lint successfully was the work of Eli Whitney, a Northerner who had come South in 1793 to teach school. While he was stopping at an estate in Georgia, his attention was called to the "extreme difficulty of ginning cotton," and he set to work. In ten days he completed a model. Later refinements did not essentially alter its principles. The cotton was placed in a hopper, one side of which was pierced by slots too small to allow the passage of the seed, but large enough to let the wires, or teeth, set upon a revolving cylinder on the other side come through and seize the fibers. The cotton thus passed through the grating, while the seeds fell to the bottom of the hopper. The lint was then removed from the first cylinder by another brush-studded cylinder, which ran in the opposite direction at a greater speed. Whitney took another Yale graduate and one-time tutor in the South into partnership with him. They planned to establish ginning mills throughout the South and to charge, after the fashion of the colonial gristmill, a toll in cotton for cleaning the grower's harvest. They proceeded too slowly. Rumors of the invention spread; a mob broke into their shop in 1793; and the principles of the gin were embodied in the improved machines of rivals. The Whitney associates spent years in the law courts, but eventually the returns from their machine canceled their expenses in defending their patent. Whatever may have been the personal misfortunes of the inventor, the South was liberated. The short-staple cotton could now be prepared cheaply and easily for the market.

The South at once plunged furiously into its cultivation. In the Georgia and South Carolina coastal plains, indigo was abandoned and even rice fields were transferred to the new staple. Cotton penetrated northward into North Carolina, and Virginia tobacco planters saw in it a profitable substitute for their declining tobacco. While outriders of its advance reached the Mississippi before the War of 1812, cotton consolidated its hold upon the Piedmont of the Carolinas and Georgia. It was upland cotton. So rapid and absorbing was its progress that this formerly grain-growing region had to import its food supplies for a time. Then the stream shifted southwestward around the end of the Appalachian Mountains. The second war with England removed the Indian barrier to western settlement, and like northern crops before and since, cotton poured westward. Its mobility in this direction was like that of the rest of American farming.

As cotton swung around the mountains into the lower South, it found unsurpassed soil advantages in two areas. The first, the "Alabama Black Belt," began in south-central Alabama and curved upward into northern Mississippi. This Alabama-Mississippi district was partly forested and partly open, and its soil was a heavy black or brown loam. The second district lay along the Mississippi River and its affluents. These broad bottom lands had been built up for ages with silt carried down by the rivers. In the United States there was probably not a soil more fertile, and its depth made that fertility practically inexhaustible. Its fitness for cotton culture was further demonstrated by the tendency of the plant to grow a longer fiber. So cotton cultivation spread northward from the junction of the Red River and the Mississippi along the river valleys and bayous into eastern Arkansas and western Tennessee. Even these conquests were not sufficient, and the migrating cotton plant moved forward to Texas. The promoters and early settlers of that region were enthusiastic about its soils. One wrote back to Georgia in the effete East that "the best lands in Alabama, Mississippi, and Louisana are far inferior to the lands of Texas." The soil on the lands near the falls of the Brazos was "at least fifty feet thick," and weeds twenty feet high grew upon it. With the exception of the black waxy prairie, the Texas lands, however, were not the equal of the alluvial river districts farther east. So it was that by 1830 these new areas strode ahead to superiority. Thirty years later Mississippi, Alabama, Louisiana led the cotton parade. Georgia was the first eastern state to place. Texas and Arkansas preceded South Carolina. Of the western states Mississippi alone produced over twice as much cotton as Georgia and South Carolina together. Like wheat and corn, cotton had developed a western empire.

The place of cotton in the life of the whole nation was impressive. In 1792, the year before the invention of the cotton gin, the annual production of the country was somewhat over 6,000 bales, reckoning five hundred pounds to the bale; in 1794, the year after the invention, production had increased by 10,000 bales. From then on the increase was rapid until in 1859 production reached its highest prewar level of 4,508,000 bales. These were absolute figures. The southern planter inclined to comparisons observed on the eve of the Civil War that his favorite staple accounted for half the value of our total exports and that this figure was nearly ten times that of its northern rivals, wheat and wheat flour. Or if exports were deemed an unsatisfactory criterion he could resort to the domestic industry of the nation. The American cotton manufactory, dependent upon the southern states for its raw material, turned out an annual product whose value was half again as much as that of wool, its nearest textile competitor, and half again as much as that of the varied iron industry of the country. In the entire world there was no rival to the South as a cotton-producing area. As late as the mid-fifties the Manchester spinners, upset by a rise in the price of cotton, gave way to their customary anxieties about a cotton famine and formed an association to discover if there were not alternate sources of supply "so as to lessen the dependence of Great Britain on the United States." But to no avail. It was the contemplation of this whole picture that fired southern politicians to boast that "Cotton *is* King."

In many respects this commitment to cotton as a staple resembled a similar attachment to tobacco many generations earlier in Virginia and Maryland. Preliminary to the cultivation of the crop was a phase of self-sufficing farming when the pioneer cut down the forest, built his log cabin, and planted corn in a rough clearing. Even the fencing that protected and partially confined his livestock, the worm fence of split logs piled in angles on each other, bore the name "Virginia fence." Like the "Tobacco Coast," the Southwest was a region of big rivers flowing into the Atlantic or the Gulf. When commercial agriculture began, rafts floated the crops down to Mobile or New Orleans and later the steamboat, like the tobacco ships of colonial days, collected the cotton from plantation landings along the banks. There was an absence of villages and only the plantations, some of them deserted and gone to waste, interrupted the wilderness.

Finally the cotton planter, like his tobacco exemplar, participated in a market mechanism. He sold his crop to a factor in an interior market town, for example, Montgomery, Alabama; this local factor sold it in an export city like Savannah, Mobile, or New Orleans to a southern factor, who then sold these shipments to a cotton broker in New York or, more likely, Liverpool, which became the largest cotton market in the world. This northern or English broker, who represented the seller, sold in turn to a broker representing the manufacturer. This linear mechanism took the responsibilities of collecting information on sales, shipment, and prices; of arranging for transportation; and also of advancing money or credit to the planter who usually did not have sufficient means to wait until his crop was grown and marketed. On the security of his delivered or promised crop, the planter borrowed from the factor; and the factor, on the security of a crop in prospect or in transit, borrowed from a bank. Thus northern or European capital or credit financed the cotton crop. Finally slave labor produced cotton, as it had tobacco.

Plantation or Farm?

The Colonial era demonstrated that labor bound to the master by contract, as was the indentured servant, or by ownership, as was the slave, was the most practicable for exploiting a country where land was cheap and plentiful and labor was neither. Another prerequisite for the profitable use of captive workers was a year-round routine to keep them busy. The tobacco, rice, and indigo staples of the South had met these conditions exactly. When introduced, sugar and upland cotton fell into the same pattern.

Sugar planting began in January, when fresh canes were set in the old fields. Then followed two months of incidental work, repairing roads, fixing the levees, and cutting wood. With the warmer weather corn was planted, and the summer was spent in keeping down the weeds and stirring the soil in the corn and cane fields. In September the corn crops were harvested, staves were cut and barrels made, and everything was prepared for the cane harvesting, which came late in October. This was a hectic period. Large gangs cut down the cane and others transported it to the sugar mill. Here it was ground between rollers, and the juice was first clarified by lime and heat and then boiled again and again until it was ready to crystallize. There was a great press about all operations, because the cane had to be harvested before the arrival of the frosts. The mill, working in double shifts, set the pace for the harvesting gangs. When a frost was actually imminent, however, every place except the fields was deserted. There the canes which were to be used next year as seedlings were cut and laid in shingled formation on the ground, and the rest of the crop was harvested and strewn in the furrows until it could be carted off to the mill. By the time that these canes had been picked up and crushed, and the juice clarified it was the end of December. Then the new year stood at hand with a renewal of its routine. Here was a process carefully worked out which utilized its labor force to the full.

Cotton afforded similar opportunities. The first months of the year were devoted to preparing the fields for the planting. If necessary, new grounds were made ready by cutting the trees, grubbing out underbrush, and rolling logs. These new fields were generally planted in corn as a preparation for cotton. On the fields which were given to the staple the seedbeds, three to five feet apart, were rounded up with the plow. Then came the planting season. It was generally the practice to plant as much corn as cotton. The latter was the cash crop, the former supplied the principal grain for the slaves and fed the hogs which were slaughtered for pork, hams, and bacon. The acreage of each crop was determined by the amount a hand could harvest. Just before the Civil War ten acres in cotton and ten in corn was a practical allotment for each field slave. In March the corn was planted. The cultivation of cotton began in April, when the top of the seedbeds was opened by a furrow, and the cotton seeds were strewn in rather thickly and then covered with earth. The cultivation of these two crops interlocked nicely. The slaves were shifted from one to the other. The cultivation of corn was simple enough, but cotton was a tender and exacting plant. The beds had to be hoed and thinned frequently and the ground cultivated with a plow to keep down the weeds. And there were insect pests. The Mexican boll weevil had not yet invaded the United States, but worms, insects, and parasites seemed to lie in wait to attack cotton at every stage of the proceedings.

When the harvest season came, the corn was the first object of attention. The leaves were stripped and the ears picked. Then came the cotton. Its harvesting season was prolonged because the bolls ripened at different times—first midway on the plant, then at the ends of the lower branches, and finally at the top. If the cotton were left too long in these ripened bolls wind and rain might drag it out and dirty it on the ground. So the hands were sent through the fields as often as there was something for the picking. This process did not require strength as much as diligence and skill. The cotton in each boll was held in four or five compartments. A single clasp of the fingers could clear out all the compartments. Some pickers used only one hand, but the more skillful kept both going at once. The actual amount picked by individuals increased through the years. On a Mississippi plantation in 1859 three champion pickers averaged 300 pounds a day, and the average of everyone, men, women, boys, and girls, was 157 pounds. As the last statement implies, every age and both sexes worked in the cotton fields when the bolls were white. After the baskets were full they were emptied, and the cotton was carted away to be ginned.

Every large planter had his own ginning equipment housed in a ramshackle two-story edifice. On the first floor was an upright shaft leading to the machinery of the gin on the second floor. This shaft was spun by a long horizontal beam fitted into it at right angles, to which mules or horses were hitched and then driven around in a circular path. After the gin came the press. In this apparatus the cotton lint was placed in a rectangular receptacle, whose dimensions determined those of the individual cotton bale, and then it was crammed down by the pressure of a lid forced by a large screw, which worked through a block above the box and was turned by animal power. The harvesting and its accompanying ginning season were generally completed by December, but in the western cotton regions the fields were often white with unpicked cotton until March or April. In cotton, as in sugar, there was an all-year routine which utilized the labor force to the full.

While the use of indentured servants declined, the general characteristics of American agriculture assisted in the employment of Negro slaves. South as well as North found it unprofitable to follow a tiresome and careful agricultural technique. Land was plentiful, and the natural fertility which it contained should be used without questioning. So the southern planter year after year set out the same fields with cotton. The only rotation which was followed at all was that of corn and cotton, but this rotation, since it was not based upon scientific principles, was of limited value. In such wasteful practices the Southerner had an advantage, for cotton did not exhaust the soil as rapidly as the northern crops. Eventually, however, new fields had to be opened, and the old fields were turned over to an unhindered growth of weeds, brambles, and thickets. As in the North, the use of fertilizers as soil amendments was restricted. A Kentucky boy wrote later of his experiences: "In my youth I never knew manure being put on the land. When, about 1855, my father began the use of it, he was much laughed at." Cottonseed, whose decomposition would have enriched the soil, was neglected. In 1807 the town of Sparta, Georgia, had to adopt an ordinance compelling each owner of a cotton gin to remove the refuse about his machinery before May "so as to prevent its unhealthy putrefaction." When the lands of the large-scale producer or of those who aspired to be such wore out, the customary response was to pull out family, slaves, and equipment and move to Alabama, Mississippi, or beyond, where fresh lands were available.

In the production of the southern staples there was not only competition between the new and older centers of production but a competition throughout the entire South between different units of production—the farm and the plantation. The farmer carried on small-scale operations and a more generally rounded agriculture. The farm owner and his family might be the only laborers upon it, or the farmer might hire help or buy a few slaves to work with him in the fields. To draw a sharp line between plantation and farm means a resort to abstractions. The plantation was a large-scale enterprise. How large? Perhaps a minimum of twenty slaves, the number an owner could manage. Primarily, it produced agricultural staples for market. Visually the traveler might insist upon the presence of Grecian columns as the test of a plantation. Actually many planters' homes were so unpretentious that in the North they would be called farms.

The plantation did not encompass all southern sections or all southern cotton growers. Free whites as well as black slaves lived and worked there. In 1860 the white population of the fifteen slave states was 8 million; the Negro population was some 4 million. Of the white families, only a quarter owned slaves and many of this limited group owned only one or two. Most Southerners, then, were in the small slave-holding or nonslaveholding classes. They deserve our attention.

Although deductions must naturally be made for such whites as were artisans, traders, and professional men, the great majority of this other South were farmers of one sort or another. They fell into two great classifications. At the lower extreme were the "poor white trash." This class was characterized by a variety of appellations—"piney woods" people, "hillbillies," "sandhillers," "clay eaters"—some of which refer to their habits, others to their locale. The most significant areas in which the poor whites were concentrated were, first of all, the great pine-barren belt of Georgia which runs diagonally across the state from northeast to southwest between the Georgia uplands and the coastal plains. In Mississippi there was a distinct pine-barren district extending north and south through the state east of the Pearl River. Other poor whites were scattered about the pine woods and sand hills which are spotty topographical features of South Carolina, Alabama, and Florida. These areas did not have the rich soils which plantation staples sought; nor had improved transportation connected them with distant markets. The poor whites obtained their food from a scraggly patch of potatoes and corn, and in greater abundance from fishing and hunting. "Wild hogs, deer, wild turkeys, squirrels, raccoons, opossums—these and many more are at

[the] very doors [of the poor whites]; and they have only to pick up 'Old Silver Heels,' walk a few miles out into the forest, and return home laden with enough meat to last them a week." Their homes were equally primitive. "A few rickety chairs, a long bench, a dirty bed or two, a spinning wheel," "a skillet, an oven, a frying pan," were the contents of their rude log cabins. Lazy, shiftless, ignorant, they were despised by the planter and the farmer and even looked down upon by the Negro. In the light of modern research, their vices were due as much to the ravages of the hookworm disease as to defects of character. Dirt eating, clay eating, rosin eating, were simply symptoms of the advanced stages of this debilitating ailment.

But the author of *Social Relations in Our Southern States* wrote in 1860, "The Poor Whites of the South constitute a separate class to themselves: the Southern yeomen are as distinct from them as the Southern Gentleman is from the Cotton Snob." Whether he owned few slaves or none at all, the southern yeoman followed a more varied agriculture which made his farm more self-sufficing than the plantation and involved less exchange of staples for bought commodities. He worked in the fields, even with his slaves if he had them; and the latter were on more friendly terms with him than they would be with an overseer or a large owner. His dwelling was neither the dirty cabin of the poor white nor the veranda-enshaded mansion of the planter. It was a comfortable but rudely constructed log or frame house; for the slaves there were no elaborate "quarters," only a simple cabin.

Though farm and plantation were everywhere intermingled, some areas had a heavier concentration of one or the other. In South Carolina and Georgia farms were concentrated along the eastern edge of the uplands, in Mississippi in the eastern part of the state. But the greater number were in the Border states and in the rounded salient thrust southward from the Border states along the mountain ranges of the Appalachians. In Missouri and Tennessee plantations clustered in the rich bottomlands of the rivers, particularly the Mississippi, and in Kentucky in the limestone areas; elsewhere in the Border states slaveholdings were small. A similar condition prevailed in the western portion of Virginia and the Carolinas. Since this whole region had a climate unsuited to southern staples, its white farmers grew cereals and raised livestock. Their economic differentiation from the rest of the South had interesting political results during the Civil War, for in this area Missouri and Kentucky remained loyal to the Union, West Virginia split away from the Old Dominion, and in eastern Tennessee and western North Carolina opposition to secession and the Confederacy was widespread. A third southern area in which the farmer predominated was the old plantation district of colonial times, the Chesapeake Bay region of Maryland and Virginia. Here by 1860 the number of slaves was diminishing, the number of free blacks was increasing, and the farm was supplanting the plantation.

On the other hand since the cultivation of both sugar and rice involved a heavy capital investment, these crops lent themselves inevitably to the plantation system. The vital factor in the production of sugar was the sugar mill, for the amount of the crop which could be harvested depended upon how rapidly the cane could be ground and crystallized before the frosts set in. In view of the existing lack of communications every planter had to have his own sugar mill. To depend upon a neighbor's mill was folly, for everyone was working his own plant to capacity during the harvest season, and no one would run other people's crops through at the expense of his own. The sugar mills, moreover, became increasingly expensive. Steam engines were introduced to furnish power, and the pans for boiling and evaporation were improved. Plantations under the circumstances tended to enlarge. The investment for an equipped sugar plantation of 750 acres and 160 slaves was about $200,000.

The Rice Coast of the Carolinas and Georgia also had a plantation economy. Here small-scale operations were hampered because the owner had to turn over the conduct of operations to overseers while he fled to higher ground to avoid the summer malarias. If an overseer had to be employed, his expense would be less if he managed a large plantation. A rice plantation required various specialized occupations, coopers to make the barrels, millers of the "Rice Machine and Mill," boatmen, bird-minders to scare the rice birds from the crop, as well as the common laborers. Probably no plantation could be successful unless it had a hundred acres planted in rice, and this acreage, on the computation of one hand to every five acres, involved a slave force of at least twenty field hands. Most of the plantations were much larger. That of William Aiken, one-time governor of South Carolina, had fifteen hundred acres which could be flooded. Two-thirds of these were planted with rice; the remainder with corn, oats, and sweet potatoes. The threshing machine by which the kernels were separated from the stalks was steam-driven, but the mill which pounded off the hulls was driven by the tide. The labor force was composed of 700 slaves. The investment in 1849 was $380,000.

Cotton production was not inevitably committed to the plantation structure. Indeed at first the hope was entertained that cotton would tend "to fill the country with an independent industrious yeomanry." A widespread realization of this anticipation never came, for the plantation became increasingly dominant in the production of this staple. The median average slaveholding (half the holdings were smaller and half larger) in 1860 in Louisiana was 49.3; in Mississippi 35; and in Alabama 33.4. Among the other states only South Carolina could equal these concentrations. In certain selected cotton-growing counties in the first two states the median holding ran from 87 to 125. On the other hand in the Piedmont region of Georgia and North Carolina the smaller unit of the farm originally seemed to have advantages. But even in these regions the plantation emerged. In 1800 in Oglethorpe County, in the uplands of Georgia, the whites outnumbered the slaves 2-to-1; there were eight nonslaveholding families to five families owning slaves; and the average holding was five slaves each. By 1860 the Negroes outnumbered the whites; the number of nonslaveholders had decreased more rapidly than that of the slaveholders; and the average holding was slightly over twelve slaves.

The tendency toward the plantation system was due to several factors. This larger unit had some advantages in the purchase of goods for consumption, the division of labor, the adoption of better practices, and in the sale of its products. Cotton growers sought out the better lands—hence the pull to the Southwest—and cultivated their holdings with a relatively larger labor force. Operations of this scale were the quickest way to wealth and so social and political influence. Nevertheless old ways persisted. Even in 1850 the cotton crop was produced on estates which were manned on an average by a slave force of six farmhands, and the larger units did not rival the plantations of the rice and sugar regimes.

Costs and Consequences

Long before John Maynard Keynes devised his first formula or computers ejected mathematical answers to programmed queries, economists speculated whether slavery paid. Like Keynes, these thinkers were British and hence outside the slave-plantation system; unlike Keynes, they had the advantage of being contemporary with the "peculiar institution" of the South. The conclusions of these economists gave the general impression of being based on *a priori* thinking. Slaves laboring under compulsion could not have been as efficient as free laborers whose gains were relative to their energy and motivation. Since idealistic and humanitarian considerations tinged an issue which people felt was fundamental, slavery when it left the realm of speculation for polemic became a matter of partisan and frequently shoddy reasoning. As the pro-slavery–anti-slavery debate continued in North as well as South, one group emphasized the exploitation, the brutality, and the unfairness of the system; the other, asserting that slavery was not so bad, seemed bent on discrediting the free labor system and bemused with the possibility of substituting an authoritarian organization of labor—with "no problem of unemployment, and . . . no lockouts, blacklists, and strikes." Whatever its form, the controversy over the profitableness of slavery unfailingly touched the nerves of guilt and pride which in this matter lay so near the surface. Painful distortion resulted.

Even today the Department of Agriculture has problems in inducing farmers "to keep books"; those who are able and willing to do so are a selected group. Before the Civil War it is doubtful if many southern farmers were accurately informed about the whole of their costs and gains. At best, most operated upon fragmentary information and upon some rule of thumb springing from their own observations and experience. Obvious were the costs of subsistence. Per slave perhaps these leveled out at twenty to twenty-one dollars a year. The slave lived in a cabin—probably no worse than the log cabin of the pioneer, except that it was older. His clothing was hand-me-downs from the master; or the planter distributed coarse dry goods, "Negro clothes," which might have been manufactured on the plantation and which, in any case, were made into garments by the slave women. Corn and hogs and, perhaps under favorable circumstances, a garden plot of his own furnished the slave's food. The owner may have had to meet some expenses for medical care and for taxes.

Unlike a free laborer, the slave represented an initial investment for the employer; the master had to pay for his rearing or purchase him outright. Theoretically this investment was a wasting asset, for the slave's productivity usually ceased after thirty years of work. Investing in a slave was not a wasting asset if the natural increase of the slave population furnished workers for use or for sale. By shifting items of expense to accord with the approved practices of modern accounting, it is possible to arrive at quite different conclusions about the "profitability" of slavery from the same set of figures for the same landholding. There are frequent complaints over the meagerness of evidence: I am impressed by its abundance. Another curiosity of the whole debate about slavery is that those who say the owner was the victim of his greed and ignorance are often dismissed as southern "apologists."

The size of the crop and its price gave the slaveowner his income. The average field hand, it is calculated, could "make" three and a half to four bales of cotton a year, perhaps twice this number on the best lands. The price for cotton, of course, varied. In the early nineteenth century, the price usually averaged over 10 cents a pound; after the panic of 1837 it fell as low as .068 cents in 1845. "Flush times" returned in the second half of the fifties. In 1860 when the average price was a fraction over 11 cents, the price of a prime field hand was $1,800. Such prices for slaves were declared "incredible," and some explained the phenomenon on the ground of a temporary dementia.

Some southerners felt that high prices for slaves were due to a discrepancy between the supply and demand. The number of potential slaves was, it is true, comparatively inelastic, since they could not be produced automatically in response to market demands like commodities. Foreign importations had been cut off by the closing of the slave trade with Africa through a national law in 1808 and a later enactment which made the slave trade piracy. There was always some smuggling of African Negroes into the United States, but it was inconsiderable. The increase of the slave population therefore depended upon the birthrate among the native Negroes. The number of slaves counted in every census increased from 1790 to 1860;[1] the percentage increase, usually lower than that for whites, declined absolutely in the thirties and fifties. As contrasted with other slave populations in history, the American one was not dying out. Indeed over the years the United States had developed areas which specialized in slave production, a secondary "staple crop." The economic development of the Border states, Maryland and Virginia and, to a lesser extent, Kentucky and Missouri, produced a slave population larger than could be profitably utilized there. An internal slave trade between these districts and the rice, cotton, and sugar regions consequently grew up. The trade was distasteful to the slaveowners in the Border states, but economic necessity triumphed over personal choice. Some firms dealt in slaves as a business. Their purchasing agents journeyed through the country with an eye open for likely Negroes between ten and thirty years of age and bought from individuals or at auction. The Negroes were then assembled at some depot and dispatched to a slave market in the lower South. Many slaves made the journey by boat along the coast, others went overland at the rate of twenty-five miles a day, the men walking and the women and children riding in wagons. The trade met with social disfavor, and those who participated in it were the object of popular contempt. Its extent is difficult to determine. After 1815 the coasting trade annually carried south five thousand Negroes. Perhaps half of these were accompanying their masters to new plantations; the rest went to the South for sale. In these ways the slave population was redistributed to those areas where it could be used to the most advantage.

Under the conditions of an agriculture producing staples which were constantly encroaching upon new areas of high fertility, slave labor was profitable. At least that conclusion seems most compatible with the behavior and attitudes of producers of crops in the South. Aside from the statistics, the changing attitude in the South toward slavery furnishes

[1] THE SLAVE POPULATION IN THE UNITED STATES

1780— 697,624	1830—2,009,043
1800— 893,602	1840—2,487,355
1810—1,191,362	1850—3,204,313
1820—1,538,022	1860—3,953,760

Source: U.S. Bureau of the Census, *Negro Population, 1790-1915,* p. 57.

additional evidence. Jefferson felt it was a great evil; and as late as 1832 a speaker in the Virginia Assembly declared that slavery was "the heaviest calamity which has ever befallen any portion of the human race," and a bill which would have indirectly hastened manumission was defeated in the legislature by only one vote. Thereafter the declining zeal in the South for manumission was an index of the profitability of slavery. But whether or not the "peculiar institution" meant great gain for the master and an endurable existence for the slave, the slave considered an irrelevance. Andrew Carnegie was fond of telling the story of an Ohio judge's interrogation of a Negro fugitive. The runaway granted he had plenty of food and clothes, good shelter, a kind master, and he did not have to work very hard. Why then, the judge asked, did the slave run away? The fugitive replied that the place he had left was open, and the judge could go down and take it—and forthwith resumed his flight to Canada.

The Achievements of Agriculture

Lack of detailed statistical records makes it impossible to measure precisely the achievements of American agriculture in the period between the Revolution and the Civil War. Nonetheless some scholars have calculated that the gross value of production in constant prices increased roughly four times between the census dates of 1800 and 1850. Since population grew at approximately the same rate, it may be inferred agriculture kept abreast of national needs for food and fibers by increasing the cultivated area and the number of workers. After 1840 or 1850 agriculture picked up speed. Its gross product in 1860—43 percent greater than in 1850—appreciably exceeded the growth rate of population. Increased productivity per capita had now to be taken into account. Improved transportation, the growth of home and foreign markets, the decline of self-sufficing farming, the shift of agriculture to the more fertile soils of the West, the wider use of machines and fertilizers—in fact the whole cluster of general and specific factors already dealt with —contributed to the forward spurt of agriculture. But this whole calculation, including explanations, is in a state of constant revision and the conclusions are now indeterminate.

Had these changes undermined Jefferson's vision of the Americans as an agricultural and virtuous people? The larger number of Americans piled up in cities was particularly menacing. Outside the tables of statistics the old stereotypes still persisted. American attitudes attributed exceptional lustre and merit to "the industrious and intelligent pioneer," in the words of Franklin Pierce, and, in some instances, of later historians. Nor did the tumultuous events of 1860 and 1861 challenge the

primacy of this conception. In the North Abraham Lincoln had the
political appeal of descending from a pioneer family; he was born in a
log cabin, he hailed from Illinois, and he was acclaimed as the "rail-
splitter." When the Southern Confederacy came into being, it chose
Jefferson Davis, a plantation owner who had made a model enterprise
of his Mississippi acres, as its President.

Internal Improvements and Domestic Commerce

Plans and Prospects

Early in 1808 Albert Gallatin, Secretary of the Treasury in the administration of Thomas Jefferson—the latter an evangelist of a central government with limited powers—sent to the Senate a report on the roads and canals of the United States. The document was a factual catalogue of what existed; it was also a detailed diagnosis of what was still needed to complete a national system of improved transport and a recommendation of national measures to attain this end. Gallatin displayed a considerable insight and a proper appreciation of priorities. At a time when domestic commerce and travel proceeded predominantly by water in sailing vessels, he thought that in the West the Federal government might aid the construction of a canal around the falls of the Ohio at Louisville; and on the East coast it might aid short canals, for instance, the Chesapeake and Delaware, linking up rivers and bays to provide safer navigation along an interior coastal waterway. His additional suggestion of a highway from Massachusetts to Georgia seemed needlessly grandiose.

Gallatin nonetheless accurately perceived that the hard core of the transportation problem was a connection between the communities on the Atlantic coast and the Great Lakes and the Mississippi-Ohio system of the West. The great obstacle was the Appalachian mountains, which were roughly 110 miles wide, almost uniformly two thousand feet above sea level, "preserving throughout a nearly equal distance of 250 miles from the Atlantic Ocean." Since it was impracticable to cross this barrier by canals, as canal technique was currently practiced in Europe and England, the best solution was to improve the navigation of certain eastern rivers—for example, the Potomac, the James, or the Susquehanna-Juniata—as far westward as feasible and then connect these terminals by an artificial road to the headwaters of a paired western river. By an "artificial road" Gallatin meant one built to avoid grades of over 5 percent, graded to shed water, and paved with a layer of small crushed stone or gravel.

While the United States might import the technology of turnpikes and canals, Gallatin was far from sure that the devices the English and Europeans had chosen for their ownership, construction, and operation were applicable here. European nations had generally left these improvements to private enterprise and private capital. The choice had worked because "these countries were possessed of a large capital," and "a compact population creates an extensive commercial intercourse within short distances." In America, on the other hand, there were so many competing needs for the limited supply of capital and population was so dispersed that "permanent works" of internal improvement, traversing long distances, were not likely to offer a hope of return. Yet Gallatin observed, "the community is nevertheless benefited by the undertaking." To this dilemma, the answer was financial assistance from the Federal government.

Into this genial solution the specter of constitutionality intruded. This consideration did not bother Englishmen, Frenchmen, Hollanders, or even Chinese. Gallatin thought the issue was not likely to be decisive in America, though the Federal government would have to get the assent of any state to a public work undertaken within its borders. Perhaps a shadow of misgiving on this score shaped his preference for the form of Federal assistance. Though the Federal government might build the improvement, Gallatin thought a subscription to the stock of a corporation already chartered for that purpose by a state "appears the most eligible mode." At a time when returns from taxes were comfortably filling the Treasury, Gallatin anticipated the Federal government might feasibly appropriate $2 million a year for ten years to complete the projects mentioned in his report.

Like many state papers of that Administration, the report was overly sanguine. Though European engineers and builders were providing a level of technical competence, it was far from certain that their American counterparts could muster such technology. Though Congress in 1802 had created the Corps of Engineers and located it at West Point to "constitute a military academy," the school, which was to become the great teacher of civil as well as military engineering, did not amount to much until 1820. Nor was there a substitute elsewhere. Still, Gallatin was certain that in America "the want of a practical knowledge is no longer felt." He also was politic enough to realize the obstructive role of local pride and local self-interest in the selection of routes: indeed his report proposed to placate the hostility of relatively unbenefited regions by a Federal donation of $3 million. He even sublimated logrolling and particularism into a delusive consensus: "The national legislature alone, embracing every local interest, and superior to every local consideration is competent to the selection of such national objects."

However eager Gallatin was to promote the national welfare by internal improvements, he was foresighted enough to realize the program of Federal assistance depended upon peace; war would make privileged demands upon the Treasury. While the War of 1812 and its protracted preliminaries frustrated his proposals, other developments contributed to making impracticable and perhaps unnecessary his great design. As for roads, the era of artificial highways had begun long before the report, and its development was generally carried forward by other aids than Federal donation. So slow is the preparation of government reports that it is not surprising Gallatin never mentioned the steamboat, "invented" —to stretch the word and the fact—by Robert Fulton in 1807. Fulton appears in Gallatin's reports only as an advisor on the relative efficiency of highways and canals.

The Turnpike Era

The road network the new nation took over from Colonial days was inadequate. What roads there were had been constructed to supplement waterways or perhaps to connect places of considerable population. In the eastern portion of the country these highways radiated from the commercial cities—Boston, Providence, New York, Philadelphia, Baltimore. Farther inland the roads ran down from the interior to some water's edge. The system, if one could lose one's sense of humor sufficiently to call it such, was localized. The planning, construction, and care of roads was generally left to local authorities, who were not particularly interested in the development of through routes. The prevailing ignorance of the principles of road engineering and the lack of capital were additional hampers upon improvement. In its elemental form a road consisted of a cleared path through the trees and nothing else. If further refinement was demanded, the road was crowned high with dirt and edged by a gutter. Over such roads the transportation of passengers was alone profitable. Freight commerce was confined either to short distances or to products such as whisky and peltries, whose value was high in proportion to their bulk. As late as the War of 1812, if a wagon load of goods was sent overland from Augusta, Maine, to Savannah, Georgia, the journey required 115 days and the freight charges on the load were $1,000.

Many states saw in the private turnpike corporation, a device which the British had used to improve their highways, a means of overcoming the handicaps which lay heavy upon American land transportation. In

1792 Pennsylvania chartered the Lancaster Turnpike to run from Philadelphia to Lancaster, "the largest inland town in America." This company raised the funds for the improved highway through the sale of its stock to investors; secured a right of way through the exercise of eminent domain, a privilege granted by the state; built at the cost of $465,000 a road surfaced with crushed small stone; and sought to recoup its expenditures and make a profit through tolls charged at gates seven miles apart. The business methods of this earliest turnpike, like that of its numerous imitators, aroused popular hostility. Road-making had previously been a governmental function; now it was surrendered to private individuals with the right to invade private property and charge tolls. The financial experience of the Lancaster Turnpike also foreshadowed that of turnpikes in general. The cost of construction far exceeded the original estimate; additional levies had to be made upon the stockholders; in 1807 the management reported that the stock was at last at par but that it had never earned more than 2 percent profit.

A rage for the construction of improved roads, however, swept the country. In his report Gallatin described the sixty-seven companies in the State of New York, where "a greater capital has been vested on turnpike roads . . . than in any other"; the progress of New England, particularly Massachusetts, where excellent thoroughfares radiated from Boston to Newburyport, Providence, and other places; and the extensive projects in Pennsylvania and Maryland for tapping the commerce of the western regions. "South of the Potomack, few artificial roads have been undertaken." Gallatin was writing, as it turned out, on the eve of the first turnpike era. For in the eastern states the golden age of the turnpike, in terms of usefulness rather than in number of charters, was from 1810 to 1830. To tempt private capitalists to invest in these enterprises most states gave turnpike corporations a monopoly on the route traversed; the exercise of eminent domain in securing the right of way and construction materials, such as gravel; and sometimes a subscription to the capital. In Pennsylvania, for instance, the state had by 1822 subscribed $1,861,542 out of a total turnpike capitalization of $6,401,474. In the uniformity and generosity of the last practice, Pennsylvania tended to be unique. In most states, however, charters specified rates of toll or maximum percentages for earnings in order to prevent extortion from users.

By 1830 other means of transportation—canal, railroad, and public highway—superseded the turnpike. The constant movement of population into new areas, however, and the discovery of new varieties of road surfacing explained the appearance of a later turnpike era in western states and the rebirth of the craze in the older regions. The plank road, for instance, made of woods as varied in staying power as hemlock and white oak, had an immense vogue in the late forties and early fifties. Though this innovation was not the whole explanation, states as diverse

as New Jersey and Ohio reached the peak of turnpike incorporation in
that period.

In the matter of turnpikes and public roads the individual states
tended to follow a policy as exclusive and as belligerent as modern
nationalism. Each state fought for its economic interests or those of its
metropolis, be it Portland, Maine, or Baltimore, Maryland. Such competition spurred enterprise; it did not necessarily build a national system.
Those with wider horizons had often advocated that the Federal government undertake to provide essential internal improvements, including
highways. Early in the century men of such vision thought for a while
they had found a way around the scruples of strict constitutionalists.
Thus, when Ohio was admitted to the Union a percentage of the money
obtained from the sales of her public land was set aside for building
roads. This decision Franklin Pierce later justified "as what would be
done by any prudent proprietor to enhance the sale value of his private
domain," in this case, the public, government domain. In 1802 it was
decided to devote a part of this fund to the construction of a roadway
connecting Ohio with the Atlantic. The logical route geographically was
from the Ohio River to some river flowing into Chesapeake Bay, for
here the distance across the Appalachians to saltwater was the shortest.
Finally in 1811 local jealousies were appeased and the road was laid out
to extend from Cumberland on the Potomac through the lower western
corner of Pennsylvania to Wheeling on the Ohio. The statute prescribed
the width of the roadway, the shape of the roadbed, and the surfacing
of stone. In the same year the first contracts were let for its construction
and in 1818 it was opened for traffic to its western terminal. The cost of
construction, $13,000 a mile, had bought a stone-surfaced road with
substantial bridges, but so great was the traffic that the road wore out
rapidly. Congress, while debating the delicate question whether it was
entitled to repair its own creation, voted the road's extension westward
through the state capitals of Ohio, Indiana, and Illinois, and some
selected a final terminal at St. Louis. This projected National Road,
however, was never completed; by the fifties the national government
had surrendered to the states through which the National, or Cumberland, Road passed the pieces lying within their jurisdictions, and the
completion of the Baltimore and Ohio Railroad made the National Road
an anachronism. Meanwhile the finished eastern portion benefited eastern
cities such as Philadelphia and Baltimore, which early made connections
with it, rather than New York, which found access difficult.

No matter how they had been sponsored or financed, improved
roads developed an immense wagon traffic. Private carriages or stage-
coaches might attain greater luxury or speed, but the Conestoga wagon,
dragged by six horses, was the mainstay of the highway. Freighting
companies were chartered which owned several wagons, employed

numerous drivers, and operated on regular schedules. An observer estimated that twelve thousand wagons arrived in 1817 at Pittsburgh from Baltimore and Philadelphia. And Wheeling rivaled Pittsburgh just as Baltimore rivaled Philadelphia. An interesting feature of this traffic was its concatenation with the traffic down the Ohio and the Mississippi. Owners of flats, who had sold cargo and boat alike at New Orleans, took ship northward for an Atlantic port and invested their money in fine goods which were taken overland by wagon and then sold along the western rivers. Thus a curious triangular trade developed, whose angles coincided with the West, New Orleans, and some eastern city.

Improved roads, as Gallatin had foreseen, did not make the investors in turnpike stocks rich. Very few such enterprises earned more than 2 or 3 percent; most were failures as investments. But their contributions to the community were, within limits, substantial. They reduced rates. It is difficult to state averages. Passenger fares in the twenties were approximately 5 cents a mile. As for the more important freight business, the competition of the eastern cities had forced down charges on a hundredweight of goods from Pittsburgh to Philadelphia from $9.50 in 1817 to $6.50 in the following year. But these unusual rates were still prohibitive. To move a barrel of flour from Pittsburgh to Philadelphia cost $13.00. Very few bulky articles could stand such freight charges. Although manufactured articles paid for their transportation, agricultural products like wheat and flour could not be gainfully carried more than one hundred and fifty miles. A ton of goods could be moved across the Atlantic almost as cheaply as from Philadelphia to Lancaster.

The Steamboat Era

Questions of constitutionality and the division of powers between the state and national governments were less pressing in the case of natural waterways. Nonetheless, in the location of lighthouses and buoys, the improvement of rivers and harbors, and the determination of what were or were not "navigable" waters, constitutional issues intruded. These related matters took on new urgency with the invention of the steamboat. For these new power-driven vessels were a comparatively uncomplicated means for developing transportation and promoting community prosperity.

On August 9, 1807, the *Clermont* left her dock at New York City, paused in the stream while her paddle wheels were adjusted and then steamed slowly northward up the Hudson. Arriving the next day at Albany, she had covered the one hundred and fifty miles in somewhat over thirty hours, a rate of speed not quite twice that achieved by some of our contemporary women swimmers on the same course downstream. Nevertheless the *Clermont* inaugurated a revolution in transportation. It was not one of invention. Foreigners had earlier devised steamboats and both the boiler and the engine of the *Clermont,* built by Watt and Boulton, were imported from England. From time to time Americans had also placed on eastern rivers boats moved by steam power in one way or another. But Fulton, the designer of the *Clermont,* had the advantage of association with Robert R. Livingston, a New York landed grandee, politician, and steamboat experimenter, who had secured a monopoly from the New York legislature granting him the exclusive right to navigate its waters with steam vessels provided a vessel of certain weight and speed was operated successfully within a certain time. Thus the *Clermont* assured to Fulton and Livingston a twenty-year monopoly of the waters of New York State and the Hudson placed the steamboat upon a route which had commercial advantages.

The steamboat's wider employment really began in the fifteen years after 1815. For one thing, the Fulton and Livingston monopoly, although not exceptionally oppressive, was successfully challenged by rival promoters and apostles of equalitarianism. Eventually, in 1824, the Supreme Court of the United States discovered in the case of Gibbons *v.* Ogden that the grant was an unconstitutional invasion of the right of the Federal government to regulate interstate commerce. For another thing, between 1815 and 1830 a definitive trend had been given to the power mechanism and shape of the eastern river steamboat. The engine, which could burn coal, had the low-pressure boilers and large cylinder of the Watt-Boulton prototype; a walking beam transmitted the motion to the large paddle wheels concealed in decorated houses; the hull was shallow and long with a main deck broadened by guards to the outer edge of the paddle wheels; and a layered structure of decks built up an ever higher wooden superstructure. The whole ship was strengthened by two trusses, hog-frames running its length, and was held together by ingenious arrangements of struts and ties. Robert L. Stevens, New Jerseyite and son of a distinguished inventor, introduced many of these innovations.

Until the railroad came, heroic efforts pushed small river steamers—Charles Dickens described one in 1842 as "a warm sandwich, about three feet thick"—into the upper shallows of the eastern rivers. Actually their main employment was on the lower reaches, or as water links in a communication system, like that between New York and Philadelphia, or on such splendid arteries as the Potomac and the Hudson. In the East, the latter was without a peer. A cavalcade of vessels connected the lower ports with New York City or ran the through route to Albany. Competition and consolidation unrolled a business drama in which Commodore Vanderbilt and Daniel Drew, to mention no other titans, secured fortunes and a schooling which they later applied to railroads. In the year ending July, 1851, the Hudson River boats carried 950,000 passengers.

Here, as elsewhere, steamboats by their regularity and convenience took over the passenger trade from stagecoach and sailing vessel. They also carried high-class freight. As the power source for a river tow the steamboat likewise contributed to the carriage of bulk cargoes. After the opening of the Champlain and Erie Canals, huge areas of barges, four or five abreast and half a mile long, were pulled by some decrepit and antiquated steamer so slowly that the movement was scarcely perceptible. Still, the rates as well as the speed were low; on the Hudson the former fell to 0.7 cent per ton per mile.

Soon the steamboat ventured out from its Hudson River nursery to the adjacent waters of New York Bay and Long Island Sound. By the thirties a series of lines connected the metropolis with New Jersey and the ports of southern New England. On the other side of Cape Cod Boston had regular service with the ports of Maine; on the Delaware steamboats fanned out from Philadelphia; and Baltimore and Norfolk were connected by a line running the length of Chesapeake Bay. But the conquest of the longer routes came more slowly—in the late forties and fifties. Of course, New York was the leader; after 1846 she had regular connections with Charleston and after 1849 with New Orleans. Though such voyages, like those across the Gulf of Maine from Boston, were subject to the same dangers as ocean navigation, the vessels that traversed them were more like riverboats than transatlantic liners. Whatever the fitness of their design, coastal steamers, operated in lines and on regular routes, began to alter the patterns of coasting commerce.

Before the steamer's arrival the chief ports of the Atlantic littoral had developed elaborate networks of sailing packets or regular traders, oftentimes with regularly scheduled sailings, between themselves and with the minor ports whose commerce they naturally wished to appropriate and enjoy. Both types carried passengers; the whole bewildering variety of finer freights—grocers' goods, textiles, iron ware, local products; and bulk commodities, if necessary to fill out the hold. On the whole, however, tramp sailors or vessels on charter picked up the last sort of cargo. When steamers invaded the coastal traffic, they at once appropriated the sailing packet business between the larger ports. The bulk of the coastwise traffic, however, continued to move under sail. There were a multitude of ports untouched by steamer lines but still with business enough to keep a packet or regular trader busy. Nor did all the trades of the coast require despatch of carriage or promptness in delivery. Bulk cargoes primarily sought low costs of transportation, which sailboats offered, since American yards turned out vessels cheap to build and operate. For the coasting trade with its shallow harbors and rivers and with its landlocked bays and sounds, the schooner increasingly proved the fittest carrier. This vessel drew little water, and its fore-and-aft rig was more quickly shifted than that of a square-rigger, and two and three masts kept the sails so small they could be handled by a small crew. By 1860 the schooner was the coaster par excellence.

Some of the commodity trades originated in the South. That region sent northward the rice of the Carolinas, sugar and molasses from Louisiana, timber from Mobile, naval stores and tobacco from many ports, and from New Orleans the grain and flour of the Northwest. But the mainstay was cotton. By 1850 more cotton was received in New York than in any other port in the country except Mobile and New Orleans. Providence, Philadelphia, and Boston also received extensive shipments. From the Potomac, Chesapeake, and Delaware vessels carried corn, wheat, and flour to northern and southern markets. But as time went on coal dominated the commerce of this middle region. Shipments depended upon the location of supplies, the adaptation of stoves and boilers to the use of anthracite, and the construction of internal improvements to bring coal from the interior to the seaports. The bituminous coal deposits of this country had been tapped in the eighteenth century; the popularization of anthracite occurred between 1815 and 1830. As canals were opened into the coal regions of Pennsylvania and Maryland, a flood of coal descended the Lehigh, the Susquehanna, the Schuylkill, and the Potomac to Baltimore and Philadelphia. This coal was shipped coastwise to New York, in spite of the canals built to carry it by inland routes, and to New England in sailing vessels which had brought northern products to Philadelphia or Baltimore. In 1822 the tidewater shipment of anthracite from Philadelphia totaled 200 tons; in 1850 it had increased to 1,075,000 tons. In exchange the extreme Northeast could furnish lumber, ice, and stone when bulk products were in question.

Unhappily, the amount of this commerce along the Gulf of Mexico and the Atlantic was as unmeasured in the days of the Republic as in the Colonial era. That by 1850–1860 it was the largest single item in America's domestic trade seems, nonetheless, a defensible surmise.

As soon as settlement crossed the mountains and drove a wedge of communities and farms across Tennessee and Kentucky, the pioneers relied upon the western waters, the Tennessee, Cumberland, Ohio, and Mississippi, as avenues for taking their products to market. Whatever the intentions of the nation which controlled the mouth of the Mississippi, these western Americans insisted upon the free navigation of that river and upon a right of deposit at New Orleans, where the goods could be transferred to ocean vessels. To carry their goods thither, they built strange, frontier merchant marines. To a later day the distinctions between various craft seem obscure, and undoubtedly the classifications were blurred, since so many builders were amateurs and the needs were so various. Flatboats, roughly shaped vessels, sometimes partly roofed over to make an ark, differed from "Kentucky" or "Ohio" flats, massive vessels covered throughout and roomy enough to carry a cargo of two to four hundred barrels or to transport settlers down river; barges, large vessels with masts, disputed the aristocracy of the river with keelboats, lighter, more graceful vessels carrying between fifteen and thirty tons, which had a keel for better balance and strength and a runway along each side upon which the crew walked when poling the ship upstream. Most of the vessels cost little to build. A farmer could construct a flatboat for his own produce, and a group of farmers might build a larger vessel.

These craft were laden with western produce and sent with the current southward. At New Orleans after the cargo was unshipped the vessels were sold for lumber. The crews then took passage for some eastern port or else returned home across country on foot. Upstream traffic was negligible, for few products could stand the expense of shipment. It cost one hundred and twenty dollars to get a ton of goods from New Orleans to St. Louis. But keelboats did make it. Manned with a crew of about thirty men, they fought their way upstream by towline, oar, or pole. Although a daily advance of ten miles by such exhausting methods was a fair average, packet lines of barges and keelboats were established on the Ohio and between Ohio River ports and New Orleans. There the rising receipts from the old Northwest revealed a substantial growth in trade. In 1798 such goods were valued at $975,000; by 1816 the total had increased to something over $8 million. This traffic was carried southward by nearly six hundred barges, twice as many flatboats, and six steamers.

For in the meantime this last method of navigation had been domesticated on the western waters. In 1809 Nicholas J. Roosevelt of New York, who was associated with Fulton and Livingston in perfecting the steamboat, made a preliminary survey of the Ohio and Mississippi from Pittsburgh to New Orleans; and in 1811 he launched the *New Orleans* at Pittsburgh. She had a carrying capacity of one hundred tons and had cost about $38,000. In November when the river was high enough, she steamed away for New Orleans, and early the following year she reached her destination. The eastern investors were gratified and looked forward to easy profits, since they had secured a monopoly grant from the Territory of Orleans, later Louisiana. In the following year the *New Orleans* entered the service between Natchez and New Orleans and earned $20,000 on her investment. The monopolists forthwith put additional boats on the Mississippi and Ohio and enterprising rivals, among whom was H. M. Shreve, later one of the most famous of river captains, decided to take their chances in this adventurous business. By 1815 steamboats had demonstrated their ability to sail from New Orleans to Louisville, Pittsburgh, and beyond; two years later the Fulton-Livingston monopoly collapsed largely because of the impossibility of enforcing it; and by 1818 a burst of boat building encouraged by the huge profits got under way. In 1821 the tonnage of steamboats arriving at New Orleans for the first time exceeded that of flatboats, barges, and other primitive vessels.

There were many similarities between river vessels on eastern and western waters and between the conditions which shaped them. Since both traveled shallow waters, the hull was comparatively flat-bottomed with a deck only a little above the water line; it was long, to provide a sufficient bearing on the water surface without increasing too greatly its resistance; side paddle wheels, which aided maneuvering, propelled both. There were also differences. Since the western partner had to make landings along the shore, the bow was built into a square-toed platform over the sharp prow concealed beneath it. With its shallow hull, the engines and the boat's quarters could not be in the hold but were piled skyward. Well forward on the first deck the engines and horizontal boilers were placed with the doors of the latter opening toward the bow to get the full effect of the draft. These engines were not the large, low-powered, finely finished ones of the eastern steamer. They were the American type of high-pressure engine, light, compact, noisy, inexpensive, and capable of delivering the surge of power required to buck a strong current or crawl over a sandbar. They were connected directly to the crankshaft of the paddle wheels rather than through a walking beam. Aft of this machinery was the second-class cabin, where the deck passengers traveled. The "scene of filth and wretchedness that baffles all description" presented by these quarters was forgotten on the upper deck, where the first-class cabin passengers had an airy and gorgeously decorated great cabin and luxurious staterooms. The whole was topped with the hurricane deck over thirty feet above water on which was the pilothouse and over which towered the two tall smokestacks.

The navigation of these inland waters was dangerous. One hazard was the vessel itself. The high-pressure engine had alarming potentialities for explosion, especially when their captains used steam "of a most dangerously great elasticity" on maiden voyages and in races with other boats. Explosions of boilers, often followed by the burning of the vessel, were only one source of danger. Shoals and bars were numerous and they shifted overnight; snags, "sawyers," and "planters"—water-logged timbers below the surface of the river or whole trees anchored in the silt by their branches but with the trunk swinging free—would rip open the delicate hulls of the vessels. A calculation placed the number of vessels lost by 1850 at 1,070, whose aggregate cost was over $7 million. The number of casualties was 2,269 killed and 1,881 wounded. No wonder Philip Hone reflected:

Steam, this powerful agent . . . has become a substitute for war in the philosophical plan of keeping down the superabundance of the human race, and thinning off the excessive population of which political economists have from time to time expressed so much dread.

Calhoun was too sanguine when he asserted that the average life of a steamboat was nine years; four or five years would have been a more accurate estimate.

In spite of their fragility, in spite of the fact that navigation except on the Mississippi south from Cairo had for all except small boats a seasonal character—spring and fall were the most favorable times—the steamboats offered advantages to passengers and shippers, particularly in upstream navigation. They increased greatly in effectiveness and capacity. Some of the boats in the twenties could carry about two hundred tons on eight feet of water; by 1860 some were carrying twelve hundred. They quickened their speeds. Whereas in 1815 it had taken twenty-five days for the voyage from New Orleans to Louisville, the prebellum record, made in 1853, was four days, nine hours, and thirty minutes. These record breakers traveled day and night and averaged nearly fourteen miles an hour. More customary were trips of four-and-a-half to six days. While speed increased, fares decreased. At first this new method of locomotion was expensive—the cabin fare from New Orleans to Louisville ranged in the early years from $100 to $125. But competition reduced this figure and it became possible to take the journey by mid-century for from $12 to $25. Deck fares fell from $8 and $10 to $3. Freight rates fluctuated wildly depending upon the season, the scarcity of cargo, and the number of competing vessels. In the forties De Bow, making out a case for river transportation probably underestimated the averages when he stated that they were between 0.5 cent and 1.5 cents per ton per mile. Compared to the rates on wagon routes, these were astoundingly low. The extent of the western fleets can be grasped only in figures. In 1811 the first steamboat was launched upon the Ohio; in 1860 there were 735 steamboats in service on the western rivers. In carrying northwestern produce to New Orleans, the steamboat probably did not displace the flatboat, on which downriver rates were generally lower. But steam had changed the western waters into a channel for two-way traffic.

These navies built a cavalcade of ports. Pittsburgh, Cincinnati, Louisville, and St. Louis had an export and import trade and steamship arrivals and departures which would have done credit to any Atlantic emporium. New Orleans, at the "mouth" of the river ninety-eight miles from its real union with the Gulf, was classed with London, Liverpool, and New York as one of the great commercial cities of the world. She was the destination of two sorts of western produce. Since the Ohio River was before 1820 the chief wedge of settlement driven into the trans-Appalachian wilderness, it is not surprising that in 1816, fully 80 percent of the products arriving at New Orleans came from the Ohio valley or from the Mississippi north of the Ohio. The roll call of commodities reflects the pioneer economic organization of the West: flour, beef, bacon and hams, corn, lard, oats, pork, peltries, whisky, apples, and potatoes. Southern products were tobacco and cotton. The value of these shipments classified under forty items was $8,042,540. In 1852 the variety of the commodities was more extensive, the classification more exact, and the amount greatly enlarged. The value of shipments in 1852 reached the total of $108,051,708. Even more significant than these absolute figures was the relative proportion occupied by their various constituents. In 1852 the value of cotton passed that of all other products combined; by that date sugar and molasses, items which were purely southern in origin, occupied a position higher even than tobacco. Meanwhile the receipts of flour and wheat and other western products remained practically stationary in value. New Orleans was becoming a southern port.

The reasons for this astonishing reversal in the currents of trade were in part the course of settlement, which had poured into the Southwest and had carried the cotton kingdom from the shores of the Atlantic to those of the Gulf of Mexico. They were in larger part the result of the construction of lines of communication between the Atlantic Northeast and the Middle West. In spite of the steamboat, upstream traffic from New Orleans never assumed the impressive proportions of that downstream. Coffee and sugar and molasses, with the occasional addition of some bulky machinery, were the chief long-distance shipments. The Northwest was supplied with cloths and fine manufactures from the Atlantic seaboard by way of the inland lines of communication. New Orleans was an export rather than an import city.

The Eastern Canals

At a time when it seemed Americans could pick and choose among several improved means of transportation, Gallatin had quite largely devoted his long report to artificial highways or canals. In his examination of their potentialities for connecting the commercialized urban East with a growing largely agricultural West, he had had to acknowledge grave impediments—with one exception. The Hudson, or North, River "breaks through or turns all the mountains. . . . A few miles above Troy, and the head of the tide, the Hudson approaches the waters of Lake Champlain and the Mohawk those of Lake Ontario." This observation required no prophetic gifts. Others had observed the same favorable situation. In the 1790's New York State chartered two private companies to improve and develop these routes. They had failed. But with every year the compulsion to overcome this failure grew stronger. New York

City stood isolated at the mouth of the Hudson. The trade of the Middle West flowed southward to New Orleans when it did not move eastward over the Cumberland Road to Philadelphia and Baltimore, New York's deadly rivals. Even within New York State the southern counties looked toward the same markets, and Lake Ontario and Lake Champlain traded with Montreal. The explanation for these preferences was the high freight rates to New York City. It cost one hundred dollars to ship a ton of goods there overland from Buffalo.

The identity of the man who "built" the Erie Canal to redirect these channels of commerce has been a battleground for partisans, but in the perspective of a century there is little difficulty in selecting De Witt Clinton, mayor of New York City, governor of the state, and canal commissioner. Clinton had the wit to realize that European experience had demonstrated the futility of improving a river if the stream was not large enough for independent navigation. Currents were variable, the depth available for vessels depended upon the season, and the towpath was either too high above the river or submerged beneath it according to the heaviness of the rainfall and the flooding of the stream. Better by far to construct a canal parallel to such a river and use its waters to keep the level set in the canal itself. In the second place, a private corporation had proved inadequate for the task, since its funds had been insufficient and its affairs badly mismanaged. If the work was to be undertaken it would have to be at the expense of the state, aided if possible by the Federal government. The latter did not cooperate. Jefferson thought the Erie was a fine project which "might be executed a century hence," and then looked nearer home at a canal westward from Washington.

After disheartening vacillations, caused in large part by local jealousies, New York in 1816 and 1817 passed the necessary legislation. The financial expedients were complicated and burdensome, for a state with a population of less than 1.5 million undertook the construction of two canals—the Lake Champlain Canal was constructed simultaneously with the Erie—whose combined cost was estimated at $7 million. To meet these expenses the credit of the state could be used for borrowing purposes, and to meet the interest and principal of this indebtedness a canal fund was created. Into this reservoir various trickles of revenue were diverted—money obtained from the land donated to aid the canal, of which a gift from the Holland Land Company was the largest, taxes levied on the manufacture of salt, taxes laid on all persons who traveled stated distances on the Hudson River steamboats, proceeds from certain lotteries, taxes on sales at auctions, appropriations from the state, and finally all tolls collected when the canals were built.

Then came the physical task of constructing the canal. Western New York was a wilderness, and the central region was one of unhealthy marshes. The pioneers at Panama in a new engineering era confronted no greater difficulties. In the absence of sanitary precautions and modern medical knowledge, agues, bilious fever, and typhus attacked the workers and occasionally halted the work. The primeval forest had to be hewed down and the roots grubbed out. The digging, furthermore, had to be done without the aid of modern excavating machinery and without the supervision of trained engineers. Such were not to be had in America. After the failure to secure an English engineer, two of the three great sections were entrusted to James Geddes and Benjamin Wright, both of whom were lawyers who had practiced surveying on the side. They developed their engineering talents as the work progressed. In fact the canal was a school of engineering. One of the subordinate engineers, Canvass White, started as a surveyor, then went to England, where he tramped two thousand miles of towpath observing every feature of canal construction, and returned in time to aid the building of locks and works with his diagrams and to discover with the help of others a waterproof cement equal to the best of Europe.

On July 4, 1817, the first spadeful of earth was turned. In 1825, this "Hellespont of the West" was completed and elaborate state and civic celebrations marked the triumph. Somehow they fell short of the achievement. For the total length of the canal from the harbors which were built at Buffalo to the basins at Albany was 363 miles; its greatest height above sea level was 566 feet, and the total lockage made necessary by ascents and descents to conform with the topography was just a little less than 700 feet. The canal itself was nothing but a big ditch; its prism was 40 feet wide at the top, 28 feet wide at the bottom, and 4 feet deep. As an engineering feat the canal was unexampled in America. Although the gates were of wood, the locks were built of stone and on the average could be passed in the short time of four minutes; its aqueducts, fills, and mechanisms impressed even European visitors. Furthermore the canal was built well within the time limit estimated by De Witt Clinton; the state had borrowed $7,411,770 to construct both canals and their construction had been attended by a happy absence of wastefulness, extravagance, and corruption. A contemporary narrator was justified in his superlatives: "THEY HAVE BUILT THE LONGEST CANAL IN THE WORLD IN THE LEAST TIME, WITH THE LEAST EXPERIENCE, FOR THE LEAST MONEY, AND TO THE GREATEST PUBLIC BENEFIT."

The effects of the Erie Canal upon the development and history of the United States ramify almost into infinity. Perhaps it is best to begin with a statement of traffic and the money returns in sheer dollars and cents. In the first year, in which it was operated for only part of the season, 13,110 boats and rafts passed through the canal and the tolls collected equalled one-seventh of the original cost. This was impressive. Yet twenty-five years later the tonnage carried on the Erie was 1,635,089;

the tolls collected in that year were $2,993,125.93.[1] The cost of original construction had been met several times over. New York, dizzied by the spectacular promotional results of the Erie, proceeded to authorize the construction of a number of canals as feeders to it—a state-wide system— and later began the enlargement of the Erie itself. But more important was the result of this record upon the seaboard rivals of New York. Though they could hardly hope to rival her in reaching the Great Lakes, they had compensations. In 1825 the Great Lakes region was comparatively undeveloped; the Ohio valley was the real heart of the West. Both Pennsylvania and Virginia thrust the bulk of their territory to the very banks of the Ohio, and Maryland, although cut off from that river by the others, possessed a part claim to one of the inevitable routes of approach, the Potomac. Finally, the commercial cities of Philadelphia, Baltimore, and Richmond were nearer Ohio than was the metropolis on the Hudson.

Of all these competitors undoubtedly Philadelphia was made the most unhappy by the Erie Canal, for the barrier of the Appalachians and the absence of rivers running east-and-west seemed to veto its construction of any effective rival. Something, nevertheless, had to be done. As a result of the organized activity of the merchants, bankers, and publicity experts of Philadelphia, the state legislature in 1826 passed a measure for a canal between Philadelphia and Pittsburgh. As the work progressed modifications of the original scheme were introduced which created the most remarkable transportation system in the United States and one of the most remarkable in the world. From Philadelphia a railroad traversed the eighty-one miles to Columbia on the Susquehanna. From Columbia a canal ascended the Susquehanna and then traveled westward along the Juniata to Hollidaysburg, where the 2,291 feet high Allegheny ridge had to be surmounted. The device chosen was the Allegheny Portage Railroad, which mounted each side of the ridge with five inclined planes interspersed with level stretches. Stationary engines pulled the vehicles up the inclines; horses pulled them on the level tracks. In this fashion cars or cradles with canal boats were raised from the Juniata and finally let down on the other side into the Conemaugh at Johnstown, whence a canal continued along the routes of various rivers to Pittsburgh. The work proceeded rapidly under the direction of engineers trained on the Erie Canal, and in 1834 the Pennsylvania Canal was opened for use.

Although the route was shorter than the Erie Canal, transportation over it was more difficult and more expensive. It had 174 locks against the 88 on the Erie, the expense of its three transshipments was equivalent to that of fifty miles by canal, and all transportation companies had to own both canal boats and cars and maintain several sets of depots and

---

[1] By 1882, when tolls were abolished, the Erie had collected $120,692,400.75.

agents. The route carried nearly every European visitor to the United States, but its record as a freight carrier was much less impressive. The total through freight, for instance, weighed at Hollidaysburg in 1844 was only one-fifth that carried in the same year by the Erie.

The Virginia and the Maryland routes are indissolubly connected with the name of George Washington. Owning western lands which he desired to increase in value and realizing the political importance of some tie binding together a country severed by the Appalachian ranges, he investigated various routes and wrote to the governor of Virginia in 1787, "It has long been my decided opinion, that the shortest, easiest, and least expensive communication with the invaluable and extensive country back of us would be by one of the rivers of this State, which have their sources in the Appalachian mountains." To prove the practical nature of his convictions, Washington became the president of the first companies chartered to improve these means of communication. The final value of his foresight was demonstrated when for over seventy years Maryland and Virginia worked together or separately to utilize the rivers —the James and the Potomac which Washington had thus designated.

The James River project was entirely a Virginia enterprise. After years of futile attempts to improve the navigation of this stream above Richmond, Virginians became impatient to have some connection with the western states. Virginia "has been living on Glory!—her past Glory—breakfasting, dining, and supping on it," while others grasped the prize. Finally, in 1832, the James River and Kanawha Company was chartered. Three years later this corporation decided to parallel the James with a canal, build a railroad from the terminus over the mountains to the Kanawha, and to improve that river to the Ohio. To supplement the subscriptions of private investors the state and the city of Richmond made contributions to the enterprise. Then began the customary tale of endeavor and disappointment. The James River Canal aroused sectional and political jealousies. There was a quarrel between the adherents of the railroads and of the canal project. As usual, the expenses of construction were far above the estimates, and money had to be borrowed at high rates of interest. By 1851 the canal had been pushed some fifty miles beyond Lynchburg. Meanwhile some poor improvements in the Kanawha River were constructed. Although the rail connection between the two was never achieved, the Kanawha turnpike running northwestward to that river from a branch of the James served for a small traffic.

A canal along the Potomac route involved a tangle of jealousies. The states immediately concerned were Virginia and Maryland, but the most favorable routes to the Ohio after leaving Cumberland went northwest through Pennsylvania. The number of towns and cities aspirant to commercial greatness further complicated the situation. Baltimore, Washington, Georgetown, and Alexandria were all closely involved. To make matters worse, there was a bitter controversy about the methods of communication—canal or railway. Even the splendid Potomac route was barred by the ridge of the Alleghenies, whose passes were all over two thousand feet above sea level. Utilization of the route illustrated in a precise fashion all the phases of transportation development. The first design was the Patowmack Company, chartered by Maryland and Virginia, aided by subscriptions from both, presided over by George Washington, and planning the improvement of the waterway. By the twenties friends of the project had converted it into the Chesapeake and Ohio Canal and, taking advantage of the current enthusiasm for waterways, had won financial assistance from the national government and from the cities the canal was designed to benefit. But as time passed Virginia lost interest since the canal was on the Maryland shore; Maryland lost interest for Baltimore merchants preferred to invest in the Baltimore and Ohio Railroad; and the railroad and the canal hampered each other by their struggles for precedence along the route and for the favor of subscribers. In 1850 the Chesapeake and Ohio Canal staggered into Cumberland on the upper Potomac eight years behind the railroad. The Ohio, on the other side of the mountains, was still unattained.

The Waterways of the Northwest

Except on the east, the Old Northwest was bounded by waterways. The Mississippi above St. Louis traversed its western reaches, the Ohio washed its southern edge. Both of these routes through their connection with the main river and New Orleans were natural avenues for commerce and transportation. On the other hand, the utility of their northern boundary, the Great Lakes, really waited upon the breaching of Lake Erie by New York's big ditch. Even then, though these vast inland seas presented unique possibilities for navigation, their use was greatly retarded by minor disadvantages. First of all, the lakes were not properly connected. The only channel between Lake Erie and Lake Ontario passed over Niagara Falls; the St. Mary's River fell sharply several feet in its course from Lake Superior to Lake Huron; and between Huron and Erie were the flats of Lake St. Clair, where a tortuous, shallow channel wound back and forth between acres of wild rice. The lakes, too, were subject to sudden and violent storms, and the lack of sea room compelled sailing vessels to make for harbor rather than run out the gale. Good harbors did not exist, and the mouths of affluent rivers which provided the natural sites for improved harbors tended to silt up even when jetties and walls were built to form a protective basin. Improvements by dredging and canals were delayed at first by the thinness of settlement and later by the Congressional conviction that the lakes were merely gigantic frog ponds and that state funds should finance harbor improvements. Although a canal had been early constructed through Canadian territory around the Niagara barrier, Michigan did not complete a canal through its territory around the St. Mary's Falls until 1853–1855. Navigation was then possible from the tip of Lake Superior to the sea.

Although the *Walk-in-the-Water,* the first steamboat in the Great Lakes above Niagara Falls, was launched in 1818, commerce on the Great Lakes was not important for several years. As on the Missouri River later, the early steamboats derived their cargoes and revenue from the fur trade. But the opening of the Erie Canal brought a revolution. In five years the tonnage, steam and sail, entering Buffalo increased six times. Before 1800 there was hardly a vessel on the lakes larger than an Indian canoe; in 1860 the merchant marine of the northern lakes aggregated 463,123 tons, of which 90 percent was under sail. For the prewar era was the one of the lake schooner, whose grace and usefulness made her the peer of the Atlantic coastal carriers. Like her eastern cousins, the lake schooner carried bulk cargoes—lumber, grain, and after 1855, ores from Lake Superior. Relative tonnage figures, nevertheless, certainly underestimated the importance of steam. Until the railroads encircled the more eastern of the Great Lakes, the passenger steamers, mingling splendor and squalor, carried travelers, businessmen, and immigrants along these inland seas; propellers, using less fuel and better adapted for passing the interlake canals, were freight carriers; and tows helped long lines of becalmed or wind-baffled schooners in straits and harbors. In 1851 the value of the Lakes' freight carriage was estimated at $326 million. A single item in the total of our domestic commerce, it nevertheless was equal to nearly three-quarters of our total foreign trade in that year. Such a development the Erie Canal had made possible. But the construction of western canals had, likewise, been an important contribution.

In 1818 Governor De Witt Clinton was writing to the projector of a canal in Indiana, "I have found the way to get into Lake Erie and you have shown me how to get out of it. . . . You have extended my project six hundred miles." The New York governor exhibited a similar cordiality to the proposals for an Ohio system of artificial waterways, and he was the dignitary selected by the state to turn the first shovelful of earth on its first through canal. Clinton's personal enthusiasm reflected the interest of New York, particularly New York City, in these western canals. For although the Erie Canal and the Great Lakes might be in the main avenue of commerce, a series of feeder communications which would pour into it the surplus produce of the Old Northwest was necessary for complete success. Such supplementary canals were even more vital to the northwestern states. Though the central and southern portions of these states generally had access to river transportation and to New Orleans, they perceived disadvantages in the latter place. Agricultural products shipped to that city often found the market glutted. An Ohio committee on canals wrote:

> To leave one's property at New Orleans is to abandon it to destruction; to wait for higher prices is to incur the dangers of an unwholesome climate. One must ship his flour or sell at a sacrifice—oft-times at a price that will not pay the cost of freight and charges.

An alternative market would have the desirable effect of competition. The committee calculated that if the flour shipped southward from Cincinnati to New Orleans in 1818–1819 could have gone via canal to New York there would have been a saving in freight rates of $364,000, which would have given the farmer an increased profit. The magic wand of internal improvements would produce prosperity.

For the construction of canals the northwestern states had undoubted natural advantages. Between the Great Lakes region, on the one hand, and the Ohio and Mississippi basins, on the other, there was no formidable divide, and by easy portages a canoe could be carried from the short streams flowing into the Lakes to the longer rivers flowing into the Ohio or Mississippi. In Ohio one logical route led southward from the Cuyahoga flowing into Lake Erie at Cleveland either to the Muskingum, which joins the Ohio at Marietta, the oldest settlement in the state, or along the rich Scioto valley to Portsmouth. Near the western border of the state the Maumee and the Miami suggested a connection between Cincinnati and Lake Erie at Toledo. Indiana was bisected by a remarkable diagonal highway. Between the headwaters of the Maumee in the northeast corner of the state and the Wabash, which eventually entered the Ohio after serving as part of the boundary between Indiana and Illinois, there was a low marshy portage of but eight miles. A similar trivial barrier separated the headwaters of the Chicago River, emptying into Lake Michigan, from an upper branch of the Illinois, which eventually joined the Mississippi River. Here was the possibility of connecting at one stroke the great north-and-south artery of the Mississippi with the Great Lakes. Furthermore, the territory through which these channels passed was rich in the natural materials necessary for canal construction, wood and stone.

The difficulties confronting the utilization of these routes had already been suggested by the history of the eastern canals. Some of them were political. Each section was jealous of the others and eager to gain for itself the demonstrated advantages of internal improvements. In spite of these sectional handicaps, the routes for canals were selected with great wisdom, and their engineering and commercial feasibility was later demonstrated by the fact that the railroads, constructed by presumably canny private capitalists, followed the same lines. In Ohio two trunk canals were constructed. The eastern one, the Ohio Canal, connecting Cleveland and Portsmouth, included both the Scioto and Muskingum valleys, and a western one, the Miami Canal, connected Cincinnati and Toledo directly. These canals crossed the great agricultural districts of the state. In Indiana and Illinois, although the construction of the Wabash Canal and the Illinois and Michigan along the routes mentioned above had been early authorized and undertaken, the latter was not finished until 1848 and the former, the longest canal in America, until 1853.

Financial handicaps dogged nearly all these western undertakings and few really paid for themselves. They were nevertheless, of service for a time, and the greatness of the Lake cities—Buffalo, Cleveland, Toledo, and Chicago—was largely due to the trade which they created and developed.

The Commerce of the Canals

The new canals became almost at once the avenues of travel and of emigration. Packet boats pulled by four horses and with frequent relays introduced speed for the first-class travelers. On the Erie Canal through packet boats moved at the rate of four miles per hour. Fare on these vessels was three or four cents a mile. Expeditious and cheap as this new means of travel was, it was a hardship which the squeamish did not enjoy. The roof was low, and crowded under it were the quarters for the crew, the ladies' cabin, the main cabin (which did duty as the men's dormitory at night), the bar, and the kitchen. Daytime might be made endurable by sitting on deck or walking along the towpath, but night was a different story, for the passengers were herded into berths in a room which lacked ventilation. The bullfrogs and the mosquitoes of the American swamps effectively banished any possibility of sleep in surroundings which in summer constituted a "Turkish bath."

But the canals were more important for the stimulus which they gave to westward settlement.

> Then there's the State of New York where some are very rich,
> Themselves and a few others have dug a mighty ditch,
> To render it more easy for us to find the way
> And sail upon the water to Michigania
>   Yea, yea, yea, to Michigania.

Westward movers who thus celebrated in song their means of emigration traveled on line boats, which Horace Greeley once described as "cent and a half a mile, mile and a half an hour." On the lakes they secured a cheap passage on some old steamer and then changed at some lake port to canal boat or wagon transportation. This tide of emigration, which carried westward New Englanders or New Yorkers who had earlier stemmed from New England, included the foreigner. It was estimated that nearly 30 percent of the immigrants landing at New York settled in the various states which were served by the Erie Canal and its western connections.

But the most important function of the canals was to transport goods. They enabled people to live in these newly settled areas by carrying away their produce and by returning with the necessities and the comforts which a new country required and which it could not produce for itself. In this quickened and enlarged domestic commerce, lower freight rates were the fundamental factor. On the Buffalo-New York route, for instance, freight charges by wagon had once averaged 19.2 cents per ton-mile; between 1825 and 1850 over the canal and the Hudson they had fallen to only 1.68 cents per ton-mile. Canal transportation thus made possible the carriage of bulky products, grain and livestock, stone and timber. The *Scioto Gazette,* describing in 1830 the effect of the Ohio Canal upon an inland Ohio town, said it "has reduced the price of salt from 87 to 50 cents a bushel, and reduced carriage on every article imported from abroad in a corresponding ratio. It has advanced the price of flour from $3 to $4 a barrel, and wheat from 40 to 65 cents per bushel."

Though the commerce on the James and Kanawha, the Chesapeake and Ohio, or the Pennsylvania "main line" might serve as illustration of the interchanges between seacoast and interior accomplished by the canals, the Erie was the best illustration. Before 1830 receipts at its Buffalo terminus from the West were small, for the canal at first secured its greatest cargoes in western New York, a region whose development it greatly hastened. But by 1835 the construction of the Ohio canals began to make a midwestern surplus available for eastern markets, and the trade through Buffalo commenced. Lumber products were usually the first commodities sent by any new western district to Buffalo. Then came a tide of grain—by 1840 the receipts from the West surpassed those from western New York—and shipments of pork, beef, and other food products. Lumber, grain, and meat, indeed, remained the great trades from the West.[2] They bulked larger than the commodities traveling from the East, but the latter were the more valuable. They were the mélange of manufactured or exotic articles required by the new settlements. Their enumeration—dry goods, boots and shoes, hardware, machinery, paper,

2 ARTICLES SHIPPED EASTWARD BY THE CANAL FROM BUFFALO

	1835	1850
Flour, bbl.	86,233	984,430
Wheat, bu.	95,071	3,304,647
Corn, bu.	14,579	2,608,967
Provisions, bbl.	6,502	146,836
Ashes, bbl.	4,419	17,504
Staves, no.	2,565,272	159,479,504
Wool, lb.	140,911	8,805,817
Butter, Cheese, Lard, lb.	1,030,632	17,534,981

Source: I. D. Andrews, *Report on the Trade and Commerce of the British North American Colonies and upon the Trade of the Great Lakes and Rivers,* p. 92.

drugs, medicines, sugar, molasses, coffee, tea, tobacco, salt, fish—reads, with few exceptions, like the manifests of the inbound cargoes of our foreign trade at an earlier period. From 1836 to 1853 these eastern exports multiplied nearly ten times in value.

Since the ambitious projects of Virginia and Maryland never really reached the West, the Pennsylvania main line and the Erie with its western feeders were the magnets which twisted into new directions the lines of commerce within the Old Northwest. By the forties the attraction of the Mississippi was yielding to that of the East.[3] By the late thirties the handling of wheat and flour at Buffalo surpassed that at New Orleans. For a time this increase in northern commerce could be regarded as an addition to New York's traffic created by new transportation facilities rather than by a subtraction from New Orleans' total. But there was no debate when New Orleans began to lose the Ohio valley. In 1845 only 5 percent of Cincinnati's flour shipments went south, while 68 percent moved north and east over railroads and canals. The remainder was shipped up the Ohio, presumably to the railheads of the Baltimore and Ohio and the Pennsylvania Railroads, the symbols of "northern enterprise." St. Louis, which took the place of Cincinnati as a purveyor of northwestern supplies to New Orleans, began in the later fifties to sense the magnetism of the rival northern route with the completion of the Ohio and Michigan Canal and the arrival of railroads at Mississippi or Missouri river ports from Chicago or other eastern cities.

Although the complete defeat of New Orleans in the Ohio region was postponed until the day of railroads, citizens of the Crescent City began to be alarmed at the unnatural tendency of commerce to defy the laws of gravity and to flow uphill. *De Bow's Review*, Southern protagonist of the Mississippi route, demonstrated conclusively that ton-mile rates on the river were only 0.5 to 1.5 cents, on the canals 1.5 cents exclusive of tolls, and on the lakes 3 cents. But the distance down the river was longer, the rates of insurance were higher, the liability of products to deterioration through climate was greater, the ocean rates from New Orleans to Liverpool were nearly twice those from New York, and with the larger ocean vessels it was more difficult to navigate the wearisome stretch from the Gulf up the river to New Orleans than to enter New York harbor.

3 THE RIVAL COMMERCES OF NEW YORK AND NEW ORLEANS IN 1851

A. Comparative value of property sent from the seaboard to the interior via the Hudson and via the Mississippi:

Years	Hudson	Mississippi
1841	$56,798,447	$30,768,966
1851	80,739,899	38,874,782

B. Estimate of comparative total value of articles landed at tidewater via the different routes in 1851: *Hudson*, $53,727,508; *Mississippi*, $108,051,708.

Source: Adapted from I. D. Andrews, *Report on the Trade and Commerce of the British North American Colonies, and upon the Trade of the Great Lakes and Rivers,* pp. 895–897.

The Railroads

The essential elements of the railroad—a track of steel rails laid upon transverse wooden ties set in a ballast of crushed stone or gravel, and the steam locomotive—are so simple in an age of mechanical complexity that it is hard to realize the slowness and the difficulty of their evolution. The railroad, in fact, united two unrelated developments. The first was the invention of the prepared roadbed, the second was the application of the steam engine to locomotion. As early as the seventeenth century in England plank roads had been built at collieries for the transportation of coal to tidewater, and in the next century attempts to protect these planks with iron had led to the invention of iron rails with flanges to keep the wheels on the tracks. Over such railways cars were hauled either by men or by horses, or, with the proper grades, they might coast down by gravity and be brought back under animal power. The only effect the invention of the Watt and Boulton steam engine had upon these roads was to suggest that a series of inclined planes might be constructed to surmount the steeper grades and that cars could be hauled up by a stationary engine at the top. Railroads which embodied some or all of these features were numerous in England and had even been built in the United States for short distances to carry gravel, stone, or coal from the mine or quarry to a lower level.

Meanwhile inventors had been experimenting with means for driving vehicles by steam. Since the Watt and Boulton condensing low-pressure engine was too bulky for such use, both Englishmen and Americans had sought other types of engine with considerable success. Finally in the late twenties George Stephenson demonstrated the right to be called the creator of the steam railroad. Although his achievements were made possible by the experiments of his predecessors and the contemporary assistance he received from others, the basis of his success was his own scientific study of transportation, which demonstrated to his mind that the locomotive to be successful must run upon a fairly level prepared road in order to avoid the resistance produced by steeper grades. Employed as engineer for the Liverpool & Manchester Railway, he prevailed upon the owners to allow him to apply his theories of construction. Incident to the construction he helped build an engine, the *Rocket,* embodying the forced draft and the multitubular boiler to keep up the steam pressure, which on a trial trip in 1829 attained a speed greater than twelve miles an hour. By the end of 1830 this all-purpose line (for it carried passengers as well as freight), using the steam locomotive, had been thoroughly tested. "With the Liverpool and Manchester line, the railroad era really began."

Americans watched these trans-Atlantic developments with curiosity and eagerness; for here and there in their own country they had already built short railroads on which cars coasted down inclined planes or were drawn by horses. By the end of the twenties the more foresighted were convinced that the new means of transportation had obvious advantages. Unlike all waterways, the railroad did not freeze in the winter; unlike canals, it might penetrate terrain which lacked the water resources and natural channels for artificial waterways. In 1830 there were seventy-three miles of railroad in the country, and a steam locomotive imported from Great Britain had already traveled on American track. From then on construction was rapid. For two decades the states along the Atlantic seaboard were the chief centers; in 1850 they had approximately 80 percent of the nation's mileage. Then with a rush the railroad leaped the Appalachians; a network of shining track was built through the old West and crossed the Mississippi into the first tier of states beyond. Indeed the railroad had practically caught up with the frontier. In 1860 of the national total of 30,635 miles, nearly half was in the states west of the mountains.[4] Even the railroads of the East were in a sense western, for cities great and small along the Atlantic coast, while they were developing rail connections with each other and building up immediate hinterlands, were also raising their eyes to the horizons of the West and dreaming of annexing its mounting commerce to their prosperity and growth. Like the canal, the railroad was a weapon of urban imperialism.

In the East, after a moment of prudent hesitation, Boston embraced the new means of transportation. She had need of some avenue to commercial salvation, for her deadly rival, New York City, threatened to seize the trade of western and even central New England. The projection and completion of the Erie Canal, by which New York tapped the West, was cause for further alarm until the more cunning Yankees conceived of hitching the Erie to their cause by a canal across Massachusetts to Albany. A report to the Massachusetts legislature asserted that such could be built for some $6 million. It was obvious to other schemers that if the Berkshires could thus easily be surmounted the Green Mountains

[4] RAILROAD MILEAGE IN THE UNITED STATES

	1830	1840	1850	1860
New England states	3	446	2,633	3,660
Middle states	70	1,510	2,972	6,353
Trans-Mississippi West		62	93	2,175
Southeast		988	1,578	5,463
Old Southwest		133	300	3,392
Old Northwest		199	1,303	9,592
Total U.S.	73	3,328	8,879	30,635

Source: Compiled from *Hunt's Merchants' Magazine* (1851) and Henry V. Poor, *Manual of the Railroads of the United States for 1868–1869.*

N.B.: "To know railroad statistics is to doubt them." George R. Taylor, *Trends in the American Economy in the Nineteenth Century,* p. 525.

and the White Mountains were no insurmountable barrier, and soon New England was crisscrossed with imaginary artificial waterways.

Fortunately, no definite step toward construction of these arteries was taken. News of the success of English railways filtered to this country and their superior adaptability to the New England terrain was so obvious that the railroad party in Massachusetts triumphed over the canal partisans, and in 1830–1831 the state legislature began to charter railroads which were actually built. One of these pioneer enterprises, the Boston and Worcester, was pointed toward the Erie; even before the former's completion in 1835, the Western Railroad was chartered to extend to the Massachusetts state line, there to connect with a line from Albany. In 1841 the road was completed. It had more than a regional importance, for its successful passage of the Berkshires showed railroad promoters and builders everywhere that the railroad could climb. Nonetheless, Boston capitalists and merchants, far from satisfied with this achievement, promoted and financed roads that it was hoped would reach the West by Montreal or by a port on Lake Ontario. They were also enthusiastic over the construction of end-to-end roads which were paralleling the Erie Canal through the heart of New York State and they invested in them. The success of Boston's western connections alarmed rival cities. The grain products of the West went directly to New England without detours through New York City, and the New England manufacturers consigned their products directly to western merchants instead of utilizing the forwarders of New York and Philadelphia.

In the South, as in New England, topography discouraged canal building. The rivers, particularly in the Piedmont, followed such narrow valleys or gorges that the parallel construction of canals was expensive; the freshet proportions of rivers after sudden rainfalls threatened canal works; water seeped away from canal beds through the porous soil. These handicaps the railroad avoided. Consequently a series of southern ports, from Norfolk and Richmond to Charleston and Savannah, either as yet undeveloped or anxious over their declining commercial glory, turned to the railroad as a means of growth and redress. Charleston was the most alert. Chafing at the realization that the navigation of the Savannah River gave Savannah a better means of reaching the cotton-growing Piedmont, and that the trade of the Georgia city prospered as that of their own languished, the Charleston chamber of commerce secured from the legislature in 1828 a charter for the South Carolina Canal and Railroad Company. Ignoring the alternative first offered by its title, the corporation chose to construct a railroad from Charleston across the state to the head of navigation on the river of their rival and thus puncture its commercial lifeline. Surveyors and promoters found the country between the termini an easy one; the road of 136 miles was opened for traffic in 1833; three years earlier one of the first locomotives used in the country,

The Best Friend of Charleston, had been tried out on a portion of the route and had demonstrated the usefulness of steam power. At the time of completion the railroad was the longest in the world. In the elation of the early thirties, it was natural to project extensions into the Cotton Belt and perhaps even northwestward into the grain regions of the Ohio valley. The cereal and livestock areas would send a down traffic to the cotton belt, the cotton belt would send a down traffic to Charleston, and that city would become the entrepôt for all the manufactured products desired for this great region. Charlestonians in convention assembled therefore resolved that "the period has now arrived when the work can no longer be neglected without a criminal supineness and fatal disregard of our own best interests, as well as the duties which we owe to ourselves, and to posterity." But the costs were staggering. After the panic of 1837 and the cotton collapse which followed, the enterprise sank beneath the waves of liquidation. Meanwhile Charleston's first railroad had been pushed westward across northern Georgia.

The meaning of these portents Savannah at first disdained to notice. But in 1833 she struck back with a railroad of her own. The Central of Georgia Railroad and Canal Company, paralleling Charleston's enterprises hardly fifty miles away, moved westward from Savannah into the interior of the state. Soon the competitors saw it was to their advantage to reconcile their rivalries and induce Georgia to charter and build a western connection for both. In 1836 the state legislature obligingly ordered the survey and construction of the Western and Atlantic. Outwitting the Appalachians, it was to begin at some point in southeastern Tennessee on the Tennessee and end at some point in northwestern Georgia on the Chattahoochee, indefinite termini which later developed into Chattanooga and Atlanta. Though it met with the customary financial difficulties, the road was opened to traffic in 1851. The Virginia ports reached Chattanooga somewhat later over a more unsatisfactory route. Thus the Western and Atlantic gave Georgia the first western connection in the southern states and made it the kingpin of the whole southern railroad system.

These railroads threatened to alter the historic channels of southern commerce. By 1850 they had connected the interior cotton belt with the Atlantic seaboard and alarmed Mobile and New Orleans. Even before the completion of the Western and Atlantic, the cotton receipts at Charleston rose from 261,000 bales in 1848 to 438,000 in 1849, and Savannah's increased from 255,000 to 391,000. At the same time receipts at New Orleans fell off nearly 100,000 bales. The Gulf cities grudgingly acknowledged the necessity for a railroad counterattack. Mobile and New Orleans both projected railroads northward to the Ohio River to beat off the invasion from the East, whether it came from New York or Charleston, and New Orleans dreamed of a railroad to the Pacific. The latter ambition was unrealized until the eighties. The roads to the Ohio after discouragement and delay were completed just before the Civil War. If the truth must be told, the real beneficiary of southern construction was Atlanta, once a spot in the wilderness, but by 1860 a flourishing commercial center of ten thousand inhabitants.

In the Middle Atlantic states the completion and success of the Erie Canal was of central importance. As we have seen it sharpened the desires of New York's rivals to reach the West—to that extent its influence was beneficial. On the other hand, success brought disadvantages. Complacent over their possession of the magnificent Erie, New Yorkers too long remained blind to the superior advantage of railways. Instructed by the experience of their northern neighbor and dazzled by the Erie, Pennsylvanians chose to reach the West by the inefficient "main line" rather than by a railroad. Even in Maryland where the leading Baltimoreans succeeded in committing their city to the Baltimore and Ohio Railroad, since a canal along the Potomac would not reach Chesapeake Bay at their wharves, the state for decades was schizophrenic, dividing its allegiance and resources between canal and railroad. Moreover, once the states had financed and built their canals, railroad competition would reduce the returns from them and thus perchance throw a financial burden on the taxpayers. The states had vested rights in an antiquated system of transportation. As a curious by-product of this dilemma, legislation in New York forbade railroads paralleling the Erie to carry freight or, if they did, compelled the payment of tolls to the state, and opinion was hostile to other railroad enterprises proposing to connect the Hudson and Lake Erie. In Pennsylvania, the charter of the Pennsylvania Railroad taxed the enterprise to recompense the state for the loss of revenue on the state waterways. Nevertheless the financial strength, the agricultural and industrial resources, the density of population, the strategic situation and driving energy of the region enabled the Middle Atlantic states to surmount all complications. Their railroads were the trunk lines which, uniting with others west of the mountains, formed the broad zone of trunk-line territory from the Atlantic to the Mississippi.

In this area the Baltimore and Ohio played for railroads a pioneering role very much akin to that of the Erie for canals. Chartered in 1827, the B & O got under way at a time when railroad engineering was in its infancy and it was still a question whether the horse or the locomotive would furnish the motive power. Even when these technical doubts had been settled and engineers had been trained on the job, the road pressed slowly westward along the Potomac. States, hostile or eager, harassed and cajoled it; court battles with the Chesapeake and Ohio Canal threatened to block its route; and financial disaster descended again and again upon it. Finally, at the end of 1852, surmounting the Appalachian barrier, it at last reached the desired western terminus at Wheeling on the

Ohio. The "main stem" of the road was 379 miles. In the railroad race Pennsylvania and Philadelphia were laggards. Concentrating every effort on the expensive state works and plunged into financial darkness by their eventual collapse, it was not until 1846 that a genuine alarm at the success of others led to the chartering of the Pennsylvania Railroad to run between Harrisburg and Pittsburgh. From the former terminus the state railroad extended the line to Philadelphia. Once under way, a driving energy pictured subscriptions to the stock as a patriotic duty and thrust the rails across the state with an engineering daring that conquered mountain difficulties. The road was opened in 1852. Five years later in a legislative *coup d'état* it purchased the state's main line.

New York's two trunk lines were curiosities. One, the New York and Erie, or Erie, Railroad, projected and chartered in the thirties, was to give the southern tier of counties in New York State some compensation for the Erie Canal and wean them from dependence upon Philadelphia and Baltimore. To fulfill the last purpose the road was forbidden to make connections with railroads from other states, and its constructors chose the unusual gauge of six feet to hinder the interchange of traffic. After years of tortured history the Erie Railroad was completed in 1851 to Dunkirk on the Lake, and President Millard Fillmore, a New Yorker in the White House by succession, took the trip celebrating the completion of "this great work of art." Since the state now suffered a railroad to challenge the canal, the legislature withdrew the protective prohibitions upon the railroads in the cross-state carriage of freight. Two years later, in 1853, a special enabling act permitted the fourteen local railroads ambling between Albany and Buffalo to coalesce into the New York Central after an interchange of stock. The thralldom which waterways still held over the New York mind was revealed by the fact that the eastern terminus of the Erie Railroad was not at New York, but on the western bank of the Hudson well above the city; and though two railroads east of the Hudson connected New York with Albany, neither crossed the river by a bridge to the New York Central.

As this recital has demonstrated, the through routes from the East forced their way to the edge of the West in the early years of the 1850's. The railroads already in the area had tended to follow the pattern of the canals, connecting the Great Lakes with the Ohio and Mississippi. There was a north-and-south trend in these enterprises. The sudden eruption of the newcomers from the East gave a wrench to the pattern. For these eastern railroads now raced for distant western termini, which in turn reached out an iron handclasp. The way was easy. Physiography was not a severe tyrant. The rolling terrain and the prairies offered a greater variety of routes than where river valleys and mountains shaped inevitable lines of communication. Moreover, the West, less thickly settled than the East, did not impose on the railroad network the discipline of serving established centers of population or industry. The whole region boiled with the ferment of construction. In the South an extension of the Western and Atlantic came down to the Mississippi at Memphis in 1857, and southern eloquence marveled at the completion of the only through east-and-west route in the region. North of the Ohio this achievement and celebration was multiplied many times as the railroads shot toward or away from the ambitious cities fringing the old Northwest: Cincinnati, St. Louis, Milwaukee, Chicago, Detroit, and Cleveland. After a herculean battle, two roads from the East secured admission to Chicago in 1852–1853 and trains over the Erie and the New York Central could now reach the booming Lake metropolis. The Pennsylvania Railroad, not to be outdone, followed a few years later. In 1857 the Baltimore and Ohio pushing westward struck hands with a connection driven eastward from St. Louis. After-dinner enthusiasm described the valleys and mountains between Baltimore and St. Louis "as level'd and made straight, for the swifter march of the armies that shall achieve the Industrial Millenium."

Meanwhile St. Louis, Milwaukee, and Chicago fanned out their roads to engross the trade of the Missouri and the upper Mississippi. In the distribution of prizes St. Louis and Milwaukee were left to envy or to sulk. Chicago made itself the real northern terminus of the Illinois Central, a railroad chartered in the thirties and reborn with a Federal land grant in 1850 to commence at the southern tip of the state and traverse as it moved northward the fat interior counties of the state. Chicago pushed westward across the Mississippi in 1856 over the first bridge south of St. Paul. The railroads of Iowa and of northern Missouri were a part of the Chicago network. In short, Chicago's strategic location, not far from the lower tip of Lake Michigan and at the end of a canal from the Mississippi, made her the railroad capital of the Middle West.

Railroad Problems and Achievements

The construction of the American railroad network was a gigantic experiment. Like the construction of the American canals, it involved the gradual acquisition of experience, the independent solution of problems, and the adaptation of European precedents to American circumstances. The conditions of railroad construction in a new country introduced a modifying influence of great importance. A scarcity of investment capital made it desirable that construction should be as cheap as possible, and the building of railroads through a country whose traffic possibilities were potential reinforced this consideration. American railroads were therefore built with grades that Europeans would have leveled, with curves that they would have straightened, and with materials that they would have despised. The penalties for this temporary construction were the constant repair or entire reconstruction of roads and a railroad accident list that led observers to believe that the railroad "go-ahead" age was indifferent to the loss of life.

Referring to the American railroads of 1837, an English observer asserted, "There are hardly two railways in the United States which are made exactly in the same way." Indeed, it was possible to find in a single railway, such as the Baltimore and Ohio or the state works of Pennsylvania, successive forms of construction which revealed railroad history as stratifications do geological development. At first patterning upon European experience, Americans used a solid construction. The rails were heavy pieces of granite laid on a stone substructure in the earth and protected at the inner edge by a plate rail; or square granite blocks, sunk into the right of way, were used as support for wooden sills, upon which wooden rails protected by a plate rail were in turn laid. Such roads were too inelastic, and the constant pounding of the train quickly wore out the iron plate rail and the rolling stock alike. Even when a lighter roadbed was devised, the use of wooden rails protected by a thin metal strap or plate rail presented difficulties. The rail was apt to tear loose at the end and curl up through the car, and it wore out quickly. All forms of construction were upset by the action of frost and portions of the roadbed had to be relaid each spring.

In England many devices had been used for keeping the cars on the rails. In some cases the flange was on the rail itself. But in 1789 an "edge rail" was patented by which the rail was set on edge and the flange placed on the car wheel. Early in the nineteenth century such rails had been proposed in this country by John Stevens, prophetic advocate of steam for water and land transportation, but it remained for his son, Robert L. Stevens, in the thirties to work over the edge rail into the T rail and lay such rails on the Camden and Amboy Railroad in New Jersey. Gradually American railways came to use such iron edge rails; wooden ties were laid transversely in sand or gravel without stone or wooden subsills; and the rail was fastened to the ties by an iron chair or by spiking through an iron plate. American railways were light and the short iron rails wore out rapidly.

Railway equipment was also fashioned by the new country. As in England, experiments with various forms of power had been tried. The Baltimore and Ohio used a sail car, which Philip Hone found in 1830, "the wind being strong from the north west," went off "with great rapidity a short distance, . . . a very pleasant mode of traveling." On some of the early roads horses were first used either to pull the cars or to work a treadmill engine. Apparently the first railroad engine to run on the tracks of a regular railroad in this country was the *Stourbridge Lion*. Imported from England, it had a short trial on the Delaware and Hudson in 1829. Though importation continued, American ironworks and machine shops were soon trying their hand at building the locomotive. Most of the early engines were too heavy or too rigid for the American roadbed. Taking advice from others, John B. Jervis, engineer and innovator, devised a front truck of four wheels attached to the body of the engine by a swivel. The weight of the engine was spread more evenly upon the track and the loose truck enabled it to conform to the curves. In 1832 these principles were embodied in the *Experiment,* the first American-type locomotive. With the aid of the "equalizing beam," another American invention which permitted the driving wheels to rock on a fulcrum without twisting the superimposed power plant, the locomotive was able to surmount the inequalities of a track which would ordinarily have derailed it. American locomotive works, like the Norris and the Baldwin, by 1860 had manufactured engines weighing twenty-five tons and capable of sixty miles an hour. The American engine had become so famous that it had been exported to England, Austria, and Russia.

The success of the railroads in the face of stage, wagon, and canal boat which they aimed to displace depended upon convenience, speed, and rates. An old stage driver recalled a fellow driver once saying,

. . . something that impressed itself on me very strongly, while he was running a very fine stage, with six beautiful white horses, and his opponent running very poor horses. He said one day: there, sir, I will take my coach, and run it with my team straight from here to heaven, and he will run his straight to hell and I will run empty and he will run full; and all at half price. It is the price in the end that governs.

The railroads found little difficulty in winning the passenger traffic. They were fast; they set their fares at the outset lower than their rivals, and by 1855 the average passenger fare was approximately two cents a mile. The average fare, it must be remembered, was usually the fare nobody paid.

As for freight rates, a period of experimentation was needed before the untried possibilities of the railroad as a freight carrier could be ascertained. At first rates were high. Freight classifications did not distinguish properly between bulky products of a low value per unit of weight and manufactured articles of higher value. The possibility of through long-distance traffic at low rates was not realized. As late as 1848 the board of directors of the Pennsylvania Railroad was unwilling to encourage a coal traffic over its properties because coal could not profitably stand existing rates of carriage. The coal should be left to the canals; "railroads must be used exclusively for passengers and light freights." Experimentation, often through the granting of rebates to special products or favored shippers, more sanguine conceptions of money-making possibilities, a competition compelling railroads to scramble for their share of the business and carry products at low prices to meet the railroad's fixed costs—all this put a new face on affairs. By 1855 freight rates per ton per mile perhaps averaged three cents; five years later two cents was not exceptional.

By the fifties the coming triumph of the railroad should have been clear to the discerning. It is true that in 1852 rails carried roughly only one-seventh of the tonnage transported within the nation.[5] But this was early in the decade. Before its end railroads had come with a rush, and many of the gaps and inadequacies in the railroad network were at last removed. Though the trade along the Atlantic coast and on the Mississippi was only partially or indirectly affected by railroads, canals were shutting up shop from New England to Pennsylvania and Ohio. Even the patriarchal Erie felt the pressure. By the end of the decade it had lost to the railroads passengers, general merchandise and manufactures, animal and dairy products. It retained its domain over forest products, corn, wheat, and flour. The total tonnage carried by the Erie Railroad and the Central was very near that carried by the canal. No wonder the friends of the latter talked wildly of means for "Rescuing the Canals from the Ruin with Which They are Threatened."

Financing Internal Improvements

The construction of transportation improvements strained the financial resources of the nation. Little wonder, therefore, that promoters and builders of turnpikes, canals, and railroads resorted to a multitude of financial devices. As we have seen, this national search for expedients turned early in the 1790's to the private corporation as a means of building and maintaining turnpikes. Previously governmental bodies had built highways; now a group of investors, animated by the hope of direct or indirect gains and perhaps by a civic glow, was given a state charter to do so. For a time in the late eighteenth and early nineteenth centuries turnpike charters, along with similar grants for toll bridges, constituted the most numerous group of charters granted by state legislatures. In short, along with banks they educated Americans to the use of the corporation for the attainment of economic aims.

5 COMMERCE CARRIERS, 1852

	Tons (Net)	Value
Coasting Trade (includes rivers and lakes)	20,397,490	$1,659,519,686
Canal Commerce	9,000,000	594,000,000
Railway Commerce	5,407,500	540,750,000
Aggregate	34,804,990	$2,794,269,686

Source: I. D. Andrews, *Report on the Trade and Commerce of the British North American Colonies and upon the Trade of the Great Lakes and Rivers*, p. 905.

As profits proved less generous than anticipated and the need of the community just as great, it was natural for government to come to the assistance of such enterprises, to "interpose its superior credit," as the phrase went, through the sale of its securities and the investment, as we have seen, of the proceeds in the stock of the turnpike corporation. Unlike the mixed corporations in the banking field, where a strong motive for state participation was gain, the chief reason for state assistance to turnpikes was promotional. Their construction would advance the economic progress of the community. As it turned out that was the one consolation to the states, for their turnpike stock shared the same sorry returns which private investors received.

The canal era introduced a somewhat different situation, though the need for investment funds was just as insatiable. To be sure there was a continued resort to the private corporation to raise money, construct the works, and operate the enterprise. Under such arrangements the canals of New England and New Jersey came into being; and of the major enterprises earlier noted, the Chesapeake and Ohio, the James River and Kanawha, at least in one incarnation, were corporations. To encourage canal enterprises, the state gave favors and often granted, for instance, a banking privilege to buoy the less attractive enterprise; or the state changed these corporations into mixed ones by its own participation or by permitting cities and towns to invest therein. Of the $188 million invested in canal construction before 1861, state and municipal governments provided 73 percent. The promotional reasoning, much the same as that in the case of turnpikes, was reinforced by the truisms that canals were more expensive undertakings than highways and that the canals in question were long-distance rather than local enterprises. In a few instances the storm of arguments in behalf of government assistance forced its way through the crevices in the constitutional and other arguments against national participation. In the mid-twenties Congress subscribed $450,000 to the Chesapeake and Delaware Canal Company; and in 1828 it appropriated $1 million to purchase stock in the Chesapeake and Ohio, that "great national project," in which the national government was the largest stockholder.

The really novel feature of the canal era, however, was the general decision to finance, construct, and operate these enterprises as public works. Here the example of the Erie Canal and New York was overwhelming. Pennsylvania, Ohio, Indiana, Illinois, and Virginia followed the same program. Sometimes the earlier failure of private or mixed enterprise to accomplish things hoped for was a partial reason for the policy. Favoring arguments, not always consistent with each other, went beyond this explanation. The state must undertake these risks for its own development, rather than ask individuals to do so, and at the same time the state was likely to enjoy such high profits on its investment that taxes could be reduced. Only the state could bring together the funds for such huge undertakings; and yet if the task were given to a corporation it would become a dangerous monster. State works would give employment, stimulate industry and agriculture, enhance the value of landed property, and quicken commerce. As the clamor died down, the promotional idea emerged as overriding and the realization that state credit could alone raise the required millions was a hard fact. In 1838, some time before the appropriations and expenditures had reached their zenith, the total state debt for canals was $60,202,000. Pennsylvania was the leader with a figure of $16,580,000; New York had invested $13,317,000; both Ohio and Indiana had debts for this purpose of over $6 million; Maryland was close behind.

Although these state works received no money from the national government the War Department aided by providing army engineers, a resource almost as scarce as capital, to make surveys. In the twenties Congress likewise turned to the national domain as a means of financial assistance. Sales of such lands had provided funds for the Cumberland Road and for assistance to western states in road building. Now land grants were given to the states for canal enterprises. Ohio, Indiana, and Illinois received 3,258,806 acres for their cross-state canals. In 1852 Michigan received 750,000 acres for the St. Mary's Canal at the Soo. The last grant could be selected "from any lands within the State, subject to private entry." From these and other grants emerged the standard procedure of bestowing upon the state alternate sections from a strip of the public domain five miles wide on each side of the canal; the Federal government retained the remaining sections. The canal thus passed through a checkerboard ten miles wide in which the red sections belonged to the state and the black to the nation. Such land grants were an admirable compromise method of Federal aid, for the opposition to them was allayed by the prophecy that the reserved sections would so rise in value as to compensate the government for its benefactions. Such land grants were not a liquid asset. Their rise in value and their profitable disposal depended upon the construction of the canal. On the Illinois and Michigan Canal their eventual sale paid for 90 percent of the original cost of construction, an exceptionally favorable outcome.

Much of the private or state stock issued for canals was bought by eastern capitalists and merchants who were interested in the extension of trade to the Northwest. But the Atlantic seaboard made demands upon its own investment capital for its expanding industry and particularly its own internal improvements. European capital was, therefore, for the first time called upon to finance American development in an extensive fashion. England was the chief contributor, for her citizens with surpluses secured in trade, industry, and agriculture were desperately seeking some sound investment. The state banks of the South, described in a later chapter, were one outlet. The projects for internal improvements in the North were equally attractive. English canals had been extraordinarily profitable, and their American prototypes were coining money. State securities, moreover, were highly regarded because the United States government had paid off its own debt in 1835 and English investors, unacquainted with the political dualism of America, did not always distinguish between the state and the Federal governments. These American securities found their way into the hands of British investors through American banks and the English banking houses, like Brown Brothers and the Barings, which were already specializing in financing American foreign trade. Often state loans were placed directly in England by agents of the various state governments. Nearly a third of the total securities for canal construction were purchased by foreign banking houses, principally in Great Britain. The securities of Pennsylvania and New York constituted a little over half the indebtedness.

Unfortunately, the financial history of most public works did not duplicate that of the Erie. Pennsylvania and Ohio most closely approximated it, for they forced the main systems through to completion. The builders of some western canals followed a more pernicious plan. In Indiana and Illinois the commissioners of internal improvements either were compelled by the legislature or chose of their own accord to begin constructing all the projected works at once and in scattered localities. In 1838 the governor of Illinois described such a procedure as cutting up "the whole system of railroads into so many parts, disjointed and disconnected one from the other for the time being, that it would appear in the attitude of a 'jointed snake,' which had been whipped into so many pieces that some of them would be decayed and rendered useless before they could crawl to each other's relief."

When the panic of 1837 ushered in five years of acute financial stringency, the defects of these methods were apparent. Some states had no completed system of public works earning money to meet the interest on their investment; nor could they float new loans to complete their internal improvements and thus place them upon a paying basis; others lacked sources of taxation adequate for their floating debts. By the early forties eight states were unable to continue the payment of interest. Ohio, by herculean efforts, kept out of their company. A movement for repudiation met with partial success in Michigan, which refused to recognize a portion of its debt. Pennsylvania and Maryland by governmental economies, taxation, or the funding of arrears of interest resumed payments on their debts before the end of the forties. Indiana and Illinois worked out compromises with their creditors paying their debts from taxes, the sale of land grants or of the works themselves, and from such revenues as the finished canals finally yielded.

Even before this debacle of public enterprise, the sudden burst of railroad incorporations in the early thirties hinted a return to the conceptions of the turnpike: chartered companies were to finance and operate the transportation system. The financial difficulties of the states during the early forties hastened this reorientation. Although the number of transportation companies never dominated the charter field as it had in the turnpike era, railroad corporations became the most important in the nation. As time went on the size of their capitalization made them the largest business enterprises in state after state, and their issues were the pabulum which kept the stock exchanges of the nation active. Railroads were the leaders in devising new forms of securities. When sales of stock no longer provided the resources to construct or enlarge their enterprises, the railroad builders issued preferred stock with a prior lien on dividends. Short-term borrowings on notes gradually evolved into long-term borrowings or railroad bonds, secured by a mortgage on the property. When even this method of "financiering" was inadequate, the chief promoters or the contractors "interposed" their superior personal credit, taking the road's securities as collateral. Imperceptibly, this last service developed into the construction company, not an engineering but a financing device.

The reappearance of the corporation, however, did not mean the end of governmental assistance. That the states had incurred debts of $42,871,084 for railroads by 1838 clearly demonstrated their continued participation in transportation enterprises. In spite of exceptions, like the Western and Atlantic, few governmental bodies built, owned, or operated railroads. The favored means was the mixed corporation. In contrast with an earlier era when state assistance predominated, large subscriptions to such enterprises were now made by cities, towns, and villages. Smarting under losses during the panic years, popular pressure forced amendments to state constitutions either limiting the size of the state debt or prohibiting loans of state credit to private enterprises. Since such restrictions were neither instantaneous nor universal, the state governments continued to play a part. In some jurisdictions governmental assistance, whatever its source, was episodic, given to projects of exceptional financial formidability, or in periods of financial crisis as after 1837, or for roads whose immediate construction seemed a matter of life and death. From Massachusetts, where the Commonwealth aided the Western to the tune of $5 million, through New York, which donated to the New York and Erie, to Virginia and Maryland, where both subscribed to the Baltimore and Ohio, the story was the same. From Portland, Maine, where the city invested $2 million in the Grand Trunk, to Philadelphia, where the municipality contributed $4 million to the Pennsylvania Railroad, and to Baltimore, which subscribed $3.5 million to the Baltimore and Ohio, it seemed as if only Boston and New York City remained untouched by the contagion. In some states, usually southern, financial assistance approached the paper dignity of a system. Localities of states contributed a major fraction of the capitalization of railroads selected for assistance, or matched dollar for dollar, or authorized a grant of so many thousands a mile.

The national government for a while in the twenties and thirties aided railroad surveys and construction by furnishing its trained engineers. Such assistance was even provided for private corporations. Through the forties no assistance of any sort was forthcoming. Then in 1850 Congress authorized the traditional contribution to transportation, a land grant. The recipient was the Illinois Central, whose interests Stephen A. Douglas, Senator from Illinois, now took in hand. He was the first statesman of the railroad age, for he both understood and spoke its language. Adroitly he mollified the various theoretical and sectional objections to the proposed donation, and his manipulation was aided by the increasing liberality shown in the disposition of the public domain. The epochal grant for the Illinois Central resulted. The national government was to transfer to the State of Illinois for every mile constructed by the Illinois Central "every alternate section of land, designated by even numbers, for six sections in width on each side of said road and branches." The other sections were reserved to the national government and were to be sold at a double price, $2.50 an acre. In case the granted sections were preempted, the squatter could pay the price to the state, or the state could indemnify itself by other sections within fifteen miles of the railroad. The total grant aggregated approximately 2,595,000 acres. After 1856 the grant for the Illinois Central, at the time an exceptional case, formed the pattern for a habitual government policy. State after state received assistance.

In view of the widespread assistance from governmental bodies, the claim has been made that government funds provided the major share of railroad funds. This seems unlikely. In their timing, nonetheless, such contributions were of critical importance. Without them some roads would have been built later; others not at all. The government provided the venture capital. On the other hand private investors probably met the bulk of the railroads' needs. These funds came from the eastern financial centers, by the fifties better braced to meet the emergency, and from Europeans who had generally forgotten their disillusioning purchases with state securities issued for internal improvements. In 1853 the total of railroad stocks and bonds held abroad was estimated at $52,100,100. After their experience with state tardiness and faithlessness in the forties, these foreign investors naturally preferred to buy the issues of corporations rather than of states.

Costs, Gains, and Losses

Though there were frequent controversies over the feasibility or wisdom of details, the states almost without question controlled or regulated transportation. Charges and services were so vital to the welfare of the community that they could not be entirely surrendered to determination by competition. Besides, as we have seen, the shade of monopoly hung over transportation enterprises, whether they were monopoly grants of a route to corporations, as was universal in the case of turnpikes and occasional in the case of early railroads, or a "state work" from which the legislature wished to fend the competition of a corporation. To turnpike and railroad the legislature had also given that attribute of sovereignty, the right of eminent domain. Transportation enterprises were affected with a public use; they were not private and beyond the pale of state surveillance and direction.

State regulation and management was facilitated by financial participation. Theoretically, in mixed enterprises states might have appointed state directors to which the corporation, in view of the state's investment, would have to listen. Usually states neglected this device; if they employed it they did so inefficiently. For public works the state alone could determine policy. Here, too, there were grave breakdowns. Boards of canal commissioners were poorly selected and confined to a narrow area of administrative discretion. State legislatures and sometimes even constitutional conventions meddled in management. Timidity alternated with extravagance; wide vision with local interests; rigidities were everywhere.

In the formal area of regulation, the turnpike era was the forerunner of the railroad one. The individual charters or the rarer acts of general incorporation regulated rates with great particularity for every sort of animal and vehicle. A common supplementary device was a percentage limitation on the returns upon the investment. Turnpikes had to keep records and present them for official review. All this was repeated when the railroads arrived. In some states, as in Massachusetts, charters placed a percentage ceiling on returns and allowed legislatures to reduce rates if a higher profit was secured. In other states, as in New York, the legislature laid down maximum passenger fares on a mile basis. Railroads were to make annual reports to some state body. As time went on, legislation moved into other areas. Charters had specified capitalization, now general laws applied safeguards—or so they were regarded—to the issue of new kinds of securities. When the novel agency of transportation disclosed through accidents a horrid capacity for the destruction of property and lives, legislation determined the size of train crews, provided for warning devices at crossings and on locomotives, and prescribed cautionary running rules. When railroads could not agree upon terms of connections and rates for their joint business, the state interfered in these matters also. The locus of power in this process was the legislature, its railroad committee, and occasionally small administrative groups appointed for special purposes. Even before the Civil War these arrangements proved too clumsy and inflexible and a few states, mostly in New England, had appointed railroad commissions with limited powers.

Yet this groping and development failed to reveal whether public works had paid. The conventional wisdom asserted the test must be whether the return from tolls, as on canals, met the cost of operation and the interest on the state's investment. Most of the $188 million invested in canals before the Civil War failed to meet these criteria. But contemporaries and later commentators have thought the operational costs and the states' investments inadequate and, consequently, unfair measures. Modern "benefit cost analysis" would lead to different and controversial conclusions. It is perhaps not too imaginative to estimate the tonnage carried by "successful" canals and calculate the savings on its carriage compared to the costs of wagon transportation. Under these assumptions of modern benefit cost analysis it would appear that the benefits conferred by the ten successful canals exceeded the costs for the entire system. These bets were off after railroad competition reduced costs of carriage below those prevailing on most canals except exceptionally well-located ones. A deeper test in modern benefit cost analysis is the developmental aspect of internal improvements. Landowners benefited when their property rose in value as improved transportation poked over the horizon; cities grew along the new routes and at their termini. Even before the railroad the beginnings of a regional specialization within the country created an agricultural empire in the Midwest, a staple empire in the South, and a base for manufacturing in the East.

Since all this specialization led to national efficiency, should the counterweight of dollars-and-cents losses for investors on the other end of the scale tip the balance? Certainly, the clamor raised by investors and their persistent efforts or those of their agents, for example, the Barings, to have the states meet their financial obligations showed that those who had lost their money were not consoled by modern benefit cost analysis. Chronologically they couldn't be, since they lived in times that can't qualify as "modern."

The argument here summarized is ingenious and perhaps a needed counterweight to the contumely scholars have occasionally visited upon the system of "public works." But for all its erudition, it sometimes seems to identify rhetoric and busyness with accomplishment. The market for transportation chose the railroads, most of which were built with private funds, and the outcome revealed its judgment of need and profitability was superior to that of the government.

vii
Foreign Commerce

Neo-Mercantilism at Home and Abroad

Strangely enough those antagonistic instructors of the American people, Jefferson and Hamilton, came to approximately the same conclusion about the desirable role of foreign commerce in the economy of the new nation. They seemed to agree that a commercial world in which each nation specialized in the productions or occupations for which it was most fitted and then exchanged its goods or services was the most efficient. With a fond, perhaps sophistical, farewell glance at a "system of perfect liberty to industry and commerce," Hamilton concluded that "system [was] far from characterizing the general policy of nations . . . the United States can, indeed, without difficulty, obtain from abroad the manufactured supplies of which they are in want, but they experience numerous and very injurious impediments to the emission and vent of their own commodities." Jefferson, generally more prone to desire American self-sufficiency, thought the United States should, in principle, prefer to stimulate navigation and commerce "by throwing open all the doors of commerce and knocking off the shackles." But as "there is no great probability that Europe will do this, I suppose we shall be obliged to adopt a system which may shackle them in their ports as they do us in ours." These two Founding Fathers were already testifying to the observation made years later on the tariff by Grover Cleveland, "It is a condition which confronts us, not a theory."

In short, the new Republic after Independence confronted the commercial and navigational systems of France, Spain, and England. Geographically the systems of the first two were not confined to France or Spain in Europe; each had a colonial empire of islands in the Caribbean and, in Spain's case, one that also stretched with the exception of Brazil from the Mississippi to Cape Horn. The Americans were most acquainted with the British system for they had, in colonial days, been a part of it. Now they faced uncertainties in the British West Indies, in Canada, and in the British Isles. From there they had once drawn most of their manufactured goods through the shipment of staples to the

British market or the despatch of bills of exchange and coin wrung from their West Indian trade. Great Britain did not reimpose her commercial system upon the late rebellious colonists without reflection. William Pitt, a convert to the liberalism of Adam Smith, led one group which would have established commerce between the United States and Great Britain and her colonies on a basis of commercial generosity. The opposition to Pitt's measures was aroused and marshaled by Lord Sheffield, whose *Observations on the Commerce of the United States,* published in 1783, was a severe arraignment of commercial liberality as dangerous and unnecessary. On the first count, Sheffield argued preference would support the British marine, a nursery of seamen; on the second, the former colonies could not unite for reprisals and blackmail, since the central government of the Confederation did not possess the power to take common action. The Sheffield party mustered so much strength that Pitt's proposals did not prevail: instead other arrangements governed the new situation which followed the Revolution. To the exasperation of the United States, Great Britain saw no reason to settle the changed relationship by a commercial treaty; very much as if she were still the mother country she regulated it by acts of Parliament and Orders-in-Council.

In the commercial policies of western European nations preference and prohibition touched nearly every imaginable feature of vessels and cargo. These commercial measures usually closed to vessels flying a foreign flag the carrying trade between colonies and mother country and between ports in the latter's coasting trade. Since their empires were to be self-sufficing, the European systems hampered foreign vessels in trading with their colonies. In the homeland, customs duties along with a multitude of port charges gave preferences to vessels of the home country and sometimes to goods brought in such vessels. Customs duties likewise were lower on goods brought from the colonies than from other sources—a form of imperial preference; and sometimes the home market for domestic producers was preserved by outright prohibitions on imports or prohibitions except under special circumstances. The English Corn Laws, for instance, which dated from the fifteenth century, permitted graduated imports of grain as the domestic price rose. Usually this mass of statutes and orders allowed foreign vessels to bring in the goods which their nation had grown or produced. This freedom was less a tribute to the logic of international specialization than a realization that if the exception were not made reprisal measures could be easily taken. In estimating the justice or expediency of this neo-mercantilism after the Revolution, Americans should heed the caution of Hamilton, "It is for the nations whose regulations are attended to, to judge for themselves, whether, by aiming at too much, they do not lose more than they gain."

For a while the question was academic. "Man proposes, God disposes." In 1793 a world war broke out; it lasted for twenty-two years, a period which constituted a distinctive era for American foreign commerce. For this struggle with its overriding necessities soon breached mercantilist restrictions everywhere, and exceptions and evasion became standard policy. Not even the perspicacious author of the *Observations on the Commerce of the United States* could have foreseen the events which were so soon to upset his reasoning and recommendations. The opposing poles of this world war were France and Great Britain, for the latter entered the conflict in 1793. The military and naval situation soon became fundamentally simple. The British navy controlled the seas and exercised such restraint upon the commerce of her enemies and of neutrals as she thought would lead to ultimate victory. The Battle of Trafalgar (1805) put a definite seal of success upon this naval predominance. Meanwhile Napoleon's armies and military genius had won on land a supremacy as unrivaled as that of England on the sea. Neither antagonist seemed able to wreck the other. At the close of 1806, however, Napoleon, master of the Continent, attempted to dislocate England's economic organization by his Continental System. Briefly, it attempted to deprive Britain's industry of markets by closing to her products such countries of the Continent as Napoleon possessed or controlled. Markets lost, British factories would shut down, unemployment would increase, the inflow of gold into Great Britain from foreign nations to pay for their purchases from her would diminish, and this economic upheaval would bring England to terms. To enforce this scheme the French emperor issued a flood of decrees, and to combat it the English poured forth a stream of Orders-in-Council. These various pronouncements bore with such extreme hardship on merchants and shipowners of the United States that the government of this country had to protest their execution and then enforce its threats with tangible measures. Short of war, the only alternative was economic pressure, or so it seemed to Thomas Jefferson, and in December of 1807 Congress passed an Embargo Act designed to drive the European nations into submission by closing our trade to them. No vessels were to leave any American port whatsoever. With variations of emphasis and with interruptions this policy lasted until its only feasible alternative, war, was declared against Great Britain in 1812. The years 1814–1815, crammed with peace treaties, put an end to this chaotic period.

With the merchant fleets of France and her ally, Spain, swept from the seas, and those of England swamped with worldwide responsibilities, the United States became the great noncombatant, and, taking refuge in such statements of international law as gave the greatest play to neutrality, the American shipowner, merchant, exporter, and importer embarked upon a career of prosperity. The services of a neutral shipper and supplier were so indispensable that, for the moment, European nations and their colonies abrogated exclusive trade laws and navigation acts and threw the closed trades open to the Americans. Great Britain's shipping interest in alarm secured the revival of a so-called rule of international law, the Rule of the War of 1756, which declared that trades closed in time of peace could not be reopened in war. This prohibition Americans evaded by carrying goods to the United States and then reshipping them, consecrated by this process of neutrality. American vessels consequently brought commodities from France and Spain, passed them nominally through a loading and unloading process in the United States, and then reshipped them to the West Indies. They reversed the process on the return voyage. The same pressure of circumstances broke the dikes of the British system. So desperate had become the position of their colonies in the West Indies that their governors invited the import "of flour, bread, wheat, rice, or grain of any sort, staves, headings, shingles, or lumber of any sort, horses, horned cattle or livestock of any kind" from the United States or elsewhere in United States vessels, and admitted other articles whose importation had been previously forbidden. Within a year the number of American vessels employed in the trade with the British West Indies increased thirteenfold; exports to the islands increased four times and imports nearly three times between 1795 and 1807. For the United States, the reexport trade in most of these years exceeded the exports of American merchandise. The volume of exports of coffee and sugar, for instance, reached spectacular levels. The United States grew no coffee and little sugar. This total explosion of foreign trade was very profitable for American shipowners. In 1807 American vessels carried 92 percent of the nation's foreign trade. Freight rates were high; vessels didn't have to wait around for cargoes. Supplementary occupations, like marine insurance, flourished. A contemporary concluded, "We seemed to have arrived at the maximum of human prosperity."

In economic history maximums have the disconcerting habit of suddenly becoming minimums. When Jefferson tried to punish England and France for their violation of our neutral maritime rights by excluding their commodities from American markets and by cutting them off from the American sources of supply, American commerce shrank. When the Jeffersonian policy of peaceful coercion failed and war took its place, the decline of American trade and shipping continued to the vanishing point. The British had an overwhelming control of the sea and blockaded the American coast or parts of it apparently at will. In 1814 the value of merchandise exports fell to $8 million, about one-thirteenth of what it had been in 1807; the value of merchandise imports fell to $16 million, about one-ninth of what it had been in 1807.

New Trades

Meanwhile, even before the period of "maximum human prosperity" American merchants and shippers had begun breaking the commercial habits of Colonial days and undertaking new trades with energy and audacity. In some instances, the Napoleonic wars were the occasions for these experiments; in others, they simply played a favoring role. In any case, Americans shipped products straight to northern Europe and brought back commodities without shipping via the metropolis of Great Britain. When American vessels invaded the Baltic, they explored the Mediterranean. The flag of the new Republic appeared in the ports of the small Italian states, at Trieste and elsewhere in the Adriatic, and finally in the eastern reaches of the Mediterranean, at the ports of Egypt and the Levant. In northern Europe American vessels resorted to the great ports of Hamburg and Bremen, still the "Hansa Towns," the heirs of the Hanseatic League, and Russia.

Nearer home, indeed at America's doorstep, lay the Spanish Empire, and farther along, Brazil, a Portuguese possession. To her vast rich areas Spain theoretically applied the policy of excluding the products and vessels of foreign nations. In 1797, since the European conflict had destroyed her commerce with them, these restrictions were lifted; evasions had always been frequent. American privateers operating from Latin American bases and American whaling vessels putting into port for repair or provisions had already blazed the way for the American trader. A Philadelphia vessel in 1798 began American commerce to the region of Rio de la Plata, the great estuary between Argentina and Uruguay; somewhat later American ships were officially noticed in Venezuela, and after 1808 they were legal visitors to Brazil, whose commerce had been opened to all nations by the emperor of Portugal, a refugee there from Napoleon. At the same time, in the wake of the whalers, Americans rounded Cape Horn and traded with the ports of the Pacific coast. Our commercial success, however, was greatest in Cuba, Puerto Rico and the present Colombia and Venezuela. Though the Spanish monopoly was ostensibly reimposed after the Napoleonic period, the struggle of the Spanish colonies for independence soon led to its abrogation. Both those loyal to the motherland and those in revolt threw open the ports in their control in order to secure supplies.

Nowhere were the advantages of withdrawal from the British colonial system greater than in the case of trade with the East Indies. From the commerce of this immense region stretching from the eastern coast of Africa to China and including innumerable islands, the American colonies had been excluded. The East India Company, the instrument of British imperialism in the Orient, had a monopoly of this domain.

But the Revolution was hardly over before the Americans began to invade the East Indies. The *Empress of China,* sailing from New York, but supplied in part with capital from Philadelphia, arrived at Canton in 1784; her return four months later to Philadelphia moved American merchants to the "opinion that this commerce can be carried on, on better terms from America than Europe. . . . We may be able not only to supply our own wants, but to smuggle a very considerable quantity to the West Indies."

As a newcomer to the Oriental trade the United States confronted the colonial systems of European nations. But, influenced by some sea change, these were more mellow and generous than in the Caribbean. The French government in 1784, opening its ports on the Indian Ocean, gave us access to its important islands and to the few stations still retained on the Indian peninsula. The Dutch treated us no worse than they did any European nation. Spain manifested no objection to American commerce with her colonies, and in British India, by a commercial treaty in 1784, the Americans enjoyed preferences in import and export duties and other privileges accorded to no other nation except Great Britain. Years later a British statesman ascribed the earlier liberality of policy in this area to "possessions of such vast extent, such a dense population, such abundant resources, such facilities for active commerce, and such means of circulating and promoting wealth." In short, restriction was impractical. To the parts of Asia and Africa on the Indian Ocean which were left untouched by the preemption claims of European nations the American trade in the early nineteenth century surpassed that of all European nations combined.

In China the Americans confronted a Chinese rather than a European commercial system. The Empire, cherishing quite justly an indifference and suspicion toward foreigners, confined commercial operations with them to Canton and regulated details with minute care. The Americans, like other foreigners, were subjected to this regime. Their vessels were entered and cleared in the same fashion; theoretically they paid the same heavy taxes; and American supercargoes and merchants were compelled to deal with the dozen or so hong merchants to whom the government had given the conduct of the trade with occidental outsiders. This situation tended to identify American policy at Canton with that of the European merchants. On the other hand, these merchants, particularly the British who alone surpassed us, were commercial rivals. American policy accordingly vacillated. It sought Chinese good will as a makeweight against British preponderance, but it sympathized with the European desire to break down Chinese exclusion. Consequently, when the Opium War, fought by Great Britain against China, resulted in the Nanking Treaty of 1842, opening four additional ports, establishing a uniform customs tariff at lower levels, and abolishing the hong, or merchant, monopoly, Americans were relieved when the Chinese insisted that these favors be extended to the traders of other nations. Indeed, some seventy years later this most-favored-nation treatment was definitely transformed by the Americans into their own policy of the Open Door.

The East Indian trade, nevertheless, aroused some misgivings. Since this country had few goods desired by Oriental consumers, specie had to be exported to pay for the imports of nankeens, silks, chinaware, and teas. Such fears were not entirely mercantilistic, for specie was collected with difficulty in the United States. But the Canton market was eager for furs with which to line the heavy garments worn by the Chinese aristocrats. Suddenly at the close of the eighteenth century new and accessible resources of fur-bearing animals were discovered. One area was the Pacific Northwest. In 1788 Captain Gray, dispatched by Boston merchants in the *Columbia,* reached that dangerous coast and started a trade which was to create the Boston "Nor'westman" and convince the Indians of that region that Boston and the United States were synonymous. Meanwhile another Boston vessel had discovered that sealskins, obtained at the Falklands or other islands of the southern hemisphere, could be sold in China. Such furs were less valuable than the glossy black skins of the sea otter of the Northwest, but they were easily collected by crews who landed on these deserted shores and clubbed thousands of the awkward creatures to death. Running westward with furs, these vessels would complete their cargoes at the Hawaiian or Fiji islands with sandalwood, used alike for incense and furniture, and with food delicacies esteemed by Chinese epicures.

By sailing east other commodities for exchange at Canton could be secured. An American vessel, taking on board at some Atlantic port a mixed cargo of foodstuffs from South America and the West Indies and reexports from the Orient, would depart for the islands off the African coast and for the Mediterranean, there to pick up specie for the Chinese trade or to exchange its cargo at Gibraltar or in the Levant for the opium of Turkey. Then it might sail, with stopovers for trade at the Cape of Good Hope, Mauritius, Calcutta, and Bombay, to Canton to exchange the accumulated cargo for silks and teas. Or the vessel might proceed from the United States to England and, to the despair of the British skipper, take on British cottons which were sold in Canton at cut prices.

The East Indian trade was an exotic, a commerce of specialties, with the possible exception of tea. But the Americans during the Napoleonic years were never able to dent the British hold on its carriage, although Congress subsidized the business and half the tea imported to America was sometimes reexported. The profits from these long and speculative voyages to the Orient were high; they supported the passing glory of small ports like Salem, and built up large fortunes, like that of "King Derby," which when put to other uses pushed the American economy ahead.

Merchandise Trades

From Independence to the end of the Napoleonic Wars, American foreign commerce hardly knew what a year of normal experience was. The immediate readjustment after 1815 was hectic, but then a more stabilized pattern slowly emerged. Until 1860 there was comparative peace, with the exceptions of the Mexican War on this continent and the Crimean War of 1854–1855 in Europe: both were essentially minor interruptions. After 1815 the Europeans reimposed their nationalistic systems of restraint or control. But in the forties and fifties Great Britain hurried to free trade. Merchants, desiring to stimulate exports, manufacturers seeking lower costs on raw materials, the masses won by the cry of "cheap bread," civil servants disdaining the irrational complexities of the old statutes, idealists identifying freedom of trade with a logical economic order and international peace—all formed a highly effective phalanx in favor of a new order. Rarely have pressure groups been better organized, better informed, and better led. Timely events, like the Irish potato famines of the mid-forties, aided the cause of the new order. Parliament repealed the Corn Laws, swept away the system of imperial preference, fell belatedly upon the Navigation Acts, the first of which dated from the fourteenth century, and threw open all trades, even the coasting one, to foreign vessels. On article after article duties were swept away. Finally, in the Cobden Treaty of 1860, France and Great Britain agreed upon the reduction and removal of duties on the trade between the two countries and engaged "to confer on the other any favour, privilege, or reduction in the tariff of duties of importation on the articles mentioned in the present treaty which the said power may concede to any third power." In short, tariff reductions were to be generalized for all nations.

Though the timing among nations varied, the free trade movement was international. In the United States, for instance, after 1815 the government progressively abandoned the regular application of preferences, which had been in operation for the American merchant marine since 1789. In that year a series of enactments had restricted registry under the American flag to American-built vessels; had given cargoes imported in American ships a reduction of 10 percent from the regular duties; had levied a tonnage duty of fifty cents per ton upon all foreign-built and foreign-owned vessels entering our ports, thirty cents per ton upon American-built foreign-owned vessels, and only six cents per ton upon vessels owned in the United States; and had virtually excluded foreign vessels from the coasting trade.

Now an act of 1815 authorized the President to repeal all discriminations—both tonnage and customs—against foreign ships "bringing the produce or manufactures of the nation to which such foreign ships or vessels may belong" whenever he was satisfied that the discrimination enforced by that foreign nation against the United States had been withdrawn. Within four months a treaty to this effect had been made with Great Britain. This was a minor achievement, since these agreements did not free from discrimination the carrying business when vessels of one nation were loaded with the products of another; nor did they open trade between the United States and the colonies of European nations. After a series of retaliatory steps Congress in 1826 authorized the President to suspend discriminations upon vessels entering our ports with commodities from any foreign country provided similar concessions were made by other nations. Two years later, after difficult negotiations, a commercial treaty with Great Britain fulfilled in large measure the liberal intentions of this legislation. British ships and cargoes from her colonies could enter American ports without paying discriminatory duties; on the same terms free ports in the British colonies were opened to American vessels and most American products, and American vessels could carry colonial products from them to any destination outside the British Empire.

Concurrently Congress was dealing directly with customs tariffs. Thus the session of 1789 saw the passage of the first national tariff act, to raise revenue and to protect American industry. Since the range of the duties for the latter purpose was low, the achievement fell short of its intentions. It made little difference. The Napoleonic wars soon introduced a measure of actual protection which no legislator would have dared propose or vote for. Then between 1815 and 1833—in the latter year a measure effected a progressive reduction of duties—the protective system secured its greatest popular support and most extreme legislative embodiment. The harsh experience when America was cut off from European production during the war years gave a new cogency to the argument for self-sufficiency; a dreaded flood of cheap imports sharpened the genuine and verbal alarm of American manufacturers; and a collapse of agricultural prices convinced American farmers that they must consent to a tariff in order to develop a home market as substitute for those lost with peace, first in Europe and later in South America. Higher duties in fact have been a common American response to depression and anxiety. The decade of the twenties was such a period. Although the reduction planned by the act of 1833 was temporarily reversed by a measure in 1842, four years later the Walker Tariff Act, christened for the Secretary of the Treasury, a professed disciple of free trade, introduced eleven years of moderate protection. In the fifties also the United States and Canada experimented with a reciprocity treaty. In 1857, a tariff of general application introduced a moderate protection lasting until the eve of the Civil War.

The purposes voiced in measure, debate, and argument were not always the cool calculations of economic loss or gain. Of one tariff, passed in the ultra-protective era, a Virginian representative said quite justly, "The bill referred to manufactures of no sort or kind, except the manufacture of a President of the United States." Nearly every enactment marred the purity of theoretical design as it compromised the interests of cotton growers or importers, both hostile to protection, with those of assorted industrialists. Nevertheless, beneath these specific and sometimes superficial stresses, tariff legislation served continuing purposes. It was a source of revenue. Indeed, over the long span from 1789 to 1860 taxes on imports furnished the largest share of the government receipts, with the single exception of 1836 when returns from land sales exceeded them. It was a means of protection to industry, though most students of the question admit that the phenomenal growth of American manufacturing in those years was in larger measure due to other causes. Still, from time to time, the solicitude of tariff makers for some goods stimulated certain enterprises.

Finally, as the decades after 1815 passed, it became clearer and clearer that in the developing international order Great Britain was sovereign. She was not only the citadel of free trade, she was the world's greatest manufacturer, greatest trader, greatest foreign investor and banker. She had the largest navy and the largest merchant marine. For this international order, she set the pattern of the gold standard, private enterprise, international peace, and material calculation.

The roster of American imports revealed this British primacy. In view of the national preoccupation with farming and, to a less extent, other extractive industries, the United States imported manufactures. As late as 1855–1859 manufactures ready for consumption were 47.4 percent of our imports, and semimanufactures an additional 12.3 percent. But these embracing and dull categories describe little. Judged by monetary value, textiles, cottons, woolens, silks, and linens were the chief merchandise imports. The cotton factories of Lancashire provided an overwhelming proportion of the cotton goods shipped to America; the mechanized linen industry of Great Britain had substituted its output for the old handmade linens, many of which had come from Germany; but Great Britain's supremacy as an exporter of woolens, although still apparent, had been somewhat diminished by France. The latter country was the chief producer of silk goods for the American market. The leadership of England was even more marked in a second category of imports, iron and steel products—a disorderly aggregate of many items, by themselves unimportant, but collectively large. Hoop and sheet iron, nails and anvils, anchors and cables, mill saws and tailors' irons, bonnet wire and sickles, jostle one another without significant appeal except for the specialist. In this classification, however, the outstanding importations were cutlery and rolled bar iron. The merits of Sheffield cutlery and Birmingham iron goods were a tradition among American consumers, and the cheapness of bar iron or wrought iron rails, manufactured by new technical methods in Great Britain, was not duplicated in Europe or in America. England's railmakers were willing to sell their product on credit; and the first step many railroad promoters took was to sign a contract for English rails, often paying for them in the securities of the railroad. All in all, from 1815 to 1860 Britain accounted for somewhat more than 33.3 percent of total American imports. France supplied another 9 to 18 percent.

Not western but southern Europe, Africa, and the East and West Indies furnished the wines and liquors, the spices, the nonalcoholic beverages, and the exotic condiments which made daily life worth living. Of these tropical or semitropical products, the imports of tea had not a "tea-party" hastened the Revolution—were the mainstay of Oriental commerce. But with the twenties American taste shifted to coffee. American imports were literally collected around the world. Arabia and the Dutch and British East Indies furnished the finer varieties, but the Caribbean area and Brazil really supplied the American market. The trade with Brazil was phenomenal. At the beginning of the nineteenth century it did not exist; but by 1860 importations from Brazil hovered around 200 million pounds. "Rio" coffee, whose somewhat cruder flavor appealed to the frontier nation—its greatest consumption was in the trans-Appalachian region—became the chief nonintoxicating American drink. The New World, too, supplied other tropical beverages and foodstuffs. Sugar and molasses, sometimes imported from the Far East, came predominantly from Brazil and the Caribbean. The spectacular imports from Puerto Rico and Cuba suggested that these islands were already swinging into the sphere of American concern. Cuba and the West Indies furnished a high of 28 percent of American imports in the early twenties and a low of 17 percent thirty years later.

With the exception of cotton, the export trade of the United States in the first sixty years of the Republic's life was a continuation of colonial commerce. For, according to the *Commercial and Navigation Reports*, exports still fell primarily into three classifications, "Products of the Sea," "Products of the Forest," and "Products of Agriculture." The fourth category, "Manufactures," consisted of numerous small items—soap, furniture, lead, snuff, nails—articles which even in the Colonial era had formed a part of our huckstering commerce. But by 1860 America was to demonstrate that some of her coarser cotton fabrics could meet the competition of the world. Sent to the less developed regions of the world, the value of American cotton fabric shipments had increased from $1,318,183 in 1830 to $10,934,796 in 1860; but even the latter figure was not as great as the value of cotton goods imported into the United States from Great Britain. No American industry concentrated on foreign trade as did the ironworks of Birmingham or the cotton factories of Lancashire.

Though the products of the sea had been a mainstay of colonial commerce, they had a relative unimportance in the Republic. New England ingenuity might invent new methods of catching mackerel and cod and create a fresh fish industry, but foreign markets stagnated or declined. For a few decades the whaling industry, with New Bedford as its chief port, sent oil for the lamps of Europe, the Caribbean, and the heathen Chinee. But the discovery of petroleum in 1859 harpooned this maritime calling at last. As for lumber products, the West Indies and the Mediterranean still needed American specialties, and the naval stores of tar, pitch, and turpentine had a steady European market.

Over the exports of some agricultural staples, the same decorous and familiar air, a hangover from the Colonial age, persisted. In the export of others a remarkable expansion took place. Pork, bacon, hams, and lard, once fit only for the colonial slave markets in the Caribbean, now more skillfully and carefully packed or cured, began their invasion of the United Kingdom and even the kitchens of western Europe. In colonial days the West Indies and South America had been a market for American wheat and flour. In 1860 Brazil was still our greatest customer. But the Latin American nations were not a dynamic market and some of them after the Civil War were to become competitive producers to the United States. In Europe, France and Germany were self-sufficient and, along with the new producers in Russia and the Near East, they could and did supply the British market more cheaply than America—except in special circumstances. After the Irish famine of 1846 American exports to Great Britain shot upward; and they did so again during the Crimean War. In 1847 American shipments accounted for 40 percent of England's imports of wheat and flour; then this figure declined. Looked at another way, at no time after 1821 and before the Civil War did the grain trade compose as much as 20 percent of the total value of exports.

Everything paled before cotton. People had once refused to believe that the United States could become the international producer of this staple. Before 1780 British spinners had imported their cotton from the Levant, and after that date they found more important sources of supply in the West Indies and Brazil. In fact, it was not until 1802 that the exports of American cotton to Great Britain exceeded those thither from the West Indies. But from that year the supremacy of the United States was unquestioned. Rivals such as Egypt or the West Indies might appear dimly on the horizon, and the English cotton manufacturers might grow gray with apprehension at the thought of a cotton famine brought about by a dependence upon a single source of supply, but the comparative advantages of cheap western lands and the increasing efficiency of American slave labor could not be equaled anywhere else.

For the cotton trade, the year 1860, occurring as it did just before the Civil War, affords an admirable point of summary. The cotton industry of European nations was dependent upon American production. Russia, Germany, Austria, Holland, and Belgium all obtained their supplies from the United States. The largest single Continental consumer, France, imported from us nearly all the 240 million pounds spun and woven by the cotton industry of her northern provinces. But Great Britain was the magnet which drew all cotton to her. Her annual demand, approximately 1 billion pounds, was three times that of the cotton textile industry in the United States. England's cotton industry, concentrated in Lancashire and spilling over a bit into neighboring shires, had over 440,000 workers dependent upon its prosperity. Liverpool, the economic capital of this district, was the greatest cotton port and market in the world. And three-quarters of England's cotton imports, the prop of this structure, came from the United States. Finally, if cotton and other southern staples were added together the South contributed two-thirds of the exports of the United States. The southern producer of cotton was absolutely dependent upon his foreign market. In the period 1856–1860 nearly four-fifths of the crop was exported.

As this recital suggests, western Europe and the United States exerted a reciprocal attraction upon each other's trade. The North Atlantic routes became the chief ocean highway of the world. The tendency was furthered by the increasing concentration of foreign trade at a few ports within the United States. Whereas in 1790 overseas commerce touched every harbor from Portland, Maine, to Savannah, Georgia, and the exports from the chief commercial states exhibited an astonishing equality, by 1860 smaller ports, like those in New England, had to submit to a regional hegemony and a single leader. And among the great rivals, Baltimore, Philadelphia, Boston, New Orleans, and New York, the last had emerged essentially without a peer. This outcome had many explanations: the superiority of a natural harbor, the development of a coastwise traffic to distribute and assemble goods, banking facilities to extend credit and auction sales to give buyers flattering prices, and the enlargement of the hinterland by canals, for example the Erie, and by railroads. Still the achievement of New York was such that many like the author of *Moby Dick* were perplexed by "your insular city of the Manhatoes, belted around by wharves as Indian isles by coral reefs—commerce surrounds it with her surf. . . . Tell me does the magnetic virtue of the needles of the compasses of all ships attract them hither?"

Judged by monetary values, the merchandise foreign trade of the United States multiplied approximately eighteen times between 1790 and 1860. The entries for the earlier years are far from accurate and then or later, since they were not in standard dollars, did not wholly show inflationary or deflationary values. With somewhat greater precision, the figures demonstrate that over the period the value of imports usually exceeded that of exports. This "unfavorable balance of trade," to use the mercantilist vernacular, had to be redressed by other international transactions because the experts agreed that their totals must be in balance. In the decades in question, the shipment of gold was of considerable importance only in the fifties after the California gold discoveries. Immigrant remittances, money sent back home by those who had arrived in this country earlier, was a contributory factor about the same time. Year in and year out, however, the sums borrowed abroad by Americans or those paid in freight money to the American merchant marine by foreign shippers were more decisive.

Investments and Credits

The amount of foreign investment in the United States before the Civil War is a matter of guesswork, punctuated by an occasional and partial investigation. In the early part of 1803 the total of American indebtedness held abroad may have been $75 million. About a third of this sum was short-term; the rest was in public securities, issued by the national government and held in Holland and France as well as in Great Britain. On the whole, the movement of securities across the Atlantic slowed up until the early twenties. The end of the Napoleonic wars found English investors with "an increase in disposable capital" seeking an overseas outlet, since "the interest of money is always highest in the least advanced communities." In 1822 these funds poured into the Erie Canal. In the thirties foreign investment in canals and in state banks, which in the South were financing the expansion of cotton cultivation, took on the proportions of a speculative boom. In 1843, two years after the boom collapsed, Congress estimated that foreigners held $150 million out of a total public debt of $279 million, most of which was in the liabilities of the states. Probably in no other period in the nineteenth century did foreign investment play so relatively large a part in the American economy. After a reversal of the trend in the early forties, foreign investment resumed more cautiously. In 1853 American securities held abroad probably totaled $222 million. This inflow of funds, more extensive than the counter current of interest on them, helped in the fifteen years before 1837 and in the 1850's to facilitate the excess of merchandise imports previously remarked.

British banks and merchant firms—Revolution or not—continued to provide the short-term mercantile credits for American commerce. Such credits in 1789 were estimated at $25 million. By 1836 they had risen to $85 million and by 1853 to $155 million. These were peak years. In times of depression the figures were much smaller. Whatever their total, such loans financed not only the direct trade between the United States and Great Britain but also trade between the United States and Europe, South America, and the Far East. The sterling bill was an international currency.

This English credit financed the American import trade. For forty years or so after the Revolution the American merchant continued the colonial practice of importing from abroad and selling to jobbers; these jobbers resold to retail country storekeepers. Since the customary period of settlement by the last was once a year, from harvest to harvest, and sometimes less frequently, the American importer perforce conformed to the same arrangements. Consequently, English export houses consigned their goods to the American correspondents on credits which occasionally ran for fifteen months. The latter discharged their indebtedness by the shipment of goods or by bills of exchange drawn on shipments to other firms in England or in Europe. Between 1825 and 1830 these arrangements were enlarged and extended. A "credit bridge" of impressive proportions was built between the United States and Great Britain. By now American importers had such a reputation for business integrity and importance that they sent their representatives abroad to purchase supplies and opened with English banking houses accounts upon which they could draw. These houses, about eight in number, located in Liverpool and London, combined the functions of commission merchants and bankers. The two largest houses concerned with the American trade were Baring Brothers and Brown and Brown. Upon these houses the American importer drew bills of exchange for his purchases. In other words, British, rather than American, capital supported the structure of American imports.

The credit system was equally important in the American export trade. The American commodities destined for foreign markets—rice, flour, and cotton—passed through an extended series of middlemen before they reached their destination. Take cotton as a case in point. The most important figure among the middlemen who handled it was the factor, usually resident at some southern port or some interior point where cotton was collected. For a commission he sold the cotton of his client. Since the planter, moreover, had most of his capital tied up in land and slaves, the factor stepped in to provide the funds for planting the crop and continuing its cultivation. This loan might be advanced in cash, but more often it was in the form of supplies purchased by the factor for the plantation and forwarded to that destination. On these advances

the factor charged interest. When the crop was made, the planter transferred it to the factor. In turn, the factor generally sold the cotton
through a broker to representatives of northern houses resident in the
South or to agents sent south by them. The seller received his payment
in a bill of exchange upon a northern house, which he could discount
at the bank. The northern house, a commission firm, had undertaken
its southern purchase if foreign trade were involved for the account of a
British commission house at Liverpool, and the former drew upon the
latter by a bill of exchange. The Liverpool house employed a broker on
commission to sell its product to representatives of the Lancashire manufacturers and drew upon him for credit. The broker in turn might provide the credit or might secure it from an English bank, usually one of
the eight Anglo-American houses. In any case, the chain of credit ended
in Great Britain. It was obvious, incidentally, that these marketing
arrangements influenced cotton cultivation as much as soil and weather.

The American Merchant Marine

The American Revolution cut the American merchant marine
out of the benefits once enjoyed within the British navigation system.
But the abnormalities of the years of Napoleonic conflict had, as we have
seen, postponed damaging effects. At least until 1807 American vessels
had fattened on the neutral trade they were carrying and the high
freights of the period. In these years the proportion of our foreign commerce judged by the value of cargoes carried in American vessels, practically never fell below 85 percent; to show that this was no accident
the decade of the twenties maintained an average of 90 percent; a gradual
decline then set in, but even in 1850 approximately 72 percent of our
trade was still carried by American vessels. An army of explanations has
been mobilized to account for this prosperity of the American merchant
marine. Many have advanced the discriminatory character of American
policy. But they forget that the purpose of this legislation was not to
create advantages for the American merchant marine but to secure an
equality of competition between nations. Unfortunately, moreover, the
periods of greatest American discrimination do not synchronize exactly
with the periods of greatest prosperity for the merchant marine. The
superior place held by the American marine is better explained by the
economic advantages which it enjoyed; and the wisdom of American
navigation policy in this period lay in its effort to give these advantages
full play.

In the Colonial period American shipbuilders had the advantage
of proximity to the materials—white oak and white pine—they used in
their vessels. Americans could build vessels more cheaply than could

their English competitors along the Thames. Although in the first half of the nineteenth century American shipyards had to reach out to less accessible supplies, they still had a comparative advantage.

The South, in spite of its admirable timber resources, exhibited again its absorption in agricultural staples and was compelled to see its timbers freighted northward to the centers of this maritime industry. Maryland and Pennsylvania had their innovating ships' architects and won a reputation for vessels of a high finish. But as the years went by, shipbuilding tended to concentrate at New York, Boston, and along the Maine coast. The first two centers had the big yards which could afford to organize their labor forces into specialized groups and buy machinery for working and handling the wooden pieces. In 1855 New York had thirty-one shipbuilding establishments; one of its firms, that of W. H. Webb, was probably the most prolific builder in the country; the city specialized in turning out large ships—clippers and packets. By this time the once important yards, scattered along the rivers, saltwater streams, and shelving shores of southern New England, were in eclipse. But Boston's big enterprises mirrored those of New York City, and the skill of her designers and builders of clippers recognized no superior.

Meanwhile Maine became the builder par excellence of general cargo, deep-sea ships. Her supplies of timber were ample and easily conveyed to the seaboard by a magnificent river system, her coast furnished countless harbors, and no attractive alternative like manufacturing ever weaned her from the sea. By 1850 towns from Machias to Kittery were engaged in building vessels, and a whole seaboard population was dependent upon the various crafts of the sea—ship carpenters, sailmakers, calkers, riggers, ropemakers, shipsmiths. Her trained labor supply gave her an added advantage. Of all the Maine centers Bath became the largest shipbuilding town in the Union, and her shipbuilders, the Houghtons, the Pattens, and the Sewalls, not only were pioneers in the development of new types but carried their craftsmanship to its highest development. New York might be the greatest port in the country, but the ships which lined her wharves were not always built there. Of the one hundred vessels registered there in 1850, three-quarters were built in New England, and of this large fraction Maine provided somewhat over one-half.

American designers and builders had the adaptive ability to devise vessels suited to their special commodities or trade routes. During the Napoleonic wars, for instance, a premium was placed upon speed as one means of escape from privateers and war vessels, and American design was undoubtedly influenced by these considerations. Smugglers and slavers, as well as privateers, brought into being the "Baltimore clipper," not a ship, for she was brig-rigged or schooner-rigged, but with a better-modeled and faster hull than her predecessors. After 1815, as the Atlantic basin became a great trading community with the carriage of commodities and even persons in bulk, American designers were presented with a further opportunity. American shipping firms conceived the idea that business was large enough to support a line of vessels sailing at regular intervals. In this faith a group of promoters established in 1818 the Black Ball Line, a "packet line" with monthly sailings from New York to Liverpool. It would have been extremely difficult to make these lines profitable if they had not carried eastbound cargoes of cotton assembled at New York by its coasting trade with Charleston, Savannah, Mobile, and New Orleans.

The first packet line was followed by a host of picturesquely named competitive imitators, who ran not only from New York to Liverpool but also from other Atlantic ports to other European destinations. The pressure of competition stimulated the continual improvement of packet ships. The first vessels of the Black Ball Line were from four hundred to five hundred tons burden, and as such they represented the maximum size which builders in the previous era had commonly accepted as safe; driven across the Atlantic, in the first nine years of their existence they averaged passages eastward of twenty-three days and westward of forty. The size and speed of these vessels gradually increased until in 1845 they began regularly to exceed a thousand tons and make faster records. A second cousin to the packet was the combination vessel for passengers —immigrants coming West—and freight—cotton outbound for Europe. These were organized in lines, but their sailings were irregular and slower. To the packets and regular traders the English were compelled to surrender the sailing supremacy of the North Atlantic.

Suddenly between 1848 and 1850 a conjunction of events opened a new trade for the sailing ship. The "Gold Rush" to California stimulated an immense demand for passenger accommodations around South America to the gold fields and for the carriage of commodities which could be sold at fantastic prices in San Francisco. This intercoastal route was restricted by law to American-registered vessels. In 1849 England repealed her navigation laws, and foreign vessels could then carry tea from the Orient to the exacting English market. Consequently a vessel could find a cargo for a voyage nearly around the world. The American response was the big and fast sailing ship.

The origin of the clipper was diverse. But the first large vessel which brought its distinctive features together in unmistakable fashion—three square-rigged masts; a long hull tapering from a bow no longer rounded, but concave, to a finely modeled stern; a narrow beam farther aft than in previous models—was the *Rainbow,* designed by a ship draughtsman, John W. Griffiths, in 1845. The master artist of the clipper ship was Donald McKay, Nova Scotia born, New York and Newburyport trained; his greatest vessels were launched from yards in East Boston. And they bore names which expressed at once a builder's pride and a sailor's confidence—*Flying Cloud, Sovereign of the Seas, Great Republic, Lightning*. These vessels made sailing records on the race courses of the world, and one of them, the *Lightning,* in her first voyage across the Atlantic logged in a day 436 miles, the greatest day's run ever made by a cargo ship under sail.

The speed and fascinating beauty of the clipper ship and the more solid performance of the regular packet must not obscure the fact that the burden of American tonnage was transported in smaller and less graceful conveyances. The bulk of the business was heavy freighting to Europe and to South America. For the cotton trade the American designer developed special types with a bluff bow, high deck-houses at bow and stern, a broad, flat bottom to pass the shallows of the Mississippi River below New Orleans, and swollen sides to give a larger cargo space. These vessels were usually operated on charter. The lines were modified for general freighting, but the vessels were still full-bowed and broad-beamed. It was the humble freight vessel which furnished the backbone of the merchant marine.

It is difficult to generalize about the ownership of vessels, for so many methods were demonstrated in practice. Vessels were often owned in shares which represented a fractional part of the value, sometimes as small as one sixty-fourth; many shipbuilders built for themselves, as the phrase went, and controlled the operation of their own vessels; captains might purchase vessels and conduct an individual business; but probably the dominant method of ownership down to 1815 was the persistence of the colonial type, the merchant-shipowner, who owned vessels, assembled the outgoing cargo in his own store, and sold to retailers by auction or some other way the product which his supercargoes or captains had picked up around the world. These merchant princes were the wealthy men of the early Republic as they had been of the colonial era. "King" Derby of Salem was but one of the many millionaires created by the commerce of that port. John Jacob Astor was not only a fur trader and real-estate owner, he engaged also in foreign trade. Stephen Girard of Philadelphia, an immigrant from France, pursued his trade in every port of the world and left at his death in 1831 a fortune of $7 million, one of the first in the country to be devoted to private philanthropies.

But the growing regularity and volume of commerce gradually made this union of functions unnecessary, and the public carrier, operating either on a regular schedule like the packet ship or secured by a charter like the freight sailing vessel, began to carry the bulk of the commerce. The latter practice began as early as 1800. Even Stephen Girard, who owned a fleet of six vessels, carried on the bulk of his operations in chartered holds. If a date must be chosen, 1815 marks the emergence of the public carrier, although in certain trades like those to the Orient, the Mediterranean, and South America, the traditional merchant-ship-owner hung on until the Civil War. But before his disappearance he had done much to create the glory of the American merchant marine. Compelled by circumstances he explored new routes, developed new trades, and took great chances. His courageous enterprise was one reason for American superiority.

In the men who ran the vessels Americans had another advantage. Perhaps until 1820 Americans, bred to the sea, continued to form a majority of the crews, and the first foreigners who were supplied to replace them, British and Scandinavians, were all good sailors. But the packet boats and clippers were run by nondescript crews who were "learned the ropes" with a brutal discipline. The officers always remained an able lot. The sea held out in early America the prestige of social position and the hope of gain and promotion. An American boy, shipping for a voyage or two before the mast, was soon started upward through the ranks of petty officers to a captaincy, and the rewards of that position were great. Shipowners paid officers good salaries and stimulated zeal and carefulness by setting aside ship space in which officers could adventure a small cargo. On the packet vessels through various sources of income the captains often made the large salary of $5,000 a year. Under these various temptations, a sea calling appealed to able Americans. These officers drove both ship and crew. Day and night sails were carried in high winds that caused other vessels to furl canvas; ropes were padlocked to keep crews from letting the sails go in a gale which seemed to them dangerous; American clippers left port when others were delaying for favorable weather. And the captains ran their vessels with smaller crews than their rivals. Under these advantages, the American ships secured the best rates and the quickest cargoes.

The superiority of the United States in the days of wood and of sail was, however, menaced by technical inventions in which Great Britain, not the United States, took the lead. Although an American, Robert Fulton, perfected the steamboat, the utilization of the new motive power on the high seas was Great Britain's achievement. In 1838 Philip Hone, a New Yorker, although he had previously doubted if a steam vessel "overburthened with the weight of machinery, with a burning volcano in her bowels" could "ride on the crested billows and sink again into their dark, deep caverns," chronicled in his diary the arrival on the same day of two British steamboats. One of them was the famous *Great Western,* registered 1,340 tons. The paddle wheels which such vessels employed for propulsion were not well suited for ocean navigation. In 1845 there arrived in New York harbor another British vessel, the *Great Britain,* an iron steamer "propelled," in Hone's words, "by the Archimedean screw instead of paddles." Five years later a British shipowner started a regular line of iron vessels, screw-propelled, between Great

Britain and Philadelphia. These new vessels not only utilized a superior means of propulsion but also substituted iron for wood. This was a great advantage. Vessels with larger carrying capacity could be constructed of the new material; the hold possessed a greater rigidity and could be modeled in finer lines; the whole ship was drier, safer, and faster. In 1854 Lloyd's Register Association, the great insurance concern, only reflected the situation when it charged a higher rate upon American wooden vessels than upon British iron ships. To pay the higher premium the wooden vessel had to charge higher freights.

Freight rates also played another important role as an item in the balance of payments. Unluckily, documented series of freight rates for the trade routes of America are lacking. By constructing an index of rates based on other routes, making allowances for distance and multiplying the rate by the size of the cargo—again a fluctuating measure—totals of a sort can be ascertained. Net United States shipping earnings suddenly shot upward to their peak—$20 million—in 1840; they remained on a substantial plateau during the late forties; and, with the exception of three years, continued by and large at the same level during the fifties. By 1860 they were back at $18.4 million. This net balance served throughout as the most important item enabling the foreign commerce of the nation to offset its negative trade balance of merchandise exports and imports. Whether they could maintain this role as the merchant marines of the world turned from wood and sail to iron and steam and rates fell—as they did during the fifties—was the critical question.

Since the international carriage of goods was a competitive activity, the nations concerned resorted to competitive policies. Great Britain had aided the extension of her steam marine to the Mediterranean, Indian Ocean, and South America by contracting to pay to favored lines an annual subsidy for the carriage of the mails. In 1840, probably to challenge the American sailing packets, it inaugurated a similar policy for the Cunard Line to Halifax, Boston, and later New York. Perhaps by copying a policy it can be checkmated. At any rate, the American Congress in the late forties inaugurated a subsidy program and in the fifties aided in a generous fashion the Collins Line from New York to Liverpool. The competing Cunarders won higher subsidies from Britain; accident and extravagance overwhelmed its American rival, and governmental dissatisfaction led to the cancellation of the Collins subsidies in 1858. The heart of the matter was, however, the greater cost of the American vessels. By the end of the fifties American advantages in building wooden vessels were no longer decisive. The British iron industry, much more advanced than ours, could turn out plates for hulls at lower prices, and, joined with British engineering, manufacture engines more cheaply. British yards with skilled workers in abundance manipulated these new materials more advantageously than did we. These newcomers took over the passenger and immigrant trades of the North Atlantic; sailing vessels glutted the California trade; and the Civil War interrupted the cotton trade and led American owners to transfer their vessels in one way or another to foreign flags. Together these factors accounted for the declining role of American vessels in American foreign trade. In 1855-1859 they carried 74 percent of the value of the goods imported and exported from this country; in 1866 the figure was 32.2 percent.

Undoubtedly, foreign trade in the period between the Revolution and the Civil War was an important factor in the economic expansion and growth of the United States. It was the avenue by which investment and immigrant workers and consumers migrated to this country; the foreign market supplemented the domestic; the trade as a whole stimulated other transforming forces, for instance, urbanization and regional economic specialization. But an evaluation of the primacy of its influence again and again confronts the central fact that it exerted its major force customarily through cotton exports. Although in the forties and fifties, shortages of grain in western England led to a considerable expansion of American exports of wheat and flour, this foreign trade remained of minor importance. Outside agriculture there were whole areas of economic activity untouched and uninfluenced by foreign trade. A foreign trade in cotton cannot bear the whole burden of explaining American growth. Southern contemporaries thought otherwise; they boasted of its strategic omnipotence. Historic development has shown they were wrong. Hamilton, in discussing the relative worth of agriculture or manufacture as a national objective, had pointed out decades earlier that a foreign market was "casual and occasional" and that the likelihood of nations suddenly changing their commercial policies increased the uncertainties. Foreign commerce lived up to his anticipations. The sudden surges of exports and imports, the blossoming of trades one day only to wither the next, the speculative inflow of investments—were all cases in point.

viii

State and Nation in Banking and Finance

Emergencies and Answers

The colonies entered the Revolution with a political case formulated with such persuasiveness and force as to inspire admiration. It had the quality of timelessness. Their military operations, vexed though they were with frequent defeat, were carried to eventual success by the French alliance and the fortitude of the army and its Commander-in-Chief. Five years after the war was over the financial arrangements of the nation had a past filled with effort and frustration, a present without a system, and a future which was unpredictable. Yet within four years the Federal Constitution and a flurry of state papers and statutes had introduced arrangements which in many respects could be said to be in advance of their times.

The Federal Constitution, written and adopted in 1787–1788, established a more effective central government than had the Articles of Confederation. Furthermore, the specific provisions of the document cleared the way for national action on matters of finance. The Republic received the power to "lay and collect Taxes, Duties, Imposts and Excises, to pay the Debts and provide for the common Defence and general Welfare of the United States" and to "coin Money, regulate the Value thereof, and of foreign Coin." Conversely, the states were forbidden to "coin Money; emit Bills of Credit; make any Thing but gold and silver Coin a Tender in Payment of Debts" or without the consent of Congress, lay any "Imposts or Duties on Imports or Exports." George Washington, the first President; Alexander Hamilton, the first Secretary of the Treasury; and Congress proceeded to utilize these enumerated powers to the full; from other provisions of the Constitution, they inferred authorizations for additional financial undertakings, notably the establishment of a national bank. In 1819 in McCulloch *v.* Maryland the Supreme Court set its approval upon the constitutional justification for the exercise of this power. On occasion the learned justices were also compelled to interpret the specifically stated financial clauses of the Constitution. Somewhat touched by the radicalism of the Jackson era, the Court in 1837 declared that, although states could not emit bills of credit, banks in which the state was a stockholder could do so, provided such bills were not made legal tender. The convenient constitutional silence on the question of whether the Federal government could make paper money legal tender was another matter. Hamilton thought the spirit of the Constitution forbade it. But after the Civil War the Supreme Court disagreed with him.

Governmental Indebtedness

During these years of beginning, the hard core of government indebtedness had been the war debt incurred during the Revolution. To meet necessary martial expenditures the Congress of the Confederation had not had the power to levy taxes. Though it could make requisitions upon the states, these were rarely and reluctantly honored. Nor were the colonies, taken separately, either willing or politically able to tax heavily within their own jurisdictions. The Revolution was in part a protest against taxation. One alternative was loans. However, not until the revolutionists had demonstrated some possibility of success or until alliances brought about a common interest in victory was it feasible to market securities abroad. By the end of the war the foreign debt was $7,830,000; in 1790 when the new nation placed its fiancial house in order, the total, with new borrowings and arrears of interest, was $11,710,000. The French and the Dutch were the chief investors. Since loans in the domestic market required an accumulation of free funds which probably did not exist in the required quantities, a large share of the national indebtedness represented government certificates given in payment for supplies. Interest payments fell behind. In 1790 Hamilton estimated the domestic debt at $40,414,000. The states, which had likewise borrowed in behalf of the common cause had, Hamilton presumed, revolutionary debts, principal and interest, of $25 million.

These sums, considerable as they were, had been quite inadequate for the task at hand. Within a week of Bunker Hill the Continental Congress began issuing "bills of credit." The good faith of the government was pledged to their redemption; in large measure they were made legal tender in payment of debts. Actually they became irredeemable paper money. By 1780 when the central government had issued $241,552,000 and the states an almost equal amount, Congress made an attempt to supplant its old issues by a new one. The exchange was to be at the ratio of 40-to-1. Neither simplicity nor soundness resulted. Nonetheless, the central government in the postwar period avoided a continuation of paper issues. Finally, in 1790 when this period came to an end, Congress accepted as subscription to its new stock its own earlier emissions at the ratio of 100-to-1. In essence this writing-down of the value of the currency was taxation. The losses of note holders were contributions to the government. As a system of taxation paper issues had the merit of bearing upon a wide constituency and operating slowly over a considerable period of time. Such a serene view of events, however, was possible for few contemporaries. The expansion of the currency during the Revolution was the chief, though not the only, cause for a galloping inflation, which raised the price of commodities and changed the real value of contractual arrangements. From these tumbling confusions some individuals were able to wrest a gain. Those unable to increase their incomes or incapable of skillful speculation were the sufferers. With frequent resort to such epithets as "greed," "avarice," "hoarding," and "monopoly," Congress and the local governments embarked upon price fixing. The ineffectiveness of these measures and the stagnation of trade which accompanied them soon caused as much discontent as the original grievances.

Consequently, when the new government of the Republic confronted the formulation of fiscal policy, it confronted a condition and not a theory. The government owed money, and its securities, the evidence of its indebtedness, were selling for only a fraction of par. To Hamilton these securities were contracts between the government and its creditors. It seemed to him a matter of honor for the government to fund its debt with new securities, dollar for dollar, and for reasons just as cogent to assume the debts of the states. Funding was also a matter of wisdom.

The political advantages need not detain us. From the process of funding and assumption Hamilton also foresaw desirable results for the private economy of the nation. Government securities, properly funded and paying interest, answer "most of the purposes of money"; they are "equivalent to payments in specie." The country lacked money. With the debt funded, merchants, farmers, and manufacturers would have new resources; interest on money, "always in a ratio to the quantity of money," would be lowered; lands would increase in value and be more easily sold. In brief, the debt could be used to stimulate the economy. He called upon British experience as evidence that "the proper funding of the present debt will render it a national blessing." Whether the process of incurring indebtedness should become standard operating procedure, Hamilton was not certain. In some exigencies, such as war, debt creation was inevitable. Sometimes he implied a wider justification for this policy. "In a country which, like this, is possessed of little active wealth, or, in

other words, little money capital, the necessity for that resource must
. . . be proportionately urgent." Elsewhere Hamilton expressed his fear
of government "prodigality" and asserted the creation of debt must
always be accompanied by measures for its repayment.

Though Hamilton was fond of playing with abstractions and long-
range forecasts, he was presumably satisfied with the short-run accomplishment of funding the existing debt. Congress passed the requisite
statute in August, 1790. In the course of these legislative operations a
disagreement arose between Hamilton and Jefferson. It is not clear that
their ideological gap was as wide on funding as it was on some other
issues. There was a difference in tone, however. Jefferson feared a public
debt for moral reasons.

In the course of time the Jeffersonian outlook prevailed, partly because of its ideological appeal and partly because general opinion and
constitutional decisions permitted the national government a rather
limited range of functions. When Jefferson became President he inaugurated a policy of governmental thrift and began paying off the
national debt. As this policy endured and operated, revenues poured in
from the customs, even under the low tariffs of the forties and fifties;
and sales of public land, a device for living off capital, supplemented
them. At times Congressional committees complained of the incon-
veniences of an overflowing treasury; and the national debt in the mid-
thirties was for all practical purposes momentarily extinguished. In an
atmosphere of partisanship, panic, and confusion Congress distributed
the Treasury surplus to the states, many of which used this windfall
for banks, canals, and education. In only twenty-one of the years between
1791 and 1860 did the expenditures of the national government exceed
its receipts. These unusual years generally came after the depressions of
1837 and 1857, when revenues fell off, or in times of war. The immediate
governmental response to such urgencies was to maintain the tax level
—the tariff of 1842 was an exception—and pare expenditures, and as soon
as the emergency passed begin paying off the debt. This policy was
financially orthodox. "No statesman," said Buchanan in 1858, "would
advise that we should go on increasing the national debt to meet the
ordinary expenses of the Government."

Whether or not those who governed states and localities could be
called "statesmen," they were generally able to incur debts for a much
wider range of activity than that of the Federal government. States
could and did issue bonds for internal improvements, notably banks and
canals; municipalities built public works, reservoirs and aqueducts, laid
out and constructed streets, and aided railroads—all by incurring debts.
As a result, while the Federal gross debt in 1860 was $64.8 million that
of states at the same date was more than four times that amount, and
the gross debt of municipalities was three times as large as the Federal.

While here and there a voice was raised in favor of continuing these expenditures in depression as well as in prosperity—"their sudden arrest and the discharge of probably ten thousand laborers now employed on the public works . . . would extend throughout the whole community, and with fearful aggravation, the losses and sufferings that as yet have been confined in great measure to the mercantile class"—a majority opinion apparently concluded that the whole experiment was the result of departure from sound principles. In the forties and fifties as states revised their constitutions they were apt to include limitations on the size of state debts or prohibitions of state investment in a variety of enterprises. Those who much later held different conceptions of fiscal management were prone to regret these discarded opportunities: "one of the most dynamic economic functions was taken away from the states for many years to come."

The Metallic Currency

Another tangle inherited from Revolutionary, indeed Colonial, times was that of the metallic currency. Buttressed by undoubted constitutional authorization, the national government acted with system and intelligence to replace the motley assembly of coins accumulated chiefly through the channels of foreign trade—the English guinea, crown, and shilling; the French pistole and crown; the Spanish pistole, "real," and milled dollar; and Portuguese coins of different varieties. Congress in 1792 took the first remedial step when it established a mint and a currency. This act, for whose details Alexander Hamilton, the Secretary of the Treasury, was largely responsible, established a decimal metallic currency whose unit was the dollar. Hamilton rejected the idea that this coinage should be restricted to a single precious metal, since it was likely "to abridge the quantity of circulating medium; and is liable to all the objections which arise from a comparison of the benefits of a full, with the evils of a scanty, circulation." Gold and silver were, therefore, to be minted, but since the two metals were clearly not of equal value he calculated a coinage ratio of 15-to-1 for their relative weights.

For nearly fifty years the metallic currency of the nation, established by these early acts and modified by later legislation, collided with one aspect or another of Gresham's Law. This statement of certain economic tendencies bears the name of a sixteenth-century London merchant who did not even formulate it. It has been briefly and therefore only approximately phrased, "Cheap money drives out dear money." Some of the difficulty arose from the attempt to circulate the two metals on a parity.

One market for them was the mint, where value relationships were fixed by law; another was the bullion market, where prices were determined by supply and demand. Furthermore, the mint valuation in different countries was not identical. Owners of the precious metals will utilize them in the dearest market. Hamilton's ratio of 15-to-1 proved to overvalue silver at the mint: silver was accordingly presented for coinage, and the possessors of gold, even if it were coined in the United States mint, either exported it or sold it in the open market for silver. Consequently, in 1834 and 1837, new coinage laws fixed a new mint ratio, essentially 16-to-1. Since this new ratio overvalued gold, the country was for all practical purposes placed upon a gold basis. Eventually even the silver coins necessary for small transactions were melted down and exported. As for metallic currency, the country got along with a polyglot collection of worn silver coins from abroad and a gold currency based upon some gold production in the southern states and importations from abroad.

In the fifties man and circumstance began a new era. One act established a subsidiary silver coinage, whose proportion of precious metal was arranged to make the pieces useless for export, and another act withdrew the legal tender quality from all foreign coins. The reign of the dollar sign was now complete. This legislation was in turn made possible by the discovery of immense gold supplies. In 1848 gold was discovered in California, and in 1851 production in the state reached $56 million. In the same year gold was discovered in Australia, and the "goldbugs" rushed to the land "down under." The gold production of the world in the decade 1851 to 1860 was $1,332,981,000—greater by 8 percent than the total production for the first fifty years of the century. As for American production, the balance of international payments was such that the nation retained within its borders a large share of the precious metal. Gold coinage at the mint rose from $3,775,000 in 1847 to $83,395,000 in 1861. The new tide of gold, sweeping through the channels of trade, also transformed the currency situation of the world.

Perhaps in some primitive community or one so inspired by Spartan simplicity as to censure economic growth and material acquisition, gold and silver might be made to suffice for the purposes of trade. In America there was always a considerable and influential group of Americans who felt that gold and silver were the only true and the only constitutional money; the states could make no other legal tender. The central government had no explicit constitutional permission to issue paper money; if paper were issued, it must be backed dollar for dollar with bullion. From time to time this attitude, perhaps strengthened by prudential reasons, resulted in statutes and orders prescribing that all dues and customs and returns from land sales, with many exceptions, must be paid to the United States Treasury in specie or cash. This hard-money philosophy seemed to strengthen as the decades passed. In his Farewell

Address in 1837 Andrew Jackson announced, "The Constitution of the United States unquestionably intended to secure to the people a circulating medium of gold and silver"; his ally, Thomas Hart Benton, Senator from Missouri, bore the significant sobriquet of "Old Bullion"; and Jackson's spiritual heir, the Secretary of the Treasury, in 1853 expressed the pious hope that the gold output of the decade would so increase that the nation might yet return to a purely metallic currency. To this outlook, as fundamentalist in its way as some thinking about the national debt, Hamilton had hardly given the dignity of discussion. It was "visionary," and history had shown it was a drag on the growth of intelligent commercial nations. It was surely incompatible with any planned progress, for the supply of the precious metals cannot be increased or decreased at will. In short, the hard-money school would have chained the American economy to nature's bounty or niggardliness.

The First Bank of the United States

In most controversies, political and academic, the formulation of an attitude is quite as apt to be against as for something. Thus the hard-money philosophy was a reaction in large measure to banks and their "paper" system. When the nation was getting under way, there were within its borders three banks—all chartered during the Confederation period. Although one of these, the Bank of North America in Philadelphia, had a national charter, Hamilton thought the nation's banking system needed a stronger and a more national institution. But some doubted that the Constitution granted the new government the specific power to establish a bank. In the end, Hamilton was compelled to embark upon a considerable exegesis to handle this difficulty. To the national government the Constitution delegated *express* powers; for instance, to coin and borrow money, to collect taxes and pay its debts, and to regulate trade. By *implication* the Federal government also had the power "to employ all the means which relate to these matters to the best and greatest advantage." The bank was one of those means. Eventually, in McCulloch *v.* Maryland, the Supreme Court adopted this reasoning.

The essence of the Hamiltonian case was that banks enlarged the circulating medium for the benefit of industry and commerce by creating and loaning credit. The visible evidence of these transactions might be checks drawn upon a sum loaned by the bank and entered upon its books as a deposit to the credit of the borrower. Actually, though this form of credit or circulation was understood by some in the United States before 1800—Hamilton mentioned it in passing—its wider use and advocacy came later. By 1850 deposit liabilities of this sort constituted

perhaps half the loans of banks; by 1860 these liabilities were the chief
instrument of lending. In the period between the Revolution and the
Civil War, note issues were the predominant form of credit advance.
Bank notes were more acceptable than checks. Printed in unit values
rather than written for specific sums, they were passed from hand to hand
and did not require frequent recourse to the banks; and bank notes
could be used for most of the small payments which a primitive country
required. Both notes as well as checks added to the money supply, for
it was not necessary for the bankers to keep a dollar in specie to redeem
every outstanding dollar, since all notes were not presented simultaneously for redemption, nor were all deposits at once drawn upon for their
full amount. Essential to this operation was popular confidence in the
banks and in their specie reserves, which, according to Hamilton's conjecture, should be in the proportion of two or three dollars of notes to
one of gold and silver held for redemption.

Banks loaned credit, whether in the form of deposits or notes, on
various terms. Commercial banking, a comparative novelty in late
eighteenth-century America, made its loans for short periods, perhaps
sixty days, and did not renew them. Such loans financed the sale of
crops, the movement of goods, and other short-term operations. They
arose, it was said, from actual transactions in course of development.
Banks run on these mercantile principles had to have a reserve of specie
on hand to redeem their notes promptly; their loans, because they came
due at frequent intervals, were highly liquid. But the usefulness of these
short-term loans in an immature, but developing economy was limited.
If banking could create and loan credit, why could it not with equal
safety do so for those long-term permanent improvements by which an
enjoyable profit might be derived from the potential resources of the
nation? Improved means of transportation, whether turnpikes, canals,
steamboats, or railroads, involved heavy investments. Manufacturing
required funds for machinery and for plants. This creation of capital
for investment might well be on behalf of the state when the government
rather than private persons undertook to finance enterprise. Such loans
had to be for long periods. In short, the banks had through demand
deposits to create capital for permanent investments. The value of the
property—securities held as collateral, for instance—was the asset behind
the loan. Since banking thus "melted down" property into currency,
specie reserve was hardly necessary. Unhappily, bank notes and checks
usually had to be redeemed when presented at the bank; and fixed or
capitalized property could not be converted suddenly into coin through
sale or mortgage. Such property was not there to be shoved across the
counter.

When Hamilton was perfecting his plans for national development
he included as one item the national chartering of a bank to take the

place of the Bank of North America. He disliked, as we have noted, the inadequacy of that institution. Abstractly, it would have seemed logical to vest banking powers in the Treasury, which collected the government revenues that might have served as a basis for note issue, and which was a department of government and under Hamilton's direction. He rejected the possibility. "To attach full confidence to an institution of this nature, it appears to be an essential ingredient in its structure, that it shall be under a *private* not a *public* Direction, under the guidance of *individual interest,* not of *public policy.*" The institution otherwise would pay too much heed to "public necessity," and would embark upon inflationary policies. Finally, "What nation was ever blessed with a constant succession of upright and wise Administrators?"

On the national stage the apparent answer to this rhetorical question was that the directors of a quasi-private bank could provide what national officials lacked. In any case, Congress in 1791 granted a charter to the First Bank of the United States. The Bank was a powerful mechanism. Its charter guaranteed that the national government would incorporate no rival. It was to last for twenty years. Its capital was placed at the immense figure of $10 million, one-fourth of which was to be paid in specie and the remainder in the securities of the United States. In this fashion Hamilton monetized a part of the national debt as he had planned in his funding bill. Though the government was to subscribe $2 million, this sum was only to assure specie for the institution and to permit the government to participate in its profits. The admirers of Hamilton have usually concentrated their idolatry upon his funding of the public debt. They rank it with the Emancipation Proclamation. Considering the immaturity of the American economy, the founding of the First Bank was as long a stride. Hamilton had a precedent in the Bank of England, which as late as 1945 was both a private and a central bank; and he had observed the experience of the Bank of North America and lived through the inflation of Revolution. Thus instructed, he elaborated a novel scheme. He seems not to have been troubled by the possibility that the duplication of governmental fiscal agencies, Bank and Treasury, might create a rivalry, or even a hostility, between them. Eventually, in the days of the Second Bank this happened.

Almost all simple descriptive terms for the First Bank are somewhat misleading. It certainly was an agency of the national government. It operated under a national charter; it loaned money to the government; though not the sole repository, the Bank held the major share of government deposits and moved such funds from place to place at its own expense; and it aided the government in foreign exchange operations. The Bank's operations and even its mere presence had profound consequences for the private economy. In addition to its main office in Philadelphia, the nation's capital in the nineties, it established eight branches in the chief commercial ports and oversaw their activities. It collected the largest specie reserve in the country, and through this fund and its large capital managed to regulate the discount and note issues of private and state banks. As lender it came to the aid of the nation's banks in emergency. Nevertheless, it aroused antagonisms. Its monopoly frightened democrats; its Federalist character and personnel chilled some political rivals; its "paper circulation" antagonized those who believed solely in the precious metals; personal distastes added bitterness to the struggle. In 1811 by a majority of one, Congress refused an extension of the charter. For an interval of five years private banks and those chartered by the states constituted the system of the nation.

The Monster of Chestnut Street

From the moment the national government disestablished the First Bank, powerful businessmen and politicians embarked upon a campaign for the charter of a successor. Whether they would have succeeded or not without the War of 1812 is doubtful, for during the second conflict with Great Britain there was a repetition of the financial disorders which had occurred during the first. The banks outside New England had so expanded their note issue and were so drained of coin that they had announced their inability to redeem their obligations in specie. Again the government was in financial difficulties. The treasury notes it issued—though they bore interest, were receivable for government dues, and were to be redeemed at a later period—became toward the end of the war perilously like continental currency. The administration sold loans at high rates of interest or at values well below par. In an orderly fashion a national bank might serve as escape from this confusion and bankruptcy. The Second Bank of the United States—the "BUS," in the alphabetical verbiage of its day—was chartered in 1816.

It had similarities to its predecessor. Again there was the monopoly privilege of twenty years; the subscriptions of private investors were to be a quarter in specie and the remainder in government securities; to the enlarged capital of $35 million the government was to subscribe a fifth. There were also contrasts. So valuable was the banking privilege esteemed that the corporation was to pay a bonus of $1.5 million to the national government for it. A fifth of the directors, of whom there were twenty-five, were to be appointed by the President of the United States with the consent of the Senate. As it turned out, two of the Bank's three presidents were successively chosen from this panel of government appointees. One of the latter, Nicholas Biddle, ruled the institution from 1823 to 1836.

As a central or controlling bank the Second Bank was better equipped than the First had been. Its capital was larger, it operated by

1830 twenty-eight branches, and it was the sole depository of government funds. Furthermore, Nicholas Biddle, its president, was one of the great bankers of his generation and a pioneer, albeit partly an unconscious one, in the art of central banking. Scion of a distinguished Pennsylvania family, Princeton graduate, patron and practitioner of the arts, he was essentially the scholar of literature, law, and economics. By dealing in domestic and foreign exchange with considerable ingenuity, he kept the notes of his bank at uniform value throughout the nation. They constituted a quarter of the total circulation. As creditor of the state banks, a position he maintained, Biddle could press for payment either in specie or in notes of the Second Bank or bills of exchange. He could thus influence in considerable measure the loan policy and note issue of other banks. In these and other ways Biddle turned in a superior performance as a central banker.

A central bank should be able to effect an expansion or contraction of credit. Through the issue and contraction of notes Biddle attempted to do so. In the absence of the lavish statistical data now available for policy determination in this matter, he relied upon such indices as the rate of foreign exchange, the movement of specie in America's foreign commerce, and the amount of specie in his vaults. He kept a reserve of one dollar for each three dollars of notes. The note issues of the new bank were always convertible; their circulation was rarely curtailed or impetuously expanded. The Second Bank's dealings in domestic exchange aided both private and government business; it became the leading dealer in foreign exchange in the United States and the chief agency for marketing American public securities in Europe. It sought, as far as its powers permitted, to restrain booms and avert catastrophic declines in business and prices. To the distress of the bank's stockholders, Biddle tried to run the institution not for maximum profits, but for the benefit of the economy. At least, such were the features of his administration until, badgered and bewildered by the attacks upon the bank and himself in a political struggle for which he was ill-fitted, he deviated from his own standards and developed an illusion of personal indispensability.

For the existence and operations of the Second Bank stirred discontent in regions, individuals, and interests. All that was needed for a blaze of hostility was a strong-minded leader to combine the combustibles and blow on the flames. Andrew Jackson played this part. He questioned the morality or expediency of all banking operations. As he once informed Biddle, "I do not dislike your Bank any more than all banks. But ever since I read the history of the South Sea Bubble I have been afraid of banks." This heresy seems no deeper than that expressed a few decades earlier by John Adams, "Every dollar of a bank bill that is issued beyond the quantity of gold and silver in the vaults represents nothing, and is therefore a cheat upon somebody." Yet Adams is venerated as a statesman and Jackson despised as an ignoramus.

Contributory assertions swelled the angry tide of protest. Bank notes could not possibly provide a stable or uniform currency. This paper system led to speculation, and aristocrats, since they were given privileges, grew richer at the expense of the producers. It was charged that the Bank of the United States never raised a pumpkin. That the National Bank was a monopoly made it all the worse. Benton, Jackson's lieutenant, expressed this discontent as he roared in the Senate, "All the flourishing cities of the West are mortgaged to this money power. They may be devoured by it at any moment. They are in the jaws of the Monster! A lump of butter in the mouth of a dog! One gulp, one swallow, and all is gone." Perhaps the real cause of all the clamor was a nostalgic allegiance to the simpler ways of the Republic—before the arrival of a modern credit economy and a monster corporation run by a Pennsylvania arisotcrat and college graduate—to the days when productive manual work enabled men to make a living and acquire an incorruptible character, to a morality above speculation and extravagance, to the time commerce was independent of a bank in which foreigners owned a majority of the stock, to governmental ways "under a Constitution framed by the sages and patriots of the Revolution," to use the Jacksonian phrase. Appealing as the manipulation of these symbols was, it did not touch those who disliked the Bank because it checked their zeal for expansion. These did not want "no bank"; they wanted more banks or different banks, ones that would lend more generously on the prosperity of the future. Spokesmen of this sort were not agrarians clinging to ancestral ways, but merchants who had not secured bank charters for themselves, bankers like those in New York City eager to wrest financial dominance away from Philadelphia, and a new class of businessmen and speculators, East and West, on the make. These interests preferred state banking systems, and to their support they could summon the provincial loyalty of states' rights. For Biddle's bank not only controlled the state banks but it also competed with them.

All this hostility took a host of forms. By its constitution Illinois, for instance, forbade any banks but state banks within its borders; other states attempted exclusion by statute. But the favorite method of discrimination was heavy taxation upon "foreign" banks. Maryland levied a tax of $15,000 upon the Baltimore branch of the BUS; Ohio and Tennessee taxed each branch $50,000; and Kentucky was the most extreme with a tax of $60,000. After some preliminary diffidence on the part of the Bank, cases involving these taxes were brought before the Supreme Court, and that body, presided over by John Marshall, in two famous decisions—McCulloch *v.* Maryland (1819) and Osborn *v.* The Bank of the United States (1824)—swept aside as unconstitutional these barriers which the states had attempted to erect. When Andrew Jackson became President of the United States in 1828, the whole bank issue became inextricably entangled with party and personal politics. Jackson announced that he would not approve the recharter of the Bank and carried his point in the ensuing bank war. In 1836 the Second Bank of the United States ceased to exist. Eight years later Biddle died, discredited by the failure of the bank for which he had secured a Pennsylvania charter. His foes thought he should have died in the penitentiary. One of the most imaginative and ingenious big businessmen of his day, he had the fatal defect of not realizing he was operating in a political setting.

Finally, in 1846, by enacting a bill for an independent treasury the national government formally withdrew from central banking. The decision thus taken was not formally reversed until the Federal Reserve Act of 1913. In the large sense, these early and promising steps toward a modern system were discarded because they were premature. Our polity was federal; our economy was agricultural. As soon expect from this setting a successful central bank, as anticipate from the poets of the young Republic an epic for a nation that as yet had no history.

The rest is postscript. As the Bank died, the Federal government put its funds in state-chartered banks, some of which were founded to secure those funds. All banks, whether depositories or institutions merely relieved from supervision, enlarged their activities. Credit expansion and speculation were rampant. This result of their own policy dismayed the hard-money men. Benton lamented, "I did not join in putting down the Bank of the United States to put up a wilderness of local banks." It took some time to find a solution for these dilemmas and to induce the nation to accept it. Under the subtreasury system the government was to build its own depositories and store its funds in them. Furthermore, all the receipts of the government from duties, taxes, sales of land, and other sources were to be paid in gold or silver or in treasury notes issued under the authority of the United States. All outgoing payments were to be in specie. Though banks might fail, government finance or government hoarding would be soundly based on specie. The national government was, in short, to divorce itself from banking. John Quincy Adams wrote incredulously:

A Divorce of Bank and State! Why, a divorce of Trade and Shipping would be as wise to carry on the business of a merchant. A Divorce of Army and Fire-Arms, in the face of an invading enemy, a divorce of Law and a Bench of Judges to carry into execution the Statutes of the Land, would be as reasonable!

Nonetheless, this was the policy of Jackson, his supporters, and his followers. Enacted first in 1840 it was repealed a year later. The statute of 1846 reestablishing the system endured.

But as Adams and others had foreseen, a complete separation of the national government from banking was impossible. Individuals, in order to obtain specie for the payments to the government, would present notes for redemption to the banks; the government competed with the banks in the accumulation of specie, which ultimately underlay the credit granted to private enterprise. Of course, partisans of hard money rejoiced. But a sympathetic Secretary of the Treasury pointed out that the Independent Treasury might "exercise a fatal control over the currency, the banks, and the trade of the country, and will do so whenever the revenue [of the government] shall greatly exceed the expenditure." But the small scale of government finance, the gold discoveries in California, and the occasional purchase of government securities by the Treasury, restoring specie to circulation, prevented complications before the Civil War.

Varieties of State Banking

By the end of 1791 when the First Bank of the United States obtained its charter, there were 6 banks in the country; in 1811, when it went out of existence, there were 88. In 1816 when the Second Bank was incorporated, there were 246 banks in the nation; twenty years later when Jackson triumphed 713. By 1860 the number was 1,562. Such figures demonstrate the hastening multiplication of banks once the restraining hand of a national institution was removed. They reflect much more: the impact of an expanding economy upon banking and the changes in state banking policy. For in the period between 1783 and 1862, the year of the National Bank Act, the spectacular history of the First and Second Banks was an interlude. State banking policy and banks chartered by the states, year-in and year-out, provided the enduring banking structure.

As the eastern states, the first to do so, laid down the lines of their banking systems in the late eighteenth century, they were still under the spell of monopoly. Each one proceeded to charter a bank of considerable magnitude in its metropolis. The Bank of North America in Philadelphia was the first instance. Within a decade the chief seaport cities had similar institutions. Though explicit grants of monopoly were not made, their titles, Bank of New York, The Massachusetts Bank at Boston, The Bank of Maryland at Baltimore, and the provisions in some instances that they should be the depository of state funds, reveal an implicit assumption of monopoly. The system, however, soon disintegrated. Even in the chief cities, merchants who could not get credit or who hoped to cut in on the profits of the banking business, and groups in the community—small storekeepers, artisans, and mechanics—not served by mercantile banking institutions sought and obtained charters for rival institutions. Small seaports set up a clamor for banks of their own; interior towns voiced a demand for "country banks," as they were later called. By 1810 the idea of state, regional, or even community monopoly was probably well on the way to disintegration.

The idea was soon reborn in the Northwest. In their constitutions Indiana, Illinois, and Missouri explicitly provided for a state monopoly of banking; their legislatures could charter no others. The recent charter of the BUS was the cogent explanation and example for this development. In the thirties legislation gave flesh to these constitutional provisions. Each state had a central bank with branches or offices. Those that confined themselves to short-term paper, as in Illinois and Indiana, survived into the fifties. Then they succumbed to the drive for a free incorporation. In the United States twenty years was apparently the normal life expectancy of monopoly privileges.

Whether the banking privilege was a monopoly or not, it was a nearly universal practice for the state to participate in the banking business by investing in bank stock. In the national field, the charter of the First Bank set the precedent. Apparently its example inspired others, for soon in Massachusetts and Pennsylvania the state governments were insisting that existing banks make room for a government stockholding or that new ones permit it from the beginning. The example spread north and south along the coastline. The chief motive was to participate in a profitable enterprise and through bank dividends reduce the state taxes. Soon it was realized that the privileges were so valuable that banks would pay bonuses to the state for renewals and alterations of old charters or for the granting of new ones. Biddle's incorporation of the Bank of the United States was won from Pennsylvania by a bonus of $4.5 million, temporary loans to the state of $1 million, and a permanent loan of $6 million. Such windfalls could be used for specific or general purposes. To some extent, state investment was also an avenue by which the state could have a voice, through the choice of directors, in the conduct of the corporation.

In the East state representation generally turned out to be ineffective, for in that area the sale of state securities was not essential to getting banks under way. Local or European capital was available, and the states eventually made their investments from state revenues. On the other hand, the banks in the western states could not rely upon private investors nor the states upon sufficient income. State loans were essential. In the monopoly state systems of the Northwest, the states provided at least half of the banks' capital and the state appointed the president and at least half the directors. Though the hope of making money from an investment operated there as in the East, the ambition to promote the welfare of the state and to control the business methods of the bank was just as significant. In the lower South such institutions took the form of property banks or plantation banks. Starting in Louisiana, in the twenties they spread by contagion to the regions where plantations, slaves, and the growing of staples promised new wealth if expansion could only be financed. These banks were mercantile, issuing notes and loaning them on current transactions. They were also mortgage banks. The private stockholders subscribed to them by tendering mortgages on their lands; they thus secured the right to borrow from the bank up to a certain percentage of their mortgaged property. When the bonds based on these borrowings and issued by the banks failed to secure a market, the state was induced to give its own bonds to the bank for sale or guarantee the bank loans. These state securities were generally sold abroad. Some of these institutions were mammoths. The Union Bank of Mississippi, for instance, originally had a capital of $15.5 million, to be secured by the sale of bonds issued by the state. This process of state investment in mixed corporations, partly state and partly private, was but another evidence that banking corporations were business enterprises saturated with a public interest.

The cessation of state investment was gradual and seems to have been frequently dictated by sheer economic necessity. Some states had either ceased the practice or liquidated their holdings before the panic of 1837. That cataclysm had shattering repercussions. To secure funds to meet its obligations, often incurred for other purposes than banking, Pennsylvania sold its bank stocks in 1843. Over the land banks of the South hovered a universal chaos. Planter borrowers could not meet their payments of interest and amortization; the states could not pay on their securities. Of the states which had financed these systems, three met their obligations by an execution against property and heavy taxation. Mississippi elected a different path. At first the state legislature announced that to repudiate its bonds was "a calumny upon the justice, honor, and dignity of the State." But by 1842 state dignity and painful necessity had been reconciled by the discovery that the whole banking transaction had been contrary to the state constitution. A committee of the legislature took high grounds: "The low and grovelling consideration of dollars and cents has nothing to do with the merits of the question. . . . Higher and holier motives than mere pecuniary considerations actuate them. They have determined that they never will submit to an invasion of their Constitution by either foreign or domestic foes." In other but more realistic words, the purchasers of the state's securities would not get back their money. In the fifties, as we have seen, the states in the Northwest likewise abandoned government financing of banks.

Meanwhile a conjunction of events in the thirties set in train a movement destined further to divorce the state governments from banking enterprises. One element in the situation was the ferment of the Jacksonian era with its dread of monopoly of the wrong political coloration, its suspicion of private or "soulless" corporations, and its hostility to banks. The resulting policies, it should be repeated, were not always those that the presidential godfather of the era, Andrew Jackson, would have approved. In any case the current of democratic opinion now demanded that banking become a "business," that it be "free," that it be opened to any individual or association of individuals—for the hated word "corporation" was cunningly avoided—who conformed to certain general stipulations. In addition to this argument for equal rights, the disestablishment of the BUS and the depression of 1837 seemed to justify a series of new banks to redress the absence of currency. Fundamental all along was the desire of Americans to invest in a business presumably profitable like banking and the widespread American craving for capital creation through banking operations. These varied forces came to a head simultaneously in Michigan and New York. The first passed a free banking law in 1837, the latter in 1838. Since Michigan was a frontier community just emerging from territorial status, New York's measure was more important. By 1861 free banking laws had spread to all portions of the Union.

The technical details established by the new system were of importance. Banks were to deposit with a state official public securities, state or national, which might be purchased with a small down payment, and mortgages. They were to receive in return the bank notes whose issue would constitute their circulation. With a shout promoters fell upon these devices. Banks multiplied; note issues soared. Perhaps the West was the more extravagant. According to the free banking plan, if the notes were irredeemable, the state officials could sell the deposited securities. But the bank would be out of business. So whenever they could the bankers set up shops in the wilderness or on an Indian reservation or at some forgotten crossroads—all localities which noteholders bent on redemption would have difficulty in finding. Even if the office were located, it would open only a day or so a week or a few hours a day. Requirements for specie reserves were met by whisking mobile reserves about from institution to institution just in advance of the examiners. This was the heyday of the wildcat bank. Fraud, inexperience, laxness, led to a flood of failures. Later regulatory legislation did something to remedy defects. The idea of free banking persisted. The corporation or association became less the agency of the state and more the weapon of the individual. As one legislator complained of free banking, "It was founded on the fallacious assumption that the business of banking should be conducted solely with a view to private gain and in total disregard of the public interests."

At the same time the fundamentalist wing, the hard-money crowd, were sure that the correct solution was an absolute prohibition of banks. Then there would be neither corporations nor bank notes. As arguments against both, a theoretical preference for a bullion currency was less impressive than actual experience with the bank failures, specie suspensions, and the worthless notes of the late thirties and forties. Where they were powerful enough to carry out their program without compromise, for example in some western states, these purists proceeded in state constitutions to forbid the incorporation of banks. Texas took the lead in 1845; four other states followed suit; Oregon closed the trend in 1857. In spite of the absolutism of these arrangements, private banks or companies chartered for nonbanking purposes carried on a banking business in one fashion or another, and the notes of banks in other jurisidictions poured across the boundaries. In this respect, as in others, prohibition did not prohibit.

Banking Regulation

Only incidentally has this description of the form of the banking system and of the direct participation of the state in it dealt with banking regulation. Except where solons cleaned the slate by dispensing with banking altogether, the former process was continuous and unquestioned as to right. Individual charters and general legislation were alike the means of its exercise. As in the case of all corporations, legislative ingenuity coped as best it might with qualifications of bank officers, details of capitalization, and the powers and duties of stockholders. There were limitations on interest rates and directives to banks run on mercantile principles that they must make a portion of their loans to farmers. But a primary concern in every jurisdiction was how to make banks safe or, in a narrower sense, how to assure their ability to meet their obligations to depositors and noteholders. Conceivably merchants, brokers, and other men of wealth might through their positions be well enough informed to avoid such losses; the worker, artisan, and farmer had neither the opportunity of forming a judgment of the worth of the bank notes he received for wages or produce nor the independent position enabling him to refuse the unsound ones. Every bank suspension, it was universally observed, bore with peculiar hardship upon the poor and industrious classes. Here and there, in partial and diffident fashion, legislation frowned upon "accommodation" paper or tried to arrive at some safe ratio between the amount of circulation and of the capital which was to provide the specie reserve.

In 1829 New York, again a banking pioneer, established a safety fund system by which all the banks became jointly liable for the debts of an insolvent one. By installments each was to pay into a common bank fund 3 percent of its capital; this accumulation was a sort of joint insurance. By the same act New York inaugurated a thorough and regular inspection of the banks by a Board of Bank Commissioners. In this state as elsewhere there had been previously requirements for reports and occasions for examination. New York introduced system and expertness. This was the greater contribution of the act of 1829, for the safety fund neither worked satisfactorily nor inspired wide imitation. Bank commissioners became commonplace. Somewhat more slowly, a few states realized the necessity of providing in the banks a specie reserve for notes and deposits, even though such requirements hampered the expansion of the currency for which so many Americans thirsted. Chastened by the banking collapse of the late thirties, Louisiana in 1842 required that the cash liabilities of its banks "be represented by one-third of the amount of such responsibilities in specie and at least two-thirds in satisfactory paper, payable in full at maturity and within ninety days." Since New Orleans was its metropolis, the state was in part a commercial one and could undertake this experiment. Later, particularly after the closings and losses in the panic of 1857, a few other states groped toward similar solutions.

Voluntary Banking Systems

When Congress in 1846 finally decided to build a wall between bank and national government, a national banking system by statute was, of course, impossible. No state, whatever it might do for itself, could erect a national substitute, and common action between all states was currently out of the question. Nonetheless, commercial transactions were on a regional and national basis. Agricultural materials moved toward the populous centers of the East and of Europe. Manufactured articles were in turn purchased there and shipped back. Inevitably these interchanges created at Boston, New York, Philadelphia, Baltimore, and New Orleans—to mention no others—a series of trading centers. Buyers and sellers, borrowers and lenders, met there. Their banks and other financial institutions had great areas tributary to them. Consequently, the commercial habits and practices of numberless individuals and institutions built, if not a national, at least regional banking systems. These were *de facto* rather than *de jure*.

New England had such a system. Early in the nineteenth century Boston had a dual system of paper currency. The city banks furnished notes which circulated at par because they could be redeemed easily; the country banks furnished "foreign" money which circulated at a discount because it could not. The city banks were distressed because their own note issues were restricted by this competition; the Boston merchants were angered because they had to shoulder the discounts on the "foreign" money they secured in the course of trade. By 1824, after a considerable period of trial and error, the Suffolk Bank emerged as a redemption agency for most New England bank notes. If any bank kept with the

Suffolk a permanent fixed deposit and a redemption fund, the Suffolk would not call upon its members to redeem their notes in specie, but would accept notes of any other sound New England bank. If any bank would not consent to this arrangement, its notes were presented regularly and insistently for redemption. So successful was this clearinghouse arrangement that by 1857 five hundred banks were members of the system and New England enjoyed a bank-note currency which, however various its origins, circulated everywhere at a common value. So profitable was the procedure for the Suffolk Bank that in the late fifties a rival was established. The Civil War and national banking legislation made both banks unnecessary.

In New York strenuous efforts, both voluntary and legislative, never achieved the elimination of discounts on the notes of country banks, even those within New York State. Nevertheless, since New York City became the great commercial emporium of the nation, there was a steady flow of money toward it and the resulting rate of domestic exchange was usually in its favor. Outside banks could make profits by selling exchange upon New York; in order to follow this practice they kept balances in the New York banks. Thus the funds flowed into the city's banks from banks in New York and from neighboring states, from institutions in the West and in the South. State legislators, often grumbling, authorized these balances, if they were in cash, to be counted as part of the reserve of the local banks. In 1860 bankers' balances in New York were set at $25 million, heavily concentrated in a few city banks. Even before the Civil War the latter were in the habit of putting these out at loans on a demand basis, largely upon security collateral.

These arrangements joined with others to reveal the triumph of certain conceptions in the field of government finance and banking. In view of the many jurisdictions and institutions entrusted with policy and act, that triumph could be neither uniform nor clear-cut. Ideas discarded in one place were picked up in another; trends in one direction were countered elsewhere by trends in another. On the whole, however, the idea of monopoly gave way to that of competition. Governmental enterprise gave way to the enterprise of individuals. The state regulated, but it ceased to participate.

The Phases
of Industrial Production

The Report on Manufactures

Hamilton was not a modern, but in his policies he certainly relied upon methods which could be so described. His first step in shaping policy was a "study." Thus at the end of the 1780's he undertook, partly by a questionnaire device, to survey the state of industry in the United States. Since he had a small bureaucracy in the Department of the Treasury, he directed it to conduct inquiries and to channel the information to him; his personal acquaintance with manufacturers in the Middle Atlantic states and elsewhere gave him additional knowledge about the industrial situation in that region. The facts thus collected underlay his famous Report on Manufactures, which he communicated to the House of Representatives in 1791.

With an imprecision which would alienate modern statisticians, he itemized seventeen areas, ranging from leather goods to gunpowder, in which industrial advance had already been marked and where potentialities were gratifying. Though his definitions were not always exact and his distribution of examples rather haphazard, he enumerated three systems of production. One was manufacturing "in a household way": its end products were usually textiles of wool, cotton, and linen, or mixtures thereof: "It is computed in a number of districts that two-thirds, three-fourths, and even four-fifths of all the clothing of the inhabitants are made by themselves." A second type was the manufacture of other goods "carried on as a regular trade," that is by artisans or "artists," some of whom were itinerant, while most worked in their own shops. Thirdly, he noted, many other articles, though "strictly speaking manufactures . . . are immediately connected with husbandry," such as flour, pot and pearl ashes, and naval stores. If Americans themselves did not

213

add value to their raw materials through their own enterprise and skill, they could and did obtain the articles through importation. Such articles were repeatedly characterized as "finery," and the process of importation as "extravagance."

Hamilton's estimate of the "maturity" of American enterprise was generally sanguine; nonetheless, its achievements he regarded as inadequate. A "further extension" was necessary "for national independence and safety." The United States must be "independent [of] foreign nations for military and other essential supplies." Somewhat larger ends were also at stake. The Americans should enjoy "the opulence to which their political and natural advantages authorize them to aspire." Hamilton in his report on the National Bank had already given the same idea somewhat sharper verbal definition with the phrase "national wealth." This concept, vaguely stated and never measured, was not mere political "pie in the sky." Hamilton had before him, as in the case of the Bank and the debt, the pattern of what England had accomplished.

The Industrial Revolution in England

The Industrial Revolution was not an institution like the Bank or the debt, but an event as inescapable in a college course as Aristotle or the amoeba. Unhappily, while the last two are definable, the Industrial Revolution is so nebulous that many economic historians have denied its existence. In spite of their reservations, it is clear that during the second half of the eighteenth century in England a series of mechanical inventions altered methods of production. In the making of textiles these machines reformed the fundamental operations of spinning yarn by using jennies, water frames, or mules, and were weaving yarn into cloth on power looms. Cottons rather than woolens was the more innovating industry. Coke had replaced charcoal in the smelting of iron, and a puddling and rolling process worked the carbon out of these cast-iron pigs, turning them into the less brittle wrought iron. Inventors perfected the steam engine and this new device pumped water out of mines, ran machinery in factories, and eventually moved steamboats and steam trains. It is also clear that by the 1830's observers of the contemporary scene were definitely conscious that an important transformation had taken place.

Though more is gained than lost by accepting the conventional idea that the Industrial Revolution consisted of the changes in production wrought in the seventy years from 1760 to 1830, reservations must be made. In the first place, the swiftness and extensiveness of the transformation in industry seems revolutionary only when this period is contrasted with the years preceding it. The heightened tempo of industrial change begun in the eighteenth century had continued and increased. In the second place, the ideas underlying the inventions can easily be traced back to an earlier period, and the factory and even capitalism predated 1760. But every period has to have its antecedents. Hamilton in his report did not extend his example of British industrialization back to the scientific explosion generated by the ideas of Francis Bacon or Isaac Newton, nor to the "industrial revolution" between 1540 and 1640 in England and elsewhere. On the contrary he was thinking specifically "of the cotton-mill, invented in England, within the last twenty years."

Another example of Hamilton's genius as a statesman was his recognition that a practical example was more likely than the words of a state paper to persuade Americans of the practicality of extending the industrialization of the country. Two weeks before Hamilton submitted his report to Congress, the legislature of New Jersey had incorporated "The Society for Establishing Useful Manufactures," more conveniently known then as the "SUM." With a projected capital of $1 million the concern proposed to manufacture an array of products from paper to brass wire. Whoever originated the society, Hamilton ardently sponsored it. A large share of the capital, $100,000 out of $500,000, was subscribed; a mill site was purchased by the falls of the Passaic; a town, now Paterson, was laid out; and factories with machinery were built. Nonetheless, the SUM failed because it was an attempt to tilt against the fundamental economic conditions of a new and an agricultural nation. Labor of a sort was secured from immigrants and women and children, but the first were often impostors or ignoramuses. Wages were higher than those paid by foreign employers. The subscribers of capital had neither the power to stay through times of adversity nor the knowledge of how to direct such a business; nor could they find engineering talent to construct so vast an enterprise, or managerial talent to run it. In a large sense, an observation of an anonymous English writer penned years before applied to this effort:

> But it is not enough that a few, or even a greater number of people, understand manufactures; the spirit of manufacturing must become the general spirit of the nation, and be incorporated, as it were, into their very essence. Knowledge may be soon acquired; but it requires a long time before the personal, and still longer time before national, habits are formed.

The Paterson experiment represented a reversal of hopes. It was a premature enterprise. Hamilton in his report had foreseen the handicaps upon the growth of American manufacturing and had speculated upon the means to overcome them. Actually, problems of markets, technology, government aid, the supply of capital and of workers, all intermingled to frustrate the Paterson experiment. It is impossible to isolate a single cause for the SUM's failure.

Technology

Nonetheless, through the difficulties of the first manufacturers —as in the SUM—there ran a common tone: the machines wouldn't work and management couldn't find anyone to provide remedies or guidance. In other words, the Industrial Revolution rested upon a technological base and upon know-how, both of which were lacking in this country. The answer, superficially easy, was to import these requisites from abroad, and Hamilton had commended this solution. The English had anticipated such a threat. In 1781 Parliament extended the laws of 1774 which imposed a penalty of £200 and twelve years imprisonment for exporting machinery used in textile manufacturing. In 1782 an additional act imposed a penalty for enticing out of Great Britain men with knowledge of the new processes of manufacture. These prohibitions were actually inoperative. For instance, Samuel Slater, later hailed as the "Father of the Cotton Manufacture of America," came to this country in 1789, evading the English laws against the emigration of artisans.

Slater had been born in England in 1768 and had served an apprenticeship which acquainted him with the improved methods of spinning cotton. He had an exceptional knowledge of cotton mills and the machines in them. His attention was directed toward the possibility of transferring the new methods to America by the announcement of premiums offered by societies or states in America for the introduction or construction of the new cotton machinery. Slater sailed secretly for the United States in 1789. Upon his arrival in New York he obtained employment in a small cotton enterprise, but was dissatisfied. He soon learned that Moses Brown of the great Providence trading family was interested in perfecting power spinning "so as to be useful to the country." Slater—this "young man," as Brown dubbed him—made a business arrangement with Brown and came to Providence. For nearly a year he was engaged in perfecting the machinery and getting it into working order. The previous machines he discarded as impossible to improve, and in their place he built from memory two carding machines and a water frame of twenty-four spindles, with some other equipment. He had some difficulty in constructing workable machines from his models. This equipment was set up in a fulling mill at Pawtucket where there was waterpower. By 1791 he had hired the small labor force that was necessary and had begun the successful spinning of cotton yarn upon the water frame. This achievement was announced in an advertisement in the Providence *Gazette:*

Cotton Manufactory
To Be Sold By
Almy and Brown
At their Store . . . A Variety of Cotton Goods,

manufactured in this Town, among which are . . . Cotton Yarn of various Sizes, spun by Water, suitable for Warps or Stockings, superior in Quality to any spun by Hand, or upon Jennies. Those who are engaged in manufacturing Cotton, either in Factories or in Families, are invited to make Trial of its Quality, and those who wish to encourage the Manufactures of their Country, to lend their Aid to establish in it this useful Business, by wearing Cloth of its own Manufacture. . . .

N.B. Cotton, and Cotton and Linen Goods, of all Kinds, are dyed and finished at their Dye House, by an experienced Workman from Europe.

The first Slater mill proved to be one nursery of the American cotton industry. The members of the original partnership, Almy, Brown, and Slater, did not retain a permanent alliance. But Browns and Slaters and their relatives by descent or marriage built new mills in Rhode Island and Massachusetts near Providence. The employees of the Slater mill went out to aid in the founding of other enterprises patterned upon it as far away as upper New York State. Though he was an innovator and a carrier of innovations, Slater had limitations. His ideas of a labor force were socially regressive. In terms of business, he rejected the power loom. Spinning was his specialty.

Even ideas about machinery are not respecters of national origin. Americanization of the power loom was in large measure the work of an American, Francis Cabot Lowell, a Harvard graduate and one-time merchant. Traveling in Great Britain in 1811, he stood for hours before the machines in the Lancashire cotton mills and asked operatives a thousand questions. When he returned to this country he pooled his observations with the practical talents of a machinist, Paul Moody. By 1814 they had perfected the power loom. One of their business colleagues later recalled "the state of admiration and satisfaction with which we sat by the hour, watching the beautiful movement of this new and wonderful machine, destined as it evidently was to change the character of the textile industry." Utilizing the loom and other machines, these New Englanders built at the waterpowers along the Merrimack and other rivers a north-of-Boston cotton industry quite different from that in Rhode Island. Operations were integrated in large-scale establishments; the labor force employed was different.

The migration of other trained workers continued to be of critical moment for many other American industries. Four years after Slater, two brothers, the Scholfields, brought to this country from Yorkshire a knowledge of a power-driven carder which performed some of the first steps in cleaning and compacting wool fibers. The introduction of this machine was in fact analogous to the introduction of spinning machinery for cottons.

As all students of ancient cultures know, the metal industries are so fundamental as to provide the very name, if not the dates, for those cultural periods. In England the basic iron industry had moved from charcoal to coke as a fuel for smelting. Pig iron smelted from coke could be used successfully in castings; but it was still too brittle for shapes which had to withstand certain strains. Here the English had invented puddling and rolling. The puddler stirred the hot iron, softened by heat from fuel consumed in an adjacent compartment; the iron, removed from the furnace, was then rolled between revolving grooved rollers, which squeezed out impurities and shaped the metal. None of these improved methods had been brought to the United States. In 1840, however, the Lehigh Coal and Navigation Company signed a contract with David Thomas, a Welsh artisan, to come to this country and introduce improved methods of smelting. He used anthracite, "natural coke," as a fuel and melted down the furnace charge of anthracite and iron ore with a blast of air heated by the furnace and blown under a higher air pressure. Larger furnaces and lower fuel costs per ton of pig iron effected economies. Such smelting establishments appeared in Pennsylvania east of the mountains and adjacent to the anthracite deposits and waterpowers. Thomas ultimately became the first president of the American Institute of Mining Engineers and another figure in the procession of foreign "fathers" of American industries. Meanwhile, knowledge of the British practice of puddling and rolling had come to this country and had been installed in ironworks throughout Pennsylvania; the puddling furnaces could use coke from bituminous coal since, though it contained sulphur, it did not come in contact with the ore. Just before the Civil War an American, John Fritz, substituted for the two-high rollers the three-high rolling machine, through which the metal passed back and forth without reversing the rollers. Fritz in turn became a president of the American Institute of Mining Engineers; but he was never the "father" of anything.

The derivation of technology from England or elsewhere was doubtless sensible and necessary, as Hamilton recognized, but some Americans resented this dependence. In 1810 the brother of Francis Cabot Lowell wrote him, "We have invented more useful machines within twenty years than have been invented in all Europe." He did not specify what inventions he had in mind. Perhaps he was drawing comfort from the American progress in the reproductive metal industries.

In the manufacture of firearms Americans made their greatest contribution in industrial practice. A gun was not a single piece of metal; it was an assembly of pieces. Gunsmiths or armorers took the parts, which had generally been cast, shaped and finished them with hand files, and then fitted them together. This method of making guns was inefficient in the first place; and it made their repair an individual item. The idea of applying machinery to the manufacture of identical, and hence interchangeable, gun parts had certainly been conceived in France in the late eighteenth century. How widely or well these precedents were known in America is uncertain. But the warlike posture between France and the United States in the 1790's made the rapid production of muskets essential. The national armory at Springfield, Massachusetts, was put to work, and contracts were let to private contractors. The most famous of the latter was Eli Whitney, at loose ends from his failure to make a business gain from his cotton gin and desperately in need of credit. He had no factory, no armorers, and no experience in making guns. In 1798 he contracted to deliver 10,000 muskets which he intended to manufacture on a "new principle." In the following year Simeon North, a farmer turned scythe and pistol maker, received a government contract for pistols. Whitney slowly installed his system at a village outside New Haven. North manufactured his pistols at Berlin and later also at Middletown. The two experimenters thus worked within a few miles of each other.

Although Whitney described his methods as unique, it was apparently other private armsmakers, for example, the Colt Works at Hartford, and the government arsenals which during and after the national emergency of the nineties made the greater contributions to what became known as "the American System" of manufacture. Machines, run by comparatively unskilled workers, made the various parts of the gun with such precision that they could be assembled into a workable finished product. Here the principles of the division of labor into specialized tasks and the use of machines to make interchangeable parts capable of assembly into finished products converged to create a system which filled representatives of the industrialized European nations with admiration and envy.

The system was then applied to other articles. For example, Chauncey Jerome thus built his cheap clock with brass works. In 1848 another American, A. E. Dennison, defying the tradition of centuries of artisan production, established the American Watch Company at Waltham, Massachusetts, and attempted the manufacture of watches by machinery. He was eventually successful. The sewing machine, patented in 1846, was produced within a few years by the same American methods. The gun industry through the first half of the nineteenth century had remained the greatest stimulus to the invention and perfection of high-speed, largely automatic machines: lathes which could form irregular shapes; the turret lathe, which could perform upon a piece of metal a succession of boring, cutting, and other tasks; and the "universal milling machines," which could cut grooves or gears. After 1850 the sewing machine industry was the one which raised mechanical problems and demanded answers. The versatility and originality of the power tools of the machine tool industry formed a reservoir of talent and experience from which manufacturers of a host of other products—hardware, tools, agricultural implements, and the like—could draw solutions for their operational problems.

The sources of technological advance and invention are in large measure a mystery. Their history in America reveals that higher learning —Francis Cabot Lowell was a graduate of Harvard, and Eli Whitney of Yale—was no barrier to invention; that it was a prerequisite is equally uncertain. Slightly educated workers, like Samuel Colt and John Fritz, made immense contributions. English merchants sent here in the fifties to observe American industry commented, "Every workman seems to be continually devising some new thing to assist him in his work." In part such up-to-dateness was feasible because invention was not a spectacular breakthrough; rather as a "package of inventions," it consisted of the removal of bottlenecks and imbalances in production or the introduction of small modifications. An agricultural background in which individual and ingenious farmers sought to ease their labors by improvements, and the ubiquity, at least in the North and the West, of public common schools assured at least literacy and perhaps some acquaintance with general scientific principles. These social factors were as likely as economic considerations to explain the national talent for tinkering and devising.

Markets

Both agriculture and manufacturing responded to the growth of the market. This theme has been often repeated, though the definition of the market has often varied. Hamilton thought of the market as a geographical area; at least that seems the upshot of his endorsement of internal improvements and of what England had accomplished in this respect. In the United States the decade 1850–1860 brought to a peak the market operations appropriate to a pioneering nation. Merchants in the South and in the West depended for their purchases upon wholesale markets in the great cities of the Atlantic coast: first Philadelphia and Baltimore, later New York. Coastal transportation and improved land transport to the head of the Ohio River explained the early success of the first two cities; its favorable position as an importer, and the Erie Canal and the Great Lakes, coming a little later, cemented New York's preeminence. In any case, western and southern retailers journeyed like migratory birds once a year to northern entrepôts. The goods they bought there, whether imports or domestics, were supposed to be superior to those purchased nearer home—at least they were fashionable and metropolitan. They were also cheaper, for they were sold under fiercely competitive conditions, and the eastern cities had the resources and institutions to give the necessary long credits. With the ubiquity of railroads just before the Civil War, this pattern of buying broke down. Goods could be ordered and shipped at any time and "drummers," salesmen from the eastern wholesalers, now moved west and south to sell to retailers by sample and display.

But the market cannot be comprehended in terms of square miles or even in terms of population. It was a political creation. On this score the Federal Constitution was exceptionally prolix. To Congress it gave the power to regulate foreign commerce and domestic commerce. All duties were to be "uniform" within the United States. "No State shall lay any Imposts or Duties on Imports or Exports" or any "Duty of Tonnage." Taxes levied by the states on commerce for sanitary and other police purposes were circumscribed. These provisions came before the Supreme Court in various cases. In the twenties Justice Marshall, particularly in Gibbons *v.* Ogden, staked out a whole area for Federal regulation. Bickering over whether the national government's powers were exclusive and paramount, and over the definition of "regulate" did not, however, entirely die away.

Markets are also a matter of the consumer's taste, and taste in turn depends upon variables of need, preference, costs, and custom. By and large the American purchasers, or large numbers of them, were content or compelled by circumstances to buy standardized goods and were not too fussy about refinements, style, and finish. These were helpful preconditions to industries starting under difficulties. The American railroads wanted rails at a low cost; the result, as Abram Hewitt, native ironmaster, observed was that "The vilest trash which could be dignified by the name of iron went universally by the name of the American rail." In woolens Americans who could afford the best imported their broadcloths from Great Britain; others bought "cassimere," a not so highly finished fabric, which could be turned out with fancy designs in large quantities on the power loom. Lower and coarser still were the varieties designated "Negro cloths." The same name was applied to coaser cottons sent to the slave market of the South. A dealer in Richmond wrote the Lawrences, "Such as you color for this market for the future let them be large figures and lively colors as they are worn only by the mulattoes and blacks and they are fond of anything that is dashing." Rarely were the consuming expectations of slaves consulted. Their work shoes were brogans, more crudely and never custom-made. The Massachusetts shoe industry, working toward the centralization of shoe-making in a factory with a minimum of machinery, responded to this stimulus.

Time after time the West, the land of frontiers, furrows, and hard work, created a mass market which eastern industry expanded to supply. Gold and silver seekers, for instance, did not have the time or chance to be fussy about shoes or have them made to order. They wanted a sturdy work boot. "Californians" had to be ready in relatively large shipments to meet sailing dates. More and more Massachusetts shoemakers accordingly concentrated their workers in central shops, divided the tasks, and adopted the sewing machine, perfected for shoes in the early fifties. The Texas Rangers and the Mexican War, furnishing an unexpected market for the six-shooter, rescued Samuel Colt, its inventor, from oblivion and made him a millionaire. Colt's revolver was made at the works of Eli Whitney. The gold diggers of California required shovels; and the Ames family of southeastern Massachusetts expanded the factory for making their light shovels and thus increased profits into a fortune large enough to outlast many misadventures. The founder of the Ames concern, incidentally, had received his training at the Springfield armory.

Most of these enterprises advanced because of the invention or improvement of the machine tools which fashioned and shaped metal. In a broad sense, the category of machine tools should include foundries, which gave a form to metal by pouring fluid into moulds, and forges, where metal was shaped under a hammer. But these processes produced only intermediate shapes. Finished products were another matter. The manufacture of screws involved a spiral thread and a slot for the screwdriver; other metal pieces had to be bent and ground to be fitted together. Still others had to have holes drilled in them. These operations had to be measured with precision, and the manufacture of such measuring implements was a prerequisite. Originally, as in the cotton industry, those who established and equipped a factory had an auxiliary room or plant to manufacture the machinery. As they accumulated machines and the knowledge of how to use them, these machine shops began making machines for different or outside uses. The shops attached to cotton mills, for instance, often became the largest producers of locomotives. Armories, whether public or private, which had to shape the smaller parts of a gun preliminary to its assembly, became centers from which were dispersed power lathes, which could turn out irregular shapes or perform many operations upon the material without stopping the machine and repositioning the work, or universal milling machines, which could accomplish spiral-milling operations and cut gears. The presence in New England of men who invented these machines scattered machine shops along the waterpowers throughout the region before the Civil War. Visitors from Great Britain, really the center of the machine-making profession at that time, were impressed by the imagination and skill with which the American machine tool industry devised machines for single, specialized operations and put them to work.

Capital and Management

Machines, materials, and mills—to mention no other items— required money. Hamilton in his Report on Manufactures and in his

reports on other subjects therefore paid considerable attention to the
capital requirements of industry. The difficulties were genuine; manufacturing, only one temptation to investment, had to compete for funds
with land, government securities, and internal improvements. As usual,
Hamilton was sure that it could. Foreign capital would flow into this
country's industrial enterprises. The monetization of the public debt,
"the operation of public funds as capital"—a favorite theme—would provide a means other than cash for investment; the establishment of the
National Bank and other banks would facilitate by creating credit "an
absolute increase of capital"; some promising industries in his inventory
did not require "large capitals."

As things turned out, of course, unexpected occurrences upset some
anticipations and fulfilled others. Investments in American industry from
abroad did not amount to much. But, on the other hand, the catastrophic
interruption of international trade during the Embargo and the War of
1812 left American merchants with genuinely large fortunes which they
could no longer invest in commerce. Seeking other outlets they turned to
industry. Francis Cabot Lowell and his colleagues exemplified this
significant development. The par value of shares in their corporations
was commonly $1,000. More rudimentary than corporations were partner-
ship arrangements to which the partners might subscribe in kind, one
partner might contribute land, another waterpower, another skill, and
still another labor. In more sophisticated and impersonal forms the
partnership persisted in business throughout the nineteenth century. In
that century's first half, nonetheless, the corporation, as it had in banking and transportation, finally made its way into manufacturing. The
chartered corporation was a flexible and systematic way of merging the
savings of the many into a common fund for enterprise. Consequently
manufacturing and mining corporations constituted after 1840 in most
eastern states the largest group of enterprises granted charters. There was
plenty of opposition to charter policy. The general arguments against
all corporations, that they were special privileges and tended toward
monopoly, were repeated on this occasion. In addition, opponents asserted
that manufacturing corporations were opposed to "individual enterprise,"
identified in this instance with simpler forms of ownership and organization. Individual enterprise was both more democratic and more efficient.
"No company can prosper that is exposed to the competition of individuals upon a *perfect* footing of equality. The employment of agents
and the natural carelessness of men who perform a duty with no feeling
of direct interest are such drawbacks upon profits as must in such cases
necessarily ruin a corporation."

On the other hand, legislators nearly everywhere exhibited toward
manufacturing corporations a more cordial attitude than to those in
banking and transportation. After all, the first seemed more local in

character, less menacing in magnitude, and by their very number more likely to be rivals than monopolies. These considerations, coupled with the competitive promotion of manufacturing within their borders, early induced many states to pass acts of general incorporation for manufacturing enterprises. New York led the way in 1811; New Jersey, Connecticut, and Massachusetts, among the important industrial states, followed suit before 1851. Though some of these measures were restrictive and the process of special chartering continued, a mere conformity with the provisions of a general incorporation act usually removed the stigma of favoritism and aided the formation of corporations. As manufacturing corporations, often along with others, picked up the advantages of greater permanence and of a liability for the debts of the enterprise limited to the individual stockholder's investment in it—a privilege conferred by Massachusetts legislation, for instance, in 1830—and as the amount of capital to launch an industrial enterprise grew, the corporation became increasingly popular—at least among incorporators. They were even emboldened to claim for their concerns a private character as distinguished from corporations in banking and transportation. The two last had a slightly public air; in their affairs the intervention of the state might be justified. Manufacturing corporations were "private" corporations and, inferentially, free from regulation and control. They could manage themselves.

For the question of capital raised the question of management. Those who provided the money should manage the enterprise. This was axiomatic whether investors had been farmers, artisans, or merchants. On the whole, it was fortunate the latter played a large role. Like other investors they were keen to see that their money was efficiently and prudentially used; unlike most other investors, they had experience in business affairs and business connections and probably knew more than most men about the way to profit. One of the superiorities of the partnership, it was felt, was the tighter amalgamation of the investing and managing functions, tighter than in corporations, which tended to separate them from each other or to scatter them among the heedless and ignorant many. The limited liability of the corporate stockholder made him less responsible and energetic than when he had been liable for the whole debt of the enterprise.

On the whole, American manufacturing found fewer difficulties in assembling capital than in matters of technology and markets. Manufacturing tapped directly the savings of individuals, primarily Americans; it tapped indirectly and increasingly the accumulations of institutions, one of which was the savings bank. The pattern and purpose of this type of bank came from abroad in the first years of the nineteenth century. Philanthropy was the motive for American imitation. Those with small incomes, the thrifty and the poor, should have a place to deposit money where it would earn interest. In 1860 in the United States there were 278 savings banks, whose deposits were nearly $150 million. Since safety was a primary objective for small investors, state statutes generally limited the investment of the assets of savings banks to government securities and mortgages on land and gave general priority to bonds over stocks. Gradually practice and legislation grew freer on these matters. While investments in industries became permissible, they were frequently limited to enterprises in the same state as the bank. As firms grew older and enjoyed business successes, they relied for growth capital less upon the sale of stock and more upon long loans—often for seven years or so— from banks and also upon the reinvestment of their own earnings. Research at the present moment has not been extensive enough to state with precision the relative percentages of these contributions.

The Role of Government

In certain instances, notably in arms production, the government played a decisive role. It furnished a large market for stands of arms, and its policy of advancing money or credit provided the capital resources for enterprises, like those of Eli Whitney, to get under way. Finally it had established its own armories at Springfield and, less importantly, at Harpers Ferry. While Hamilton was silent on some of these specific interventions, he moderately endorsed the government arsenals, "As a general rule, manufactories on the immediate account of government are to be avoided," . . . but there seemed to be "an improvidence in leaving the essential implements of national defence to the casual speculations of individual adventure."

Nonetheless, in his many reports Hamilton recommended various government policies that set a framework for industrial growth. The national policies towards banks, internal improvements, and immigration could speed industrialization; that he omitted a discussion of corporation law and certain other factors was perhaps due to the fact that power to act in these areas lay with the states. That the very existence of government aided industry probably seemed to him too banal for reassertion. He was, however, fertile with specific suggestions "for public encouragement": bounties for the production of selected articles; premiums for the recruitment of skilled artists; the importation of plans and machinery; and, finally, an increase in the existing tariff on nails, liquor, cotton and woolen fabrics, and glass, to mention no others. The tariff would truly protect infant industries, like the "precious embryo" of a woolen factory at Hartford, against the competition of foreign-made goods. A late high priest of Republican doctrine, who also edited Hamilton's papers, hailed these proposals as laying "the foundation of the protection policy in the

United States." Since Hamilton argued his case in "plain, business terms," it was very wholesome reading "and cleared the mind from cant." The commentator had to grant that it lacked uniformity and steadiness "in application."

The first tariff act, that of 1789, many of whose duties Hamilton had worked to raise, was a necessary means of gathering revenue for the government; as a means of protecting industry it fell short. It made little difference. The Napoleonic wars soon introduced a measure of actual protection which no legislator would have dared propose or vote for. Then between 1815 and 1833—in the latter year a measure effected a progressive reduction of duties—the protective system secured its greatest popular support and most extreme legislative embodiment. The harsh experience when America was cut off from European production during the war years gave a new cogency to the argument for self-sufficiency; a dreaded flood of cheap imports after the War of 1812 sharpened the genuine and verbal alarm of American manufacturers; and a collapse of agricultural prices convinced American farmers that they must consent to a tariff in order to develop a home market as a substitute for those lost with peace, first in Europe and later in South America. Higher duties, in fact, have been a common American response to depression and anxiety. The decade of the twenties was such a period. It was then that Daniel Webster, Congressman from Massachusetts, who had hitherto advocated the unencumbered trade he thought his mercantile constituents wanted, became a convert to protection and the spokesman for manufacturers. It was then that Henry Clay from Kentucky popularized in a single philosophy—the "American System"—the idea of the home market created by industrial growth; protection for certain agricultural products, for instance, wool and hemp; and the expenditure of the funds thus secured for internal improvement. In the thirties the pressure of Jacksonian ideology and its followers compelled a retreat from high protection. Although the reductions planned by the Tariff Act of 1833 were temporarily reversed by a measure in 1842, the Walker Tariff Act, christened for the Secretary of the Treasury, a professed disciple of free trade, four years later introduced eleven years of moderate protection. The tariff of 1857 extended this period until the eve of the Civil War.

The purposes voiced in measure, debate, and argument were not always the cool calculations of economic loss or gain. Of one tariff, passed in the ultraprotective era, a Virginian representative said quite justly, "The bill referred to manufactures of no sort or kind, except the manufacture of a President of the United States." Nearly every enactment marred the purity of theoretical design as it compromised the interests of cotton growers or merchant-importers, both hostile to protection, with those of assorted industrialists. Nevertheless, beneath these specific and sometimes superficial stresses, tariff legislation served continuing purposes. It was a source of revenue. Indeed, over the long span from 1789 to 1860 imports furnished the largest share of the government receipts, with the single exception of 1836 when returns from land sales exceeded them. It was a means of protection to industry, though most students of the question admit that the phenomenal growth of American manufacturing in those years was in larger measure due to other causes. Still, from time to time, for some goods the solicitude of tariffmakers gave a real stimulus to production. Perhaps its general effect was psychological. Hamilton bewailed the timidity in trying new ways of doing things, the fear of failure, the want of experience as handicaps to establishing American industry. A tariff, demonstrating the government was on the side of experiment, gave reassurance and hope.

When Came the Brave New World?

An enumeration of individual industries or of the factors operative in general industrial advance has a disadvantage. While it may map the affluent streams, it neglects the broad river into which they all flowed and to which they all contributed. Ideally, "quantitative data and statistical analysis" should accomplish this second task. Actually data of this sort for the years before 1860 or a little earlier are spotty or unauthoritative. The historian tends therefore to turn to "qualitatively identified events" to set the time, the course, and the extent of industrial change. Hamilton's Report in 1791 was stimulating; it foresaw the time when American industry would provide the prosperity, or "opulence," enjoyed in the enterprising nations of western Europe, but it could neither provide nor guarantee arrival at that destination. Change was neither neat nor uniform. In America "the shift away from the production of goods in household to those made in shop or factory was uneven in time and in place, in the country as a whole the transfer was rather generally completed before the close of the third decade of the nineteenth century." In instances, the advance was sudden and spectacular. In 1820 the number of spindles, the conventional measure of capacity in cotton factories, had been a little less than 200,000; in 1831 it was 1,246,703. The percentage increase was 652.3. Capital employed in industry in a rough way was $50 million in 1820 and $1.8 billion in 1860. The industrialization of the country was indirectly mirrored in the behavior of prices. As long as production was centered in localities or neighborhoods a wide discrepancy between the price indexes in different markets was apt to result; a degree of harmony of these indexes would attest the nationalization of the market. For five urban centers wholesale price indexes show a wide discrepancy before 1850 and "a sharp increase in the measure of harmony in the succeeding decades." The tendencies which these various examples show should not imply that an even more marked industrial growth did not follow the Civil War, or that any of these periods had a growth which was automatic or inevitable.

Historical scholars differ over the decades in which the industrial pace picked up a breath-taking speed. Some have gone back to the rather old-fashioned date of 1807. Certainly, contemporary observers who had once believed the country should remain an agricultural nation had noticed a change after the War of 1812 and had begun to shift their philosophical position. Jefferson, once a stalwart agrarian, noted in a letter in 1816, "Within the thirty years which have since elapsed [from my earlier statements], how are circumstances changed!" He concluded, "We must now place the manufacturer by the side of the agriculturist." The next year along with Adams and Madison he accepted honorary membership in the American Society for the Encouragement of Domestic Manufactures. War and industrial growth both put a peremptory premium on adjustment to the practical.

The Labor Market, Labor Conditions, Grievances

Recruiting a Labor Force

The new factories required workers. Hamilton in his Report on Manufactures, while admitting their scarcity, had canvassed with characteristic hopefulness, the sources of supply. Skilled workers could be recruited through immigration, for the material and religious advantages of the United States would tempt "foreign artists" to this country. In a measure these anticipations were realized, for there was a considerable emigration of artisans from Great Britain and Ireland. Some of them were scamps, who sold a knowledge and skill they did not have; others, like Slater and the Scholfields, were the agents by whom industries were transferred to the United States. Such immigrants, however, did not furnish the unskilled labor force which ran the new machines. They were the aristocrats of labor, the foremen or overseers or even the manufacturers. From the twenties more ordinary immigrants became numerically important parts of the industrial army. Their invasion alarmed the native worker, and the native-American movement of the fifties capitalized on the competition of the European laborer, with his alleged lower standards of living and his necessitous condition, to fan into flame an anti-foreign campaign. The papers of this party and those of the workingmen attacked the capitalist who imported cheap labor in order to pay lower wages or to break strikes, and called for legislation which would protect the American workingman against the pauper labor of Europe just as the manufacturer was protected by the tariff against its commodities.

Although the labor force was long predominantly American, industrial managers found they had to counter the allurements agriculture held out to most natives. The comparative ease of undertaking farming offered a career without dependence upon a master and in which the worker, subject to the demands of the market, could order his own work.

In brief there was a limited reservoir of male unskilled labor to draw upon for nonagricultural employment. One solution was the subdivision of labor and the use of power machinery; these innovations made it feasible to employ women and children; as one of the advocates of the new system wrote, they could become the "little fingers . . . of the gigantic automatons of labor-saving machinery." Women had always manufactured. They had done spinning and weaving in the home, and they had been helped by children. The translation of these operations and this labor force to the factory was simple; besides it opened the door to an El Dorado. Their work would increase the national wealth. Hamilton in 1791 wrote, "Women and children are rendered more useful, and the latter more early useful, by manufacturing establishments than they would otherwise be." Individuals, as well as the nation, benefited from the labor of women and children, for while the farmer tilled his fields, his wife and children might be earning in the factory.

Nor was the sole advantage a material one. Puritan thinking—and it was by no means confined to New England—had looked upon work as the path to righteousness. Now new possibilities of salvation through labor were available. Employed in factories, women "would be kept out of vice" and children would be given not only vocational training but moral education. Accustomed in their formative years to the habits of industry, they would grow up to be serious and industrious citizens. Finally, poverty might be abolished through the factory system. Widows and children and those who were otherwise helpless might find in the new industry a way of employment which would give them independence and free the community of their care. Hamilton, who held a rather acerb estimate of American industriousness, thought Americans were a rather indolent people, a tendency enhanced by the seasonal character of agriculture. Manufacturing, he felt, would induce a superior diligence and discipline. As a consequence of all this, the early factory promoters from Samuel Slater to Francis Cabot Lowell were not regarded as the exploiters of the community, but as its benefactors.

The "Advantages" of Child Labor

The proportion of women and child operatives employed in the new factories varied from industrial district to district. But, from the first, child labor predominated in the textile regions south of Boston. The original labor force of Samuel Slater's water-frame factory was a young one. During the first week of January, 1791, he had at work nine operatives, seven boys and two girls, all of whom were between seven and twelve years of age. Unfortunately, as factories grew more numerous the statistics of child employment became fewer and vaguer. It was not until the census of 1870 that a fairly complete enumeration of employed children was made. But such figures as are available for the first part of the nineteenth century show the continued concentration of child labor in the textile regions that stemmed from the Slater enterprise. In 1831, of Rhode Island's cotton-mill labor force of 8,500, 3,472 were children under twelve years of age. The other states where child labor was prevalent—New York, Connecticut, and New Jersey—made no approach to this figure or percentage. Southern New England's preeminence in this respect was due, in the first place, to Slater's example. He brought to this country not only a knowledge of the English machinery but also an acquaintance with its labor policy. Since the early English cotton factories were run by children, Slater followed the same policy in his own factories. The spinning processes characteristic of the region also led to the greater employment of children, for one adult operative and two child assistants tended a machine.

These child labor forces were not, however, recruited as in Great Britain. Rarely were children transferred from the poorhouse to the factory; nor was the apprenticing of children successful. Rather the family system of employment predominated. Newspapers in the industrial regions were filled with advertisements which illustrated its prevalence. A typical advertisement in the Providence *Manufacturers' and Farmers' Journal* of January 14, 1828, read: "Families Wanted—Ten or Twelve good respectable families consisting of four or five children each, from nine to sixteen years of age, are wanted to work in a cotton mill, in the vicinity of Providence." There were several advantages to the family system. Since the children and their families were not separated and the parents could protect the morals of their offspring and discipline their waywardness, the arrangement helped to break down the American prejudice against the evil conditions of child labor in the English factories, gave stability and order to the mill village, and exempted the employer from all responsibility for the care of his employees outside the mill. That was a parental obligation.

Although children were put to work in the factory at very tender ages, very few were younger than seven. Probably most of the children were between the ages of ten and twelve. They worked the same number of hours as adults, from eleven to fourteen a day. Their tasks, however, were the lighter ones. Girls put empty bobbins upon the machines and removed them when they were full; boys carried boxes of bobbins from place to place; children pieced broken threads upon the mule. Children simply policed the machinery. While Moses Brown was gratified that his and Slater's system resulted in "near a total of saving of labor to the country," at least one contemporary observer was impressed by the disadvantage of confining young spirits and bodies within noisy, ill-ventilated, poorly lighted factories. In 1801 Josiah Quincy visited one of Slater's establishments. He wrote that the attendant was

> . . . very eloquent on the usefulness of his manufacture and employment it supplied for so many poor children. But an eloquence was exerted on the other side of the question more commanding than his, which called us to pity these little children, plying in a contracted room, among flyers and coggs, at an age when nature requires for them air, space, and sports.

There was a touch of sentimentalism in Quincy's argument. A firmer case rested upon the conflict of child labor with the American creed that children should be educated not only as workers but as future citizens. Obviously, the children in the factories had neither time nor opportunity to learn to read and write. Nearly everyone recognized that such a situation was a danger to a democratic society. Apparently manufacturers admitted the validity of the argument. Samuel Slater founded a Sunday school not for the religious training but for the secular education of his little children. It met on Sunday so as not to interfere with their daily labor in the factory. Other Rhode Island manufacturers established evening schools for the same purpose and reason. In 1813 Connecticut, probably inspired by the traditions of the apprentice system, compelled proprietors of manufacturing establishments to provide for the education of child operatives. These arrangements did not answer the need. Children working six days were obviously not eager for learning on the seventh, nor were those working fourteen hours a day likely to benefit much from evening instruction. In both Massachusetts and Rhode Island there was agitation for the passage of laws which would compel children to attend school for at least a fraction of the year. In 1836 Massachusetts required all children under fourteen years of age to have three months' schooling in the year preceding their employment. Four years later Rhode Island, whose problem was more intense, passed a diluted imitation of this law. In 1848 Pennsylvania took a further step with an act which forbade the employment of children under twelve years of age in textile factories.

More significant than such feeble legislation was the fact that in the debates between the supporters and opponents of such legislation the employers were on the defensive. They affected to believe that they gave children work as an act of charity to keep them and their families from want. Or else they pictured themselves as besieged by parents who demanded jobs for their children. In factory as on farm, a parent's children were his labor force. Factory policy enforced this attitude. Large families with many children were sought in factory advertisements; space in factory tenements was determined by the number of children who worked in the factory, not by those who attended school.

Woman's Work

In 1860 women constituted 20 percent of factory workers. Three industries were conspicuous for feminine employment: boots and shoes, men's ready-made clothing, and cotton textiles. In the first 40 percent of the total employees were women; in the latter two industries about 60 percent. The employment of women in cotton factories was the real novelty. For here women left their homes and worked under factory discipline. Observers were particularly impressed by the north-of-Boston region, where throstle spinning facilitated the employment of women. This modification of an English method did not require as much physical strength, and its spinning was continuous; the spindles ran much faster and with less breakage of the fibers. Untrained workers like farm girls could run these machines, and the investment of capital in the machines was justified by their productivity. In 1831 80 percent of the workers in Massachusetts textile mills were women, and at special times and places the percentage was higher. Most of these women were in their late teens or early twenties.

The employment of young women was a deliberate policy on the part of the industrial pioneers in the large cotton factories north of Boston. Their proprietors, without subscribing to the details of the Jeffersonian vision, were sure that America could avoid the miseries and corruption of European countries; and these owners were acquainted through observation with many of the abuses of early industrialism in England. They did not see why their factories or factory communities should imitate those alien enterprises. The Waltham capitalists, as Appleton later wrote, "could not perceive why this peculiar description of labor should vary in its effects upon character from all other occupation. . . . It was not perceived how a profitable employment has any tendency to deteriorate the character." Finally, to recruit workers, who felt much the same way, the owners had to dispel the impression that factory work was degrading and immoral. So they created the "Waltham system." This system was in turn applied at Lowell and then copied in most of the other textile centers of that area.

Only persons of good character were employed in the mills. The Lowell Manufacturing Company in 1836 stated that it would not "continue to employ any person who shall be wanting in proper respect to the females employed by the company, or who shall smoke within the company's premises, or be guilty of inebriety or other improper conduct." Girls were discharged for laziness, for lying, for profanity, and one factory at least had a rule providing for the discharge of people who attended dancing school. It was natural when so much attention was paid to morality that church attendance should be expected of operatives. The keepers of the company boardinghouses were required to report operatives who did not attend divine worship, but only one company taxed its operatives to support a church. Requirements were made of even the highest operative. Overseers in charge of the workrooms were selected with greatest care. Most of them were married men, and many of them were teachers in the Sunday schools which the religiously inclined operatives attended.

The companies provided boardinghouses for the workers and in most cases compelled them to live there unless they had families in the city. The companies paid the board of the operatives to the keepers of these houses. They were often women whose character was vouched for by decent widowhood and a few small children, and they were supposed to run their establishments with the strictness of a girls' school or a nunnery. They were to keep a watch over the habits of their wards and expel undesirable callers. Doors were locked at ten P.M., and no girl was admitted thereafter without a very special excuse. The same careful oversight followed the operatives to the factory. Near the door sat the overseer at his desk, and no girl was to leave the room without his permission.

This elaborate protective system was crowned by the blacklist. Whenever an operative was honorably discharged she was given a paper to that effect. If an operative was dishonorably discharged, her name and offense were entered upon a book and the unpleasant news was "sent around" to the other mills. Occasionally the names of culprits and their misdemeanors were sent to other textile centers. Without an honorable discharge it was impossible for a worker to secure other employment in textile mills. People were blacklisted for offenses ranging all the way from prostitution to fixing looms incorrectly. Furthermore, an honorable discharge was not granted by a Lowell mill unless the operative had worked a year and had given a proper notice of withdrawal. The factory owners wanted to discourage the rapid turnover of their labor force. More effective than such disciplinary action, however, was the character of the girls themselves. They were their own most successful moral police.

In its first bloom the Waltham, or Lowell, system undoubtedly created unusual factory conditions. Visitors to Lowell were favorably impressed by the flowerboxes at the windows of the factory, by the bits of verse or scriptural quotations which the operatives tacked upon the looms to memorize as they worked, by the full attendance of workers at the Lyceum when Emerson spoke, by the girls' societies for studying French and German and for debating, by the "Improvement Circle" which published the *Lowell Offering*—filled with nostalgic descriptions of country life, Cinderella stories of the operative marrying the rich young man, and some verse of moderate merit—and by the educated and modest demeanor of the operatives. In fact, the girls went to Waltham and to Lowell because it was the equivalent of an education. Home industry was breaking down, and other occupations such as teaching had not yet been opened extensively to women. Restless energetic young women wanted freedom and the chance to make money. One of them wrote:

> In plain words,
> I am a schoolma'am in the summer time
> As now I am a Lady of the Loom.
> . . . inside these factory walls
> The daughters of our honest yeomanry,
> Children of tradesmen, teachers, clergymen,
> Their own condition make in mingling.

Some of these "ladies of the loom" were eager to show that women could take a place in the world and make their own living. They were not permanent operatives. If work was slack they would return to the parental roof until business picked up again. At the end of four or five years, after a glimpse of the world and with a smattering of culture and a little money, they would return to their schooling, go back to the farm, or marry. The hardships of industrialism did not bear heavily upon such as these.

About 1840 the pretty features of this industrial idyll began to fade. On the one hand the textile centers north of Boston began to develop a class of permanent factory operatives. The girls who earlier had come to the mills in Lowell as to a boarding school began to go elsewhere. Miss Farley, the editor of the *New England Offering,* the successor to the *Lowell Offering,* wrote that she saw "the Great West open for our girls away there, with all this clamor for teachers, missionaries, and wives." The owners of the mills found it so difficult to recruit farmers' daughters close at hand that agents were dispatched to northern New England and were paid premiums for the girls whom they secured. These newcomers tended to form a permanent operative class, since they lived so far from home that it was not easy for them to leave the industrial centers. At the same time immigrants began to displace the native workers. In the late forties Irishwomen, who earlier had done the cruder manual tasks about the mills, began to tend machines. The result was the recruitment of an operative group from "the Irish and low-class New Englanders," as Miss Farley described them. Between 1849 and 1859 the percentage of foreign-born employed in a typical, large-scale New England cotton factory increased from 31.84 to 52.53. Meanwhile the character of the employers had altered. The pioneers of these textile enterprises, with their sense of paternal responsibility, were leaving the scene; and their places were taken by capitalists and absentee stockholders whose major interests were dividends and profits. In their hands the Waltham, or Lowell, system became an efficient and dread agency for punishing revolt and preventing change. Through the blacklist discontented spirits were deprived of a livelihood.

Behind the blacklist lay the pervasive control of the industrial cities by the corporations. In Lowell many overseers in the mills were also aldermen in the city; the clergy were well aware whence the support for the churches came; employees who voted the wrong ticket were told they would lose their jobs; people were afraid of expressing sympathy with "reform" lest they offend the corporations; and the press was used to influence opinion in Lowell and elsewhere. Even the workers' papers, the *Lowell Offering* and its successor, the *New England Offering,* were fathered by the corporations. With few exceptions their articles viewed the Lowell system optimistically, a literary slant helped by the fact that Miss Farley, one of their later editors, was not working in the mills, but looking back at them through the haze of reminiscence.

Factory Wages

Before 1860, as since, there was a wide spectrum of wages. Agricultural workers, the largest fraction of the labor force; skilled workers, like carpenters; unskilled workers, the "gorilla type," to use a later phrase, on docks and railroad building; "ladies of the loom";—all had different wage levels. Some workers were paid for piecework, and others were paid by the day. Wages differed from place to place and region to region. Neither employers nor employees kept long-run records of what was paid. Finally all wages were affected—in an irregular fashion, to be sure—by unemployment, by changes in the cost of living, and by the forms wage payments took. Since a cluster of large cotton mills north of Boston kept records of wages over the years, summaries of their accounts conveniently give an idea of the amounts and trends of factory wages. Even here, however, reservations are plentiful.

The phenomenon of mass unemployment attracted the cotton textile industry's attention for the first time in the depression years after 1819. The numbers involved are a matter of surmise. In the cotton-mill sample, however, 309 days "were determined to be the usual number of days worked in a normal full time year during the period 1825–1860." This steadiness in employment was partly due to the fact that managers preferred running their mills to closing them down. The recruiting and replacement of workers was difficult enough in any case, and the loss of acquired working skills was another disadvantage. If mills did close down farmers' daughters returned home to "help out"; and laborers in towns and villages usually had a small truck garden, some poultry, and a pig to keep away want when money wages ceased or were pathetically small.

In any case, actual annual earnings per worker amounted to $161.51 in 1825 and had risen by 1860 to $191.52. The most marked nominal fluctuation had been a decline in the early forties. If, however, vacillations were interrelated with changes in the cost of living—real wages—the greatest declines had been in 1835–1837 and 1850–1858. If the quality of the "found"—offered in the way of rent and meals in the factory boarding-houses—did not deteriorate, workers made indirect gains during periods of rising prices, for the companies paid a fixed sum for each worker to the operators of these establishments.

These north-of-Boston factories, when they paid their hands cash wages, usually once every four or five weeks, introduced an innovation which was unusual elsewhere as late as 1850. Much more common was the "store order" or "truck system" under which the worker was paid by an order entitling him to purchase goods to a certain amount in the store owned either by his employer or by a merchant with whom the former had made some arrangement. Occasionally the workers were paid with a share of the products which they had manufactured. All these arrangements had a natural origin. The putting-out system had grown around a storekeeper who paid the workers in commodities when they brought in the finished products; many early factories were erected and operated by those who were at the same time retail or wholesale merchants; in a country where currency was scarce, barter or "payment in kind" was a necessity. However justified the store order system was originally, it became a means of making profits for the manufacturer and of exploiting the workers. Employees were forbidden to trade except at the company store, and when they arrived at the employer's store or at the one with which he had made contractual arrangements, they found the price of goods was usually marked up to make greater profits. Often fraud increased these excess profits. Since the store order system prevailed in Fall River, it applied to Hannah Borden, one of the Borden family and a star weaver in their mills. Sensing that she was being cheated, she was able to compel an accounting because of her family position, only to discover that she had been charged for various articles of male wearing apparel which ladies of the loom were not then in the habit of wearing. It was conservatively calculated that under the store order system the real value of wages was on the average reduced at least 25 percent.

We do not know with precision who was dependent on the factory girl's earnings. Evidence seems to indicate they went to the worker for her self-support. Elsewhere the meaning of individual wages might be distorted by the fact that wages were generally pooled with those of others in the family group. The family system of employment in Rhode Island and southern Massachusetts illustrates this generalization. A classic example of this arrangement was the contract made between Dennis Rier and a Lancaster, Massachusetts, cotton mill:

1815, Jan. 27, Dennis Rier, of Newberry Port, has this day engaged to come with his family to work in our factory on the following conditions. He is to be here about the 20th of next month, and is to have the following wages for work:

Himself	$ 5.00
His son, Robt. Rier, 10 years of age	.83
Daughter, Nancy, 12 years of age	1.25
Son William, 13 years of age	1.50
Son Michael, 16 years of age	2.00
	10.58
His Sister, Abigail Smith	2.33
Her daughter Sally, 8 years of age	.75
Son Samuel, 13 years of age	1.50
	4.58

House rent to be from $20 to $30. Wood cut up $2. per cord.

Rier's own wage was probably inadequate for the support of this group, but when the wages of his relatives and little ones were added to his own he probably made shift to get along.

"Work, for the Night Is Coming"

Throughout the country at the beginning of the nineteenth century the normal working day was from sunrise to sunset. Factory operatives had long days. In Fall River Hannah Borden went to the mills and had her looms working at 5 A.M.; she took an hour for breakfast at 7:30, worked from 8:30 until noon, when she allowed half an hour for dinner, and then worked until 7:30 in the evening; all in all she tended looms thirteen hours a day. At first such factory operatives worked fewer hours in winter than in the summer, when "good light" lasted longer, but later the introduction of artificial illumination helped to even out these irregularities. The average time worked, however, remained high; in the Lowell mills in 1839, twelve hours and thirteen minutes. As if the hours of industry were not long enough, factories sometimes prolonged them by various devices. The chief stratagem was to start the machinery in the morning by "solar time" and stop it at night by clocks which were several minutes slower. This was euphemistically described as "factory time." In this way between twenty and twenty-five minutes were added to the length of the working day.

At first long hours seemed natural to nearly everyone, for the farmer in his fields, the clerk in the store, the woman in the home all worked from dawn to darkness, and factory work differed very little in intensity from that in these other occupations. The moral outlook of the community also approved tlhe custom of long hours. Religion stressed the duty of industry and diligence; leisure was equivalent to idleness, and idleness was a temptation to vice. Finally, the new factory masters felt that long hours were necessary in order to earn money on their investment. Machines were much more expensive than tools, and their cost could be recouped only if they turned out many items through continuous and rapid operation during a long day. Later the employers discovered that the long hours were demanded by the operatives themselves. They gathered at the factory gates long before they were lifted, cut short their meal hours, and could hardly be turned away from the machines at night. The explanation of this excessive devotion to labor was the low piece-rates. Factory operatives who wanted to make high wages had to labor long hours.

At first the advantages of children's and women's labor were so commonly and widely esteemed that there was little tendency to treat the hours of these workers as a separate problem. This refusal to make distinctions contrasted sharply with the contemporary situation in England, where legislation for the protection of these dependent groups was being enacted. Although little legislation was passed in this country, public opinion was prepared for action by debate and controversy. The need for educating children had, as we have already seen, resulted in laws which required some months of schooling for child factory-workers. Massachusetts had passed the first legislation. This state took the next step in 1842, when it passed a law fixing the length of the working day at ten hours for children under twelve years of age employed in factories. The argument for this legislation seems to have been the need for enforcing the earlier statute on education and also the realization that the long hours which children were required to work "must be permanently injurious to their health." About 1850 other states began to pass similar legislation. All these acts were laxly enforced.

As for women a vehement controversy began as early as the thirties over the effect of the hours of labor upon their health. Opponents of the long hours asserted that the hot ill-ventilated factory rooms, saturated with moisture and cotton lint, so weakened the workers that after a few years in the factory they went home to die. On the other hand, investigators declared that the factory by its training in regular habits and the requirements for physical exercise actually benefited the health of the women workers. They went home from the factory after a few years stronger than when they had come. Elisha Bartlett, M.D., of Lowell, wrote in 1841 *A Vindication of the Character and Condition of the Females Employed in the Lowell Mills*. The overseer of one spinning room in which fifty girls were employed thus classified his charges: " 'Looks well,' 25; 'rosy,' 9; 'fat and looks well,' 4; 'looks healthy,' 2; 'very healthy looking,' 2; 'fat and rosy,' 2; 'fat and pale,' 3; 'thin,' 2; 'pale,' 4." This analysis was hardly scientific. It was not until 1849 that an impartial appraisal was made by Dr. Josiah Curtis in a report given before the American Medical Association. He made mathematical calculations of the amount of air required by each person and then discovered that even in the best Lowell mills his standards were not approximated. He concluded, "There is not a state's prison or house of correction in New England where the hours of labor are so long, the hours for meals so short, and the ventilation so much neglected as in the cotton mills with which I am acquainted." Yet in Massachusetts there was no separate movement to regulate the conditions of women's labor. Nor was there anywhere else. The drive for shorter hours, the ten-hour day, was designed to benefit all workers.

The Ten-Hour Movement

Just why ten hours should have been picked by the laborers as the proper working day is difficult to discover. At any rate, after a time it seemed to the workers that "ten hours well and faithfully employed is as much as an employer ought to receive, or require, for a day's work; and that it is as much as any artisan, mechanic or laborer ought to give." This was the resolution of the "mechanics and others assembled" in New York City in 1829 to remonstrate against any further increase in the hours of labor. This resolution expressed more than the conviction of the workers; it was evidence that in the late twenties a ten-hour movement was under way. Indeed, in this matter New York craftsmen were a little belated. Skilled workers in Philadelphia had already launched a campaign for this objective with the argument that a longer day than ten hours was physically disadvantageous and gave no time for self-improvement, and they had met with partial success. In Boston, however, a strike for the ten-hour day collapsed.

In the early thirties the ten-hour movement gained renewed impetus because employers, anxious to make money during the years of prosperity, worked their laborers hard and because the latter effectively resisted. In 1835 a ten-hour campaign swept the country. The workingman's appeal for such a working day did not stress its necessity for the physical welfare of the laborer or even a possible gain in efficiency which would compensate the employer for giving shorter hours. Although both of these conditions were mentioned, the real war cry was the benefit of leisure for the workingman. It would give him time for moral and mental improvement. Particularly was this necessary in a democracy where the worker had the ballot and he should be allowed to prepare himself for its intelligent use. Although such assertions were undoubtedly advanced to win public sympathy, they apparently represented a genuine conviction on the worker's part. The slavery of long hours was a barrier preventing that equality of opportunity and of station which the common man in the era of Jacksonian democracy felt was his inalienable right. Strikes sputtered along the eastern seaboard.

One measure of their success was the response to the agitation for a shorter working day mounted by artisans and mechanics employed on government work. They were not particularly successful in their petitions to Congress or to the Cabinet heads under whose jurisdiction they were employed. In 1836 workers in the Philadelphia Navy Yard hit upon the idea of appealing to the President. They were so successful that others followed their example. In 1840 Martin Van Buren, a President whose political career had been made years before by a campaign for the extension of the suffrage to the common man of New York, issued an order directing that on the public works of the government all workers, "whether laborers or mechanics, be required to work only the number of hours prescribed by the ten-hour system."

The early movement for the ten-hour day had been undertaken by the mechanics, artisans, and handicraftsmen whose occupations had been untouched by the machine and the factory system. Their success had not affected the factory workers, who still worked from twelve to fourteen hours a day. Occasionally such operatives felt that they could stand it no longer and had a "flare-up" or "turn-out" for the shorter day. Since such demonstrations were generally failures and strikes proved futile, factory workers sought to obtain the ten-hour day by legislation in the various states. Such legislation was pushed for by a campaign of propaganda, and then pressure upon the legislature, especially through enormous petitions. Although more subtle methods have now replaced this form of lobbying, the labor organizer of the forties brought it to a high degree of perfection. Although such methods were novel, no new arguments for the ten-hour day were advanced by this factory agitation. A Lowell petition of 1842, for instance, asked for such a law because

. . . it would, in the first place, *serve to lengthen the lives of those employed,* by giving them a greater opportunity to breathe the pure air of heaven, rather than the *heated* air of the mills. In the second place, *they would have more time for mental and moral cultivation,* which no one can deny is necessary for them in future life.

The first state legislature to surrender was New Hampshire. Petitions from the industrial centers began to assail the legislature in 1845, and two years later they had become so numerous that an enactment was passed whose first section declared "that in all contracts for or relating to labor, ten hours of actual labor shall be taken to be a day's work, unless otherwise agreed by the parties." The labor press was jubilant. Horace Greeley, examining the law with the detachment of a New York editor, declared it to be a "milk-and-water" enactment. He was right. That conditional

phrase "unless otherwise agreed by the parties" was an exception as wide
as all outdoors. Before the law went into effect the Nashua and Manchester corporations announced that they would discharge all employees
who did not sign special contracts for longer hours. There were indignant
mass meetings of operatives who pledged their "lives and sacred honor"
not to work more than the "legal number" of hours. This was mere
whistling against the wind. Discharges crushed such opposition, and the
blacklist followed obstinate operatives not only in the New Hampshire
industrial centers but even to Lowell.

A second hollow victory was won in Pennsylvania. As a result of
agitation the state legislature passed in 1848 a labor statute which tangled
together regulations of child labor and the ten-hour day. Ten hours was
to be a "legal day's labor" in textile and paper factories. The act, like
its New Hampshire predecessor, had a saving clause making exceptions
for special contracts. These the employers insisted the employees would
have to make. Pennsylvania cotton factories operating on a ten-hour
basis, they said, could not compete with New England's twelve-hour
industry, and to add a spur toward the acceptance of special contracts
they threatened to transfer their mills to a "western Lowell" somewhere
in Virginia. The operatives in the western part of the state, unimpressed
by these arguments, struck to enforce the legal day of ten hours. But
eventually they went back to work upon an agreement which recognized
the ten-hour day but reduced the wages by one-sixth.

Massachusetts was the chief factory state of the Union, and there the
agitation for the ten-hour day was most intense. The first petitions came
from Fall River and other centers, most of which were south of Boston.
Then Lowell joined in the fray. The number of such documents annually
increased. In 1845 these reached a climax when petitions signed by 2,139
persons were presented to the legislature. Stimulating this flood of
petitions were various organizations and individuals. In some industrial
centers an ephemeral group might be collected for this purpose. In
Lowell the women operatives were organized in 1845 into the "Lowell
Female Labor Reform Association." Its ultimate goal was the better
organization of society, but for the moment it devoted itself to uplifting
the moral and intellectual level of the operatives, repelling slanders upon
their good name, holding socials, and working for the ten-hour day as a
means of securing leisure for the operatives' improvement. Its creator was
Sarah Bagley. A striking contrast to the sweet Hannah Farley, she harassed
the Lowell capitalists with her sharp tongue and her mordant wit. The
Female Labor Reform Association and others united with the New
England Workingmen's Association, an organization interested in utopian
ends, to sponsor the ten-hour day. Aid was also contributed by a vigorous
labor press. Under such direction the petition procedure was systematized,
discordances among demands for the ten-hour day were harmonized; and
in 1846 petitions with ten thousand signatures were presented.

Meanwhile, the Massachusetts legislature was compelled by the clamor to make an investigation of the factory system. A committee of the House responded in a report mingling reprimand and unction. It found no cause for so unusual a procedure as state intervention in business affairs. It pointed out that "labor is intelligent enough to make its own bargains, and look out for its own interests." State legislation would put Massachusetts factories at a disadvantage in competition with those of other states. Even if mill conditions were bad they could not possibly damage operatives such as these farmers' daughters. The committee did, however, find abuses, but these should not be remedied by the legislature. "We look for it [the remedy] in the progressive improvement in art and science, in a higher appreciation of man's destiny, in a less love for money, and a more ardent love for social happiness and intellectual superiority." The operatives refused to accept such consolation; Sarah Bagley announced that her testimony had been misrepresented; the Lowell Female Labor Reform Association deplored the findings of the legislative committee and petitions continued to pour in—all to no avail. One of the reasons for the failure of this well-directed and enthusiastic ten-hour campaign in Massachusetts was the fact that the leaders were unwilling to accept empty legislation like that in New Hampshire or Pennsylvania; and another was the prestige and influence of the corporations in the Massachusetts legislature. Probably the most important factor in their defeat was the conservative Puritan tradition of Massachusetts, which valued diligence as an aspect of godliness.

But the war for shorter hours was not without its victories. In 1847 the Lowell corporations, in deference to public opinion, lengthened the "nooning" period, thus cutting out twenty minutes of work and reducing the average day to just under twelve hours. Though in 1853 they cut the length of the working day more substantially, their mills did not attain the ten-hour average in any month of the year. In the rest of the country, however, hours had been greatly reduced since the first of the century. Years later the so-called Aldrich Committee of the United States Senate, using samples for a fair range of industries, concluded that in 1840 a day's work averaged 11.4 hours; there was so little change during the next decade that the average for 1850 was 11.5; in 1860 it had declined to 11. Though some handicrafts, like the building trades, had won the treasured 10 hours, workers in cotton and woolen factories still labored 12.2 and 12.7 hours a day respectively.

Labor Organizations

Factory workers were not the first to organize into associations to protest against their conditions of labor or to seek better conditions. In fact, the first strike of textile workers did not come until 1828, and textile workers' unions were never very effective. The first union came in the trades. These workers were not protesting machinery because mechanization was a matter of relative indifference to them. In a fashion reminiscent of the old days of craft guilds and of masters, journeymen, and apprentices, these skilled laborers were distressed at the new ways in which their callings were being organized. Outsiders with capital and a knowledge of the wider markets were competing with each other to supply goods cheaply. They employed boys, apprentices, women, and children—"greenhorns all"—to perform the simpler tasks which flowed from a division of labor; they cheapened the product. The control of the trade was passing from the "members of the profession" into the hands of "capitalists." In spite of this radical-sounding rhetoric, these trade unions were rarely permanent. They came into existence to handle some particular grievance. When the members of one trade joined with those in another they usually formed a city trades' union. In the thirties these organizations broke out of their urban chrysalis and established the "National Trades' Union," a federation of the local groups. It held three annual conventions, passed resolutions, and expired.

However customary organizations of national size and their methods of coercing employers may seem in the twentieth century, unions were a disquieting novelty in the United States of the late eighteenth and early nineteenth centuries. It seemed to employers and to others that trade unions obviously violated the common law which forbade combinations and conspiracies to injure others. In quite typical fashion, therefore, labor quarrels were transferred to the courts for legal, if not trade, adjudication. The first criminal conspiracy trial in the country occurred at Philadelphia in 1806. It sought to appraise the organizations, methods, and aims of the Philadelphia cordwainers. The counsel for the union, appealing to the American shibboleths of liberty and democracy, pictured the employers as attempting to oppress the poor worker. The prosecution, on the other hand, described the employers as the defenders of the liberty of those individuals who wanted to work and as "the guardians of the community from imposition and rapacity." But they had more potent appeals to self-interest. Prices would be increased if higher wages were paid, and the industrial position of the city was menaced. It was no wonder that the jury accepted the judge's charge that "a combination of workmen to raise their wages may be considered in a twofold point of view: one is benefit to themselves . . . the other to injure those who do not join the society. The rule of law condemns both." This decision struck the laborer as a ridiculous travesty of justice and fact:

Shall all others, except only the industrious mechanics be allowed to meet and plot; merchants to determine their prices current, or settle the markets, politicians to electioneer, sportsmen for horse-racing and games, ladies and gentlemen for balls, parties, and banquets; and yet these poor men be indicted for combining against starvation?

Decisions in later cases avoided the extreme assertions of this early one, for judges tended to emphasize not so much the mere unlawfulness of the combination as the unlawfulness of the methods it adopted and the object which it had in view. The courts usually discovered that in its methods and purposes the union was injuring something or somebody —the employer, other employees, the state, trade, or commerce—and hence was illegal. But in 1842 Commonwealth *v.* Hunt gave the Massachusetts Supreme Court and its Chief Justice Lemuel Shaw, a great American jurist, a chance to pass on the issue. The alleged injury had been an attempt by Boston cordwainers to enforce the closed shop. The workers' lawyer declared the common-law crime of labor conspiracy was "part of the English tyranny from which we fled." Justice Shaw's decision, while incidentally validating the legality of the closed shop, went on to greater matters: the legality of labor unions, their purposes and methods. Toward the close of its opinion the court said,

We think, therefore, that associations may be entered into, the object of which is to adopt measures that may have a tendency to impoverish another, that is, to diminish his gains and profits, and yet so far from being criminal or unlawful, the object may be highly meritorious and public spirited. The legality of such an association will therefore depend upon the means to be used for its accomplishment. If it is to be carried into effect by fair or honorable and lawful means, it is, to say the least, innocent; . . . if by falsehood or force, it may be stamped with the character of conspiracy.

This decision became a predecent for other courts. It definitely recognized the legal right of labor unions to exist. Furthermore, by refusing to punish the demand of the laborers for a closed shop it legalized an existence which was not circumscribed but broad and free.

The Struggle for Status

There were many varieties of belief and many choices of action within the labor movement. Wages and hours were not the only hard-core issues, nor strikes and coercion the only means of action. The American worker shared in the idealism of his general environment. He wanted the dignity of his work and of his person admitted and, although he did not insist upon an equality of property and possession, demanded the equality under the law and the equality of opportunity which a democratic country should afford him. The labor movement was, in brief, concerned with the status of the worker. The avenue to that end was politics. But should the worker join with other reformers in a "separate and distinct" party? Or should he work through existing political organizations? Or should he give up these alternatives and strive through utopianism for a more perfect society?

By the decade of the twenties the course of industrial change had gone far enough to create in the eastern urban centers a working class distinct and self-conscious enough to realize the discriminations under which the "producer" was laboring. The laborer felt that the law courts were too expensive for the poor man and that the state was creating monopolies in transportation and banking which made rich men richer and poor men poorer. He objected to the state militia system, which snatched every man from work for a period of training and compelled him to equip and find himself during this interval. The system by which debtors could be thrown into jail for inability to pay their creditors bore with special hardship upon the working classes and the unemployed. In 1829 the Boston Prison Discipline Society estimated that 75,000 persons were imprisoned on this charge in the ill-ventilated, unsanitary, crowded jails of the nation, and that a large proportion of this number owed sums of but a few dollars.

But the greatest social concern of the labor movement was the school system. Free, public, nonsectarian schools to which the worker could send his children did not exist throughout the nation. To be sure, most New England states had a public school system, but some workingmen objected to the "ecclesiastical air" of these institutions, and poor parents in any case had to put their children to work. In the Middle Atlantic states the educational system was a hodgepodge of sectarian schools and schools run by philanthropic societies, such as the Public School Society of New York City, to provide education for those who could not pay for it. About the former there was an atmosphere of religious dogma; about the latter there was the taint of poverty. In the middle states the number of children who were not in any school was amazing.

This condition the workers hoped to remedy. A report written by Philadelphia workingmen in 1830 declared:

> When the committees contemplate their own condition, and that of the great mass of their fellow laborers; when they look around on the glaring inequality of society, they are constrained to believe, that, until the means of equal instruction shall be equally secured to all, liberty is but an unmeaning word, and equality an empty shadow, whose substance to be realized must first be planted by an equal education and proper training in the minds, in the habits, and in the feelings of the community.

The monopoly of education by a specific class created castes, and the lack of education among the workers perpetuated their inferior status. Consequently the working-class movement poured forth a rich variety of educational schemes. Some were indigenous to the workers; others were grafted upon the movement by outsiders. In some instances emphasis was placed upon manual and vocational training, but the workers still felt that they ought to be allowed to share in the educational fare of the aristocrats. Compulsory attendance was advocated. And there was no doubt in the laborer's mind that the state should provide free education for all classes.

Since by the twenties the liberalization of the suffrage requirements in the American states put the weapon of the ballot into the hands of the workers, they began to form political organizations, elaborate programs, and nominate candidates. Most of these organizations developed in the eastern cities from the strikes which were waged for the ten-hour day. Most were short-lived. In some cases they were destroyed by internal dissensions. In others they fell a prey to the practical politicians, who directed idealistic agitation of the workingmen to their own political ends. After 1834, moreover, the labor union movement swung away from political measures for social ends to strikes for higher wages. Mounting prices and American prosperity made the change in emphasis both necessary and effective. Although the political movement failed for the moment, it had profound ultimate consequences. Its program slowly converted popular opinion, and state legislatures gradually repealed the laws for imprisonment for debt, swept away the provisions for militia service, and established public common schools.

In the decade of the forties the labor-union movement returned to this preoccupation with status. One reason for this emphasis was the business situation, for after the panic of 1837 genuine continued prosperity failed to return until the California gold rush of 1849. In this period of hard times economic action through the strike for limited ends such as hours and wages was difficult. But a greater reason for the emphasis upon the worker as a citizen was the realization that the new American industrialism was a challenge to the American dogma of equality. An assembly of Boston workers declared:

It is our belief that the same causes of evil and suffering are operative in this country, that, in the Old World, are developed to giant magnitude, and are crushing the producers of wealth to the very dust, and that unless a speedy change can be effected in our social condition the time is not far distant when the laborers of the United States will be as dependent, as oppressed, and as wretched, as are their brethren in Europe.

There was a frantic search for an escape from the inevitable. This was true even in such movements as had their origin among the rank and file of the workers. But the utopianism of the forties can be traced more generally to the reformers who were clamoring to show the worker the avenue by which he could be free and if necessary push and pull him along it. As Horace Greeley, one of this tribe, pointed out, it was easier to get ten thousand people to work for the workingman than to get him to work for himself.

From the welter of programs and platforms two emerge as symptomatic of the industrial malaise. One was Association—or "Fourierism," as it was called after its originator, Charles Fourier, a French thinker and pioneer socialist. The Fourier philosophy was transported to America by Albert Brisbane, a wealthy young man who had no firsthand knowledge of working-class conditions, but compensated for this difficulty by an extreme dogmatism. In 1840 he published *The Social Destiny of Man, or Association and Reorganization of Industry,* which put the master's teachings in a language which Americans could understand. Fourier's or Brisbane's ideas then appealed to the sympathies and aspirations of Horace Greeley. The columns of his various newspapers proceeded to explain this new method of production and exhort their readers to embrace it.

Fourierism in its American form planned the establishment of ideal communities called "phalanxes." Association had such a wide appeal to the intellectuals of America that more than forty phalanxes were established in the United States. For one reason or another, all were failures. This outcome must not hide the background of protest. One of the Fourierists wrote in 1850 that the real question was not unemployment, low wages, or long hours, but that "The laborer does not belong to himself, has no right to be, and exists upon sufferance. He is emphatically a wage slave. Herein is the fundamental evil to which he is subject."

If Association was an escape from the evils of the present by a flight forward to the future, Agrarianism proposed the desired change by a back track to an earlier America. The chief prophet of this gospel was George Henry Evans. Evans, English-born, had come to this country in 1820 and for years as a labor editor was the spokesman for radical ideas. In 1844 he aided in the establishment of the National Reform Union to spread his philosophy. In an address to the people of the United States in 1844 this organization pictured the onrush of machine industry with so efficient and complete a technical equipment that the number of laborers required to produce commodities was greatly diminished. Unemployment and low wages were the results. There is the possibility of wrestling "with this monster," but

As well might we interfere with the career of the heavenly bodies, or attempt to alter any of Nature's fixed laws as to hope to arrest the onward march of science and machinery. The question then recurs—the momentous question: "Where lies our remedy? How shall we escape from an evil which it is impossible to avert?" . . . Our refuge is upon the soil, in all its freshness and fertility—our heritage is on the Public Domain, in all its boundless wealth and infinite variety.

To land, in Evans's mind, man had a natural right just as to air, water, and light. These rights were equal and they could not be disposed of by their possessors. As for practical measures, Evans and his disciples felt that the public domain should be given, not sold, to those who were landless. Although these settlers might be forbidden to sell or mortgage their land, an exception might be made if the land were resold to other landless persons. Since the public domain seemed inexhaustible, their system of escape might well last for a thousand years. He urged as a protest against industrialism not the phalanx, but the use of political pressure to secure legislation; he had as an objective not the ideal community of the future, but the use of the public domain to perpetuate what he fancied was the ideal America of the past.

But the Agrarians miscalculated the emergency as badly as the Associationists, or the simon-pure Jeffersonians for that matter. Although under the terms of the Homestead Act of 1862 the national government practically gave away the public domain to actual settlers, it was an expensive business for the eastern industrial worker to reach free land in the west and start a farm, and by 1890 the frontier was gone anyway. For years before the passing of the frontier the American labor movement wistfully continued to turn to the West as a means of its salvation—but only as an afterthought. Even by the middle of the nineteenth century, whatever a fringe of dreamers or resolution-passers might assert to the contrary, the workers realized that the here-and-now of their jobs was the main problem. Near the head of an address to the journeymen printers of the United States issued by a convention of such workers in 1850 were the words, "It is useless for us to disguise from ourselves the fact that, under the present arrangement of things, there exists a perpetual antagonism between labor and capital. The toilers are involuntarily pitted against the employers." Although conditions were much better in the United States than in Europe, this statement justly recognized one result of the industrial transformation in America.

Conjectures on the Contours of Change, 1790–1860

While narratives may describe what happened within the American economy in terms of changes of details, they cannot summarize or generalize these changes. The last is the task of measurement. Experts in this field customarily use the gross national product (GNP), which has been disarmingly defined as "the heap of finished goods and services produced each year." Since the GNP is customarily stated in financial figures, the estimates must make adjustments for the changing value of money; consequently the estimates are reduced to "constant prices," with the price of a chosen base-year stated as 100. Even then the statistical totals may have only a limited usefulness unless they are placed on a per capita basis. For instance, the marked per capita increase in the agricultural sector in the pre-Civil War years may well have been due to a decline in the number of agricultural workers coupled with the maintenance of former levels of output. A final difficulty is the meagerness of statistical data for certain periods. One commentator has concluded, "Our usable statistical record does not go back beyond 1839—and the data have already been stretched to the utmost for the forty years before 1879." Clearly the task of measurement is intricate and strewn with inferences, assumptions, and differences of opinion.

There is, however, considerable agreement that the years of neutral trade and domestic prosperity in the last decade of the eighteenth and the first of the nineteenth century gave the country a growth rate superior to the Colonial era. A long interruption accompanied the international involvements from 1807–1815. There is less agreement in conjecture and calculation for the twenties and early thirties. Before the panic of 1837 the annual per capita product growth rate was perhaps close to 2.5 percent. Then, after a decade of readjustment, a third acceleration in the growth rate took place. One author came to the conclusion, making many adjustments, that the rate of growth per year after 1839 ranged between $1\frac{5}{8}$ percent and $1\frac{3}{4}$, but never attained 2 percent. This was "a personal judgment."

National totals of this sort iron out the fate of individuals. Using this approach and different statistics, one scholar has concluded the average American in 1860 was better off than his counterpart in 1840, and the American of 1840 better off than the average American of 1800. By 1840 the income level in the United States was "clearly above that of France." By 1860, if not earlier, per capita income in the United States was already "equal to that of Britain." The pupil had equaled the master.

The Railroad Business

The Civil War

Initially, the middle period which we have just traversed was so called for purely chronological reasons. In terms of economic change, however, it was a period of transition, or rather of preparation. It began the changes which underlay the great forward leap in the late nineteenth and early twentieth centuries. Not only did productivity increase at a faster pace than previously but an alteration in the way material things were made or handled was so extensive that the United States in 1915 would have been quite unrecognizable to those accustomed to pre-Civil War days. The changeover of centuries, so often a convenient breaking point for historical calculations and narratives, in 1900 made no real break in this process of transformation except insofar as 1899–1900 constituted a peak for one of those long upward swings of fifteen to twenty years in economic growth. Popular and political attitudes towards business and industry also seemed to shift about the turn of the century, but the change of direction was a coincidence and more superficial than real. Theodore Roosevelt and Woodrow Wilson, the successful evangelists of the "Square Deal" and the "New Nationalism" were born, educated, and reached young manhood in the nineteenth century and their scheme of things by and large recapitulated its dominant values.

The initial effect of the Civil War was to impede rather than further the transformation, here brusquely characterized. Just before the war the economy was resuming a spectacular long swing of expansion after the brief setback of the panic of 1857. The Civil War dropped a massive bar across this trend. Easily available statistics provided the surface evidence of the interruption. Whereas in 1860 the nation's railroads laid down 1,500 miles of track, in 1863 the total sank to a low point of 574. Changes in the production of pig iron were somewhat less startling. With the exception of 1864 the annual gross tonnage was less than 1 million;

and in 1861 it touched a low point of 653,000. The cotton famine, consequent upon the evaporation of the cotton trade, prostrated cotton manufacturing and a railroad serving a New England cotton region had to find consolation in the fact "its territory had contributed proportionally more men to the public service, since the war began" than more heavily populated areas. On the other hand a new market stimulated in the North agricultural production: in wool, which filled the gap left by cotton, and in wheat. Farm gross product in current dollars rose from $1,484,000,000 in 1860 to $2,542,000,000 in 1870.

Since the Civil War was really a conflict between nations, a more tangible and human instance of its results was directly visible in the measures both took to wage it. One of the tests was financial. The Federal Union after flailing about paid for the war by taxation; levies upon production, incomes, and inheritances, supplemented the more conventional returns from the customs tariffs. Since all these sources were inadequate, the government took to borrowing through the sale of securities and through the issue of paper money, perhaps better regarded as a tax since, as that money declined in value, its holders took the consequences. The Federal debt reached its peak at $2.8 billion, an amount thirty-three times greater than the prewar debt and equal to more than half the national income. At the command of the victors the Confederate debt of $2 billion was repudiated after the war. In the North the financial measures cleared the way for the fingers of government influence to reach into every nook and cranny of debt management and monetary policy. Although increased government influence was generally not the avowed intention of the measures taken, it was their effect.

The Civil War laid hands on men as well as dollars; it transferred them from the occupations of a nation at peace to a career of killing, rapine, and systematized destruction. The levies upon manpower are imprecise, as lists of personnel were kept carelessly and duplication of entries was commonplace. After wrestling with the complications one commentator surmised that "presumably eight-hundred thousand at one time or another served in the armed forces of the seceded States." After contemplating the confusion of records in the North he chronicled the exceptions and then, giving up, stated no totals. Another source "assumes" there were 2.3 million on the Union rolls during the war. Customarily, immigration would redress such drains upon the civilian labor force. But this recourse did not materialize. The immigrant stream, already slowed by the panic of 1857, fell sharply in 1861; and when immigration picked up in the last two years of the war it resumed at levels usual in the late forties. Despite the expulsive factors at work in their native countries, foreigners were no longer attracted on the same scale and rate to the United States because its image as a country at peace and prosperous, without high taxes and national conscription, had become so blurred.

A period of reconstruction followed the war. It was a time of immense perplexities and complexities. As after all wars, there was an underlying attempt to get "back to normalcy," a phrase President Harding later contributed to the vernacular. The economy with a resilience and an ability at self-adjustment which postwar statesmen were usually loath to acknowledge, much less rely on, rapidly resumed its growth. Pig-iron production in tons increased between 1850 and 1860 only 50 percent; it doubled between 1865 and 1875; production of coal increased 100 percent in the former period, in the latter 145 percent. The mileage of railroad track laid down was twice as long in 1865–1875 as in 1850–1860. New industries, like shoes and men's ready-to-wear clothing, in which the Civil War hastened factory production, grew apace. The war's retardation of industrialization had been a short-time phenomenon. The panic of 1873 slowed things down, but the forward march was resumed. After bumping over a depression or two—that of 1893 was the more severe—economic activity, or gross national product, reached a peak in 1899. The postwar average rate of growth in commodity output was almost half again as large as the prewar one.

People and Policy

Although commodity output grew faster than population, the latter factor was not divorced from the former. In the end the aggregate of people's needs constitutes the market for goods and services; people also provide the labor force for farm and factory with which technology, in spite of all its cunning and skill, cannot entirely dispense. In 1860 the population of the United States was 31,443,000; it passed the 75 million mark in 1900 and the 100 million mark in 1915. While these absolute figures were impressive, the increase of population in terms of percentages was slowing down. Whereas before 1860 the percentages from census to census were always above 30, they fell generally into the 20's over the decades until 1910. The next decade, that of World War I, witnessed a precipitous falling-off from 21 to 14.9 percent.

In 1860 native-born whites and Negroes constituted 86.7 percent of the total population; in 1920 this percentage was 86.4. Following the surge of immigration in the prosperous early eighties, there had been a percentage increase of the foreign-born in the American population. But the figure had soon fallen back to the more conventional level. These persisting averages did not reveal that the crude birthrate in the country had been declining steadily over the decades. By 1916 former President Theodore Roosevelt, alarmed at the prospect of "race suicide," was warning his fellow citizens that each married woman should have more children. Otherwise, he predicted, "the race will not go forward. . . . I do not want to see us Americans forced to import babies from abroad."

Whether Americans were geographically more mobile than other peoples is debatable. They tended to think of themselves as so. In any case, after the Civil War as before, the tides of internal migration operated to distribute and redistribute the population again and again. Since this migration was tied to figures which the Federal census provided only once every ten years and censuses before the present century were usable only in terms of the states where people were born and where they later resided, many currents, short-run ones in distance or time, were overlooked or underestimated. In the large scale, the pattern of migration carried people westward. Between 1880 and 1920 California and Oregon, as contrasted with most eastern states, received in every decade more in-migrants than they lost by out-migration. Meanwhile in the heartland of the American West, states like Iowa and Missouri, Indiana and Illinois, began to run a consistent deficit migration. The pull of the Far West began to depopulate the old West. On the whole population shifted towards the edges of the country. Meanwhile a more novel population movement rotated about a north-south axis. The lower South from South Carolina to Louisiana with the exception of Florida lost more migrants than it gained. Negroes, moving from a farm culture attended by various forms of social and political discrimination, constituted an element in this stream; but white farmers, also under disadvantages, preferred to take chances on the beckoning industries of the North and East. The South often complained that its status was "colonial"; in terms of migration, that word was ill-chosen.

Meanwhile within the gigantic continental aggregate of the United States, there was migration into the cities. The census complicated its measurement by changing the definition of a city's size from 8,000 to 2,500; and political necessities involving annexation of smaller units into "metropolitan areas" or "greater" something-or-others introduced further uncertainties. In 1860 one out of every five Americans lived in a city; by 1920 every other American was an urban rather than a rural dweller. At the former date there were no cities of a million or more inhabitants; by the latter date there were three. Cities grew from immigration and from domestic migration. Not all the in-migrants came from American farms; towns, villages, and smaller cities also contributed. In any case, as far as migration was concerned, urbanized industrialized Eastern states like New York, New Jersey, and Connecticut, had a fairly persistent in-migration.

These population displacements had profound effects upon transportation, agriculture, finance, and industry. Whether the resulting transformations had as much effect upon policy as did the ideas held by men of what the state could and should do was not a simple question. The Civil War by its very outcome discredited, when it did not shatter, the premises and range of measures associated in the northern mind with "rebellion" and with the South. During Reconstruction the Thirteenth,

Fourteenth, and Fifteenth Amendments to the Federal Constitution placed upon the activities and policies of the states limits that if they had been proposed before the Civil War would have brought an uproar of protest against the tyranny of the central government. States' rights did not disappear from the dialect of politicians or from the strategic weapons of political maneuver, but the central government was, if you please, more central and more powerful. Charles Francis Adams, Jr., President of the Union Pacific Railroad System, grumpily reflecting upon the transitory fame of statesmen, admitted that most Americans would acknowledge Thomas Jefferson as the author of policies most typically American. Then added Adams, "Not a trace of Jefferson's contributions to our system remains." No peer of Jefferson, or of Hamilton for that matter, was in a position after the Civil War, as after the Revolution, to formulate a grand design for the nation. But Justin Morrill who sat for Vermont in House and Senate from 1854 to 1898, "the longest period of continuous service in the United States Congress so far recorded," author of tariff and land-grant college bills, surely had claims to speak for his times, though he came from an agricultural area. In 1890 he expressed a vigorous dissent to "the idea . . . that nothing should be done by any people through legislation to change or to elevate and increase their industrial power." Coming from a practical and influential statesman, this generalization carries more weight than the formulations of theoreticians, like Herbert Spencer, or judges, like Stephen J. Field. In the light of Morrill's attitude it is incautious to characterize the post-Civil War period as one of laissez faire.

Though Morrill was a Republican, the identification of post-Civil War economic programs with any party is a simplification perilously close to nonsense. The years when either party controlled both the Presidency and the two houses of Congress were few indeed. Both major parties were aggregates of interest groups and the like-minded joined hands across nominal partisan boundaries. Distintegration within Democratic and Republican parties assumed at times major and critical proportions. In 1896 the Populist program almost took over the Democratic party. Characteristically, William Jennings Bryan, who led this Silver Crusade, spoke in his classic "Cross of Gold" oration not only for the discontented masses but also for the "broader class of business men," by which he meant wage earners, professional men in small towns, merchants in "crossroads stores," farmers, and miners. Semantic magic could go no further. Sixteen years later Theodore Roosevelt chose to tear the Republican party apart by the formation of a new one, the Progressive. The former President had once been content to have a member of his cabinet inform the Union League Club of New York that Roosevelt was "the greatest conservative force for the protection of property and our institutions"; now he dominated a national convention, seated under a banner reading "Pass Prosperity

Around." The fact that both Bryan and Roosevelt were defeated gives a certain consistency to these many contradictions and ironies.

In 1791 Alexander Hamilton was pleading that national advantage would be better served if the predominant agricultural occupations of the country were tempered by some admixture of manufacturing. By the time of the Civil War this prescription, whether measured by the numbers involved in various occupations or by the contributions of various occupations to national output, had been measurably fulfilled. The decades which followed continued the trend. The agricultural sectors declined in importance and the industrial state grew and consolidated its gains: the typical American implement was no longer the plow, but new generators of power, whether gasoline or electricity; the hero of the crowd no longer the farmer, but the industrialist or the financier. These surface changes were but symbols of a transformation of the whole of American civilization.

The Completion of the Railroad Network

An examination of the causes of this overturn should place the responsibility upon improved means of transportation. Whereas the first half of the century had largely depended upon navigable waterways, canals, and wagon hauls, the encroachments by the railroads began in the fifties to pick up speed. Extending rapidly into the western regions, the railroads soon outran the course of settlement and changed the technique of pioneering. It was now possible to travel with comparative ease into the midst of the government domain, to secure provisions and supplies while the land was put under cultivation, and to grow specialized products for markets in the United States or in Europe. Coupled with the inducements of the government land system, the railroads settled the West with the rapidity of a prairie fire. While this change was taking place in the western regions the railroads facilitated the concentration of manufacturing in the eastern United States and the distribution of manufactured commodities to a national market. With the processes of exchange thus enlarged and quickened both in manufacturing and in agriculture, there appeared an elaborate marketing organization—with salesmen, clerks, brokers, middlemen, advertisers, wholesalers—whose growing importance has been one of the most significant economic facts in the twentieth century. In the railroad world first appeared the problems of business organization which have dwarfed technical changes in importance. The capital requirements for railroad finance were so great that the investment banker found here one of the first openings for his activities and later his control; the stress of competition was from the outset felt so sharply in railroad construction and operation that experimentation with new forms of business organization and consolidation was early undertaken; and finally the connection of the railroad with the prosperity of the whole community was so vital that the national government was compelled to interfere in the operations of private enterprise.

In the railroad age after the sixties railroad pioneering, a stage already completed in the East and the old West, moved into the western half of the nation. There were similarities—and differences. For now rails and locomotives entered an area largely unsettled and partly in a stage of territorial organization. Except for the wagon train, the pony express, the stagecoach and such sidewheelers as had applied Misissippi steamboating to the Missouri, Sacramento, San Joaquin, and Columbia, there was no previous system of transportation. Neither the Indian nor the buffalo had quit the region. If the words could be appropriately applied to so modern a mechanism, the construction and operation of the railroad in this last West had an air fresh and primal.

In view of the widespread fascination during the railway age for connecting bodies of water by railways, it was not surprising that the daring project of a Pacific railroad should occur as early as the thirties to individual dreamers. It was not until the next decade that the project gained weight and dignity. Then it was taken in hand by Asa Whitney, a New York merchant engaged in the China trade. In 1845 he presented a memorial to Congress suggesting the construction of a railroad from Lake Michigan to the mouth of the Columbia. The supreme advantage of its construction would be a new and direct route to the Orient, which would divert through the central states and New York the fabulous trade of the Far East. This vision appealed to the imagination of sanguine Americans. Here at last was a means of outwitting the geography of the Northwest Passage and the Isthmus of Panama, and satisfying the search which was as old as Columbus—"Sail to the West and the East will be found." Such aspirations received further point when the gold rush to California and the agricultural migration to Oregon created settlements in the Far West separated by a gap of unsettled territory from the nation to which they belonged and of whose government they formed a part.

In 1853 the practicability of a railroad had so impressed Congress that surveys were authorized. Reviving an earlier practice, government engineers traversed these western areas and discerned five practical routes. Rivalry among the cities along the Mississippi and the Great Lakes for the eastern terminus of the road and the larger sectional controversy between North and South postponed action. As far as building the railroad was concerned the pessimistic prophecy of a California Senator proved shrewed: "If any route is reported to this body as the best those that may be rejected will always go against the one selected." The Civil War finally made possible a decision, for it removed from the National Congress the proponents of the southern routes and gave an impetus to a railroad connecting the loyal segments of the Union. The northern route of Whitney was impracticable from a business point of view, since it ran through an uninhabited country. The logic of the situation dictated the Platte route, which stages, freighters, and the pony express were following to the West. In 1862 Congress passed an act to aid the construction of the first transcontinental railroad.

The major portion of the construction was entrusted to two large companies. One was the Central Pacific of California. This company had already been incorporated by four Sacramento merchants—Leland Stanford, Collis P. Huntington, Mark Hopkins, and Charles Crocker—and others. They were then men of moderate financial resources, but the first left behind a heavily endowed university and the second a fortune which in a nephew's hands was spent for a priceless library of manuscripts and rare books. The second company, the Union Pacific, was incorporated by the Federal act of 1862. Roughly speaking, the Central Pacific was to build eastward from Sacramento and the Union Pacific was to build westward from some designated point. Eventually the Central Pacific group secured a terminal for their road at San Francisco. As for the Union Pacific, an "initial point" was finally selected on the hundredth meridian near Fort Kearney from which the road could depart westward over the plains. Connections with lines to the East were to be constructed either by the Union Pacific or by other corporations.

Not until after the Civil War did the work begin in earnest. Then a feverish activity characterized the undertaking, for the government had offered by later acts such financial and material assistance that both segments of the road were eager to obtain for themselves as large a share of the grants as possible. The Central Pacific had a severe task through the mountains, and the securing of material and of labor was difficult. Railroad equipment was shipped around Cape Horn, and Chinese were imported to grade, lay ties, and spike track. The Union Pacific found fewer difficulties of terrain, but it had problems. Not until 1867 was there a railroad connection to bring supplies to the "initial point." The company finally secured its laborers from demobilized officers and soldiers and from the "wild Irish." Eventually, on May 10, 1869, the two roads were brought together at Promontory Point, Utah, although it took a legislative enactment to effect this junction and prevent both from building parallel lines to get the government bounty. The nation paused to celebrate the event. As the last spike was tapped home the telegraph carried the blows of the sledge, bells were rung, cannon fired, speeches delivered, and verse published. In this literary flood Bret Harte's poem, chronicling the dialogue of the two engines "facing on a single track, half a world behind each back," alone was worthy of the occasion.

"The country," wrote the editor of the *Nation* in 1883, "can never feel again the thrill which the joining of the Central and Union Pacific

Line gave it." This nostalgic reflection was elicited by the completion of another transcontinental, for in the early eighties many a wedding of the rails marked the fruition of decades of dreams and expenditures. In the extreme South, New Orleans at last got her transcontinental, but hardly through her own efforts. Fulfillment came from California. When the little group of capitalists interested in the Central Pacific failed to unload that enterprise upon investors, they used the Southern Pacific to secure a practical monopoly of California's railroads. First pushed eastward to seize the natural gateways into southern California, the road was later extended across the southwest to St. Louis and New Orleans. Meanwhile the Atchison, Topeka and Santa Fé, a local road in Kansas without grandiose ambitions, moved westward along the route of the old wagon trade to Sante Fé and then, after crawling across the deserts of New Mexico and Arizona, bludgeoned and negotiated a way to the ports of southern California.

For the area north of the equator of the Union Pacific–Central Pacific, Congress launched the Northern Pacific to fulfill the dream of Asa Whitney. The charter had many vicissitudes until Jay Cooke, with the halo of his Civil War successes still about him, undertook in spectacular and, as it proved, disastrous fashion, to finance the road. Some years after his failure, Henry Villard, a German immigrant who fashioned a career from political reform, newspaper reporting and high finance, seized the road by a financial *coup d'état* and, skillfully fitting it in to his transportation monopoly of the Northwest, completed the Northern Pacific to termini on the lower Columbia and Puget Sound. A decade later, in 1893, another immigrant "empire builder," James J. Hill of Canada, completed the Great Northern. This outgrowth of a little line, which Hill had originally purchased to further his forwarding business between the Mississippi and the Red River of the North, connected Duluth and St. Paul with Seattle over a route singularly free from excessive grades and curves. One more route was to follow suit. In 1909 the Chicago, Milwaukee and St. Paul, chartered in the midcentury to enable the "iron horse" to "drink at Lake Michigan and slake his thirst at the Mississippi," reached Seattle and Tacoma on Puget Sound.

The construction of these western railroads created a new series of railroad centers. Duluth contended with St. Paul and Minneapolis; Kansas City undermined the dominance of St. Louis. On the Pacific coast the battlegrounds were divided. The Northwest of Oregon and Washington was geographically and economically so separated from California that only one north-and-south railroad connected them. In the former area Portland on the lower Columbia would naturally expect to draw the resources of that basin to her merchants and shippers. On the contrary, Seattle, cut off from the Columbia by the Cascades, developed more rapidly, for the close interaction of railroad traffic and ocean commerce on the

Pacific directed the preference to the better harbors afforded by the cities of Puget Sound. In California the rivalry between San Francisco and Los Angeles was notorious. Between the railroad centers on the Pacific coast and those along the Mississippi, the Missouri, and the Great Lakes only one center of importance had developed—Denver. Although the Union Pacific passed her by, a group of energetic local capitalists spent decades transforming her into a railroad center in spite of opposition.

By 1915 the trans-Mississippi West had roughly half the mileage of the country. The achievement was impressive but misleading. The region really saturated with railroads remained the Northeast. In 1915 the states with the highest proportion of mileage to area were in order New Jersey, Massachusetts, Pennsylvania, Ohio, Illinois, Indiana, and Connecticut. Expressed in another way, the roads within "Eastern Territory," which according to the boundaries drawn by the Interstate Commerce Commission lies north of the Potomac and Ohio and east of Lake Michigan and a line from Chicago to East St. Louis, carried over twice as many passengers and tons of freight as did those in the Western District. Furthermore, within the former territory railroad mileage, in spite of the network built before the Civil War, multiplied by nearly four times between 1860 and 1951.[1]

The Expansive Force of Competition

Without question the most important spur to construction in the railroad age was competition. One phase of this rivalry was governmental, for state competed with state and metropolis with metropolis.

[1] RAILROAD MILEAGE IN THE UNITED STATES

	1870	1880	1890	1900	1910	1915
New England	4,494	5,977	6,831	7,512	7,016	7,937
Middle States	10,577	15,147	20,038	22,360	24,207	24,371
South Atlantic	6,481	8,474	17,300	21,917	27,940	30,573
Old Northwest	14,701	25,109	36,976	41,138	45,705	45,295
Old Southwest	5,106	6,995	13,342	16,211	22,770	23,527
Southwestern	4,625	14,085	32,887	37,529	51,772	53,941
Northwestern	5,004	12,347	27,294	32,164	39,437	41,447
Pacific	1,934	5,128	12,031	15,485	23,256	26,720
Total	59,922	93,262	166,703	194,321	242,107	253,811

New England: Maine, New Hampshire, Vermont, Massachusetts, Rhode Island, Connecticut
Middle States: New York, New Jersey, Pennsylvania, Delaware, Maryland, District of Columbia
South Atlantic: Virginia, West Virginia, North and South Carolina, Georgia, Florida
Old Northwest: Ohio, Michigan, Indiana, Illinois, Wisconsin
Old Southwest: Alabama, Mississippi, Tennessee, Kentucky, Louisiana
Southwest: Missouri, Arkansas, Texas, Kansas, Colorado, New Mexico, Oklahoma
Northwest: Iowa, Minnesota, Nebraska, North and South Dakota, Wyoming, Montana
Pacific: Washington, Oregon, California, Nevada, Idaho, Arizona, Utah

Even the smaller cities, for whom an approach to the West had once been only a dream, now proceeded to put together or build the most impracticable routes toward this El Dorado, as misled as the Spaniards who centuries earlier sought the City of Gold in mid-America. Every community with a single railroad wanted another, in order to secure the lower rates and other benefits of railroad rivalry; and places without any railroad whatever realized by this time that the advent of the railroad meant economic salvation and its absence atrophy. The railroad corporations were prey to the same impulses and enthusiasms. There were a few strategically situated lines, at least so it was charged, that renounced ambition and sat back to enjoy the flood of dividends. Such were exceptions. Most railroads were driven to irresistible expansion, either by leases, acquisitions, or construction. If a new traffic suddenly materialized, oil in western Pennsylvania, copper in Michigan, or coal in West Virginia, they must share in it. Beyond their farthest railheads beckoned the tantalizing will-of-the-wisp of "new resources," "undeveloped areas," "future waterpowers." Of course the strong and the aggressive grasped for these opportunities. So did the weak and the improvident with the added stimulus of desperation. For any addition of carriage and revenue would, it was thought, head off bankruptcy and turn business failure into success.

Some even perceived that the very nature of the railroads stimulated among them the most extensive and virulent form of competition in the United States. In the first place, railroad executives and observers realized that the investment in the roadbed and terminals of a railroad was fixed in any case, and that the operating expenses did not increase proportionately to the amount of traffic carried; a certain minimum of costs for construction and maintenance was necessary. As a consequence the railroad was desperately eager for traffic volume, and it would continue operations under any circumstances which promised a return. Deficits on some traffic would be borne if they could be recouped on others; periods of extended loss would be undergone in the hope of future profits. In the second place, the competitive area was not limited to the mere rivalry of parallel lines. The Industrial Commission of 1900 commented upon the

. . . extreme fluidity of freight . . . once loaded upon a car, it appears to make little difference whether the distance hauled be 500 or 1,500 miles. Twenty-five years ago there were twenty competitive routes between St. Louis and Atlanta, varying in length from 526 to 1,855 miles respectively. . . . Freight transported from New York to Denver may be carried more than 3,100 miles via New Orleans, as against 1,940 miles direct, one route being 62 per cent longer than the other.

These competitive phenomena first appeared on a large and devastating scale in trunk-line territory where in the mid-fifties the Baltimore and Ohio, the Pennsylvania, the Erie, and the New York Central were reaching out for the same western traffic and desiring to carry it to the Atlantic seaboard. As early as 1855 the president of the Pennsylvania in his annual report chronicled efforts made by the railroads to prevent the "ruinous competition" for passengers and to supersede with some form of harmony the "army of drummers and runners, spread over the country and paid by each company." The events of the fifties were but a preliminary skirmish to the larger conflict which began in the sixties and grew steadily in intensity for nearly forty years. For one thing, new commodities were involved, as the railroads demonstrated their ability to transport bulky products. The quarrel was no longer over passenger traffic, but over the carriage of coal, oil, grain, and animal products. To get their share in these through traffics or to prevent their diversion to others, the great trunk lines, it was apparent by the mid-seventies, were breaking out of the mold which had shaped them as feeders for one municipality. From this welter New York and Chicago stood out as of supreme importance.

Whatever its earlier allegiance, each road now sought through construction, purchase, or lease some entrance to New York City in the East and to Chicago and St. Louis in the West. Even to the New York roads the former task was not always easy. The Central achieved it under the leadership of one of the great railroad kings of the era, Cornelius Vanderbilt. At the time of the Civil War the "Commodore," then nearly seventy years old and in possession of a fortune of $20 million, was drawn into a railroad career which began with a speculation and ended with the creation of a great system. By 1864 he had consolidated the two lines between Albany and New York City and emerged from the speculative flurries to which the stocks of these concerns were subjected in Wall Street with enormous winnings. He began the purchase of stock in the New York Central Railroad, and in 1866–1867 the dominant stockholders persuaded him to perform with it a legerdemain similar to that of his other roads. He did so. In 1869 the road was consolidated with its New York connection and a single concern ruled from there to Buffalo. Alarmed by the possibility that his trunk-line rivals might cut him off from Chicago, the Commodore now proceeded to bring under his dictatorship the necessary western connections. On his death in 1877, he had a through route of 953 miles from New York to Chicago. At the same time he had compiled a personal fortune of $100 million, relaid his track with heavy rails, built sturdy bridges, scrapped defective equipment for better, and reduced the running time between New York and Chicago from fifty hours to twenty-four. The death of the Commodore did not end the progress of the Central. His son, William H. Vanderbilt, less flamboyant than his father but just as able, and the House of Morgan continued the expansion of the road. In 1915 the system owned and operated 14,491 miles of track. Its lines were stretched from St. Louis to Boston and from Detroit to Cincinnati.

Meanwhile a similar growth had taken place for similar reasons on the other trunk lines in the northeast competitive territory. As for the Erie, from the Hudson to Dunkirk on Lake Erie its possession by a gifted *plunderbund* more interested in stock manipulation and personal enrichment than running a railroad, for years stalled operational achievements. Finally, in 1880, through lease and construction the Erie secured an entrance both to Chicago and to Cincinnati and was in a position to compete with its rivals. Farther south the Pennsylvania Railroad had been more steadily aggressive. In 1869 it leased a connection with Chicago, and in the following decade it began an expansion which extended its tracks in the West to St. Louis and in the East through New Jersey to New York harbor. Feeders were pushed south to the Ohio and the Potomac, north to a row of ports on the Great Lakes. Then early in the twentieth century at a cost of $100 million it tunneled the Hudson to New York City, erected an echoing basilica for a station, which has now been obliterated for a sports arena, and tunneled the East River to Long Island, whence it secured connections with the New England lines by the magnificent Hell Gate Bridge. In 1915 its system aggregated 11,823 miles. Meanwhile the Baltimore and Ohio, stung by the same competitive goad, forced an entrance into Chicago with memorable difficulty in 1874 and then fought its way with construction and lease north and east from Baltimore to Philadelphia and New York. Like the Erie, it looked across the Hudson to Manhattan.

Outside trunk-line territory, competition was at work in the same fashion and to the same purpose, expansion. In the South the thinness of traffic and the economic disorganization following the Civil War inspired the railroads with the same ruthless spirit which bankruptcy had induced in certain northern lines. In the West the vastness of the territory, the size of the railroads, and the need to control strategic canyons and passes as a location for one's line made the competitive struggle for independence and power through construction a battle of the gods. Thus construction and expansion were spurred by the desire to avoid dependence upon associates who at any moment might prove faithless or to prevent competition. The Atchison, Topeka and Santa Fé, which in its original design touched neither the Mississippi nor the Pacific, was under the necessity of expanding to Chicago, the Gulf of Mexico, and into Mexico and California. The Union Pacific when it discovered its western outlet, the Central Pacific, was in the control of a transcontinental rival, the Southern Pacific, built a short line to Portland, Oregon, to protect itself and also to develop the trade of the Pacific Northwest.

Mere growth, however, proved no charm against the evil eye of competition. Indeed it heightened the severity and anguish of the disease by increasing the strength of the sufferers. Certainly, they needed every resource when a competitive seizure fell upon them. Almost any incident might bring one on. In trunk-line territory, for instance, the arrival of the Baltimore and Ohio in Chicago in 1874 so elated its president that, trumpeting defiance in his new freedom, he announced that "like another Samson, he could pull down the temple of rates upon the heads of these other lines." Two years later Vanderbilt brought on another affray, because he saw no reason why the Baltimore and Ohio should be allowed by an agreement to charge less on grain traffic between the West and the seaboard. Although the Baltimore and Ohio had a shorter route, the Central had a road with an easier grade. The Baltimore and Ohio's attempt to secure a connection into New York City in the eighties precipitated a conflict in rates with the Pennsylvania. As late as 1888 the Grand Trunk made a bid for a larger share of the dressed-beef traffic from Chicago, and soon all the roads were carrying this article in trunkline territory at a loss. In such engagements the bankrupt roads or those on the verge of that disaster had an advantage. They had everything to gain and nothing to lose. Rates, of course, sank like a plummet. During the war of 1874 the freight rates on grain from Chicago to New York fell from 60 cents per one hundred pounds in December, 1873, to 30 cents in March, 1875. Passenger fares from Chicago to New York and Boston fell from $22 to $15. The chief hardship of the rate war fell upon the railroads; for rates were cut below the cost of handling the business, and dividends were imperiled. The public, moreover, was not always benefited, for the vacillation of rates unsetled orderly business. Sooner or later the disease became so severe that the railroads adopted the curative measures of agreements or arbitration. But these were only of temporary efficacy.

The competitive struggle also shaped the rate system, the magnitude of investment in the railroad network, and the ethics of railroad operation. One well-nigh universal outcome was the rebate, a reduction from the published tariffs which the railroads granted to corporations or individuals in order to secure their traffic patronage. Mutations of this simple and almost universal privilege, embodied in rate jugglery, billing, and service charges made rebating a fine art. Perhaps the rebate system had once had a justification. It enabled railroads to experiment piecemeal in lowering rates; and later these reductions were often generalized for all shippers. By the railroad age this excuse was overshadowed by grave disadvantages. Rebates were given to those who had the power and the unscrupulousness to demand them; more insignificant and more squeamish shippers were at a disadvantage. As a matter of fact, the railroad became the irresponsible arbiter of the success and failure of individual businessmen. It occupied the same unofficial position in regard to communities. Localities served by competing railroads enjoyed low freight rates; localities without this benefit had their rates maintained at higher levels or even jacked up to make good the losses in traffic carried from competitive points. What the traffic would bear was the principle in rate making.

Reputable railroad managers did not relish the exercise of these secret and arbitrary powers. One of them testified in the mid-eighties to a Senate committee:

> The railroad managers . . . no longer controlled their own business. Under the threat of losing freights they were forced to make concessions which they knew were wrong. They were annoyed by applications which it was impolitic to refuse, and met with suspicion and charges of treachery from the very men who were being made rich by rebates, yet feared that someone else might be getting better rates. . . . No wonder that railroad managers accused each other of fraud and deception. Men who in all the other relations of life were blameless winked at falsehoods, and dallied with deception, not because they were morally debased, but actually because they knew not the way out of the toils.

Competition also led to an overinvestment in railroad facilities; sometimes thinly concealed blackmail compelled this extravagance. There were specialists who promoted parallel or competitive roads to sell as soon as they were built or even earlier to the enterprise already in existence. A group of these brethren paralleled Vanderbilt's line from Buffalo to Chicago; Vanderbilt opened a ruinous rate war upon this upstart, but eventually he purchased the line at a price which it was rumored was so high that he thought the road laid with rails of "nickel plate." The story may be true or not; the name survived. Later another group of capitalists determined to repeat the operation farther east, paralleling the Hudson River Railroad by a road on the river's west shore and building a line from Albany to Buffalo which would be visible all the way from the tracks of the New York Central. At the same time, 1883, reversing roles, Vanderbilt was projecting a line which was to parallel the main line of the Pennsylvania Railroad. This tangle was eventually unraveled when the Pennsylvania bought off its competitor and Mr. Vanderbilt purchased the West Shore Railroad.

But these were simply the showy and episodic outcroppings of a continuous process. Two roads were built where one would have sufficed; three where two were quite adequate. Less realized but probably more important was the increase in fixed charges effected by leases. The owners of strategic or nuisance lines dominated negotiations for such contracts, wringing from the lessee the last penny in the payment of interest on their road's bonds and a guaranteed dividend upon their stock. An insider on the New York, New Haven and Hartford, the victimized road of many such holdups, wrote in 1900:

> The New Haven has always been prone to underestimate the value of a competitor, and as a result of the delay, in very many instances, has paid a tremendous price, when, with very little effort, the competition could have been stopped at its inception and with very little expenditure. The road has been extremely

fortunate in being so rich it could afford to pay the prices it has for its acquisitions, but is there not a limit beyond which even a property like the New Haven can go?

Overbuilding and overleasing overexpanded both plant and the fixed payments upon it. According to one canon, rates must be adjusted to provide an adequate return upon this overblown structure.

Consolidation Is the Life of Trade

Even before the Civil War, railroad owners and managers attempted by agreements to abate the more grievous forms of competition. Roads sharing in the same routes and traffics would together set rates and apportion traffics and territories. Such undertakings were predominantly local in character. From time to time roads operating in a larger area would send their officials to a railroad convention where through talk and exhortation they sought to reason each other into the adoption of a common policy. On these occasions some hard-headed or benighted disputant, with an individual view of his corporation's advantage, usually prevented the attainment of harmony. After the Civil War these amateur endeavors gradually evolved into the pool, an institution for which there were English precedents. Broadly defined, a pooling agreement usually set an elaborate rate structure and then sought to divide among the members the available traffic upon some percentage basis. Uniform rates would then be maintained because there was no advantage in violating them. Although some attempts were made actually to send traffic over the roads in proportion to their allotments, this arrangement was difficult. Generally, therefore, any road could carry all the traffic it wished; but if it exceeded its quota, the receipts, after a deduction was made for haulage, were divided among the other roads. In actual operation these schemes became very difficult to enforce. The roads which carried the traffic disliked paying sums to those which didn't; there was a strenuous competition for greater allotments; new roads appeared and demanded to be taken into the agreement. Although fines for violations were imposed and an impartial chairman kept the books and transferred the proceeds from one railroad to another, the operation of these pools was continually breaking down. Ruinous rate-wars would then intervene and compel their restoration. At least such was the general experience of pools in the West, South and above all in trunk-line territory, where in 1877 the through routes established the Joint Executive Committee and appointed as its impartial chairman Albert Fink, a German immigrant, a practical railroad man, and a pioneer in the field of railroad economics and statistics. He was the "Napoleon" and "czar" who was to hold the roads to an harmonious policy.

That his strenuous labors as a railroad Sisyphus fell short of success was due to the inherent weakness of the pooling device. For one thing, such agreements were extralegal and the members could not resort to the courts to enforce them. Lacking these sanctions, the pools depended upon the sense of obligation and estimate of self-interest exhibited by individual railroad managers. This was a feeble reed. The hope of making money by violating agreements was too strong for whatever sense of honor dictated their observance. The unscrupulous, indeed, often signed these agreements with the idea that by violating their word they could enjoy a very considerable interim of profit taking before more honorable railroad men began their own infractions. Even if the managers acted in good faith, they found it difficult to control their subordinates. Charles Francis Adams, an experienced railroad official and railroad commissioner, gave a human insight into this unpleasant business:

The freight agent and the passenger agent is under a terrible strain all the time. He is working for his living. He is judged by results. All the time he has to meet the sharpest of sharp practices. If he is successful, and gets what is called his "share of the business" that is all right. . . . If he does not get his "share of the business" he is apt to be told some day that his services are no longer required. Accordingly, he will have recourse to every conceivable evasion. "Smartness," as it is called, thus becomes the quality most highly prized, especially in subordinates. Honesty and good faith are scarcely regarded. Certainly they are not tolerated at all if they interfere with a man's getting his "share of the business." Gradually, this demoralizing spirit of low cunning has pervaded the whole system. Its moral tone is deplorably low. . . . That healthy, mutual confidence which is the first essential to prosperity in all transactions between man and man, does not exist in the American railroad service taken as a whole.

After 1887 when the Interstate Commerce Act explicitly forbade pooling and the nineties when a series of adverse decisions under the Sherman Anti-Trust Act hampered the use of the device, it was obvious that some other form of consolidation was required. The chaos of bankruptcy through which the railroads had passed during the decade of the nineties afforded everywhere the opportunity for an era of actual consolidations. As road after road was reorganized, it became possible for the stronger roads to invest in the weaker ones or to provide the funds necessary for financial readjustment. The years of golden prosperity after 1898 introduced a period of giddy consolidation. Such immense railroad systems were formed that it was hoped they would be immune from the dangers of competition. In some cases these dangers were to be removed through the domination of a traffic territory by a single road. The Boston and Maine and the New York, New Haven and Hartford had thus divided New England between them. Or else several roads might be united through the ownership of one another's stock and through representation on one another's board of directors. In this fashion, a harmonious policy which became known as a "community of interest" was established.

On every side, the growth of this policy was illustrated. The Pennsylvania Railroad, buying into the reorganized Baltimore and Ohio, owned by 1906 nearly half of its preferred and over a third of its common stock, and various Pennsylvania vice-presidents sat in succession on the board of directors of the Baltimore and Ohio. On their part the Baltimore and Ohio and the New York Central were buying into feeders of disturbing trunk-line competitors. And in the West shone the dazzling sun of Edward H. Harriman, the greatest exemplar of the community of interest program. His life coincided with the American formula of success in which both luck and shrewdness played a part. He started as an office boy in a Wall Street house, saved money, purchased a seat on the Stock Exchange, cultivated the friendship of the right people in society and business, made more money, and in the eighties became a director and finally guiding genius of the Illinois Central. He managed it so effectively and established its credit so soundly that after 1893, when the Union Pacific was in course of reorganization, he compelled the banking house which had undertaken that task to permit his participation. Once on the board of directors of the transcontinental, he made extensive stock purchases and secured an absolute control by 1900. The next year the Union Pacific purchased the holdings of the late C. P. Huntington and others to gain control of 45 percent of the Southern Pacific's stock—a dominating holding in view of the scattered ownership of the remainder—and Harriman became the latter's president. These acquisitions gave him a stranglehold on the Pacific coast, with three important exceptions: the Atchison, Topeka and Santa Fé in the Southwest, and the Northern Pacific and the Great Northern in the Northwest. After some skirmishes with the Santa Fé, Harriman convinced that road it should operate its lines in harmony with his. Two of the directors of the Union Pacific were in 1905 elected to the board of directors of the Santa Fé, and Harriman and his associates meanwhile purchased in the market approximately 14 percent of its capital stock.

Meanwhile a community of interest was secured in the northern zone after a struggle for possession which became an American financial epic. As we have seen, James J. Hill was the overlord of the Great Northern; Hill and J. P. Morgan controlled the Northern Pacific after a reorganization in the nineties. Then these allies each secured an interest in the Chicago, Burlington and Quincy. The motive for this acquisition is controversial. It afforded a connection with Chicago for the Hill roads, and it made it possible to divert the Mississippi traffic to the Northwest over the Hill lines and thus increase freight revenues. Both aims strengthened the competitive power of the Hill-Morgan systems, and the Chicago, Burlington and Quincy, reaching westward as far as Denver, was a portentous invader of the Harriman provinces. When the latter was refused a share in these arrangements, he began to purchase stock in the Northern Pacific; Hill and Morgan, tardily alerted to what he was doing, eventually tried to head him off. The contest which ensued in Wall Street was insane. On May 9 stock of the Northern Pacific ran up in an hour from $350 a share to $1,000 a share, and none was to be had at that price. The simple fact of the matter was that the speculative fraternity had been selling stock that they did not possess and were now trying to purchase it in order to fulfill their contracts. Unless some arrangement was made the number of bankruptcies would be appalling. In compromise lay salvation.

In 1901 the Northern Securities Company was chartered by the State of New Jersey. This concern was a holding company whose capital stock of $400 million was exchanged for all the stock of the Northern Pacific and a great majority of the stock of the Great Northern Railroad, both of which, be it remembered, controlled the Chicago, Burlington and Quincy. The directors of the Northern Securities Corporation numbered fifteen; three of these directors were also directors of the Union Pacific Railroad, and Harriman, who was naturally one of the three, was also a member of the executive committee of the Northern Securities Company. By this single stroke the Harriman lines—Union Pacific, Southern Pacific and Illinois Central—aggregating nearly 21,000 miles, and the Hill lines, aggregating 20,000, were brought under the benign aegis of the community of interest idea, and competition west of the Mississippi was effectively limited.

In 1904 the Supreme Court, as we shall see, ordered the dissolution of the Northern Securities Company. The Union Pacific, however, still retained a stockholding of $22 million in the Great Northern and the Northern Pacific; from the sale of its other holdings in these roads it obtained a profit which it now proceeded to invest in other railways. Harriman made large purchases of the securities of the New York Central and Hudson River Railroad and poured the money of the Union Pacific like a flood into the Baltimore and Ohio, so that by 1906 over 18 percent of its stock issue was owned by the former railroad. For a time it seemed the elimination of competition might be accomplished through a railroad despot. Apparently he believed it possible—on terms. Before the Interstate Commerce Commission in 1907 this small, nervous man, concealed by glasses and a big mustache, in response to the query, "Where is that thing going to stop?" replied, "I would go on with it. If I thought we could realize something more than we have got from these investments, I would go on and buy some more things." He felt that only the law prevented the concentration of every transcontinental road in his own hands. Before his more grandiose conceptions were realized or his boasts made good, Harriman died in 1909. Undoubtedly the greatest railroad man of the United States, if not of the world, he built his consolidations and held them together by personal power. His death in any case would have brought some recession. Meanwhile the government was proceeding to demolish the vast aggregation he had constructed. The steady pressure of the law destroyed the ties between the Union Pacific, on the one hand, and the Great Northern–Northern Pacific, on the other.

Consolidation, nevertheless, had gone too far to be suddenly reversed. Harriman's example had been followed by numerous imitators. In 1900 the Industrial Commission calculated that a quarter of the outstanding stock of railroads was owned by other railroads, a figure which represented a considerable increase from the middle of the preceding decade. By 1906 this proportion had increased to a third. These interlocking stock ownerships were supplemented by a series of interlocking directorships. Connections between railroads were at the same time taking place through the medium of the investment banking houses, which supplied the funds for railroads and controlled their operating policies in varying degrees. In 1912 the firm of J. P. Morgan and Company owned stock, among others, in the New York Central and Hudson River Railroad; the New York, New Haven and Hartford; the Northern Pacific; the Erie; and the Atchison, Topeka and Santa Fé. Partners of the firm were also directors in these and other railroads, and in many cases the latter's stock was voted by a voting trust in which the firm was heavily represented. As the years went by, stock ownership in railroads became more dispersed. The importance of large holdings by individuals or families declined. But the process of consolidation through ownership, lease, interlocking stock ownership, and holding companies continued.

Changes in Technique and Operation

While the railroad network was building and its organization shifting from competition to consolidation, a series of innovatons bestowed upon it a new scale and efficiency of operation. Some of these changes were technological. To be sure, the familiar American phenomenon of temporary and flimsy railroad construction was repeated in the new areas of the trans-Appalachian and of the trans-Mississippi West. Here lack of capital for investment in a permanent roadbed, the possibilities of speculative profit from an undeveloped country, the haste of construction—all contributed to the repetition of conditions which had characterized early American experimentation with the railroad. With the growth of population and the development of commerce, however, the American railroads passed through reconstruction after reconstruction until they compared in excellence and permanence with their European prototypes. Nevertheless, the conditions of American railroads were so different that unique distinctions remained. The long distances covered by American railroads, the mobility of population, the carriage of bulky products—coal, lumber, and the like—and the difficulties of the terrain put railroading upon an unusually large scale of operation in this country.

The weight and size of the American rolling stock illustrated this tendency. American passenger cars were larger and heavier than those of European countries. Development in this direction was compelled by the innovations of George M. Pullman, who in 1864 constructed his first sleeping car—the "Pioneer A." It was so large that the roads which used it had to cut down their station platforms and alter their bridges. The later creations of Pullman, the diner and the "palace" or parlor car, were in the same tradition. Freight cars—coal cars, flatcars, and boxcars—all increased in capacity and weight. In the sixties freight cars had a normal capacity of 7.5 tons; by 1915 boxcars on American railways fell primarily either in the classification between 30 and 35 tons or that between 40 and 45 tons capacity. Increasingly locomotives were differentiated for the services they were called upon to perform, passenger or freight, but all increased in size and weight. In the sixties American builders turned out an engine with six driving-wheels, "the Mogul," and then with eight drivers, "the Consolidation." Later ten-coupled engines were constructed.

From the myriad improvements which have made these increases in size and power possible—telegraphic operation, automatic signals, gigantic bridges of steel and concrete—it is possible to select two of fundamental significance, the steel rail and the air brake. In the fifties railroad men believed that the iron rail had reached the limit of its usefulness. Heavier rolling stock was impossible because it would destroy the roadbed. In the same decade Sir Henry Bessemer brought to perfection the improved methods of making steel which bear his name, and the English rolling mills began turning out Bessemer rolled steel rails. Their general use was retarded for a while by the expense of manufacture in this country. In time prices descended to ever lower levels. Over $100 a ton in gold in the early seventies, they hit $17.62 in 1898. By the end of the eighties most of the railroads had been relaid with the Bessemer rail. This rail was from eight to fifteen times as durable as its predecessor and it could support a much heavier traffic. In the nineties the use of the "open-hearth rail," manufactured by an even superior process, began.

The other improvement vital to American railroad progress was the invention of an American, George Westinghouse. The weight of trains and the speed of their operations were severely limited by the difficulty of bringing the cars to a stop. In 1868 Westinghouse took out the first of a series of patents for an air brake—a series which was not to come to an end until 1907. All of his brakes relied on a complicated appliance, "the triple valve." His first brake was the "straight air-brake," which operated the brakes on all cars by air, compressed at the engine and sent the length of the train through an air line. It did not operate perfectly, however, because the last cars were stopped more tardily than those at the front of the train. By the seventies he had taken the first steps on a different principle, and after his failure at the classic Burlington Brake Trials, 1886–1887, he feverishly perfected the automatic air brake which was standard equipment for twenty years. This automatic brake had an air-pressure reservoir on each car, and the air in the brake line was kept at a constant pressure; when the engineer reduced the pressure by a valve, the reservoir on each car set the brakes so quickly that there was no swinging or jerking by the rear cars of a long train and passengers in the last coach were not in danger of being thrown the length of the car. The adoption of this and other improved devices was, however, often compelled by state and, at the turn of the century, by national legislation as a part of the safety movement that characterized the era.

With the decline in the construction of new railroad lines after 1900 the period of dynamic changes in railroad technique seemed to come to an end. The day of great inventors, like Stephenson, Jervis, Westinghouse, was over. In the nineties, nevertheless, some railroads began experimenting with electric power as a motive force. Perhaps successes on urban transportation lines inspired them, but expenses of installation proved heavy. Diesel power—which in the 1930's "smashed the old roadblock of steam"—and the general failure of railroads to cope with competition from other carriers limited the application of electricity.

Nor were all the operating advances of this era engineering ones. In spite of their snarling competition, railroads cooperated to create a national system. By the eighties most railroads had abandoned their insistence upon peculiar gauges and 4 feet 8½ inches had become the recognized standard. Most roads were relaid to conform to it. In the same decade, in 1883, the American Railway Association adopted a scheme by which the country was divided into four time-zones, roughly 15° in width, between which the difference of time was to be an hour. The advocates of "God's time" were outraged, but timetables were regularized. Somewhat later the provinciality, jealousy, and chaos displayed by the railroads in handling the freight business of the nation was modified. In 1889, largely at the insistence of the government, the country was divided into three great districts, within each of which classifications of commodities were uniform for all roads. Railroads also worked out arrangements for the interchange of freight cars on a mileage or a per diem basis, and thus freed the shipper from his dependence upon the fast freight-car lines which had developed during the sixties to prevent the necessity of transshipping freight when it passed from one railroad to another and to introduce into commerce that immense convenience, the throughway bill.

The completion of the railroad network, technical and operational improvements, and the desperate competition for business and traffic brought about in the thirty-five years after the Civil War an almost un-believable reduction in freight rates. In 1867 they had averaged, using the rather unsatisfactory "revenue per ton per mile," 1.925 cents; in 1900 they were 0.729 cents. They hovered for the next fifteen years in the neighbor-hood of this figure. More illuminating than such averages was the re-duction in so critical a specific rate as that on grain from Chicago to New York: this fell from a high of 83 cents in gold per hundred pounds in 1865 to 9.6 cents in 1914, the lowest figure for the whole period. Passenger rates did not decline in comparable fashion. The Civil War and the years that followed apparently brought about some increase over the fifties; at least in 1882 "the revenue per person-mile" was 2.447 cents. By 1900 it was down again to 2 cents and by 1914 just a little under.

The Government Largess

Mountains might be flanked by passes and technical difficulties solved through invention, but neither of these achievements actually brought the railroad into existence. Capital somehow had to be enlisted to finance the surveys, purchase the right of way, do the grading, lay the rails, and finally purchase the railroad equipment and keep it rolling. To obtain the necessary capital had been peculiarly hard in early American history, and the conditions surrounding the construction of the railroads often heightened that difficulty. The projects which were entertained and set in train ceased to be purely local ones, involving a limited investment, and became transcontinental in aspiration. Many were built in advance of population and of traffic. Still the problem was met and met mag-nificently. In 1868 the cost of the railroads in the United States was estimated at $1.6 billion; in 1915 the value of their stocks and bonds was $21,128,000,000. Such accomplishment depended on foreign as well as American capital, on government as well as private funds.

Government poured forth its largess. For at least a decade after the Civil War it seemed as if the enthusiasm and generosity of the earlier period of public aid, the thirties, had returned from some limbo to the American scene. So every governmental unit not prohibited by some constitutional restraint seemed eager to furnish credit to the railroad. The feckless habits of Civil War finance provided a general background for this extravagance. In the southern states the reconstruction of eco-nomic life required railroads and, since private capital was inadequate and timid, states issued their own securities or guaranteed those of private corporations. Too often individuals rather than the community were enriched by this process. In the North the general prosperity of railroads during the war had erased the memory of their financial difficulties during the fifties and fired enthusiasm for their extension. Experienced states like

Massachusetts reembarked upon a policy of state aid and continued promotional investments. Local governments from Maine to Milwaukee gave assistance. The amount of these aids and investments has never been accurately determined. A government investigation in the 1930's concluded that by the end of 1927, states, counties, and cities had loaned $88,486,743 to railroads, guaranteed or endorsed railroad securities to the extent of $48,503,425, and subscribed to railroad stocks and bonds $157,689,080. Since this report made no distinction by date, it is impossible to tell what proportion of these sums fell in the period between 1860 and 1915. The same difficulty handicaps any distribution of losses among decades. For losses there were. Railroads, for instance, repaid about 60 percent of the first sum mentioned in the above series. We know also that many southern states, beginning in the seventies, repudiated their debts, debts in part incurred for railroad building. Thus the history of the forties was recapitulated.

As the railroad age got under way the chorus demanding Federal aid grew louder. Luckily, the Illinois Central and other land grants furnished easy precedents for policy at the very moment the need was even more pressing. Consequently, in 1862 and 1864, the measure of government assistance was enlarged by the acts providing for the first transcontinental project. An atmosphere of uncertainty hangs over the reasons for the government's generosity. The capitalists interested in the project financed a large lobby in Congress whose activities have never been disclosed, but the magnitude and daring of the project and its location through the territories rather than the states and through the "American desert" go far to explain Congressional liberality. The corporations involved, to whom the grants were now made directly, were authorized to take for each mile of the railroad constructed ten alternate sections of land on each side of the track. In addition to land the government granted a loan of national bonds. The amount for a mile varied according to the assumed difficulties of construction—$16,000 in the plains, $32,000 in the basin between the Rockies and the Sierra Nevadas, and $48,000 across those mountain chains. The reason for the innovation of financial aid was the belief that the road could not penetrate the difficult terrain without assistance additional to the land grants, the revenue from the sale of which in an unpopulated country was necessarily a future one. In a loose and ambiguous fashion the government attempted to protect its investment. Those thirty-year government bonds, upon which it was compelled to pay the interest, were to be a mortgage upon the railroads; their interest and principal were to be repaid by the railroads and every year the railroads were to apply "5 per cent of their net earnings" to the discharge of their debt to the government.

The financial assistance given by the Union Pacific and Central Pacific acts was not a precedent followed for many roads. In fact, it was limited generally to connections or branches of that project. But the land-grant policy was pursued with mounting generosity. In the territories the most liberal grants sometimes gave twenty alternate sections on each side of the track and, in case some of these sections were already in private possession, extended the indemnity limit to sixty miles from the railroad. In these and other instances the railroads were to carry troops and government property at reduced rates. The provisions of these acts were generally interpreted leniently by Congress or by the General Land Office, which was trusted with their execution. Writing in 1883, a critic of the policy pointed out that Congress allowed many railroads to retain grants although they had not fulfilled the requirements of construction within a certain period, that the General Land Office interpreted the indemnity clause for the benefit of the railroads in a manner contrary to the intention of Congress, and that in dealing with the actual settler possessing claims to land presumably granted to the railroads, the same office acted as if "every presumption is against him, and no mistake is ever made in his favor." The total acreage of the grants is a matter of dispute. From the national government, directly or indirectly, railroads were granted approximately 223 million acres; by 1943 they had secured final patents for 180 million. Between a fifth and a quarter of the total area of both Minnesota and Washington was granted to railroads.

As far as the national government was concerned, the period of assistance to railroad building came to an end in 1872, when the last land grant was made. The panic of the next year and the Granger movement of the seventies slowed assistance from local governments—state, county, and city. New state constitutions forbade the loaning of public credit to corporations or else hedged such procedure about with difficult conditions. Restrictive legislation or constitutional provisions were also passed by the states to curb the activities of local bodies. Today only limited survivals of this practice are legally possible. The reasons for a reaction against the once eagerly accepted policy of government aid are to be found in its results.

First of all, the effect of the policy of government aid upon the government was frequently deplorable. Although the railroads built under state aid often failed to pay dividends or were not constructed efficiently, the states still had to pay the interest and principal of the bonds which they had issued. When repudiation did not follow, heavy taxation and impaired municipal and state credit went in the train of local aid. As for the national government, the United States fortunately emerged from the loan of its securities without a major loss. After years of litigation in the courts, several prolonged Congressional investigations, and the well-founded fear that the railroad adventurers who ran the aided roads would use the roads' income to pay dividends and finally force a foreclosure by which the first mortgage holders would receive the property before the second lien of the government became operative, the loss in interest and principal on all government loans was approximately $11,014,000; the amount repaid was $167,755,000. Undoubtedly, the land-grant policy of the government stimulated fraud in Congress and in the General Land Office, and the resulting corrupt alliances between individuals in government and in business was one cause of the degraded political morality in the period after the Civil War.

More important than the effect of government aid upon the donor was its effect upon the railroads. Since the land secured from the government was a valuable resource only if it could be sold to settlers whose payments would furnish funds for financing the roads and whose products would furnish a traffic, the land-grant railroads often embarked upon extensive promotion and colonization projects. The Illinois Central fixed prices of five to twenty dollars an acre, gave six years' credit, advertised its lands extensively in the East and published a guide to them in Germany; the Santa Fé land department kept immigration agents in Europe and transported thousands of Mennonites free of charge from Europe to Kansas; and the land department of the Northern Pacific tried to colonize groups of Civil War veterans and of English, Swedes, Finns, Norwegians, Bohemians, and Russians upon the plains of Minnesota and Dakota. Such activity illustrated the reversal of old pioneering conditions, where the settler pushed ahead of the means of transportation. How much financial assistance the railroads received from their land grants and their efforts to settle them varied from railroad to railroad. One careful estimator places the total at half a billion dollars. In a sense these figures are irrelevant. The real function of the land grant was to furnish the railroads with a property which they could hypothecate as collateral for credits. In some instances this possibility led to the promotion of railroads for the sake of the land grant, to carelessness about construction costs, to extravagant capitalizations and eventual losses to investors. On the other hand, without government aid many of these roads would not have been built as early as they were and the development of the country would have taken place more slowly. One further reservation: less than 8 percent of the mileage of the country was constructed with the assistance of Federal land grants.

The Private Capitalist and the Railroad

Whatever the form of government aid, it was designed as a temptation to the investment of private capital, the chief reservoirs of which were in the eastern states and in Europe. In the East fortunes built in other fashions, particularly in foreign trade and in merchandising, were swung to the new means of transportation. John Murray Forbes of

Boston, who was interested in railroad connections east and west of Chicago, had received his training and his early start in the China trade; he enlisted the financial support of others enriched by the same means. The original capitalists of the Illinois Central included a group of merchants, some of whom traced the beginnings of their wealth to the same source. Intermingled with the group of merchant investors was another composed of successful railroad men who reinvested their money in new and promising undertakings. In Forbes's enterprises Erastus Corning, an Albany hardware merchant and first president of the New York Central, was heavily committed. Among the investors in the Northern Pacific was a large Pennsylvania Railroad group which included Thomas A. Scott, vice-president, and J. Edgar Thomson, president of the Pennsylvania.

In turn the eastern capitalists attempted to secure funds from their European connections. Forbes incessantly pointed out the advantages of American railroad investment to his European correspondents. When the great banking house of Jay Cooke and Company agreed to act as financial agents for the Northern Pacific, Cooke hoped to sell $50 million out of an $80 million bond issue to European investors. He approached the Rothschilds, who refused the proposition, and then the loan was peddled around Europe to one banking house after another in Holland, England, Austria, and Germany—all without success, although journalists were flattered with gifts and bankers were wined and dined on an elaborate scale. The failure of the Cooke promotion was not, however, typical. Dutch, German, and above all, English capital flowed into the securities of American railroads—although the regularity of such investment was violently interrupted by panics or by the occasional disclosures of the folly of the American promoters. Some roads like the Illinois Central were for a long period controlled by foreign stockholders, and for a time, 1890-1896, a majority of the stock in five of America's early roads, including the Pennsylvania, was held abroad. In 1914 foreign investment in railroad securities, $4.17 billion, was approximately a fifth of the railroad capital outstanding at that date. Whether the funds came from the East or from Europe, the railroads of the West and South were largely constructed and operated by absentee capitalists.

As the railroad age got under way and the plain style of building a road through the issue and sale of stock was discarded for more complicated methods of financiering, not all railroad managers, capitalists and investors by any means were animated by the simple ambition of constructing a needed public improvement and running it in sober fashion for operational returns. Fascinating vistas of quick and more certain gain opened in other directions. One was the construction company which evolved naturally from the earlier practice of paying off the contractor in the securities of the enterprise and of relying upon the superior personal credit of officers in time of emergency. In the post-Civil War era, these emergency arrangements became a regular reliance, whether or not they were needed. A small group, usually large investors and officials, formed a construction company and then contracted, often with themselves as representatives of the road, to finance the latter's construction, for a construction company was a financial, not a building, concern. This group then furnished current funds as they were needed and took in return the securities of the road. The famed Crédit Mobilier of America, the construction company for the Union Pacific, thus received government bonds, first-mortgage bonds of the railroad, land-grant bonds, and common stock—the last three items, particularly the stock, at figures less than their face value—and then raised the funds needed for construction by selling these securities or by borrowing upon them. Calculations as to the profit secured by the Crédit Mobilier differed from investigation to investigation. The most recent sophisticated appraisal estimates "the upper limit of profit" at $16,501,760.22. All things considered, including the completion of the road six years ahead of schedule, this sum was "justifiable." But the construction company, as used there and elsewhere, encouraged extravagance and corruption when men in one capacity had the possibility of making money by awarding contracts to themselves in another; saddled the railroad with the burden of a large capitalization upon which it either must or was supposed to earn dividends; and created stock whose face value was far greater than the actual money payments made for it.

The construction company was only one of many devices for speculation. Since bonds by common understanding generally built the road, the value or equity of the stock was largely surmise. If it were disposed of for less than par, the process capitalized either favoritism or a haunting suspicion of its essential financial soundness. If capitalization were increased with the expectation that a consummated merger or amalgamation would bring higher profits, hopes were capitalized. Or perhaps the directors might simply manufacture stock as an incident to their speculative battles on Wall Street. The result of these and other procedures was "watered stock," or "stock inflation," which represented no monetary or other actual investment. *Poor's Manual* in 1885 thought that a little less than one third of the capitalization of the nation's railroads in that year represented water.

Another avenue of private gain was the lease, and less frequently its sequel, the amalgamation. Individuals or a ring would purchase at a usually low price the securities of the desired enterprise; forthwith these securities would be given a more pleasing value by an advantageous exchange for the stock of a higher-toned railroad or by a lease to the latter. Sometimes this was a legitimate procedure, but more often it was a purely speculative one.

In any discussion of such practices it is difficult to secure a sense of proportion. It is wise to remember that a railroad president like Charles Francis Adams, Jr., who conscientiously labored to revive the Union Pacific by sound practices, should be placed against Jay Gould, whose malevolent touch ruined so many concerns. There were directors who scrupulously refrained, because of their fiduciary position, from speculating in the stock of their roads just as there were those who made a practice of doing so. The Pennsylvania Railroad, which followed sound financial policies, was a makeweight to the Erie, which had for many years violated them. Some construction companies were necessities; some stock dividends represented income plowed back into the railroad; railroad stocks might be wringing wet, but bonds in many railroads were copper-riveted investments which careful legislation or administrative ruling permitted savings banks, insurance companies, and trustees to own. Nonetheless, speculation and the overexpansion of the railroad network, in part the result of competition, set off many of the business panics which swept the nation in the railway age.

Long before 1857 observers were predicting that the hectic outburst of railroad building in the early fifties would be disastrous; and the panic of 1857 was the answer. The fearful prostration of the panic of 1873 was set in train by the collapse of Jay Cooke, who had miscalculated the willingness of the public to purchase the securities of the Northern Pacific. The panic of 1893, although less closely connected with railroad overexpansion, followed the railroad growth of the eighties. After these cyclones had blown over, the wreckage of railroad systems littered the business world. In the six years 1893-1898 the courts foreclosed 67,000 miles of railroad—about one-third of the total mileage of the country. Among the failures were such great systems as the Union Pacific, the Northern Pacific, the Erie, the Baltimore and Ohio, and the Atchison, Topeka and Santa Fé.

One feature of the collapse of the nineties was the increasing recourse to bankers for assistance in obtaining the funds necessary for reorganization. Bankers, to be sure, had been previously concerned in the financial arrangements of the railroads, as the connection of Jay Cooke and Company with the Northern Pacific witnessed, and had indeed exercised some influence over the railroads for whom they acted as financial agents. In the case of a grant of aid for reorganization purposes the necessity for a sharper control seemed to exist. If a great banking establishment like the House of Morgan was to market the new securities through its prestige, some guarantee that the funds so obtained were used wisely was required. This might be exerted through placing a representative of the banking house upon the board of directors or through a "voting trust"—a few trustees appointed by the bankers to whom the voting power of the stock was surrendered for a period of years. In this fashion the House of Morgan in the period of reorganization became an influence in the affairs of many railroads. This development of "banker's control" was pregnant with possibilities for the future.

State Regulation

Throughout the period before the Civil War there was a spluttering debate on whether it was either feasible or wise to rely upon competition to govern the railroad world. Neither the question nor the frequent variant upon it, the degree of competition, received a definite answer. Meanwhile the states by charter provisions, statutory legislation, and the rulings of commissions regulated railroad practices. When the Civil War was over, the debate was resumed. Now, as a result of experience both here and abroad and of observation, railroad men and economists proclaimed with greater certainty that the railroad was by nature a semimonopoly and that competition, where it did exist, was not universally beneficial. The alternative was cooperation between railroads. But it was quite impossible to win public permission for the railroads to do this themselves. Fink's failure to legalize the pool demonstrated that. On the other hand, public regulation of railroad "abuses" by the devices hitherto employed was incompetent and uninformed. One answer was a new form of state railroad commission. Massachusetts set one pattern. Her commission, established in 1869, was given general powers to investigate railroad practices and to consider complaints presented by an individual shipper or locality. The grievance might be the unreasonableness or inequality of rates, discrimination, defective service. The commission issued findings; it could not compel obedience. It relied upon public opinion and the possibility of appealing to the legislature for a statute to bring the railroads to terms. This was no idle threat. The charters of practically all Massachusetts railroads allowed the state to alter, amend, or repeal them, and the state supreme court had convincingly supported the doctrine that the railroads were public corporations, created solely for the good of the public. A personal reason for the success of the Massachusetts way was the fact that Charles F. Adams, Jr. was a member of the Commission in its first ten years of operation.

In the western states the abuses of early railroad construction and operation were peculiarly aggravated. The railroads were dilatory in fulfilling the conditions upon which the Federal land grants had been issued; states, local governments, and individual farmers had invested in railroad securities which like as not now failed to pay dividends; otherwise railroads were financed by absentees who were foreigners whether they lived in the East or in Europe; railroad rates were high, for they failed to retreat rapidly from the inflationary level of the Civil War; and discriminations, particularly the incomprehensible higher charge for a short than a long haul, were rife. These specific grievances were all sharpened by the agricultural prostration following the Civil War. Farmers, since they could not easily prevent the overproduction of agricultural commodities, sought instead a legislative remedy for their ills. As a weapon for their program, they took over the Grange; ironically, for the Grange, or the Patrons of Husbandry, had been established in 1867 by Oliver Hudson Kelley, a New Englander, a Minnesota dirt farmer, a clerk in the Agricultural Department at Washington, as a secret organization to elevate farming through education, discussion, and social contacts. The Grange frequently asserted that it was not a political party or party organization.

It was impossible, however, for an organization with a membership early in the seventies of perhaps a million, to refrain from using its power in behalf of ends urgently desired by farmers. Undeterred by a strict construction of political self-denying ordinances, meetings of state granges in the Northwest advocated, as means of preventing the abuses of the railroad, Federal assistance to a Great Lakes–to–Gulf waterway or else the construction by the Federal government of a railroad from the Mississippi to the Atlantic seaboard. Either of these schemes would introduce rock-bottom and genuine competition. In the states they sought either through commissions or through legislation a more stringent regulation of railroad practices. Thus in Illinois they first inserted into the new state constitution of 1870 an injunction that "the General Assembly shall, from time to time, pass laws establishing reasonable maximum rates of charges for the transportation of passengers and freight" and "shall pass laws to correct abuses and to prevent unjust discrimination and extortion in the rates of freight and passenger tariffs." Three years of experimental legislation ensued before a statute of 1873 conquered inadequacies.

An existing board of railroad and warehouse commissioners was to draw up a schedule of maximum rates for passengers and freight, and upon the railroads was placed the burden of showing that these rates were unreasonable. This commission of three members no longer had to wait for complaints from shippers, who might be prevented by fear of the railroad from parading their grievances. Upon its own initiative it could "investigate and ascertain whether the provisions of the act are violated" and "immediately cause suits to be commenced and prosecuted against any railroad corporation which may violate the provisions of this act." However typical of Granger legislation these Illinois laws were, they were unique in their survival. In Iowa, Minnesota, and Wisconsin regulation was so extreme and so careless and the hostility of the railroads was so effective that the Granger laws were repealed or modified in the later seventies. In Illinois the railroads were hostile enough. They endeavored to obey the law in a way to make it obnoxious or ridiculous and attempted to educate the people and the legislature to the necessity of repealing the legislation. When their campaign failed, the enforcement of the laws was fought year in and year out through the hierarchy of the courts.

It is not necessary to examine the detailed decisions of the Illinois courts, for the cases arising under the legislation of that state were united with cases from other states and decided by the Supreme Court of the United States in 1877. The first of these Granger cases, Munn v. Illinois, involved warehouse charges; its principles, however, were immediately extended to the railroad regulations just described. The majority of the court dismissed the pleas that such legislation violated the Fourteenth Amendment by taking property without due process of law and declared that the warehouse business was "clothed with a public interest" and could be regulated. Whether the rates established under such regulation were reasonable, was for the legislature, not the court, to determine. "We know that this is a power which may be abused, but that is no argument against its existence. For protection against abuses by legislation, the people must resort to the polls, not to the courts." To the objection of counsel that the regulation of warehouses was a regulation of interstate commerce, which was solely within the power of the national government, the court asserted that, "until Congress acts in reference to their interstate relations the state may exercise all the powers of government over them, even though in so doing it may indirectly operate upon commerce outside its immediate jurisdiction." In the railroad cases these principles were applied, and the railroads' defense that their charters were contracts and were being impaired by this legislation in defiance of the constitutional prohibitions was swept aside by the Supreme Court, which pointed out that these charters had been secured under general incorporation laws which allowed the state to amend, alter, or repeal them.

Although the Supreme Court might admit that the people had the right to pass such legislation, conservatives did not subscribe to its necessity or its wisdom. Railroad presidents talked wildly about the "confiscation of private property." A. T. Hadley, then a lecturer at Yale, felt sure it violated the immutable laws of trade; and one magazine writer, linking together the Pittsburgh riots of 1877 and the Granger laws in the Middle West, gave it as his considered opinion that the Grangers had "turned Communist" and begun "spoliation." It is impossible to tell whether the Granger laws despoiled the railroads. Many of these laws were too quickly repealed; the effects of those that escaped repeal cannot be disentangled from other important factors. Their influence upon public policy was profound. Other states of the Middle West and of the South in the late seventies and eighties reflected the Granger agitation on a smaller scale and passed less thoroughgoing legislation. Finally, in

1887, the Granger railroad philosophy, perpetuated by other organizations, united with other interests to force the passage of national legislation—the Act to Regulate Commerce.

National Regulation

Soon after the Civil War it became apparent that railroad regulation was a national task. As the commerce over these new avenues of communication became increasingly interstate, Congressional debates on the constitutionality of national regulation showed that the constitutional theorists were aware of the new emergency, and the flood of petitions pouring in from the western states gave impetus to more practical activity. The burden of the Granger lament was the exorbitant freight rates on bulky products shipped from the interior to the Atlantic seaboard. At the same time some reformers and shippers in the East were seeking national legislation "to control and limit by law, within proper constitutional and legitimate limits, the rates and charges of existing lines of transportation." By 1874 the anti-railroad movement had wrung from a select Senate committee the voluminous Windom Report on transportation routes to the seaboard. The committee declared the heart of the railroad problem to be the provision of "cheap and ample facilities" for the interchange of commodities among the different sections of the country. As permanent measures it suggested state legislation to prevent stock watering and national legislation to prohibit the consolidation of parallel or competing lines. The problem of *"cheap* transportation is to be solved through *competition."* In order to preserve real competition the committee suggested the construction and operation by the national government of a double-track freight railroad from the Mississippi to the Atlantic, but placed greater emphasis upon the improvement of waterways which, "when properly located, not only afford the cheapest and best-known means of transport for all heavy, bulky, and cheap commodities," but "are also the natural competitors, and most effective regulators of railway-transportation."

Before any further steps were taken the drive against the railroads assumed a different guise. Old issues had disappeared, for in the later seventies trunk-line competitive warfare and the extension of the railroad network had provided "cheap and ample facilities." Now "the paramount evil" was, according to the Cullom Report, made by a Senate committee in the eighties "unjust discrimination between persons, places, commodities, or particular descriptions of traffic." While local rates, where competition did not exist, remained at the old levels, rates between competitive points were slashed, and the discrimination of a greater charge for a short than for a long haul became frequent. The new transcontinental railroads demonstrated this phenomenon on a large and flagrant scale. The lavishness and injustice of personal rebates increased. Although every investigation uncovered their existence, reproaches were ignored by railroads and shippers; and some concerns, like Standard Oil, brazenly continued to furnish new illustrations. The widespread character of these evils made the attack against the railroads national rather than sectional. While the embattled farmers of the West were attempting in the eighties to revive some of the Granger legislation which had been repealed, eastern manufacturers and shippers were equally determined upon protection against discriminations. Some railroad officials and many investors also sought national regulation as a substitute for some of the radical proposals under consideration and as a means of ending the competitive chaos in the railroad world. Railroad executives with strategically located enterprises and a hard-core preference for competition held back; but others wanted to call in the government to prohibit abuses and to police self-regulatory measures. The alternative was a harmony imposed by bankers or other strong leaders, or else the survival of the fittest in some sort of amalgamation. The Congressional committee which reported the Act to Regulate Railroads acknowledged:

> Not a few of the ablest railroad men of the country seem disposed to look to the intervention of Congress as promising to afford the best means of ultimately securing a more equitable and satisfactory adjustment of the relations of the transportation interests to the community than they themselves have been able to bring about.

Little wonder the majorities for the act of 1887 were impressive.

Also known as the Interstate Commerce Act, the railroad act derived its provisions from previous legislation and from the experience of the country with railroad abuses. The act declared that all charges were to be just and reasonable; and it forbade rebates and personal discriminations of every sort. Railroads were forbidden to charge greater compensation "for the transportation of passengers or of like kind of property under substantially similar circumstances and conditions, for a shorter than for a longer distance over the same line, in the same direction, the shorter being included within the longer distance." The Interstate Commerce Commission (ICC) was authorized to make exceptions to this principle after investigation. All pooling and traffic agreements were prohibited. The railroads had to make annual reports to the ICC on their financial condition and their operation. The enforcement of the act was given to the Interstate Commerce Commission consisting of five members whose terms were to be for six years. Complaints were to be made to this body; its decisions were to be issued in the form of orders to the carriers; if one of these remained obdurate, an appeal was to be made by the Commission to the courts for a writ compelling obedience.

For a few years after its establishment the Interstate Commerce Commission secured the cooperation of the railroads. But when this era of harmony inevitably ended, the commission was hampered by the clumsiness and delays of its procedure. It operated upon complaints by shippers. If a railroad saw fit to resist an order of the ICC, that body had to obtain an order from the courts. The courts reheard the entire case and took new evidence. Then the case drifted through the hierarchy of courts until it came to the Supreme Court. On the average, appealed cases required four years for settlement; delays twice as long were not infrequent. Then through judicial interpretation the powers of the commission were greatly limited. It retained its authority to prevent personal rebating. But in 1897 two judicial decisions struck down other activities. In one the Supreme Court found that while the ICC could determine the fairness or reasonableness of rates in the past and order redress, the Act to Regulate Commerce did not give it "the legislative function of prescribing rates which shall control in the future." This decision, of course, prevented even passably thorough rate regulation. A few months later the Supreme Court in another case accepted a railroad's plea that competition between places and railroads could justify a charge for a long haul lower than that for a short one even under the definitions of the Act to Regulate Commerce. In truth, the act contained so many ambiguous objectives and had consciously adjourned so many disputes to the courts that it is likely the Court was expressing popular intentions rather than defying them. Perhaps the Interstate Commerce Commission lacked the stature to formulate a convincing philosophy for railroads. His appraisal of its members led Charles Francis Adams, Jr., President of the Union Pacific, to conclude, "Our country is just about half civilized and the average public man belongs to the uncivilized portion." In any case, the courts, given a differently phrased measure, were far from reluctant to fall upon the railroads. They relentlessly used the Sherman Anti-Trust Act of 1890, forbidding "every contract, combination, or conspiracy" in restraint of interstate trade, to dissolve some of the most ambitious pools, protectively christened "associations," in railroad history. "Competition," said the judges, "is the grand rule which governs all the ordinary business pursuits and transactions of life. Evils, as well as benefits, result therefrom."

In the present century Congress passed a series of enactments which gave both a new thoroughness and a new turn to the regulatory process. In 1903 a new statute defined rebates more precisely. Prodded by Theodore Roosevelt and "decent railway men," to use Roosevelt's accolade, Congress made the proof of discrimination before the courts easier by declaring that any departure from published tariffs, taken alone, was a misdemeanor, and some years later removed the clauses by which the railroads had escaped the prohibition of the long-haul and short-haul practice.

Like most problems, that of the railroads didn't go away. The Roosevelt Administration, originally rather indifferent to it, grew more interested when various government agencies mapped the close connection of rates and discrimination with the growth of big business in meat packing and petroleum: shippers still complained of extortionate rates, and many railroad officials continued to invite national action to solve the evils of competition and put a stop to the divergent and hostile policies within the states. "Let the Government regulate us," said A. J. Cassatt, President of the Pennsylvania Railroad and one of the great apostles of the "community of interest" idea. Though Roosevelt thought legalized pooling was "the best possible regulation of rates," he sensed its political impossibility and favored granting the Interstate Commerce Commission the right upon complaint to set a just and reasonable maximum rate. If the ICC had the power "to make the maximum rate that which the railroad gives to the most-favored shipper, it will speedily become impossible to favor any shipper." Perhaps this rather backhanded way of getting at rebates was a concession necessary to get the Hepburn Act of 1906 passed. That act also covered pipelines, express or shipping-car companies, terminals and services. After a long quarrel and intricate maneuvers it provided a compromise on judicial review. The Interstate Commerce Commission was given the power to issue its own orders; the railroads, not the Commission, had to resort to the courts; and while the Federal Circuit Court might set aside these orders, the Commission's report "shall be *prima facie* evidence of the matters therein stated." Appeals from the Circuit Court were to go directly to the Supreme Court and were to have precedence on its docket. The Attorney-General was to conduct the formal prosecution in such cases. The railroads were still allowed to charge the old rate pending adjudication of the new. Four years later a supplementary act declared that the ICC in prescribing reasonable rates and regulations for the future, could suspend any change in rates or practices proposed by the railroads for ten months, during which reasonableness of the change could be determined. The burden of proof of reasonableness was placed upon the railroad.

Admittedly these were technicalities. But procedures are principles. Before 1906 the task of national regulation was conceived primarily in terms of remedying past rates and practices. After 1910 the Interstate Commerce Commission was permitted to shape policy for the future. However haltingly, the Hepburn Act let the government into the area of setting prices. To exercise its significant new powers the ICC gained wider authority to compel reports, examine railroad books, and finally in 1913, in the Wilson Administration, to undertake a physical valuation of railroad property. Such an appraisal was thought to be an essential preliminary to sound rate-making.

The concept that rates should be based not upon watered stock but upon real value was not a simple one. Original cost, reproduction cost new, reproduction cost less depreciation, and other values and elements of value might be the test for real value. Before the test for real value and other policies were worked to any rational conclusions, World War I intervened. Within a few months freight congestion and its accumulated problems were too great for solution by existing government agencies or by private carriers, unwilling or unable to see the problem of transportation as a unified one. Only a new agency would be able to provide the extension of the facilities and new equipment; only a new agency could give increased wages to meet the increased cost of living and also increase rates to underwrite these advances. At the end of 1917 Wilson took possession of the whole transportation system of the country, coastwise and inland water transportation as well as railroads, and placed them all under the Secretary of the Treasury as Director-General. This move was not influenced by the principles of the nineties when the Populist party had called explicitly for government ownership and operation of the railroads. Rather on this occasion Wilson might well have said as Cleveland did on another, "It is a condition that confronts us—not a theory."

Survivals and Renewals

As the Wilsonian order demonstrated, railroads even at the end of the railroad age had not entirely displaced water transportation. Nonetheless, their victories had been substantial. Most river traffic went under. At the very moment when a government report was announcing in 1877 that the "Mississippi river is still and will always continue to be the most important avenue of commerce between the West and the South," the railroads were carrying the larger share of the grain and flour of the Northwest; and within a few years, instead of floating downstream, cotton went by rail to the Atlantic or the Gulf ports or made the whole journey by rail to the Northeast, crossing rather than following the Mississippi. By 1905 the total receipts and shipments by rail at St. Louis, once a river port rather than a railroad center, were more than one hundred times those by river. If the Mississippi capitulated to the railroad, it is not surprising that the other rivers did. The upper Mississippi and the Missouri and the rivers of the Pacific coast ceased to be significant carriers, and eastern streams sank to the level of carrying excursionists on the one hand and petroleum, lumber, sand, and gravel on the other. Practically the only surviving traffic of importance was carried upon the Ohio and the streams which united to form it. Coal was its salvation, for the mines along the Monongahela could dump their dusty cargoes directly into barges and it could be unloaded at the user's or merchant's yard on the lower streams without transshipment. But even this success meant twilight for the steamboat as well as the old ports it served. Pittsburgh and tugs and tows were the symbols of the new era on the western waters.

Even before 1860 the canals had begun to go under in New England, Pennsylvania, and Ohio. Some of the more strategic canals lived into the twentieth century. But only the willingness of the states which owned them to cut tolls and make up deficits from other funds made such endurance possible. Sacrifices of this order kept the Illinois and Michigan in operation. Although its offspring were dying all about it, the patriarchal Erie Canal still survived. Even if it was steadily losing tonnage to the railroads, its low rates acted as a check on the freights charged by them. The canal partisans prevailed upon the state to make the canal a "free" one with the abolition of tolls in 1882. It did little good. In 1900 only 5 percent of the tonnage reaching New York from the interior came by the canal and the Hudson. Once again desperate, the protagonists of water and the foes of railroads persuaded the state to build a barge canal at a cost of over $100 million, a project not completed until after World War I.

Such was the history of most waterways, natural and artificial. There seemed a mystery in all this, for in the late nineteenth century the all-rail rate on wheat from Chicago to New York per ton-mile was nearly four times as much as the ton-mile rate by water. Those suspicious of railroads suspected skulduggery. Other interpreters asserted that the success of the railroads was due to their natural superiority. Canals froze, rivers varied in depth and concealed hazards to navigation, railroads were the faster means of communication. There were variants to these advantages. Insurance rates for the carriage of goods by railroads were so low that they were assumed by the railroad, while the shipper by canal or river had both the annoyance and the expense of insuring his own shipments. Railroads could go anywhere. Spur tracks ran to the doors of factory or grain elevator and diminished the inconvenience and expense of teaming. Finally the country had so grown away from waterways that auxiliary hauls to them were longer and more expensive. In truth, American history was not unique in chronicling the victory of the railroad over the waterway. European experience had been similar. Where waterways had persisted, as in Germany, France, and Belgium, natural conditions were extremely favorable and preferential legislation checked the natural outcome of railroad competition.

To this general proscription of waterways the Great Lakes were a startling exception. Total shipments increased between 1889 and 1916 from 25 million to over 125 million short tons, and in the latter year one-third of the nation's merchant marine was employed on these waters. Great Lakes ports had a waterborne commerce greater than that of the traditional cities along the Atlantic seaboard. One reason for the success of the Lakes in the face of railroad competition was their location in a region producing bulky commodities admirably suited to water transportation. It was harder for the railroads to monopolize the grain traffic from Minnesota and the Dakotas to the Atlantic seaboard than it had been from Illinois and Iowa. At the same time the discovery and exploitation of the vast iron ranges around Lake Superior provided an eastward commerce in the ore consumed by the iron and steel industry at the other end of Lakes Erie and Michigan. Return cargoes, although not equal to the eastward commerce, were supplied by coal. Since coal and iron constituted over four-fifths of the traffic tonnage on the Lakes in 1916, they determined the lines of commerce. There was comparatively little local traffic except on Lake Michigan and Lake Erie; the chief lanes of lake commerce were from Lake Superior ports to those on Lake Erie, and the greatest lake ports were the two termini—Duluth–Superior and Buffalo.

A second explanation for the success of the Lakes was the continually evolving technical equipment. After the eighties sailing vessels declined and the steam vessel became the dominant carrier. At the end of the Civil War the average propeller had weighed 231 tons; by 1920 the typical carrier had a tonnage between 3,000 and 7,000. The cargoes were heavy, and the vessels were adapted to them. Hulls were long boxes with slightly shaped ends and straight sides; the wheelhouse and the engines were placed at the fore and aft extremities; the cargo space between was approached by a series of uninterrupted hatches. The docks fitted the vessels. Grain was shot down through batteries of spouts, coal and iron were dumped through chutes. Machinery likewise speeded the unloading process. Endless conveyors lifted the grain out of the hold, and a series of shovels, carrying both scoops and operating cabs, like the magnified tentacles of some restless insect, dipped out the coal and iron. With waits at terminals reduced through efficiency, vessels could make trip after trip and multiply their usefulness and cheapness. Like other transportation marvels, the Great Lakes vessels were generally owned and operated by railroads, great industrial concerns, like United States Steel, or large shipping corporations.

Another survivor of the waterways era was the coasting trade, both on the Atlantic and the Pacific. Larger and larger vessels, now built of iron and steel and usually driven by propellers rather than paddle wheels, were launched in every decade to provide for the overnight passenger comfort or the luxury which railroads did not yet provide. In the carriage of bulk cargoes, there were losses, like that of cotton which took to land, and gains, like that of petroleum which sought cheap marine transportation. And the old standbys were standbys still. On the Atlantic coast lumber moved northward from the yellow pine belt of the southern states and coal from the rising ports of Hampton Roads and the traditional shippers of Baltimore, Philadelphia, and New York. On the Pacific the great new forest empire of the Northwest shipped its products southward from northern California, the Columbia, and Puget Sound; petroleum from California made the return journey. To carry these bulk cargoes builders, particularly those in the eastern yards, created the great multimasted schooners; their acme, the *Thomas W. Lawson* of 1902, had seven masts and a steel hull and was of 5,218 gross tons burden. Actually as early as the eighties the tugs with tows of specially built barges or cut-down sailing vessels were exhibiting their operational savings. By 1910, if not earlier, these carriers, as prosaic as freight cars, had taken over the bulk trades. Their affinity with the railroads did not stop there. For railroads ever since the Civil War had been buying into the lines of coastal steamers in the Atlantic–Gulf of Mexico commerce or founding and developing them. The consolidation movement at the turn of the century brought these as well as independents into larger aggregates, big business saltwater variety.

Although waterways ceased in general to be its rivals, the railroad had to meet other challenges. On land the first serious competitor developed from the attempt to solve the problem of urban transportation. Horse busses gave way to horsecars; horsecars gave way to cable cars; and in the late eighties a new transportation device, the electric car, demonstrated its efficiency upon the thirteen miles of the street railway system of Richmond, Virginia. The familiar phenomena connected with a craze for a new method of transportation at once appeared. It seemed to be a simple and inexpensive matter to put a motor under the old horsecar, string a wire above the tracks, dismiss armies of stablemen and hostlers, dispense with horses and barns, and make money. The arrival of the electric car also coincided with the heyday of nineteenth century promotion. The golden day for plunder in the railroad world had set, and now a group of buccaneers turned toward the rising sun of electric railways, or "public utilities," as they were called. In New York, Philadelphia, and Chicago such groups controlled the political organizations which gave franchises and operated in business upon the dictum of C. T. Yerkes, one of their number: "The secret of success in my business is to buy old junk, fix it up a little, and unload it upon other fellows." A host of other promoters organized trolley lines, extended them rapidly, brought about incorporations or consolidations swimming in watered stock, paid dividends when companies did not earn them, and neglected to make proper charges for depreciation.

Even in the fifties, as horsecar lines crawled toward the suburbs, the railroads were alarmed at the loss of passenger traffic and, as the mood stirred them, uttered either defiance or lament. Later, as these horsecar lines became electrified and were formed into systems, they became even more efficient competitors. In only one of the years between 1901 and 1908 did new construction amount to less than a thousand miles. A few years later Ohio and Indiana among the states had the longest mileage. Though Pennsylvania and New York had considerable trackage, the interurban electric railway was outstandingly a middle western phenomenon. As it turned out, the new method of transportation had a short boom. Construction was accompanied by an unbelievable optimism. "Hopes were capitalized, hopes were sold." When decline set in after 1910, the companies themselves ascribed their ills to the extravagant demands of their employees, the high cost of materials, and the exactions of public regulation. Amateurism in management, the ability to carry only passengers and light freight, and heavy overhead costs made the electric railways poor competitors, but more important were the traffic inroads made by the automobile.

In the 1890's there was a national rebirth of interest in good roads. The strongest impulse for this movement came from the farmers who were increasingly aware of the high costs and other disadvantages that 2 million miles of dirt road imposed upon their economic activity and their social life. In the nineties the Populist movement enabled the farmers to organize for political activity, and the establishment of rural free delivery of mail in 1897 created an army of lobbyists for good roads among rural-free-delivery carriers and officials in the Post Office Department. This phalanx of agitation and support was primarily concerned with the improvement of post and farm-to-market roads.

The barriers to change were numerous. Finances came from local taxes and those who paid taxes customarily "worked them out" under supervision of local road commissioners. Favoritism, inertia and ignorance, and a disinclination to improve through routes were the result. Probably the nation had been better prepared to cope with these difficulties a century earlier. Besides farmers, other supporters joined the good-roads army—bicyclists, or "wheelmen," as they were called, and Americans who had been abroad and seen the magnificent national highway systems in some European countries. Not all these new allies wanted farm-to-market roads; they sought a system of hard-surfaced roads connecting cities and large towns. Also in the nineties states like Massachusetts and New Jersey established state road commissions and appropriated money for the construction and maintenance of state systems. But the West and South wanted a national program; they didn't want highways for "joyriders," as the new breed of urban automobile drivers had been christened. In 1916 Congress enacted a Federal Aid Road Act.

The Federal government was to transfer funds to states for improved roads; and the states were to match this aid dollar for dollar. The Federal government through the Department of Agriculture in cooperation with the Postmaster-General was to designate the roads to be aided. In 1923 Federal expenditures for post roads were $169 million.

The automobile industry played little part in the formative period of the movement for good roads. The railroad, on the other hand, was an enthusiastic participant. Its spokesmen, with an air of splendid certainty, foretold it "an idle dream to imagine that auto-trucks and automobiles will take the place of railways in the long-distance movement of freight and passengers." The railway station, as it had been with horse-drawn conveyances, was the "natural terminus for roads." Even before 1916 doubts had dimmed this assurance. In that year motor vehicle registration reached 3,617,957 and the Federal Aid Road Act refused to limit its appropriations to farm-to-market roads. Still, when Charles Francis Adams, Jr., wanted to aid a fellow historian, Frederic Bancroft, to go from Washington to Baltimore, Adams sent his car and chauffeur to drive Bancroft only from his home to the Washington railroad station.

xii
The New Industrial State

After Appomattox the United States resumed the momentum toward industrialization which had been so marked for two decades or so before the Civil War. Fortunately, a demonstration of this transformation need not depend upon dollar values of product, which fluctuate widely. Fortunately, also, enough figures of quantities produced are available to construct an index of manufacturing production. One such formulation concludes that manufacturing productivity multiplied twelve times from 1860 to 1914. Indeed, the United States in this period became the most powerful industrial nation in the world.

Of course the vicissitudes of American political history have had considerable influence upon the rate and the direction of this industrial transformation. For one thing the nation had passed through two wars—the American Civil War and the war with Spain. While the second was essentially a "bow-and-arrow" conflict, "a splendid little war," relatively without direct influence upon the nation's industrial growth, the Civil War lasted four years, involved millions of men, and took place within the national territory. The older view that the Civil War stimulated industrial development is no longer held without reservations; the spectacular spurt forward once the war ended leads to the inference that the factors for an industrial transformation were latent in the economy and only needed freedom and certainty to clear the way for their operation. Aside from war, the policies of the national government in regard to currency and business regulation have also had a direct effect upon industrial history. In the realm of policy peculiar importance, if not sacredness, has attached to the protective tariff. The era of modern protection, as we shall see, came in with the Civil War; it was not seriously modified until the eve of World War I. This long reign of protection, however, did not greatly influence the general course of our industrial development. There were instances of its benign effect—the tinplate industry, the silk mills, beet-sugar manufacturing—but even in these industries other factors have to be taken into consideration. As for our fundamental industries—meat packing, food preserving, lumbering, coal mining, petroleum, iron and steel, automobiles, electric equipment—the tariff was negligible. There were more fundamental explanations for the industrial power of the United States.

One explanation was the sheer growth of population and its redistribution between urban and rural areas. The latter process practically compelled an expansion or rebuilding of American cities. Construction is a broad term that can cover public utilities, like sewers and electric railways, or business and industrial buildings. The rise in the value of "nonfarm residential construction" is a simple illustration of the trend. For the five-year period 1869–1873 the average value per year of gross construction was $220 million. The same average for 1912–1916 was $1.26 billion.

The American people, not as individuals but as masses, constituted, with the exception of Russia, the greatest free-trade market in the world, and this free market was made accessible on a national scale to manufacturers by the improved means of transportation constructed during the railroad age. From the increased population was recruited in turn the army of laborers who were to man the country's machines and run its offices. Finally, the American people occupied an area packed with natural resources.

Natural Resources and Their Use

In 1860 American industry was dependent upon the natural resources most easily exploited by the simple economic organization of a frontier nation—"the products of the field and of the forest." By 1914 American manufacturing had not sloughed off this chrysalis. Yet the merest glance at the industrial scene showed that the chief features of the industrial state until recently were provided by other industries, most of which had come into being after the mid-nineteenth century. They were the heavy industries, the ones with prolonged and indirect systems of manufacturing, requiring large fixed investments and generally turning out producers' rather than consumers' goods. Of primary importance were the industries which provided extrahuman power. With the resources—coal, oil, natural gas, and water—for these power industries the United States was generously endowed. An equally fundamental industry was that of iron and steel; the cornerstone of this industry rested upon natural resources of coal and iron. Dependent in turn upon the steel and other metal industries were the other giants of the industrial state—the electric, the machine, and, somewhat later, the automobile industries. In short, at each hand American industry now depended not so much upon growing things as upon metals and minerals, even sand and gravel, all capital supplies in the bank of the earth.

Coal was one illustration. In 1860 the country mined 14.61 million tons; in 1914 nearly thirty times as much. In this period American coal —whose production surpassed that of Great Britain, the motherland of the Industrial Revolution—was the main source of power, the chief fuel, and, it may be added, the commodity that provided half of the tonnage carried by the American railway. At first anthracite had the leadership. Its deposits, localized in five counties of northeastern Pennsylvania, were all discovered and utilized before 1835. Their association with the Wyoming, Lehigh, Schuylkill, and Susquehanna river valleys and their location near the most thickly settled parts of the United States gave them means of transportation and a market. After methods of burning it had been perfected, anthracite served as a fuel for industrial establishments, for locomotives, and for steam vessels, and its annual production generally exceeded that of bituminous coal until the decade of the seventies. By the twentieth century the output of anthracite mines was apparently stabilized and used predominantly for domestic purposes.

The place of anthracite was usurped by bituminous coal, which secured the ascendancy in 1870 and increased its output until in 1914 its tonnage was over four and a half times that of anthracite. By far the largest proportion of bituminous coal was used to raise steam under boilers, either in industrial establishments or in railroad locomotives; but in addition it yielded gas, after processing, for lighting and heating operations; it filled the bunkers of ocean and Great Lakes vessels; and, coked, it was an essential in the new method of smelting iron. Of the several varieties of coal blanketed under the word "bituminous," the United States had the greatest deposits in the world. They were scattered throughout the nation from Puget Sound through the Great Plains and Corn Belt to the Appalachians. The greatest producing areas, however, were the Appalachian fields underlying the plateau which runs nearly from Lake Erie into northern Alabama. The Appalachian coals, generally speaking, were of superior quality; the industrial centers were near at hand—these were the reasons for the fields' usefulness.

Throughout the later nineteenth century there was really no fuel that could challenge coal. In this period petroleum, which was eventually to become a challenger, was primarily an illuminant. In the fifties those in search of a substitute for whale oil succeeded in distilling from certain bituminous coals a usable coal oil, kerosene; they perfected its distillation process, encouraged the large-scale manufacture of lamps to burn it, and developed a method of distributing it through grocers. All of these innovations cleared the way for a business dependent upon petroleum, which it was hoped would provide a more abundant and less costly base-product for kerosene. Through a complicated chain of events, abounding with crises and coincidences, an oil company drilled the first commercial oil well near Titusville, Pennsylvania, in 1859. Thus began a new era in the modern world. The new method of obtaining petroleum was so successful and the demand for kerosene so great that into western Pennsylvania poured a tide of speculators and fortune seekers. Farmers grew wealthy either as producers or as the surprised owners of this treasure trove; wells were driven recklessly and oil ran to waste for lack of transportation facilities; the oil town sprang into existence with its tatterdemalion houses, stores, saloons, and houses of prostitution; Wild-west order prevailed. This pattern of hasty, reckless living was repeated with variations as new centers of production were opened up. At the end of the century the business took a new turn. The invention of the internal combustion engine placed a premium upon the gasoline which the early producers had either wasted or mixed, as far as inflammability would allow, with kerosene. The discovery that heavier oils could be burned if sprayed under pressure created a market for fuel oil first in railroad and marine transportation—where the oil's lesser bulk and automatic stoking furthered its use—and later in industrial plants and even for domestic heating. By 1900 the total production of oil in the United States over all the previous decades had been about a billion barrels; over the next fifteen years it was 2,612,956,000. By then petroleum and natural gas were furnishing about one sixth of our annual power output, a percentage considerably greater than that of water-power.

These wider uses sometimes preceded, sometimes followed the opening of new centers of production. The Appalachian field, smudged through western Pennsylvania, West Virginia, and eastern Ohio, was the first field of importance. In 1885 production in the Lima field in northwestern Ohio was undertaken and, uniting with a neighboring segment in Indiana, this new area produced for a time over one third of the oil in the United States. In the late nineteenth century, field after field swung into production, although in nearly every case discoveries or earlier drilling had taken place. California, stimulated by the example of Pennsylvania, had an oil craze in the sixties and began important production in the nineties. In 1901 the Gulf fields were opened when a well in southeastern Texas was blown in with a flow of between 5,000 and 10,000 barrels a day. This new development spread eastward into Louisiana. Other fields crowded in Illinois and southwestern Indiana and into the Wyoming district in the Rocky Mountain region. Finally, in 1911–1912, the gigantic midcontinent field—northern Texas, Kansas, Oklahoma, and parts of Arkansas—came into production. All this feverish expansion fell well within the lifetime of John D. Rockefeller. He saw the discovery, the development, and the progressive decline of the Appalachian field, the rise of California to a position of primacy, and then its surrender to the midcontinent field.

Iron, together with coal and petroleum, was the third great resource of the industrial state. Deposits were scattered nearly everywhere, but their utilization in industry depended upon their physical or chemical properties, the ease of mining, and upon either the proximity of the coal employed in smelting or the cheapness with which iron could be transported to the furnace districts. Although the previous mining areas around Lake Champlain and in the mountain nucleus of the Border states continued to furnish ores, sometimes into the twentieth century, new resources built the post-Civil War industry. In the eighties the development of the remarkable deposits of the Chattanooga-Birmingham region, where the ores were closely interleaved with coal—whose high sulphurous content was a handicap—got under way. The real revolution in the iron industry was the discovery and exploitation of the Lake Superior iron district. In 1844 a party of government surveyors in the upper peninsula of Michigan discovered iron near what is now Marquette, and a year later other explorers beheld "a mountain of solid iron ore, 150 feet high." This early description gave the name "ranges" to those iron deposits, for they were found along ridges, hills, and occasionally mountains. The development of the region waited upon transportation improvements, for the area was remote from the coal deposits and the eastern markets. But the Great Lakes were at the doorstep, the continued improvement in the canals at the "Soo" encouraged large-scale transportation, railroads were built inland through the forests and swamps from the shores of Lake Superior or Lake Michigan to the iron deposits. Extensive mining operations began in the seventies or eighties. There were four ranges: the Marquette range lay south of Lake Superior, to the west of the present port of Marquette; the Menominee bordered that river and built an outlet at Escanaba; the Gogebic straddled the Wisconsin-Michigan line; the Vermilion was a hundred miles due north of Duluth. Then in the nineties came the Mesabi. This new field, slightly to the south of the Vermilion, was nearer Duluth and had an area equal to that of all the other four ranges. The dominance of these mines mounted until in 1919 they produced nearly 85 percent of the iron of the country. This extraordinary achievement was due to three factors. Extraction was easy, particularly in the Mesabi region; transportation was organized with such efficiency that the ores were laid down at the eastern lake ports at low prices; and the mines produced high-grade ores of many varieties. No country then had their equal.

Generally, the natural resources located east of the Mississippi River were discovered upon private property. In every case the owners of these resources did nothing to create them and in most cases did not realize their existence. In fact, this land had usually been alienated as agricultural land by the colonies or under the provisions of the public land system of the national government. Now untold wealth descended upon the unsuspecting owners, and the theory of private property was so little questioned that they were not disturbed in its possession or enjoyment. The fantastic results of this arrangement were conspicuously demonstrated in the oil "game," an industry which deserved that vulgar appellation. In the sixties dazed Pennsylvania farmers became wealthy, and after 1910 sleepy-eyed Indians repeated the experience in Oklahoma. Some might utilize their wealth wisely, but since "Lady Luck" was the goddess presiding over the scramble, the "Coal Oil Johnny" who lit cigars with bank notes became the extravagant symbol of the industry.

The natural resources upon the government domain in the unsettled West might have been disposed of by some intelligent plan, but for forty years after the Civil War Congress displayed neither the willingness nor the ability to deal with the question. Rather it shilly-shallied, passing special acts, vaguely worded, abounding in exceptions, and economically unsound. Coal lands were dealt with in a series of acts, the most important of which in 1873 provided for sale at prices varying from ten to fifteen dollars an acre; Mineral Land Acts of 1872, applying to other than coal lands, provided for their sale after a certain amount of exploitation and development at prices from $2.50 to $5.00 an acre; and the Timber and Stone Act of 1878 sold land chiefly valuable for timber and stone and unfit for cultivation for at least $2.50 an acre. In every instance this legislation aimed at the transfer of these natural resources to private hands. Even in this lavish process Congress was inefficient or careless. Startling exceptions were often made. The states of Minnesota, Michigan, and Wisconsin were exempted from the Mineral Land Acts, and the iron deposits of the Lake Superior region were, therefore, sold at even lower prices. Railroads received natural resources in their land grants; many of the timber lands were given by the government to the states as "swamp lands" and then transferred to the timber corporations at a pittance; and the Homestead Act and the Preemption Act, designed to create a nation of small farmers, were used to secure the resources for which Congress sought special treatment. The confusion of national policy and the rapacity of private individuals everywhere bred corruption.

The basis of any intelligent land policy was the classification of the land in the public domain and a special treatment based upon its value. The first effective step was taken in 1879, when the Geological Survey was established and authorized to make a land classification. In 1891 a second step in the new policy was taken in the passage of the Forest Reserve Act, which authorized the President to withdraw forest areas from entry. In these districts lumbering was carried on under special provisions. This policy of withdrawal was applied to mineral and coal lands by Theodore Roosevelt, a vigorous champion of the conservation movement, and by Taft. The actual value of these attainments remained, however, in doubt. Withdrawal was in many cases simply a postponement of action; the final disposition was important.

To the exploitation of these resources their owners or lessees brought a zeal fired by the hope of profits and by the fear that rivals would get ahead of them. An era of intense competition ensued. Where the battle was stayed through semimonopoly, as in the Vermilion iron range or the Lima-Indiana oil field, an orderly and efficient development was possible. These instances were exceptions. Nearly everywhere the owners skimmed the cream of the resources. In timber cutting the best trees or those of a favored species were selected; valuable timber was wasted in slash. Once the lumbering was completed no precautions were taken against forest fires, which raged for square miles through the lumbered areas, charring the standing timbers, killing growing trees, and in some cases actually destroying the soil itself. In the extraction of oil the aim was to run off the oil in the oil sands through wells on one's own property before a competitor could tap the same underground resource. Offset wells were first drilled along the property lines in order to expedite this race for robbery. As a consequence oil fields were plugged with far too many wells; wells were located with an utter absence of adaptability to the needs of the field; overproduction was so great that prices crashed and low-grade consumption uses were stimulated; oil in some of the gusher fields was stored in great earthen lakes where it seeped into the soil, lost its valuable qualities by exposure to the sun or was washed away by rain; the natural gas, accompanying the oil, was allowed to dissipate into the atmosphere. The figures of some of these debaucheries are astonishing. Yet a western oil journal put it, "What do we care if millions of barrels of crude oil are wasted and billions of cubic feet of natural gas go up into the air? After us the deluge!"

This rapid exploitation undoubtedly created an almost unparalleled inrush of material prosperity. Yet it was a mathematical certainty that the process could not continue. The National Conservation Commission of 1909 asserted that with the increasing rate of production the coal supplies of the country would approach exhaustion before the middle of the next century, that the high-grade iron ores would not "last beyond the middle of the present one," that petroleum faced the same future, and that in timber production there was already a stringency calling for immediate measures. This pessimistic inventory, however, failed to appreciate that in the past national resources had on occasion been considered "exhausted" and that human inventiveness had often outwitted limitations imposed by circumstance.

Technical Changes—Coal, Oil, Steel

Abundance of natural resources was, however, not enough. The economic development of the United States since 1860 has been due to the fact that raw material has been rapidly converted into goods through improved machinery. The age since 1860 may have been the "age of coal and iron" or the "age of petroleum" or the "age of electricity." It was unquestionably the "age of the machine."

Technical advances in the actual extraction of the material resources which nourished the industrial state were most uneven. Most coal and iron mines were underground; their exploitation required shafts, tunneling and shoring. The coal and ore had to be torn from the rock which grasped it, broken sufficiently for loading, and hauled and elevated to the surface. All these tasks belonged to the craftsman with his drill, powder, skill, and strength. To such work it seemed impossible to apply factory and machine methods, for as the *Coal Age* put it, "We cannot bring the work to the mechanism, but we have to move the mechanism to the work. . . . We have a factory which is always demolishing its own walls, and is faced with the herculean task of supporting the load of some hundreds of feet of overburden." Nonetheless, shaft mining was mechanized. From the eighties on, compressed air drove power drills; in the next decade machines undercut the seam of coal, the first step in its loosening; and in the twentieth century electricity took over the task of lighting and hauling. The most spectacular innovation was the decision in the early nineties to use steam shovels to shove aside the overburden of earth and then excavate the granular ores of the Mesabi range in open-cut or strip mining. In these immense, ugly man-made valleys the designers of the new method laid railroad yards and introduced the locomotive. In 1915 open-cut mines provided two-fifths of the output of iron ore.

The extraction of petroleum from the earth also required the new application of old methods. E. L. Drake, a spurious "colonel" and former railroad conductor, who drilled the first oil well at Titusville, demonstrated that the equipment once used in boring salt wells could work successfully for petroleum. A heavy drill suspended from the derrick was churned about in the hole by a donkey engine attached to the other end of a walking-beam; and as the drill punched its way downward, the well was lined with pipe to prevent the loose earth and water from seeping in. The later changes in this apparatus were chiefly in size. Only in the twentieth century was the rotary drill invented. Its use was confined to certain soils and rocks. This instrument was rotated through the earth like an auger, and liquid mud, forced down through the stem, spurted out at the cutting edge and carried the loosened material to the top of the well. With such an instrument the driller could reach the oil sands in weeks rather than in months, and greater depths could be obtained.

Greater progress characterized the transportation of these raw materials to the point where they were used or refined. The carriage of coal was, of course, a phase of the railroad development. The transport of iron ore from Lake Superior to Pittsburgh combined in deft perfection rail and water transportation. A steam shovel scooped the ore into cars; the cars, hauled to Duluth or Superior, ran onto the decks over pockets into which the contents of the cars were discharged when their bottoms folded outward. Chutes led the ore from the pockets into the hold of an ore vessel. At a Lake Erie port the vessel was unloaded by automatic machinery and the ore placed again in railroad cars; at Pittsburgh these cars were unloaded by dumpers which turned the cars on their sides and cascaded the ore into bins; finally skip cars carried the ore to the top of the blast furnace. "By the turn of the century," an admiring analyst has written, "the transport of Lake Erie ores had become an intricate ballet of large and complicated machines."

For petroleum a completely novel transportation system was invented. During the boom days in western Pennsylvania, barrels, wagons, and boats had made shift to carry the petroleum from the wilderness to the consuming centers; then railroads were pushed hastily into the oil country and the tank car was invented. The final solution was the pipeline. During the Civil War the use of pipes to carry the oil from the wells to the railroad sidings had been undertaken. The idea of the pipeline was soon extended; pumping stations were placed along it to force the oil over grades; and in the late seventies the first trunk line was carried over the Appalachian Mountains. This feat demonstrated the feasibility of long pipelines, and a network was laid down to the refining centers and constructed in the new fields as they were developed. By the twentieth century they were also carrying gasoline from the refinery to the consuming centers. Such lines constituted an important part of the nation's transportation system. In 1914 a trunk line carried oil from the mid-continent field to the Standard refineries at Bayonne, New Jersey—a distance of fifteen hundred miles.

The final step was the refining, or smelting, process. Although it may be stretching meaning to apply these words to coal, the consumption of coal in boilers and the coking of it in ovens were not revolutionized until well into the twentieth century. As for petroleum, the wresting of usable products from the raw material was in essence a simple process of distillation. When heated, the various elements passed off at different temperatures; the lighter gasoline first and then the kerosene. The so-called straight process sufficed as long as kerosene was the chief product desired. Only in the iron and steel industry did the early years of the industrial state witness a revolutionary break with the past. Steel, of course, had always been manufactured, but the expense caused it to be produced in small quantities and for specialized uses. Before modern civilization, draped over a framework of steel, was possible, the cost of production had to be lowered. The answer was a further extension and perfection of the indirect process by which the ore became steel after being made into pig iron.

The first step in that process was at the furnace or smeltery. In the smelting operation the decade after the Civil War witnessed the continued decline of charcoal as a fuel and the disappearance of the iron "plantation," the forests which had once provided the raw material. Anthracite which provided a high enough heat if fanned by a hot blast gave way to coke. The sulphurous taint of ordinary bituminous coal, the source of coke, was missing in the Connellsville coals of western Pennsylvania. Because of its physical characteristics coke gave a hotter and quicker fire than anthracite. After 1860 no startlingly new principles were introduced in the furnaces in which the new fuel was piled with the limestone and the ore for smelting. But these furnaces did increase in efficiency and in size. Stronger blasts and higher temperatures were employed; the dimensions of the furnace and its attendant apparatus were enlarged; and a greater quantity of pig iron was produced. The modern furnace was an industrial Laocoön of skyscraper specifications; a conglomeration of gigantic cylinders, surmounted by towering stacks, and tied together with thick coils of pipes and flues. When the Lucy Furnace in the Carnegie works went on blast in the 1870's the factory produced 70 tons of smelted iron a week; by the late 1890's "hard driving" produced over 100,000 tons a year. In 1894 the United States permanently surpassed Great Britain in the production of pig iron, and in 1906 she more than equaled the combined production of Great Britain and Germany.

Although a portion of the iron run from the smelting furnace was made directly into furnished cast articles, most of it was manufactured into steel. Modern steel is an iron which has been cleansed of silicon and other impurities, and in which the carbon content is between 1 and 2 percent and is well combined with the other elements. Since this carbon content is less than that of cast iron and is not crystalline and separate, steel lacks brittleness and combines strength and malleability. The inventions which made large-scale steel production possible came in the fifties. Henry Bessemer, an Englishman of an inventive turn of mind, publicized in 1856 his discovery that hot pig iron could be cleaned of its deleterious elements, carbon and silica, if a blast of air were forced through it, for the oxygen consumed the impurities. Further experimentation was necessary before the exact conditions under which the process worked were appreciated. Robert Mushet, an English metallurgist, for instance, drove all the carbon out and then replaced it to a precise percentage with spiegeleisen. Bessemer, like Arkwright, emerged with a title and a fortune. Probably before Bessemer's discovery an ironmaster in Kentucky, William Kelly, had happened upon the same process. However satisfactory this fact may be to national pride, it instigated patent litigation, for Kelly had a patent on the process, Bessemer had one for the machinery, and Mushet another for his recipe. Eventually these patents were consolidated in this country.

Meanwhile a laboratory had been set up at the Wyandotte ironworks near Detroit, investigations into the qualities of iron ores were conducted, and in 1864 steel was produced by the Kelly-Bessemer methods. After a delay for further experimentation, the Bessemer process, a very inexpensive one, swept into use during the seventies. A pear-shaped converter was filled with molten iron, air was blown through, and when the color and length of the flame issuing from the mouth of the converter were right, usually after ten or twenty minutes, spiegeleisen was added and the machine tilted to pour forth a stream of spitting steel. The early Bessemer process was known as the "acid process," for the converter was lined with an acid material. Such converters throve on the Lake Superior ores, but they could not cope with phosphorus-bearing or sulphur-bearing irons until two Englishmen during the seventies substituted a lime or magnesian lining and gave their names to the new method. The Thomas-Gilchrist, or basic, process not only removed the phosphorus from the iron but blended it with the lining to form a phosphate by-product which was commercially valuable.

The acid and the basic processes were applied to both the Bessemer and the open-hearth method of making steel. The open-hearth process has been named the Siemens-Martin process after its German and French inventors. In their process, pig iron, scrap iron, old steel, and ferromanganese were piled into the shallow bowl of the furnace, and the whole was cooked by heat which was outside the molten mass. The process was longer than the Bessemer. In the late nineteenth century it was thought the better controls in the open-hearth process accounted for its superiority. Bessemer steel had a tendency to fracture under sudden shock, it was claimed, and manufacturers of finished products, like car axles and structural steel, specified open-hearth steel. The basic open hearth could use slightly cheaper materials. Nowadays with more sophisticated chemical knowledge, it is maintained that the Bessemer process by using oxygen as fuel makes it impossible to control the nitrogen content of the product and thus prevent a deleterious hardening or ageing of the steel. In any case, in 1908 open-hearth steel surpassed for the first time the production of Bessemer. Meanwhile in steel-making as a whole the same story of international leadership was written. In 1880 the United States surpassed Great Britain in the production of Bessemer steel; and twenty years later she achieved the same victory in the production of open-hearth steel and went on to overwhelming leadership.

A brief narrative of the chief inventions in the primary steel process must not be so short as to conceal the fact that the American industry, after the Civil War as before, did not rely solely upon native American genius. It borrowed from abroad by the importation of skilled artisans; by an examination of European technology either in person or by perusal of learned journals; or by the acquisition of patents. Amidst constant bickering about the effectiveness of protective tariffs, iron and steel generally sought and obtained some protection from the government, and certain industries—the tinplate industry for one—owed their establishment to the operation of such protective measures. By the nineties, however, Andrew Carnegie, the greatest of ironmasters, was praying that the government would stop tinkering with the tariff and leave industry to its own strengths. In his field these were considerable. The United States had, on the one hand, abundant resources strategically located and, on the other, an insatiable and extensive market. For one thing, after the Civil War the railroads were laid with steel. The first steel rails in the country for commercial use were rolled in 1867, and only two decades later they had displaced iron on old and new railroads alike. Rolled steel plate first superseded iron in locomotives, and in ocean and lake vessels. After the nineties the market was dramatically expanded by the development of the American tinplate industry, whose product, when made into cans, found novel and generous consumers in the oil industry and in the canned-food industry of the country. The cheap steel nail made the iron nail an antique; and the wire industry, transposed to a steel basis, made miles of barbed-wire and woven-wire fence to enclose the western prairies. Steel shapes, standardized in design and production, facilitated the rapid construction of bridges not only in the United States but across the rivers of the world. Then came the skyscraper and the huge factory, whose skeletons were frameworks of steel. Toward the end of the period the historic connection of our metallurgical industries with transportation was reaffirmed by the construction of steel passenger and freight cars and by the reliance of the automobile upon steel alloys. These were but the major demands. Practically steel drove puddled iron, wrought iron, and cast iron from even their smaller fortresses.

Electricity

Within the industrial state, economic change could hardly be measured by masses of figures alone. Qualitative factors were involved, for the distinction of the era lay not so much in the improvement of old ways of doing things as in the manufacture of new products. As a workingman compared 1883 with 1878 he commented, "We get many things now we did not have then."

Of these new industries, born by the hundreds in the industrial state, the electrical industry because of its size, the pervasiveness and variety of its social and economic results, and its problems was unique. Since the days of classical Greece and Rome, philosophers, scientists and other men of a curious turn of mind had been slowly accumulating knowledge about the baffling phenomenon of electricity.

In the first part of the nineteenth century electricity left the field of mystery and stunt and was applied in this country to communications. The first practical application of electricity came in the field of communications when Samuel F. B. Morse in the 1830's invented with the help of others the telegraph. An electric battery was sufficient to power his apparatus, and fittingly a new language of dots and dashes—the Morse code—served to transmit public and private news and to ask questions. Fittingly enough, also, the first ceremonial message transmitted over an experimental line between Baltimore and Washington financed by the national government was "What hath God wrought?" The world of learning and technology is still providing an answer. Meanwhile the spread of the new service was unexampled in rapidity. By 1848 the "magnetic" had sent words as far as St. Louis; by 1861 a telegraph, subsidized by the government, spanned the continent and outmoded the Pony Express; in 1866 Cyrus Field, a retired American paper manufacturer, financed with English assistance the first permanently successful Atlantic cable. Its laying was a stirring drama of human patience and persistence.

In 1876 Alexander Graham Bell exhibited at the Centennial Exposition in Philadelphia a telephone which transmitted the human voice and other noises over wires. Bell was a Scot, educated abroad, who came to this country in his twenties. His interest in the science of acoustics as a means of training the deaf had sparked his career as inventor. Once invented and improved the telephone spread rapidly. The first exchange was opened in 1878; the White House by the middle of the next decade had a telephone, which Grover Cleveland regarded with some disfavor; and in 1892 the American Telephone and Telegraph Company inaugurated with much ceremony a long-distance line between Chicago and New York. In 1887 there were 170,000 subscribers; in 1917 over 11,716,000 telephones were in use. No wonder Arnold Bennett remarked, "What startles and frightens backward Europeans in the United States is the efficiency and fearful universality of the telephone." Without it the tempo of modern American business would be impossible.

Until 1880 the electrical industry had been concerned chiefly with communication. But with incandescent lighting and the use of electrical power for transportation and industry, electricity began a new era. These novel demands required electric power in a full stream beside which the current used by the telegraph or the telephone was a mere trickle. Inventors of electric lights and of motors were consequently as concerned with dynamos and transmission as they were with their immediate apparatus. Electric lighting came first. In the first decade of the nineteenth century Sir Humphry Davy produced an arc between two pieces of charcoal. Later experimenters tinkered with the arrangement of these carbon pencils, the automatic formation of the proper gap between them, the prevention of rapid deterioration, and in the seventies arc lighting was placed upon a commercial basis. It was realized, however, that the new instrument gave too brilliant a light for domestic use and was far too expensive. This dilemma enlisted the attention of Thomas Alva Edison. The drama of his life, typically American in its ambitions, in its scientfic bent, and in its rise from train boy to the "Wizard of Menlo Park," has tended to obscure the contributions of predecessors and contemporaries. Incandescent lamps had been designed before Edison turned his attention in 1877 to the problem of devising a filament which would be inexpensive and durable and whose decomposition would not blacken the inside of the bulb. In this quest he had the assistance of a laboratory and field force and his own remarkable thoroughness of procedure and fertility of resource. Like other inventors, he had to build a dynamo suitable for his purpose. Then in a vacuum bulb he employed a platinum filament. This was too expensive. Finally on October 21, 1879, he turned current into a filament of carbonized sewing thread. The resulting glow lasted forty-five hours. The world was now ransacked for a better element; six thousand vegetable growths were tested; finally a carbonized bamboo filament was found most satisfactory.

In the domain of electrical power George Westinghouse, air brake inventor, was the victor over Edison. To be sure, the latter in 1882 built the first central station, the Pearl Street Station of New York City, and distributed its current to the eighty-five buildings which were wired for electric lighting. This pioneer station set precedents in its generators, connections, and distribution system, but it produced a direct current. Such a current could not be transported long distances because of the cost of the wiring; in fact a mile was the limit of profitable distribution. But Edison remained the partisan of direct current. On the other hand, George Westinghouse became convinced that the future belonged to alternating current. In company with William Stanley he built generators and transformers to make its use practicable. The transformer stepped up the voltage, shot it along a small wire to great distances, and then a second transformer stepped it down to any voltage at the other end. He likewise purchased the patents of Nikola Tesla, a Serbian immigrant, for a simple reliable motor using alternating current, and his organization brought it to perfection. Westinghouse apparatus illuminated the World's Fair in 1893, and in 1894–1895 his principles were adopted in the installation at Niagara Falls, which transported power over the incredible distance of twenty miles. The alternating current victory was complete.

While this battle between alternating and direct current was on, electricity was applied to the field of transportation—the electric trolley and the electric locomotive—and then to the field of industry. The modern use of the electric motor to turn machinery began in 1893, when several were installed in a South Carolina factory. The electric motor proved ideal for machinery. The exact power ratio for each machine was now obtainable; the motor could be cut off and on as necessary; factories, since the interior distribution of power was now feasible without the weight of shafting and clutter of belts, became lighter and airier than the many-storied work prisons of the nineteenth century. We have already seen how the employment of electricity had helped transform mining operations. In the fifteen years after 1902 electrical energy for industrial uses was multplied nearly sixteen times. Its flexibility and its dependability and its ease of distribution emancipated American industry from the rigidities of water or steam power. The rationalization of industrial processes was now feasible.

Meanwhile the electrical industry had returned to its first triumph, communication. Scientists in the late nineteenth century had decided that many forces moved in waves. If these could be actuated, amplified, and controlled, telegraphing and telephoning could dispense with wires, and messages, perhaps even images, could be sent through the air. Reliance was put originally upon a stream of electrons, particles in the atomic cluster. By heating an electrode to incandescence, these investigators and inventors released from it a tiny flow of electrons; this stream, imprisoned in a tube filled with gas or drained of air, moved to an anode; by placing a grid or grids in the gap between the electrode and anode the electronic flow could be manipulated. One of the first to apply these principles was Guglielmo Marconi, an Irish-Italian who patented in Great Britain in 1896 a wireless telegraph. By 1902 he was able to send a full message across the Atlantic. Meanwhile experimenters were seeking to replace Marconi's comparatively inefficient and noisy receiving sets with instruments more capable of amplifying the tiny impulses that came over the air and perhaps eliminating some of the frequencies that made wireless telephoning impossible. The best of the resulting devices, the vacuum tube, was patented by an American, Lee De Forest, in 1906. De Forest, discouraged by his efforts to promote his invention, sold it for a fraction of its value to the American Telephone and Telegraph Company. They employed it as an amplifier in the first transcontinental telephone line, opened with great pomp in 1915. Then their engineers scurried about the American coast, the Pacific islands, and Europe, installing apparatus. At the end of the year intelligible "hellos" and conversations originating in the United States were heard across the Atlantic. Regular wireless telephone service between London and New York came somewhat later, for the application of myriad varieties of tubes and of their surrogate, the transistor, to radio broadcasting, television and computers was the accomplishment of the war and interwar periods. Forthwith electronics opened doors, detected submarines, and carried presidential fireside chats to the voters. Thus automation and the mass media jeopardized the values placed upon work and reading by centuries of civilization.

The Motor Revolution

Meanwhile the internal combustion engine had created a system of travel and transport that superseded or modified the network of railroads built in the nineteenth century and shook American habits, social and economic. Those Paul Prys, the pollsters, discovered, for instance, that more proposals of marriage were made in motor cars than in parlors or on front porches, the traditional arenas for this chivalry. These attainments were strictly twentieth century. For it was not until 1913 that the number of motor vehicles registered in the United States crossed the million mark and not until 1916 that the national government began the planning and financing of a national highway system. These twin events signalized the end of a period of experimentation. It had begun in the later decades of the nineteenth century when Europeans had invented the internal combustion engine, driven by gas exploded by an electric spark, and had harnessed this power plant to the carriage. Why the Americans were so laggard in these inventions is something of a mystery. Perhaps the identification of speed with sport and with keeping horses was closer in Europe. There the automobile started out as a plaything for the aristocracy. This context was not lacking in America when Henry Ford in the nineties put together a horseless carriage running on bicycle wheels and powered by a motor which consisted of a piece of gas pipe and a flywheel of wood. Later Ford decided he would concentrate on a cheap car made "for the masses" or "the farmer." "The way to make automobiles is to make one automobile like another automobile, to make them all alike. Just like one pin is like another pin when it comes from a pin factory." The Model T of 1907 achieved this goal. To attain the desired cheap price Ford and his partners five years later began experimenting with the conveyor-belt system for assembling magnetos. In 1914 full assembly-line production had reduced the time for chassis assembly to 1 hour and 30 minutes from the 12 hours and 28 minutes necessary for stationary assembly. In 1920 every other motor vehicle in the world was a Model T Ford. If it were not for certain highly idiosyncratic methods for shifting gears and producing a spark, this vehicle might have been called standard.

After World War I a series of technological refinements and accessories popularized even further the new mode of transportation. The car was given a miniature electric plant which powered the ignition, lighting, and the self-starter. The last was of supreme importance, for hand cranking involved so much strength, skill, and danger that women were infrequent drivers and the winter use of the car involved a fatiguing and perilous spinning of the engine. Another handicap, the fabric tire which wore out quickly and was expensive, was superseded by casings which lasted longer because of their chemical compounds and lower pressures, the latter contributing in turn to increased riding comfort. The open vehicle, which in spite of its "one-man top" and sides gave little protection, was replaced by the closed car. This model, once an expensive custom-made rarity, became the mainstay of the industry. The enclosed room on wheels facilitated all-weather and all-season use. Speed increased as engines grew more powerful and fuels graduated into the category of "high-test." Furthermore, the application of mass production to the automobile for years progressively lowered prices. In 1904 the Ford car sold for $1,200; in 1924 the Model T touring car without self-starter was priced at $290. Though automobile prices after the early thirties greatly increased, installment purchasing and the secondhand car business set an army of purchasers rolling. The right to a car became as inalienable as that to life, liberty, and the pursuit of happiness. Indeed, it was synonymous with them.

Although the bicycle preceded the automobile as a stimulus to improved roads, the history of the modern highway system is closely interlocked with motor vehicles. For the wider use of the automobile depended upon engineering innovations, the most elementary of which was a hard-surfaced road, upon the construction of through routes, and upon the coordinated planning of a national road network. A start had been made by some states, particularly in the East, which had placed state agencies above the town and county authorities once solely responsible for the construction and maintenance of roads and had made state appropriations for a state highway system. Then in 1916—an important supplementry act came five years later—the Federal government reentered the field of highway construction which it had abandoned nearly a century before, by matching state appropriations in various proportions with Federal grants-in-aid. In return the national government insisted that the states establish highway departments and maintain the aided highways. The Secretary of Agriculture, in cooperation with these highway departments, was to select a main system of interrelated highways.

The airplane, a contemporary of the automobile, developed more slowly and in a quite different fashion. For tardiness the explanation was simple: the immense inventive and engineering problems of flight. Though men had dreamed for centuries of conquering air, it was not until 1903 that two Middle Western bicycle repairers, Orville and Wilbur Wright, flew in any practical fashion in machines heavier than air. Their interest in this problem had been aroused in the nineties and for several years their own advance epitomized the previous long years of experimentation. They read the works of Otto Lilienthal, a German, and Octave Chanute, an immigrant American. Both of these pioneers had constructed small gliders and, launching themselves into the wind from little heights, had learned something of air pressures, the proper shape and area of wings, and the methods of maintaining balance in flight. The Wrights also read the works of Samuel P. Langley, an American scientist and experimenter. He had flown model planes with tiny engines for considerable distances, but his larger machine, built after years of preparation, tumbled into the Potomac from its launching platform "like a handful of mortar." The Wrights built gliders and learned to fly them on the deserted sands near Kittyhawk, North Carolina. Perhaps the most important contribution of their motorless planes was the improved devices for warping the wings mechanically in order to achieve a lateral stability. In their crate of wood, wire, and cloth the brothers then installed a light internal combustion engine of their own construction and in December, 1903, were able to telegraph their father that the strange contraption had left the ground under its own power, covered a distance of 284 yards, and alighted without accident. Five years later, when they demonstrated by a series of short flights in this country and in France their mastery of the air, other Americans and Europeans were also flying. No other invention has done so much to erase from the mind of man the word "impossible."

Though the quest for flight was successful, much remained to be done. The early airplanes were not fast. A man running along the ground kept pace with the Wrights's first flights, and not until 1919 did the speed of the airplane officially surpass the record of an automobile, 131.7 miles an hour, fashioned several years earlier. The use of the airplane involved, furthermore, the mastery of a new art, aerial navigation, somewhat akin to maritime navigation, though it was three-dimensional rather than two-dimensional. The first pilots looked overboard for familiar landmarks or in obscure weather ran by dead reckoning, homed to earth by the glow of city lights through the clouds, or jumped overboard with parachutes when the gas ran out. Certainty and safety had to be joined with speed if flying were to be anything else but sport and fair-weather, daytime movement.

Machines: Organization and Invention

A narrative of separate inventions may obscure general tendencies. From textile to automobiles, the American objective in the introduction of machines was to achieve a flow and continuity of operations. In iron and steel, for instance, it was wasteful to shut down furnaces, to lose and then regain the high temperatures essential to their operation; in shaping steel rails, the rail would cool off as it was clumsily manipulated through the two rollers used in the process. About the time of the Civil War a gifted mechanic installed a third roll above the others; this three-high mill, a significant innovation, rolled the rail on the way back to begin the process. Massive flows of power from steam or water powers, higher temperatures, stronger blasts, the steady flow of the assembly line —all these meant in industry after industry a larger factory. In 1859 industrial establishments employed on an average 9.3 workers and turned out a product valued at $13,429; in 1914 industrial establishments on the same average basis employed 25.5 workers and turned out a product valued at $87,916. The last decades of the nineteenth century were those of most rapid progress toward industrial giantism. The large-scale factory required higher inputs of capital in overhead and equipment. Their savings were in labor costs, achieved in lower wages per unit of production and in the more efficient organization of their labor force, the application of trained management, or in expenditures for research and development. Perhaps these were theoretical particularities, but behind them loomed the fact that the American market was large enough to make specialization and the intensive use of capital profitable. The materialization of these enterprises in turn made that market possible—as Ford had shown with motor cars.

Genuinely new departures in industrial production required not the piecemeal installation of new machines but the installation of a system. Eli Whitney had once demonstrated this in the manufacture of firearms. Decades later in the manufacture of Bessemer steel, Alexander H. Holley, the holder of an engineering degree from Brown University, determined to speed up the use of the converters, which had to be periodically stopped because the hot charges wore out the lining. He adopted a floor plan with paired converters, elevated so they could be worked on, and then devised a preferred converter bottom which could be installed from outside by an artisan without cooling the whole apparatus. This innovation, plus the accompanying machinery, Holley patented; the "standard of a Holley plant" became the mark of excellence and profit. Toward the end of the century as the cotton industry shifted from New England to the South, the northern manufacturers of cotton machinery provided prospective purchasers plans for a standardized factory, a complete list of materials required for construction, and an enumeration of the machines best-suited to produce any of the several types of yarn and fabrics. They even furnished trained erectors to install the machines and start their operation.

Apparently all an aspirant manager needed to start was the money or the credit to buy tools. But in the 1880's, as markets widened and new techniques were introduced, American mechanical engineers sensed the need for a science of management. Since the inputs of capital and labor were interrelated, not surprisingly these discussions usually focused on labor costs. Thus, wages and related labor questions were the primary interest of Frederick W. Taylor, destined to become the prophet who provided a logic and a faith for the new movement. Forced to abandon a formal education by poor eyesight, he secured employment from the Midvale Steel Company. In 1882, when he became foreman, he began to put into practice some of his ideas, but it was not until 1895 that they received public recognition. In that year he delivered before the American Society of Mechanical Engineers a paper on "A Piece-Rate System." As the title suggests, his chief interest was in methods of obtaining maximum production from workers who, he believed, were loafing or inefficient. His solution was a "scientific" analysis of the job to determine the maximum speed at which work could be done, followed by an attempt to induce the laborer to attain this maximum by the payment of a higher piece-rate for a larger output. In the following years Taylor's ideas and interests were enlarged by experience, and in 1903 a second paper before the same organization on "Shop Management" contributed little new on the labor side of production but stressed the importance of machine arrangement and factory organization. On this occasion Taylor advocated the standardization of tools and equipment at the level at which they would do their best work, the routing and scheduling of work through the factory, and consequently a greater emphasis upon the organization of the factory and a planning department. Scientific management, thus conceived, was a necessary prelude to the later increasing divergence of ownership and control within the corporation. For without this accumulated knowledge, it would have been difficult to hire and instruct competent management.

Taylor's ideas were adapted, altered, and modified by a group of followers. Not only were machine operations analyzed, but manual operations were scrutinized and more expeditious and efficient methods were suggested. Although the actual installation in factories of the Taylor system in its purest forms was limited, the influence of the ideas transcended applications. In 1911 scientific management was placed before the public in dramatic fashion when L. D. Brandeis employed it before the Interstate Commerce Commission in his brief against a rise in railroad rates; he argued that the railroads could save money through scientific management and thus avoid the necessity of the proposed increases. A bibliography of efficiency literature was created; conferences and organizations were formed to promote efficiency; colleges gave an academic benediction by offering courses in the subject; and efficiency became the war cry of a mechanically organized and mechanically minded age.

Scientific management was a single illustration of a much broader cause of American industrial development—the growing knowledge of pure science and its application to material affairs. With varying emphasis technical education sought to promote both these ends. In the first half of the nineteenth century engineering instruction had been largely confined to the United States Military Academy at West Point; but as the industrial age got under way the situation was almost immediately altered. In 1850 Rensselaer Polytechnic Institute at Troy, New York, established twenty-five years earlier, became an engineering school with a four-year course. In 1864 Columbia University established a School of Mines, which by the end of the century had conferred more than half the mining industrial degrees in the United States. Meanwhile the national government took a significant step when the Morrill Act of 1862 gave a powerful stimulus to engineering instruction by a donation from the public lands to each state for the support of a school or schools in which the "leading object shall be . . . to teach such branches of learning as are related to agriculture and the mechanic arts . . . in order to promote the liberal and practical education of the industrial classes in the several pursuits and professions in life." Most states established agricultural and mechanical colleges or universities; in other states the funds were given to private institutions which were chartered for the occasion, as Cornell University, or were already in existence. At first the students at such institutions were regarded as an inferior order of beings by cultural colleagues, but such snobbishness did not stay the colleges' development. They enlarged the scope of their curriculum to include branches of engineering other than civil; they gave a more thorough grounding in theoretical science; they appealed to a practical-minded age; and eventually Francis Amasa Walker, the creator of the modern Massachusetts Institute of Technology, surveying his world, pronounced it good. "In schools of applied science and technology as they are carried on to-day in the United States . . . is to be found almost the perfection of education for young men." Roles were reversed, the protagonists of Latin and Greek were put on the defensive. Nor was technical engineering confined to institutions of collegiate grade. Specialized schools for certain industries, like textiles, were established, and technical or vocational training was introduced into the grades and high school. In 1917 the national government joined the movement in a small way by appropriating sums, to be matched by the states, for instruction in "trade, home economics, and industrial subjects." While the act soft-pedaled the second of these items, the instruction as a whole was to fit the youngsters for "useful employment" and was to be "practical."

Much of this public and private development was confused and at cross-purposes. Sometimes it groped toward fundamental matters. Historically and logically, science and technology were not the same thing. To make a crude distinction, science was systematized knowledge, usually verbal; the scientist drew his livelihood from a court or a university. Technology, on the other hand, concerned itself with the useful; its practitioner was a working man, a mechanic, an engineer. Actually, in America such "philosophers" of the Revolution as Paine and Franklin believed science could be useful to men; at the same time science had not reached a stage where it could offer much help to the farmer, the merchant, or artisan in the ordinary course of his business. After the

Revolution the convergence of science and technology was uneven. The iron industry remained the stronghold of empiricism. Its folk hero was the robust ironmaster, John Fritz, largely self-educated but the inventor of the three-high mill. After he had constructed a machine he would direct, "Now let's start it up and see why it doesn't work." In such a context Carnegie's employment of a trained chemist in 1870 was certain to occasion surprise. As late as 1897 the manager of a steel works in Chicago dismissed one of the "world's leading metallographers" and sent him fleeing to Harvard University.

On the other hand, the electric industry, although it had its origin in science and Edison employed a mathematician to make the long calculations for the application of Ohm's law to the operation of the incandescent lamp, did not become science-dominated until it assimilated electronics in the twentieth century. Suitably enough in 1900 General Electric had supplemented the consultant scientist with the establishment of a research laboratory under the direction of an American chemist trained in Germany. In the same decade the American Telephone and Telegraph Company undertook research work.

Knowledge, in spite of its triumphs, was not everything. "The greatest difficulty in commercial life," Frederick W. Taylor once observed, 'is to get the opportunity to successfully carry out experiments." Actually, neither government nor labor was ideologically opposed to technological innovation: American business leaders, riding ahead on an expanding economy, were generally—textiles were an exception—in a position, temperamentally and professionally, to take the risks which change involved. A people born of immigrants, accustomed to exchanging environments, East for West or street for street, and undertaking within a lifetime a series of employments from agriculture to storekeeping and the assembly line, was not unaccustomed to, nor afraid of, change.

The Geography of Industrial Power

New England and the Middle Atlantic states together formed the historic center of American manufacturing. The Industrial Revolution in its transit from England had first alighted there. Waterpower had driven its mills and factories; capital acquired in trade or industry nourished its development; a native population, supplemented by arriving immigrants, manned its machines; a system of roads, canals, and later railroads, leading inland from the coast, and the ocean itself distributed the products of this region. On the eve of the Civil War the factories and shops of this region produced practically every variety of manufactured goods made in the nation and employed a majority of the workers engaged in manufacturing. In general it still retained an industrial preeminence when World War I arrived. To be sure cotton textiles since the nineties had begun to drift southward, but the woolen industry was even more heavily concentrated in the Northeast than before. Great iron and steel works, dependent to a considerable extent upon imported ores, gave the region a share of this magnificent industry, and the manufacture of finished products, from hardware to the new electrical equipment, either remained or settled in the Northeast. The region had the greatest markets, an ample labor force, and available capital.

Still this historic industrial area was conducting essentially a holding operation. The great expansion of industry after 1860 was in the northern half of the great interior valley, particularly in the five states of the old Northwest. In 1860 manufacturing was just touching the region; in the next fifty-five years it transformed it. Railroad lines were constructed; population swarmed; and the natural resources of the country were at hand in the oil and natural gas of Pennsylvania and Illinois, in the omnipresent coal fields, in the forests of the Great Lake states, in the unequaled Lake Superior iron ranges; and it was still the center of American agriculture. It was the last factor that first accounted for the region's industrial growth. With the refrigerator car and the cold-storage packing plant, Chicago became the packing center of the nation; the enterprise of Minneapolis millers and waterpower made that city the flour capital; and the agricultural market drew westward manufacturers of reapers and wagons.

Natural resources not derived from agriculture—petroleum, gas, lumber, coal—also made the Middle West an industrial empire. But it was the Lake Superior iron deposits that gave her world leadership in the metallurgical industry. Since more coal than ore was required in smelting and refining, these operations moved eastward to the river valleys of eastern Ohio and western Pennsylvania, to the southern shore of Lake Erie, and to the Chicago-Milwaukee district. This western area also became the home of the motor car. In its pioneer days the automobile was manufactured in New England and New York, and the pull of the market ought to have been sufficient to keep the manufacture there. But as early as 1905 Michigan was already the center of concentration. The supremacy of this state and of Detroit was explained by their nearness to raw materials—wood and iron—their previous specialization in carts and wagons and experimentation with marine gasoline engines, the myriad of small shops which could make machine parts, and the generous audacity of their businessmen, who took chances on the industry.

In the Far West of the Mountain and Pacific states and in the South, the first years of the twentieth century brought spectacular increases in industrial activity. But the achievement in both areas was far short of that already described for other regions. In the Far West industry was generally closely connected with the primary development of natural resources—lumber, petroleum, minor metals, and a small iron and steel industry. In the South the potentialities of a steel industry were slowly realized, in part because the ores of the Chattanooga-Birmingham area were not chemically suited to the acid process. On the other hand, the dream of decades, to bring "the spindles to cotton," was on the eve of final realization. Local and outside investors provided capital; the mill villages with their paternalism and services drew workers from farms and southern highlands much as Lowell had done from New England homesteads eighty years earlier; cheaper wages for workers producing standard fabrics undercut northern producers just as surely as the more modern mechanization of southern mills undercut the older equipment of the industry along the Merrimack and the Fall River.

Although the United States was often identified with a machine culture, manufacturing was actually highly concentrated. In both 1869 and 1909 twenty-seven states contributed less than 1 percent apiece to the national total of value added by manufacturing. In the same years New York and Pennsylvania were the leading industrial states; and in 1909 Massachusetts was more important industrially than any southern or midwestern state with the exception of Illinois. The headstart of the Northeast, along with special circumstances, accounted for the continuation of its leadership. Nonetheless its percentages were declining. In the twenty years after 1869 industry surged into the old Northwest; in the twenty years after 1889 the South made the most spectacular advances. In the Far West only California and Texas seemed to be progressing. Though the process of displacement and shift was far from immediate, it seemed inexorable. Industry moved into or toward the largest aggregates of population.

In 1880 the President of the American Society of Mechanical Engineers commented the American textile industry made goods so cheaply "that the very beggars in our metropolitan cities and the 'tramps' sleeping in our fields, . . . wear a finer fabric than kings could boast a century ago." Journalists and politicians, then and later, were usually ready to see about them "a golden age" or "a millennium." Not everyone, however, was satisfied as the United States accumulated "firsts" in industrial production, built the "longest transportation routes" in the world, and people crowded into the world's "largest" city save London. Groups in the community felt they endured inferiorities or did not participate on equal terms in the race for wealth. In all likelihood these were minority opinions and voices. At intervals, however, the economy took sudden downturns; panic widened and could no longer be confined to the mere censure of a banking or business system that appeared vulnerable to such reverses. These depressions varied in severity. Major crises, like those after 1873, 1893, and 1907, shattered values, inflicted bankruptcy and unemployment, and let loose a flood of agitated and apprehensive talk about revolution and the disintegration of the capitalistic order. Some critics found consolation in the dream of returning to the Middle Ages, where cities had cathedrals and craft organizations and where vestiges of the struggle for gain and for things fell away. Others, of a more impatient temper, looked forward, after an apocalypse of destruction, to the emergence of a new order, giving to each "according to his need" and erasing the injustices and anxieties latent in industry and in capitalism. Instead the nation undertook the eradication of visible abuses and the removal of particular grievances.

xiii
Big Business
and Popular Response

The Regime of Competition

Like the railroads, the American industrial domain was governed without question by the private capitalists: their pride in bigness, progress, ambition for power, and desire to make money inspired them to launch enterprises, often risky, and then to expand their area of success and control. There was, however, one painful disadvantage to this arrangement: competition created uncertainty, introduced brutal ruthlessness into business operations, and diminished profits. Industrial competition had always existed, but it increased both in scale and in intensity after the Civil War. The spread of railroad systems broke down the protection against competition erected by distance, and created a larger market. The increasing size of industrial establishments intensified competition. So much capital had been invested that the owners could not afford to let it lie idle, nor could they easily transfer it from one industry to another. Within limits, therefore, business was run at a loss rather than not at all. Furthermore, a succession of crippling panics of exceptional length continually put business success on trial. The best-known index of wholesale prices calculated for all commodities, with 1909–1914 equalling 100, rose during the Civil War from 89 to 185, declined to a low of 68 in the mid-nineties, then rose slowly until the eve of World War I. It is hard to tell whether the erosion of prices by its inexorableness or by its vacillations was more responsible for revealing the strengths or weakness in the economic structure.

The competitive features of America's economic expansion inevitably aroused admiration. Read the account of the first decade of the Bessemer

319

process in this country, written by Captain William R. Jones, the great iron and steel maker of the Carnegie group. The managers of the steel works were eager to demonstrate the capacity of their plants and the skill of their workers. When they made records some dispatched jubilant telegrams to friends or rivals; others worked on in secret, relying upon rumor to magnify their achievements. This "strong but pleasant rivalry of the young men who have assumed control of the works" and "the *esprit de corps* of workers" who were not "content until the rival's record is eclipsed" had all the simple appeal of youth at play. But the stakes of such joyous sportsmanship were economic survival in the face of those who would take it away, pecuniary gain in the face of those who sought to deny it. It was a grim business. Speaking for himself and probably for others of his generation, H. O. Havemeyer, president of the sugar trust, gave the Industrial Commission a frank education in 1899. "Business is not a philanthropy. . . . I do not care two cents for your ethics. I don't know enough of them to apply them. . . . As a business proposition it is right to get all out of a business that you possibly can."

From the many solutions proposed for dealing with "cutthroat," or "destructive," competition, for this was the vernacular of the country, businessmen preferred combinations, mergers, amalgamation, "whatever their name or sign." For one thing businessmen could create such combinations with a minimum of help from others, for example, the state. Profits for the creators and members of such organizations came from several directions. The combination could be capitalized at a figure larger than the sum of its parts by issuing watered stock which could be sold to investors and outsiders with financial advantage to those on the inside. The ruinous effects of competition could be avoided, for the consolidation might diminish the number of competitors, or obtain a monopoly or semi-monopoly or stabilizing position in the industry, or effect economies and savings which would enable it to make more money as a competitive unit. At times these considerations operated with peculiar cogency. First let a depression spread ruin and chasten competitors; then let a period of ensuing prosperity stimulate the market for stocks; this was the recipe for an era of consolidations. Thus, in 1899 the capitalization of new industrial consolidations reached the unusual sum of $1,866,000,000; in 1901 it was $1,632,000,000. "Nothing like this wave of mergers [1897–1903] has ever been seen again." Though it was a period of bigger firms, size could not dwarf the generation of business leaders who gave the new forms to American industry. Between the Civil War and World War I, giants strode the business earth; they were legends partly because they were men of immense accomplishment and partly because those who hated what they did found it politically expedient to personalize complicated and impersonal issues by calling them "robber barons."

Contradictions in Coal

The vital importance of railroads in the history of American business has been demonstrated again and again in the course of competition and consolidation. It was in fact through the railroads that the anthracite coal monopoly was created. The railroads serving the anthracite region of Pennsylvania desired to stabilize an unsettled industry, so run by an army of small producers and restive employees that "their joint delusions, the waste, inefficiency and negativism stamping the industry, the attendant disruptions of production and the loss of markets, . . . [had] become insufferable." Anthracite roads like the Pennsylvania and the Delaware and Hudson thought they had found an answer in the ownership of mines—which thus became captive shippers—and in large-scale operations. After the Civil War the Philadelphia and Reading under the leadership of the charismatic Franklin B. Gowan—it is hard to filter any candor from his histrionics—acquired a coal estate of 100,000 acres through a subsidiary and forthwith went bankrupt. Pools which attempted to apportion coal traffic among carriers and thus avoid glutting the market generally broke down. After 1900 an exceedingly workable community of interest had taken their place. Small and competing railroads had been leased or purchased; interlocking stock ownerships and interlocking directorates wove a web among the anthracite coal railroads; and the Temple Iron Company, in which five anthracite railroads, carrying nearly 72 percent of the total shipments, owned stock and were represented by directors, met frequently to apportion the business among its five members. The Pennsylvania and the Delaware and Hudson, anthracite roads outside this organization, cooperated with it. Independents were removed from the field by contracts made in perpetuity between them and the roads. There was an anthracite monopoly. Nonetheless the wholesale price of anthracite, $7.86 per ton in 1865—it had been $3.39 four years earlier—fell to $2.98 in 1895, whence it recovered to approximately $5.00 on the eve of World War I.

Bituminous coal had a history with a different outcome. As in anthracite there was an army of operators, and the expenses of mining were so small that little capital was required to commence operations. Every period of prosperity and rising prices brought in the "snowbirds," the "country banks," the fly-by-nights of the industry. As the twentieth century wore on, large holdings were created. Industries like the Bethlehem Steel Corporation, United States Steel Corporation, Ford Company, public utilities, and railroads bought and operated mines to supply their own demands. Aside from these "captive mines," large coal companies— Consolidation Coal Company and Pittsburgh Coal Company—entered the industry. There were faint traces of combination through holding companies, interlocking directorates, individual stockholdings in many concerns, but most observers laid the undoubted misfortunes of the bituminous coal industry to its violently competitive character.

Petroleum Pioneers in Big Business

Coal was an old industry; petroleum was new in 1859. Fittingly enough the latter produced the era's most eminent protagonist of bigness: John D. Rockefeller. Necessarily he was a pioneer and, the times being what they were, others, when they were not excoriating him, imitated him. First a bookkeeper who saved on a modest salary, later a partner in a commission produce-house which made money during the Civil War, Rockefeller in 1865 cut loose and embarked wholeheartedly upon the oil-refining business. Cleveland, where he lived, was a promising center for this industry, for the city was near the Pennsylvania oil fields and situated astride the great east-west avenues of transportation. By 1870 various partnerships in which he and others were interested were incorporated as the Standard Oil Company of Ohio, with a capitalization of $1 million. Although it was the largest oil refiner in the United States, the situation was an unhappy one. Just as everyone could start a coal mine, everyone, with luck, could drill a well. In the late eighties there were approximately 14,000 producers in the Pennsylvania region alone. At times a flood of crude would break prices disastrously. Some of this was to Rockefeller's advantage. Some was not. But in refining, the field in which he had embarked, the disadvantages were obvious. In his words, "the butcher, the baker, and the candlestick-maker began to refine oil . . . the price went down and down until the trade was ruined"; it was necessary "to bring some order out of what was rapidly becoming a state of chaos." Rockefeller dreamed of some vast merger of refiners as the remedy for this depressed condition.

Almost incidentally he first sought his end under the aegis of the South Improvement Company, a corporation with very wide powers chartered by the Pennsylvania legislature in 1871. The next year many of the largest refiners in the country, including the Rockefeller group, and representatives of three great oil-carrying railroads, the Pennsylvania, Erie, and New York Central, formed under its terms an alliance for their mutual benefit. It was a railroad as well as a petroleum undertaking. In order to prevent the roads from competing for the carriage of crude and refined oil, the organization apportioned shipments among them and the oil men acted as eveners in distributing this business. In return the refiners received such railroad rebates that few outsiders could hope to survive in business. The members of the scheme had rebates on their own oil and products; they also received a cash rebate on all the shipments made by their rivals; and finally they secured waybills of all rival shipments—waybills which gave a knowledge of the amount of their competitors' business and the people with whom it was done. Although this scheme was drawn up with the greatest secrecy, details leaked out and a roar of disapproval coupled with pressure by injured parties forced the railroads to announce "equal and open rates to all."

During this turbulent interval, Rockefeller proceeded rapidly to acquire refineries in Cleveland and elsewhere; in the former place he obtained the bulk of refining capacity, usually by purchase through stock or cash at a valuation set by his representatives. With some evidence behind it, an impression prevailed that Rockefeller used his favored position with the railroads to coerce the sale of his competitors in refining. His own explanation of his success was that "the conditions were so chaotic and uncertain that most of the refiners were very desirous to get out of the business." In any case, he had his rebates too, for the railroads, in spite of their pronouncements gave rate concessions to Standard Oil. Rockefeller later regarded this situation with high good humor. He told the story of the Boston merchant who announced, "I am opposed on principle to the whole system of rebates and drawbacks—unless I am in it." Undoubtedly the jest accurately described the contemporary situation. Rebates were universal and businessmen, whether in steel, sugar, tobacco, hardware, or oil, shipped under this favored arrangement.

Over the years Standard Oil enhanced its competitive power. One weapon was the control of transportation. The early success of the organization had been aided by rebates from railroads, but now these favors were menaced by the construction of pipelines. Quick to appreciate the urgency of the situation, the Standard built or leased lines, competed for the shipments of oil, and then consolidated in one way or another the competing interests. By 1879 most of the pipelines in the Appalachian field were brought together in the United Pipe Lines Company, in which the Standard held a controlling interest. It thus had a practical monopoly of pipeline transportation, which it could utilize both against the oil-well owner and against the independent refiner. To escape this monopoly these interests had undertaken the construction of a pipeline across the Appalachian Mountains to connect the oil producers with eastern railroads not involved in the rebate agreements and later with the seaboard. Against this Tidewater Pipe-Line Company the Standard struck by the construction of its own lines, by a whispering campaign against the financial solvency of the concern, by purchasing the refineries to which the Tidewater sold oil, and by struggles in the courts. Eventually, in 1883, the two rivals signed a treaty of peace recognizing the *status quo;* the Standard did 88.5 percent of the business and the Tidewater the remainder.

A second weapon was marketing organization. Apart from the foreign market where American oil had no competition until the close of the century, the Standard moved rather slowly and haphazardly in creating a disciplined or centralized marketing organization. Beginning in the mid-eighties it accelerated a program of building bulk stations to which kerosene was delivered in tank cars and from which tank wagons delivered to retailers. The Standard purchased marketing companies or enlarged its holdings of stock in the larger ones. Everywhere operations were carried on efficiently and economically, and everywhere this marketing agency gathered information and opened fire in competitive warfare if occasion demanded. If the former activity was often indistinguishable from industrial espionage, Rockefeller was ready with explanations. Unethical actions, if they did exist, were individual rather than corporate. "An occasional employee . . . acted in connection with the business or perhaps in conducting his own affairs, in a way which might be criticized. Even in a comparatively small organizaton it is wellnigh impossible to restrain this occasional man who is overzealous for his own or his company's advancement." However they obtained their information, agents of the Standard used it to approach retailers and other consignees and threaten a price war unless purchases from rival organizations ceased and patronage was given to the Standard.

The price wars were the grand engagements in the long campaign of competition. In fact, they were one of its justifications in the mind of the public, for they meant lower prices. But such performances were not to the taste of John D. Rockefeller. He regarded with great disfavor the individualistic businessman who was a law unto himself. "He was the one man who had to sell at less than cost, to disrupt all the business plans of others in his trade, because his individual position was so absolutely different from all the rest." Since the business world, however, was governed by these "natural laws of trade," it was inevitable that even in the petroleum industry there should be price wars. Rockefeller wished to avoid these disturbances, so independents usually found that as long as they did not attempt to increase their share of particular markets beyond 15 or 20 percent, they could count upon avoiding price competition. If they were daring or imprudent, the Standard brought to bear its unparalleled technical efficiencies and its access to a national market where losses in one area could be recouped by gains in another. Meanwhile all over the country the price of kerosene fell. In 1863 the wholesale price without tax had been approximately 45 cents a gallon; by the mid-nineties it was 6 cents.

Always Rockefeller moved ahead as the apostle of order in the industry. The incalculable must give way to the rational, strife to cooperation. With power and persuasion he converted other refiners. By the mid-seventies generally through the transfer of stock in the Standard Oil

Company of Ohio, whose capitalization was recurrently enlarged for this purpose, the Rockefeller group had acquired refineries in Pittsburgh, Philadelphia, New York, Brooklyn, and Baltimore. In 1879 the Standard controlled 90 percent of the refining in the country. In that very year S. C. T. Dodd, counsel for the Standard, one of the most ingenious of corporation lawyers, bent an old device, the trust, into a new method of consolidating many corporations. Three years later a higher form evolved. Under a trust agreement the stockholders surrendered their securities to nine trustees and received in return trust certificates. As owners of these certificates they elected the trustees, though the original nine were designated in the agreement. The trustees were to establish new corporations, if they saw fit, elect the directors and officers of all the companies whose stock they held, and "exercise general supervision" over their affairs. Though they thus controlled corporations, the trustees were not a corporation. No legislative act, no charter had given them birth or powers. Imitators in other industries rushed to copy this unique conception. It was not for long. In the nineties the law frowned upon this scheme so severely that a new method had to be discovered.

Whether by accident or by design the State of New Jersey came to the rescue of the harassed consolidators. Most states had generally forbidden corporations to own the stock of other corporations except by special enactment. New Jersey transformed exceptions into a system. In 1889 she amended her corporation laws to read: "Any corporation may purchase . . . the capital stock of . . . any other corporation or corporations of this or any other state, and while owner of such stock may exercise all the rights, powers, and privileges of ownership, including the right to vote thereon." Business wise men read the meaning of this star in the East. The Standard Oil Company of New Jersey, already in existence, increased its capital stock in 1899 from $10 million to $110 million. This new stock was issued in exchange for the stock of the constituent concerns, which refined oil, produced crude oil, owned pipelines, carried on marketing operations, sold natural gas. The holders of the stock in the New Jersey concern elected its directors, who controlled the policy of the subordinate concerns, for which the New Jersey company held and voted their stocks. The line between this holding company and the trust was indistinguishable. The directors of the New Jersey company simply took the place of the trustees; that they were practically identical is disclosed by a comparison of the personnel of the two boards. Of the fourteen directors in the New Jersey company in 1907 six had been trustees in the trust of 1882.

Under the aegis of the holding company the Standard group enjoyed its golden age. In the piping of petroleum the concern had practical monopolies in the Appalachian, Lima-Indiana, and midcontinent fields. In production a single Standard refinery used more crude oil than the

seventy-five independent refineries in the country. The Standard produced 87 percent of the refined products. In marketing there was the
same story. The Standard marketed easily over 80 percent of the American product both in this country and abroad. And how the money rolled
in! From 1897 to 1906 the annual dividends on its stock, according to the
Bureau of Corporations, fluctuated between 30 and 40 percent. While
balance sheets and public reports seemed to award the wreath of success
to Standard Oil, actually this great aggregation was slowing down in the
first decade of the twentieth century. While it remained a large producer
in old fields, the entry of large new fields—California, midcontinent, and
Gulf coast—exceeded the Standard's resources and administrative energy.
By 1911 figures of the organization's control of production and of refinery output had both slumped to 60-65 percent. Standard's competitors
were supplying 70 percent of the fuel oil, a third of the gasoline, and one
quarter of the kerosene distributed in the domestic industry.

Integration in Iron and Steel

Although an apostle of international peace, Andrew Carnegie
was the warrior of the iron and steel industry. This young Scotchman,
climbing the ladder of American success from bobbin boy to superintendent on the Pittsburgh division of the Pennsylvania Railroad, had
amassed a small fortune and knew the right people on the Pennsylvania.
Among his many investments were those in ironworks—fabricating railroad bridges, wheels and axles for railroad rolling stock, and iron rails.
He did not invade the furnace phase of the industry until 1870. More
slowly impressed than his associates with the power of steel, he became
in the early seventies a wholehearted convert and poured his money and
energy into the construction of the J. Edgar Thomson Steel Works twelve
miles north of Pittsburgh. They were designed by A. L. Holley, the
engineer who gave the American steel industry its typical magnitude and
layout; the plant was cannily named after the president of the Pennsylvania Railroad; and it was run by the redoubtable ironmaster Captain
W. R. Jones. In 1875 the works made its first blow and rolled its first rail.
The new step was a profitable one. The Pennsylvania Railroad not only
purchased its products but gave it rebates (a privilege which the Baltimore and Ohio was also insistent upon sharing), and the plant, managed with technical efficiency and executive skill, poured forth a great
volume of steel at a lowering cost of production. Competitors were
aghast.

Until the eighties the Carnegie enterprises exhibited few differences
from the Standard Oil. Carnegie had received rebates from the railroads
and had purchased competitors—the Homestead Works—as Rockefeller

had done. The Standard, although controlling the refining, transportation, and marketing of oil, had until 1888 largely left the production of the crude oil to other individuals. Somewhat earlier the Carnegie companies sought to control their raw materials, to integrate the industry. First were the supplies of coke. Carnegie consequently sought an alliance with Henry Clay Frick and bought into the Frick Company. Frick, through an early realization of the superiority of Connellsville coal for coking and through audacious borrowing, became the undisputed "coke king of Connellsville." Through his association with Carnegie he became the directing genius of the whole Carnegie organization. The second step was the control of iron ore. The Carnegie Company like others purchased its ore from various Lake Superior ore companies. Although Andrew Carnegie preferred to continue this arrangement, Frick and other advisors overcame his reluctance and forthwith the group made long leases of Mesabi ore-bearing lands. When it proved to be impossible to get rate concessions on the carriage of their raw materials, they established their own fleet of ore carriers on the Lakes and through purchase and construction obtained a railroad line between Conneaut on Lake Erie and Pittsburgh. Laid with heavy rails and running over low grades, the Pittsburgh, Bessemer and Lake Erie completed an efficient and economical transportation system. It is not surprising that the *Engineering and Mining Journal* in January, 1897, after surveying the efficient integration of the Carnegie properties, came to the conclusion:

> This company is not only in a position to make steel cheaper than any other producer; it is so situated as to be absolutely in control of the market, and make the prices of steel what it will. . . . The situation is not altogether a comfortable one, and many are looking anxiously for the result.

However startling may have been the creation of the Carnegie power, it did not have a monopoly of the method of integration. During the nineties promoters, businessmen and bankers were assembling various aggregates. When the members of these groups who made finished products of steel began to furnish their own ingots or buy them from business allies instead of from his works, Carnegie, in a role completely congenial to his genius, talked widely and well. It seemed that his company planned the construction of mills making wire rods, tubes, and steel sheets. He guilelessly asked:

> Why should steel makers make plates for other firms to work up into boilers, when they can manufacture the boilers themselves? Or beams and girders for bridges, when they can turn out and build up the completed article, or plates for pipes when they can make pipes? I think the next step to be taken by the steel makers will be to furnish finished articles ready for use.

To carry to the limit the policy implied in this quotation would have unloosed a competitive war which would have cut prices and profits to the bone and would have bankrupted concerns lacking the financial stamina and natural resources of the Carnegie group.

From such a gloomy prospect steel men and bankers alike recoiled. A search for ways of peace revealed a larger consolidation as the best solution. Carnegie was anxious for a retirement in which to study and to spend his gains for philanthropies. The banking house of J. P. Morgan, already heavily committed to investments in the steel world, was eager to prevent industrial warfare. It undertook the necessary negotiations. In 1901 the United States Steel Corporation, incorporated as a holding company in New Jersey, was launched with a capitalization of $1.4 billion. This industrial giant illustrated compactly every motive for consolidation. Economies through integration were secured, competition was avoided, and the incorporators made money by a process which Andrew Carnegie had once described, "They throw cats and dogs together and call them elephants." In view of the prices paid for the constituent concerns and the hopes capitalized, the securities of the United States Steel Corporation inevitably were heavily watered. The Commissioner of Corporations later estimated that the total capitalization of the concern exceeded the value of the property as determined by an "historical analysis" by $726,846,817. Opponents and supporters of the United States Steel Corporation argued violently as to the justice of this stock-watering, but it undoubtedly brought an immediate advantage to the owners of the properties included in the consolidation. Among others who benefited by the formation of the concern was the syndicate headed by J. P. Morgan and Company, which underwrote the securities. The syndicate was recompensed in stock from the sale of which it made a profit over and above expenses and cash advances of $62.5 million.

After 1901 United States Steel continually strengthened its industrial domain. New concerns were purchased. The most conspicuous acquisition was the valuable Tennessee Coal and Iron Company, a producer in the Birmingham-Chattanooga region and the owner of vast reserves of coal and ore. This was purchased during the panic of 1907 with the assent of President Roosevelt. At the same time the United States Steel Corporation continually enlarged its holdings of coke and ore through lease or purchase. It erected new mills, of which the metamorphosis of an empty spot on the shores of Lake Michigan into the steel city of Gary was, of course, the most dramatic. To its competitors, for they still existed, the United States Steel meanwhile preached the gospel of cooperation. For a time pools and associations were utilized, but after the panic of 1907 E. H. Gary, chairman of the board of directors, inaugurated his famous dinners where high-powered steel men got together. One of the diners commented, "He exhorted us like a Methodist preacher at a camp meeting." The gospel according to Gary maintained, "It is good law and good morals to endeavor . . . to maintain to a reasonable extent the equilibrium of business, to prevent utter demoralization of business and destructive competition." Above all "avoid violent fluctuation," seek "stability." The hearers told each other what they were doing. The dinners worked only fairly well except in arousing public suspicion, and the device was dropped in 1911 when the government brought suit against the United States Steel Corporation. Ever since 1901, however, the prices that "Big Steel" had charged on rolled products were known to its competitors through the Pittsburgh-plus system—prices at Pittsburgh plus the freight—no matter whence the product was shipped to the purchaser. The prudent recognized leadership when they saw it.

The Electrical Industry

The electrical industries exhibited almost at once a high degree of concentration. Since the first telegraph line had been constructed by the national government, there was the possibility of government ownership for this new instrument. Morse desired it. When Congress proved either indifferent or preoccupied, private capitalists, inventors, politicians, officials and employees of the government post office, and promoters chartered companies and threw lines about the country. These were immensely profitable if they possessed a monopoly of messages; financially sterile when faced with competition. In the late fifties a process of consolidation began, although many speculated skeptically how a "consolidation of failures [is] to escape failure?" By the end of the Civil War the Western Union Telegraph Company had purchased its last great rival and in the act once more issued a flood of watered stock. The monopoly seemed invulnerable. It granted telegraph privileges to Congressmen and political bosses and its exclusive contract with the Associated Press enabled it to still newspaper criticism. But the possibilities of competition had not been killed. The process of blackmail, exemplified by the railroads, was cheaper in the case of the telegraph, for the construction of parallel lines was less expensive. Chance-takers built first to threaten and then to sell out to Western Union. The adroit Jay Gould in alliance with other railroad men performed this magic twice in the seventies and eighties; the second time he sold out for five or six times the value of his properties. Then John W. Mackay, the silver-mine king, took hold of the Postal Telegraph Company and built a great concern of transcontinental lines and cables across both the Atlantic and the Pacific Ocean. Although in 1916 there were twenty-six companies in the telegraph business, practically 98 percent of the commercial service was handled by companies affiliated with either Western Union or Postal

Telegraph. For a time the telegraph and telephone were closely affiliated. Postal Telegraph was the largest stockholder in the American Telephone and Telegraph Company, and the latter for a few years after 1909 controlled the Western Union.

Patent ownership gave the telephone from the beginning the possibility of monopoly. And the owners of the Bell patents sternly determined to protect their rights at any cost. Within a quarter of a century there were six hundred patent suits. Some of them were minor engagements; others shook the patent office, the legal world, and the stock market. In every case the Bell companies were victorious. Then at the precise moment in the early nineties when their early patents expired, the Patent Office, suddenly deciding to be a kindly Mercury, brought tidings of great cheer; after fourteen years of delay it granted them a patent on an improved transmitter. Other branches of the government sought in vain to overthrow this decision. Meanwhile stock had been watered and the telephone empire had been organized. The Western Electric Company manufactured the instruments; the American Telephone and Telegraph Company constructed long-distance lines and provided service; and the American Bell Telephone Company leased its instruments to local companies. These permanent contracts arranged an annual rental for the equipment and provided that the parent company should hold stock in the subsidiaries.

In the nineties there was a renewed outburst of competition. Under the second presidency of Theodore N. Vail, who first came to the company from the United States Railway Mail Service, this threat was met by simplifying and centralizing the structure of the central company, now the American Telephone and Telegraph Company, and by purchasing and incorporating within it many of the competing companies. Vail also cultivated public good will. When the government expressed disapproval of the alliance with the Western Union in 1913, the telephone company disposed of its holdings, promised to acquire no more competing companies, and offered to cooperate with the independents in long-distance service. Since then the Bell company and the independents have delimited their areas. In 1917 the Bell system had 7,326,000 out of the nation's 11,716,000 telephones.

Edison and Westinghouse were the pioneers of electrical power. From each developed a gigantic manufacturing concern. In 1878 when Edison was struggling with his incandescent lamp, he formed the Edison Electric Light Company and various financiers—including J. P. Morgan and Henry Villard of Northern Pacific fame—were associated with him. Several years later Edison's interests were consolidated into the Edison General Electric Company under Henry Villard. Finally in 1892 the General Electric Company was established. It combined the Edison companies with the Thomson-Houston Company, an extremely important

New England concern owning valuable patents. In this process of combination Edison sold out his holdings and the subsequent growth of General Electric was due to other technicians and financiers. George Westinghouse, on the other hand, built up his businesses in a more personal fashion. He contributed the funds for growth himself or solicited them from his friends. In 1891 the Westinghouse Electric and Manufacturing Company consolidated his previous interests. A few years later General Electric and Westinghouse entered into an agreement which recognized the patents of each company and "the right, subject to certain exclusions, to a joint use thereof." For decades the two dominated the production of generators, transformers, motors, and control apparatus. Nevertheless, there has been no monopoly in the production of electrical apparatus. Thousands of small concerns were manufacturing specialties and part lines, and there was even competition between the full-line manufacturers, Westinghouse and General Electric. This competition, however, was not always in the crude form of price cuts. The General Electric Company, with its huge reserves, its uninterrupted flow of dividends, and its financial alliances, rivaled the United States Steel Corporation, the General Motors Corporation, and the American Telephone and Telegraph Company. To this rival, whatever the theoretical possibilities, Westinghouse did provide "an effective competitor."

General Electric and Westinghouse did not generate and market electric power; they simply sold the machines which would do so. The advantages of converting a power generated by the thrust of water or steam into a force—be it light, heat, or motion—which could move over the channels of wire to the place of work were almost instantly appreciated, and the glittering demonstrations of the Columbian Exposition and the Niagara Falls installation convinced the ardent that here was the way to wealth. Between 1902 and 1920 the net production of electrical energy by central stations multiplied ten times. Industrial establishments and streetcar installations could also generate electricity in their own power plants or they might purchase power generated in central stations owned by others and sold commercially for any purpose the purchaser might have in mind.

As in most untried enterprises, the path of investment and management was not smooth. The original capital costs were high. A system of accounting which would correlate rates and costs had to be formulated and since electric power could not be stored, discovery and cultivation of overlapping markets to even out the "load" were essential. Since electric power came of age at a time of political and economic reform, proposals for public ownership, usually by municipalities, or for government regulation were inescapable. Massachusetts and Wisconsin each established public utility commissions in 1907. Public utility corporations also turned to the big manufacturers for managerial advice and assistance. Just as the early railroads expected locomotive and rail manufacturers to take railroad stock in payment for the equipment they provided, promoters of electrical public utilities expected the manufacturers to give financial assistance. General Electric, for one, established in 1904 the Electric Bond and Share Company to hold the stocks of operating companies. Before disaffiliation some twenty years later, Electric Bond and Share became the largest holding company in the industry. Compared to the degree of centralization in other contemporary businesses, ownership in public utilities remained diffused and fragmented. Geography, nonetheless, might sometimes facilitate a local or regional monopoly. The largest cities, for instance, offered the greatest advantages for the building of large central stations and of extensive systems of distribution.

Motors: The Big Two

As in all new industries, the competition in the manufacture of automobiles was peculiarly feverish. Since technical changes were so rapid that manufacturers could hope to produce a taking car which would sweep the market in a single year, and since the amount of capital required for starting business was small, the field was alive with "manufacturing gamblers," "plungers," "skimmers." Every depression or reversal killed them off. Fortunately for the industry and the nation, trade associations in the automobile industry modified the most glaring disadvantages of competition. First of all, standardization was accomplished. Although the makes of cars had an individuality in inward and outward appearance, the thousands of small working parts were standardized, and varieties were reduced to a few necessary types. Then in 1915, when patent legislation threatened to retard the progress of the automobile industry, most makers through the National Automobile Chamber of Commerce signed an agreement by which the patents of one party were made available to all others without the payment of royalties. In addition patents were acquired for the common use of members. But the consolidators wanted more than this. As one of them put it:

Many of us thought that the industry was beset with difficulties and so came the desire to some of us to form a combination of the principal concerns . . . for the purpose of having one big concern of such dominating influence in the automobile industry, as for instance, the United States Steel Corporation exercises in the steel industry, so that its very influence would prevent many of the abuses that we believed existed.

As it turned out two concerns gave big business to the industry. One was General Motors. This corporation, chartered in New Jersey, was the creation of William C. Durant. Durant's early years as a drugstore clerk and patent medicine salesman showed his talents for salesmanship and the appeal of his personality. Later he had made a remarkable success as a wagon manufacturer, and from that business he had been called to revive the fortunes of the Buick Company. He was successful. The Buick may be regarded as the nucleus of General Motors. Durant then began a career of giddy expansion. He purchased all sorts of automobile concerns on the theory that the future might belong to even the most bizarre of them, but by 1910 he was placed on the sidelines while the bankers rescued his organization from bankruptcy. Meanwhile he purchased another small automobile factory and began the manufacture of the Chevrolet. With his customary wizardry he transformed this concern into a big business and secured the alliance of the Du Ponts, chemical manufacturers with capital, not only for this enterprise but for the recapture in 1916 of the General Motors Company through the purchase of its stock in the open market. Though financial misadventures later sent Durant into exile and gave to Morgan and Du Pont the control of the corporation, it became an industrial giant, manufacturing cars at all price levels.

Meanwhile Henry Ford grew on his own prosperity. By 1907 he controlled the majority of the stock in the Ford Motor Company. Expansion and integration were the war cries. Ford's own plants began the manufacture of parts; blast furnaces and foundries were built; paper and glass factories controlled; timber lands, waterpower sites, coal mines, iron deposits were purchased; railroad lines knit together many of these properties. It was apparent that the automobile field was the preserve of the giant corporation. The benefits of large-scale production, the wide-flung nature of marketing agencies, and the sheer force of momentum gave them an advantage. In 1915 Ford and General Motors manufactured just under 50 percent of the national output. In view of the fact, however, that Ford produced nearly five times as many cars as his rival and that his lead was more marked than it had been a few years earlier, perhaps the motor industry should be described in terms of the "big one" rather than the "big two."

These achievements of bigness were spectacular: to their advocates they were "inevitable," to many outside observers they were "dangerous." Whether they were typical is another question. A correct answer faces many variations in the definition of "monopoly" and the absence of detailed studies. Empirically the construction of railroads and the multiplication of motor cars has lowered transportation costs and had broken down regional and local markets, more easily monopolized than the national one. The well-known multiplication of competitive units in trade and service industries, a fact of urbanization, gives one kind of bias to speculation, while the declining percentage of agricultural activity in the national economy and the consequent reduction of individualistic production gives another. Brooding over these and other factors one student concluded that competition declined "moderately" from the Civil War to the end of the century and thereafter it increased "moderately."

The Security Business

Be that as it may, there is no doubt that after the Civil War the corporation became the dominant form of business enterprise. Once largely confined to banks, insurance companies, and transportation agencies, corporations now crowded individuals and partnerships out of manufacturing, spread from large concerns to tiny ones, and invaded even the field of construction and retailing. Wherever three or four persons engaged together in a common business a corporation was born. Between 1860 and 1914 an index of incorporation showed their multiplication by nearly sixty times. Many factors explained this phenomenon. For one thing, state after state eased the act of incorporation by statutes laying down general rules through compliance with which any promoter could establish a corporation, enlarged the corporation's privileges—the holding company was a case in point—and granted the directorate a power of decision and management less curbed by the oversight or obstruction of stockholders. But a shameless rivalry in chartering was not the whole explanation of the fever for incorporation. Shareholders had a limited liability for the debts of their concern; the sale of securities gathered together in a mighty stream a thousand trickles of investment funds; and promoters, consolidators, and bankers made money through the sale and manipulation of securities.

For as the deluge of securities mounted, the marketplace in which they were bought and sold was broadened and its methods, technical and institutional, improved. In 1869 boards of competing brokers were consolidated into the New York Stock Exchange and in spite of competitors this modern Wall Street remained the security exchange of the country. The fodder coming to its mill exhibited the familiar sequence. Throughout the later decades of the nineteenth century railroad securities were its favorites and the great banks loaning in the call money market refused to lend on other collateral; at the turn of the century a few industrials were on inferior terms allowed to join this aristocracy. Two decades later they enjoyed a superior respectability. Undoubtedly the Stock Exchange gave a continuous appraisal of security values and expedited transactions between buyers and sellers. But it also provided facilities for gambling on the prices of securities through methods understood by the expert and mysterious to the uninitiate. Public criticism mounted. And even the experts grew discontented when they were cheated by other insiders. So there were waves of reform. At one time or another the Stock Exchange passed rules for adequate and regular reports from corporations listed on its board, discouraged fictitious transactions, and punished "reckless or unbusinesslike dealing." Outsiders were not, however, willing to trust the Stock Exchange to purify itself. The New York legislature passed some regulatory legislation; national action, often demanded, was continually deferred.

Not every corporation listed its securities in the Stock Exchange, nor did those quoted on the board always obtain funds through public offering of securities. In large part the methods of financing industry current in the early days of the Industrial Revolution persisted. The launching of an industry often required small funds; growth was financed out of profits. Thus the original investment in the petroleum business by Rockefeller and Clark in 1862 was only $4,000. As their business activities extended, the large profits were plowed back into the enterprise. No exact notion of their extent can be secured, but in a single company, the Standard Oil Company of New Jersey, the capital was increased from $3 million to $625 million between 1882 and 1922; about four-fifths of the increase represented the reinvestment of profits. In the twentieth century Henry Ford repeated this traditional story of growth. The capital stock of his third concern was $100,000, but only $28,000 was ever paid in cash. Other manufacturers sold him parts on thirty to ninety days credit, and since the purchasers paid a deposit on orders and cash down when delivered, Ford often sold the cars before his bill from the parts manufacturer had to be paid. Within fifteen months the Ford company paid 100 percent in dividends. These profits financed his customary expansion; if he built gigantic new plants he either failed to reduce prices or raised them slightly for the moment. Between 1904 and 1923 the net worth of the company grew from $100,000 to $359,962,000. Nor were Rockefeller and Ford exceptions.

If established companies issued new stock, the law generally compelled them to offer existing stockholders the first opportunity to make additional subscriptions. But the sale of bonds in all corporations and of stocks in new companies was generally effected in the first instance through the investment banker. Strictly speaking, he was simply a middleman who arranged for the sale of securities, issued by a corporation or a government, to the purchasers—individuals, estates, banks, insurance companies. He could perform this function alone or with others in a syndicate. His charges were in many forms—cash, stock, commission, fixed payments. Whatever form underwriting might take, the investment banker became of central significance in the industrial state.

The Civil War enormously stimulated a business hitherto largely unspecialized and in spite of the connections established between American and European bankers, largely localized in character. But now to handle the securities issued by the government during the Civil War and to refund them and the temporary debts after the war, banking houses expanded their organizations. New partnerships were formed, and new alliances were made with agencies overseas to sell the "governments" to European investors. In origin many of those early investment houses naturally sprang from mercantile businesses, since the handling of goods required a large amount of capital and their importation had led to the establishment of financial ties with foreign banks. Thus Alexander Brown & Sons of Baltimore, the oldest investment banking firm on the American continent, gradually specialized in the marketing of securities after having commenced business as an Irish linen importer. Thus, too, the firms of J. and W. Seligman and Kuhn, Loeb and Company grew from clothing and merchandising companies. Even the House of Morgan had merchandising as a remote ancestor. To be sure, John Pierpont Morgan, who came to this country in 1857, was not a counter clerk or peddler, but the firm which he represented, J. S. Morgan and Company, had been established in London by George Peabody, an American who had made his money in dry goods, and was named after Junius S. Morgan, also an American and a former dry goods merchant. Merchandising, however, had no connection with Jay Cooke, appropriately christened the "Tycoon" by his associates, and, as we shall see, the banker who organized the sale of government securities during the Civil War on a colorful and effective basis. After the Civil War he was compelled to allow rivals to participate in the "jamboree" of refunding, and their association introduced the word "syndicate" to American banking practice.

Earlier Cooke had perhaps introduced the practice by underwriting with seven others an issue of Pennsylvania Railroad bonds. The form of security was significant, for in the seventies government financing tapered away and railroad financing took its place. To be sure, Jay Cooke was ruined by the association as the Northern Pacific carried him down in 1873. But other banking houses, associated with the Union Pacific and the Pennsylvania, had prospered. Morgan also entered the field. His first great coup was in connection with the New York Central when W. H. Vanderbilt, the son of the Commodore, employed Morgan to sell part of his holdings abroad in order to avert popular hostility and prevent the depression of the American market when the stocks were placed on sale. In the nineties, when railroad reorganizations were thick and fast, Morgan had the prestige and experience to carry out such operations. Roads like the Baltimore and Ohio, the Erie, and the Northern Pacific felt the touch of his magic. At the end of the century the industrial field gave new opportunities to the investment banker. Thus Morgan became involved in the promotion of steel consolidations forced by the threats of competition from Carnegie, and finally he was either persuaded or compelled to undertake the formation of the United States Steel Corporation in order to stabilize the industry.

Jay Cooke and J. P. Morgan and the others were private bankers; their concerns were partnerships. But it was possible also for incorporated banks to market securities. Biddle's Second Bank of the United States, for instance, had been the channel by which American securities had reached European purchasers. In the later nineteenth century banks again emerged as dangerous and perhaps surreptitious rivals to the private banker-underwriter. Finally the practice was regularized by the creation of security affiliates, owned by the same shareholders as the bank and directed in harmony with it. Although the First National Bank of New York pioneered with this mechanism, establishing the First Security Company in 1908, the National City Bank was a more significant illustration of the complete process. In 1881 James Stillman, a cotton merchant who owned railroad and bank shares, became its president. He brought to the institution the advantages of a friendship with William Rockefeller, a member of the Standard Oil group; and in the nineties the great resources of the Standard Oil companies and their overlords began to find an outlet through the National City Bank. It was the "Standard Oil Bank." Stillman aggressively sought alliances with other luminaries in the business world. At first repelled by Harriman, he later "went right after him," regarding him as the next great promoter after the Standard Oil group. The Rockefeller, Standard Oil, Harriman, and City Bank alliance controlled railroads, metals, copper and iron, entered the public utility field, and from time to time pained Morgan by its aggression and success. Competition might be avoided by a community of interest. Various enterprises indeed brought the two groups together. The flotation of the United States Steel Corporation required their joint efforts; the racket about the Northern Pacific in 1901 had been stilled by an agreement which involved the two parties; and after 1907 these occasional notes of peace became a continuous harmony when J. P. Morgan and Company purchased $1.5 million of the stock of the National City Bank and J. P. Morgan, Jr., sat on its board of directors. As in railroads and industry, community of interest replaced competition. Before 1908 the National City Bank had joined with the House of Morgan in only one underwriting enterprise; by 1912 they had participated in sixty-seven common operations, aggregating in all over $1 billion.

Bankers' Control

Previous to the Civil War, investment banking in this country had been not only a small but a passive occupation. The investment banker was simply a merchant. But as he actually formed companies and aggressively sold their securities, he became interested in the institutional purchasers of his products—banks and insurance companies. Alliance with the former was more important, for not only did they purchase securities for their savings and trust accounts but they furnished the short-term loans which underwriters required until the securities they were marketing were sold, and they had large sums of money in the call market available for security trading. Thus after 1875 the House of Morgan was closely allied with the First National Bank of New York; in 1912 it was, with the exception of the bank's president, the largest shareholder, and three of Morgan's partners sat on its directorate. The First National Bank and the House of Morgan in turn controlled other banks which controlled other banks. As for insurance companies, Jay Cooke had organized and managed one in order "to lay out anchors for the obtaining of money." Morgan was so eager to tap this great reservoir of savings that in 1910 he purchased $51,000 par value of stock in the Equitable Life Assurance Company for $3 million. As an investment this yielded him one-eighth of one percent, but the concern then had assets of $504 million.

As the banker cast aside his passive role, he was driven irresistibly to a greater interest in the enterprises whose securities he marketed. The relationship between Cooke and the national government at the time of the Civil War ironically illustrated the process. In order to secure issues for his house, Cooke had to maintain friendly, often dishonest relationships with both the Congressional and executive branches of the government. Twenty years later J. P. Morgan learned in his reorganization of the Baltimore and Ohio that he must retain some control over the concern whose finances he rehabilitated; otherwise it might relapse into evil ways and impair the estimate of Morgan's intelligence held by those who had purchased stock from him. On the other hand, there were often advantages for the corporation in continued association with the banker; his financial advice was valuable and new security issues could be marketed through him. Bankers either exercised control through a voting trust or began to sit on the board of directors of their clients and dependents. In 1912 the House of Morgan, the First National Bank, and the National City Bank held in all 341 directorships in 112 corporations with aggregate resources or capitalization of $22,245,000,000. Among others, their representatives answered directors' roll calls on the Atchison, Topeka and Santa Fé, the Great Northern, the New York Central, the Northern Pacific, the Southern Pacific, General Electric, Pullman, United States Steel, American Telephone and Telegraph, and Western Union.

This network of directorships and stock ownership, tying together railroads, industries, public utilities, and banks, concentrated in the financier an immense power. Occasionally they denied its existence. In 1913 J. P. Morgan and Company announced that the concentration and merger movements in banks were due to the necessity of meeting the financial demands of large-scale businesses, that bankers held directorships in other concerns as a duty, not as a privilege, and declared, "It is preposterous to suppose that every 'interlocking' director has full control in every organization with which he is connected, and that the majority of directors who are not 'interlocking' are mere figureheads." On the other hand, investment credit was essential to the industrial state, and the masters of capital thus exercised a power of life and death. Manufacturers outside their orbit trembled lest they be engulfed. Henry Ford, whose thoughts on the subject were not always lucid, arraigned the bankers, and annual conventions of the National Association of Manufacturers listened to abusive oratory on the subject. Undoubtedly the banker brought a new viewpoint. He was interested in commissions, in promotions, in uninterrupted profit, in market values, in financial stability, and in industrial cooperation. His contacts with men and materials of production were at second hand. All this marked so great a change from the days of the pioneer industrialists that observers christened the twentieth century the era of finance capitalism. At least the bankers thought the world good. George F. Baker, president of the First National Bank, although he felt in 1912 that the concentration of credit had "gone about far enough," said, "In good hands I do not see that it would do any harm . . ." and "I do not believe it could get into bad hands."

The Attack on the Trusts

The evolution toward business bigness challenged deep American folkways and transformed what were often at first only doubts and questions into active antagonisms. For after all here was monopoly, the ancient foe. As one critic surveyed the general scene of the eighties and nineties, "Business motivated by the self-interest of the individual runs into monopoly at every point it touches the social life—land monopoly, transportation monopoly, trade monopoly, political monopoly in all its forms, from contraction of the currency to corruption in office." As this sentence suggests, the discontent of those decades was not focused upon partial areas of business consolidation but was an attack upon the industrial order and its results. The dissection of the trust problem— analysis is too orderly a word—raided the terminology of feudalism and despotism for definitions of limitless power. Men described as "kings," "pashas," and "barons," usually linked with the word "robber," ruled the business world. The acquisition and piling-up of wealth was also alarming. Extravagance, ostentation, idleness all seemed to portend a decay of the American character and morality. Theodore Roosevelt was coining an appropriate slogan when he scolded the "idle rich." William Jennings Bryan struck a similar note when he gave his basic (as politicians would now call it) speech on "the Man and the Dollar," declaring, "In the determination of our questions, we should find out what will make our people great and good and strong rather than what will make them rich." Many Americans were pragmatic and observant enough to perceive that bigness was related to efficiency and that an economic order in which prices fell could hardly be identified with the extortion of monopoly blackmail. So the opponents of bigness pursued their campaign against the trusts on social, ethical and religious bases. To shatter the concentration of business enterprise would remove the danger with which aggregated economic power threatened democratic government and would throw down the barriers preventing small men from entering business callings and, what is more, succeeding in them. This was the philosophy of a "nation of villagers."

Not surprisingly, measures against monopoly embodied a good measure of confusion. While legislation and Congressional investigations if the committees pressed hard enough against witnesses, who were frequently evasive and often dishonest, might unearth the facts about the trusts, the selection of a feasible program against monopolies was another matter. States and territories nevertheless attempted legislation and by the time the Sherman Anti-Trust Act was finally passed by Congress, in 1890, fourteen had constitutional provisions and thirteen had laws of an anti-trust character. The Federal anti-trust act bore ironically the name of Senator Sherman, chairman of the Senate Committee on Finance, who had little to do with its provisions. The first two sections of the act require quotation in full:

Section 1. Every contract, combination in the form of trust, or otherwise, or conspiracy, in restraint of trade or commerce among the several States, or with foreign nations, is hereby declared to be illegal. Every person who shall make any such contract or engage in any such combination or conspiracy, shall be deemed guilty of a misdemeanor, and, on conviction thereof, shall be punished by fine not exceeding five thousand dollars, or by imprisonment not exceeding one year, or by both said punishments, in the discretion of the court.

Section 2. Every person who shall monopolize, or attempt to monopolize, or combine or conspire with any other person or persons to monopolize any part of the trade or commerce among the several States, or with foreign nations, shall be deemed guilty of a misdemeanor, and, on conviction thereof, shall be punished by fine not exceeding five thousand dollars, or by imprisonment not exceeding one year, or by both said punishments, in the discretion of the court.

Although the Sherman Act appeared to be clear and definite, it was so only on the surface. Since the legally erudite believed there was no Federal common law, the anti-trust act simply put into a Federal statute the rules of common law. These were hardly precise. The common law against monopolies had been variously interpreted in England from the time of Cromwell to that of Queen Victoria. Though there was thus doubt at the core of the matter, something was clearly made a crime with penalties, something was made a statement of public policy. As Sherman said in debate, Congress should establish "general principles" and by construction the courts would make the distinctions. The hard-headed, however, were alert to point out the contradictions in enforcing a competitive order. Senator Platt of Connecticut, for one, questioned the assumption that

. . . all competition is beneficent to the country and that every advance in price is an injury to the country. Unrestricted competition is brutal warfare, and injurious to the whole country. The great corporations of this country, the great monopolies of this country are every one of them built up on the graves of weaker competitors that have been forced to their death by remorseless competition.

As the national government experimented with the application of the Sherman Anti-Trust Act and the courts passed down decisions, a decade of perplexity ensued. The first important case involving an industrial trust was the E. C. Knight case in 1895. The facts were clear. The American Sugar Refining Company, through the purchase of four Philadelphia refineries, controlled 95 percent of the refining of sugar in the country. The government sought to annul these purchase arrangements as contracts in restraint of trade. The Supreme Court declared that the

. . . contracts and acts of the defendants related exclusively to the acquisition of the Philadelphia refineries and the business of sugar refining in Pennsylvania and bore no direct relation to commerce between the states or with foreign nations. . . . Commerce succeeds to manufacture, and is not a part of it.

Although the ineffective preparation of the government's case somewhat explained this extraordinary decision, such judicial hairsplitting convinced the ordinary observer that the act was useless.

Though the learned judges soon discarded this artificial distinction between manufacturing and commerce, though they asserted "every contract" meant "every contract," the status of the act was entirely unsatisfactory. Its interpretations had been most contradictory, the most important cases decided under it had been those involving labor unions and railroads, certainly of minor interest to the framers of the act, and no important trust had been brought to book. The exact apportionment of the responsibility for this outcome is difficult. The Department of Justice did not have the machinery or the funds to conduct extensive investigations into corporations and had no precedents as to the best methods of pleading cases. Neither the Cleveland nor the McKinley Administration was aggressive enough against big business to disregard court rebuffs. In the last analysis the Supreme Court had to bear the major responsibility for its own decisions.

The Roosevelt Administration determined to implement the Sherman Anti-Trust Act and to infuse new energy into its enforcement. Though Roosevelt saw the trust problem partly as an administrative one of investigation and of new regulations, he determined upon a spectacular assault upon some outstanding monster. The Northern Securities Company, which, as we have seen, amalgamated the railroads in the northern trans-Mississippi zone was selected for the test. The choice was a dramatic one. The corporation had just been created, and corporation counsel felt a holding company was legally impregnable. The bankers of the concern were much alarmed. Morgan departed for the White House in a quest for certainty and James J. Hill wrote plaintively, "It really seems hard, when we look back on what we have done . . . in opening the country and carrying at the lowest rates, that we should be compelled to fight for our lives against the political adventurers who have never done anything but pose and draw a salary." In 1904 the Supreme Court gave its decision. By a majority of 5-to-4 it declared the Northern Securities Company illegal under the Sherman Anti-Trust Act. The fact that it was a holding company, that the corporation was the creation by a single state, was brushed aside. The effect of the Northern Securities Company was to diminish the free competition which Congress felt was beneficial to the people. Though the immediate practical effects of the decision were negligible, the ardent opinion of the importance of the decision held by Roosevelt and others was not extravagant. It did apply the Sherman Act to big business and show that the government had the power to control it. Suits were forthwith initiated against the American Tobacco Company and the Standard Oil Company of New Jersey, gigantic combinations, the latter of which in the popular mind was the incarnation of the whole trust movement.

In 1911, during Taft's Administration, the Supreme Court passed down its decisions in these two cases. Verbally they were of immense importance, for the judges apparently gave new meaning to the phrase "every contract, combination in the form of trust, or otherwise, or conspiracy." For a decade or so the majority of the Court had said again and again that "every" meant "every." Now the majority, but not the same one, guided by the Chief Justice, asserted these words were meant to have the meaning of common law at the time the act was passed. Resorting to a somewhat different common law than that hitherto used, the Court declared that only restraints of trade which were unreasonable were prohibited. Defining the second section of the act, which was "the complement of the first," Justice White wrote,

   . . . the criteria to be resorted to in any given case for the purpose of ascertaining whether violations of the section have been committed, is the rule of reason guided by the established law and by the plain duty to enforce the prohibitions of the act and thus the public policy which its restrictions were obviously enacted to subserve.

This test did not exempt from the operation of the law the two corporations at the bar; they were dissolved, though with little immediate effect upon the renewal of competition.

As for the "rule of reason," some contemporary critics complained that it introduced judicial legislation; other contemporaries, including the President, asserted the new rule made little practical difference. All the restrictions and restraints legally condemned before 1911 were unreasonable and would have been forbidden afterwards as well. In a sense, both observations were sound. Though the Court upheld, as it always had, the regime of competition, it exercised a baffling and frequently frustrating discretion in determining what was and what was not consistent with that purpose.

The "Square Deal" and the "New Freedom"

Roosevelt, though he used the Sherman Anti-Trust Act, was not convinced that it embodied the right policy toward big business. Mr. Dooley, the Irish saloonkeeper of Finley Peter Dunne, sensed a typically Rooseveltian current of thought in the President's first message to Congress in 1901:

"Th' trusts," says he, "are heejous monsthers built up be th' inlightened intherprise iv th' men that have done so much to advance progress in our beloved counthry," he says. "On wan hand I wud stamp thim undther fut; on th' other hand not so fast."

As the years went on, Roosevelt's fundamental caution led him to make frequent distinctions between the "good" and the "bad" trusts. Consolidation was the result of the economic process; it brought blessings in overcoming the wastes of competition and introducing efficiency. Instead of dissolving corporations by a purely negative statute, the government should supervise and regulate them to prevent abuses such as monopoly "achieved through wrong," artificial raising of prices, artificial restrictions on productivity, and the elimination of competition by unfair or predatory practices. In a characteristic salvo, he declared, "We are against crooked business, big or little." Such was the summation of his thought and experience embodied in his "Confession of Faith," the speech accepting the nomination of the Progressive party in 1912.

In that campaign Woodrow Wilson was the victor over the ebullient

Teddy. Once Wilson had obliquely condemned government regulation of
business as "socialistic" and expressed the belief that the evils of business
could better be remedied through courts and the civil and criminal law
than through commissions. But before he became President of the United
States, he deserted these earlier dogmas and put himself in tune with the
flood tide of reform. His policy was best expressed in the collected speeches
which he entitled *The New Freedom*. He pictured the growth of combination and of combinations of combinations through community of
interest and through banking alliances.

> A trust is an arrangement to get rid of competition, and a big business is a
> business that has survived competition by conquering in the field of intelligence
> and economy. A trust does not bring efficiency to the aid of business; it *buys
> efficiency out of business*. I am for big business, and I am against the trusts. Any
> man who can survive by his brains, any man who can put the others out of the
> business by making the thing cheaper to the consumer at the same time that he is
> increasing its intrinsic value and quality, I take off my hat to.

To the objection that the restoration of competition failed to "observe the
actual happenings of the last decades in this country; because they say it
is just free competition that has made it possible for the big business to
crush the little," Wilson replied, "It is not free competition that has done
that; it is illicit competition. It is competition of the kind that the law
ought to stop, and can stop—this crushing of the little man." Wilson
claimed that the prohibition of unfair competition would actually liberate
the energies of the people by giving to "outsiders," small producers and
investors, the chance to show their true worth. Although this thinking
seemed to smack of the "good" and "bad" trust creed, it differed essentially from Roosevelt's thought in its interpretation of the past, in its emphasis, and in the policy to be pursued. Like Roosevelt, Wilson had
abandoned the mere idea of trust busting. Unlike Roosevelt, he regarded
the state of competition as more normal than that of monopoly and he
proposed to regulate the methods of the former rather than the practices
of the latter. The policy was to be preventive rather than curative.

In 1914 a Democratic Congress to which Wilson gave vigorous and
continual leadership passed the Clayton Anti-Trust Act and the Federal
Trade Commission Act. The latter act established the Federal Trade Commission (FTC)—whose resemblance to Roosevelt's proposals even Wilson
could not talk away—to be composed of five members. Designed to make
more effective the operation of the anti-trust laws, the Commission was
given broad investigatory and administrative powers, including the power
to issue orders preventing unfair methods of competiton which Section 5
of the act significantly called "unlawful."

It was hoped that the convenient vagueness of this phrase—"unfair methods of competition"—would be an adaptable instrument in the hands of the Federal Trade Commission and the courts for dealing with changing business situations. But the Sherman Act had likewise been vague and the desire of critics, including those in business, for definiteness in anti-trust legislation was one reason for the Wilsonian program. So the Clayton Act embarked upon definitions, but came to port awash with a curious cargo of futile prohibitions. In the first place, price discrimination between purchasers of a commodity was prohibited "where the effect of such discrimination may be substantially to lessen competition or tend to create a monopoly." This prohibition was also seasoned with plentiful exceptions for differences in grade, quality, quantity, transportation costs, selling costs. Secondly, exclusive contracts by which the purchaser or lessee agreed to deal only in the goods of the seller or lessor were prohibited when the effect "may be substantially to lessen competition or tend to create a monopoly." Thirdly, one corporation might not acquire stock in another when the effect "may be substantially to lessen competition . . . to restrain . . . commerce or tend to create a monopoly." But corporations might purchase such stock for investment, and corporations might own the stock of subsidiaries formed for legitimate purposes. Finally, after two years from the passage of the act "no person at the same time shall be a director in any two or more corporations, any one of which has capital, surplus, and undivided profits aggregating more than $1,000,000," other than banks and common carriers, "if such corporations are or shall have been theretofore, by virtue of their business and location of operation, competitors, so that the elimination of competition by agreement between them would constitute a violation of any of the provisions of any of the antitrust laws." These last two provisions groped against interlocking stock-ownership and interlocking directorates.

The Democratic platform of 1916 pledged the party to "remove, as far as possible, every remaining element of unrest and uncertainty from the path of the businessmen of America, and secure for them a continued period of quiet, assured and confident prosperity." Like many platforms, this statement was silent about specifics—in this instance, taxation. A large segment of opinion maintained that in levying taxes the national government should be guided predominantly by its need for revenue. The divorce of revenue measures from their effects had proved impossible; and Congress, rather than enacting a tariff "for revenue only," had used the tariff as a measure to protect American enterprise. In addition to these economic considerations, there was a pervasive ideology that revenue acts should tax the "luxuries" consumed by the rich rather than the "necessities" of the poor. While French wines presented a clear instance of the former, definitions became blurred when, for instance, it came to sugar. In times of national emergencies, such classifications of necessities were submerged by an overmastering need for revenue. Such, indeed, had been the case in the North when the Civil War spawned an array of financial measures. Almost automatically Congress enacted a tax on personal incomes above six hundred dollars. In the postwar reappraisal of these hasty measures, the income tax was dropped, largely because of difficulties in administering it. Nonetheless, some economists and some politicians in the West and in the South discerned in an income tax a crude means to redress the injustices of the industrial order, as they diagnosed them. An income tax would put a stop to the concentration of wealth, and if it applied to incomes above an exemption of four thousand dollars, it would tax only "the surplus over and above that amount necessary for good living." As if to consecrate his remarks, one advocate of the income tax reminded his hearers that he was speaking on the anniversary of the birthday of Thomas Jefferson. Although the need for additional government revenue in the nineties, not great in any case, could have been met in other ways, the equalitarian drives of the time insured the insertion of an income tax in the tariff of 1894.

Soon thereafter the Supreme Court invalidated the income tax as a direct tax not authorized by the Federal Constitution. Within fifteen years a conservative Senate leader introduced an amendment to the Constitution allowing Congress to levy income taxes. Congress passed the proposal and enough states had ratified it by 1913 to add the Sixteenth Amendment to the Constitution. In the same year the Wilson Administration took advantage of the government's new power by passing an income tax law as part of the revision of the tariff. After an exemption of $3,000 the "nominal" tax was 1 percent; the maximum surtax was 6 percent on incomes of $50,000 or more. These levies were on personal incomes; the tax on corporations was a straight 1 percent on net income. Partnerships were significantly exempted from this exaction. It took a war—not long in coming—partially to reveal how the income tax could be used for social, economic, and political purposes and how taxes could be automatically raised or applied to other sources of revenue. Compared to the potentialities of the Sixteenth Amendment, the protective tariff was a pigmy.

The Money Question

The Civil War

Since the Republic had not fought a man-sized war for half a century and the Civil War turned out to be a novel sort of conflict, the early failure to appreciate its possible burdens was perhaps understandable. It was also unfortunate—unfortunate in a military sense and unfortunate in the field of finance which provided, as the phrase went, "the sinews of war." Governmental expenditures shot upward. Their annual total, which had been $63,131,000 in 1860, had mounted to $1,297,555,000 in 1865. The auspices for an effective financial answer to this situation were not favorable. Since the depression of 1857 the Federal budget had run a deficit; the Republicans, who now had to conduct the war, were an untried administration and an untried party; and the civilian officials, including Secretary of the Treasury Salmon P. Chase, who formulated financial policy, were as unprepared in their field as their military counterparts were in battle. Indeed, it was not until the close of the war that Treasury and Congress, instructed by experience and aided by victory, coped adequately with realities. In the end, the measures taken, both the improvised and the foresighted, set for half a century the American patterns of money and banking, silver coinage being the one important exception.

To meet its requirements for income the Federal government turned belatedly to taxation. The tariffs on imports were raised and raised again. An elaborate system of internal taxation was devised: taxes on liquor and tobacco, licenses for occupations, sales taxes upon industrial and agricultural products, and an income tax. The overall practice, succinctly described by a contemporary, was "wherever you find an article, a product, a trade, a profession, or a source of income, tax it." In spite of this dragnet, total tax receipts during the war were roughly only a quarter of the total sum of Federal loans. The latter were issued in bewildering

347

variety. Some were comparatively long-term government bonds. Early in the war the government issued the "five-twenties," callable in five years and maturing in twenty; a later loan, the "ten-forties," was christened in similar fashion.

The early call dates reflected the habitual American belief, at least as old as Jefferson, that government debt should not extend to later generations and should be reduced in times of peace. These securities became attractive to purchasers after issues of paper money promised a speculative gain from buying government tax-exempt bonds with depreciated paper dollars; the interest on the bonds, and perhaps the principal, was payable in gold. Furthermore, the marketing of these securities was entrusted to the superheated salesmanship of Jay Cooke and his employees. Cooke was an apostle of the Union and abolition; he also received a commission on his total sales. Cooke organized a vast army of salesmen, conducted an advertising campaign mingling God, justice, and patriotism, and sold millions to large and small subscribers alike. These innovations and this experience launched "Our Modern Midas," as an enthusiast saluted him, on his career as America's first conspicuous investment banker. In addition, the Treasury poured forth a series of short-term notes, some running for three years, bearing interest, and sometimes possessing the quality of legal tender. It was thought these would be held by investors; actually they formed a part of the circulating medium.

Whether or not these issues were paper money, the legal tenders, or "greenbacks," as they were called from the color of the ink in which they had been printed, certainly were. Within ten months of Fort Sumter, early in 1862, the national government resorted to financial measures reminiscent of the American Revolution and the Continental Congress. Congress permitted the Treasury to issue $150 million in fiat money, which was to be "legal tender in payment of all debts, public and private, except duties on imports and interest on the public debt." These notes bore no interest. Nor were they redeemable in gold or silver. The only conversion which they had was an exchange, at the request of the holder, for government bonds bearing 6 percent interest. Over a step so momentous there was a searching debate. Opponents with considerable cogency questioned the constitutional power of the government to issue paper money and with frequent recourse to historic example, including the Revolution, pointed out its inflationary dangers. Every objection was beaten down with the sincere cry of "necessity." No opposition delayed later legal tender acts. Instead the last of the acts in 1863 limited or withdrew the convertibility into government bonds and left the question of redemption until the end of the war. Along with other legal tenders the greenbacks unloosed an inflation which increased the cost of the war to the government by perhaps $589 million. Inflation was due to many factors and was probably as "inevitable" as the issue of greenbacks, which was one of its causes.

During the debate over paper issues some Congressional voices supported the new currency with traditional anti-bank arguments: at least the legal tenders were not bank notes, they were the money of the national government. Such an attitude promised ill for the hope, clearly and stubbornly held by Secretary Chase, of substituting for the chaos of state bank notes a uniform circulation issued by institutions under national charter. "We must have an exclusive national currency," he wrote privately. "The state bank currency must be driven out of existence." In spite of indifference and hostility to his proposals, the preoccupation and passions of wartimes were so engrossing that the argument from "necessity" worked in their behalf. Favorably instructed by New York's previously described free banking act, Chase proposed that the note issue of the national "associations," for such these banking corporations were ingenuously christened, be based upon the bonds of the national government. By conferring, in effect, a potential banking privilege upon these securities Chase incidentally enlarged the market for them. As further protective coloring, the national banks were to secure their supply of notes from the Comptroller of the Currency. Apparently pains were taken not to remind the suspicious of "the Monster of Chestnut Street."

In 1863 Congress passed a national bank act; in the following year this statute was so rewritten as to be in fact the charter of this new system. Existing state banks or new groups could alike secure a national charter. These alone could issue bank notes, for in 1865 a statute put a punitive 10 percent annual tax upon all other bank notes. The basis of the note issue was government bonds. For the former, the act set a total circulation at $300 million, half apportioned among the states according to their population and the other half according to the demands of business. Against these notes and also against credit currency or deposits, the national banks were required to hold a reserve either in "lawful money"—for example, the greenbacks—or in specie. In the smaller places this reserve was 15 percent; three-fifths of this reserve, however, might be deposited in national banks of "reserve cities," originally eighteen in number. In cities so designated, national banks were required to keep against their deposits a reserve of 25 percent, half of which might be on deposit with banks in a "central reserve city," New York. Here national banks also had to maintain 25 percent reserves. The whole ingenious structure was subject to careful examination by Federal officials.

When Appomattox finally stilled the civil strife, the nation confronted financially a strange mixture of ruin and promise. In nearly every bank in the country specie payments had been suspended since December, 1861, a failure forced in large measure by the government's departure from the gold standard. Legal tenders of the greenback variety were outstanding to the amount of $433,160,000. The business of the country was conducted with paper; the price level was stated in terms of paper dollars, badly depreciated in terms of gold. In April, 1865, $100 in greenbacks would have brought $64.73 in gold; the low point of exchange, in July, 1864, was $35.09. Gold was still required for foreign balances, for customs duties, and for interest payments on the public debt. Gold had become a commodity traded on an exchange of its own at daily fluctuating prices. The national debt had increased from $64,844,000 in 1860 to $2,755,764,000 in 1866. For the former date the debt per capita was $2.06; for the latter $75.42. To measure the gross debt as a percentage of the national income, only figures for a ten-year period rather than for a prewar or postwar date are available. Between 1859 and 1869 this percentage moved from 1.3 to 37.3.

Complicated and burdensome as these various financial problems were, it was the postwar period which made their solution so difficult and explosive. As we have seen, the years between the Civil War and the twentieth century were ones of shattering economic change. Industry became the ruler of the economy, and new forms of business concentration ruled industry. Farmers and wage earners, confronted with the necessity of bewildering adaptations, chafed at the most galling of all inferiorities, a failure to share in the new wealth and a loss of power to direct social and economic affairs. Nor was their restlessness eased by general business conditions. Once the flush of postwar prosperity faded, the economy entered a prolonged downswing, not really dissipated until the late nineties. Within this period two of the four great American depressions, those of 1873 and 1893, fell. The discontented struck back, as we have seen, against the railroads with the Interstate Commerce Commission and against big business with the Sherman Anti-Trust Act. Certainly, the money battle was as central to the period as either of these statutes, and it was probably more emotional.

The Public Debt

The first postwar task was consideration of the public debt—greenbacks, short-term notes of varied descriptions, and the longer-term loans. As time went on, a large group, groaning at the immensity of the burden, proposed to discharge it, principal or interest or perhaps both, through the issue of legal tenders. Their proposal, however, is more appropriately considered in connection with the greenback crusade. Needless to say, it hardly appealed to those of traditional temper. The debt must be paid and it must be paid in conventional fashion. To tolerate a national debt was to tolerate a "mortgage upon the property and industry of the people." At least this was the estimate of Hugh McCulloch, Secretary of the Treasury in this critical period. A national debt was immoral for it encouraged extravagance; it was un-American, for it created a monied aristocracy; it was "anti-republican" for it increased the patronage in the hands of the executive, filled the country "with informers and tax gatherers" and made "rigid national economy almost impracticable." Such was the McCulloch indictment. It was authentically Jeffersonian. So he proposed to refund the short-term notes with long-term securities, refund the long-term securities at lower rates of interest, and pay off the debt with surpluses and sinking funds. The policy prevailed.

As the decades passed, it met with extraordinary success. A flood of revenue enriched the Treasury. As we shall see in a later connection, since no fundamental reduction was made in the tariff structure, the customs revenues poured in. On the other hand, though the internal taxes and excises were gradually repealed and lowered—the income tax, for instance, ceased after 1872—the amounts annually collected on liquor and tobacco and other articles remained large. Indeed, returns from internal revenue were as novel in this period as the contemporary decline in the receipts from land sales. However accumulated, a treasury surplus resulted. Bonds were called at their earliest date and additional amounts purchased in the open market at a high premium. Secretaries of the Treasury laughingly surveyed their difficulties; Grover Cleveland puzzled over the evils of a surplus revenue; and politicians with an eye on the voters advocated increased expenditures for pensions and for rivers and harbors. By 1893 the debt had fallen to a low point of $961,432,000.

Thereafter depression years accumulated small deficits; the Spanish-American War brought a token increase in military expenses; and that the nation could shoulder expenditures for the construction of the Panama Canal, in the neighborhood of $400 million, was a matter of national gratification. In the early years of the new century the debt reached a quiet plateau, a little lower in 1915, when Armageddon had engulfed the world, than in 1898 when America finished its "splendid little war" against the Spaniards. In 1915 the debt was $1,191,000,000. The per capita debt was $11.83; expressed as a percent of the national income the figure was 3.7.

The Rag Baby

In his policy for funding the Treasury notes issued during the Civil War, Hugh McCulloch had a conservative outlook; those notes were not permanently to form a part of the nation's money circulation. His attitude toward the legal tenders was equally orthodox. Rejecting the primitive hard-money principles of Jackson and of Benton, he was nonetheless sure that the only sound paper currency was one convertible into coin:

By common consent of the nations, gold and silver are the only true measures of value. They are the necessary regulators of trade. I have myself no more doubt that these metals were prepared by the Almighty for this very purpose than I have that iron and steel were prepared for the purposes for which they were being used.

In short, the greenbacks were to be brought up to a specie standard. In proportions never made quite explicit by those in authority, some were to be withdrawn from circulation. Some proposed the Treasury cremate them, others that the Treasury hold them in reserve. The unwithdrawn greenbacks were to be funded by redemption with government bonds bearing interest—a feature the greenbacks lacked.

Though the policy had wide support, the Civil War debates over the greenbacks gave warning that it would arouse opposition. For in the greenbacks many sensed the possibility of a currency managed not by the bankers but by the national government. Money as the measure of value and exchange was not the creation of God's ordinance, but of legislation. This legal currency could be expanded or contracted at will; its amount would be based not upon a relatively inflexible reservoir of precious metals, but upon "population," the "business needs" and "activities" of the country. Instead of preventing overissues beyond "a safe and just point" by tethering the paper currency, as bank notes had been restrained, to coin and "lawful money" some thinkers proposed the interconvertibility of legal tenders and government bonds.

As these choices indicated, the greenback problem was not one of simple alternatives, for some interests might dislike both greenbacks and bank notes; nor was it detached from debt management nor the uneven impact of depression and prosperity. The movement in behalf of greenbacks, for instance, gained momentum during and following the depression of 1873. Historically, as we have seen in Jackson's time, farmers and workers had been inclined to prefer coin or bullion to bank notes or other forms of paper. What they esteemed "sound money" was more apt to result from a contraction of the legal tenders and a turn toward specie. Professional classes in receipt of salaries or other forms of fixed income were better served by contraction than its opposite. Academic economists and the Protestant clergy both preached the doctrine of hard money and identified a hankering after the greenbacks as the equivalent of sin and "heresy."

The business community was far from united on the greenback question. Cooke, the puissant investment banker, expressed one school of thought:

Why should this Grand and Glorious Country be stunted and dwarfed—its activities chilled and its very life blood curdled by these miserable 'hard coin' theories—the musty theories of a bygone age. These men who are urging on premature resumption know nothing of the great & growing west which would grow twice as fast if it was not cramped for the means necessary to build Rail-Roads and improve farms and convey the produce to market.

Those who were betting on the growth of the country wanted a currency system which would ease borrowing and development and which would minister to their sanguine expectations by a rise in the level of prices and a fall in interest rates. Those who held property for sale, be they farmers with wheat or merchants with dry goods, dreaded a deflationary policy. Particular groups, like the ironmasters of Pennsylvania and elsewhere, wanted the indirect protection greenbacks gave their industries; if those who imported rails were compelled to use greenbacks to purchase gold at a high premium, railroads would prefer to patronize domestic producers who accepted legal tenders without bothering about gold and its relative standing. Bankers were divided. Country bankers, who needed currency for loan purposes, opposed the contraction of greenbacks. City bankers, more apt to loan demand deposits subject to check, gave preference to their interest as creditors and favored contraction. Quite rightly, the *Nation,* surveying the confused scene, concluded the "debtor class" lived in large mansions, "on Beacon Street, Fifth Avenue, and Chestnut Street, with huge safes stuffed full of stocks and bonds, but especially stocks."

There were many variants to the greenback philosophy. Only a few voices suggested that the government enlarge its expenditures to relieve unemployment, create deficits, and meet these deficits with paper money. Far more general was the idea that this "lawful money," this "people's currency," should be used to handle the immense burden of government debt lowering over the country. Taking their cue from the ambiguities and silences of the various loan and currency measures during the Civil War, these money crusaders proposed to pay the holders of government securities in greenbacks unless the face of the bond stipulated coin. Some thought only the principal should be thus discharged; others added interest to principal; there were distinctions between different loans. All this seemed eminently fair, since the bondholders had purchased government securities with depreciated money and the currency good enough for the plow-holder ought to be good enough for the bondholder. Such slogans hardly appealed to bondholders. In their eyes greenbacks were a rag baby of censurable parentage. The proposal also affrighted the custodians of the Treasury, who asserted that the government, at least by implication, had promised and advertised payment in coin. To revoke the contract would, they felt, thus destroy public confidence in the credit of the government, a credit which must be kept unimpaired for future borrowing in future wars, a whole string of which McCulloch foresaw. In 1869, after the triumphal election of Grant, Congress pledged the faith of the United States to the payment in coin or its equivalent of all the obligations of the United States.

The problem of the existing greenbacks remained. In 1866 the Treasury had undertaken contraction. A statute authorized the Treasury to retire $10 million of these notes within six months and thereafter not more than $4 million a month. After the total had thus been somewhat reduced, Congress in 1868 stopped further withdrawal. In 1875, however, Congress permitted the reduction of legal tender notes to $300 million contingent upon an expansion of the bank-note currency; declared that the remaining greenbacks would be redeemable in gold after January 1, 1879; and provided for the sale of government bonds to secure a fund for greenback redemption. The reduction of legal tender notes to $300 million was not achieved, however, for an act of 1878 changed this amount to $346,681,016. The same act stipulated that when the greenbacks were redeemed they were not to be cancelled, but were to be reissued by the government in the course of its operations. In spite of such vacillations, on the selected day, January 1, 1879, the Treasury had accumulated enough gold to redeem the greenbacks if they were presented. The reserve and the promise sufficed. The premium on gold disappeared and the dual price quotations with it.

The bare recital of these legislative and administrative measures reflects only palely the contemporary uproar over resumption. Farmers and organized workers had joined the melée, particularly after the panic of 1873. Eventually the Greenbackers organized their own political party and made a considerable showing—usually exaggerated—in the Congressional campaign of 1878. Then the movement declined. Successful resumption deprived it of an issue. Furthermore, a new and, as it proved, more appealing method of inflation rose on the horizon of American politics.

Free Silver

At the very moment of resumption, Francis A. Walker, an American economist, government servant, and later president of the Massachusetts Institute of Technology, was writing:

Merchants and economists rightly visit their severe condemnation upon all schemes for "scaling down debts" by means of paper inflation. Is it any the less reprehensible morally—is it not even more a blunder economically—to adopt measures which must seriously aggravate the pressure of all existing obligations, public, corporate, and private throughout Christendom?

Walker was a bimetallist through international action. While a program of bimetallism was sure to anger greenback zealots, who identified specie with "barbarism," bimetallism probably won wider popular support than paper money. Silver was a precious metal, and its supply was limited by unforeseeable factors of discovery and costs of extraction; a silver coin was a coin from a mint and not the easy issue from a printing press. Furthermore, silver had the stamp of Americanism. Alexander Hamilton had argued for bimetallism, Andrew Jackson and Thomas Hart Benton had believed in hard money; in the 1830's the national government, as we have seen, had set the mint ratio for silver at approximately 16-to-1, a ratio which so undervalued silver that it was not generally presented for coinage. Historically, if not logically, the silver dollar became the "dollar of the daddies." Many in the post-Civil War generation wanted it back, for in 1873 Congress had, in the course of monetary legislation, almost routinely dropped its coinage.

In the next year or two, foreign events changed the world position of silver. Foreign countries limited or abandoned their silver currencies. In the American West new mines were opened and poured a flood of silver into the channels of trade. The price of silver naturally fell; and when the mine owners looked to the government for a purchaser, they discovered the demonetization of silver. The act of 1873 was converted into the "crime of 1873," passed presumably at the instigation of an English corruptionist and the Jewish international bankers, all favorite stereotypes in the drama of conspiracy. Actually, a handful of Treasury and Mint officials along with John Sherman had foreseen the flood of silver and wished to remove, unostentatiously, the complication raised by this issue to specie resumption. An agitation for the recoinage of silver belatedly sprang up. In 1878 Congress passed the Bland-Allison Act, which provided for the purchase and coinage by the government of from 2 million to 4 million dollars' worth of silver monthly. The alternative to this act in the words of "Silver Dick" Bland, Democratic Congressman from Missouri, was "issuing paper money enough to stuff down the bondholders until they are sick." In the administration of the measure the caution of gold bugs prevailed. The Treasury purchased the minimum amount of silver. The silver dollars which were coined usually stayed in the vaults, while silver certificates, representing those deposits, circulated. Certificates, silver dollars, legal tenders, all were interchangeable on demand into gold.

During the eighties the currency battle continued in a lower key. In the South and West agricultural organizations, borning, dying, coalescing, finally became "alliances" and advanced varied political programs. That of the Southern Alliance in 1889 reflected well enough the hopes of the debtor farmer. Its financial planks called for the free and unlimited coinage of silver and the substitution of greenbacks for the national bank notes. Its solution for agricultural marketing difficulties was the subtreasury system. In every county with an annual agricultural production worth $500,000 the United States should, the platform urged, establish warehouses and a subtreasury. To the former the farmer was to bring his grain or cotton for storage; from the latter he was to receive legal tender notes up to 80 percent of the local current value of his deposited crops and a certificate of deposit. These certificates were to be sold within a year to millers or other consumers for the difference between the going price and the sum the farmer had received from the subtreasury. The purchasers could secure their commodity from the warehouse by paying the sum that the subtreasury had advanced to the farmer plus an annual interest charge of 1 percent.

From the alliances the tide of agricultural unrest flowed after 1890 into the Independent, or Peoples', parties which were multiplying in the western states with the fecundity of grasshoppers. Kansas was the center of this social revolt, and its prophetess was Mrs. Mary E. Lease, Kansas lawyer and mother of four children. She was the author of the famous advice to the Kansas farmers "to raise less corn and more *hell!*" and her verbal visions often included an earthy analysis of the farmer's plight.

Wall Street owns the country. It is no longer a government of the people, by the people, and for the people but a government of Wall Street, by Wall Street, and for Wall Street. . . . We were told two years ago to go to work and raise a big crop and that was all we needed. We went to work and plowed and planted; the rains fell, the sun shone, nature smiled, and we raised the big crop that they told us to; and what came of it? Eight-cent corn, ten-cent oats, two-cent beef, and no price at all for butter and eggs—that's what came of it. . . . The people are at bay, and the blood-hounds of money who have dogged us thus far beware!

Two years later thirteen hundred delegates met at Omaha. They established the Populist party as a national organization and on July 4, 1892, drew up a second "Declaration of Independence," which thus indicted the state of the nation:

The people are demoralized. The newspapers are largely subsidized or muzzled, public opinion silenced, business prostrated, our homes covered with mortgages, labor impoverished, and the land concentrated in the hands of the capitalists. . . . The toils of the millions are stolen to build up colossal fortunes. From the prolific womb of governmental injustice we breed the two great classes—tramps and millionaires.

The financial measures advanced by the new party were inherited from the alliances and other groups. They demanded a legal tender currency issued without the mediation of the national banks through the subtreasury or a better system; they sought the free and unlimited coinage of silver at the ratio of 16-to-1; they advocated that the circulating medium be increased to not less than fifty dollars per capita. They sought a graduated income tax. After political jockeying, the Populists nominated General James B. Weaver for the Presidency. In spite of his irreverent nickname, "Jumping Jim," Weaver was a splendid figure. A Civil War veteran, a born orator, he had crusaded as a Greenbacker and as an Independent with courage and with conviction. His book *A Call to Action,* printed in 1891, is an excellent illustration of the philosophy of the western revolt. Although both the major parties threw sops to the inflation movement in the vague approval of some form of bimetallism, the Populists secured a million votes in the election. They carried five states—Colorado, Idaho, Kansas, Nevada, and North Dakota. They failed in the southern states, the other center of discontent, because their party labored under the charge that in splitting the Democrats it would cause Republican or Negro domination and the return of reconstruction days.

Meanwhile the silver forces had wrung from Congress a partial victory, the Sherman Silver Purchase Act of 1890. The need which explained its passage was not the hardship of debtor farmers and exploited workers, but the need of the Republican leadership to secure the passage of a protective tariff by conciliating Senators from the silver-producing states. The new statute, superseding the Bland-Allison Act, provided for the purchase of 4.5 million ounces of silver per month at the market price. Since this amount was practically the total output of the silver mines of the country, the act greatly increased the currency. Other provisions of the act, weasel-worded, apparently intended that the silver Treasury notes might be redeemed in gold. The test whether the nation could remain on the gold standard came two years later, grew sharper during the panic of 1893, and was not eased until 1896. Since government revenues were inadequate, the Treasury had to meet government bills in part with gold. Since individuals and banks, their confidence in the currency weakened, sought gold or needed it to meet international balances—a situation due in part to the same insecurity—greenbacks and Treasury notes were presented to the Treasury for redemption. In these critical years the gold reserve, which practice had set at $100 million slipped again and again below that figure. To stay the calamity Cleveland in 1893 forced the repeal of the Sherman Silver Purchase Act and later sold four bond issues, with a face value of $262 million. Part of the gold to make the subscription to the bonds was withdrawn from the Treasury through the redemption of paper money! The paper money in turn was paid out to meet government expenses. An endless chain was in operation. The spectacle fanned the fury of the silverites; and the bargains the administration had to make with the bankers, including Morgan, who took the third loan and imported gold, assumed the air of a conspiracy "to bully the people" into submission.

For the currency question had become a religion. It was preached in every schoolhouse, on street corners, in hired halls, and at farmers' picnics.

That gospel found its bible in *Coin's Financial School* by W. H. Harvey. This paper-covered volume, selling for twenty-five cents, was first published in 1894. Its story starts on May 7, 1894, when Coin steps on the platform of the Art Institute of Chicago, "looking the smooth little financier that he is," to begin his school in which journalists, merchants, bankers, and politicians, or their sons, seek instruction. It ends with a magnificent reception to Coin several days later at the Palmer House. The body of the book is given to Coin's argument in favor of bimetallism, his devastating answers to objections from the audience, and to crude pictures illustrating the lecturer's points. Analogy is a favorite method of Coin's dialectic. If the government could raise the price of horses by purchases in the open market, could it not by the same means raise the price of silver? The arguments were easily understood, and the whole book had such an air of reality that many must have believed that there really was a Coin and that he held his famous school.

The election of 1896 presented the issue to the nation for definite settlement. The Republican party under the tutelage of Mark Hanna declared for the gold standard. The Democratic party stole the Populist financial program and won the allegiance of most Populist members. The platform of the Democrats focused upon the money issue as paramount and declared for the free and unlimited coinage of silver. William Jennings Bryan swept the convention by his plea for silver coinage and became at once the leader and the nominee of the new Democracy. Rarely in national history has a campaign been fought with such sectional and class bitterness. The conservative opinion of the East regarded Bryan as a veritable "antichrist." After a summer of intense excitement McKinley defeated the Bryan crusaders. Vachel Lindsay, years later, sang a fitting requiem:

> Boy Bryan's defeat.
> Defeat of western silver.
> Defeat of the wheat.
> Victory of letterfiles
> And plutocrats in miles
> With dollar signs upon their coats,
> Diamond watchchains on their vests
> And spats on their feet.
> Victory of custodians,
> Plymouth Rock,
> And all that inbred landlord stock.
> Victory of the neat.[1]

[1] Reprinted with permission of The Macmillan Company from COLLECTED POEMS by Vachel Lindsay. Copyright 1920 by The Macmillan Company renewed 1948 by Elizabeth C. Lindsay.

Although Bryan carried the South and most of the western states, he lost the old Granger center of discontent, the Middle West. This was the greatest reason for his failure. The region had become partly industrialized, and it had developed a more balanced agriculture which did not feel so sharply the depression of the nineties. Its economic interests lay with the East rather than with the frontier and the South. The year 1896 marked thus an end of an epoch. McKinley's election and the shift in the balances of foreign trade seemed to promise the Treasury would ride out the storm. An increased production of gold throughout the world, already under way through new methods of production and refining or through new discoveries, inflated the currency. A series of favorable harvests dulled the edge of western discontent. There was an interim of prosperity. In 1900 the Gold Standard Act declared the gold dollar the basic monetary unit with which all other forms of money were to be maintained at a parity. To redeem the government's paper money a reserve of $150 million in gold was set aside. It could not be used for ordinary expenses. If redemption drew the reserve below its legal total the redeemed notes were withheld from circulation. Thus settled, the money question in its cruder aspects disappeared for thirty years.

The National Bank System

During the prolonged struggle about money, the cry was sounded again and again that governmental policy was contracting the currency and that the amount in circulation was inadequate for the nation's business. The proof of this assertion, if one were provided, was the decline in prices and the resulting hardship of certain economic groups. As usual, the causes for a decline in prices were numerous. Technological changes, as in steel, lowered costs and prices; new low-cost areas of production—for instance, wheat fields in the trans-Mississippi West or Russia, or new findings of petroleum in Pennsylvania—worked to the same end. The fiercely competitive character of an individualistic economy meant that industrialists and farmers could not keep reductions in costs for themselves. As for the money stock, the amount in circulation with few exceptions increased after 1869: whether it increased as rapidly as the need for it was a matter of conjecture and controversy then and since.

While gold and silver were both increasing, even more significant was the increase in bank money. Since note circulation was now a prerogative confined to the national banks, these new issues took the place of those formerly put out by the state banks. By 1873 the amount of state and national bank notes in circulation was $338,789,000. A decline then set in, and in 1891 the figure was $123,916,000. Be it recalled that government bonds were the foundation under such issues. As the Treasury funded issues and purchased bonds in the open market, it shrank the base for note circulation. Superficially those who complained of contraction had here ammunition for their case. Actually, the constantly growing practice of loaning not notes, but a demand deposit on the bank's books which the borrower drew upon by check, should, if contemporaries had appreciated the change, have drawn all the fire from the charge. While note circulation declined, deposits in national banks more than doubled, and deposits in all banks multiplied nearly three times. Early in the twentieth century amendments to the National Bank Act and the enlarging government debt made possible, as it turned out, an expansion of the note issue as well. In 1912, on the eve of the Federal Reserve Act, bank notes totaled $708,691,000. Meanwhile deposits in all banks had shot ahead. In 1866 deposits were roughly twice the amount of notes, in 1912 twenty-eight times the sum of bank notes. In the latter year the total of bank deposits was $19,719,188,000.

The figures of deposits also demonstrated that the expectations of the creators of the national banking system had not been wholly realized. They had planned that the national banks would form the national system, and the state banks would disappear. For a few years after the Civil War these hopes seemed on the point of realization. In 1868 1,640 out of 1,887 banks were under national charter. Their strategic importance in matters of capital, deposits, and note issues was overwhelming. Then a reversal set in. The comparatively large capitalization of national banks prevented their spread to many small communities; their inability to finance agricultural operations and to loan on land made them useless for many parts of the South and West. To undertake these neglected and other functions, the state could still charter institutions which, if they were unable to issue notes, might still collect savings, make loans, discount paper, and thus create deposit currency. By the eighties the founding of state banks, particularly in the South and West, gained speed. After 1900 these new state institutions faced a new competitor, the trust companies. State-chartered, such corporations were originally devised to act as "the recipients and trustees of funds in large and small sums, held for account of widows, minors, and others." Gradually they developed a general banking business. Usually the operations of state banks were less rigidly controlled and supervised than those competing under a national charter. Consequently, in 1900 the national government had to come to the aid of its system. Capitalization requirements for national banks in towns of 3,000 or less were reduced from $50,000 to $25,000. Though a temporary stay toward state incorporation ensued, the total picture was not greatly altered. In 1912, when the number of national banks was less than half that of state banks and trust companies and they still had a monopoly of note circulation, their loans and discounts were $5,973,754,000 out of $14,626,772,000 and their deposits $8,064,193,000 out of $19,719,288,000. In short, even the halfway steps taken toward a national system of banking were farther from realization at the beginning of World War I than at the end of the Civil War.

If the independent Treasury sought to influence the nation's economy, whether for good or ill, it had to function in a stilted, indirect, and perhaps even illegal fashion. For, as we have seen, this system had been established in the decade of the forties to divorce the national government from the banking business. After the Civil War the monetary decisions of the national government and the resulting administrative response of the Treasury presented this conception with a genuine dilemma. If the Treasury persisted in aloofness the banking structure might well go under. For, be it remembered, in order to redeem the greenbacks and to meet the principal and interest on the public debt, the government built up large gold reserves. Importers always had to pay customs duties in gold, and since tariffs were high and expenditures usually less than income, surpluses generally piled up in the government's vaults. In some years the government seemed likely to engulf the gold of the country; at all times there was little correlation between the rhythm and amount of government receipts and expenditures and the business needs of the nation. As gold flowed into the Treasury, bank reserves diminished and bankers perforce curtailed credit and raised interest rates. The government therefore attempted to prevent these disadvantageous fluctuations in the money market by putting gold into circulation through the purchase of government bonds. Finally, during the administration of Theodore Roosevelt, the Secretary of the Treasury of the United States shattered the tradition of Jackson and Van Buren by announcing, "The money of the country belongs to the people, and Treasury operations must be made subordinate to the business interests of the country." Defying the intent of the law, he made generous deposits in banks rather than in government vaults.

Although government policy failed to put its hands on the levers directing the course of the economy, as the rejection of the greenback currency, the partial realization of a national bank system, and the continuance of the Independent Treasury all demonstrated, private enterprise followed a course toward national centralization. As we have seen, individual banks far down in the hierarchy could keep a portion of their reserves in banks in central reserve cities. Though in 1887 St. Louis and Chicago also received this designation, the reserves of the nation continued to be concentrated in New York, and, as time went on, in a few banks. By 1910 six great banks had 73 percent of national bank balances; the National City Bank alone held more than all banks combined in 1875. As before the Civil War, these funds were loaned at call with securities as collateral. In time of crisis it was thought these loans could be quickly liquidated through sales on the stock market. Actually, at such moments the market often fell too rapidly to perform this benign function, and the reserves of national banks were utilized to finance trading in securities.

Panic after panic demonstrated the unsoundness of these arrangements. For instance, in 1907, when financial terror came although the nation then had the largest supply of gold in the world, the country banks began calling back their reserves from the bankers in the reserve cities; these banks had either to collect their loans on the call money market or sell the collateral; the reserve city banks hesitated to elect the latter process, for it caused them terrific losses and drove the security markets even lower; instead they partially suspended specie payments by using clearinghouse certificates to settle balances between themselves and by rationing cash to their depositors. Although the banking structure was largely saved, the leadership and cooperation which accomplished it were improvised and worked in the face of the anarchistic selfishness of the banks, each of which, chasing liquidity, clung like a leech to its own reserves and was loath to aid other banks lest it be itself destroyed. In fact, the situation was largely saved by the decisiveness, prestige, and power of J. P. Morgan. He took command and decided which banks should be rescued and how it should be done.

The Federal Reserve System

Indeed, the panic of 1907 gave spur to the many movements for banking and currency reform. Currency, it was said, was not flexible in amount. It should not be rigidly based upon the size of the government debt, as in the case of note issues, or upon the amount of gold and silver as were various "certificates" or "notes," but upon the business of the country. The banking system, it was charged, was disjointed; reserves should be massed and marshalled at danger points by a central command and banks should act to save the structure and not themselves. It was easy enough to diagnose defects. To overcome state particularism, quiet the traditional dread of a banking "monster," assign direction to private or public officials or both, and apply on a large scale innovations in banking method required political leadership of a high order. Fortunately, a considerable period of investigation and education preceded the enactment of the Federal Reserve Act in 1913. This prelude should not detract, however, from the ingenuity of its solution.

First of all, its sponsors rejected a single central bank, although experience in European industrial countries had made such an institution a precedent, which the big bankers of the nation urged America to imitate. But the opposition of Jefferson and Jackson and of the people toward the First and Second Bank of the United States cast a minatory shadow across the minds even of twentieth-century statesmen, particularly those who were Democrats; the more recent unearthing of a "money trust" by the Pujo Committee convinced many Americans that the monopoly of credit must be destroyed; and the ingrained localism of a nation, continental in extent, was further argument against undue centralization. Instead, the nation was eventually divided into twelve Federal Reserve districts, whose boundaries were required to have "due regard to the convenience and customary course of business." In each district there was to be a Federal Reserve Bank. These were to be government banks in that the Treasury was to deposit Federal funds in them; they were to act as fiscal agents of the government; and government officials were to share in their management. They were also to be bankers' banks. Their whole capital was to be subscribed by the member banks. All national banks were given the alternative of becoming member banks or surrendering their charters; other banks were invited to join. Each Federal Reserve Bank was governed by a board of nine directors, of whom the central authority at Washington, the Federal Reserve Board, appointed three and designated one to be chairman; the banks elected the remaining six. Lest the large banks dominate, the banks were divided into groups based upon capitalization and each group could elect two directors; a bank, no matter what its size, possessed only one vote. The member banks were required to place their entire reserves in the Federal Reserve Bank of their district. Thus the New York banks, or Wall Street, were supplanted as the holders of bankers' balances.

The Federal Reserve Board, the "capstone" of the structure, had advisory and administrative powers, many of which were intended for common action in financial emergencies. Whether the government or the bankers were to appoint the members of the Federal Reserve Board would decide, in large measure, the public or private character of the "Fed." After Wilson quietly asked protesting financiers if they would place appointees of the railroads on the Interstate Commerce Commission, the Administration view prevailed. The Board consisted of the Secretary of the Treasury and the Comptroller of the Currency, *ex officio,* and five others, appointed by the President—who was to show a "due regard to a fair representation of the different commercial, industrial, and geographical divisions of the country"—and with the consent of the Senate. To the American Bankers' Association it seemed that bankers' control "was a guarantee against political control and it was equally a guarantee against incompetent management—two important respects wherein the pending system is lacking." As it turned out, the compromises of the act were so skillfully worked out that the method of appointing directors to the Federal Reserve Board seemed an irrelevance. The initiative of individual member banks in making loans provided the impulse to granting loans. Member banks loaned Federal Reserve notes which they received through the regional Reserve Bank after borrowing from it a like sum. The security for such an interbank loan was gold, gold certificates, drafts upon other banks, or notes, drafts, and bills of exchange "issued and drawn for agricultural, industrial or commercial purposes, or the proceeds of which have been used, or are to be used for such purposes." Except in the case of agricultural paper the loan must not run more than ninety days.

A second tie between the member banks and their superiors was forged by the requirement that the former keep against their own deposits a member bank reserve or deposit with the Federal Reserve Bank of their district. Against demand deposits country banks had to keep a reserve of 7 percent, reserve city banks 10 percent, and central reserve city banks 13 percent. These reserves the member banks built up by depositing gold, currency including Federal Reserve notes, checks on other banks including those issued by the Federal Reserve Banks, and notes, drafts, or bills of exchange as defined above and discounted by the Federal Reserve Bank. These reserves were not static; they were constantly fluctuating as they were used in the course of business; they could not fall permanently below the minimum required by law. Since it was clear that the member banks borrowed from the Federal Reserve Banks, the statute limited the capacity of the latter to lend by requiring them to keep against all circulating Federal Reserve notes a gold reserve of not less than 40 percent and against all member bank deposits a reserve of 35 percent in lawful currency.

Though there were many subtle fashions in which the Federal Reserve Board and the Federal Reserve Banks might exercise control over currency and credit, the chief weapons at their command were two. One was the discount rate. Under ordinary circumstances, it was thought, they could contract credit by raising the rate at which the Federal Reserve Banks rediscounted the paper presented by member banks or expand credit by lowering the discount rate. In order to reenforce discount policy the Federal Reserve Banks were authorized to buy and sell in the open market certain forms of paper and United States government securities. The latter proved more important. If a Reserve Bank bought securities the check would be deposited by the payee in a member bank, which would deposit it with the Federal Reserve Bank, where it would be added to the member bank's reserve. With more ample reserves the latter could follow a more liberal lending policy. A sale of government securities by the Reserve Bank would operate in reverse fashion and to the opposite end—a contraction in credit. The implications of this power were hardly appreciated at the moment of its bestowal.

Although there was a chain of command along which directives and exhortations, permissions and prohibitions, might travel, in the end the headquarters and the members of the army remained independent, outside, as it were, policy set by the Federal Treasury or the President of the United States. Such had not been the aims of currency philosophers and agitators for over half a century. Nor did the result mean, even by inference, that the big bankers had had their way. They did not get the powerful central bank entirely divorced from political influences that they had wanted, although they got reforms. Perhaps the administration of the act would shape the banking world of actuality nearer their hearts' desire. The Federal Reserve Act was only a statute, and amendments, frequently dictated by emergencies, always gave an opportunity for the change which might be an improvement.

The Farmer in the Machine Age

Published in 1868, Guyot's *Elementary Geography* declared, "Tilling the soil, called farming, or agriculture, is the principal business of the people in nearly all the States." For a decade or so thereafter this remained true, but by 1870 the balance between those engaged in agriculture and those in other occupations was trembling, and at some moment within the next ten years for the first time in American history farming employed less than half the working force. In 1910 the non-agricultural labor force was twice the agricultural. In brief, farming had become a minority "interest."

This profound shift in American economic life reduced agriculture, so it was said, to a position of inferiority. The repercussions upon government policy were bound to be far-reaching, for the concern of government with farming had been early, continuous, and extensive. The reasons ran a wide gamut. Food and fibers were essential to life, and a healthy agriculture was thus the base of national welfare and strength. Both the isolationist and the jingo sensed the fact. For centuries, furthermore, agriculture had been esteemed a more virtuous occupation than others. If no Jefferson now arose to rehearse with sophistication that old conception, William Jennings Bryan from the American heartland was there to celebrate with sentimentality "the pioneers who rear their children near to Nature's heart, where they can mingle their voices with the voices of the birds—out there where they have erected schoolhouses for the education of their young, churches where they praise their Creator, and cemeteries where rest the ashes of their dead."

Nor could those who guided the destinies of the Republic or those who passed the laws in its several states afford to turn a deaf ear to agricultural demands. In jurisdiction after jurisdiction historic constitutions or statutory systems of apportionment and representation gave a disproportionate influence to the rural regions; and in the United States Senate, with its equal delegations from all states, agricultural blocs had at least a negative power. In those unofficial bodies which play so great a role in democratic government, the interest or pressure groups, the farmers in the years after the Civil War attained new skill and influence. The agricultural societies of an earlier day gave way to the Grange, whose influence upon railroad legislation has already been chronicled. As the Grange waned, the Alliance movement of the eighties grew to power, formulated a political and economic program and called upon "producers" to unite at the ballot box to elect governments "that will work in the interest of the many against the exactions of the few." Then came the Populist uprising of the nineties and Bryan's defeat.

In 1902 from the resulting disintegration there emerged in the Northwest the American Society of Equity and in the Southwest the Farmers' Union. Both societies were founded by newspapermen. Of the two, the Farmers' Union proved so effective it absorbed Equity and lived on to become the most militant of large farm organizations after World War I. Toward the very end of the period the Non-Partisan League set the prairies afire in the Dakotas and elsewhere. These successive incarnations of farmers' aspirations and needs were far from agreeing with each other. They might unite in endorsing "the Golden Rule," but their attitudes toward governmental aid and intervention ranged from a suspicion of "political farmers" to an advocacy of a limited state socialism.

The Land System and Western Settlement

This historic national policy toward agriculture was, of course, its land system. To make that land system more effective the government had since midcentury embarked upon land grants to railroads. Now the Civil War gave opportunity for a further phase of both programs. In 1862 Congress had, as we have seen, chartered the Union Pacific and showered assistance upon it. In the same year Congress passed the Homestead Act. Representing the fulfillment of agitation which had sought for years to throw the lands "wide open," the act granted to "any person who is the head of a family, or who has arrived at the age of twenty-one years, and is a citizen of the United States, or who has filed his intention to become such" a quarter-section of the government domain—an area of one hundred and sixty acres. The final possession of this land was not given, however, until the grantee had "resided upon or cultivated the same for a period of five years." This was the important reservation to government generosity; the only other, the payment of registration fees, required a sum of money which was merely nominal.

Apparently the Homestead Act sought to enforce the traditional purpose of the American land system. It was entitled "An Act to secure Homesteads to actual Settlers on the Public Domain," and a section of the bill reenforced this title by declaring that the entry of the land must be made by the settler "for the purpose af actual settlement and cultivation."

But in reality the Homestead Act did not adjourn existing legislation nor effect that wholesale democratization of policy which it implied. Sales of land continued for years under the preemption and other laws; the huge grants to railroads and to states removed great areas from homesteading; and the last section of the Homestead Act allowed the commutation of the settlement requirement by permitting the grantee to purchase his quarter-section at the minimum price, generally around $1.25 an acre, after an interval of six months. Free land was more sloganeering than reality; sales, direct or indirect, remained for three decades the important method of disposal. Through these means after 1862, as before, wealthy and skillful landowners dotted great estates across the map of the West. One Irish engrosser owned 250,000 acres in Illinois, Missouri, Kansas, and Nebraska; a bonanza farm in the Dakotas contained 100,000 acres; and ranch syndicates, often provided with foreign capital, owned millions of acres west of the Mississippi.

The Homestead Act envisaged the average, workable American farm as one of one hundred and sixty acres. Such a calculation was justified by agricultural experience in the humid regions where the old land system had developed and was reasonable enough in the first tier of states west of the Mississippi and a little beyond. Here the technique of farming worked out in the forests and the prairies of the nearer West could still be applied. But when the prairie merged into the Great Plains along a line wavering between the ninety-eighth and one hundred-and-first meridians, the traditional agricultural technique was shattered. The new region did not vary superficially from the old, and settlement spread over its eastern edges time and again only to be withered back by the climate. The average rainfall on the Plains ranges from ten to eighteen inches, and these averages do not reflect seasonal variations, which may sink below the minimum. Agriculture of the eastern type could not thrive year-in and year-out in such a region.

West of the Great Plains the tide of pioneers found mountain ranges whose valleys and whose intermountain plateaus were semiarid or contained the finally delimited "Great American Desert"—all regions obviously unfitted for customary agriculture. Then came the states of the Pacific coast, a patchwork quilt of incredible climates depending upon the altitude and the lay of the land toward the sea. In the north the Willamette valley reproduced, to be sure, a forested land and a setting of weather akin to that which the pioneer had left farther east. But the Puget Sound basin had a forest which was almost unconquerable; the central valleys of California, the Sacramento and the San Joaquin, have an average rainfall of from five to twenty-five inches; the coastal regions of southern California have a temperature suited to exotic agriculture and a rainfall chiefly winter-seasonal. To meet these new conditions agriculture had to make a readjustment through irrigation, through dry-farming, through new crops. The land laws which underlay agriculture faced a similar necessity. Where irrigation was possible, smaller holdings were often expedient; where irrigation was impossible, dry farming or grazing was an alternative to traditional cultivation. The old unit of one hundred and sixty acres did not conform to either of these situations.

Adaptation of the government land system proceeded tardily. An intelligent policy required an adjustment for specific types of farming, distinctions among agricultural regions and the sizes of holdings: such an equilibrium in turn required a knowledge of soil and climate conditions and agricultural possibilities. The Homestead Act worked well enough until 1880 in certain parts of the West; it failed to cope with the situation in the Great Plains, in desert regions, and on forest lands. Lacking omniscience and alertness, Congress in 1909 doubled the Homestead allotment to three hundred and twenty acres in certain western states, and in 1916 allotted holdings of six hundred and forty acres on "stock-raising" land, a grant still too small for that purpose. Neither of these laws was designed for irrigable land. The government policy toward its desert land represented a characteristic evolution. In 1877, by the Desert Land Act, the government sold at $1.25 an acre six hundred and forty acres of desert land to individuals who would irrigate it within three years; when the ambiguous phraseology of this enactment led to both fraud and failure, the Carey Act of 1894 provided for the cession of public lands to the states provided that they undertook their settlement and irrigation; finally the Federal government, by the Reclamation Act of 1902, entered the business of constructing irrigation facilities for the government domain. The government was driven to undertake this national irrigation policy by the demands of the western states, by the large capital resources required for the projects, and by the picturesque desire to redeem the desert so that the "comfortable homes of happy and contented people [might] spring up where before had reigned the cactus, the rattlesnake, and wild desolation." In the years that followed, government engineers and agricultural scientists solved many of the technical problems of irrigation agriculture, but the settler had continual difficulty in meeting the cost of the land, which he often purchased at exorbitant prices from speculators, and also of the irrigation works, whose cost of construction he was presumed to repay over a period of years.

In spite of deficiencies, the government land policy transferred the usable land in the western regions to private ownership. The public domain shrank, population increased, and the frontiers of the East and of the West filled in and advanced to meet each other across the Great Plains and the Rockies. By 1890 the frontier lines of settlement, two inhabitants per square mile, had consolidated and observers in government service and out were declaring that the frontier was no more. The people who accomplished this miracle of settlement when "free land was receding at railroad speed" were first of all the native Americans lured westward by the prospect of better lands or greater fortunes or pried loose from the East by failure. As they always had, immigrants also joined the mighty throng: Germans, Scandinavians—"What a glorious new Scandinavia might not Minnesota become!" wrote Fredrika Bremer in 1850—and later Finns, Czechs, Japanese, and Mexicans. But in general these agricultural migrations from abroad declined after 1890; the "new immigrants" from southern and eastern Europe found industrial employment. Be that as it may, the West was settled and the era of cheap and abundant farmland came to a close. The effect of the closed frontier upon forms of ownership, methods of production, farm costs, and the price of land was profound.

American Tenancy

The comparative disappearance of cheap or free land joined with other factors—farm improvements, better roads and community services, and inflation, generally associated in one way or another with war financing—to increase land values. This generalization had not applied between the Civil War and 1900, a period during which the average value per acre of farmland, reflecting the decline of agricultural prices, held fairly steady. But with the twentieth century a nationwide tendency toward higher values for farmland set in. Between 1900 and 1910 the average value per acre of farmland approximately doubled: between 1910 and 1920 the figure increased another 75 percent. The first two decades of the twentieth century were often christened the farmers' "golden age." Nor was this designation sheer nostalgia. When land was expensive it could no longer serve as the basis for the cheap production of agricultural products. The farmer's overhead, represented by land values, was a mounting cost of agriculture. In short, under the new conditions agriculture was not an occupation to be undertaken lightly or without resources. The change menaced in several ways the favored American concept that he who worked the land should own it or vice-versa. A separation of management and ownership would dim the agricultural virtues of independence, self-reliance, and individual responsibility which the nation cherished so highly. It might even be bad for the land, as well as for the cultivator. As it happened, in 1880 the census for the first time devoted itself to the forms of land ownership. Its disclosures challenged the old ideals. In 1880 one-quarter of the farms of the country were cultivated by tenants who did not own the land. By 1900 that percentage was 35.5. Then, as the rate of change slowed, the figure mounted to 38.2 in 1920.

Tenancy predated the census of 1880, even in pioneering areas of abundant lands. For many reasons individuals in different circumstances preferred originally to rent rather than own land. Settlers who rented could look over the area for the best lands for later purchase; as age slowed down sires, their male heirs would enter into a temporary tenancy for the land they expected to inherit; men carrying on professions would rent the property they had purchased as insurance against insecurity; widows who didn't want to guide plows along furrows rented to men seeking farms. Tenancy was a means of mobility and adjustment; it didn't involve a permanent landless peasantry, for it was a ladder leading up and down. Tenancy was a protean arrangement as shifts in time and between crops suggested. The tenant farmer's concentration on staple crops—wheat, corn, cotton—was a general characteristic. If the owner furnished the seeds, the work animals, and the farm machinery he received a larger share of the crop; in such circumstances leases were short and the rent was on a share-and-share basis. Cash renting, depending upon soil, situation, crop, and the proportion of the means for farming furnished by the parties, was rarer.

In the South the necessity of providing a substitute for slavery after the Civil War gave tenancy distinctive characteristics and extensive application. The dream of forty acres and a mule, cherished by many Negroes and some whites, evaporated because the government, if for nothing else, could not constitutionally expropriate enough private lands for them; on the other hand, white employers failed to make a go of the wage system and to work the Negroes in gangs under white overseers. Too "many negroes began to desire to get off by themselves and run one or two horse farms." Consequently, "the large landowners . . . began to place their tenant houses all over their farms and rent to their tenants." If the landlord provided land, quarters, seed, fertilizer, tools, work animals, livestock, the worker shared the crop, to which he had no title, on a half-and-half basis. He was a "cropper," and the Supreme Court of Georgia declared in 1882 that his case was "rather a mode of paying wages than a tenancy." If the worker owned mules and implements, he might be a "share tenant," paying for the rent of the land with one-third of his corn and one-fourth of his cotton; or he might be a "standing renter," paying a fixed amount of cotton, no matter how much was produced.

As of old, the method of marketing a crop determined the ways of cultivation. At the beginning of the crop-year, the owner or tenant sought an advance on the crop from a merchant, to whom, in accordance with laws passed in the sixties and seventies, the cultivator gave a crop lien. Because of the risks involved, the merchant would charge high rates for his advances and also exercise a rigid supervision over the workers whose liens he held. These arrangements allowed industrious Negroes, if they were lucky in their merchants and landlords, to become independent landowners. At the other extreme, the Negro who was continually in debt was reduced to a stage of peonage indistinguishable from slavery. Behind the facade of tenancy the plantation system continued in the South. Its labor force remained dependent in an extraordinary degree upon landlord, merchant, and banker. Class lines were drawn more sharply in the South than in any other agricultural region.

Even in a system so subtle, formalized, and useful, the old and new were mixed. For one thing, the tenants were increasingly white. In 1920 the latter constituted 61 percent of all southern tenants excluding croppers; about 56 percent of croppers were white. On the other hand, tenancy dictated the continuance of the one-crop regime—cotton. The merchant or landowner sought its cultivation. Since cotton always had a market, he was sure of some return from his debtor or tenant. The merchant desired the single crop because it kept the tenant more dependent upon the store for goods than did general farming.

With some historical justification Americans regarded tenancy as foreign and hence undesirable. As Theodore Roosevelt declared in 1907:

> Nothing is more important to this country than the perpetuation of our system of medium-sized farms worked by their owners. We do not want to see our farmers sink to the condition of the peasants in the old world, barely able to live on their small holdings, nor do we want to see their places taken by wealthy men owning enormous estates which they work purely by tenants and hired servants.

There was more to these aversions than mere sentimentality. In the South tenants were apt to move every season; in the North they rarely rented the same property for ten years. They took little root in the social institutions of their neighborhoods. Since owners rarely paid compensation, tenants made few improvements on the farms, and they allowed buildings and the soil itself to deteriorate. Erosion was more prevalent on tenant farms than on owner-operated farms.

The agricultural wage earner completed the agricultural labor force. From available enumerations taken at different seasons of the year and defining "laborers" differently, it is impossible to say whether their number increased or decreased over the decades. The number in 1920, 2,883,000, was about what it had been ten years earlier and was also 25 percent of the total currently employed on farms. These agricultural wage earners fell into many categories. At one extreme was the "hired man" of fiction and poetry who lived the year around on the farm and married the farmer's daughter. Socially accepted, independent in attitude, many-skilled, he was an American type who bewildered Europeans and even southerners. A Harvard economist wrote in 1916, "probably nothing like him ever existed before and may never exist again."

Of increasing importance were the farm laborers who found employment on the big ranches and the bonanza wheat farms of the trans-
Mississippi West or the migrant and casual laborers required as additional
workers during the critical harvesting period for many crops. Some were
old crops like wheat—"hoboes" to the number of twenty thousand invaded Kansas for the harvest of 1920—or old callings like sheep shearing.
Others were the new crops which refrigeration, canning, and new dietary
tastes now placed upon a specialized and intensive production basis. In
the East the vegetable, berry, and fruit crops recruited armies of Negroes
and urban dwellers, including women and children. The foreigner also
played a great part. In the Far West orchards, vineyards, hops, berries,
and sugar beets required additional labor. In the nineteenth century
gangs of Chinese and later of Japanese, operating under "bosses," hired
out for these tasks. Even when others joined them, they were males, foot-
loose or single. The family labor system waited generally until World
War I. For such as these, wages were lower than in industrial employment.
The rootlessness and hardships of their lives and the lack of promise, for
here was no prelude to ownership, were additional disadvantages. Not by
accident did the Industrial Workers of the World in the twentieth century
find recruits among the agricultural workers of the West.

The Westward Movement of Cattle and Sheep

The westward movement influenced agricultural migrations,
the price of land, the increase of tenancy. It also dictated the history of
the American staples. The areas of their production shifted toward the
West and, after the frontier was closed in the nineties, tended to a more
stable localization.

The livestock grazer was the outrider of agricultural advance. Following the hunter and the trapper and preceding the plowman, he sought
always the open range. The area of this promised land had usually been a
constricted one. But suddenly after the Civil War it expanded across the
western half of the continent and included at its greatest extent in 1885
over 1,355,000 square miles, an area equal to that of western Europe and
a part of European Russia. In this vast domain the great herds of buffalo
were on the point of extinction, while their food supply, the grasses of
the prairies and of the plains, was still unimpaired as a food resource.
The disappearance of the buffalo facilitated the herding of the Indians
upon reservations. Finally, the construction of the transcontinental railroads provided an outlet for the herds of cattle, which could be pastured
on the wild grasses and shipped to the consuming centers of the nation.
At the same time the growth of modern packing and the use of refrigerator cars expanded the market for dressed beef. The result was the

cattle country, which left a heritage popularized in the "western" of the movies, but chronicled more accurately in the literature of Owen Wister and Will James and the folk songs of the cowboy.

The source of the cattle industry was Texas. That state's mild climate made it an admirable breeding district, the range produced luscious grasses, and the Spanish land system with its large grants made possible the keeping of great herds. Even before the Civil War cattle were driven north from Texas to Illinois to be fattened. After that conflict Texas cattlemen began driving their herds northward to the widespread tentacles of the oncoming railroads. This contact generated the cow towns, Marshall, Dodge City, Abilene, Ogallala, where buyers, ranchers, cowboys did business and celebrated their transactions with amusements reminiscent of the mining camps or the railroad construction towns. Meanwhile came a discovery that cattle could not only live through the winters on the northern plains but emerged fattened and ready for the butcher's block. The cattle could get at the forage where high winds blew the snow from the tops of the knolls; the little valleys furnished protection; early in spring, nutritious grasses burst from the south slopes. A northern area extending as far as the Canadian Northwest was added to the cattle kingdom.

These two regions were linked together by "the long drive." It started in Texas after the roundup, when the calves were branded and the selected cattle were cut out for their journey. Cowboys now pushed the cattle north, with an eye out for marauders and stampedes, until they came to the cow towns. Here some of the cattle might be sold for immediate shipment. Most of them, however, were marched onward to the northern ranches, which in some cases were the property of the Texas ranch owners. In the late seventies and early eighties these operations assumed the guise of big business. There were great cattle corporations which adopted seductive titles—the American Pastoral, the Western Ranches, the Matador Land and Cattle Company—issued securities to the tune of nearly $22.5 million and sold a good share of them to foreign investors. For a time such concerns made high profits; but in the late eighties they began passing dividends, and today only a few remain.

The passing of the range industry was due to as many factors as its creation. One was the cheapening price of fencing wire. Ranchers anxious to save hiring help began to enclose large areas of the public domain. These fences running for miles cut across the drives and compelled expensive detours. Of course they were illegal, for no law allowed such large-scale appropriation of government land, but they were maintained by shotgun diplomacy. Finally came the farmer. He was the mortal enemy of the cattleman, for his enclosures were legal; and, as a homesteader, he had the support of the government. Other causes of the cow country's decline were the quarantines which the northern states placed upon Texas cattle, prohibitions dictated alike by a desire to prevent the spread of cattle diseases and by a desire to prevent Texas competition with their own cattle producers. Behind all these factors was that of overproduction. In spite of a voracious demand, the price of beef cattle declined with the multiplication of the western herds. The prairie and the plains became so overstocked that their native forage was no longer adequate for the support of the animals.

After 1890 the cattle industry was built upon new bases. One of these was the remainder of the open range in the Far West. The cattle bred and grown on these acres were fattened along with native-bred cattle in the Corn Belt, which lay to the East. In the nineties Iowa, for instance, began the extensive fattening of cattle bought outside the state. In the country as a whole the number of cattle increased more rapidly than the population until 1900; since then there has been a relative decline. Meanwhile the center of beef cattle production moved steadily westward. In 1850 it was Lexington, Kentucky; in 1920 it was near Ellsworth, Kansas.

Although the Civil War temporarily halted the decline of sheep herded in eastern flocks, wool production definitely moved westward after 1870; and after a short passage through the prairie states reached its final habitat, the Far West. There were two sheep frontiers. Descendants of the old Spanish herds moved northward from New Mexico to California, from California to Oregon, and then from the coast eastward into the Rocky Mountain region. During this migration they were continually improved by breeding with merinos. Meanwhile sheep had been driven from the eastern portion of the United States. Continually crowded out by farmers who turned to cereals and other products as more profitable, sheep husbandry concentrated increasingly in the Rocky Mountain region from Montana to New Mexico. Yet even in this last refuge homesteading in the twentieth century led to a decline in the flocks. In 1920 Texas, once famous for longhorns, had more sheep than any other state. Whatever the dislocations, American sheepherders were apparently able to produce in competition with wools from the newer centers of the world—Australia, New Zealand, South America. In the American West were huge areas of government land, and sheep were such close croppers that they could find a living on grazing land which would not support other animals. The flocks were moved about from district to district to take advantage of the different rainfalls and altitudes. Yet even in the West there was a swing away from the production of wool. The improvement in means of transportation has made it possible for this area to market mutton, and the sheep growers of the West in the twentieth century were duplicating the experience of the eastern sheep growers after 1880; they were shifting their attention from clip to meat, or seeking a dual-purpose animal through a new breed. In the eastern part of the country, with the exception of a small area in the Ohio valley, sheep husbandry had completed this transformation.

The Cereals Move West

After the herdsman came the American farmer. In his advance into the trans-Mississippi West he followed the pioneer tradition of sowing wheat and other grains; wheat was the American cash crop. In 1859 the chief center of production was the old Northwest, and Illinois was the leading state. Thirty years later the supremacy of the trans-Mississippi region was unquestioned, for Minnesota and California led the whole parade. By 1919, although the Middle West was still an important producer, the prairie states were the wheat empire. Kansas, "wheat king," grew twice as much wheat as Illinois, the second in production.

Infinite variations of climate, soil, and history made this wheat migration possible. Before 1860 the American wheat farmer specialized almost exclusively in the soft winter wheats. When the early settlers in Wisconsin and Minnesota attempted to utilize these varieties they found they winter-killed with discouraging frequency. The alternative was spring wheat, occasionally cultivated but generally despised. Its yield was smaller than that of winter wheat and, maturing late, it was more liable to rust and other devastating diseases. By the 1850's Iowa farmers, however, had met the problem of winter-killing by shifting to spring wheat. At the end of the century the introduction of durum wheat extended the wheat area into the dryer areas of the Dakotas. In the corn and winter wheat belt which sprawls from Pennsylvania to Kansas there was a similar adjustment as wheat spread westward. By the end of the seventies, however, the hard red winter wheats from southeastern Europe, whose varied names revealed their origins, demonstrated an ability to withstand winter-killing and drought at the western edge of the area. Their high gluten content made admirable flour. Eventually this "Turkey Red" and its improvements made Kansas the greatest wheat state of the nation. Here were a cool growing season, a hot harvesting one, a fertile soil, and a state where corn could be rotated to perfection with the smaller grain.

California was the first important wheat state in the Pacific West. For two decades, 1870–1890, bonanza farming in the central valley made it a great wheat area. Then the larger profits promised by fruit and truck growing put an end to the interlude and brought the Pacific Northwest into prominence. In the interior Columbia basin after 1890 came the last wheat frontier. Here was a lava soil of incredible depth and richness, spring rainfall which made for rapid growth, and a summer so dry that the ripened wheat could stand for weeks in the stalk and be harvested by the most efficient machinery without an intervening drying in the shock or barn. The heaviest wheat yields per acre in 1920 in the chief wheat states were made by Washington, Oregon, and Idaho. Richly endowed as these districts were, the constant growing of wheat had exhausted the soil and led to a demand for more varied farming.

Unlike wheat, corn was a peculiarly American crop. Its acreage surpassed that of any other crop. Since it is grown nearly everywhere, corn production has never exhibited the intense regionalization of wheat. Nevertheless, the conditions which favor its growth have produced a specialization. It requires a long growing season with hot days and hot nights and rainfall particularly in the month of July. These conditions were not found north of the line of 66° mean summer temperature nor in an area of less than eight inches mean summer rainfall. Corn requires a fertile soil which is easily cultivated, for the plant is dependent upon human care to keep down the weeds. Before 1859 within this area the center of corn production had moved northward, and in that year the three leading states were Illinois, Ohio, and Missouri. Although Illinois continued to be one of the great producers until 1919, the center of corn production moved westward, and Iowa became the supreme corn state of the nation. Although corn was grown in the winter wheat area and was the exclusive cereal of the cotton kingdom, there was a definitely delimited corn belt which began in central Ohio and extended into Kansas, after engulfing the whole of Iowa. So fat was the land that the region rejoiced in the title of the most productive food-growing area in the world.

Since there were few exports of corn, the uses of this grain were also American. Only 10 percent of the crop fed human beings directly. Rather it was the staff of life for livestock. It was estimated in 1921 that nearly 75 percent of the crop was fed on farms to work animals, hogs, and cattle. The centers of hog production and of cattle fattening were, therefore, intimately related to the centers of corn production. There were in 1920 as many beef cattle in the Corn Belt as there were on the Great Plains and three-fifths of the commercial hog crop was produced in the same region. Indiana, the leading hog-producing state at the outbreak of the Civil War, had been displaced by the invincible Iowa.

The New and the Old South

Corn and hogs were also southern products. But they were not characteristic staples like tobacco, rice, sugar, and cotton. The first of these, tobacco, in 1860 was predominantly a Border state industry; in 1920 it still remained so. From 1870 until after World War I Kentucky was the chief producer; before that Virginia had been. One variety, Burley tobacco, discovered in 1864, was manufactured into chewing tobacco; it required rich soils and heavy feeding. Its rival, the flue-cured Bright tobacco, was utilized in the manufacture of cigarettes, which in the twentieth century were first emancipated from the taint of effeminacy and then adopted by the new women smokers. The growth of this yellow leaf on poorer soils created a new tobacco area in southern Virginia and northern North Carolina. As for rice, the influence of the Civil War was unmistakable. Actual devastation came to many plantations on the Atlantic seaboard; disuse ruined others; and the aftermath of war, with impoverished planters and chaotic labor systems, prevented any rebuilding. When important rice production did recur in the 1880's, it was on the Gulf coast of southwestern Louisiana and southeastern Texas. Here were rich prairies traversed by sluggish streams which could be used for the essential irrigation. Farmers from the Northwest introduced the large-scale mechanization they had used for wheat. In the decade 1909–1919 similar conditions in eastern Arkansas produced a rice industry, and one of the marked successes of irrigation was the increase of rice production in the Sacramento valley of California. Such a migration set in startling contrast the extinction of the original rice centers, the Carolinas and Georgia.

The American cane sugar industry was necessarily confined to the rich bottomlands of the Mississippi River in southern Louisiana. The ruin effected by the Civil War could not, therefore, compel a migration of the crop to new regions of production within the United States. The greatest handicap inflicted by the war was the abolition of slavery, for the cultivation of sugar was a capitalistic enterprise requiring the gang labor of a large number of workers. It was not until the nineties that the industry reached the production levels of pre-Civil War days. After that it exhibited the most astonishing variations. The Louisiana crops, grown only because of tariff protection, satisfied but an infinitesimal portion of the domestic demand. Meanwhile in the nineties the production of beet sugar had been undertaken largely as the result of a propaganda campaign conducted by the Department of Agriculture. After fifteen years of zealous effort beet sugar surpassed cane sugar production; thereafter its lead was unchallenged. Although there were plenty of lands and climates suitable for its growth in this country, it was localized beyond the northeastern edge of the Corn Belt, particularly in Michigan, and in Colorado, California, and Utah, where the beets were grown under the ideal conditions of cool days with abundant sunshine and water supplied by irrigation at the right periods. A California authority declared, "The growing of beets is not agriculture, but horticulture." The process from growing seed to topping the beets was strewn with fussy tasks requiring monotonous and careful hand labor. The beet sugar industry was the indigo industry of the twentieth century. It could be maintained only by tariff protection.

It is a relief to turn from such an exotic crop to one which flourished naturally in the United States—cotton. After the Civil War the South returned inevitably to its cultivation. There was a demand for the staple, and southern development had trained both white and colored labor in its cultivation. Not until 1876 did the production equal that before the Civil War. After that date cotton production increased rather steadily until in 1914 it was three times that of 1876. This increase was accomplished in two ways. The first was the spread into new western areas, for Texas particularly was fitted for the crop. Her black waxy prairie was probably equaled in richness only by some of the bottomlands of the Mississippi River; she started under less of a handicap, since her area was comparatively untouched by the Civil War; her labor force was more efficient, since it was dominantly white and not composed of former slaves with a rudimentary preparation for self-reliant agricultural operations. The prairies and then the plains were most fitted for mechanized production. In 1920 half the cotton crop was grown west of the Mississippi River. One unexpected blessing of this dominant area was its dryness. The boll weevil did not thrive there as in the humid regions of the East. This well-known pest invaded the United States from Mexico in 1892 and thirty years later was causing annual losses of $300 million. Weevil damage did a great deal to slow the revival of cotton culture in the old South, a region unexpectedly brought back into major production after the Civil War. The chief explanation for this recovery was the discovery that with fertilizers cotton could be grown on the exhausted lands of the eastern states and even in soils whose composition had been deemed unfavorable. For fertilizers the eastern states had available not only the cottonseed but also deposits of marl and phosphates. In addition, large use was made of commercial fertilizer.

The Milk-Can Nucleus

A cow or two kept for milk and butter was as general in pioneer American farming as were the few hogs that accompanied the wheat or cotton grower in his westward migration. Specialized milk production and butter making appeared when the industrialization of the East created an urban market, and when improved transportation enabled the adjacent areas to ship perishable products. In 1860, therefore, the dairy industry of the country was primarily eastern; but the westward movement of dairy products had already begun. New Englanders, moving into northeastern Ohio, carried their agricultural traditions with them, found the climate unsuited for stable crops and the land adapted to grazing, and by 1860 had converted the Western Reserve into "Cheesedom." After the Civil War the dairy industry marched on to transform eventually even the agriculture of Minnesota and the eastern portion of the Dakotas. It moved into a belt where corn and winter and spring wheat encountered the hazards of weather or pests, or where after a brief interlude of pioneer farming the settler turned to some agricultural adjustment which would enable him to stay in business. The urbanization of the old Middle West provided the markets for this development. But adjustment was not easy. The shift to dairying required a considerable investment of capital for the herds and greater agricultural skill. Besides it was more confining to the farmer.

That dairying was a more permanent form of agriculture was shown by census figures of 1920. New York, the leading milch-cow state in 1860, was still second, and Ohio was sixth; Wisconsin was, however, the first. The transformation in that state followed the startling decline of wheat growing; by 1890 it was practically completed. The leaders in the movement were easterners, New Yorkers who had been bred in the dairy tradition and carried west a knowledge of its methods and worth. One was W. D. Hoard, later governor, but first editor of *Hoard's Dairyman* and evangel of the new dispensation, an experimenter, and an inspirer of experiments. The Wisconsin Dairymen's Association, founded in 1872, secured new markets for cheese; short courses at the agricultural college in the University of Wisconsin turned out trained dairymen and cheesemakers; and professors of that institution made invaluable contributions to the industry. The "tester," invented by Professor S. M. Babcock and given by him to the industry, devised exact measurements for the butterfat content in milk and thus simplified the factory production of butter and gave a norm for breeding. Finally, the foreign element in Wisconsin —Germans, Bohemians, Scandinavians—bred in a more careful agricultural technique, were willing to undertake the agricultural transformation of the state.

Roughly, the dairy industry was located in what the regionalists called the hay and pasture region of the United States. Where the terrain was too rough for tillage or the soil unfavorable, permanent pastures were fenced in for grazing. The other land was used to grow crops necessary to supplement the pasture or to feed the animals during the season when it was not available. Hay production continued to be improved by the introduction of new cultivated grasses, of which the most important was alfalfa. Although an unsurpassed feeding crop, it was originally confined to regions that had the necessary dry season for curing and winters that the roots could survive. Later breeding improvement created a crop more difficult to winter-kill, and artificial dryers met the problem of weather. The Dairy Belt raised corn, an essential in cattle feeding. The usefulness of this cereal was greatly extended by the importation in the seventies of silage practices from France and Germany. In the silo, fermentation generates certain acids which prevent decay and make the shredded stalks and leaves tender and succulent. Finally, the dairy industry has been profoundly affected by the centrifugal separator, introduced from Sweden in 1882.

Machine Agriculture

Before the Civil War American farmers had been driven to extensive employment of machinery in a desire to cultivate a larger area and to avoid the higher overall labor costs apparently inherent in large-scale cultivation. The same tendency continued in the modern period and for the same reason. Indeed, that reason was intensified in the twentieth century, when industry became more efficient and the rewards which it offered either in wages or salaries or in social conditions were more enticing than the prospect of becoming an independent farmer. Invention was spurred to meet the emergency.

In the harvesting of small grain the reaper was at last brought to perfection. McCormick and Hussey, as we have seen, had constructed successful machines before 1860, but their earlier models did not complete the process. The grain after it was cut lay on the table behind the cutting-edge until it was raked off by a man who walked beside the machine or rode upon it. Numerous inventors, challenged by this deficiency, perfected self-raking machines of considerable ingenuity or constructed frameworks enabling workers mounted on the machine to bind the grain by hand. Others had turned their attention to the possibility of a mechanical binder using straw, wire, or twine. The first two materials proved unsatisfactory, but in 1878–1879 John F. Appleby patented the first successful twine binder—a combination, needless to say, of his own originality and the ideas of predecessors. Soon after the chief features of the modern harvester emerged. In the Far West, where the ground was hard, the dryness cured the grain in the stand and the stalk grew short, a header decapitated the wheat, and later united with the mechanical thresher to perform every operation from cutting the grain to bagging the kernels. In the earlier days these huge combines took on gigantic proportions. A gasoline engine ran the threshing machine, and thirty horses pulled the apparatus through the fields. Moving slowly over the sunbaked, heat-quivering prairies, devouring the grain as they went, these machines were the acme of agricultural mechanization.

The invention of the mowing machine for hay was intimately associated with that of the reaper. For a time inventors sought to devise a machine which would perform both operations. By 1860, however, it had become a distinct and practical machine, the first of a mechanical plant which later included hayrakes, tedders, stackers, loaders. The great American crop, corn, was less quickly subdued to the reign of the machine. Perhaps the necessity was less urgent. The corn crop did not need to be harvested in a limited period; at first the stalks were not cut down, but were consumed in the fields by the livestock; the ears could be husked at leisure, and the kernels could be eaten off the ears without shelling. The invention of the silo and the increasing sale of corn, as well as the high cost of labor, encouraged inventions. Most of the successful machines came in the later part of the nineteenth century. By then corn planters had been devised which overcame the unique difficulty of planting corn in hills rather than in drills; corn harvesters were built which cut the corn in the field and bound it in a shock; corn huskers and shredders performed for maize what the threshing process did for wheat.

The effects of machinery upon agricultural production varied from region to region. In 1920 machinery was most concentrated in the spring and winter wheat regions and in the Corn Belt. In South Dakota, for instance, the value of implements and machinery on each farm averaged $1,500. On the other hand, the mechanization of agriculture had not affected the harvesting of fruits or vegetables; its greatest failure in a staple production was cotton. In 1920 the value of farm machinery on the farms of the Cotton Belt averaged $215. Negro labor was unskilled in the use of machines; the small holdings retarded mechanization; low wages provided no stimulus for a substitute for hand labor; and, finally, there was the nature of the cotton plant. Its bolls came to maturity at different times and so a field had to be picked several times and with discretion.

While machines may have turned fields into factories for certain crops and in certain regions, machines remote from farms, also had a specific impact upon farming as a business or a calling. The refrigerator car influenced livestock raising as much as the prairies; machinery for producing cottonseed oil and corn syrup gave a new use for agricultural products; the manufacture of flour through successive grindings and the substitution of rollers for stones, processes both imported from Europe, enabled mills to handle hard wheat; the factory production of cheese, butter, and condensed milk and factory canning ranked with the growth of scientific agriculture in their influence upon dairying and truck farming.

The Structure of Agricultural Research

Improved farming methods had been adopted before 1860, but they were far from universal. In part, this was due to the speculative and tentative character of the new agricultural science, which in many instances was little better than granny's lore. The New York State Agricultural Society was perfectly willing to publish in 1843 a prize essay on injurious insects which recommended treating the grain fly with "all pungent odors . . . that most offensive of all odors, the one proceeding from the skunk, has been tested and highly recommended as a preventive."

Even when more thoughtful agricultural recommendations were made, the conditions of American agriculture, an abundance of free land, worked against the adoption of improved methods. These two barriers, however, were naturally overcome as the public domain was whittled away and as the body of exact agricultural knowledge was coincidentally increased. In the latter process 1862 was an *annus mirabilis*. In that year the Department of Agriculture was created and the Morrill Act was passed; both acts were fundamental to the amassing of agricultural knowledge and its diffusion throughout the nation.

The first appropriation by the Federal government in aid of agriculture was in 1839 to the Commissioner of Patents "for the collection of agricultural statistics, and for other agricultural purposes." Although the amount was increased, the agitation for a fuller recognition of the agricultural interests of the country continued; and finally, in 1862, Congress passed an "organic act" establishing "the people's Department." It was still a Cinderella of politics, for the head of the Department was not a member of the President's Cabinet. It was not until 1889 that the office was ennobled with full executive dignity. The Department, however humble, was "to acquire and diffuse among the people of the United States useful information on subjects connected with agriculture in the most general and comprehensive sense of the word, and to procure, propagate, and distribute among the people new and valuable seeds and plants." As appropriations multiplied and the Department graduated in the late eighties from its pioneer era of political appointments, scientific prima donnas and empire builders, and discarded confused purposes, it became a central organizer for investigations throughout the country and an important agricultural research institution in its own right.

The second achievement of 1862, the Morrill Act, had as its background the educational ferment of the fifties, which sought to supplement the classical curriculum and aristocratic educational institutions with more practical subjects and more democratic places of learning. State legislatures petitioned for grants of public land to aid such undertakings. Agricultural societies and progressive educators perfected and popularized plans, and it was the happy fate of Justin S. Morrill, one-time small-town Vermont merchant, later a Representative, to sponsor in Congress a bill embodying the contributions of many others and to give it his name. The Morrill Act established in each state

. . . at least one college, where the leading subject shall be, without excluding other scientific and classical studies, and including military tactics, to teach such branches of learning as are related to agriculture and the mechanic arts . . . in order to promote the liberal and practical education of the industrial classes in the several pursuits and professions in life.

As the means to this end, the act turned to the American resource, the government domain. To each state or territory to become a state was given 30,000 acres of public land for each Senator and Representative in Congress. Though the land was generally located in the western states, the endowment varied. New York received 990,000 acres; Alabama actually obtained only 24,000 acres. These lands were to be sold by the states, and the money obtained was to be invested in securities "yielding not less than five per centum upon the par value of said stocks." This fund was not to be spent for buildings, although up to 10 percent might be used for the purchase of a site for an experimental farm. Annual reports were to be made of experiments and improvements, and these were to be distributed to all land-grant colleges.

The total grant given by the original Morrill Act was equal to the area of Maryland. But in the conversion of acres into money the states were not always fortunate. By the Morrill Act the college had to be established within five years, and many states were thus in haste to sell their lands. Such lands, however, came into competition with the land sales of railroads and with the donations of the Homestead Act. Ohio's land were sold for 50 cents an acre. New York was more fortunate, for here Ezra Cornell, a moneyed man, member of the legislature, interested in education, took most of the state's grant at 60 cents an acre, sold the land gradually, and turned over the surplus to the state land-grant institution—Cornell University. Some of the lands, located in the white-pine belt of Wisconsin, were sold for more than $16 an acre; Cornell's endowment from land sales was about $5.5 million. In the disposal of the endowment the states followed several practices. In some states the money was given to a separate agricultural college; in others the fund was used to establish the new agricultural and mechanical colleges which dot the land from Florida to South Dakota; and in still others it was turned over to endow departments or schools in existing or new universities.

The early history of these colleges was crammed with crises and change. The inadequacy of their financial support was overcome by further appropriations on the part of the national government and by an even larger measure of support given by the individual states. Another difficulty was the elaboration of a curriculum. At first the new studies tended to assume a protective coloring. The course was a four-year one leading to a bachelor's degree, and was freighted with a great many non-professional studies—algebra, trigonometry, English and other languages, logic, and some variety of history. The agricultural instruction was originally a one-professor job. He was the "agricultural chemist" inherited from an earlier day and was expected to teach all there was to know about soil, fertilizer, feeding, and dairying. But the task of instruction soon exceeded one man's capacity, and devolution set in. One subject after another split off, and all too often levies were made upon the ancient languages for a nomenclature to describe them. A frequent criticism of the schools was that they were too theoretical, that they turned out very few "dirt farmers," that bachelors of agriculture exhibited an unwillingness for agricultural life. Gradually it was recognized that the diffusion of new knowledge to actual farmers must be accomplished by some other educational device. The agricultural colleges turned out the teachers, the demonstrators, the organizers, the research students. In an effort to redirect some of these trends, the so-called Second Morrill Act of 1890 specified its appropriations were "to be applied only to instruction in agriculture, the mechanic arts, the English language and the various branches of mathematical, physical, natural and economic science, with special reference to their application in the industries of life."

The history of the earlier Morrill Act had also demonstrated the necessity of agricultural experimentation to discover new facts and to test theories. European nations, notably England, had answered necessity by the establishment of agricultural experiment stations. Connectictut happened to be the first state to make appropriations directly for this purpose. Since the middle of the nineteenth century Yale College had been a pioneer in instruction in agricultural chemistry, and S. W. Johnson of the Yale Scientific School successfully led the agitation which secured the establishment in 1875 of a state agricultural experiment station financed by a private gift and state appropriations. After other states had followed Connecticut's example, there was an insistent demand for the nationalization of the movement, and finally, in 1887, Congress passed the Hatch Act. Under its provisions $15,000 was appropriated annually from the money derived from the sale of public land to each state and territory for the establishment of an agricultural experiment station. For years these stations, too, wrestled with the necessity of solving severely practical problems and spreading useful information. But by the twentieth century they were freed from their dependence upon the revenue from the sale of land and given appropriations for original research on long-time projects "with a view to the discovering of principles and the solution of the more difficult and fundamental problems of agriculture." To be sure, much of the new knowledge acquired here and elsewhere was trivial and misdirected, much of it but the application of scientific jargon to empirical methods followed for years by practical farmers; but as the instruments of research were developed, scientists, farmers, and other students made the United States a leader in the international process of fabricating a scientific agriculture.

The Achievements of Agricultural Science

The improvement of animal breeds, begun before 1860, continued with more exactness and efficiency after the Civil War. In the cattle industry the stockmen of Texas bred up their nondescript herds of longhorn Texas steers with importations of Herefords and other improved breeds. Improvements in dairy cattle were even more remarkable. Although the old hope of obtaining a dual-purpose cow serving as a milker in life and a beef animal at demise was never abandoned, more attention was given to milking qualities. Most modern breeds—Holsteins, Jerseys, Ayrshires, Guernseys—had been imported before 1860. After the Civil War stockmen and owners, devoted to particular breeds, established cattle clubs or associations and maintained herd books where parents and progeny of pure-blooded animals were registered. Much of this activity was a form of agricultural snobbishness or commercialism. Later more attention was paid to production records than to pedigree, and romantically named cows gave down yearly their startling totals of milk. Finally owners of ordinary herds equipped with milk scales and Babcock testers were able to apply tests to their own cows and eliminate poor producers.

Meanwhile researchers investigated the best methods of raising and feeding livestock. In their arrogance, human beings were apt to regard a proper diet as essential only for man. But studies in nutrition were just as useful for other animals, and the testing of theories was more scientific, less willful. W. O. Atwater, a pupil of Johnson's and one of the founders of the Connecticut experiment station, conducted experiments in the relation between foods and animal vigor and invented a calorimeter to measure the calories. His work received the acclaim of European investigators; nor did the later discoveries of vitamins supersede his contributions. A livestock manager became unwillingly a dietician. He had always been a veterinarian, for animal disease could sweep away the investment of money and months of labor while man looked helplessly on. But bacteriology and a knowledge of other invisible organisms provided new vistas of explanation and hence methods of control. Success was not universal. But investigators of the Department of Agriculture were in the eighties at last able to explain the involved causation of Texas fever, which was spread by ticks that had bitten infected cattle; the young ticks hatched from the eggs of these ticks inherited the disease and then transmitted it, months later, to healthy cattle. A dip was devised to kill the ticks without killing the cattle. Where causes and cures could not be discovered, disease was fought by other methods. In the 1880's the Bureau of Animal Industry was given the power to establish animal quarantines; over the years its powers were enlarged until, after compensation to the owners, it could slaughter suspected animals. Only in this fashion was the mysterious hoof-and-mouth disease of hogs and cattle eradicated from the United States. The Department of Agriculture which had begun as a research agency ended as a regulatory body.

Plants were more easily improved than animals. One method, the introduction of new and improved varieties from abroad, was energetically continued, particularly when the doctrine of national self-sufficiency fired the imagination of politicians and officials in the Department of Agriculture. Ludicrous failures, like the attempts to grow tea in South Carolina, could not obscure real successes. The agriculture of whole regions like California was based upon importations. The Spanish colonial period introduced olives; but American efforts after 1850 were responsible for the raisin grape, the prune, and the Brazilian navel orange—the last an outstanding success. Staple crops benefited. Corn was indigenous, untouched by alien influences. But the introduction of Egyptian cottons into the Southwest and that of Acala cotton, comparatively immune to the boll weevil, from Mexico were landmarks in southern agriculture. The immigration of wheat has already been mentioned. Stimulated by the success of hard red wheats, Mark Carlton, a wheat fanatic, traveled about eastern Europe collecting and importing improved varieties. Entirely apart from importation, sudden mutations or natural hybridizations of all plants were continually changing both native and foreign species. Alert American farmers, noticing these variations, selected the seed of the better specimens for further cultivation. Artificial breeding came more slowly in this country than in Europe, but in the twentieth century, when genetics finally became a science, Americans made contributions of the first order.

One objective of breeders was plants relatively immune to attack by disease and insect. But in the nineteenth century other methods of defense were perfected. Europeans had discovered that many diseases were due to fungus growths, and in the eighties a French professor in an attempt to curb the downy mildew of grapes finally perfected the bordeaux mixture, the standard fungicide. Twenty years later an American scientist in the Department of Agriculture, E. F. Smith, insisted, in spite of European disdain, that other plant diseases were due to bacteria and proved his discoveries. No single cure-all was, however, forthcoming. As for the insect pests, the first step in any attack was the detailed study of their life cycles and habits. Scientists had been building this knowledge for centuries, and practical farmers had been dosing plants with chemicals for years, usually with no results. In 1865 a writer in the *Practical Entomologist* declared, "If the work of destroying insects is to be accomplished satisfactorily, we feel confident that it will have to be the result of no chemical preparation." Yet within two decades Americans had developed arsenical insecticides for gnawing insects and devised a kerosene-soap emulsion which killed sucking insects on contact. It was less expensive and perhaps more "natural" to assign the slaughter of insects to their usual enemies, birds, other insects, parasites. Since two-thirds of America's insect enemies were probably immigrants from abroad, this new method of approach involved searching the world for natural enemies, breeding them, and freeing them in the United States. The gypsy moth, the browntail moth, and the boll weevil were fought in this manner. Entomologists like to contemplate their complete success in saving the citrus industry of California in 1888 merely by introducing and acclimatizing the Australian ladybird beetle.

Attacks of disease and insects were less injurious when the plant itself was strong. Fundamental, therefore, were the methods of cultivation. Scientific concepts of this matter were in 1860 far too simple. The gospel according to Liebig declared that the question was largely one of the chemical elements needed for plant life, and soil experts felt that if the rocks from which the soils were formed were known a proper basis of soil and crop relationship was established. Gradually scientists realized that soils evolved; not only their origin but weather and crops determined their character. Nor was plant growth merely a matter of chemistry. The physics of the soil was important. So manure, for which Liebig expressed a rather poor opinion, was necessary because it conserved soil moisture and improved its texture. Furthermore, the biology of the soil was important. Practical farmers, for instance, had long observed that leguminous plants, such as clover, fertilized the fields; a chemist showed that they increased the nitrogenous content of the soil; and European investigators from 1877 to 1890 were able to prove that this process was accomplished by microorganisms working in the soil or in the root nodules of legumes. When all reservations were made, however, nitrogen, potash, and phosphates remained the essential plant foods. Their combination in artificial fertilizers was a landmark in modern history. The United States drew one essential material from the nitrate beds of Chile, another from the great potash deposits of Germany, and a third from its own phosphate rocks. The annual value of artificial fertilizer— a poor measuring stick—increased over nine times between 1879 and 1919. Its use in the southern states of Georgia, North Carolina, and South Carolina, its greatest consumers, enabled them to remain cotton producers; in the Middle Atlantic states truck and fruit gardeners employed it in their intensive agriculture; and it stimulated the crops on the fertile farms of the Middle West.

Agricultural Education for the Farmer

But all this knowledge was so much "book farming" unless the dirt farmer could be infected with it. Short courses at the land-grant colleges were devised for him and were placed in the winter when he could attend them. In the eighties the University of Wisconsin offered the first of such courses which has had a continuous history, and its example was followed by other institutions. It was realized at the same time that agricultural instruction of a simpler sort ought to be given in secondary schools. To meet this demand the University of Minnesota had established on its campus a sort of agricultural high school. In the early part of the twentieth century this movement for earlier agricultural education was furthered by other states or by private philanthropy and hastened when popular desire compelled the high schools throughout the country to break away from the classical discipline and to establish departments whose subjects had a more immediate relationship to the typewriter, the plow, and the turning lathe. Eventually the inevitable appeal for financial help was sent to Washington, and in 1917 the Smith-Hughes Act appropriated money to aid the states in vocational education in agriculture, trade, industries, and home economics, including the preparation of teachers.

In a country where zeal for education is united with a fervor for results, these devices seemed inadequate for scattering knowledge broadcast and converting people to its usefulness. Education had to be taken to the farmer. In the first fifteen years of the present century boards of agriculture in the several states financed, and the Federal government advised, farmers' institutes. In their methods, mingling enthusiasm and scientific agriculture, these institutes resembled the pre-Civil War agricultural societies. Though they grew and prospered in terms of numbers, the Federal government, after the passage of the Smith-Lever Act in 1914, substituted for them a system of county agents.

The county agent, as idea and actuality, had several sources. The most significant contributions were made by Seaman A. Knapp, a versatile New Yorker. Driven to Iowa by poor health, he was successively farmer, stock raiser, editor, professor, and president of the Iowa State College of Agriculture. Undertaking the development of lands in Louisiana, he discovered farmers were hostile to new methods until they had been demonstrated successful, and that demonstration was difficult to initiate, since the price of experimentation might be financial loss. Early in the twentieth century he was able to secure financial assistance from localities, from the United States government—which assigned Knapp some money from boll weevil appropriations for "bringing home to the farmer on his own farm information which would enable him to grow cotton despite the presence of the weevil"—and from the General Education Board, the philanthropic dispenser of the Rockefeller oil fortunes. Agents were appointed to supervise the demonstrators and to carry the gospel to others. In 1908 Knapp declared that for success the work "requires at least one agent in each county." Meanwhile in the North extension work had progressed to a similar conclusion. In New York State, for instance, local efforts and contributions provided precedents and experience. Finally the legislature passed a law for a state system. The initiative was supposed to come from the farmers in the county, who were to form a county farm bureau and who, along with the state and county, were to contribute toward its expenses. The executive and educational head of the county farm bureau was the county agent. Projects were to be outlined by the State College of Agriculture and the State Department of Agriculture. Other states followed suit. County agents all over the country were leading lives as harassed as those of the country doctor, as they jounced over their bailiwicks in Fords, conducted field demonstrations, made programs for institutes, imported outside specialists, and tried to be the agricultural "leaders" that their superiors were always exhorting them to be.

The Smith-Lever Act, nationalizing the office of county agent, provided a base fund of $10,000 for each state and additional amounts to be distributed among the states on the basis of their rural population and to be matched by the states. These funds were to be administered by land-grant colleges in cooperation with the Department of Agriculture; the funds were "to aid in diffusing among the people of the United States useful and practical information on subjects relating to agriculture and home economics." The administration of this act naturally determined its policy and its methods. Many business interests ancillary to agriculture, for example, International Harvester, Sears Roebuck, and the railroads, had favored the county agent system as a middle-of-the-road device for stabilizing agriculture and farm policy. More to the point at hand, David F. Houston, the Secretary of Agriculture, had been greatly impressed by personal observation of the county agent demonstration system, and the Department consequently announced that it would not sanction the use of the Smith-Lever funds for farmers' institutes, short courses, or correspondence. They were to be used instead for state and county agents and traveling specialists in such subjects as dairying, poultry, engineering.

The Farmer as Seller

The economic development of the United States since 1860 hastened the transition from self-sufficiency—always a relative matter except in certain times and places—to commercial agriculture. The railroad opened distant markets and destroyed the household as an industrial unit producing its own goods. The industrial community, city or town, constituted a domestic market for agricultural products. The growth of agricultural knowledge and the spread of agriculture across the continent joined with these other factors to put a premium on specialized farming. Consequently the farmer became a cog in a commercial machine whose revolutions took place beyond the horizon. Naturally, he did not always understand the significance of these changes and he tended, like anyone else, to regard the remote and uncontrollable with suspicion. If the state of agriculture was prosperous, he was content to let well enough alone; if it were depressed he subjected the system of which he was a part to detailed and hostile scrutiny. Alterations made in the system were apt to be more rewarding than the application of scientific principles to agriculture, since bumper crops by their very abundance often further reduced the price of agricultural products. But it was not easy for the farmer to find a quick remedy for his ills. Commercial agriculture was a highly competitive occupation. The thousands of wheat or cotton growers could not concert to control their output or the prices at which it was sold. On the other hand businessmen in industry and marketing were combining and merging, and the resulting "big business" was restraining competition. As a competitor the farmer was left unprotected in a world of privileged monopoly. At least that was a frequent lament.

Those who wanted an immediate solution for low prices turned in this period, as they had in earlier ones, to the simple recourse, an increase in the quantity of money. On the whole the farming regions, though opinion there was not unanimous, furnished in the late nineteenth century and after, the voters for the greenbackers, silverites, and other apostles of inflation. Frequently they supplemented their doctrines of financial management with ingenious campaigns for reducing the costs of marketing and securing thereby for the "producer" a greater share of the final price. From the hosts of agencies responsible for these unfair conditions, the farmer visited the heaviest opprobrium upon the railroad. The rates it charged and the service it gave determined the vital statistics of agriculture as surely as they determined those of manufacturing. The farmer's attitude toward the railroad, as voiced by Granger and Populist, merged into the larger national movement for extensive governmental control over the transportation system, a movement whose achievements have already been described. Other enemies were the "hordes of profit-taking middlemen." Their variety was legion, for the methods of marketing agricultural products differed in complexity and inclusiveness. But most significant for the period in question were the appearance and development of exchanges for the marketing of agricultural commodities. Such exchanges first dealt with the staple crops of the country, cotton and wheat; these had a world market and could be easily graded and stored. As means of refrigeration, storage, and grading were perfected, the method was extended to other products ranging from lard to eggs.

Trading on these exchanges set a continuous price for the agricultural commodity in question. A grain farmer of the Northwest would take his wheat to the country elevator erected at a railroad siding by local or outside capital. The price paid by the country elevator was the price then ruling in the primary grain market minus a deduction for freight and other charges, insurance, and profit. In effect this meant the quotation for wheat on the Chicago Board of Trade. For in 1848 the Board of Trade was established as a place primarily for the purchase and sale of grain, and a decade later Chicago was boasting of being the largest primary grain market in the world. In the marketing of cotton the Civil War destroyed the factor system of the plantation era. Now cotton was usually first purchased by the local merchants who had staked growers to a living while the latter "made" the crop; from the country merchant it was purchased by "cotton buyers and shippers," for thus wholesale firms located in the interior markets or ports of the South were denominated; the buyer and shipper sold to domestic mills or to their brokers or to importing merchants abroad, who sold through "selling brokers" to the "buying brokers" of the English mills. But the price was determined fundamentally by the quotations on the cotton exchanges, of which the most important, the Liverpool Cotton Association and the New York Cotton Exchange, were formed in 1870. The setting of prices at these exchanges was made possible only by the standardization of products, the provision of grain elevators or warehouses, and by a revolution in means of communication. The telephone, the telegraph, and the transatlantic cable carried the slightest tremors in these central markets to the remotest general store in Texas or grain elevator in the Dakotas.

Some of the transactions on these exchanges concerned the sale, purchase, and delivery of commodities for cash. But more important, numerically and intrinsically, were the sale and purchase of contracts for the future delivery of the products. This dealing in grain futures began informally in the forties, for a Chicago paper of those years announced that "several sales of corn 'to-arrive' were made in May, and in the following September it is said that [what] corn arrives is principally on contracts." The practice of future trading developed rapidly in the course of the Civil War, and in 1865 the rules of the Board of Trade officially recognized its existence. Trading in cotton futures commenced in the confused aftermath of the Civil War, when great demands, small crops, and wildly fluctuating prices led purchasers to seek stability through future contracts. The successful laying of the first Atlantic cable and the shipping of cotton by steamship facilitated the movement. The establishment of the New York Cotton Exchange was due in large part to the desire to systematize trading in futures.

Trading in futures performed an invaluable service for those who really owned commodities. Country elevators might see the profit from their storage and handling of grain wiped out if they had to sell their grain at a lower price than they had paid for it. A spinner of cotton goods who had purchased his raw material early in the season would be at a profound handicap in the sale of his finished goods if competitors had bought their supplies at later and lower prices. Elevator owner or cotton manufacturer, each could insure himself against loss by selling at the time of his original purchase contracts for future delivery at the current price. If prices went down before the contract was met he lost on his first cash transaction, but gained on his future sale; if prices went up he made his profit on the cash transaction rather than on the future contract. This process of hedging could be applied to selling as well as to purchasing and to nearly every stage in the marketing process. Trading in futures for hedging purposes, however, constituted only a part of the total transactions in futures. Speculators who neither owned nor cared to own agricultural commodities, but simply liked to match their estimates, wits, and manipulations in a gamble with fellow traders upon the probable course of prices also dealt in futures. A professional lingo of "selling short" and "going long" was created to describe their practices.

Professional economists and participators in the marketing process were always ready to point out the benefits accruing to society from these elaborate arrangements. They resulted in the establishment of standards; they daily brought together all the information about crop production and human needs; they assembled and stored products bearing the risk of insurance and interest; they financed crop movements, for the producer was paid at once by the first purchaser, who borrowed from the local bank or other middlemen. All these borrowings with their interest charges were passed along through the whole series of middlemen and banks without burden upon the producer; even the gambler in futures removed the burden of speculative risks from the shoulders of legitimate commercial enterprise. In spite of the overwhelming clarity of these explanations, the American farmer was not always convinced that the marketing system worked in this benign fashion. In the first place, purchasers of agricultural products on occasion combined to prevent competitive bidding. Country elevators were consolidated into "lines," which pooled the wheat to be bought; grain-dealer associations fixed a common price; and at the primary grain market of Chicago the great terminal elevator companies, the chief buyers in the market, operated often in agreement. The situation was as alarming as in the Chicago stockyards, where the five great packers cooperated in setting a price. Nor was trading in futures wholly advantageous. The process of selling short depressed prices, or at least that was the hope of those who indulged in playing this side of the market. Economists might prove that the fluctuation in prices was less severe after the establishment of trading in futures than before, but this did not alter the fact that from day to day prices were changed not only by the differing judgment of brokers but by manipulation.

Farmers who generally regarded themselves as independent men of property thought one remedy was the provision of their own marketing facilities. They turned to cooperation. Marketing enterprises of this sort achieved their first success in dairy products. Indeed, cooperative cream-

eries and cheese factories owned by farmers' capital hastened the industrialization of this branch of agriculture. Then farmers conceived the
idea of building and constructing their own grain elevators, but few survived mismanagement and the effective hostility of the existing elevators.
Cotton growers in the South selected existing firms to handle their product on commission and built their own warehouses. All in all, by 1900
there were somewhat over eighteen hundred farmers' business organizations engaged in marketing, mostly in the western Middle West. By 1920
there were approximately eight thousand, engaged largely in the marketing of grain, livestock, fruits and vegetables, and dairy products. Their
success was partly due to state legislation exempting them from general
incorporation laws. Such laws permitted cooperatives to give each member a vote regardless of the amount of his stockholding and to pay dividends based on patronage rather than on earnings. The movement was
often aided by commission men in the larger markets who were being
squeezed out by other buyers. Although there were significant exceptions, the larger number of cooperative enterprises were local. They did
not affect the great primary markets. In the early twentieth century,
however, the American Society of Equity and the Farmer's Union were
considering the setting of minimum prices and their attainment through
cooperative warehouses or elevators; and the Non-Partisan League
sought the construction of state-owned elevators, an idea as old as the
Populists.

Perhaps it was easier to induce the government to regulate marketing. The Granger movement of the seventies turned to the passage of
state legislation controlling warehouse practices and prices. Then and
later there was a shrill demand for a legislative prohibition upon trading
in futures. In the twentieth century the American Society of Equity and
the Farmer's Union both realized that assistance from the national government was necessary for the success of their plans. They were content
for the moment to press for the establishment within the Department of
Agriculture of an Office or Bureau of Markets to investigate different
systems of marketing farm products and the demand for such products
in the various sections of the country. Although such a proposal aroused
little enthusiasm among Department officials, still astigmatic to questions of distribution, it was embodied in legislation in 1912 and 1913.
The dam was now broken. In the next few years the government passed
legislation enforcing standard grades in grain and cotton contracts, establishing government supervision for warehouses, and empowering the Secretary of Agriculture to control the packing yards and manipulation and
trading in grain futures. These multifold tasks were transferred to the
Bureau of Markets. Thus, once again what the government began by
investigating it ended by regulating.

The Farmer as Purchaser and Borrower

The farmer as businessman was purchaser as well as seller. Since land, buildings, and equipment had to be bought and usually bought on credit, the farmer was concerned with the general price level and with the price of borrowing. The first to his mind was apt to be set by the trusts and monopolies. In the late nineteenth century the Mc-Cormick monster, the "harvester trust," aroused his anger; in the twentieth century the fertilizer trust joined the company of the damned. So the farming regions, when they were not finding escape through the direct mail-order house, furnished part of the evangelism behind the Sherman Anti-Trust Act and stimulated the investigations of the Bureau of Corporations or its heirs into the price of things that farmers bought.

Ofttimes farmers advocated or resorted to more drastic remedies. Here, as in selling, cooperation was the magic wand. Thus, in the seventies the Granger leadership, in order to answer the realistic query of farmer-members as to "what money is there in the movement," first sought to have local agents buy directly from manufacturers and wholesalers; later they stressed the founding of cooperative stores upon the principle of the Rochdale stores in Great Britain. In spite of exceptions, this early cooperative movement collapsed, for inefficient managers were employed, credit was extended too liberally, and the individualistic American farmer was incapable of the patient and long-time loyalty required for such undertakings. The aspiration to buy cooperatively was inherited by the successors of the Grange and occasionally realized. By 1920 farmers were buying through cooperative associations fertilizer, fuel, cement, and seeds. Perhaps 1 million members participated in such arrangements. Sometimes these merchandising activities were supplemented by farmer ownership of manufacturing enterprises. From the days of the Grange to those of Equity, farmers tried their hands at farm-machine works, twine mills, and fertilizer plants. In the twentieth century a few of these enterprises were highly successful.

As businessman the farmer was borrower. He needed short-term loans to buy seeds, livestock, and frequently provisions to carry him through the interval until crops were matured and sold at market. Always more important than any other forms of agricultural borrowing, these loans were in some ways akin to those granted by banks for commercial operations. There were also differences. Agriculture was based upon a slower turnover, corresponding in the case of crops to the seed-harvesting period, and in the case of livestock to the period of fattening. Before the spread of banking facilities to the farming regions such loans were usually obtained from the local retail merchants or from agents who sold farm equipment. In the South this arrangement had become a determining part of the agricultural system. In the North its hold was not so universal or tenacious; but it had profound disadvantages everywhere. The cost of such credit was high, often amounting to 15 or 20 percent, and the prices of the goods for which such credit was generally advanced were excessive. In Wilson's administration the legislation of 1913 establishing the Federal Reserve System sought to make bank credit more available for farm operations by allowing agricultural paper to run for six months rather than three. A decade later it was given nine. Even though banking facilities with much cheaper rates were thus available, the less dependable and efficient farmers could not meet the business requirements of these institutions and continued their parasitic and expensive dependence upon store credit.

The farmer has always required long-term capital. He needed money for fencing, buildings, and for machinery; he needed money for land purchases, even at a time paradoxically when government land was "free." For capital investments the farmer borrowed on mortgage. Figures of such indebtedness for the early decades are not dependable. Between 1890 and 1920, however, the mortgage debt on farms occupied by their owners multiplied nearly four times. A larger figure, the total farm mortgage debt, rose from $3,207,863,000 in 1910 to $8,448,772,000 in 1920. Loans by individuals were always the most important source of these funds. Even farmers loaned to farmers, for they understood this method of investment. Banks were inadequate for the task because they did not spread rapidly to the West; and also the national banks under the act of 1863, profiting by the experience of the earlier unstable institutions, forbade loans on real estate. Yet easterners, dazzled as well as the pioneer by the pictured development of the West and attracted by the high rates of interest, were impatient to loan money. Western investment companies were formed to meet the situation. A common type sold to eastern investors debenture bonds based upon the security of farm mortgages; others simply acted as agents in the transfer of the mortgages between lender and borrower. Even eastern farmers loaned to western farmers. In 1889 citizens of New Hampshire had $25 million invested in western mortgages. As the country settled into stability, insurance companies conducted a careful investment of their capital in such securities, and state banking systems which could perform a similar service appeared.

Nevertheless, there was still a complaint against the system by which mortgages were written. It was charged that the interest rates were too high; numerous unnecessary fees were charged; five years, the period which mortgages were allowed to run, was too short a time for a farmer to pay off the mortgage from income; and renewals involved new expenses and commissions. Although these accusations had point, the causes of oppressive mortgage conditions were less the malevolence of financiers than gambling upon land values by farmers and money lenders

398   *A History of American Economic Life*

and the incalculable risks of agriculture. Mindful of their disadvantages, however, farmers' movements campaigned for state-financed loans to farmers, an object achieved in the Dakotas in 1917–1919. On the national scene the Wilson administration at the time of the Federal Reserve Act gave notice that it would sponsor a rural credits act. Such a measure was enacted in 1916.

It is easy to get the impression that throughout the decades since 1860 agriculture had been a sick industry. The shrinkage in the number of farmers compared to the increase of workers in nonfarm occupations, the achievements of an industrial society, set on a hill rather than under a bushel, have both contributed to this impression. And the statements of political programs also colored this image, for the spokesmen of farmers emphasized the misery, the discontent, and the inferiority of their constituency. Actually, the accomplishments of agriculture were tremendous. The land in farms more than doubled between 1860 and 1915; the nation's migrant farmers created an agricultural empire beyond the Mississippi. Agricultural employment in the twenty years after 1860 increased 52 percent; in the three decades ending in 1910 a further increase of 30 percent brought the absolute figures to a peak. Beginning in 1870 investment in lime and fertilizer (in terms of 1910–1914 dollars) mounted "phenomenally" to $90 million in 1900; average annual expenditures for tools, implements, and machinery were nearly ten times as great in 1900 as they had been during the Civil War, itself a period distinguished for farm mechanization.

As farmers put more acres under cultivation, enlarged their herds, and applied more resources to their operations, an increase in output occurred. An index of gross income from total farm production increased from 40.2 in 1869 to 106.6 in 1915. Agriculture, like manufacturing, covers a variety of occupations. In both endeavors, some wane, while others spurt forward dramatically. Just as whale oil declined before petroleum, the commercial production of hay fell as horses ceased to pull streetcars and the tractor began to displace the team on the farm. In the twentieth century, just as the automobile changed the contours of manufacturing enterprise, the rising popularity of citrus fruits shattered the conventional patterns of agricultural priorities. While taste, fashion, and technology changed, the percentage of agriculture devoted to growing raw materials—cotton and tobacco—remained relatively unchanged; shifting ideals of masculine and feminine beauty and the growth of the sedentary city diminished the importance of staple foodstuffs and markedly increased the consumption of dairy and poultry products. At the same time production of proteins through meat products relatively held its own.

Though agriculture in some ways resembled industry, divergences remained. Agriculture faced inelasticities that industry did not. Agricultural production could not spurt ahead or slow down as quickly. The farmer must plan a routine of rotations and other changes for a series of seasons; consequently, he cannot respond at once to changes in demand. That demand is relatively inelastic, for the human stomach is limited in its intake. And that intake may be reduced if large groups of people do not have the means to purchase enough to meet their wants. Agricultural prices fluctuated widely. During these years of expansion they often fell so low that hardship, loss, and destitution flooded the farm regions, as they did the frontier in the 1870's. Though nothing could be done about weather or plagues of locusts, many dreamers thought the farmers' problems could be solved by large farms, heavily mechanized and under the direction of trained managers. Whatever its theoretical advantages, bonanza farming or large-scale farming in the United States ran into difficulties. An individual enterprise for raising wheat on the flatlands of the Red River Valley in Minnesota and North Dakota, from the seventies to the nineties, could cultivate thousands of acres, employ a maximum of a thousand men, and own fleets of modern machinery; a plowman could run a furrow in one direction for a day and turn over the next day later on his way back. Conceptually and visually this was exciting. It worked when the price of wheat was favorable, but prices weren't favorable year after year. The big farms were broken up and sold as smaller holdings. The littler farmer might not make much money, but he had superior staying powers, since he was not as dependent on a cash income. But the notion that agriculture should imitate business persisted.

Meanwhile, as a whole, American agriculture proved productive and vigorous enough to supply the domestic market and, as later events proved, to feed soldiers on the battlefield and hungry civilians at peace. Those who focused on a single aspect of agricultural change might agree with J. J. Hill, the empire builder of the Pacific Northwest, who in 1909 gloomily announced, "In twenty-five years we shall face a nation with famine." Hill spoke near the end of a decade in which agricultural output per worker increased only 8 percent. This was uniquely low. In 1870–1880 the increase was 20 percent; in 1890–1900 it was 15 percent. In view of the trends a fairer estimate of agricultural performance lies in a somewhat oversimplified paraphrase of Winston Churchill's tribute to the airmen of Great Britain, "Never in the field of production was so much owed to so few by so many."

The Wage Earner Under Competition and Monopoly

Migration and the Labor Force

With the Civil War behind them, "bulls on the United States" looked forward to an era of material prosperity and national progress. Late in 1865 their mouthpiece, the *Commercial and Financial Chronicle*, was thus diagnosing the future:

After political security, there is nothing that the Republic needs so much as bone and sinew, for the development of its vast resources. . . . Having solved all problems and disposed of all doctrines and theories relative to the intention of our political system, we want flesh and blood, men, women, and children, to assist in fulfilling that intention.

This crying need for a labor force was, of course, a historic American phenomenon. The birthrate and international migration had met the need for people during colonization and the years of growth. They continued to do so, but in slightly different proportions. Between 1860 and 1920 the number of persons gainfully employed in nonagricultural pursuits rose from 4,325,116 to 30,984,765. At the former date they constituted 41.1 percent of all persons gainfully employed; at the later date 73 percent. Here was another evidence of the triumph of the industrial state.

For a brief interval it seemed that the historic reliance upon immigration might shatter in the hand. As we have seen, in the late fifties the number of arrivals from abroad declined, and the Civil War—with its pressure upon manpower for its armed forces, agriculture, and industry —discouraged an immediate migration from Europe. In an air of urgency Congress reverted in a mild way to the colonial policy of assisted immigration. In 1864 a contract labor law "to encourage immigration" exempted immigrants from the draft and permitted employers to advance the money for paying the immigrant's passage. This advance constituted a lien upon the recipient's wages for twelve months and upon any property he might acquire in this country. Although employers or agents inserted advertisements in the foreign press, recruited workers, paid passages, and signed papers, the contract labor law was more symptomatic of domestic moods than effective in inducing immigration.

The fundamental causes for immigration were, as they had always been, the opportunities in agriculture and industry. As the steamship, the foreign post, the cable, and the cheap newspaper sped communications, these advantages were brought more quickly to the attention of the European migrating masses, and their reaction was more immediate and flexible. An exceptional international mobility of labor resulted. In almost rhythmical fashion, workers flowed into America when attractive possibilities of work were presented and retreated when they were withdrawn. A glance at the graph of immigration shows that years of prosperity led to a great increase of immigration, while panic years were followed by a striking decline in foreign arrivals. These fluctuations are even more significant when account is taken of the number of foreigners departing from the United States. After the panic of 1873 the figures of departing aliens rose, until in 1877 for every 100 arriving male aliens 54 left; and in 1895, in the midst of a depression, the ratio was 100-to-78. Although apostles of Americanization bewailed these "birds of passage," their mobility reflected a crude adjustment of labor force to labor needs.

Most discussions of the wider effects of immigration upon industry in the United States have been needlessly complicated by the contrast drawn between the "old" and the "new" immigration. The "old" immigration from nothern and western Europe predominated until 1896; after that date the "new" immigration from southern and eastern Europe furnished the majority of foreign arrivals. It is not clear, however, that the effects of this new immigration upon American industry were different from those of the old. For three years, from 1907 to 1910, an Immigration Commission, created by act of Congress, investigated the problem and compiled reports. Its findings were characterized by a wistful yearning for the old immigration. Yet in 1870 in the very midst of those good old days Francis A. Walker, economist, statistician, and later president of the Massachusetts Institute of Technology, was writing:

Here [in the East] we find the peasants of Ireland and Germany engaged, painfully to themselves and often wastefully to the employers, in all sorts of mechanical operations to which they have no traditional or acquired aptitude. . . . They have fallen upon our shores, the migratory impulse exhausted, their money gone, with no definite purpose, with no special preparation, to become the victims of their place and circumstances, to seek such occupation as offers itself, to underbid native labor, to adapt themselves painfully to the conditions of our industry such as they have found them, or to join the rabble that troops after a Tweed, a Morrissey, a Hayes, and an O'Brien.

Whether of the old or of the new immigration, the arriving foreigner generally undertook the more unskilled occupations of the community. He was ignorant of the American industrial scheme and compelled immediately to make a living. The increasing mechanization of American industry offered simple tasks to the hordes of common laborers and peasants, untrained in modern industry, who poured into the country. Through the job levels of American industry there has thus been a shifting procession of different races. The coal-mining industry affords one illustration. In 1869 an English investigator found that "of the 30,000 miners engaged in the Pennsylvania coal districts, but few will be found who are not English, Welsh, or Irish," and the same generalization, if enlarged to include Germans, could have been applied to the other districts of the country. But coal mining, expanding with prodigious rapidity in the era of the industrial state, clamored for laborers. In the eighties Slovaks were first employed in considerable numbers in the Pennsylvania fields, and in the following years Magyars, Poles, and Italians, with a few from other nations, inundated the region. The iron and steel industry had a similar history. In 1875 Captain Jones of the Edgar Thomson Works was writing, "My experience has shown that Germans and Irish, Swedes and what I denominate 'Buckwheats' (young American boys), judiciously mixed, make the most effective and tractable force you can find." But such preferences were conveniently altered as the industry began its incredible expansion and the new immigrants, employed in the less skilled positions, began to transform the racial complexion of its huge workshops. In 1907 the roll of the laboring force in the Carnegie Steel Company plants in Allegheny County showed large numbers of Slovaks, Magyars, Croatians, Russians, and Italians. The Croatians surpassed the Irish; the Italians the Germans; the Roumanians the Swedes; and the Slovaks the "Buckwheats."

Any discussion of the effects of immigration upon wages, hours, and general conditions of labor is largely surmise, for it cannot be disentangled from the other factors which have shaped America's industrial development. It has often been said that the pauper immigrant with a lower standard of living depressed American labor conditions. The historian can only point out that clothing was a sweatshop industry before the Jewish immigrants of the eighties began to furnish its labor force; that the textile factories of Lowell exploited native Americans before they repeated the process with Irish, French Canadians, and Poles; that in the nineties the immigrant labor of the northern Illinois coal fields was menaced by the native American labor in the southern fields of the same state; and that in the twentieth century the living standards of foreign laborers in the cotton industry of Massachusetts and Rhode Island were threatened by the simon-pure American operatives of the southern states. The historian may further point out that the industrial development of the country since 1850 has been made possible by immigrant labor.

A second, less disputed, result of immigration was the stratification of the American laboring class along racial levels. These racial lines coincided with differences in skill and craft. In coal mining the foreman and superintendents were Americans or descendants of the earlier immigration, while the workers were foreigners; in the steel industry the skilled positions were held by natives, the lower rungs of the industrial ladder were occupied by the recent immigrants. Between the two groups there was little affinity. In the coal towns Americans would not associate with the inhabitants of "Hun Town" or "Little Italy"; in the steel industry "white men" were sharply arrayed against the inferior "Hunkies" and "Ginnies." Differences of religion, language, living conditions, aroused hostilities and antipathies which the employer often capitalized, setting race against race in the manner of the defunct Austro-Hungarian empire. Immigration has undoubtedly made difficult the labor solidarity characteristic of industrial nations with a homogeneous population.

The American wage earner has been an insistent advocate of immigration restriction and has quite rightly attributed to the employing class the opposition to such measures. The Know-Nothing movement of the fifties believed that the "capitalist" and the "money-power" were the advocates of unrestricted immigration. Later the organized labor movement felt the contract labor law of 1864 enabled employers to break strikes and lower wages. In the agitation of the twentieth century E. H. Gary, chairman of the board of directors of the United States Steel Corporation, deplored the movement for restriction. With a certain poetic justice, the argument for a protective tariff was turned by the workers against its beneficiaries. If the manufacturer was entitled to protection against the products of the pauper labor of Europe and the Orient, the laborer was certainly entitled to protection against the labor itself. The first legislative response to agitation of this nature came naturally in the eighties, when figures of arrivals spurted ahead. In that decade Congress prohibited the importation of labor under contract except for certain skilled workmen; began, by the temporary exclusion of Chinese laborers, a policy of permanent hostility to Oriental immigration, Chinese and Japanese; and tightened the provisions and enforcement of the general immigration laws. This was not enough. Finally, in 1917, Congress succeeded in passing over presidential vetoes an act requiring of every immigrant the ability to read some language or dialect. Wilson in his tart analysis of the act complained, "Those who come seeking opportunity are not to be admitted unless they have already had one of the chief opportunities they seek, the opportunity of education. The object of such provisions is re-striction, not selection."

Restrictive legislation by no means dried the streams of migration replenishing the labor armies. There were Captain Jones's "Buckwheats." This migration of country folk into town and city—the centers of trade and manufacturing—had long been marked in New England and the Middle Atlantic states. After 1860, as industrialization spread to new regions, the phenomenon was repeated. In the Middle West, traditional agricultural heart of America, population tended to shift to the busy industrial centers at the edge of the Great Lakes, just as in the East it wedged tighter and tighter into the urban districts along the Atlantic seaboard. Meanwhile in the South the rise of industry occasioned move-ments and regroupings of population. Southern similarities with the New England of an earlier century were startling, for the prejudice against factory work among the whites whom the manager elected to employ in the mills had to be broken down. Apprehensions were banished by the paternalistic system of the southern mill village, which gave the mill superintendent a large measure of control over the character and activities of his help. But most southern white farmers who were not well-to-do were willing to escape the burdens of tenancy, mortgages, and low cotton prices, either by working in the mill seasonally or moving into the mill village as a permanent operative class. Most of the cotton mills established in the Piedmont region had little trouble in recruiting a labor force from their immediate environment. By 1900, however, cotton mills began to have difficulty in securing further employees from this region. Then advertise-ments painting an attractive picture of industrial life were printed and circulated in the hill counties, and agents, sometimes accompanied by a worker as a sample, were sent to enlist workers from among the mountain whites. Resort was had, also, to the poorer farmers of the coastal plain.

Women and Children First

The search for industrial laborers cannot be approached solely from the geographical aspect because in its quest for workers the factory reached out everywhere to different classes and groups of the community. From the first it relied upon the labor of children and women. As far as the decennial census reveals, the number of child workers in the gainfully employed agricultural and nonagricultural labor force reached a peak in 1910 when 1,353,100 boys and 637,100 girls employed were from ten to fifteen years old. The decline in the next ten years was precipitous. One reason was that at the time of the 1920 census the Federal act taxing products made by child labor was in operation. More of the children employed in nonagricultural pursuits in 1920 were engaged in trade, domestic service, and clerical occupations than in the cotton factories or in the iron and steel mills. The decline of child labor in industrial pursuits was due to the invention of machinery which made unnecessary the sort of labor children could contribute and to the passage of restrictive legislation by the states. Such legislation, which in New England and the Middle Atlantic states came at last to some degree of effectiveness, was responsible for the remarkable decline during the decade 1880–1890 in the number of children employed in the cotton mills of the North.

These changes were not duplicated in the southern states, where a competing cotton industry was coming into existence. The cotton industry until recently employed the greatest number of children in this country. The South continued this tradition, for the number of children under sixteen employed in her mills increased from 2,300 to 27,500 between 1870 and 1905. The manufacturers sought operative families with children; the whole family was put to work, and the wages of the mother and the children were as essential as those of the father in maintaining the family's level of subsistence. The anachronism of this development was further exemplified when the southern factory owner, regarding himself as a philanthropist, asserted that he employed children only because of the necessities and importunities of their parents, and resisted the enactment of restrictive legislation with an air of self-righteousness. Any criticism of these arrangements irritated the touchy sectionalism of the region. A North Carolina manufacturer wrote in 1905, "I consider it a sad day for North Carolina when the emissaries of northern fanaticism, prejudice, and envy are allowed to come here and 'frame bills' to be enacted into laws for the government of the people of this great and free State."

Between the censuses of 1870 and 1920 the number of women gainfully employed in nonagricultural pursuits increased from 1,429,000 to 7,466,400. These totals alarmed conservatives, who felt that woman's place was in the home, and delighted feminists, who found here an evidence of their hoped-for emancipation. Certainly, in the half century here under scrutiny, personal and domestic service lost its historic role as the chief employment for women. Employment in the professions increased. In manufacturing women have made great advances in certain employments. While in some of the traditional occupations, like cotton textiles, they relatively lost ground, the mechanization of other industries enabled them to perform operations which did not require great physical strength or endurance. By 1920 in the food industries—bakeries, candy factories, fruit and vegetable canning—over half of the workers were women, which was natural enough, since women had prepared the food in the home; cigar and tobacco factories followed cotton mills and clothing factories as the greatest employers of women; the metal-working trades, excluding the heavy iron and steel industry, were a new occupation for women. No matter how many figures were collected, it was impossible to say whether the women workers in industry as a whole displaced men. There was some evidence that women concentrated in certain industries, men in others.

Much more dramatic than their employment in industry was the preemption by women workers of the occupations created by the invention of new methods of communication, the increasing attention paid to paper work in production and in commerce, and the growth of trade as distinguished from industry and transportation. Although the telegraph companies were slow to employ women, the telephone became almost at once a feminine monopoly. In 1870 only 350 women were employed as telephone and telegraph operators; in 1920 the 175,500 women employed constituted 93.8 percent of the telephone operators. As long as most of the stenographic work was associated with government business—legislative debates or court cases—women made little headway in this occupation; but in the 1860's women gained a foothold in the fields of bookkeeping and accounting, clerking, and stenography. The establishment of business schools and the wider use of the typewriter hastened their invasion. In 1870 there were somewhat fewer than 10,000 women employed in these occupations; in 1920 their number had increased to 1,980,000, and some of these occupations they had made distinctly feminine. Over 90 percent of the stenographers and typists were women. The third occupation in which women wage earners became important was retail selling. In 1850 even women's stores were clerked by men. Reformers who wished to improve the lot of the working girl in other employments advocated that she be allowed to enter this more desirable occupation. At the time of the Civil War women began to enter retail trade, and the establishment and growth of department stores after the seventies, by making possible a greater division of labor in retailing, increased the employment of women. In 1870 saleswomen were not separately enumerated by the census; in 1920 stores employed 349,500. Unfortunately this new occupation did not furnish the relief for an oppressed womanhood which the prophets had anticipated. Instead, employers paid women a lower wage than men, and the conditions of feminine work became a problem for the reformers of a second generation.

The inferior position of the woman worker was baldly reflected in the lower wages she received. The *Workingman's Advocate* in 1868 wrote that "women do not get, in the average, one-fourth the wages that men receive"; in manufacturing employment they were paid perhaps about 54 percent of men's wages in the first decade of the present century and about 60 percent in 1920. These lower wages were due primarily to the fact that women filled the less skilled positions at wages which men would not usually accept. Apologists justified the situation on the ground that men were heads of families, that women were temporary workers employed until they married, and that their earnings were "pin money." This may once have been true. But between 1890 and 1920 the proportion of married women among women gainfully employed in nonagricultural pursuits increased from 12.1 percent to 21.2. It was observed that even the wages of unmarried daughters generally went into the family budget. By the twentieth century women sought work from economic necessity— either to preserve or to raise the standard of living in the family unit of which they were a part.

The Status of the Wage Earner in the Machine Age

From whatever source the wage earner may have come, he was subjected after 1850 to the terms of labor imposed by the railroad and the machine. The extension of the railroad meant that labor produced for a national market; goods manufactured under certain labor conditions in Albany competed with those manufactured under different circumstances in St. Louis. Nor was the competition of commodities the only result of universal railroad transportation. Since labor itself became more mobile, wage earners from Mississippi competed with those from Chicago. Labor agitation, labor movements, labor legislation, labor practices were no longer the concern of a locality or a section; they involved the sweep of a national arena. And in this larger setting the factory and power machinery shaped the conditions of labor. Before 1850 the cotton goods industry alone had felt the full operation of these factors; now in the industrial state their influence became almost universal.

To a large extent the mechanization of American industry destroyed the handicraftsman or artisan, the master of the skills necessary for his trade, and brought the less skilled worker to greater importance. In some instances this change was accomplished without machinery by subdividing a process into simple operations most of which were performed by hand. To such subdivision scientific management later made extensive contributions. But in most cases the smaller reliance upon skill was hastened by the use of machinery to perform the separate tasks. To be sure, there were contradictory tendencies. Much unskilled labor was abolished by the greater use of cranes, conveyors, chargers, and other mechanical devices. The "gorilla type" of worker, as F. W. Taylor called him, became less essential to industry. The Industrial Revolution even heightened the importance of some skilled trades. Machine repairers, since they were the physicians of these automatic instruments, required almost professional skill. Engineers, managers, inventors, efficiency experts, multiplied to take over the tasks of planning, routing, analyzing, which the handicraftsman would once have assumed. It was certain, nevertheless, that the desire of American industry was to make greater use of unskilled or semiskilled labor, and that it succeeded. For the employer the change meant the possibility of paying relatively lower wages and a greater ease in securing workers. For the worker it meant a greater dependence upon the employer, since his unique skill, formerly acquired by a long apprenticeship, was no longer necessary and he could be taught in a few days to tend the machine. These unskilled tasks were, moreover, routinized and monotonous. The psychologists are still debating whether such automatism stifled the worker's "creative spirit" or pleasantly expressed his "motor impulses."

The effect of machinery upon the hours of labor cannot be traced accurately. A measurable starting point was provided by the length of the working day. By 1860 the movement for a ten-hour day had met with general success in the building trades and some other skilled occupations, but in the factory industries its conquest had not been noticeable. The average day the country over was eleven hours. In the next five decades this figure slowly diminished. After the Civil War the labor unions, with a sublime indifference to actual conditions, campaigned for an eight-hour day. At the turn of the century this had just been secured in a precarious and uneven fashion in the mining industry, where work underground was peculiarly dangerous and disagreeable, and it was general in the building and other skilled trades; but even Gompers had to admit in 1899 that "the average hours of labor of the American worker are about nine and one-half a day." But World War I worked a revolution in the length of the working day. In 1914 the standard hours a week in industry numbered 53.5; in 1920 they were 50.4. Perhaps at the latter date about half the factory workers in the country had the 48-hour week. But some conspicuous employments reached this goal tardily if at all. For the iron and steel industry the dogmatic dictum of Charles Schwab still applied, "Anyone familiar with steel knows that a great deal of work must be carried on continuously. There is no other way to do this. It is a practice throughout the world." Reduced to figures, this generality meant a 12-hour day for the majority of steel workers and a seven-day week for a considerable percentage.

It was a common feeling among workingmen, however, that in general the labor of these shorter hours was more intense and more uninterrupted. In many industries there was an increase in the number of machines which a worker served. It is difficult to apportion the causes of these increases between the use of improved and automatic devices and the more intensive application of human labor. But the machine industry of the twentieth century undoubtedly represented a contrast to the artisan and to the earlier factory. In the old days the rhythm of operations was determined by the natural rhythm of the worker; in modern times it was the regular and remorseless beat of the machine that set the tempo. Although machinery undoubtedly lightened heavy labor, it substituted an emphasis upon precision, attention, nervous vitality, which was extremely wearing. In spite of the numerous attempts at statistical measurement of fatigue, no very specific generalization can be made as to whether the worker was more or less tired after the eight-hour day of 1920 than after the eleven-hour day of 1860.

Such considerations dovetailed into the effects of machine production upon the health of the worker. On this point it was possible to demonstrate that male factory workers died earlier and were more susceptible to certain diseases than other males; it was not possible to explain these facts by dissociating the effects of factory employment from those of the standard of living of factory workers. Industrial accidents were, on the other hand, definitely connected with the day's work. Such figures as have been compiled show that mining was proportionately the most dangerous occupation. In 1907 the fatalities in coal mining were 3,232; in 1920 they were 2,260. The United States had the worst record of all important coal-mining countries. Railroading was the second most dangerous occupation; in 1907, 4,534 employees were killed; in 1920, 3,578. When the total calculations of industrial accidents were made in 1913, the annual fatalities were placed at 25,000, and injuries involving more than four weeks' disability numbered 700,000. This was warfare: these deaths in industry were just over half the battle deaths of the American army in 1917 and 1918. During the war the government insured its soldiers at low rates. Yet in the late nineteenth century the common law assumed that, if an employee agreed to work for an employer, the former accepted all the ordinary dangers of the industry, all the extraordinary dangers if he was in a position to know them, and all the dangers arising from the carelessness, ignorance, or incompetence of his fellow employees. Upon the laborer rather than upon the industry descended the burdens of industrial accidents.

Another definite measurement of the effect of the Industrial Revolution upon the wage earner was provided by the fluctuations in his wages. There are volumes of wage statistics for the United States, but it has been exceedingly difficult to interpret them or to draw any conclusions. The statisticians also have seized upon these figures, and the layman, after reading about medians, quartiles, weighted averages, logarithmic curves, and trends, is left with the impression of many modifying factors and damaging contradictions. From the mass of calculations, however, emerge a few generalizations which roughly approximate facts. One is that the money wages of nonagricultural workers greatly increased after 1860. One index of money wages for workers in industry, with an occasional attention to agricultural workers, rose 53 percent from 1860 to 1913. By far the larger share of this increase took place during the Civil War and the postwar years before the panic of 1873. The index figure attained in that year was not reached again until 1903. Money wages, however, by themselves are meaningless: it is what they can buy in commodities that gives them significance. Probably no wholly adequate measure of the cost of living can be secured for the United States before 1913; back to 1890 it is possible to procure prices of various retail products which entered into the worker's consumption in various weighted proportions; before that date most is conjecture. From such data as we have, real wages over the period as a whole from 1860 to 1913 probably rose less rapidly than money ones, since the index of the former increased only 43 percent. If this long time-span is broken down it reveals that real wages lagged behind from 1860 to 1873; rose more rapidly than money ones during the remainder of the century as prices fell more rapidly than wages; and held a plateau in the years that intervened before the outbreak of World War I.

A factor which completely undermined most statistics of wages in the United States was the relative degree of unemployment. Hour wages mean little unless the number of hours worked not in a week, but in a year or even several years is known. Unfortunately, the United States and the separate states did not in this period collect reasonably accurate statistics of unemployment. But although definite standards of measurement cannot be secured, it is recognized that a competitive machine civilization caused unemployment in several fashions. Men were thrown out of work through the invention of machinery or the application of improved methods to production. Commentators have comforted discharged laborers with the assertion that the use of machines would lower prices; if the demand for the product were elastic production would enlarge and eventually larger work forces would be employed; or else new occupations would be created through industrial advance. A temporary displacement was admitted. Nor had the expansion of industry been effective in preventing intermittent employment, occasioned by seasonal influences or market conditions, in industry. Even the basic iron and steel industry was associated with the fickle industries. Its blast furnaces, because of the desirability of continuous operation, constituted one of the most stable processes in the industry. Yet the number of men employed on them ranged in 1908 to 1910 from 18,545 to 46,810. It is little wonder that an investigator into the conditions of labor in iron and steel in 1910 found that among the workers "there has been no complaint so frequently made or so strongly expressed as that regarding irregularity of employment."

At periodic intervals came the trough of a "business cycle." A palsy seized industry, production was curtailed, and workers had to shift as they might until a slow cure was effected. In the nineteenth century there was no accurate means of measuring this unemployment. Even for a depression as recent as that of the mid-nineties, figures of unemployment ranged from a well-meaning estimate of 4.5 million to the informed calculation of Paul Douglas that in 1894 the number of unemployed in manufacturing and transportation was 904,000, a figure that was 16.7 percent of the labor supply in those occupations. Although many observers interpreted such distressing events as the punishment of a righteous God upon the degraded classes of the community and in the nineties regarded the pathetic "industrial armies" marching to Washington for relief as recruited from congenital tramps and criminals, the community usually assumed responsibility for easing the hardships of those who were unemployed through no fault of their own. Measures taken were usually neither efficient nor well directed but they were certainly various—soup kitchens and bread lines, shelters for the homeless, subsistence gardens, emergency committees collecting old clothes, private charities spending public money, policemen acting as relief agents and social workers, payments to the unemployed in wages, truck, and store orders, differing treatments for unemployed and unemployables. By the panic of 1914 a pattern had developed from this confused experimentation. Existing private charity organizations—associated charities—gave relief from their own funds; and governments sheltered the homeless, distributed appropriations to the poor, and sponsored public works. Relief methods were fairly objective. Impetuous impromptu organizations were discouraged, investigation preceded assistance, and efforts were made to determine the number of unemployed. The city was still the recognized unit in formulating unemployment relief measures, although three states had statewide systems and national organizations were advocating a national policy.

Finally, the trend of industrial development shattered the close relationship and neighborly contact which had existed between the employer and his employees. The growth of corporations diffused ownership among many stockholders, whose chief interest was generally profits; and the corporation together with bankers' control created absentee ownership and responsibility. To be sure, there were exceptions. In southern villages the cotton mill built operatives' houses, aided in the establishment of schools, and financed churches, and the mill owner or agent either was superintendent in the Sunday school or taught classes. The fact that the workers and the employees were of a common race and that the southern manager inherited a conception of *noblesse oblige* from the slave regime created a community of feeling. When this sentiment began to dissolve in the twentieth century the alarmed owners stopped at nothing to scotch the snake of industrial unrest which was destroying their Eden. In the North there were localities or plants where employer and employee knew and respected each other. Some businessmen still attempted to maintain the old neighborliness. Andrew Carnegie announced that he liked to be called "Andy" by his men; F. W. Taylor derided "the employer who goes through his works with kid gloves on, and is never known to dirty his hands or clothes"; and Mark Hanna felt a genuine satisfaction in talking man-to-man with his workers. While the problem of status and equality might be solved, and sometimes was, within the plant, the larger question of relations within the community remained insoluble. Most employers did not or could not live on the same street as their workers, nor were they or their wives content to patronize the same schools, clubs, or churches.

Labor Organization: Seedtime, 1850–1877

If the individual worker sought to change the conditions brought into being by the Industrial Revolution he found himself whirled about in the maelstrom of competition. He competed with other wage earners whose necessity for a job was as great as his own. He competed also with the employers for a division of the product. In the latter rivalry the wage earner was at a great disadvantage. "While corporations are the richest and strongest bodies, as a rule, in the state," wrote Judge Rogers of the Rhode Island Supreme Court in 1892, "their employees are often the weakest and least able to protect themselves, frequently being dependent upon their current wage for their daily bread." But the individual wage earner was not yet done with competition. Employers competed with each other. If one were willing to raise wages and shorten hours, he might be confronted with the lower production costs of his competitor. The most generous employer with the welfare of his men at heart could not escape this pressure. Under the circumstances it was inevitable that the worker should seek to escape the evils of the competitive system through combination. The trade union was his answer. But to form a union from hundreds and thousands of individuals, loyal and selfish, American and Italian and Polish, was a task much more heartbreaking than the organization of a merger.

For twenty-five years after 1850 leaders and workers sought to cope with the changing character of industry. They did succeed in establishing a number of genuine labor organizations on a national scale, for both the market for goods and the market for labor were extending to national limits. By the end of the sixties, twenty-nine trades had national trade unions. But in the depression between 1873 and 1877 many of them dwindled away or disappeared. A few, particularly in the skilled trades, survived. But it was noticeable that in the dynamic new industries of the industrial state the labor unions exerted little control. Before 1875 on the railroads only three of the later four brotherhoods had been established; of these the Brotherhood of Locomotive Engineers was the only one of any importance and it hearkened willingly when railroad officials recommended that the members seek to improve the "moral, social and intellectual condition of the Locomotive Engineers" rather than encourage "antagonism to your employers." In bituminous coal mining, organization was shattered by undisciplined strikes and the arrest of leaders. In anthracite the failure of a strike to prevent wage cuts broke the ephemeral but powerful Workingmen's Benevolent Association, and then in 1875–1877 Franklin B. Gowen, of the Reading Railroad, determined to identify unionism with the endemic terrorism of the anthracite region commonly ascribed to a gang known as the "Molly Maguires." By the testimony of a Pinkerton detective he was able to impress the newspapers and courts of the day if not all later investigators. A series of executions purged the mining regions of violence and union activity. In the fundamental iron and steel industry only the skilled workers were organized. In 1876 three organizations coalesced into the Amalgamated Association of Iron and Steel Workers. But the merger was a sign of weakness rather than strength, as only the Sons of Vulcan, the puddlers' union, had a noticeable membership.

The harsh realities of the workingman's life stimulated most of this labor union activity—as it always had. Unions struggled to prevent wage cuts and secure increases or campaign for a shorter working day. To be sure, what was feasible did not always concern them. For at a moment when very few industries had secured a day of ten hours, labor's mouthpieces were demanding one of eight and advancing the argument of one of their number, Ira Steward, the "eight-hour monomaniac" of Boston, as justification. Steward asserted the shorter day would aid even the manufacturer.

In the mechanical fact that the cost of making an article depends almost entirely upon the number manufactured is a practical increase in wages, by tempting the workers through their new leisure to unite in buying luxuries now confined to the wealthy, and which are costly because bought only by the wealthy.

This shorter workday was to be obtained by an educational campaign and legislation. By 1868 the national government had responded and passed an eight-hour law for government employees. Such legislation secured in the states was worthless.

Other labor leaders and reformers were meanwhile moving against the wider hardships, as they saw them, of the incoming machine age. As escape they advocated cooperation—cooperative stores in which they could purchase goods and cooperative factories in which the workers furnished the capital, managed the enterprise, and took all the profits. "The cooperative principle . . . will build all our cities, dig our ores, fill the land with the noise of the loom and spindle. The workingman . . . will become contractor, builder, manufacturer, reaping the rewards of his own industry and the profits of his own labor." All this was natural enough for men only a stage removed from the handicraftsmen who had helped themselves and given themselves employment. But practice contradicted anticipation. The cooperative factories, many of them established by the molders' union, instead of destroying the "wages system" became the personal possessions of a few laborers whose actions and outlook were indistinguishable from those of capitalist employers. They worked holidays and thought there was little use for the union. Since cooperative enterprises required capital, the union movement became involved in the financial panaceas of the era; and this concern led them to an emphasis upon political action rather than upon strikes. All this sounded like an earlier day. Indeed, Robert Dale Owen and George Evans would have felt at home at the annual conventions of the National Labor Union (1866–1872), a reflection of the National Trades' Union of the thirties.

Meanwhile, in December, 1869, nine Philadelphia tailors met in the hall of the American Hose Company and established the first local assembly of the Noble and Holy Order of the Knights of Labor. Its first Master Workman, Uriah S. Stephens, a tailor, was the real sire. Trained for the Baptist ministry, his thinking was deeply influenced by his religious heritage. As an all-round "joiner," he believed in brotherhood and had a knowledge of secret fraternal organizations and ritualistic nomenclature. He criticized existing unions as "too narrow in their ideas and too circumscribed in their fields of operations. . . . I can see ahead of me an organization that will cover the globe. It will include men and women of every craft, creed, and color; it will cover every race worth saving." Apparently he felt that a religious ritual would create his visioned solidarity of labor by shattering the barriers of prejudice and self-interest which divided laborers from one another and impressing them with a common brotherhood. To effect these objectives he drew up a secret ceremonial, the *Adelphon Kruptos*.

The note of piety and religion in Stephens was neither ill-timed nor perfunctory. Though Protestant pastor and Catholic prelate might thunder against the evils of unionism, Americans prided themselves upon being a Christian nation. Inherent in the Christian tradition was the idea of brotherhood. United with the democratic emphasis on majority rule, these ideas formed a powerful weapon in persuading individualistic workers to join their working brothers in unions and in persuading presumably hostile public opinion that unions were American. To go it alone without a union "faith" was unmanly and unsuccessful.

So the Knights were shaped to meet the needs of the seventies. While the old trade unions based upon craft lines were wilting away, this new organization arrived with the gospel that all workers were one. While the members of the open unions were being persecuted, their organizers discouraged, and union employees blacklisted, the Knights flung a protecting veil of secrecy over union membership. In fact, the disintegration of the previous labor movement cleared the way for the new one. In 1873 the local assemblies around Philadelphia were so numerous that they were formed into the first district assembly of the Order, and the membership five years later was so large and divided that the first national meeting was required for the sake of harmony and compromise. Before it met, the American labor movement entered a new phase.

The Uprising of Labor, 1877–1886

In 1877 at least one observer felt that the labor disturbances of that year deserved a book. The Hon. J. A. Dacus, Ph.D., thus described them in his *Annals of the Great Strikes in the United States:*

> This Republic suddenly startles the world; drowns the noise of strife on the Bulgarian plains, and among the Balkans, and draws exclusive attention to the social *émeute* on this side of the Atlantic unparalleled in the annals of time. Sudden as a thunder-burst from a clear sky, the crisis came upon the country. Hundreds and thousands of men belonging to the laboring classes, alleging that they were wronged and oppressed, ceased to work, seized railroads, closed factories, foundries, shops and mills, laid a complete embargo on all internal commerce, interrupted travel, and bid defiance to the ordinary instruments of legal authority. . . . It seemed as if the whole social and political structure was on the very brink of ruin. . . . But the spontaneity of the movement shows the existence of a widespread discontent, a disposition to subvert the existing social order, to modify or overturn the political institutions, under which such unfavorable conditions were developed.

Although allowance must be made for a certain journalistic breathlessness, the great railroad strikes of 1877, caused by repeated wage cuts and "doubling up," sometimes flared into open violence with troops called out, property destroyed in gigantic bonfires, and loss of life. On these occasions and on others in the next twenty years an untamed, undirected, spontaneous mass movement of the wage earners convinced an unprepared nation that European history was being violently repeated on this side of the Atlantic and that the labor problem had become American.

The beneficiary of this discontent was the Noble and Holy Order of the Knights of Labor. Purely by chance that organization in 1878 assumed a national form when the first general assembly, convened at Reading, adopted a preamble, a platform, and a constitution. The first two documents were inheritances from the past, continuing the tradition of earlier American labor and reform movements. The general statements of the preamble indicted "the recent alarming development and aggression of aggregated wealth" and justified the organization of the workers to prevent the "pauperization and hopeless degradation of the toiling masses." Some planks in the platform were more specific. They called for equal pay for equal work for both sexes, the prohibition of labor by children under fourteen years in shops, mines, and factories, the reduction of the hours of labor to eight a day for cultural reasons, the payment of wages once a week in money rather than in orders or truck, the substitution of arbitration for strikes, "the reserving of the public lands, the heritage of the people, for the actual settler—not another acre for railroads or speculators," "the establishment of cooperative institutions, productive and distributive," and the bestowal of economic and social rights upon the toilers so that they might be "capable of enjoying, appreciating, defending, and perpetuating the blessings of good government." In one of the many changes or additions made in later years to this document the Knights were told, "It is the duty of all to assist in nominating and supporting with their votes only such candidates as will pledge their support to those measures regardless of party." The attention given to these policies depended upon the personality of the Order's leaders and the demands of the situation.

Finally, there was the constitution. It embraced the local assemblies, the district assemblies, and the general assembly, and established as national officers a General Executive Board and the General Master Workman, all dignified for secrecy rather than convenience by abbreviations of the initial letters. Theoretically, the organization was an extremely centralized one. Actually, it was decentralized, for the district assemblies and local assemblies assumed an independent and often impudent air toward the General Master Workman and his fellow officers. No uniformity, moreover, characterized these subordinate organizations. A single craft generally composed a local assembly, but there were locals built around industrial plants, and "mixed locals," particularly in the smaller places, of all varieties of workers. On paper, district assemblies should have included all workers within a certain geographical unit. Actually, some district assemblies, for reasons, largely fortuitous, were in effect trade or craft assemblies; and in the eighties a proposal was advanced to include all the workers in a single craft throughout the nation in district assemblies of their own.

But in spite of its piebald organization, the Order aspired to universality. Doctors, lawyers, bankers and liquor dealers could not join it. But everyone who worked or had worked for wages was welcomed. Capitalists, merchants, farmers, belonged. It organized the skilled, the semiskilled, the unskilled; it included women in its membership; and it did not scorn the foreigner or the Negro. The *Adelphon Kruptos* was translated into French, German, and Scandinavian, and requests were made for Polish, Italian, and Bohemian versions. The Knights preached the solidarity of labor.

The next step in evolution was to discard the semireligious chrysalis of the Order. In 1879 Stephens, who had been General Master Workman, resigned, and Terrence V. Powderly was elected as his successor. An Irish machinist, Powderly was a humanitarian, a gifted propagandist, a middle-class reformer whose very appearance impressed contemporaries as unlike that of the conventional labor leader. "English novelists take men of Powderly's look for their poets, gondola scullers, philosophers and heroes crossed in love." Although he frequently failed to guide the movement of which he was the head, he often influenced it. For one thing, his opposition to the secret features of the order was certainly expedient, since they had aroused public suspicion. Allan Pinkerton, with a reckless carelessness of fact, wrote in 1878 that the Knights of Labor "is probably an amalgamation of the Molly Maguires and the Commune." The Catholic Church, which opposed secret religious orders whose vows interfered with the freedom of the confessional, was hostile to the Order. But the Knights had to organize the Irish Catholic worker. Powderly was a Roman Catholic and appreciated the difficulty. In 1881 all restrictions on the disclosure of the name of the Order, previously concealed by asterisks, were removed, an affirmation was substituted for the oath, and the scriptural passages and language were expurgated from the *Adelphon Kruptos*. Although Stephens was disconsolate and a few Protestant preachers felt the Knights had become an instrument of the Pope, the secularization of the order undoubtedly increased its usefulness to the labor movement in the decade of the eighties.

By 1881 the army of Knights had enlisted somewhat fewer than 20,000 members. Yet in 1886 the Order had multiplied to the incredible total of 702,924, the largest labor organization which the United States had ever seen. These five years of success were not due to the achievements of the Knights of Labor in cooperation or in politics. In these areas programs of action were primarily local in character, and the central organization confined itself to homilies or campaigns of education. Nor was participation in successful strikes the entire explanation. In fact, in the days of its primitive purity the Knights had been opposed to strikes; the platform of the Order in 1878 preferred discussion and agreement—which they called "arbitration"—as a means of settling disputes, and Powderly was temperamentally and intellectually convinced of the danger of striking, an attitude quite understandable in the light of labor experience during the seventies. Even though the order later made efforts to systematize the calling of strikes and provide funds for such activity, the independence of local units; the failure to collect strike funds or their diversion, if collected, to other purposes; and the persistent reluctance of Powderly and most other officials to modify their suspicion of this method —all contributed to make preparation for strikes inadequate and to furnish a vacillating direction.

In the mid-eighties, nevertheless, the Order won some prestige and some membership as a result of successful railroad strikes. Like as not the workers were organized into Knights after they had won their victories rather than before. As the outstanding labor organization in the country, the Order was the beneficiary also of an eight-hour movement which it did not wholeheartedly support. Years later Powderly, reflecting upon a growth so phenomenal that the membership once multiplied nine times in a twelvemonth, declared, "At least four hundred thousand came in from curiosity and caused more damage than good." American agriculture and politics had both provided similar organizational crazes. As the movement toward organization gained, the sensationalism of the press gave momentum by exaggerating the power of the Knights. Thus the New York *Sun* declared:

> The ability of the president and cabinet to turn out all the men in the civil service, and to shift from one post to another the duties of the men in the army and navy, is a petty authority compared with that of these five Knights [the General Executive Board]. . . . They can stay the nimble touch of almost every telegraph operator; can shut up most of the mills and factories, and can disable the railroads.

Regrouping in the Labor Movement, 1887–1893

The Knights reached their peak in 1886, but the collapse of the eight-hour movement in May of that year injured the Order ironically. Though Powderly expressed a disapproval for an eight-hour strike, the rank and file of his organization, other unions, and unorganized workers nevertheless set the first of May as a deadline for the attainment of a workday of fewer hours. Actually, the resulting general strike was confined to the great industrial centers, and in Chicago, where eighty thousand wage earners ceased work, it reached its greatest intensity. In that city other factors incited aggressive action. For three months McCormick, unwilling to be "dictated to" by the unionization of his plant, had locked out workers and conducted operations with "scabs" and Pinkertons. Finally, there were the anarchists. Although some of their leaders were European immigrants, one, Albert R. Parsons, was an Alabaman, a Confederate veteran, and a Knight of Labor. The anarchists felt that politics were a delusion, that the ideal society of which they dreamed could be brought into existence only through violence, and they expressed their conclusions in the vague exciting rhetoric characteristic of much revolutionary writing. On May 3 a battle between strikers and scabs at the McCormick reaper works was broken up by the police and four strikers were killed. One of the anarchist leaders, summoning a meeting of protest in Haymarket Square for the evening of May 4, included the appeal, "Workingmen, arm yourselves and appear in full force." In Haymarket Square the dull speeches had worn on into the night and rain had set in when a squad of police advanced to break up the meeting. Someone threw a bomb. One policeman was killed instantly, others were fatally wounded.

A wave of hysteria swept Chicago. Under conditions of popular excitement which made a fair outcome of the proceedings unlikely, the leaders of the anarchists were arrested and brought to trial as accomplices to the murder. Although the actual bomb-thrower was never discovered and a connection between him and the anarchists was never established, eight men were convicted of murder by a jury; and four were actually executed. This injustice to individual men had wider repercussions. The radical elements in the Knights of Labor seceded in anger because Powderly did not vigorously protest the injustice of the Haymarket trials. Conservatives outside the labor movement blamed the "outrage" on the Knights of Labor. Everywhere radicals were harassed, anti-labor legislation enacted, and middle-class American opinion carefully instructed to identify the labor movement with violence.

Six years later disaster overtook the Amalgamated Association of Iron and Steel Workers. During the eighties this union, aloof from the Knights of Labor, had become the most powerful craft union in the nation. But it failed to include unskilled workers, and because of inertia and employer opposition it had failed to organize the steel mills. An exception was the Carnegie Homestead Works at Pittsburgh. But here the union men gained the ill will of their employers by whining over minor grievances and attempting to restrict output. Whether or not Carnegie shared in the decision is debatable; certainly Henry Clay Frick, his lieutenant, resolved to eliminate the union from his domain. The battle came in 1892. Frick informed a Congressional investigating committee, "We did not care whether they were union or anti-union, but we wanted men with whom we could deal individually. We did not propose to deal with the Amalgamated Association . . . as we had plainly told them." But of course the ostensible quarrel was over wages. Frick meanwhile made arrangements with Pinkerton for an army of three hundred detectives, and when the strike broke these were placed on barges, towed up the Ohio and Monongahela, and brought abreast of Homestead early in the morning of July 6. An army of strikers mobilized on the bank. Who fired the first shot was a matter of dispute, but an engagement broke out between the strikers behind breastworks and the Pinkertons on the boats. By evening the latter surrendered. Although prisoners of war, they were treated outrageously by the mob, composed chiefly of women and boys. "The character of the injuries inflicted upon the Pinkertons in some cases were too indecent and brutal to describe in this report," later declared the Congressional committee of investigation. This committee quite wisely blamed the outbreak upon both parties. But the employers won. The militia was called out, martial law was declared, and the union was broken.

The great railroad strikes of 1877 had begun the period of labor uprising; the railroad strikes of 1893–1894 fittingly ended it. Eugene V. Debs, a homely middle westerner who combined the occupations of groceryman and labor leader in the Brotherhood of Locomotive Firemen, was discontented with the exclusiveness of his organization and established the American Railway Union on industrial lines. In 1894, still flushed with a stirring victory over the Great Northern Railway, the union adopted the cause of workers in the Pullman Company. The latter, on strike against a reduction in wages, the discharge of workers, and the paternalism of the company, joined the Debs organization; in June the American Railway Union forbade its members to handle all trains which included Pullman cars. As the strike spread, the public was irritated by the blockade of railroad transportation in the West and horrified at the destruction of Chicago railroad property by mobs of railroad workers or hoodlums. On their side, the railroad workers saw the General Managers' Association, representing the employers, maneuver so as to make government intervention necessary to protect the mails; they saw the government's case against the strikers entrusted to a special attorney in the pay of one of the railroads; they saw an army of special deputies sworn in by the government and paid by the General Managers' Association; they saw President Cleveland send national troops to Chicago over a protest of the Illinois governor to prevent violence and insure the carriage of the United States mail; they saw an injunction obtained from a Federal court forbid the officers of the union and "all other persons whomsoever from doing any act whatever in furtherance of any conspiracy or combination to restrain either of said railway companies or receivers in the free and unhindered control and handling of interstate commerce over the lines of said railroads"; and they saw their leaders ultimately imprisoned for contempt of court because they violated the injunction. The strike was broken, the union smashed.

In the mid-nineties, after fifteen years of exciting development, the estate of the American labor movement seemed as low as in the seventies. In 1897 the total number of organized workers, 447,000, was only slightly larger than during the best days of the National Labor Union some thirty years earlier. Less than one-tenth of the mine workers in the country were organized; the Homestead strike had destroyed unionism in the plants of the largest steel concern of the nation—a ruinous portent, since that concern was later to form the nucleus of the United States Steel Corporation and shape its policies; on the railroads the favored brotherhoods were stronger, while the majority of workers were still unorganized; and the attempt of the Knights to achieve a labor solidarity had failed. In 1890 they had only 100,000 members, and a few years later they were absorbed by the farmers' movements of the West.

Probably the chief reason for this outcome was the times. From the labor organization's point of view these were "out of joint." Periods of depression, such as those of the seventies and the nineties, may fill workers with discontent; they don't encourage staying power. The employer's business situation hardens his attitude against union demands. Struggling to keep going in the face of competition, he is more interested in cutting costs than in consulting a "social conscience," or admitting he should "recognize" the union. For labor organization depression means stagnation and breakup.

There were, as well, powerful auxiliary explanations for the doldrums of these years. Partisans of differing methods of labor organization and strategy have naturally advanced different explanations. Undoubtedly the stresses and strains of industrial unionism were one cause for the decline of the Knights. Powderly himself searchingly appraised the Order in this fashion:

> Advocating arbitration and conciliation as first steps in labor disputes she has been forced to take upon her shoulders the responsibilities of the aggressor first and, when hope of arbitration and conciliation failed, to beg of the opposing side to do what we should have applied for in the first place. Advising against strikes we have been in the midst of them. Urging important reforms we have been forced to yield our time and attention to petty disputes. . . . While not a political party we have been forced into the attitude of taking political action.

But on occasion craft unions fared no better. After all, it was the Amalgamated Association of Iron and Steel Workers, the strongest craft union in America, that collapsed after Homestead. Mere organizational defects were not, therefore, the whole explanation for the failure of labor's revolt.

More important was the fact that in the later eighties and early nineties big business enterprises were perfecting methods of dealing with labor unions. After all, the great corporations were powerful in their own right; and conscious of common interests, many industries were forming associations for the battle against unionism. Singly or together they possessed the means to protect their property during strikes and to keep it in operation. This warfare required armies. Men of vision, like Allan Pinkerton, the founder of the great detective agency, answered the call. In 1866 the Pinkertons first hired out guards to employers to protect their property during industrial disturbances. The business grew with such rapidity that within twenty-five years the Pinkertons had multiplied their offices, increased their forces, furnished men for more than seventy strikes, and gone into preventive work. One advertisement announced:

> Corporations or individuals desirous of ascertaining the feelings of their employees, and whether they are likely to engage in strikes or are joining any secret labor organizations with a view of compelling terms from corporations or employers . . . can obtain a detective suitable to associate with their employees and obtain this information.

The profits in selling protection were so great that competitors multiplied. Each had its arsenals of weapons and ammunition and recruited its forces in large part from the vicious and criminal classes of the population. By 1900 the pattern was set for the new century.

Supplementing this effective pressure was the anti-union activity of the theoretically "neutral" state. In microcosm the Chicago affair of 1894 demonstrated the variety and effectiveness of that assistance. Although troops had been employed to curb industrial disturbance before, never had they been used on so impressive or unjustified a scale. Nor had the courts been so sweeping in their proscriptions. To be sure, through the late seventies and eighties they had been beating a retreat from the generous interpretation of the common law of Commonwealth *v.* Hunt and emphasizing anew the doctrine of criminal conspiracy which condemned unions if they sought illegal ends by innocent means or innocent ends by unlawful means and held all union members responsible for the unlawfulness of either purposes or methods. Now in the Chicago affray the government supplemented these theories with the assertion that the Sherman Anti-Trust Act applied to labor union activities. The first section of the statute declared, "Every contract, combination in the form of trust or otherwise, or conspiracy in restraint of trade or commerce among the several States, or with foreign nations, is hereby declared to be illegal." Although Congress had probably not intended to proscribe labor union activity by an act designed to curb trusts and monopolies, the Attorney General of the United States and several inferior courts, though not the Supreme Court, utilized the Sherman Anti-Trust Act for this purpose.

Generally the means of preventing the criminal acts attendant upon labor quarrels had been to seek indictments for criminal prosecution; but this method was slow and injury might be inflicted by irresponsible people before the case was decided. In the eighties employers were increasingly turning to the courts for injunctions to prevent in anticipation any damage to their property. The Chicago strike in 1894 for the first time witnessed the use of the injunction on a large scale, and the Supreme Court, although it omitted to discuss the applicability of the Sherman Anti-Trust Act, placed the injunction upon a firm legal foundation. By defining property as the right of a business to continue in operation with new or old employees or to sell goods to old and new customers, the courts were able to issue injunctions not only against possible destruction of physical property but against strikes and boycotts damaging the owner's property in these intangible consumer or worker relationships. The person who violated an injunction was not punished for the crime prohibited but for contempt of court, and this procedure did not involve trial by jury but simply a hearing before the judge who had drawn up the injunction. The injunction nipped strikes at the beginning, when they were apt to be most effective; and before a final decision was made the outbreak was likely to have collapsed.

The American Federation of Labor, 1886–1920

Jay Gould remarked, "I can hire one half of the working class to kill the other half." In view of this cynical utterance, no explanation of the collapse of the Knights of Labor was complete without a knowledge of the fatal fissures within the labor movement of the eighties and nineties. As the Knights of Labor sank, the American Federation of Labor increased its membership. This was an organization primarily of skilled workers. Its constituents, the national trade unions, craft in character, had occasionally cooperated with the Noble and Holy Order, sometimes had joined it, but more usually had distrusted it. In 1881 some trade unions formed a rival organization, the Federation of Organized Trades and Labor Unions. Although the Federation was extremely feeble, the leaders of its most aggressive unions, P. J. McGuire of the carpenters and Adolph Strasser and Samuel Gompers of the cigarmakers, continued to feel their way toward a form of organization adapted to American conditions. They discarded the idea of cooperation, opposed political methods, and sought the attainment of immediate objectives by economic pressure. Strasser's testimony before a Senatorial committee in 1883 was the classic statement of this aspiration.

CHAIRMAN: I was only asking you in regard to your ultimate ends.
THE WITNESS [STRASSER]: We have no ultimate ends. We are going on from day to day. We are fighting only for immediate objects—objects that can be realized in a few years.
MR. CALL: You want something better to eat and to wear, and better houses to live in?
THE WITNESS: Yes, we want to dress better and to live better, and become better citizens generally.
THE CHAIRMAN: I see you are a little sensitive lest it be thought that you are a mere theorizer. I do not look upon you in that light at all.
THE WITNESS: Well, we say in our constitution that we are opposed to theorists, and I have to represent the organization here. We are all practical men.

The statement's latent implications for unlimited improvements in working conditions were revolutionary, but the emphasis upon "immediate objects" and practicality reassured a middle-class nation easily alarmed by the prospect of revolutionary change and the destruction of private property.

It was fortunate for the national trade unions that these principles excited the ardent allegiance of Samuel Gompers, destined to give leadership to the American labor movement until his death in 1924. For in the labor movement, as Stephens and Powderly had demonstrated, leadership was half the battle. Life and character fitted Gompers for the role. Born in England of Dutch Jewish parents, emigrant as a boy to this country, self-educated cigarmaker, he did not descend into the labor movement but grew up within it. He was admirably fitted for the democratic leadership of a wage-earner movement. He liked men, meeting, talking, and drinking with them, and he was in his own mind a practical man.

At no time in my life have I worked out a definitely articulated economic theory. As there has been need for practical action in various fields, I have always squared proposals upon the few fundamental principles that determine all my judgments. I am very frankly a partisan—a union man—not a half-hearted advocate who may be swayed either to the one side or the other. . . . I am unalterably with them [trade union laborers], yea, even to the extent of their errors, their mistakes.

"The world of selfish antagonism to the defenders and protectors of the workmen's rights and interests" felt the impact of Gompers' union gospel; so did heretics within the labor movement.

The Knights of Labor were among his first enemies. Their heresy was disclosed by a quarrel within the Cigar Makers' International Union in New York City which arrayed Gompers and Strasser against opponents who secured the backing of the local Knights of Labor. As a counter-offensive the Gompers-Strasser group secured the calling of a convention of the national unions in May, 1886, "to protect our respective organizations from the malicious work of an element who openly boast that 'trade unions' must be destroyed." When the Knights rejected an ultimatum from this group, the national unions met again at the end of the year, established the American Federation of Labor, and elected Samuel Gompers as their first president. Four years later membership of the American Federation going up met the membership of the Knights of Labor going down.

After this victory membership kept an even plateau through the mid-nineties. In 1898 began an era of spectacular increase. The years of business prosperity at the turn of the century had weakened employers' hostility. As new national unions were formed and existing ones joined the central organization, members mounted to 1,676,200 in 1904. The Knights had never succeeded like this. But the bright morning was soon gone. The membership curve leveled or declined. In 1912 it had reached only 1,848,700 within the AFL. In the same year the total number of organized workers was 2,483,500.

Then came a golden age for organized labor. One cause was a favorable political climate. The humanitarianism of the Progressive movement inspired a series of labor laws and even of favorable court decisions. A second explanation was World War I. A flood of orders from the Allies soon after the conflict broke out and from the United States after she became an "associated power" brought a wave of industrial prosperity. As prices rose, employers were able to meet the demands of their workers by transferring heightened labor costs to purchasers. When immigration fell away, the employer bid frantically for domestic workers and compromised his principles about union recognition. Finally, organized labor with remarkable canniness cast aside a natural pacifist philosophy and determined to support the war. It announced that "the government must recognize the organized labor movement as the agency through which it must cooperate with the wage earners."

To an extent the Wilson Administration harkened to this ultimatum. In 1920 the total number of organized workers had reached the astounding total of 5,110,000, of whom over 4 million were affiliated with the American Federation of Labor.

Such totals concealed an uneven achievement. In manufacturing, only 23.2 percent of the total wage earners were organized. The basic industries were untouched. In as old an industry as textiles, unions had never been important; in as new a one as automobiles, employers were bent upon maintaining their own freedom. The employers' association of Detroit chanted, "Detroit is Detroit because of the Open Shop," and Henry Ford based his labor policy upon "purely individual" relationships and the settlement of grievances "man to man." In the great barony of steel, unions had less influence than thirty years earlier. When the United States Steel Corporation was formed, the board of directors, although they tolerated already organized unions, voted, "We are unalterably opposed to any extension of union labor," and in 1910, after the workers lost a disastrous strike, this "soulless corporation," in Gompers' words, eradicated the union from its domain. Its example spread to other fields—transport on the Great Lakes, bituminous coal mining, structural steel and iron construction—related to this central industry of the industrial state.

In coal mining, however, the unions achieved great success. In 1890 rival organizations had coalesced into the United Mine Workers and before the decade was over had won in the bituminous mines of the central competitive field—western Pennsylvania, Ohio, Indiana, and Illinois—a recognition that conditions of labor were to be determined by interstate joint conference between the employers and the employees. Then they moved on to anthracite, where unionization was difficult. Racial differences destroyed labor solidarity and the employers of the "anthracite trust," when confronted with the question of unionism, replied that "anthracite mining is a business, and not a religious, sentimental or academic proposition." One of their number referred to his associates and himself as "those Christian men to whom God has given control of the property rights of the country." The union had the advantage of the leadership of John Mitchell, the conservative and devoted president of the United Mine Workers, and of popular support engendered by hatred of the anthracite monopoly. The anthracite strike of 1902 was a classic of labor history. Eventually the national government forced mediation upon the owners and the unions secured virtual though not nominal recognition. A decade later the United Mine Workers sought to organize the Colorado and West Virginia bituminous fields. The battle in the former area was notable for its fury and the abysmal ignorance of working conditions in his own companies demonstrated by John D. Rockefeller, Jr. In West Virginia judges issued injunctions on any provocation; militia occupied embattled areas; and military men administered martial law. The failure to organize West Virginia was fatal, since its nonunion mines contributed a rapidly increasing proportion of the nation's output. But in 1920 the United Mine Workers had organized over half of the workers in the coal industry.

In transportation the four brotherhoods still stood astride the railroad world. Even though their militant threat to strike for the eight-hour day in 1916 gained popular disfavor, they won their demands. On the other hand, the shop workers, yardsmen, telegraphers, clerks, and maintenance-of-way men were either grouped in minute unions or entirely unorganized. For them the Federation in 1908 established a Railway Employees' Department, but only the period of World War I and government operation of the railroads filled it with membership.

Finally, there were the wage earners of the building trades. These workers had always been extraordinarily successful in attaining organization, and the local character of the market and the handicraft nature of their work enabled them to continue their progress. In the American Federation of Labor they were the core of the craft-union group. In many of the large cities—Chicago, San Francisco, New York—the building trades were effectively organized in labor monopolies. Unpleasant disclosures sporadically revealed their labor leaders constructing personal machines through the grant of jobs, collecting personal graft from employers as "insurance" against strikes, and serving as tools in the competitive warfare between one employer and another. These "labor racketeers" and "labor czars" terrorized both worker and boss.

All in all, by 1920 labor had organized one fifth of the nonagricultural workers of the nation. This figure was far less impressive than that of Great Britain, but in view of employer hostility it was a considerable achievement. For big business shrank neither in influence nor in power during the twentieth century. Its technique for dealing with labor had become almost automatic. In time of peace the industrial giants either established their own detective forces or employed outsiders to guard their property and to keep tabs on union-minded workers and stirrings of discontent. In time of war they hired strikebreakers and employed private armies, either deputy sheriffs or operatives from Pinkerton and his imitators, to protect them in the "right to work." The courts were induced to issue injunctions, and a favorable public opinion was cultivated. The "scab," announced President Eliot of Harvard, was "a very good type of modern hero."

As labor grew powerful, employers outside the pale of big business drew together and spoke in more belligerent tones. Organized on a local scale, as at Dayton or Indianapolis or elsewhere, they became experts in "union smashing" and in maintaining their cities as "open-shop" towns. Organized on trade lines, often in the beginning to bargain collectively with their workers, they became disgusted as workers occasionally broke agreements, and they grew implacable in their hostility to unions. Thus the National Metal Trades Association, established in 1899 among the manufacturers of metal products, disavowed "any intention to interfere with the proper functions of labor organizations," but declared, "we will not admit of any interference with the management of our business" nor "deal with striking employees as a body." The Association worked out a complicated and skillful system of strikebreaking and of dealing with labor organizers. "Special contract operators" or spies were placed in the works to detect the presence of agitators; if a strike broke out, payments from a previously accumulated defense fund afforded compensation; guards were provided, lawyers hired, injunctions sworn out. The Association boasted, "No strikes of any moment have been won by the machinists' union since the organization of the National Metal Trades Association."

Unlike the Metal Trades Association, the National Association of Manufacturers embraced all manufacturers who would join. For the first few years after 1895, when the Association was organized, the tariff and foreign trade absorbed its attention, but in 1902, reflecting a tendency of the twentieth century, it became violently anti-union. According to its directors, its purposes were not so much to break strikes as to carry into effect certain principles and to resist attacks upon these principles by unenlightened workers. The "Principles" were drawn up by conventions and amended frequently. The National Association of Manufacturers was opposed to boycotts and strikes, and to interference which would prevent the employer from determining wages, the number of apprentices, and the help he should hire and fire. The open shop was its insistent war cry. From time to time these principles were interpreted by the presidents of the organization in an appealing rhetoric. One declared, "We are not opposed to good unionism, if such exists anywhere. The American brand of unionism, however, is un-American, illegal and indecent." Another president somewhat mystically asserted, "The real and ideal union is the one between employer and employee." The Association maintained lobbies, sought and obtained political influence, instructed professional men and community leaders in its vision of the proper economic system, and tried to convince the workers "that their employers are their best friends," and that "hysteria and half-baked theories cannot bring us industrial supremacy."

"Pure and Simple Unionism"

Such success as the American Federation of Labor achieved, Gompers and his followers ascribed to the organization's continued devotion to its first principles. Indeed, these labor leaders frequently referred to precedent and tradition with the zeal and awe usually exhibited by members of the legal fraternity. The first article of the official creed prescribed organization of labor on craft lines. McGuire had put the case, "Being organized on special trade lines they can act on trade matters all the more intelligently and practically as well as speedily than in mixed bodies." These crafts were generally composed of skilled white workers, although the Federation did issue charters for a few national unions of unskilled workers and authorized the formation of separate unions for Negroes. Federation officials encouraged all national unions to adopt the policies which had made British unions and a few pioneer American ones successful. In order to retain the loyalty of the worker to his organization in periods of industrial deflation and labor defeat, they urged the establishment of benefits and insurance for sickness. High dues and assessments built up strike funds controlled by the central officers. These officers, moreover, were given centralized authority over their locals and over the calling and conduct of strikes.

The strike and its companion weapon, the boycott, were but means to compel obstinate employers to recognize the union or its agents as the representatives of their workers in the settlement of grievances and the negotiation of trade agreements determining the conditions of labor. The trade agreement was the great contribution of the federation's "new unionism." Before 1896 it had been used only occasionally; now it was to be erected into a system. Such a contractual arrangement between the employer and his employees entailed considerable limitation of the employer's right "to do as he willed with his own." He wished to hire and fire on his own terms; the union counterattacked with the "closed shop" or the "preferential union shop," in which union men were to be exclusively employed or given priority.

The national or international trade unions enjoyed so great an independence in policy and action that the AFL at first seemed rather powerless. Its chief functions were to preserve order in the labor world by preventing "dual" unions and by settling some interunion disputes; it was to spread the union movement by organizing workers and by making local unions into national organizations, a purpose for which it had its own corps of paid organizers; although its strike authority was limited and it had no central strike fund, it possessed the power to levy assessments upon all its members for the support of strikes of which it approved; it represented the workers in matters of national legislation; and through its press, officers, and conventions it was the sounding board for the principles and policies of its members. As it acquired a larger income and staff, as it gained in public tolerance and even esteem, the influence of the central organization grew stronger. Here, too, the leadership of Gompers was an important factor.

In general the American Federation of Labor accepted the machine, the factory, and private capitalism. But within that framework the organization had ideas about desirable conditions of labor. It demanded healthful and sanitary surroundings; it sought in Gompers' words in 1899 a "living wage," a wage "sufficient to maintain him [the laborer] and those dependent upon him in comparative comfort commensurate with his economic and social surroundings," a convenient and dynamic abstraction. But above all the union sought security for the worker. A job must be "made" for him to banish the nightmare of unemployment. Machines, some had thought, occasioned such involuntary idleness, but the leaders of the federation realized it was fruitless to protest against the introduction of machinery. Toward the efficiency movement of the early twentieth century, however, they cherished a distrust lest it mean "the wiping out of our trade and organization," and labor protests prevented its employment in government work. The "making of a job" likewise involved union restrictions on the number of apprentices and the amount of a day's work, union opposition to piecework wages, and a whole series of unproven and intangible union restraints upon output. "Job making" inspired in large part the agitation for a shorter day's work. The dominant motive of the federation in its passionate attachment to the eight-hour day was the desire to divide the available amount of employment among a greater number of workers. Economically the idea might be fallacious, but it was persistent.

From the first the AFL had sought its objectives through economic pressure and negotiation. It opposed political methods; organized labor should have no party of its own and no alliance with existing political organizations. It was said that the Knights of Labor had demonstrated the futility of such political measures and that, entirely aside from the Knights' experience, organized labor was a minority group in the total population. Furthermore, American workers, not class-conscious, were both Republicans and Democrats. Thus political agitation would disrupt the union. A strict adherence to this outlook, however, proved difficult. When a depression like that of the nineties blunted the economic weapon or when an attractive presidential candidate like Bryan was nominated, it was hard to stay on the reservation. State favoritism for the "bosses," apparent in the dearth of labor legislation and "government by injunction," finally drove the Federation to action. In 1906 the annual convention found a way out. After describing a platform of desired legislation, it announced, "We will stand by our friends and administer a stinging rebuke to men or parties who are either indifferent, negligent, or hostile." Since this policy of "reward your friends, punish your enemies" stopped short of forming a separate labor party, the leaders of the Federation could declare their opportunist attitude toward political measures was consistent. Although in 1908 Gompers and other leaders of the AFL derided Taft and the Republican party so bitterly as to become allies of the Democrats, such activity was all "nonpartisan." In 1912 Gompers took a less conspicuous role, but he apparently regarded the election as placing in office an administration sympathetic to his program. In 1916 the American Federation endorsed the Wilson administration and its officers and worked for his reelection.

Criticism and challenge of the accepted canon came from within the Federation. Socialists expressed dissent, for although some of the more radical preferred to remain outside the Federation, which in their estimation was "a cross between a wind bag and a rope of sand," the moderates remained within its fold seeking to unhorse Gompers and to educate the Federation's membership to demand the "overthrowal of the wage system and the establishment of an industrial cooperative commonwealth." They championed a greater centralization of power within the Federation, participation in politics through a labor party, the formation of wage earners into industrial unions, and "the collective ownership by the people of all means of production and distribution." Gompers and his followers stamped out most of the socialist vision in the nineties. The expedience of industrial unionism persisted and in fact some industries, like the women's clothing industry, the brewers, and the United Mine Workers were organized along industrial lines. By 1910 the Federation itself seemed on the point of discarding the doctrine of craft unionism in its purest forms.

The IWW

Nor did the American Federation of Labor include all organized labor. Outside its boundaries remained at one extreme the Railroad Brotherhoods, at another the advanced Amalgamated Clothing Workers' Union, the efficient organization in the men's clothing industry. But the AFL's greatest enemy was the Industrial Workers of the World (IWW).

This organization was established in 1905 by radical socialists to whom Gompers and his tribe were "labor fakers" and by the Western Federation of Miners, an ably led organization whose philosophy had been forged by a series of strikes akin to revolution in the copper and metal mines of the West. Somewhat as the Knights had done, they sought a new society through the destruction of the wage system. One of their hymns, "Paint 'Er Red," expressed their rough-hewn, rowdy outlook:

> "Slaves" they call us, "working plugs," inferior by birth,
> But when we hit their pocketbooks we'll spoil their smiles or mirth—
> We'll stop their dirty dividends and drive them from the earth
> With ONE BIG INDUSTRIAL UNION!

> We hate their rotten system more than any mortals do,
> Our aim is not to patch it up, but build it all anew,
> And what we'll have for government, when finally we're through,
> Is ONE BIG INDUSTRIAL UNION!

The IWW had a stormy career of sects and secessions. The Western Federation of Miners, for instance, soon withdrew. But the IWW's methods of sudden and aggressive strikes and its resort to sabotage—the "strike on the job"—enabled workers who had little money to coalesce quickly into unions and wage an industrial conflict. The exciting and unpolished utterances of its press and leaders and its emphasis upon industrial unionism were useful in breaking down barriers between races and crafts. It appealed, therefore, to the unskilled worker, the migratory and seasonal laborer, the exploited foreigner. In the West the IWW enlisted the workers in mines, oil fields, agriculture, canning, and lumbering. When local authorities, quaking at the red menace, attempted to prevent organization and street speaking, "Wobblies" would descend upon the community from every direction, exercise their "rights," and crowd the jails until officials and people grew tired of the burden of support.

Then the organization invaded the East, appealing to workers whom the AFL had neglected. Its greatest achievement was the strike at Lawrence, Massachusetts, in 1912, when the textile mills, forced to reduce hours by legislation, also reduced wages. Here the revolutionary rhetoric of the IWW was more than matched by the unscrupulous methods used by employers and city officials to combat them. They planted dynamite in the hope that its arranged discovery might cast discredit upon the workers; police fought to prevent parents on strike from sending their children outside the city in order that they might be properly cared for; and an official of an American Federation union actually condoned the clubbing and bayoneting of women and children. The strikers won a substantial increase in wages, but apparently they used the radicalism of the IWW as an expedient—and temporary—means to this end. The IWW moved on to pastures new. World War I brought a debacle. Pacifist and socialist, the organization was easily stigmatized as unpatriotic. Popular hostility, court persecutions, and local vigilantism drove leaders and members into exile, put them into jail, or summarily dispatched them by lynch law. Meanwhile the workers to whom they had appealed might meditate with renewed irony upon the chorus of their ditty, "The Preacher and the Slave":

> You will eat, by and by,
> In that glorious land above the sky;
> Work and pray, live on hay,
> You'll get pie in the sky when you die.

Protective Legislation

Even before the Civil War certain states had taken steps toward protective labor legislation. After the conflict the movement continued. Children were one object of legislative solicitude. Massachusetts, for instance, passed a law in 1866 prohibiting the employment in any factory of children under ten years of age and requiring an eight-hour day and six months of schooling for those between ten and fourteen years of age. Not until 1879, however, was an enforceable statute enacted. Other states followed suit, but by the mid-nineties only twelve states regulated child labor in all gainful occupations. The typical statute applied to manufacturing only, set a minimum age of twelve years, fixed maximum hours at ten a day for those above the minimum age, and accepted a private affidavit that the child had reached the legal working age. One half of the states had such enactments.

Legislation protecting other wage earners was tardy. By 1874 agitation for a shorter workday for women had obtained enough momentum to secure in Massachusetts the passage of a bill providing that "no female over the age [of eighteen] shall be employed in laboring by any person, firm, or corporation in this commonwealth in the manufacture of cotton, woolen, jute or silk fabrics more than ten hours in any one day, or sixty hours in any one week." Because of the large number of women employed in these industries the act really limited the hours of all workers. By the mid-nineties a third of the states apparently had hours legislation for women, but verbal loopholes and uncertainties over constitutionality generally destroyed these acts' effectiveness. In fact, only three states had workable statutes. Meanwhile Massachusetts, to protect the health of all workers and prevent accidents, had modified in 1877 a mass of British legislation into the first factory act in America. Here imitation was rapid.

Many states even established an inspection system for enforcement. But the safety movement of the nineteenth century, like legislation for the protection of children and women, was dwarfed by the massive development of the twentieth century.

For after 1900 the slow stream of labor legislation quickened to a torrent. The American Federation of Labor was only in part responsible for this acceleration; with its ingrained aversion to politics, the AFL was often indifferent or hostile to the statutes enacted. But although the central organization might remain aloof, some national unions and many regional labor groups in state or municipality were taking positions on the battlefront. Nor could the passage of labor legislation be ascribed to the employers. Some were indifferent; more were insistent that the conditions of competition be equalized—if South Carolina would raise her standards, Massachusetts employers could tolerate the raising of theirs. But most employers expressed an innate hostility—such legislation was desirable in Utopia but not in practice. Rather the essentially middle-class Progressive movement was responsible for the floodtide of labor legislation. As Theodore Roosevelt blistered the "malefactors of great wealth" and Woodrow Wilson more chastely pleaded for a social conscience, business was placed upon the defensive. Consumers saw in the laborer a fellow victim of business enterprise. He too was "exploited," he too must be protected from the "cruelty," "greed," and "self-interest" of the industrial system. Studies provided figures of wages and hours for this passion to feed upon. Although they made sober contributions of value, their data on child labor, on night work for women, on the death and maiming of workers by industrial accident, had also an inherent "human-interest" appeal occasionally verging on sentimentality. Armed with facts and feeling, ministers, social and settlement house workers, economists, journalists, socialists and reformers, the National Child Labor Committee, the National Consumers League, the American Association for Labor Legislation, the General Federation of Women's Clubs, marched upon the state legislatures and won results.

Perforce American labor legislation was of the most diverse sorts. Since action by the national government was severely limited by current understandings of the Federal Constitution, the individual states had the chief power of legislation. The earliest laws were passed in the states first touched by the Industrial Revolution. This was one reason, along with the puritan paternalism of New England thinking, for the leadership of Massachusetts. Many western states, whose industrial population was small, passed legislation because of their freedom from tradition and their tendency to look toward the state government for action. The most backward states were in the agricultural South. The fact that forty-eight states were involved in the process both helped and delayed the process of legislation. In some states it was possible to secure more advanced measures than the whole nation would undertake; on the other hand, the adoption or retention of such statutes was hindered by the fear of competition from states with backward standards. Also, the extraordinary difficulty of enacting laws state by state discouraged both reformers and labor leaders. It was one reason for the labor unions' dislike of government action.

In the traditional field of child labor regulation the Progressive era made legislation universal. Labor unions realized that such workers could not be unionized and that their competition with adults could be prevented only through legislation. In the South, before 1900 the most conspicuous region without such legislation, local opinion, marshaled by labor unions, journalists, and clergymen, began to press for the restriction of child labor. The textile industry, in which children did most of the spinning, was alarmed; a measure excluding children under twelve years of age from factory work was characterized by a South Carolinian as "a bill to discourage manufacturing in South Carolina." Shrinking from extreme measures, the state permitted children below the minimum age to work if their earnings were required to support themselves, their widowed mothers, or their disabled fathers. Everywhere exceptions drove holes through seemingly rigorous legislation. But by 1920 the typical child labor enactment forbade employment under fourteen years of age and set an eight-hour day for workers under sixteen years of age.

Far more novel was the rapid enactment of measures for the protection of women workers. Between 1909 and 1917 nineteen states adopted such measures for the first time; twenty states made improvements and extensions of existing legislation. Hours were the chief issue. Whereas in 1900 a ten-hour day was regarded as standard, by 1919 Massachusetts was establishing a forty-eight hour week for women workers in factories, stores, and communication and transportation enterprises. Only a few years before, the treasurer of a Lowell mill had announced that he believed in a nine-hour day "when the millennium arrived, not before." In eight-hour legislation Massachusetts was not the pioneer. California had anticipated her by nearly a decade. The former regained her primacy, however, by the enactment in 1912 of the first minimum wage law for women in the United States. But the Massachusetts law was a feeble instrument. The commission for setting minimum wages was to consider not only the cost of living but also the financial situation of the industry in question and was to rely upon publicity rather than compulsion for an acceptance of its findings. Within a year eight other states passed minimum wage legislation and then the movement petered out. Protective legislation for women faced greater barriers than that for children. For one thing, the courts, as we shall see, dangled above it the Damoclean sword of "unconstitutionality." For another, the labor unions were not uniformly enthusiastic. The American Federation looked askance upon minimum wage laws as a dangerous interference by the state in wage matters better left to union agitation. Some women's groups resented the "inferiority" implied by protective legislation; and, of course, the spokesmen of reactionary business were sure to regard such measures as "subversive" and identical with sin.

The Progressive movement also busied itself with measures to ease the hardships caused by industrial accidents. No matter how thoroughly machinery was protected or workers trained, these accidents happened and the common law, usually placing the complete responsibility upon the worker or his fellows, hampered the injured man in recovering damages. In 1910 every American state had modified these doctrines, but without genuinely solving the problem. Damage suits against employers, however expedited, were slow, wasteful, and uncertain. European nations after the same experience had adopted systems of workmen's compensation which provided an indemnity to the worker or his family. After 1910 the states raced to enact such measures. Wisconsin's was the first to go into operation. In order to escape the hostility of the courts, many of these measures gave the employer the option of contributing to a workmen's compensation scheme or meeting a suit for damages shorn of the protections afforded by common law doctrines of "fellow-servants" and "contributory negligence." By 1920 forty-three states had legislation. All of the states which did not have such laws were in the South.

With workmen's compensation laws, general legislation protecting all workers petered out. Protection to male wage earners was not extensive, though over the years states had passed legislation limiting hours in designated employments such as mining, brickyards, bakeries, or public works; and two states, Oregon and Massachusetts, limited the hours of all men employed in manufacturing establishments to ten a day. In the national field Congress in 1907 had prescribed for railroad trainmen ten hours of rest after sixteen consecutive hours of work, and in 1916 passed the Adamson Act, which assured the same pay for an eight-hour day as had been given earlier for workdays of greater length.

The paucity or limitations of such laws were explained by the indifference of the Progressives and the hostility of the unions. The Progressive movement was interested primarily in the handicapped labor groups. Time and time again it was said that "the men could look after themselves." Gompers and the American Federation of Labor would have paraphrased the statement to read: the unions could look after the workers. For if union members could obtain shorter hours, better wages, and compensation for injuries through state action, what motive was left for remaining within the unions and for paying dues?

Union Activity and the Law

Committed to union measures, the AFL was concerned primarily with preventing restriction upon the union's existence or upon the methods which it could employ. It might frown upon the Oregon law, as it did, but it boiled with passion at injunctions and court decisions affecting boycotts and strikes. After the nineties the legal position of the unions was uncomfortable at best. An injunction and the doctrine of conspiracy lurked around every corner. The courts permitted strikes on hour and wage questions and primary boycotts, but strikes for the closed shop and sympathetic strikes met with judicial disfavor. As for picketing, there was disagreement, although one Federal judge declared, "There is and can be no such thing as peaceful picketing, any more than there can be chaste vulgarity or peaceful mobbing or lawful lynching. When men want to persuade, they do not organize a picket line." Labor leaders looked wistfully over the water to Great Britain, where courts rarely hampered labor activities with injunctions and where Parliamentary legislation specifically rejected the doctrine of criminal conspiracy as applied to combinations of employees, authorized peaceful picketing, and exempted the agents and members of unions from suits for unlawful acts claimed to have been committed in behalf of the union.

Without similar protection American labor was vulnerable. Early in the century two cases brought American labor leaders to the verge of panic. The first was the Danbury hatters' case. A hat manufacturer of Danbury, Connecticut, brought suit against 197 members of the United Hatters of North America. Alleging that the nationwide boycott waged by the unions against his hats was a conspiracy restraining interstate commerce, the hatter sought triple damages—$240,000—under the Sherman Anti-Trust Act. The defendants, many of whom had never heard of the boycott and rarely attended union meetings, had their homes and savings accounts attached because they were union members. In 1908 the Supreme Court sustained the damage suits and for the first time definitely asserted the Sherman Anti-Trust Act applied to labor. The hatters' union and the AFL raised the money and restored the houses but not the bank accounts to the unfortunate union members. Meanwhile the Bucks Stove and Range Company secured an injunction against the Federation because the *American Federationist,* the organization's newspaper, published the former's name on its "unfair list" and thus furthered a boycott against the company's products. When Gompers and other officials ignored the injunction, they were sentenced to imprisonment or fines, from which they escaped only on technicalities. Nor was the consternation aroused by these cases allayed by the fact that in both instances the National Association of Manufacturers was involved.

In the eyes of Gompers, the Sherman Anti-Trust Act and these decisions operated "to outlaw organized labor"; the unions consequently demanded legislation exempting them from the Sherman Act. Their drive culminated in provisions in the Clayton Anti-Trust Act of 1914. In that statute the unions received the pious comfort that "the labor of a human being is not a commodity or article of commerce." One section declared that nothing in the anti-trust laws should be construed to "forbid or restrain individual members from lawfully carrying out the legitimate objects" of labor organization; another forbade the issuance of injunctions in disputes between employers and employees "unless necessary to prevent irreparable injury to property or to a property right" and enjoined a jury trial in criminal contempt cases. Gompers hailed this enactment as "labor's Magna Carta." Cooler voices pointed out that several "weasel words"—for instance, "lawfully," "peacefully," and "legitimate objects"—had been inserted into its provisions. Actually the statute was simply declaratory of existing law.

The Constitutionality of Labor Laws

Sooner or later most labor legislation came before the courts for review, for the judiciary had to determine whether the legislature had acted within the limits imposed upon it by constitutions. The Fifth and Fourteenth Amendments, for instance, of the Federal Constitution might place through interpretation severe restrictions upon the variety and extent of labor legislation. The Fifth Amendment declared in part, "No person shall . . . be deprived of life, liberty, or property without due process of law." This provision applied solely to the Federal government. Toward the close of Section 1 of the Fourteenth Amendment this prohibition was applied to the states:

No State shall make or enforce any law which shall abridge the privileges and immunities of citizens of the United States; nor shall any State deprive any person of life, liberty, or property, without due process of law; nor deny to any person within its jurisdiction the equal protection of the laws.

But some restriction upon personal rights for the protection of society was obviously desirable even in a highly individualistic society; it has been imposed under the "police power." Like other legal conceptions, the police power had vague attributes, but considerations of public health, public safety, and public welfare—equally vague ideas—were deemed to justify its exercise.

As different philosophies in state and Federal courts gave content and definition to these concepts, confusion resulted. Still out of the ruck certain general tendencies emerged. There was little hesitation in declaring state regulation of child labor constitutional. Children were obviously not capable of making valid contracts, and they were entitled to protection as wards of the state. In the case of women the constitutionality of regulation was recognized more slowly. Early laws fixing their hours of labor were declared unconstitutional—a violation of their freedom of contract; but in 1908 the Supreme Court declared constitutional the Oregon law limiting hours to ten a day for women in industry on the ground that "her physical structure and a proper discharge of her maternal functions justify legislation to protect her from the greed . . . of man."

Protective legislation for all workers had a more uncertain history. In 1898 the Supreme Court in an epochal decision, Holden *v.* Hardy, held that the Utah statute limiting hours in mines was constitutional. The court declared it was a valid exercise of the police power; it implied that such legislation was necessary to place the parties on terms of equality in making a contract, and asserted that an action to protect the freedom of contract of employees would come with better grace from them than from their employers. In 1905 the court declared in the famous case of Lochner *v.* New York that a limitation of the hours of workers in bakeries passed beyond the legitimate exercise of the police power. Finally, in 1917, the same court declared that the Oregon act establishing ten hours as a maximum day for all employees in factories was constitutional. "It is now demonstrable that the considerations which were patent as to miners in 1898 are today operative, to a greater or less degree, throughout the industrial system." Workmen's compensation acts, at first rejected by the state courts, were ultimately pronounced constitutional. In 1917 the Federal Supreme Court declared the New York law "a reasonable exercise of the police power of that state."

The prospect before organized labor in 1917 was serene. In that year a remarkable series of Supreme Court decisions validated a number of labor laws. An evenly divided court upheld a minimum wage legislation for women; a majority approved of the Oregon Ten-Hour Act, the Adamson Act, and nearly every statutory variation of workmen's compensation. The political support of the Administration by organized labor had apparently paid some dividends. But World War I presented a new crisis. Was it an opportunity to advance? Or did it threaten retrogression?

An International Economic Order

"Rule Britannia"

In the period between the mid-fifties of the last century and the outbreak of World War I in the second decade of this, foreign trade and investment operated and developed within a framework the details of which had been foreshadowed at the end of the first half of the nineteenth century. The new period was one of peace. Although conflicts, of which the American Civil War was easily the most severe, broke out from time to time on every continent except Australia, they did not involve a clash between great naval powers; and the sea, the avenue of international trade, was comparatively unvexed by blockades, embargoes, and depredations. Generally speaking, it was an era in which private enterprise undertook and operated the processes of international economics. Government corporations and monopolies in this area were almost unknown; government regulation, control, and promotion were common enough, but compared to the mercantilist systems of earlier centuries and to the oncoming restrictions of the era of warfare and welfare in the twentieth, government "interference"—for such it was significantly and commonly called—was at a minimum. Comparatively speaking, it was a period of free trade and of free investment. Individuals and groups of individuals sold and bought where they chose and could; lent and borrowed in the same manner.

The overlord of this international system was Great Britain; its capital was London; its international police force, the British navy. Though energetic newcomers, like Germany, Japan, and the United States, had toward the end of the period whittled down her preeminence, the United Kingdom, entirely aside from her Colonies and the Dominions, remained before World War I the greatest trading nation. Her imports were 17.4 percent and her exports were 15.4 percent of the world's total in each category. She was indubitably the world's largest banker. Her long-term investments overseas were in 1913 roughly $18,656,372,000. Borrowers from all over the world turned first to her great private banks and development companies for their funds. She was the financier, furthermore, of the world's commerce. In this period the gold standard became truly international. In 1821 Great Britain adopted gold monometallism. In the seventies Germany and France had followed suit. The United States, as we have seen, ceased in 1873 the free coinage of silver at the mint and, after experiments with a modified silver coinage and legal tender paper, had by the nineties abandoned this course and taken adequate measures for the redeemability in gold of its varied issues. In the same decade even the Orient had partially adopted gold. Internationally speaking, the gold standard was a sterling standard. Though the banks in the great financial capitals—Paris, Berlin, and New York— might finance through their credits a part of their national commerce, even they turned to London for supplementary assistance. London had the markets for commodities, the purchasers and speculators to deal in them, the warehouses to store them, and the banking system with branches all over the world to provide short-term credit. The sterling bill had universal acceptability. American exporters took it in payment; American importers sought it to discharge their indebtedness. To complete the circle Great Britain had the largest merchant marine in the world. In 1914 its net tonnage of 12,415,000 was approximately 40 percent of the world's total and it carried just over half the world's commerce.

In view of this extraordinary achievement, British policy was bound to govern the conditions under which a considerable share of international economic transactions took place. As far as investment was concerned, Sir Edward Grey, Secretary of State for Foreign Affairs, remarked in 1914, "British financiers run their business quite independent of politics, and, if we attempt to interfere, they naturally consider that we come under some obligation." Though this might be the cabinet's intent and a cogent statement of the reasons therefore, the government in actuality frequently intervened by diplomacy to assure that its citizens had a chance to invest elsewhere and to win concessions esteemed profitable. In addition to this burden of promotion, the government undertook to protect the investments of its citizens from discrimination, defaults, and shabby treatment—but only on occasion. There was no rigid formula of action, unless the calculation of what seemed feasible or unfeasible in individual instances can be so denominated. As for trade, Great Britain had by 1860 completed the structure of policy which was to endure essentially unaltered until World War I. The repeal of the Navigation Acts had opened every trade, even the coasting one, to the vessels of every nation. As for tariff, Great Britain was a free trade country with duties for revenue on about a dozen articles. By a series of commercial treaties she had systematized a most liberal interpretation of the most-favored-nation clause. Concessions granted by the signers to each other were extended to third parties.

In spite of the immense prestige and importance of this example, it failed of universal imitation. Though the German government might be said like Great Britain's to have let economic considerations take their course in the matter of foreign investments, France mingled inextricably political with private considerations, public with private agencies. Nor did either France or Germany follow Great Britain, as for a time seemed likely, into free trade. After 1875 their industrialists received moderate protection, and agrarian interests, landlords and peasants, menaced by importations and falling prices, wrung from ministries almost prohibitive duties. In contrast with the more complicated devices of a later and earlier mercantilism, these tariffs were crude devices for directing or decreasing trade and the general level of duties in 1900, in spite of the drift to protection, still was lower than in 1850.

In the later nineteenth century a renewed interest in colonies, protectorates, and spheres of one sort or another seemed at first glance likely to cloud the purity of the international order here set down. The great powers of Europe, Japan, and the United States, all or severally, fell upon the dark continent of Africa, upon the storied wealth and actual poverty of Asia, and upon islands in the Pacific and Caribbean. They sought to acquire new areas and influence, or to enlarge their established positions by war, negotiations, partitions and exchanges. The motives for this empire-building were not simple. Unless the endocrinologists isolate a gland whose secretions are responsible, it is possible to give only a confused and irrational explanation for imperialistic phenomena. Statesmen and peoples rejoiced at the increased territory and population subject to their flag and embraced the opportunity to carry their way of life to backward or misguided peoples, in spite of the painful obligations involved. Amateurs in the Malthusian menace demanded colonies as an outlet for surplus population. More mundane economic factors were involved. Colonies were sought as markets for manufactured goods, as sources of raw materials, and as areas destined to be served and developed by investment capital. Some thought these prosaic objectives were difficult of realization unless the mother country and its dependencies were bound together by various preferences. These might exclude foreign shipping, give favors to investors and concessionaires showing the right flag, and encourage a reciprocal trade by assimilating the dependent area into the tariff laws of the mother country or by partially removing or lowering duties in the colony on the goods of the mother country or on the goods of the colony in the mother country or both. That this was not the inevitable result of imperialism, Great Britain demonstrated. Within her empire, the greatest in the world, there was no prohibition on the shipping of other countries. Between 1898 and 1907 the dominions gave some British products a preference; she reciprocated with none. Her colonies, with the exception of ten in the West Indies, had no preferential rates for British goods.

The American Pattern

The core of American international economic policy was the tariff. There the parallelism with Europe ceased, for in the timing of its protective measures and the extent of its protection the United States was unique. The movement got underway during the Civil War. When the exigencies of Federal finance required heavy taxation, it was natural that imports bear their burden. Since internal revenue taxes on manufacturing, often on successive processes, were greatly increased, it seemed unfair to handicap American producers vis-à-vis foreign ones unless duties on competing imports were raised as recompense. In spite of considerable statutory jockeying in the decades following the war, the new arrangements persisted essentially unaltered. The nineties, however, proved a significant ten years for the protective movement. They began with the McKinley tariff of 1890, one which again raised duties, continued in the Wilson-Gorman Act of 1894 by which the Democrats failed signally to alter the program of their rivals, and closed with the Dingley Act of 1897, jacking rates to new levels. For a tariff this measure proved to be exceptionally long lived. Finally, in 1909 and 1913, there was first a modification and then a partial withdrawal from the protective regime. In the latter year the Underwood-Simmons Act at last enacted arrangements that accorded in some logical fashion with the fact that the United States was the most powerful industrial nation in the world. By this time raw materials—wool, sugar, iron ore, hides, coal, and lumber—were on the free list and the duties on manufactured articles were lowered and simplified.

The arguments by which the general protection policy was advocated or made palatable to the groups, including consumers, outside the benefited area stressed the wisdom of protecting the tender experiments by Americans with new enterprises, like silk and tinplate, the infant industry argument which was as old as Hamilton, and moved on to the assertion that protection kept American factories running and gave the laborer a full dinner pail, a crude forecast of the full employment program of a later period. If the counter-argument that protection interfered with the international specialization of production along lines of natural advantage carried little weight, the aphorism that it conferred unnecessary advantages upon big business—"the tariff is the mother of the trusts"—helped explain the retreat from protection during the Progressive era. Beneath these verbal formulations matter-of-fact needs and pressures operated. As we have seen, the tariff was more than an expression of commercial policy, it was a means of raising revenue, indeed until the passage of the income tax amendment in 1913 it was on the whole the chief source of federal income. Thus fiscal considerations were frequently overriding. Nor was the position of the American farmer toward the tariff as simple as in some European countries. Imposts on wheat, corn and cotton were meaningless, since America exported these products and the domestic price was the world one. Levies on dairy products and potatoes afforded protection to only a limited fringe of producers in the border regions. On the other hand, shepherds of American sheep and planters of American sugar feared business obliteration without protection; the duties consequently were high, complicated, and persistent. Moreover, the equal representation of the states in the Senate gave the agricultural regions an influence disproportionate to their population. Finally, American manufacturers, whether they needed duties to survive or not, naturally preferred to limit the number of competitors for the market. The American tariff was not, therefore, a response to abstract reasoning. Logrolling, compromises, bargains, defiled the process of enactment. Though a defeated presidential candidate was greeted with derision when he asserted, "The tariff question is a local question," the observation had practical insight.

From time to time reciprocity tampered with this scheme of things. The United States gave concessions to the trade of a particular country and avoided generalizing such concessions by an interpretation of the most-favored-nation clause which differed from the one currently in vogue in Europe. On the Continent the extension of a privilege was "unconditional" and therefore applied to all of the nation's foreign trade treaties. The United States, however, adopted a "conditional" most-favored-nation clause so that concessions were granted to one nation and might be extended to others when they too made concessions. Protected by this conditional gloss, the United States and Canada in 1854 entered into a reciprocity treaty which admitted free to each area the raw materials of the other. Ten years later, at the insistence of the United States, the treaty was denounced. In 1875 a reciprocity treaty with Hawaii admitted free to this country a list of commodities of which the sugar grown by the expanding plantation economy of the islands was the most important; the reciprocal free-list on American imports into the islands embraced many manufactured articles, grain, and breadstuffs. The treaty lasted until Hawaii's annexation. In 1903 the United States agreed to reduce its duties on Cuban products, again notably sugar, by 20 percent and Cuba reduced hers on imports from the United States by 20 to 40 percent. There were occasional endeavors, and they were little more than that, to transmute these specific occasions into a general policy. The McKinley Act of 1890 placed coffee, tea, hides, sugar, and molasses on the free list, but permitted the President to impose duties upon them unless the countries from which they came gave concessions on American imports. Actually, this legislatively bestowed weapon was aimed at reciprocity with Latin America; seven agreements resulted. Its abrogation on the passage of the Wilson-Gorman Act in 1894 created resentment.

On the whole, the reciprocity program flowed from no carefully considered or consistent commercial policy. Political considerations, the desire to bring Hawaii within the American orbit, largely explained the treaty of 1875. The Cuban treaty of 1903 was ratified amidst a Rooseveltian clamor over America's "moral obligations" to the island, the "Pearl of the Antilles" in the vernacular of the Spanish-American War. In view of the multiplicity of the factors involved, it was difficult to appraise with precision the effects of reciprocity policy. For one thing, the policy admittedly gave the Hawaiian and Cuban sugar producers a preferred position in the American market and consequently stimulated their sugar production. On the other hand, the general increase in trade which everywhere followed a reciprocity treaty was only in part ascribable to the policy.

As the enumeration of the reciprocity treaties suggests, the device was often a precursor or postlude to political encroachments upon the sovereignties of others. In this field European countries had taken the lead and the United States was a late-comer. From time to time, during the decades following the Mexican War, Americans and their spokesmen had lisped the clichés of imperial expansion, but most of these verbal gropings came to little. This aloofness from overseas expansion the Spanish-American War shattered. Most Americans had not anticipated an imperialist outcome from a war fought ostensibly to make Cuba free, but a combination of quixotism, national pride, and a desire for commercial advantages led the people and President McKinley, almost to their own surprise, to acquire an overseas empire. The Hawaiian Islands were annexed during the conflict, later we secured a favored position in Cuba, the peace treaty gave us Puerto Rico and Guam outright, and ceded the Philippines to us for a nominal payment. The last were the chief booty. Undoubtedly there were altruistic motives for their annexation, but the debates in the Senate and the record of President McKinley's conversion to the policy of annexation show that the Philippines were desired as a base for commercial expansion in the Orient. These islands were to be the equivalent for us of the ports and concessions obtained by other nations in China. Manila was a coaling-station on the way to the Orient and, like the British Hong Kong, was to be an entrepôt for commerce with China.

Although the unlimited possibilities of the Pacific inspired the imagination of American statesmen, the course of American Empire was chiefly southward into the Caribbean area. The Roosevelt Administration gave vigor and urgency to the construction of the Panama Canal, tightened American control over Cuba, and acted as receiver for bankrupt governments around the Caribbean. By 1907 a treaty was made with Santo Domingo under which Americans administered the customhouses and set aside a certain portion of the receipts to pay off the nation's creditors. The Taft-Knox Administration found this "preventive action" to its liking, and Woodrow Wilson, "an idealistic President . . . became in fact the most extraordinary interventionist in Latin America in the history of the United States."

The motives for the creation of an American Empire in the Caribbean ran the gamut of imperialism—if the utterances of the statesmen responsible for it can be believed. Here, as elsewhere, Theodore Roosevelt exhibited his indifference to economic considerations and decried the huckstering aspects of imperialism. Taft announced with considerably less bounce that the diplomacy of his Administration in this area, "substituting dollars for bullets," would be "an effort frankly directed to the increase of American trade." Wilson and Bryan hoped the turbulent Latin American nations would prefer "republican forms of government" and American investments to "foreign concessionaires." All in all, strategic considerations, particularly the protection of the Panama Canal which had not been neutralized by the United States, and the desire to introduce law and order into distracted nations, were just as likely to explain the American concern with the Caribbean as were trade and finance.

Whether American territorial acquisitions dated from the turn of the century or earlier, the United States as far as possible placed them on a favored footing through tariff regulation. In general, the colonies were to give preference to American goods, and colonial goods were to be given preference in the market of the mother country. The simplest way was to include the former within the tariff walls of the latter. This was done at once with Alaska and Hawaii, and with Puerto Rico in 1902 after a delay occasioned by the American beet and cane sugar industries. In the Philippines, however, the treaty with Spain required the United States for ten years to give Spanish vessels and trade the same treatment accorded to similar American enterprises. When this restriction lapsed in 1909, various American interests—tobacco planters, cigar manufacturers, and the growers of cane and beet sugar—prevented the immediate realization of a complete freedom of trade. Almost at once most American products were admitted free to the islands while importations from other countries were burdened with duties, but it was not until 1913 that the Underwood-Simmons Tariff Act finally removed the earlier quotas on the importation into this country of Philippine tobacco and sugar.

Undoubtedly the American system bound the colonies closer to the

United States. In 1915 the United States virtually monopolized the commerce of Hawaii and Alaska, possessed 80 percent of the external trade of Puerto Rico, and in the Philippines had increased the small fractions of the early century to 50 percent of the archipelago's imports and 45 percent of its exports. In every case absolute totals had greatly increased. The American Empire as a whole purchased American textiles, machinery, flour, and gadgets; it supplied a flood of raw materials—salmon, sugar, tobacco, vegetable oils, pineapples and hemp. But this interchange of goods often inflicted competitive losses upon American producers and shaped the economic life of the colonies in directions not always favorable to the real welfare of their inhabitants. Undoubtedly the colonial system cost the American government money; even without it, the United States would have had much of their trade. Compared with the total foreign commerce of the country, the trade with our territories was tiny. In 1915 they took 7 percent of our exports and provided 9 percent of our imports.

These figures certainly demonstrated the comparative unimportance of the American Empire. The colonial possessions of our commercial rivals were larger in area, population, and potentialities. Yet the United States, in view of the commercial policy in its own possessions, could hardly demand an equality of economic opportunity in English, French, German, Russian, or Japanese dependencies. Nor was the attempt made. There were, however, vast areas like that of China where European influences had not yet hardened into commercial preferencs, though they threatened to do so, and where the United States was unwilling to copy the schemes of its contemporaries because it either held back on the ground of high principle or entered the race too late to be effective. To cope with a situation of this delicacy, European nations in the African Congo had already subscribed to an international agreement giving the trade of all comers similar treatment and in China the United States had been insisting for decades that the privileges granted to any nation by China, usually under duress, should be extended to all. At the close of the century when the decrepit Chinese Empire seemed about to dissolve into separate and perhaps exclusive spheres of influence, the United States government, with the sympathy of Great Britain if not at her suggestion, dispatched the open door notes to the countries involved. In them the American Secretary of State, John Hay, asked the recipients to undertake that in their spheres, treaty port rights would not be curtailed, that the Chinese tariff would apply to all merchandise "no matter to what nationality it may belong," that it should be collected by Chinese officials, and that within the spheres of influence no discriminations should be made in the port dues between vessels of different nationalities or in the charges on the railroads, no matter from what nation the merchandise came. When most nations had accepted this declaration, John Hay declared a

universal affirmation. But the open door, aside from its emotional usefulness proved a feeble formula. There were constant complaints, well sub-
stantiated, of its violation. In its original and narrow definition, it neither
abolished the spheres of influence nor mentioned the matter of equality
of investment opportunities. But of that, more later.

Ships and Policy

Though Great Britain's merchant marine was the unquestioned mistress of the seas, the United States just before World War I
had the third largest tonnage in the world. No figures could be more
delusive when foreign commerce was in question. The greater part of the
American marine was employed in the Great Lakes or in the coasting
trade. Great Britain and Germany both surpassed our marine in foreign
commerce; we were in the ruck with Norway, Italy, Japan, and France.
In the circumstances the portion of American overseas trade carried by
American flag ships declined. Whereas in the late fifties the percentage,
on the basis of value of cargo, was 74, in 1914 the percentage of our imports and exports, again by value, transported by American vessels was
only 9.7. The explanations for this regression were predominantly technical and economic changes in shipbuilding and ship operating, changes in
which the United States did not effectively participate. National policy
was a minor but contributory factor.

In spite of the successive triumphs of steam in the first half of the
nineteenth century, the sailing vessel after the Civil War still had its
usefulness. On the North Atlantic route between the United States and
western Europe, the most traveled ocean highway in the world, the coal
for the new means of propulsion was both available and cheap. But vessels
with long voyages to distant ports in the Pacific and the Indian oceans
were unsure either of coal or of reasonable prices. Eventually an improved
economy in the use of coal or the shortening of sea routes—the opening
of the Suez in 1869 was in this respect epoch-making—eased a dilemma
which the discovery of new coal supplies and the substitution of oil later
almost removed from consideration. These achievements came slowly, and
meanwhile bulk cargoes requiring no scheduled delivery and traveling at
low rates aided the perpetuation of sail.

The grain trade from the Pacific coast to European ports fulfilled
these requirements. As the American wheat empire moved into California
and the Pacific Northwest, a fleet of sailing vessels annually repaired
thither in search of charters to carry the golden cargoes around the Horn.
The voyage to market was fourteen thousand miles. For this grain trade
American builders in the two decades following the Civil War created a
special ship. It had some of the features of the clippers—the flat floors, or

bottoms, the great length, the easy lines. On the other hand it avoided the extreme concave bow and, although still heavily rigged, discarded the higher sails, divided the larger ones, and occasionally added a fourth mast with a fore and aft rig. All this contributed to ease in handling. These creations were larger than the largest clippers—the *Roanoke* could carry 5,400 deadweight tons—and had sailing records that were fairly comparable; in operation their labor costs were lower than their predecessors of the fifties. In spite of their superiority, they were still wooden vessels. Almost all were built in a few large yards along the Maine coast, for in this state the old craft of wooden shipbuilding took a last stand. Wages were low, attractive alternate occupations few, and the required skills and habits the possession of a considerable seacoast population. The builders, however, had to go far afield to Virginia, Maryland, Ohio, and even to the Pacific Northwest for their timber supplies, or else substitute inferior woods. Survival, even on these conditions, was impossible once wooden ships confronted first the competition of iron and then of steel sailing vessels. In the use of these superior materials British shipbuilding and the technological processes which clustered about it were superior to the American and by the end of the seventies their yards were launching flotillas while disaster swept all but a few builders on the Maine coast. Upon this disadvantage of higher costs for inferior vessels was piled the higher expense of manning and supplying American ships. On these accounts an English ship of one thousand gross tons cost $650 to $800 a month; an American $1,100 to $1,250. Toward the end of the century, therefore, our participation in the Pacific grain trade and other long trades had slid down to a small fraction of what it once had been.

This decline was a grim portent. For many of the factors accounting for it operated with even greater force in the case of steam vessels. In the midcentury these were ships of the future; by the outbreak of World War I those of the present. In 1914 sailing vessels constituted less than 2 percent of the British merchant tonnage, while their percentage of the American was just under 20. This discrepancy existed in large measure because the steamship was an exceedingly complicated product and many highly scattered operations were involved in its creation. At the end of the experimental period, say, by the late 1860's, iron had demonstrated its superiority to wood for the hull, and the propeller and the compound engine theirs to paddle wheels and more simple power plants. Low-cost building depended upon a matured iron industry, fortunately located, and upon a highly developed engineering industry. All these England had. The United States did not. To be sure, advances and adaptations were made on this side of the Atlantic. The construction of ocean-going steamers moved to the Delaware and closer proximity to raw materials, and integrated concerns with capital secured the necessary technical equipment for large-scale operations. Nonetheless, the location of coal and iron was probably more advantageous on the Clyde; wages of skilled workers were lower in Great Britain; and the cost of iron and later of steel generally higher in this country, in part because of the price policy of the "steel trust," the shipbuilder's *bête noir*. At the turn of the century vessels were 25 to 50 percent cheaper in Great Britain than here. Americans, therefore, built no *Titanic*, gross tonnage 46,489, or *Vaterland* with one of 52,282.

Meanwhile accompanying changes revolutionized the shipping business. Ownership by shares or fractional shares in the vessel gave way to great corporations issuing stock and operating on schedule their huge specialized fleets over the network of sea routes radiating from Western Europe to North and South America, Africa and the Orient. These greyhounds competed so fiercely for passengers, mail, express and high class freight that at the turn of the century, like other big business, they united in conferences and pools to fix rates, apportion ports, divide traffic, abate the nuisance of differential rates and kill off intruders by rate wars and fighting ships. At a lower level, the drab workhouse of the sea, the steam tramp, took over the bulk trades once carried by the sail freighters. In all this the United States had little part. Here as in the case of the sailing ship, American vessels cost more to build and, when built, more to man. In the category of small freighters wages in 1901 were $860 a month for nineteen men on an American ship, $491 for eighteen on a British, and $341 for fourteen on a Norwegian vessel.

Throughout the era policy toward the merchant marine never exhibited the intelligence displayed by European rivals—neither the comparative freedom of British policy nor the rigorousness of German or French. Instead, it hesitated, unable even to repeal or rationalize the somewhat contradictory inheritance of its past. Thus, the American coasting trade was closed to foreign flags. With the acquisition of colonies this prohibition was extended to Puerto Rico and Hawaii, but not to the Philippines. No unwillingness on the part of statutemakers to assimilate a distant geography into the American coastline explained this exception; instead the justified expectation that the American merchant marine could not expand sufficiently to carry on the business deterred them. Nor did Congress, though such proposals were often urged upon it, revive the differential tariff on goods imported in American vessels, a device first adopted in 1789, or long exempt American ships from the payment of tolls on the Panama Canal. Another protective measure was to deny American registry to foreign-built vessels. American operators could not buy, therefore, in the cheapest market. Even if this handicap were repealed and owners given the chance to purchase "free ships," the differential in operating costs remained. Such might be overcome through government subsidies or "contracts" for scheduled lines and by sailing and steaming "bounties" to vessels picking up business where they could find it.

Time after time proposals for all or some of these measures entered the arena of debate. The arguments varied from the sentimental to the realistic. A merchant marine ministered to national pride, promoted American trade, and with a shipbuilding industry was essential for American defense. The last assertion was given new cogency as the United States acquired its colonial empire. But little was accomplished. Before 1900 contracts had brought into being a short-lived line to Brazil, the Pacific Mail to the Orient and between California and Panama, and the American Line in the North Atlantic. Congress never enacted bounties. Admission of foreign-built vessels into American registry was not vouchsafed until 1912 and 1914, too late to be effective in the period under discussion. For so little result from so much talk and movement, the conflict in interest between shipbuilders and ship owners over free ships was in part responsible. The indifference of agrarian interests to the merchant marine and the incompatibilty of direct and open grants to private enterprise with current conceptions of the proper relation between government and business explained more. Perhaps also most Americans were content to let others carry their goods as long as they did so cheaply and fairly. A Congressional committee in 1914 after searching investigations disproved the assertion that European merchant marines discriminated against the United States. These findings as a whole assumed a world at peace. A century earlier, war had inflicted penalties upon the American merchant marine; it had also given it profits.

A Shifting Foreign Trade

The payments which Americans made to others for shipping services were one of those invisible items, along with remittances by immigrants, tourist expenditures, and interest on foreign loans, which enabled the United States throughout this period to retain its so-called favorable balance in the foreign merchandise trade. Between 1860 and 1914, in only sixteen years did the value of imports exceed that of exports; most of such instances were in the sixties and early seventies. Meanwhile, of course, the totals of merchandise exports and imports greatly increased. Between 1879 and 1913, to take available statistics and avoid the distortions of wartime trade, the value of American exports in terms of constant 1913 dollars increased from $810 million to $2,448,000,000; and the value of imports, again in terms of constant 1913 dollars, from $479 million to $1,793,000,000. In spite of this astonishing achievement the foreign trade of Great Britain and Germany before World War I still surpassed that of the United States. To both these leaders as well as to many other European nations, foreign trade, judged by the ratio it bore to domestic activity, was more vital than to the United States.

Inevitably, the nature of the commodities whose values contributed to these dollar totals reflected developments in the economies of the United States and of other nations, changes, that is to say, in conditions of supply and demand. On the latter score Europe continued to become in the latter half of the nineteenth century, as earlier, more industrialized and more urbanized. Her factories needed raw materials, her population must be fed. The policy of European nations reflected the pace of these changes. England, for instance, in 1846 had repealed the Corn Laws which had heavily taxed the importation of grain. On this side of the Atlantic as long as there were people to enter farming and new acres to be acquired cheaply or "for free," Americans could meet European requirements. Between 1850 and almost to the end of the century, agricultural commodities constituted the largest percentage, from 73 to 83, of total exports. The penetration of the western states by railroads, the lowering of transport costs to the seaboard and for ocean freights across the Atlantic worked in the same direction.

Cotton had been the dazzling exemplar of these commercial relationships. But the Civil War had reduced cotton exports to a mere trickle and encouraged British factories to seek supplies elsewhere. By the end of the period of Reconstruction in the South, in 1880, exports of raw cotton had attained quantitatively the level they had enjoyed in the golden decade of the fifties; this total grew rather steadily until in 1913 it reached a pre-World War I peak of 4,562,000,000 pounds. England, once the chief consumer of the American staple, was now joined by the cotton industries of other European nations and of Japan.

More spectacular than cotton's ability to hold a prominent place in the export trade was the enlargement of the role of other agricultural commodities. While pork and other hog products were a relatively large increment in this increase, exports of wheat began to spurt forward in the seventies and at the turn of the century had multiplied some four or five times. This inrush of agricultural products from the New World so endangered European farmers that an Austrian commentator compared the importation of American grain with that of the precious metals in the sixteenth century which ruined the mining industries of Europe and wrought a social transformation. When the distressed agriculture of Europe turned to livestock, it was soon confronted with new American competition, for the packing-house products—bacon, pork, and lard— which America had always exported were now joined by the trade in beef, first of animals on the hoof and then of dressed carcasses kept fresh by the new methods of refrigeration. European governments, at the bidding of their agricultural factions, constantly interrupted this trade by embargoes and prohibitions based upon the alleged presence of animal disease or the employment of unsanitary methods of packing.

In some continental countries tariffs clamped down on imports from America. England, on the other hand, accepted the fact of American competition. Supplies of American grain drove Russian and German wheat from the English market and American meat products captured it from European suppliers. As for her own domestic producers, England was comparatively reconciled to the necessity of transferring their labor and capital out of agriculture into other callings. By the turn of the century Europeans began to turn to other new regions—the Argentine, Australia, and Canada—for the source of their agricultural imports. Though the violent years of the twentieth century might temporarily reverse these trends of the nineteenth, they could not obliterate the record of those trends. The growth of American agricultural production had depended primarily upon the expansion of the domestic urban market, but the marginal importance of foreign demand could not be ignored. In the five years ending in 1909 exports judged by volume were as a percentage of American output 18.6 for wheat, 11.3 for corn distributed outside the United States farm sector, and 65 for cotton. They had been somewhat higher throughout the 1890's. Some time during that decade or a little later, agricultural products began to lose their preeminence in the columns of total exports.

Their decline was so gradual that by the beginning of World War I, agricultural exports still accounted for almost half. The victorious newcomer in the export column was, of course, manufactured products. Although the rough reason for their triumph was the immense increase of manufacturing within the United States, an emphasis upon this generalized explanation conceals the many delicate shifts in the roster of exports, an extremely varied collection of commodities. Originally the manufactured commodities which were exported were ones dependent for their materials in a direct primitive sort of way upon the field, the forest, or the mine. American textile and shoe exports depended on cotton, wool, and leather; exports as far apart as ships or barrels on American forests. The spectacular omen of the new industrial age was petroleum; it was at once dependent upon foreign markets. As the fields of Pennsylvania poured fourth a deluge of oil seemingly impossible either to stop or to control, refiners discovered a market in Europe where, with the exception of England, there had been a shortage of fats and oils for a generation or more. In a very literal sense, kerosene promised light. A Norwegian scholar recalled how his countrymen in the 1860's, dazzled by the light of a petroleum lamp, "could hardly tear themselves away from the wonder they saw before their eyes." How to get the product to these consumers was a problem; even to carry petroleum, with its reputation for explosiveness, across the Atlantic was a problem. At the end of 1861 the first shipload of crude reached London: to get a crew the shipper had had to get the men drunk and practically shanghai them. Exports, among which kerosene soon surpassed crude, increased nearly fifteen times between 1862 and 1866; by the mid-seventies 75 percent of the illuminating oil refined in the United States went abroad. England was the greatest consumer. Though competitive suppliers in Russia and in the Far East had at the turn of the century successfully challenged the American "oil trust," the proportion of the world market supplied by the United States in 1914 was almost half again as large as it had been ten years earlier.

Petroleum's remarkable expansion in the export trade had taken place without any governmental assistance, except for the conventional motions of promotion made by American consuls abroad. The value of exports of copper, which increased from $1 million in 1881 to $151 million in 1914, were due in part to the discovery of new deposits in Arizona and Montana and to the passage in 1869 of a protective tariff act which obliterated the important import trade and thus permitted the more powerful American producers to form a pool which disposed of its "surplus" product in foreign markets at a price lower than the domestic one.

At the end of the seventies, within the category of exports of manufactures refined petroleum, textiles and other products of animal or vegetable origin began a constant decline. By 1910–1913, metal products led the parade; and among metal products relatively complex machinery and vehicles were challenging commodities more directly connected to the processing of raw materials. The former products, be they Singer sewing machines or McCormick reapers, had always had a large foreign market. By the twentieth century the trend was clear enough for a New York banker to celebrate the American "Commercial Invasion of Europe":

> American locomotives, running on American rails, now whistle past the Pyramids and across the long Siberian steppes. They carry the Hindoo pilgrims from all parts of their empire to the sacred waters of the Ganges . . . We have been successfully meeting competition everywhere.

On the eve of World War I, the chief manufactured exports of the nation were by value iron and steel products, meats, copper other than ore, refined oils, and wood and wooden articles.

With equal directness, the import trade of the United States reflected the changed economic character of the nation. As a new country America had traditionally depended upon the importation of manufactured articles. In the quinquennium 1856–1860, finished manufactures averaged 48 percent of the nation's imports, and manufactures of cotton and wool led in our import trade. By 1910–1914 the situation was reversed. As a result of American industrial development and the imposition of skyscraping tariffs, finished manufactures constituted only 22 percent of American imports. Although the proportion of imports represented by food products had altered hardly at all in the same span of years, the increases in the absolute totals—notably of coffee and sugar—reflected the growth in population and the maintenance of our standard of living. Most significant of all, however, was the astonishing increase in the proportion of our import trade formed by crude materials—from 12 percent in 1856–1860 to 35 percent in 1910–1914. Of the five most important imports by value just before World War I, only chemicals were nonagricultural; the other imports were hides, coffee, sugar, and raw silk.

Since the domestic economy in the sixty years after the Civil War was unmistakably shifting from an agricultural to an industrial basis and the components of our foreign commerce reflected the development, there was an accompanying alteration in the relative importance to American commerce of the regions and nations of the world. These changes did not destroy the old hierarchy. On the eve of World War I, as on the eve of the Civil War, Europe topped the heap. Nonetheless, her percentage declined. In 1860 75 percent of our exports went thither, in 1914 63; at the former date 61 percent of our imports came from Europe, at the latter 44. She continued to import our foodstuffs and raw materials, and her industrial civilization and her high standard of living made her also the largest market for the American manufactured products flooding the channels of world trade. Within Europe the United Kingdom remained the prime market for American goods, the largest source of American purchases. She supplied products of her own manfacture. Many of the raw materials from the less developed portions of the globe also came to America by way of this traditional "metropolis."

While European leadership gave a certain stability to the figures of American foreign commerce, this period of transition witnessed a steady mounting in the importance of North America outside of the United States in both the export and import trade. Geographical propinquity was one explanation. So closely articulated, for instance, were the economies of Canada and the United States that by 1914 the former was the second most important nation for American foreign commerce, in spite of the fact that Canada was a Dominion of Great Britain and that the adjustment of tariff policy between her and her southern neighbor had been one long bicker of frustration. Meanwhile Asia displaced South America from third position. The mounting imports of raw materials—silk, sugar, and rubber, for instance—explained the importance of both continents; as markets they were of minor concern. Or put in another way—certainly too rational—if American statesmen had been directed solely by the criteria of international commerce, the country should have remained at peace with the United Kingdom, Canada, Germany, France, and Cuba, for these nations in that order were the five most important to the United States, tested in each instance by the combined value of imports and exports.

The Dollar Goes Abroad

There is a sound objection to the use of the appellation "debtor" or "creditor" nation. Theoretically and in practice, it is impossible to apply the terms to any nation in any long-run or embracing sense. The inflow of payments must balance the outflow of payments. Though on the surface there may be a surplus of merchandise exports over merchandise imports, the difference is accounted for by the invisible items which have earlier been mentioned. However, in terms of the investment of capital it is customary to speak of debtor and creditor countries; the former are the borrowers and the latter are the lenders. When both processes are in operation in any nation at the same time, it is the major one which determines the designation.

By this test the United States was until World War I a debtor nation. In considerable measure the funds for national expansion and development had been obtained from abroad. In 1869 long term investments by foreigners totaled $1.39 billion; in mid-1914 they were estimated at $6.7 billion. Of this total British investors furnished nearly three-fifths; the capital exporting nations of western Europe—Germany, the Netherlands, and France—somewhat over a quarter. Although a portion of these huge sums had gone into enterprises that were controlled by the investors which made them, so-called direct investments, by far the larger share was in securities issued by national, state, or local governments or by American concerns managed in America, so-called portfolio investments. As far as government securities were concerned, Europeans had repeated their unhappy experiences of an earlier period. The repudiation by southern states of the debt piled up by reconstruction governments exceeded in its classic hypocrisy a similar reaction after 1837 when states failed to meet the obligations incurred for banks and internal improvements. On the whole, foreign investors preferred to risk their funds in private enterprises. Great industrial consolidations, like United States Steel, appealed to them. The favored field, however, was railroads. In 1914, $3,933,000,000 of the $6.7 billion total was in this category.

As a makeweight to this import of funds from Europe, American investments abroad were slow in maturing. In 1869 they were probably about $80 million; by 1897, on the verge of the Spanish-American War and the debut of the United States as a "first-class power" they had increased to $684.5 million. Then with dramatic unexpectedness American investors purchased at least a portion of the government loans floated by creditor nations as experienced as Great Britain and Germany, and with somewhat lesss huzzah placed their funds in agricultural, transportation, and industrial enterprises overseas. In the brief span between the Spanish-American conflict and World War I American investments overseas multiplied five times; their total in mid-1914 was $3,513,800,000.

Such achievements were bound to elate American observers. John Hay remarked even in 1902, "The 'debtor nation' has become the chief creditor nation. The financial center of the world, which required thousands of years to journey from the Euphrates to the Thames and

Seine, seems passing to the Hudson between daylight and dark." None-theless, twelve years later the United States still remained a debtor nation. Nearly half its investments were near home in Mexico and Canada. It was far from assuming the function of world's banker as that task was understood in the exchanges and bourses of London, Paris, Amsterdam, and Berlin. To be sure, at the time of Hay's ecstatic outburst Great Britain was marketing war loans in New York; Germany, German cities, and Sweden were borrowing there; and American bankers were lending to Russia's railways. A year or so more and Japan was to finance her war with Russia and her subsequent reconstruction with millions of American dollars. But the significant feature of American foreign investment was not these portfolio investments undertaken for others, but the direct investments in American-controlled enterprises beyond the national borders. In 1914 the sums so placed were roughly three-quarters of all American foreign investments. To plot these direct outthrusts as suc-cessive, specialized frontiers in the advance of the American dollar would be largely whimsical. Usually American enterprises abroad reflected the experience and the interests of the American domestic economy and grew out of it.

Thus, long before the United States had completed its own railroad network, American engineers, promoters, and investors were aiding others —for a consideration—to build the new means of transportation. Before 1860 William Wheelwright, a Massachusetts Yankee, had built railroads in Chile and Argentina, though he had to use British capital to do it; and Henry Meiggs, a fugitive from Californian creditors and American justice, descended upon South America and as the "Messiah of the Rail-ways" proceeded with a breath-taking engineering daring to build lines through the Andean elevations of Peru. Meanwhile, as American railroads groped to the Great Lakes and the farther West, American builders and investors became interested in Canadian connections. After the Civil War Commodore Vanderbilt and others poured across the Border. At the same time the railroads of the American Southwest saw no reason to stop at the Río Grande or any arbitrary line on the map, particularly since Porfirio Diaz, President of Mexico from 1876 to 1911, was a "strong man" who preserved law and order, rehabilitated the credit of his country, and welcomed foreign investors. For many Mexican lines Americans furnished technical assistance, and provided capital and management—all to such effect that the Diaz administration in 1906–1908 nationalized some of these enterprises to forestall an uncomfortable American economic hegem-ony. Meanwhile railroad capitalists had directed their attention to China, seeking a share in the concessions located in the heart of the empire or meditating, as Edward Harriman did, the articulation of the main railroad artery through Manchuria with the Trans-Siberian Rail-way, a trans-Pacific steamship line, and his own railroad network in the

United States. Most of these ambitions were stillborn, though the government stepped in as a solicitous midwife. By 1914 Americans had direct investments of $225.1 million in railways outside the United States.

Americans, too, had been prospectors and miners. Gold and silver had tempted them to California and the Rocky Mountain states; now the search for precious metals carried them to Mexico, where American large-scale operation rejuvenated abandoned or undeveloped mines, to Canada, where one gold strike after another culminated in the Ontario discoveries of 1910; to Peru and Chile. Baser metals had their allure. For the last three decades of the nineteenth century, the supplies of domestic copper were so ample that there was little incentive to overseas enterprises. But then the emigration of copper developers and dollars began—to Mexico, to Chile, and to Peru, where American innovators were able to exploit immense areas of low-grade ores by the profitable innovations of mass production. Indeed until the later discovery of copper in Africa, Americans—the Guggenheims, Hearsts, Anacondas—controlled the most important copper deposits of the world though they were outside American boundaries. Nickel in Canada, iron in Cuba and Brazil also came within the American orbit. In short, in 1914 American foreign investments in the precious metals were $232.7 million; in industrial minerals $487 million.

Nor were the American oil companies laggard in overseas expansion though their domestic deposits were still esteemed "inexhaustible." Even in the nineteenth century Standard units or allies were producing in Peru, Canada, and Mexico, and soon they were to be at work in Rumania. In 1900 E. L. Doheny, already enriched by California discoveries, was contemplating near Tampico, a little hill "where bubbled a spring of oil, the sight of which caused us to forget all about the dreaded climate. . . ." By 1914 gushers were shooting their black gold into the air, American companies were vying with English and Dutch rivals for oil lands and official favors, the United States was importing Mexican oil, and of the total world investment by America in oil production, $143 million, the largest share was in Mexico.

Americans had been lumbermen and farmers. Why should they halt at the evergreen forests of the Northwest or the irrigated lands of California? With the twentieth century the lumbermen and the paper companies purchased and leased timber reserves from New Brunswick to British Columbia. By 1916 Canada was supplying 16 percent of the newsprint used in the United States. For decades land speculators and farmers had also crossed the boundary into Canada. Meanwhile land-hungry Americans moved into Mexico. Many took up small holdings. Others, like the Hearsts, built up immense cattle ranches, operated plantations for the growing of tropical products, or undertook to irrigate tracts of hundreds of thousands of acres. Americans had at one time owned perhaps one-tenth of the privately held rural land in the Republic. Elsewhere in the Caribbean, Americans also extended the plantation system. Toward the end of the last century a consolidation movement brought together in the United Fruit Company the interests of Andrew Preston, a Boston merchant who owned plantations in Jamaica, Cuba, and Santo Domingo, and those of Minor C. Keith, who united railroad construction with banana cultivation in Costa Rica and Colombia. The concern extended the areas devoted to sugar and bananas and owned and operated a merchant marine and a railroad system. Meanwhile in Cuba, perhaps in satisfaction of bad debts, Americans as early as the eighties began to acquire sugar plantations. In the next two decades they affected a reorganization of the industry. They built large crushing plants, *centrales,* serviced them with light railways, and collected the cane from small planters or large estates. The latter, often owned by Americans, ran into the tens of thousands of acres. By 1914 American investments in Cuban sugar were nearly five times what they had been before the Spanish-American War. Over the world American investments in agricultural enterprises aggregated in that year $355.8 million.

Of course the distributing and manufacturing enterprises, the newer features of the industrial state, reached out to overseas regions. Merchandising, indeed, frequently developed into production. The oil concerns, like the Standard, in order to market their kerosene had as early as the seventies to provide storage facilities and marketing centers abroad. Duke, once selling his cigarettes in the Orient, soon erected factories in Shanghai to make them. Harvesters, glass, electrical products, even the early Ford were produced in branch plants outside America under American auspices. By 1914 the sum invested abroad in manufacturing, $478 million was the largest single item with the exception of industrial minerals in our direct investments. It was the largest if investments in sales organizations and oil distribution were added to it.

Compared to a later period this overall achievement was but a beginning. A comparison with Great Britain's figures induces the same reflection. Americans had invested more money in Canada than in any other country; Great Britain's total was four times ours. Though we surpassed her in Mexico and Cuba, we were still far to the rear in Latin America as a whole. Needless to say, the Western Hemisphere was the area in which we would have a natural leadership.

Dollar Policy

Generally speaking, the investments made by foreigners in the United States occasioned no national policy. Though states sometimes gave such debts rude treatment and minority groups protested the alien ownership of agricultural land, this was the era when both borrowers and lenders regarded international investment as beneficial and, in any era, the United States was too powerful and stable a nation to be "exploited." As for American investments abroad, they were too inconsiderable throughout the late nineteenth century to inspire general governmental concern. In the interval between the Spanish-American War and World War I, however, administrations from McKinley to Wilson participated in programs of promotion and protection, openly and sometimes painfully summarized as "dollar diplomacy." In any case, it was not of universal geographical application. American investors in Europe and Canada, for instance, neither needed nor won governmental assistance. Rather it was designed for backward and undeveloped regions, characteristically thirsting for capital. In short, it was a policy for China and for the Central American countries and the Caribbean islands enclosing the American Mediterranean.

In the first area the "Open Door" policy of John Hay almost at once revealed its limitations. Concerned only with commodities and their treatment, it neither abolished spheres of influence nor mentioned mining and railway concessions. The intervention of American diplomats on behalf of Americans, particularly those seeking railroad concessions, did something to redress this omission. Their representations stressed the expertness and the wealth of the Americans as well as their political disinterestedness, since the United States could have no ulterior designs on the independence or territory of the Chinese. When the Chinese sometimes discriminated against the Americans or, much more likely, some great power wrung from the Chinese exclusive concessions for its nationals within a sphere of influence, the State Department and its representatives filed protests and began to define the open door, unilaterally, in a more embracing fashion. In 1909 the Taft-Knox Administration—Philander C. Knox was Secretary of State—knit the various threads together. The President announced, "The State Department will, therefore, foster the use and investment of American capital which operates for the establishment of legitimate business interests in China and for the welfare of that great empire and which gives us a legitimate standing in maintaining the integrity of China and conserving her just rights." Only confirmed skeptics, uninstructed in the high motives of American policy, will dismiss the last objective as pure hokum. Pursuant to these purposes the Administration insisted that American banking houses participate with those from other countries in a consortium advancing funds for railroad construction, currency reform, and industrial development. Finally President Wilson looked with disfavor upon the arrangement, since the guarantees protecting the loan touched "very nearly the administrative independence of China itself." The American bankers withdrew.

In the American Mediterranean the devices by which the United

States built a sphere of influence have already been mentioned. The mixture of motives behind the program ranged from the political, the strategic, and the idealistic to the economic. Though there is plenty of debate over the proper emphasis to be assigned to these various causes as well as over the question whether in any specific instance the government prodded the investors into action or the investors solicited government intervention, the economic upshot of preachment and practice was unmistakable: a preference zone for American investments. The result was paradoxical: grievous as framed by Woodrow Wilson, grievous and ludicrous as expounded by William Jennings Bryan, his Secretary of State. High associates of the latter felt his Mexican policy was tangled with the rivalry of British and American concerns, and in Colombia a Wilson-Bryan interference prevented the bestowal of a huge concession upon an English oilman, apparently with the innocent expectation that such self-denial by someone else would mark the end of the concession era. In the course of these tumultuous doings, Bryan declared to a British representative that the latter's "Foreign Office had simply handed its Mexican policy over to the oil barons for predatory purposes." To which the British diplomat unperturbed replied, "Mr. Secretary, you are talking just like a Standard Oil man." Perhaps this interchange was as good a commentary as any on the foreign investment policy of Sir Edward Grey and of dollar diplomacy. Between both there was much resemblance.

The Gilded Age and More, 1869–1919

Foreign trade, of course, is a sort of barometer for a nation's economy. Since the keeping of statistical information about this particular activity has been more careful and continuous, it furnishes perhaps a more precise measurement of economic change and fluctuations. Be that as it may, the half century following 1869 was a great leap forward in American economic development. Employing a decadal comparison of 1869–1878 with 1879–1888, gross national product (GNP) in terms of 1860 prices increased 65 percent. Between 1879–1888 and 1889–1898 the percentage was 36. In terms of its own normal performance, the economic advance of the United States was exceptionally rapid during the so-called gilded age. It surpassed, incidentally, the achievements of other western industrializing nations.

When it is realized that advances were not confined to one sector of the economy, and that agriculture as well as manufacturing was striding forward at a giant's pace, the contemporary elation over the approach of the "golden age" and "the millennial period" is understandable. We have already suggested the causes: an increase in population, technical knowledge, abundant natural resources, and the industrial intelligence of the population. Since business talent is not distributed among men in equal doses, it is not surprising that an exceptional generation of business leaders emerged.

Socially and personally they were a varied lot, ranging from an exhibitionist like "Diamond Jim" Brady to a patrician like J. P. Morgan —whose insistence that he wanted only "gentlemen," in the old-world sense, to participate in business decisions made in his library would have ruled out most of his contemporaries—from a clown like Jim Fisk to a thoughtful analyst of the role of business and philanthropy like Andrew Carnegie. Whatever their shortcomings, they were eager for power and prominence and possessed the talent for attaining their ambition by force or by persuasion. Their talent was not technical invention—Ford, Edison, Bell, and Westinghouse were exceptions—but the ability to devise and utilize new methods of business organization and operation. In taking their chances of success or failure, they usually ignored doubts and rode roughshod over opposition. But the successful conduct of their business gave them personal gratification and seemed to them the fulfillment of their social obligation. John D. Rockefeller, glorying in the fact that he made "cheap oil" and employed "people at a remunerative wage," made the apology for a generation. Most of his contemporaries accepted it.

xviii
War and Normalcy

During World War II a phrasemaker classified the participants into nations who were "peace-loving" and those who were not. Historical events then and since raised doubts whether the United States could justly qualify for the former category. To be sure, a preliminary aloofness from both world wars shortened the duration of America's participation in them. But a long interval, christened the "Cold War," followed the end of World War II; and on two occasions the United States, largely alone, took the leadership in two "hot" wars on the fringes of Asia, first in Korea and then in Vietnam. These affrays were far from nominal. The number of Americans serving in the armed forces during the Korean War substantially surpassed that in World War I, though battle casualties in the latter conflict had been considerably greater. But judged by the number and duration of conflicts she had fought since 1917 America had no peer among the industrialized nations of western and eastern Europe.

The Finances of World War I

Since no statesmen on the further edge of this period of conflict could have expected to foresee its direction nor even the alignment of participants, it would be unfair to demand precise prescriptions from Woodrow Wilson in April, 1917, as he summoned the nation's people and their Congress to declare war against Germany. From the immediate point of view, however, the President felt this "momentous" step would involve "the extension to those governments [associated with us] of the most liberal financial credits," "the organization and mobilization of all the material resources of the country to supply the materials of war and serve the incidental needs of the Nation in the most abundant and yet the most economical and efficient way possible," the equipping of the navy, particularly to fight the submarine, and the enlargement of the armed forces by a draft of "at least five hundred thousand men"; and "the granting of adequate credits to the Government, sustained, I hope, as far as they can equitably be sustained by the present generation, by well conceived taxation." The desperate situation of our associates—on short rations and with no credit for purchases—and America's sudden need to get the war machine going worked in the same direction: the greatest need was money.

William G. McAdoo was Secretary of the Treasury. He was the type of businessman liberal Presidents like to appoint to that position in order to reassure the business community. Though he had "rich" friends, he also wanted to give the Treasury "a touch of human warmth, to make it a people's Treasury instead of a banker's Treasury." Even before war came he was preparing himself as a war financier by examining the policies of his remote predecessor, Salmon P. Chase. McAdoo does not say what biographies he read and he voiced his own conclusions with a measure of reticence. Still, Chase's program had been "a hodge-podge of unrelated expedients" and seemed to have originated "from a sense of desperation." McAdoo leaves the impression that he was repelled by the Civil War experiment with greenbacks and by the government's reluctance to resort to taxation—and comparatively grateful to Jay Cooke for utilizing circus tactics in selling bonds to the people. On matters of detail McAdoo preferred to operate on his "hunch" rather than on masses of statistics and the patterns of the past.

During the war years and in the months of demobilization immediately following, the United States issued five war loans. Subscriptions to them totaled approximately $24 billion. Four loans were given the patriotic title of "Liberty"; a fifth was called a "Victory" Loan. Potential subscribers could hardly avoid a parade or a deluge of salesmanship from four-minute speakers, the "stentorian guard." "We capitalized the profound impulse called patriotism," wrote McAdoo somewhat smugly. The Treasury had an advantage over the days of Salmon P. Chase. The income tax was now constitutionally unassailable and even before April, 1917, the nation had begun flexing the particular muscles involved by raising the rates in a revenue bill in 1916. Three tax measures followed, but at a slower pace than appropriation bills. The act of February, 1919, raised the normal tax on individual incomes in 1919 from 4 percent to 8 percent; raised surtaxes to a maximum of 65 percent; increased the tax on 1919 corporation incomes to 10 percent; and levied an excess-profits tax of from 20 percent to 40 percent on net income over 8 percent on invested capital. These taxes were progressive because they increased on the larger personal incomes. In 1918 they amounted to 77 percent on increments above $2 million. One motive underlying this hitherto unexampled severity of rates had been hinted by Wilson early in 1918, "The profiteering that cannot be got at by the restraints of conscience and love of country can be got at by taxation." In the end, loans met about two-thirds of the war costs; taxes a third.

Though much emotion and many words were spent upon the differences between these two methods of raising funds, the distinction hardly justified the excitement. Though the government did not have to pay interest on the taxes it collected, both taxes and loans transferred purchasing power from control by private individuals to control by government officials. No matter from what sources it obtained money the government had new power over commodities. Since these were in short supply and were needed "at once," prices rose. In spite of McAdoo's self-congratulatory poses, government policy helped the ascent. The policy of the Federal Reserve System, just getting organized, was kept in tune with Treasury policy. To anticipate the receipts from taxes and from the sales of bonds the Treasury sold short-term certificates of indebtedness to bankers rather than to nonbank investors. Although a goodly portion of each liberty loan was used to retire these advances, the member banks had used them to borrow from the "Fed." Furthermore, to facilitate the sale of bonds purchasers were constantly exhorted "to borrow and buy" and fifty dollars down was enough to start an individual on a career of investment. The Federal debt was continually being monetized. As the supply of credit and money increased, prices rose and reached their peak in 1920. In that year an index of wholesale prices was a little less than two and a half times as high as in 1915, and the index of consumer prices had doubled. Tin Pan Alley, less statistically minded, gave consolation of sorts for the H.C.L.: "The high cost of living is only a joke, The high cost of loving is keeping me broke." [1]

Loving or living, peace or war, certain expenses of government, notably its civil costs, must go on. In war, since revenues rarely keep up with expenses, the government debt mounts. 1916 was the last of the years this sum moved along a presumably "normal" plateau of somewhat over $1 billion. In 1919 the national debt was $25,484,506,000; per capita this was about twenty times what it had been in 1916. The debt was not the cost of the war. A true estimate requires the deflation of costs to a level of constant dollars and the inclusion of other governmental expenditures such as those by the states. An item in the accounting of World War I, ambiguous in terms of definition and in terms of policy, was the money the United States loaned its allies. Roughly speaking, this sum was $9.5 billion. In April, 1917, the Allies lacked further credits for purchases in this country of military and civilian commodities. They insisted that the financial relief we at once tendered them should be regarded as a loan and

[1] From the song THE HIGH COST OF LOVING Words by Alfred Bryan Music by George W. Meyer. Copyright 1914 (Renewed) Leo Feist Inc., New York, N.Y. Used by Permission.

not as a gift. The sums were spent in this country for goods and services and they thus became an explanation for the extraordinary expansion of our export trade and an explanation for the sudden transformation of the United States from a debtor to a creditor nation. These inter-Allied debts continued into the postwar period as one of the most vexatious of international issues.

Supplies and Industry

As in most of Wilson's forecasts of the way the war would have to be organized, there was a tiny basis of experience. The Allies had turned to America as a source of supplies before April, 1917, and such concerns as the Du Pont Company had erected great plants for the production of smokeless powders; while the Bethlehem Steel Company had become in practice a captive concern meeting the needs of the Allies for steel. Even the national government had begun to nibble at the problems of industrial production through taxes or other controls. In the latter area once the country had entered the war administrative evolution picked up speed.

By March, 1918, a War Industries Board had been given responsibilities for planning and organizing war production. Some of its powers had a firm legal basis; others were based upon executive orders; a vague interpretation of these grants of power was also a convenience. Wilson appointed as chairman of the board Bernard M. Baruch. Baruch had made a large fortune by speculating in stocks and by "creative investment"; his political preferences for Theodore Roosevelt and Woodrow Wilson attested a liberalism of a certain sort; and the possession of assured wealth gave him independence and detachment. In fact he fulfilled that *beau ideal* of visionaries in that era, he was above the battle; he had no ambition or private interest to serve.

Dreading the dead hand of bureaucracy, as most civilian organizers of victory did, Baruch recruited a staff not from the big names of business but from the next lower echelon of active presidents or vice-presidents. Most of these administrators were dollar-a-year men. Through the accidents of organization and of history, fuel, and food, railroads and shipping were outside the province of the War Industries Board; other sectors of the economy, like retail trade, it chose to ignore. The Board dealt with industries fundamental to the war effort, and it represented the government, including the armed services; it formulated its policies in cooperation with boards of businessmen organized on a business basis. At the height of its powers this amalgam was directing seventy-three industries with seven thousand plants. The needs of the government and of the civilian economy were marshaled, evaluated, and the order of their priority determined. The highest rating was AA; producers with this rating were assured of getting the raw materials, particularly steel and coal, needed for their operations and also were assured of transportation for their finished products. Another weapon of the Board was price fixing. A high price was a means of stimulating production; it also increased the cost of the war and fed the public suspicion of profiteering. The Board, after investigation and consultation, set maximum prices on government purchases; these prices reflected the cost of production and a reasonable profit. The former was set high enough to keep high-cost producers at the work of essential production. Since these cost-plus prices were identical for all producers, large concerns with integrated production and high efficiency like the United States Steel Company made huge profits. The intervention of the government into the marketplace where forces of supply and demand meet, the core element in a free economy, could hardly have gone farther. "The War Industries Board," wrote its historian, "extended its antennae into the innermost recesses of industry. . . . Never was there such an approach to omniscience in the business affairs of a continent."

Assertions and generalizations of this sort do not create as living or as accurate an impression as concrete administrative decisions. In 1918 the War Industries Board came to the conclusion that the passenger automobile business was nonessential and that, in order to save steel, production of passenger automobiles should be cut back to one-quarter that of 1917. While Henry Ford had been able by accumulating materials to put himself beyond the reach of the Board, the automobile men staged the most vehement protest of the war. They claimed the decision of the Board was one "to liquidate" their industry, the third largest in the country. "What would happen to its 300,000 workers, the parts suppliers, the dealers absolutely flat out of business? the banks to which the automobile manufacturers owed money? You might as well appoint a receiver for the State of Michigan." For the Board, a member, summarizing shortages of coal, blast furnaces, and transport, wearily concluded, "It has not been one thing but a hundred and one things to bring about conditions."

Actually, against its better judgment the Board was anticipating in thought and action a wider network of controls than it had started with. The war was too short to gauge the Board's long-term success. Armies were raised; the American forces and those of America's partners were supplied; and the runaway tendencies of prices had been stayed—at least according to conjecture. Conjectural too was the estimate as to whether industry and those who governed it really attained their proclaimed objective: "production, production, production." While they probably succeeded in apportioning production between commodities essential and nonessential to war, the measures of overall output point in several directions. Between 1916 and 1920 petroleum production and refining kept abreast or ahead of demand, the annual output of bituminous coal rose from 502.5 million tons to 568,667,000 tons, and the manufacture of motorcars with the exception of 1917 increased approximately 20 percent; but cotton textiles used fewer bales of raw material, and the total production of steel ingots practically stood still. "Steel," wrote the historian of the War Industries Board, was "an epic of the war." If so, it was a pretty ambiguous one. In general, "the figures leave no real doubt that our production for the whole war period was below the normal trend of peace-time output . . . even though such a 'normal trend' can never be accurately determined."

Labor

In its concern with costs and productivity, the War Industries Board touched the fringes of labor, for the availability of labor and its price was an item entering into costs of production. Statistically the magnitude of the problem was awesome. Through voluntary enlistments and the draft the government withdrew from the civilian labor force numbers which constantly escalated as estimates of the need for manpower were revised. About the time of the armistice the government had taken from the existing labor force somewhat over 4.3 million men. With the coming of peace the armed forces were demobilized as rapidly as they had been assembled. Before the end of 1919 this process was substantially completed. Both expansion and curtailment were sudden, short, and unsettling. Of course, individuals were always growing up into the labor force and thus provided some recruits for the civilian work force. The conventional reliance upon immigrant labor proved impossible. Immigrant arrivals, which had reached a peak in 1914 of 1,218,480, were only a quarter of that figure the next year and a tenth of it in 1918. In direct and indirect ways the war was primarily responsible for this falling-off; the conflict also contributed additional arguments to an extrawar movement for a limitation upon immigration. In 1917 Congress passed over Wilson's tart veto an act imposing a literacy test upon immigrants. This policy expressed a preference, albeit a little circuitously, for the "old" immigration from nothern and western Europe over the "new" immigration from southern and eastern Europe. Newcomers from the latter areas were supposed to be less easily assimilated than Germans or Irish. Naturally the chauvinism of World War I, with its frustration at "hyphenated Americans" and the War's aftermath of alarm at Bolsheviks and Communists in Russia and, momentarily, in the heart of Europe, simply heated up and extended the blind impulse to exclusion. Congress in 1920 imposed a limit of 150,000 upon annual arrivals from Europe. This number was to be rationed among the nations according to "the number of inhabitants in continental United States in 1920 having that national origin."

No statute could stay the mobility of native Americans. Losses of migrants from outside were in some measure offset by a greater migration of Negroes from the South—a migration already under way—and by the entrance of women workers into manufacturing. The maximum number of the latter in any one year of the war was not over 100,000; usually it was less. Industry also reabsorbed the large numbers of unemployed in 1915. Workers already employed shifted about in search of high pay and easier working conditions; employers shamelessly robbed other employers of their working forces by seductive recruiting methods. An official observer of the resulting mobility characterized it as "a merry-go-round of labor," "a very dementia of mass migration which . . . turned manufacturing establishments into mere junction points where the victims of the wanderlust changed trains."

A democratic government where workers have votes is chary about resorting to any trace of compulsion in its labor policies. The Wilson administration was lucky in having Gompers at the head of organized labor. In contrast with some socialist leaders in the labor movement such as Eugene V. Debs, Gompers rejected the pacifist and anti-militarist traditions of labor and informed the speaker of the House of Representatives, "the working people will [not] fail in the performance of duty and to give service for the safety, integrity and the ideals of our country." It does not appear, however, that organized labor or its leaders ever gave a no-strike pledge. Gompers was a shrewd calculator and could use words to conceal thought. Since he realized that patriotism could be an excuse for exploitation as well as an inspiration to exertion, he apparently wanted to dig in along the line of gains the union had already made in the matter of wages, hours, and conditions of labor and insist that if this status were changed it should be done by collective bargaining with some sort of mediation at the end of irreconcilable differences. The government should rely upon organized labor as its spokesman and agent in labor policy. Different-minded and more aggressive union leaders wished to take advantage of the labor shortage to push for an improvement in labor's situation by the conventional weapons, including the strike if need be.

In the end Gompers had enough skill to walk the tightrope. On the bewildering series of boards and commissions improvised to deal with war labor, organized labor was represented. Still, the nub of the matter, as labor defined it, was not representation, but "a full measure of recognition." The government explicitly gave notice that "it cannot commit itself in any way to the closed shop . . ." When the government spoke of labor sharing in determining the conditions of work, it meant hours and wages, but not the closed shop. At the end of the war the policy of union labor had paid dividends. A reduction in the length of the working day to eight hours was apparently delayed by the war-born necessity of overtime, but annual real earnings of nonfarm employees, after adjustment for unemployment and the value of the dollar of 1914 has been made, rose from $649 in 1916 to $694 in 1918. In 1920 nonfarm real wages were higher than they had been when the war ended. Those were the days when workers—at least in the thoughts of salaried employees in manufacturing whose incomes stood still—flaunted their affluence by wearing silk shirts on the job. The most conclusive mark of labor's success was the numbers enrolled in labor unions. Totals of union members increased from 2,560,000 in 1915 to 5,034,000 in 1920. Almost 80 percent of the latter figure were in the American Federation of Labor.

The Merchant Marine

For the massiveness and complexities of the government's entrance into economic affairs, transportation provided a unique example. The simple explanation for this distinction was the fact that in this area the government had an early start. In maritime shipping the need for vessels became apparent as early as the second half of 1914. The American merchant marine was simply inadequate for carrying to foreign markets the exports of American commodities. That two of these exports happened to be wheat and cotton was of considerable political moment. American harvests of these two crops were exceptionally ample; their sale would have been one means of lifting the current domestic economic depression. All parties to the European conflict also wanted them. Meanwhile supplies were piling up at eastern ports for lack of vessels. Wilson, apparently at the suggestion of McAdoo, proposed the formation of a shipping board as a government agency to purchase ships, presumably the German vessels which had sought haven in American harbors. The President only partially thought through this problem, particularly in its overtones of international law and practice. But conservatives were having none of a solution which put the government into this shipping business, and Congress defeated the proposal.

Some of these obstructions melted away two years later as the United States hung on the brink of war or a little later toppled over it. Ships for victory were an essential. Without them the United States could not transport an army overseas or supply it; and without ships the civilian population and armed services of our associates might be starved into surrender. As the German submarine warfare stepped up, it was a close question throughout the later months of 1917 whether American intervention would be effective. In a series of measures Congress established the Shipping Board. The provisions of its enabling act sounded like a derivation from the Interstate Commerce Act; they were regulatory of shipping rates and practices. In practice, these responsibilities faded away. As the maritime situation grew more critical, the Shipping Board chartered the Emergency Fleet Corporation. Though private in form, this corporation was a government agency. Government funds purchased its stock and government millions for the construction of vessels flowed through it. By 1918 the Corporation had pretty well abandoned the construction of wooden ships to concentrate on steel; and Charles M. Schwab, president of Bethlehem Steel, took the place of an admiral as the director-general of the Corporation. A business leader of immense dynamism and ability and a gifted showman, Schwab made the Fleet Corporation essentially an independent enterprise. Shipyards and shipways were built; a working force was recruited, housed, and trained; designs for fabricating ships of standard parts were adopted; and individual workmen were put on a competitive performance basis. Anticipating the Stakhanovites, the labor heroes of the Soviet system, American riveters pushed the record of 658 rivets in eight hours to over 6,000—and then rested for several days to recover from their effort. As its maximum program, the Emergency Fleet Corporation had undertaken to build 3,148 vessels of 17.4 million deadweight tons. About 2.4 million tons had been delivered by the time of the armistice; but the momentum of its construction and operation continued into 1919 and then petered out. The American merchant marine engaged in foreign trade at the opening of the war hardly exceeded 1.5 million deadweight tons; in 1920 the figure was 13.5 million. In scoring this record there had been fearful frustrations and considerable waste, but the accomplishment in its setting "became one of the conspicuous successes of the war effort."

The Administration of the Railroads

On land the government did not need to create a transportation network. The railroads were there and so was their regulator, the Interstate Commerce Commission. The difficulty was that the system was not meeting the war emergency. One way to break freight blockades was to materialize the old dream of water transportation through up-to-date carriers. The navigational improvements of the Ohio and upper Mississippi by locks and dams had been under way for a long time; and New York State had just finished the Barge Canal, the successor of the old Erie. The chief aim of Federal agencies was to secure floating stock —tugs and steel barges—for experiments on selected routes. The whole experiment was on so small a scale and lasted so short a time as to be hardly worth assaying. Results were provisional and in the short-run unprofitable.

Since water transportation was of the past and over-the-road trucking a thing of the future, the nub of the problem remained the railroads, privately owned and operated. The railroads needed investments for improved or additional equipment; and in the operational field they needed money for maintenance and for pay raises dictated by legislative acts, union agreements, and competition for a pool of workers assured of ubiquitous opportunities for employment. Woodrow Wilson's proclamation of December, 1917, assuming Federal management of the railroads, asserted they were to be used "for the transfer and transportation of troops, war material, and equipment to the exclusion, so far as may be necessary, of all other traffic thereon." The competitive principle upon which the country had so far relied was discarded for a nationally unified system. The same document arranged for agreements between the government and the roads for a rental "on the basis of an annual guaranteed compensation above accruing depreciation and the maintenance of their properties equivalent, as nearly as may be, to the average of the net operating income thereof for the three-year period ending June 30, 1917."

The operation of the railroads was placed under the United States Railroad Administration of which the handy McAdoo was made Director-General. He generally chose from the existing executive personnel of the roads those who became regional directors of the unified system and Federal managers of the individual roads. These directors and managers all had to sever their connection with the private railroads and received their pay from the national government. The conventional directors of an earlier era could do little but meet, declare dividends not greater than the regular rate in the three years ending on June 30, 1917, and wait with such patience as they could muster the return of the railroads to their owners after the war and the settlement of accounts between the roads and the government.

Agriculture: Mobilized and Rewarded

Although in transportation prewar government policy and the breakdown of private operation combined to explain the wartime expansion of government acitvity, a similar situation did not prevail in agriculture. The Department of Agriculture "at that time, had little interest in economic activities. It was, in fact, a great scientific research and statistical institution," and its Secretary "was anxious not to have it entangled in economic problems of war production and price control." At least such was the observation of Herbert Hoover, whom Wilson in

May, 1917, appointed as food "administrator." Hoover's chief problem was "what to make of a diminished thing." Whereas in 1914 the cotton crop amounted to a little over 16 million bales, historically a record up to that time, it sank to approximately 11 million bales the next year and remained at a low level through the war. The wheat crop in 1915 was just over 1 billion bushels; the next year it sank to 684,572,000 bushels, an annual level more typical of the late nineteenth century than of the twentieth. Not only was food in short supply, but prices for it had gone up 82 percent in the two and a half years before the United States entered the war.

Hoover decided to solve each problem as it arose on an American and not a European basis. This meant the avoidance of a centralized bureaucracy with dictatorial policies. Thus he avoided a retail rationing system. Such rationing programs were cumbersome, inefficient, and relied upon the mistaken notion that to regiment consumers was better than to seek their voluntary cooperation. More fundamental than these campaigns for conservation and restraint—some of which had their silly sides—were the stimulation of agricultural production and the application of brakes upon prices. The two objectives overlapped and were frequently obtained by a single measure. The Food Administration, through the Food Administration Grain Corporation, endowed with millions of government dollars, guaranteed to purchase all grain from the growers for $2.20 a bushel; Congress tried to jack this up to $2.40 for the 1918 crop, but Wilson vetoed the bill. The "fair price" of $2.20 had been set by a committee whose chairman was the president of an eastern college; by the last quarter of 1917 the actual price was higher than the prewar average for 1911–1914, a superiority generally maintained until the end of 1919. The Grain Corporation distributed wheat to licensed millers according to quotas based on their percentage of business done in 1914–1916. The millers agreed to operate their mills at a maximum profit of 25 cents per barrel of flour. In the latter part of 1917 the price of flour fell from a previous high of $16.00 to $10.00 or $11.00 a barrel. The Food Administration attempted to transfer the benefits of the stabilization and reduction it thus achieved to the consumer, generally in the poorer classes, who bought baker's bread. The Administration required bakers to produce loaves of standard weight, to abolish the practice of returns of unsold bread, and to mingle substitute flours with wheat. These controls did not accomplish any general reduction in the price of bread. But the customary retail price of ten cents a loaf usually persisted.

Domestically the Food Administration applied stimulative prices and the resulting controls along the way to rice, cottonseed, and hogs. The policy toward sugar was more complicated, for here was a commodity grown in this country by beet and cane producers, but more considerably imported from abroad. Households consumed sugar; industries as vast as candy, condensed milk, canning, and soft drinks, required supplies; and the production of sugar in continental Europe, like that of fats, had been gravely impaired by the war. Responding to these forces, the price of sugar had risen precipitately in 1916 and 1917; and in the fall of the latter year an actual shortage developed. The Food Administration, thereupon, decided to treat sugar in a manner somewhat similar to that used for wheat. In mid-1918 it organized the United States Sugar Equalization Board with capital provided by the government. The Sugar Board contracted to buy all the sugar of domestic beet and cane producers and part as well of the essential Cuban crop. The prices were not the same in all instances, for the costs of production differed. Cuban sugar was purchased at a lower rate. These supplies were sold to users and distributors at an agreed upon markup. Though the patriotism and self-denial of retail consumers was relied upon to limit the use of refined sugar, certain "nonessential" users, like the manufacturers of candy, were allowed only a percentage of their customary needs. The deficit of candy-bars as a morale builder among enlisted personnel was an incalculable loss.

Though Hoover always implied his food administration drove with a light rein, the measures taken by the government actually affected the structure and spirit of agriculture. They did not transform either. Thus, there was only a slight diminution in the numbers engaged in agriculture as contrasted with prewar days. Addressing the food administrator as "my boy," the administrator of the draft assured Hoover, "You must have every needed boy on the farm. Leave it to me, and we will do better if there is no public discussion." While the number of agricultural producers took no spectacular upward turn during the war years, the commercial fertilizers used increased from 5,418,000 to 7,176,000 short tons. Since the manufacture of fertilizer depended in considerable measure upon the mixture of elements imported from abroad, the construction of plants to fix nitrates from the air was a safety measure. The Wilson Dam across the Tennessee River and a plant using methods largely untried in this country for fixing nitrates from the air were one response to the needs of agriculture as well as of the munition makers. Finally, farming stood on the forward edge of the "Motor Revolution." Between 1915 and 1920 the number of trucks on farms multiplied between five and six times, the number of tractors ten. While these novelties were appearing farmers expanded their acreage either by moving into frontier territories or by changing their land use. Land in farms between 1915 and 1920 rose from 917,335,000 acres to 955,878,000. Whether all these increases added up to more intensive or more extensive cultivation, the experts obscured by the diversity of their definitions.

As for the farm problem, if the ability to pay taxes after paying those on real estate is the test of success, an income tax collector in 1918 reported for Wisconsin, "The high cost of butter, cheese, and eggs has given many of them [the farmers] large incomes, part of which they owe the State." Nor was this sign of prosperity their only war gain. For the first time the government, and not the impersonal market, had administered the prices of agricultural commodities. Some sections of farm opinion had been advocating such a government policy since the days of the greenbacks.

Reconstruction: The Wilson Phase

Beyond experience with these individual facets of the economy loomed the war's total effects. At the height of the war effort, 1918, the nation probably devoted to the war a fourth of its income as measured in the value of goods and services produced or provided. This sacrifice was not shared equally by individuals or, more importantly, by classes. Unlike wages, salaries did not rise; and taxes fell heavily upon salary receivers. In spite of widespread clamor over profiteering, those who drew income from managerial positions or investments in business paid the largest share of the personal income tax and made the major personal subscriptions to loans. "Thus they bear the largest burden of war costs," concluded an economist of distinction. What was the result of the collection and expenditure of these sums? The value of goods and services flowing from "government activity" did not quite double between 1912–1916 and 1917–1921. By World War II expert observers admitted that they should add to gross national product (GNP) "national security outlays"; and, extrapolating this concept and figures back to World War I, they discovered that such outlays amounted in 1918 to $12.78 billion in current dollars.

The intervention of the government into the economy during World War I was massive; in operation it was as abrupt as it was continuous; it was also new. Would it endure? If it did not, would it leave a legacy? Those impressed at the swift day-by-day changes in the conduct of a war economy and perhaps mindful of the earlier evangelism of Wilson and his followers for domestic reform anticipated understandably that the war might bring a new era. *Forbes Magazine,* a journal speaking for business enterprise, soon after the armistice announced:

. . . business hereafter will be conducted on a higher plane than that which prevailed in the care free, money-making days before the war; we are to set a new value upon the things of the spirit, a new value upon helpfulness and co-operation, a new value upon things humanitarian, and also a new—but different—value upon mere money-making, mere accumulation of wealth on an inordinate scale.

As the words were penned, and even earlier, the United States had rejected both this ecstasy and the impulse generating it. War agencies—as important as those for industry and for food—had been designed with a built-in melting point. Their relatively small-scale bureaucracy and their cooperative spirit with private business made it easy to dismantle them when peace came. It was said that the dollar-a-year men in Washington celebrating the armistice did not return to their offices to sign the outgoing mail already dictated, but rushed to the station to entrain for their former, or for better, jobs in private enterprise. For months Americans had been singing, "Turn the dark clouds inside out, 'Til the boys come home." Now was the appointed time. Plans for gradually demobilizing the armed services and integrating the veterans into a peacetime labor market collapsed. In December, 1918, 600,000 men in the United States were discharged from the army, and in the next seven months as the American Expeditionary Force was brought home 337,000 men a month became civilians. Within a year after the armistice, demobilization was complete.

The years after the Civil War constitute in conventional textbooks a period of reconstruction. "Reconstruction" after World War I in a short-term sense was crowded into the two years between the armistice on November 11, 1918, and the election of Warren G. Harding to succeed Wilson in November, 1920. In the long-term sense reconstruction lasted through the Administration of Coolidge or Hoover.

Labor and Capital

Since the relations between labor and capital had been governed by largely impromptu measures during the war, a more self-conscious effort was later initiated to find, as Wilson put it when summoning the Industrial Conference in 1919, "some common ground of agreement and action with regard to the future conduct of industry." Representatives of labor, management, and the public were to search together for such a policy. The conference met under ill omens. A bicker among unions as to who should represent labor organizations preceded the gathering; employers were generally resentful at the concessions government had made to labor during the war. The conference soon split on the related issues of union recognition and collective bargaining. After harrowing the field of definitions several times, it was clear that the employer group wanted either the "open shop" or the association of their workers in company unions or shop councils; the workers wanted to be organized in independent unions and to bargain through "representatives of their own choosing." Though Wilson pled for the dropping of extreme positions, Gompers walked out when the employer group failed to endorse the labor position. A rump session sought to mend the rent and failed.

To speculate about public opinion is to admit fallibility. Nonetheless, there were many evidences that in the period of reconstruction labor was operating in a hostile environment. Labor leaders often seemed to misjudge this situation or be indifferent to it. At the time of the Industrial Conference unions were coalescing into a drive to organize that citadel of the open shop, the United States Steel Corporation. With the exception of union recognition, the workers' demands—for instance, the basic eight-hour day instead of the twelve-hour shift—seem in retrospect minimal. But the unions put at the head of their united effort W. Z. Foster. Foster was enough of a strategist to channel the push against steel within the limits of "business unionism," as Strasser and Gompers had defined it in their heyday; but Foster had once written a book on syndicalism which forecast in a vague and theoretical way the possibility of a governmental system along industrial lines. The directors of U.S. Steel hardly had the magic talent to foresee that Foster was later to become a leading figure in the American Communist party. But, in any case, the attempt at organization through or by "industrial unions" rather than craft unions reminded them of the dread IWW and appeared an attempt to duplicate the Russian Revolution in America. The leaders of the steel strike were "Bolsheviki"; their aims "the closed shop, soviets, and the forcible distribution of property." Whether or not this analysis reflected genuine convictions, it was highly useful in instructing and frightening a public already prone to hysteria. The strike collapsed in January, 1920.

More or less at the same time the railroad shopmen were planning a strike for higher wages against the Federal Railroad Administration. On several occasions directly and indirectly President Wilson let the wage earners know he would not tolerate any such nonsense; that workers should "think and act like true Americans" rather than as a class privileged to strike in perilous times; that there should be a truce in resorting to the strike weapon until the laws of supply and demand and the measures of the administration against high prices had accomplished something. The President counseled, "We cannot hastily and overnight revolutionize all the processes of our economic life, and we shall not attempt to do so." Fittingly enough when Calvin Coolidge, then Governor of Massachusetts, rebuked Samuel Gompers for his attempt to intervene in the Boston Police Strike of 1919 with the ringing declaration, "There is no right to strike against the public safety by any body, any time, any where," Wilson sent Coolidge a note of commendation.

Variations on the Competitive Theme

One of the difficulties of the word "reconstruction" is that it implies too systematic and designed a purpose. Instead, in reconstruction, as in a high wind, the air was full of flying fragments coming helter-skelter and with force from many unexpected directions. In 1920, purely by coincidence, the Supreme Court had an opportunity in the United States Steel case, to pass judgment upon historic anti-trust policy. President Taft had initiated this action in 1911, and finally after a long twisting journey through the courts "this super combination of overwhelming power" awaited judgment. For various reasons two of the Justices abstained from the decision. Consequently, a majority of 4-to-3 declared that the Steel Corporation had not achieved a monopoly of production or a monopoly in setting prices; vigorous and direct competition presently prevailed in the steel industry; size by itself was not an offense. Moreover, the majority ruled, to dissolve the corporation threatened "a risk of injury to the public interest, including a material disturbance of, and, it may be serious detriment to, the foreign trade." Justice Holmes, who reluctantly joined the majority, expressed the private opinion that the Sherman Act was "a foolish law. I have little doubt that the country likes it and I always say, . . . that if my fellow citizens want to go to Hell I will help them." Be that as it may, the decision seemed to set a new course across an uncharted sea. If "public interest" were to be the supreme test transient governmental decisions might well substitute some other good than the maintenance of competition as a sacrosanct policy.

Of all the fields in which reconstruction gave considerable and considered attention to the nation's war experience, transportation was the most significant. This is not to say that emotion and haste did not play a part in the outcome. On the seas, the United States now had a fleet in being, the second largest in the world, albeit with a higher percentage of small and slow vessels than that of Great Britain. On land, the United States government still operated the railroads, but it was obligated to return them to their private owners. The national government was used to legislating for the railroads at frequent intervals, and the end of the war gave an opportunity for a thorough restatement of national policy. Conceivably, the government could now nationalize transportation. But if one theme dominated postwar policy that theme was a revulsion against government ownership. The tradition of public "internal improvements," so strong in the first half of the nineteenth century, had withered back in the more immediate past from the state to the municipal level and so constituted no precedent for decision or practice during the period of reconstruction. To this generalization there was one exception. Glenn E. Plumb, an Iowan who was counsel for the Organized Railroad Employees, fathered the Plumb Plan, under the terms of which the United States would buy the railroads from their owners by exchanging its bonds for the bonds and stocks of the railroads; one estimate of the cost was $20 billion. The government was to lease the roads to a private corporation, "its sole capital being operating ability." Of the board of fifteen directors, five were to be appointed by the President, five elected by the railroads' operating personnel, and the final five by the roads' executive personnel. The board was to operate a unified system. "We would make," said Plumb, "the railroads the background for the first great experiment in industrial democracy on this side of the Atlantic." This comparison did not reassure those Americans who currently sniffed alien influence everywhere. The more moderate of these detected the example offered by the contemporary guild-socialism of the English Fabians; those without a sense of humor suspected emanations from Russia, a nation which had deserted the cause of Democracy in 1918 and which was now clumsily building a new system of society and production and where the United States was intervening militarily. The Railroad Brotherhoods, the most conservative unions in the country, and their presidents were ludicrous candidates for conspirators on behalf of communism, and the rhetoric of Plumb was more reminiscent of nineteenth-century populism than it was of Karl Marx.

Neither the government agencies nor Congress followed these deviant paths. The United States Shipping Board was convinced by war experience the nation should have its own merchant marine; according to its own and popular predilections it thoroughly distrusted continued government ownership and operation. Whether it should sell vessels for which the taxpayers had already paid at a cheap or dear price to private purchasers was a more debatable question. An act of 1920 authorized the Board to sell the government-owned vessels, or if sale were impossible, to charter them particularly to "such lines as are desirable for the promotion, development, expansion, and maintenance of the foreign and coastwise trade of the United States." World War I had marked the heyday of the tramp freighter; lines had taken its place. If neither sale nor charter sufficed, the Emergency Fleet Corporation could operate the vessels "until all vessels are sold."

As for railroads, the Transportation Act of 1920, cast in the form of amendments to the Interstate Commerce Act, seemed on the surface a continuation of old attitudes. Actually it reversed American policies. Competition, hitherto relied upon for fairness and reasonableness of rates and the expansion of facilities, had during World War I revealed disadvantages which forward-looking railroad experts had long anticipated. The railroads needed capital; investors needed confidence. The Transportation Act now placed upon the Interstate Commerce Commission (ICC) the responsibility of so exercising its powers, including that of rate-making, "as to foster, protect, and control the commerce with appropriate regard to the welfare of those who are immediately concerned, . . . and to promote its growth and insure its safety." Congress prescribed 5.5 percent as a fair return for the first two years of the act. This rule applied to the carriers as a whole and not as individual routes. A whole host of innovations, subsidiary to the new direction, altered the familiar landscape. The ICC could now control the issue of securities and determine minimum rates, its consent was necessary for the extension of lines or their abandonment. The obsolete prohibition of pooling in the Act of 1887 gave way to the requirement of preliminary authorization by the commission. As we have seen previously, attempts to enforce uniform fair rates, particularly by state commissions, had run into the dead end of differences of earning power between railroads. In 1920 the ICC was enjoined to draw up a plan for the consolidation of roads into systems with approximately equal earning power under a uniform level of rates. The commission could not compel roads to consolidate, but the latter could not do so without the consent of the former. To sweep the historical record bare, the Transportation Act exempted authorized combinations from the operation of the anti-trust laws. The Commission could compel the joint use of terminals. Finally the act set up a Railroad Labor Board, representing the railroads, the employees, and the public, to decide controversies regarding wages. The Board was a permanent board of arbitration, but its decisions were not binding. Though much of the act was never realized in practice, considering the magnitude of the interests involved and the number of accumulated resentments, it was one of the most successful steps in reconstruction.

Historically a period of reconstruction was hardly worthy of the name unless it included an amendment to the constitution. The post-World War I era was no exception. By 1919 Congress and the states completed the ratification of the Eighteenth Amendment, prohibiting the manufacture and sale of intoxicating beverages. War had reinforced the arguments of the opponents of alcohol, for the use of grain in distilling or brewing was obviously unessential in a time of cereal scarcities. The brusqueness of the prohibition amendment in abolishing an extensive private enterprise—in 1917 brewers produced 60 million barrels of malt liquor and distillers 286.1 million gallons of spirits—exhibited no novelty: the Thirteenth Amendment freeing the slave had also swept away a great private right without compensation. But the prohibition amendment committed government to an interference in the hedonistic impulses of individuals and at the precise moment when doughboys had become habituated to a different standard of values and when, according to their theory, they had not been "consulted." No other measure, with the possible exception of tax bills, gave government action so bad a name.

"Not Nostrums, but Normalcy"

One of the first signs that the period of post-war reform and innovation held no further promise came in the political field, for in the Congressional elections of 1918 the Administration of Woodrow Wilson had lost its control of the House and, as events proved, of the Senate as well. In the election of 1920 Warren Gamaliel Harding, who had a gift for political rhetoric, if for little else, had won an overwhelming victory. His verbal diagnosis of the needs of the times set the keynote for the decade of the twenties. "America's present need is not heroics but healing; not nostrums but normalcy; not revolution but restoration; not surgery but serenity." But Wilson as early as December, 1918, had informed Congress that "from no quarter have I seen any general scheme of 'reconstruction' emerge which I thought it likely we could force our spirited business men and self-reliant farmers to accept with due pliancy and obedience." Thus the policies of the nation long before the votes of Harding's triumphs had been counted had rolled like tumbleweed toward "normal" conditions.

On one occasion Harding confessed his ignorance of economic principles and his despair at his inability to find any wise man to advise him. Nonetheless, in forming his Cabinet he had been canny in appointing men of ability to State, to the Treasury, and to Commerce. Andrew W. Mellon, an unobtrusive and wealthy banker from Pittsburgh, continued to direct the Treasury under Coolidge and Hoover; in Commerce Hoover held sway until his elevation to the Presidency. By all conspicuous tests Hoover possessed great and varied capacities: a mining engineer who had translated and published a Latin treatise on that subject, an accomplished administrator who had organized the relief of starving Europeans before and after American participation in World War I as well as the domestic Food Administration during it, appreciative of the contribution scholarly fact and theory could make to government through "the formulation of large national policies to the next phase in the national development," as his scholar-administrator relation to the investigations, *Recent Economic Thought* and *Recent Social Change,* demonstrated. Paradoxically he was a bureaucrat whom most proposals to resort to political action made twitchy. Matters of finance and of commerce were central, as the Republican dynasty continued to head the ship of state back to the haven of normalcy.

The first step was to dismantle the structure of war finance. Some parts would have to be discarded; others might be saved; still others refashioned. Wilson had foreseen the necessity and appropriateness of shifting from war to a peace business. "It was idle to talk of a successful and confident business reconstruction" before the readjustment had been made; "no true friend of the nation's essential business interests can afford" to advocate a delay beyond 1920. Taxes should be stable; "they should not discourage enterprise." As it turned out the Republican party undertook the tasks Wilson had sketched. They were beneficiaries of institutional arrangements emerging from the past, in some instances a long one. With bipartisan support Congress passed and Harding signed a bill establishing for the first time a Federal Budget. The various governmental agencies and departments were to transmit to a Bureau of the Budget an annual estimate of their financial needs, the President was to transmit to Congress the resulting budget along with estimates of receipts and recommendations for taxes to deal with a projected deficit or surplus. The Bureau of the Budget was placed in the Treasury Department, but the Secretary was given no authority over it. Whether the budget was efficiently enough designed or even intended to play the role of a like-named device in the House of Commons where "Budget Day" was the moment of truth was somewhat beside the question. A nation couldn't have a budget policy unless it first had a budget. Another new agency of policy was the Federal Reserve. Just jelled into manhood by the crisis of World War I, the "Fed" inevitably served the Treasury's and the nation's needs in loan and debt policy. This governmental role was as old as the Bank of the United States and as recent as the statute establishing the Federal Reserve system. Still, there was friction. On one occasion McAdoo in a discussion of the power status of the Federal Reserve Board characterized one proposal as likely "to make the Board more obstructive than ever, and it would swell their heads."

With the change of administration in 1920, Andrew W. Mellon slowly began the inauguration of Treasury postwar policy. Some of the measures were so traditional to postwar eras that they were automatic. As after the Civil War, the Treasury was concerned with refunding short-term indebtedness for a type with later maturity and also lower rates of interest. In this area the Treasury could exercise considerable discretion, though it had to rely upon the cooperation of the Federal Reserve. The gross national debt declined from over $25 billion in 1919 to a little over $16 billion in 1930. In every year but the first the government operated with a surplus.

This achievement was accompanied by a reduction in taxation. Mellon operated on the assumption that it was wiser to reduce taxes first on the income of wealthy individuals and on corporations. This preference would stimulate production and multiply jobs. By the end of the Coolidge era Mellon's philosophy of taxation was able to operate at full throttle. "Coolidge," said Hoover, "has dignified economy to a principle of government." Consequently Congress had raised exemptions under the personal income tax; the normal tax was reduced from a range of 6 to 12 percent to one of 1.5 to 5 percent, and the maximum surtax to 20 percent. The corporation tax was reduced from 13.5 percent to 12 percent. The results which Mellon had forecast were forthcoming. In spite of changes, individual and corporate income taxes produced almost as great a percentage of total tax revenues as at the peak of the war and the proportion of the total income tax revenue paid by the upper-income brackets had increased. Whether or not this made Mellon "the greatest Secretary of the Treasury since Alexander Hamilton" is a matter of partisan opinion; it at least suggests, he might deserve being called a precursor of the "Great Society."

Agricultural Relief

Government policies of the sort already mentioned have conditioned the general economy within whose context the discrete items work. What they meant to more specific aspects of production was another question. Agriculture, for instance, had enjoyed during all the twentieth century an exceptional level of prosperity. Writers on the pre-World War I years consistently refer to them in terms of exaggeration. World War I undoubtedly put agriculture through disturbing years of transition but it had not retarded a profitable expansion. An immense market for agricultural exports opened, and after the armistice the need to rescue Europe from starvation required loans from the national government for financing a further continuation of these shipments. Farming expanded to meet the challenges. However, a sudden decline in agricultural prices began in 1920 and continued. In this emergency memories of $2.00 wheat and a government guaranteed price for hogs danced in the farmer's head like sugarplums snatched away.

Without the aid of protection and wartime inflation it was implausible to repeat explicitly the wartime program. An influential Republican Senator from Massachusetts expressed the dominant distaste for the proposal, "It puts the United States into active business. I think at this time the more we take the government out of business and the less we put it in the better." Wheat and cotton farmers who found this homily unpalatable did not have to depend upon their individual farm organizations; important individuals came to their rescue. One was George M. Peek, a wealthy plow manufacturer who had served on the

War Industries Board. "You can't sell a plow to a busted customer," was his aphorism. With the help of General Hugh Johnson, also an alumnus of the War Industries Board, Peek formulated a model to relieve farm distress. What caused the low prices of redundant staple farm products was their competition in the world market; wherever sold, they sold at a world price. Protective tariffs on imports were a delusion in raising the price in the domestic market. Consequently the government should buy the "surplus" and sell it abroad for what it would bring; with this threat removed, the tariff would be effective in raising the price in the domestic market. An ingenious feedback device would enable the benefited farmers to pay back to the government the losses and expenses of this dual price-system. Naturally the idea of a "just price" threaded through all these mechanisms. With an eye turned back to prewar days, the proposal advocated a "parity price"—proportioned to the price paid by the farmer for the goods he consumed or used in production. By the mid-twenties this plan had crystallized into an agricultural relief bill, one of many thrown those days into the Congressional hopper. The American Farm Bureau Federation, whose center of strength was in the Middle West, had taken up the causes of "equality before the tariff" and "parity in prices." Other farm organizations, beholding other paths to salvation, both derided and admired the success of the Farm Bureau Federation by christening it an "assistant government." It was not so successful as to convert Calvin Coolidge. As President he brusquely vetoed the McNary-Haugen bill embodying the Farm Bureau's proposals. Perhaps mindful of his younger days as a Vermont countryman, Coolidge preferred a measure aiding "balanced and diversified agriculture" or a program of "safe farming" rather than one in behalf of "certain groups of farmers in certain sections of the country." The act also involved "governmental fixing of prices." Once this principle was accepted it would certainly spread to a "multitude of other goods and services." "Government price-fixing . . . had alike no justice and no end. It is an economic folly." More concretely if the bill raised prices it would stimulate an increase of acreage and of crops. "The truth is that there is no such thing as effective partial control." He concluded there were "many other reasons why it [the McNary-Haugen Bill] ought not to be approved, but it is impossible to state them all without writing a book."

When authorship was in question, Herbert Hoover was more of a professional than Coolidge. As he took over the Presidency, he inherited a Republican party pledge to do something for the farmers. With his warm recollections of an Iowa boyhood, he may have had more understanding of the problems of the producers of staple crops than had a Vermonter more accustomed to "a program of safe farming." The causes of the inability of farm regions to keep "pace in prosperity or standards of living with other lines of industry" were multiple. Many dislocations dated back to World War I and its aftermath when the farming area was expanded and the value of farmland was capitalized at a high level. More recently policies in other lands with "more nearly virgin soils" and with lower labor costs undercut America in the world market. As a result there were occasional "climactic surpluses." The only solution was a "great instrumentality clothed with sufficient authority and resources." The statutory result was the Federal Farm Board, with eight members and an appropriation of $500 million for its operations. These funds were to be lent to farmer-owned and farmer-controlled cooperatives to hold crops off the market and to store them. If these measures proved inadequate the Farm Board could create stabilization corporations and loan them money to purchase and hold "surpluses occasioned by climatic variations or by harvest congestion." The board went to work with dispatch. Its chairman was Alexander Legge, millionaire president of the International Harvester Corporation, an alumnus of the War Industries Board, and a self-styled "conservative business man." Like the causes of farm distress the problems of the Farm Board were legion. Not the least of them was to meet the expectation of Hoover that the creation of the board "would at once transfer the agricultural question from the field of politics into the realm of economics."

The Rise and Weakening of Organized Labor

Whether Hoover thought a similar outcome was possible or desirable in the case of industrial labor, the absence of government policy in the area of capital and labor prevents an answer. After the spasm of strikes and labor failures in 1919–1922, unions entered a period of pessimism and relative inaction. All in all, labor had not done badly during the war; even though it failed to capture the citadel of "recognition." Annual real earnings per capita for nonfarm employees in terms of 1914 dollars, even adjusted for unemployment, rose from $672 in 1920 to $855 in 1929; meanwhile the length of the working day in hours dropped so sharply during the war that in 1919 nearly half the industrial workers worked forty-eight hours or less a week. Though the trend slowed in the twenties, the longer day disappeared. Even in the steel industry where the workers lost their strike, the pressure of public opinion and the intervention of a civic-minded stockholder with large holdings compelled United States Steel to abandon the twelve-hour shift, an improvement it had once declared "impossible."

American wage earners generally calculated the value of belonging to a union. The twenties inclined these calculations in a negative direction. Observers committed to the theory that the interests of workers and employers cannot be identical and that the correct organization of capital-labor relationships should be one of continued tension, punctuated by violence, are quite unwilling to believe that the workers' reaction to the prosperity of the twenties was the result of an objective examination of the facts; more probably it was the result of employer "manipulation" of "personnel" policies. In the swift vogue during and after the war for workers' "councils" and "shop committees" apparently there was evidence for this *caveat*. The impetus for such organizations came generally from the employers and most schemes gave them or their representatives the greater weight in making decisions. Consequently these were "company unions," "labor crushing" devices. That the motives of the employers for preferring such organizations for "collective bargaining" purposes might have included, as they did in some instances, generous or humane ones only proved that if employers were not sinister they were naive. Hard-bitten employers were against outside unions and organized groups to guarantee they wouldn't get a start. "Detroit is Detroit because of the open shop" represented the thinking of Ford and General Motors alike. However the causes be apportioned, membership in labor unions declined from the peak year of 1920. In 1930 it was 3,632,000, of which about three-quarters were in the American Federation of Labor.

The national policy toward labor in the twenties was worked out in the private sphere by the managers rather than by employees or the government. There were exceptions to this statement. The "works councils," officially favored during the war, persisted as an influence. During industrial outbreaks the courts as usual set the rules of the game. In spite of legislation, like the Clayton Act, which union labor once felt protected its activities, judges still issued injunctions against a wide spectrum of union practices and objectives. With a change in the economic climate subsequent to the panic of 1929, Congress passed the Norris-LaGuardia Act in 1932. The statute contained a statement of public policy to the effect that an individual, unorganized worker should "have full freedom of association, self-organization and designation of representatives of his own choosing to negotiate the terms and conditions of his employment"; it continued to permit courts to issue temporary or permanent injunctions in cases growing out of a labor dispute but only if a "substantial and irreparable injury to the complainant's property will be unavoidable." An investigation and determination of the facts in the case was a prelude to any such action; and the prerequisite of a jury trial, instead of judicial punishment for contempt of court, was a required postlude to violation of the injunction. The act passed Congress by overwhelming majorities and President Hoover, who had advocated a law of this sort in 1928, signed it.

Associations in Industry

The twenties were a decade characterized by the magic magnetism of business: the innovation of the principles of efficient business enterprise would save the forlorn and the disadvantaged. Few fields of policy demonstrated the aptness of this generalization better than agriculture, where farmers and their spokesmen sought salvation in measures enabling the cultivators of the earth to enjoy the blessings of a protective tariff and where producers were seeking to submerge their individual interests beneath the sea of harmonious and common action. In union there was strength and correlative and imagined advantages. Historical policy has insisted upon a different structure for industry. From railroads to oil the objective was competition. But war needs, along with economic theory, had demonstrated the wastes and other disadvantages of competition. Businessmen cringed at the dangerous vagueness and instability of anti-trust policy. They wanted to know what was allowable before they had done it and they aspired to enlarge the permissive area of common action. The answer to these perplexities was an open-price association between producers. The members of these associations—in the manner of the Gary dinners and, less exactly, the railroad pools of Albert Fink—would exchange information about output, inventories, plans, and prices. Many such associations confined themselves to promotional or advertising activities, others anticipated their members would react in a rational or sensible way to the price information they received.

Between 1915–1919 World War I gave an immense stimulus to this type of organization; the quinquennial 1925–1929 had a similar record. By this time Hoover, whose engineering imagination had been touched by the potential of associations for standardization of products and of cost accounting, had got under way in the Department of Commerce a policy of encouraging such organizations. It was a ticklish business, for the Supreme Court had served notice by several decisions that it was going to be discriminating in judging the legality of such organizations; the Department of Justice which enforced the anti-trust statutes was understandably reluctant "to go along"; the aims and desires of the parties to a trade agreement were often irreconcilable; and, of course, it was particularly hazardous from a political point of view for Commerce to get the reputation of being a monopoly-builder. The line negotiations had to follow was neither as straight nor as sharp as that testing automobile drivers under the influence. Nonetheless, Hoover's policy prevailed. When the organizers of the Cotton Textile Institute approached him for guidance in 1926, "that big man patted us on the back and said 'go to it.'" Attitudes toward competition or the lack of it could also be gauged by the number of cases initiated under the Federal anti-trust laws. By this test the Administrations in the twenties had as energetic a record as did that of Woodrow Wilson. In the last two years of Hoover's presidency, however, the number of new cases was five in 1931 and three in 1932, hardly the dimensions of a crusade.

Banking: Potentials and Purposes

Important as these facets of the economy were, none taken by itself offered the opportunity for shaping national policy as a whole. Conceivably, banking and financial policy could facilitate and attain this overview. But the Federal Reserve Act had not intended any such result. It had rejected a single central bank for a regional system with traces of common action. It was designed, as most statutes usually are, to cope with evils already experienced and thus more or less understood. It sought to combine in a system thousands of individual institutions tied to Federal Reserve Banks through the necessity of borrowing from the latter. The implement for this relationship was short-term paper representing real transactions: high rates on this rediscounting would discourage borrowing, low rates would do the opposite. All this apparatus would assure the liquidity of banking institutions, and the mobilization of resources at strategic danger points in case of panic or crisis. The Federal Reserve System was more concerned with events taking place within a short time-span than in forecasting or responding to long-term or secular trends. Rather than directing, controlling, or regulating the economy, the system responded to it.

World War I and the years immediately thereafter revealed wider horizons and more distant vistas. For one thing the position of New York as the nation's banking center and indeed one of the world's great banking centers gave its Reserve Bank—rather than that in Washington—leadership in the Federal Reserve System. The Federal Reserve Bank of New York also had an exceptionally able banker as its Governor, Benjamin Strong. Strong was a great admirer of the Bank of England and of the English banking system. He was also masterful and persuasive. Word War I had also greatly increased the number of banks which were members of the Federal Reserve System. Finally the war had tremendously expanded the size of the Federal debt; new billions of government securities were in existence. The Federal Reserve Banks and their members began dealing in these securities. Whenever these units bought a United States government obligation in the open market, the banking mechanism so operated as to increase the member bank's reserve and the combined reserves of all member banks. When a Reserve Bank sells in the open market, there is a diminution in the reserves of member banks. "Consequently, when the System believes credit conditions need to be eased, it buys in the open market"; when it judges credit should be tightened, it sells in the open market. By 1922–1923 the Federal Reserve had centralized and systematized its open market operations. The next year the Reserve initiated quite consciously an easy-money policy. The biographer of Strong says this step "was of historic importance. It was the first large and aggressive easing action deliberately taken by the Federal Reserve for the purpose of combating a decline of price levels and business activity and of encouraging international capital flows."

Another premise of the act establishing the Federal Reserve System was the desirability of the gold standard—both within this country and in the international sphere. No matter how much public opinion in this country might wish the nation to remain aloof from responsibilities for world affairs—whether expressed in treaties or in terms of "moral obligations"—it could not escape the consequences of a shattered Europe. Before the war Europe had been America's largest customer for and supplier of commodities in foreign trade; it had been the chief foreign investor in American enterprises. While the war had taken a terrific toll of life and property in Europe and the armistice had distorted political and economic relationships, World War I did not destroy or wholly reverse historic ties with the United States. Rather it exaggerated them. The value of American merchandise exports, which in 1915 had been close to $4 billion, had increased to $10,776,000,000 in 1919; though the value of merchandise imports in the same interval multiplied three times, they were still far short of exports. America's favorable international balance of trade reached staggering proportions. Even during the war, European nations had been hard put to pay for their takings; they sequestered and resold or used as a basis for credit their private holdings of American securities and shipped their gold to this country. There were some novel offsets to this deficit; military expenditures abroad, for instance, were approximately $1 billion in 1918. But these were transitory. American postwar merchant marine policy, building up an American carrying trade; the rise in income from American private investments abroad—their total was increasing spectacularly; and more directly the raising of tariffs by the acts of 1922 and 1930—all operated to make the achievement of equilibrium in international balances more difficult.

In terms of controversy and in reality, the creditor-debtor relations between governments introduced another unsettling item. Foreign nations as governments had borrowed billions from the American government. Though the former may have regretted their gallantry in insisting upon loans rather than upon a contribution to a common and perchance a "righteous cause," they soon found a verbal means of redressing their mistake. In the Versailles peace treaty, they had attempted to impose upon defeated Germany various "costs" of the war. The sum was astronomical and its collection proved as damaging to the victor as the vanquished. Thus when Germany made reparations in kind—for instance, coal—the French mining industry was not amused. But European statesmen soon advanced and repeated a syllogism in which they linked the payment of reparations by Germany to the payment of war debts to the United States: without the one, none of the other. This program hardly appealed to American sentiments. While Secretary of Commerce Hoover foresaw in some detail the disadvantages and dangers of this arrangement, President Coolidge disposed of the issue with an aphorism, "They hired the money, didn't they?" This was both accurate and popular.

Starkly considered, Coolidge's attitude was hardly workable. During the mid-twenties an American World War Debts Commission labored to paper over the cracks. It succeeded in reaching agreements with European debtors. In essence these provided for the repayment of the principals of the debts in installments extending over sixty-two years; the rate of interest over the whole period of payments varied from 1.6 to 3.3 percent. The parameters of these decisions were hardly those of the arithmetic of economics; they were political. On the one hand, as Mellon observed, it would be foolish to go to war to collect the debts; on the other hand, the United States could not be so severe in its exactions as to cause insurrections within the boundaries of the states who were debtors to us.

These debt agreements did not cut the umbilical cord between German reparations and Allied payments to the United States. At the same time the agreements were being formulated, efforts were being made to remove reparations from the realm of turmoil born of the peace treaty and kept alive by popular attitudes. By 1928 negotiations had resulted in the Young Plan, so named after Owen D. Young, president of the General Electric Company. The Young Plan set for Germany the payment of annuities somewhat lower than earlier calculations; the last of these were to cease in 1988. Through specified devices, including domestic taxation, Germany was to raise these sums; the attendant difficulty of transferring her payments was to be made via a new institution, the Bank for International Settlement, which could investigate postponements and recommend remedial measures. In effect, the Young Plan reduced reparations, coupled reparations with the payment by the Allies of their debts to the United States and to Great Britain, and through its devices hoped so to operate as to create a prosperous Germany capable of the production of a surplus of goods and services which once marketed abroad would genuinely discharge her international obligations, now more feasibly stated.

Within this context of multiple details, American and British bankers were working to reestablish the gold standard as a basis for international transactions. Wilson's Administration in the President's prenormalcy phase had taken one step by lifting the embargo on the export of gold on June 7, 1919. The next year the country began importing gold, and during the early twenties these imports attained tidal proportions because gold served to discharge trade imbalances or because gold flew to take advantage of an American sanctuary and its higher interest rates. These flights endangered gold reserves abroad and delayed the return of the international gold standard. Strong believed such a standard was necessary for stabilizing foreign exchange rates and also, indirectly, as a discipline for domestic monetary policies. "The gold standard," he felt, "is a much more automatic check upon the excesses in credit and currency than is a system where gold payment . . . is suspended and it is left to the human judgment of men to determine how much currency should be issued which they do not need to redeem in gold." Montague Norman, Governor of the Bank of England, believed the same creed and, like Strong, preferred to settle policy without governmental interference. In April, 1925, Great Britain returned to the gold standard with the pound sterling at its prewar parity with the dollar; in mid-1926 France accomplished the *de facto* stabilization of the franc. As a prerequisite to British resumption, the Federal Reserve Bank of New York extended a $200 million loan to the Bank of England and J. P. Morgan a supplementary one of $100 million. To preserve these more stable relationships the different national banking systems should have followed a rediscount policy which by its influence upon interest rates would not set in motion disturbing flows of gold. It was desirable for the Federal Reserve System to set a rate that would not be high enough to draw gold to the United States. On the other hand, domestic considerations such as inflation or speculation might make such an increase desirable. Thus, sometimes the objectives of domestic and foreign welfare were compatible; sometimes they were not. After the panic of 1929 many ascribed this disaster to the Board's failure to nip stock-market speculation by preventing in time the expansion of credit for it.

Triumph at the Brink

In the twenties economic policy actually depended upon the time and circumstances. To christen the period as one of *laissez faire* is ideologically misleading, for private enterprises and activities frequently called the government to come to their assistance or rescue; and the government was prone to respond favorably, as experiments as diverse as the protective tariff, open-price associations, and the Farm Board demonstrated. This reliance upon a mixture of motives and measures was certainly accompanied by an extraordinary advance in national prosperity. One of Wilson's military advisors, looking forward to reconstruction, had hazarded, "first there'll be a down, then an up, and then there'll be hell to pay." In a rough way events accorded with this timing. There was a sharp downturn in 1920–1921, and after 1929 the roof fell in. But between 1920 and 1929 gross national product had risen in 1929 currency from $73,300 billion to $104,000 billion or in per capita terms from $688 to $857.

It is possible to attribute this surge of productivity to an effort to redress the setback inflicted by an unusually destructive war. In any case, Herbert Hoover, accepting the Republican nomination for the Presidency in 1928 in the congenial setting of Palo Alto and Stanford, thought the dilemmas of reconstruction were over. The nation, in Hoover's words, faced a "new day," not as fetching or novel a title as that given by later actors in the political drama to their programs. Nonetheless, Hoover was as ecstatic as those who succeeded him:

One of the oldest and perhaps the noblest of human aspirations has been the abolition of poverty. . . . We in America today are nearer to the final triumph over poverty than ever before in the history of any land. The poorhouse is vanishing from among us. We have not yet reached the goal, but, given a chance to go forward with the policies of the last eight years, we shall soon with the help of God be in sight of the day when poverty will be banished from this nation.

The New Deal

Four years after Hoover had first voiced his vision of an America without poverty, he had an occasion to repeat the prophecy. Though this second time he retained the phrase "with the help of God," he failed to repeat "given the chance to go forward with the policies of the last eight years." Perhaps the loss of this "chance" in the election of 1932 explained this omission; perhaps the former President hesitated to furnish another derisive brickbat to his numerous detractors; perhaps his experience in the White House convinced him of the ineffectiveness of the measures he had taken to cope with what a report of an agency of the League of Nations had described as "a depression unexampled in severity and extent."

Saving the Banks

Even before the stock-market break of October 24, 1929, signaling unmistakably even to amateurs the end of the prosperity of the twenties, a few skeptical and discerning observers had noted omens of a change. After the crash occurred the politicos quarreled about the division of blame between foreign and domestic circumstances; and formulators of business cycle theory, in spite of the immense refinements in timing and measuring cyclical phenomena, could not agree in this instance whether such alternations of prosperity and depression were self-generating or were caused by episodic shocks, for example, World War I, outside the system. Those theorists were adventurous and competent enough to describe the phenomena which "accompanied" a downward or an upward turn. An enumeration of results might hit upon causes.

On election night 1932, as Franklin D. Roosevelt reflectively looked back with a few friends upon his recent triumph, the fall of prices and the enlarging number of unemployed seemed to him dark clouds ahead. Certainly, both of these items "accompanied" the depression. They were

495

not always measurable, for authoritative governmental statistics were sometimes lacking. The wholesale price index of all commodities according to figures from the Bureau of Labor Statistics was 61.9 in 1929, a little lower than the previous year; by 1932 it was 42.1. Particularly conspicuous among the declines were farm products, the index for which had practically halved. The consumer price index, measuring retail prices, had dropped somewhat less. But a wide spectrum of Americans, from millionaire to college undergraduate, knew through personal experience that on the "Big Board" in Wall Street the collapse of values was more shattering than that of wheat on the Chicago Board of Trade. From a high in 1929 to a low in 1932, U.S. Steel sank from $262 to $21 a share, General Electric from $450 to $13; American Telephone and Telegraph from $310 to $71. An index of common-stock prices declined a third between 1930 and 1931; and halved again in 1932. Prices are not only the cost of subsistence; they furnish the means of paying wages, of discharging indebtedness, and via profits they instill business confidence and energy. In 1929 3.2 percent of the civilian labor force was unemployed; in 1932 the percentage was 25.2. Even though the wage level had not sunk so catastrophically, the absence of work meant hardship and bitterness. Asking "Brother, can you spare a dime," selling apples on the street, or joining the "Bonus Army" in a march on Washington to demand the immediate cashing of a previous concession, a paid-up insurance policy for veterans, were degrading alternatives to starving.

If the problems posed by deflation were a heavy burden at the time of the election of 1932, they were light compared to those on the day of Roosevelt's inauguration, March 3, 1933. For nearly two years the European financial structure had been under pressure, as suspicion of the soundness of banks and of currencies darted like quicksilver around the continent. The crisis of exchange and gold withdrawals began in Austria and reached the water's edge in September, 1931, when Great Britain went off the gold standard. On the surface the United States seemed likely to resist the contagion as the country had immense supplies of gold, 36 percent of the world's monetary stock, and a foreign trade, albeit diminished, with a favorable balance. Perhaps the situation of the United States vis-à-vis the outside world was an irrelevance, but the European crises at least unsettled American composure about banking institutions and induced Americans to question the safety of their own banking structure. Banks and individuals began the customary quest for liquidity by trying to turn their assets into money. Banks began suspending. Nearly a fifth of the commercial banks in the United States suspended operations between 1929 and March, 1933. Those who had claims upon gold withdrew the metal for shipments to presumably safer havens or for hoarding. In individual states governors began proclaiming banking holidays for ostensibly trivial commemorative occasions; during these holidays limited banking operations were permissible. By March 4, 1933, the banks of the United States were all closed. At this moment, unprecedented in recent American history, Franklin Delano Roosevelt in his inaugural address announced, "Only a foolish optimist can deny the dark realities of the moment."

The "dark realities" of want, deprivation, and confusion, even if not as extreme as in March, 1933, had been apparent for months. Roosevelt in a published commentary upon his own inaugural had observed, "For many months the people had looked to Government to help, but the Government had looked away." This was hardly an accurate account of the immediate past. As far as the relief of the unemployed was at issue, Hoover preferred the voluntary giving of individuals and labored to stimulate and organize this variety of charity; if the results fell short—as they did—he felt states and municipalities, rather than the Federal government, were the legal and desirable avenues for the administration of relief. But many of these lesser governments lacked the financial resources or means of taxation to handle the burden. When the deflationary situation reached a critical point, Hoover had acted with dispatch and with discernment. In 1931, when the imperiled banking and credit structure of Europe was collapsing, Hoover proposed a year's moratorium on all intergovernmental debts arising out of the war, including reparations. Eventually the nations involved came to some agreement. The United States, foregoing for the moment the largest income, made the largest sacrifice.

At the end of the same year, as the economic structure weakened, the President proposed the formation of the Reconstruction Finance Corporation (RFC). The United States subscribed the entire stock, $500 million, of the corporation; in order to make the loans authorized by the act, the RFC could issue its obligations directly to the borrower or sell them. These obligations were to have a maturity of not more than five years, were to be tax exempt, and were to "be fully and unconditionally guaranteed both as to interest and principal by the United States." Loans were to be made to banks, to railroads with the approval of the Interstate Commerce Commission, to farm credit institutions, or to farmers through the Department of Agriculture "when an emergency exists," that is, when they could not get loans for crop production. "All loans were to be fully and adequately secured." As the emergency deepened the Reconstruction Finance Corporation served as a detour to get around principles and inhibitions. Early in 1932, for instance, an amendment authorized loans to states "for relief and work relief to needy and distressed people and in relieving the hardship resulting from unemployment"; and to finance in one way or another "self-liquidating public works"—housing, bridges, dams, and military installations—and to aid agencies financing agriculture and farmers. As a matter of fact, the RFC proved so handy and so successful that it endured until 1953. But its resources and policies may have been so limited and dilatory in the face of the magnitude and ubiquity of distress and failure that perhaps Roosevelt was justified in regarding his predecessor as a "gloomy defeatist" and the Hoover administration as a "do-nothing" administration in its dealing with the depression. In any case, looking backward at the travail through which the nation had passed, it was clear to Roosevelt on March 4 that those who had run the country had tried, "but their efforts have been cast in the pattern of an outworn tradition."

In spite of the derision Roosevelt felt for his predecessors, he inherited their problems and paradoxically adopted some of their instruments of solution. The Reconstruction Finance Corporation was an obvious example of this continuity. Roosevelt also called upon his own experience. On the national scale this had begun as Assistant Secretary of the Navy during World War I. He shared in the organization of the national effort and obviously admired it, if the frequent resort to military metaphor in his inaugural address and elsewhere is any test. In 1928 after the debilitation of a polio attack had removed him for an interval from the limelight of politics, he returned to office as Governor of New York; his terms lasted until he became President at the depth of the depression. In his gubernatorial years, he continued the policies of his predecessor and one-time sponsor, Alfred E. Smith. These programs revealed an exceptional sensitivity to the problems of farmers and to the generation of hydroelectric power under public auspices; but Republican opposition in the Legislature limited the measure of Roosevelt's accomplishment.

Finally, during the campaign of 1932, he delivered a series of topical addresses dealing with the problems confronting the nation. The single most important address on the general situation rather than specifics advanced the theory that the age of opportunity had been closed or limited since the beginning of the century: "Our industrial plant is built; . . . our last frontier has long since been reached . . . our task now . . . is the sober, less dramatic business of administering resources and plants already in hand." Whatever one may think of this subscription to a historical hypothesis, it certainly was pessimistic: it shared the disillusion of the time. As a forecast it proved unsound. But then Roosevelt's ability to generalize was not his strong point.

On the whole, Roosevelt's mind worked most effectively matching concrete, short-term solutions with concrete problems. When once confronted with the necessity of defining his "philosophy," he was startled and puzzled. "Philosophy? I am a Christian and a Democrat—that's all." He was pragmatic, experimental, and immediate. No widespread acquaintance with economic structure or theory marred his innocence. Frances Perkins, his perceptive Secretary of Labor, wrote she never saw him read an economics book. Intellectuals are prone to regard great books as shaping an era—for instance, Adam Smith ruled the first half of the nineteenth century, Charles Darwin and Herbert Spencer the second half. By Roosevelt's time John Maynard Keynes was the great shaker and mover. On a visit from England he called at the White House and was surprised that the President was not "more literate" economically speaking. For his part Roosevelt was not impressed. Keynes "left a whole rigmarole of figures. He must be a mathematician rather than a political economist." In fact, the President was a little impatient with the whole subject. As he said in his acceptance speech in 1932, "But while they prate of economic laws, men and women are starving. We must lay hold of the fact that economic laws are not made by nature. They are made by human beings."

Anyone as gregarious, voluble, and warmhearted as Roosevelt was sure to seek and, more importantly, accept advice. Among his advisors were professional associates and friends and neighbors in the Hudson River Valley, those who had served him as Governor in Albany, and, more officially, some extremely gifted members of his Presidential Cabinet. In an informal way while at Albany Roosevelt had begun consulting academicians for their general learning and specialized knowledge. By the time he went to Washington these advisors had coalesced into a small group from Columbia University who could tell the President what he sought to know or direct him to sources which would. These advisors, journalistically christened the "Brain Trust," were pictured by hostile caricaturists as gibbering idiots clad in disarray of cap and gown. This sense of shocking novelty was unjustified. Wilson and Hoover had both drawn upon academic opinion. More than most political leaders Roosevelt moved through a sea of advice. Members of the Brain Trust shifted, so did the procession of politicians. Even the family gave counsel. Some advisors were certain others were "giving a lot of poor advice." Few could tell whose ideas would prevail. In the circumstances it was unlikely that the Roosevelt administration would inaugurate any systematic design for rebuilding the nation.

Nor was that the need at the moment of inauguration. First, the banks, or those which were "sound," or "solvent," had to be reopened. Through plans and devices in large measure formulated by members of the Hoover administration, and by the first of Roosevelt's fireside chats whereby he explained banking to his fellow Americans and instilled them with "confidence and courage," this essential step was taken. Almost as urgent was the larger necessity of getting the economy rolling again. A reiterated theme in nearly every policy was the need, as Roosevelt said, "to put people back to work" and to raise prices and wages; the first would stem hardship, the second would give the country a more active market for goods and provide the means to handle more easily and more quickly the crushing burden of personal and corporate debt. Putting "purchasing power" in the hands of the people was one way to reach both objectives. Though the resulting relief measures were variously administered, the large appropriations by the Federal government far surpassed the sums belatedly distributed in "those dingy (stingy) days" of the Hoover Administration.

A few months before his election, Roosevelt in a Jefferson Day address reviewed American history and his own attitude toward the policies and personalities involved. He concluded:

> I am not speaking of an economic life completely planned and regimented . . . The plans we make for this emergency may show the way to a more permanent safeguarding of our social and economic life to the end we may in a large measure avoid the terrible cycle of prosperity crumbling into depression. In this sense I favor economic planning . . . Jefferson labored for a widespread concert of thought, capable of concert of action, based on a fair and just concert of [the] interests [of farmers, workers, and businessmen].

Apparently Roosevelt thought the President should play the "honest broker" between these interests and could thus sublimate the self-concerns of each into a shining compromise. For this role he had blind spots. One of his most loyal associates, Frances Perkins, Secretary of Labor, who had resolved in Roosevelt's favor every doubt, wrote in 1946:

> Roosevelt never understood the point of view of the business community. . . . He did not hold that everything should be judged by whether it made money, and this made the business people incomprehensible to him. . . . While he had no dislike for businessmen as such, he was always in strong opposition to the idea that business should dominate the life of the country; he felt keenly that it was unhealthy for our economy and contrary to decent principles of human development and culture.

Such reasoning, whether sound historically or not, had been associated with agrarians and with politicians. It was primitive Jeffersonianism. Politically it had its usefulness. Business could be plausibly and profitably pictured as a scapegoat.

Originally business was held responsible for the Depression. Thus Roosevelt's first inaugural announced that the "unscrupulous money-changers" had "abdicated" and had been driven from the temple. Later business could be pictured as the roadblock to the wholesome innovation or to the realization of American ideals which Roosevelt was attempting. In his acceptance speech of 1936, Roosevelt after a backward glance at the American Revolution, detected in his time "economic royalists controlling the lives, fortunes, and property of other Americans. Private enterprise, indeed, became too private. It became privileged enterprise, not free enterprise." The nation's task was to substitute "economic equality" for "economic tyranny." The nation was waging "a war for the survival of democracy. . . . I am enlisted for the duration of the war." Though some among the President's intimates were made uneasy by the extravagance of this concept and utterance, it did not seem to alienate voters. In the election Roosevelt won the electoral vote of every state except Maine and Vermont.

The Blue Eagle

But after all Roosevelt in 1936 was running on the record of the "New Deal," made according to some commentators, in the first one hundred or the first one thousand days. Not the first but the most embracing of these rescue operations was the National Industrial Recovery Act, which in the shorthand of a later vernacular became the "NIRA." The concepts and phraseology of this device were brought together in April, 1933, from a welter of confusing counsel—among the peripheral influences was the United States Chamber of Commerce! Certain braintrusters were nearer the center. So were "Barney" Baruch and Hugh Johnson, both alumni of the War Industries Board of World War I. Though the ideology of the National Recovery Administration (NRA), which the act established, can be traced as far back as Theodore Roosevelt, it stemmed more immediately from Herbert Hoover and his gospel of a partnership between industrial associations and government.

Since industry, to resort to the Rooseveltian statement of things, was subject to "over-production," "underconsumption," "destructive competition," or "unfair practices or lack of any comprehensive planning," it should be permitted, anti-trust acts or no, to establish a code to govern itself and eliminate these abuses. Such codes, established by representatives of each industry and approved by the National Recovery Administration, were also to establish maximum hours of work and minimum wages. All these devices were to increase "purchasing power, to reduce unemployment." Pursuant to these aims Section 7A of the act insisted that codes should grant employees "the right to organize and bargain collectively through representatives of their own choosing" and that an employee as a condition of employment should not be compelled "to join any company union or refrain from joining . . . a labor organization of his own choosing." Frances Perkins' comment was crisp: "7A was a problem of semantics. It was a set of words to suit labor leaders, William Green [President of the AFL] in particular." Whatever the bill's meaning, its reversal of the past pattern of reform filled some traditional reformers with alarm.

General Hugh Johnson was appointed to head the NRA. He was temperamental and theatrical. Although his nickname, "Old Iron-pants," might imply a certain façade of military toughness, a heightened sensitiveness saw every act and policy in personal terms. Speed was of the essence. Johnson had a rudimentary administrative machine at work before Congress had even passed the bill establishing the NRA. Washington was crowded with manufacturers eager to write codes which, with government authority, would compel them to abandon destructive competition and stabilize prices and profits. By June, 1933, the Cotton Textile Institute had the first code ready; some called it a "model." A minimum wage of ten dollars a week in the South and eleven dollars in the North, a forty-hour week, no more than two shifts a day—all these would combine to stabilize production and employment at the 1929 level. By the end of 1933 one thousand codes had been submitted. Since the processing of these documents was necessarily slow, while "it must go fast if a business is to do for itself and for the country the great good offered by NIRA," the NRA offered as a shortcut a standard "code of fair competition" prescribed or approved by the President. There must be "a truce on selfishness." All those who complied or drew up codes were given the privilege of displaying "the Blue Eagle" on their enterprise or their products. The subcode governing the eagle's display was as detailed as the regulations for the American flag. When the automobile industry was reluctant to sign a code, partly because of Henry Ford's preference to go it alone, Johnson asserted, "I wouldn't like to go out and sell any product in the United States that didn't have that bird on it." Ford called the Blue Eagle "Roosevelt's buzzard." A bemused brain-truster later recalled the NRA experiment: "Nothing like this, short of war, had been seen in any nation since Peter the Hermit and others incited the Crusades. It submerged all other activities of the New Deal."

By its own terms the National Industrial Recovery Act was to expire in 1935; even before that the excitement and enthusiasm had begun to ebb. At this juncture the Supreme Court ended the ecstasy by its famous decision in the case of A. L. A. Schechter Corporation *v.* United States. All the Justices, but not in the same opinion, declared the act unconstitutional. "Congress cannot delegate legislative power to the President to exercise an unfettered discretion to make whatever laws he thinks may be needed or advisable. . . ." Nor could this exercise of extraordinary powers be justified by the constitutional grant to the Federal Union of the right to regulate interstate commerce or acts "affecting commerce." The illegal acts must occur in the "flow of commerce," the regulation of wages and hours of workers cannot be justified by the fact that these matters may "affect" commerce. "The recuperative efforts of the Federal government must be made in a manner consistent with the authority granted by the Constitution to the States." The concurring opinion of two Justices commonly known as "liberal" was even more searing. To reporters Roosevelt announced that he did not "resent" this decision, though he wondered why the NIRA was any more unconstitutional than the measures taken during World War I, which had never been brought to adjudication. The decision of the Justices on the meaning of interstate commerce went back "to the horse and buggy days." Privately, Roosevelt instructed Miss Perkins, "Have a history of it written, and then it will be over."

Shifting Gears in Midstream

In spite of the sweeping character of the Schechter decision, the Court actually ruled on several provisions of NIRA in a series of cases over time and hence granted the administration a period of re-adaptation. No matter how gifted at improvisation and experiment, it had to discover a new overall philosophy for its industrial program and formulate or justify exceptions to it. By 1938, two years after his re-election, Roosevelt stated a generalized analysis of what was really wrong and proposed remedies. Whether dealing with past or future the President's message to Congress was prolix and frequently opaque. No wonder, for it had to announce a change in direction. The evil now was the concentration of economic power in the hands of big business. Powerful and "blindly selfish men" made the fundamental decisions. "The power of a few to manage the economic life of the nation must be diffused among the many or be transferred to the public and its democratically responsible government." These absolute alternatives were somewhat blurred by explanations. With many a tribute to the small businessman or the outsider, "competition" was to be restored through a more vigorous enforcement of existing, though "inadequate," laws; and tax policies must give preferences to "competitive enterprises." The basic thesis "is not that the system of free private enterprise for profit has failed in this generation, but that it has not yet been tried." In short, there was a mixture of promises and threats and a tribute to an anti-trust ideology which the associationism of NIRA had recently repudiated. The President did not so much propose action as a "study" of the concentration of economic power by a Temporary National Economic Committee (TNEC) composed of representatives from Congress and the executive departments. By 1940 TNEC had published thirty-one volumes of hearings and forty-three monographs. With varying degrees of brilliance and insight they covered a wide range of monopoly. Their recommendations as a whole were timid and inconclusive.

Meanwhile the Administration rejuvenated the Anti-Trust Division of the Department of Justice with larger appropriations and personnel and injected a greater zeal into the initiation and conduct of cases under this rubric. The concept that competition might be disastrous would not however go away. Among the many paradoxes of Roosevelt's address of

April, 1938, was the discovery, "It may be necessary to give special treatment to chronically sick industries which have deteriorated too far for
natural revival, especially those which have a public or quasi-public
character." The symptoms of this illness were the usual ones of a deterioration of the price structure, a high level of unemployment, and
perhaps a long case history of infection. Petroleum was so much one of
these chronically ill industries that NIRA had singled it out for special treatment. Section 9C permitted the President to "prohibit the
transportation in interstate and foreign commerce of petroleum produced
or withdrawn from storage in excess of the amount permitted . . . by State
law" or any authorized agency of a state. The Supreme Court had first
revealed its perversity, according to Roosevelt's light, by invalidating this
provision by a majority of 8-to-1 early in 1935. In due course statutes and
Congressional resolves authorized petroleum policies, operating within a
compact between most oil-producing states and through agencies such
as the Bureau of Mines in the Department of the Interior. These devices
brought about a balance between the production of petroleum and the
market demand for it by a complicated system of allowable quotas and
also enforced to some degree effective conservation practices. Most oil
producers welcomed this partnership with the government. Whether it
had favored big business or small producers seemed a matter of divided
judgment.

Another "chronically sick industry" was coal. In view of instabilities
extending back into the nineteenth century and the many futile efforts
at cures made by management and labor, coal had been "chronically
sick" long before the depression of the early thirties. But the collapse
of the NRA was an emergency in the here-and-now, and both the mine
owners and the United Mine Workers wanted the salvation of stabilization. Congress responded with legislation in 1935 and 1937. Among other
purposes these bills were to further "the conservation of coal deposits in
the United States by controlled product and economical mining and
marketing." These measures established a National Bituminous Coal
Commission and also enacted a code of fair practices and virtually compelled membership by a heavy tax upon producers who did not join.
Through a delimitation of ten price-areas where costs of production were
relatively similar the Coal Commission could set minimum prices yielding
a return per ton as equal as possible to the weighted average of the total
costs in each area. The Commission could also set maximum prices, if in
the public interest, which would yield "a fair return on the fair value
of the property." Workers were entitled to bargain collectively through
representatives of their own choosing, and such agreements as their representatives secured for maximum hours and minimum wages were to be
binding upon all producers if ratified by a two-thirds majority of the
latter. Although the bills had statements likely to placate the Supreme

Court, the Justices in Carter *v.* Carter by a majority of 5-to-4 invalidated both the labor and price-fixing provisions of the 1935 act. This time there were forceful dissents. Mr. Justice Cardozo stated, "The liberty protected by the Fifth Amendment does not include the right to persist in this anarchic riot." Subsequently, in 1940, a majority of the Court, relying partly upon the dissent of Cardozo, upheld the constitutionality of the Bituminous Act of 1937. In 1943 the experiment, which had been once extended, expired.

Magna Chartas Galore

One of the many ways in which an individual or policy could gain the designation of being pro-labor was the humanitarian desire to relieve the distress and ease the burdens of the handicapped and those discriminated against; historically this desire had been a main current in the stream of progressive thought. Roosevelt's political and personal career had exposed him to this influence. The persistent idea in NIRA and later enactments that the state should in a positive way further collective bargaining between employers and organized unions chosen by the employees was a somewhat different policy. Although there were many in the administration's inner circles who favored it, there were a great many who did not. In the haste and confusion attending the drafting and enactment of NIRA and the desire to attain an appearance of consensus, the President and many among his advisors may have "committed themselves, probably without realizing it, to a broad policy of intervention in collective bargaining."

Beneath the clamor, however, was a deep and continuous undertone of employer unwillingness to go along with this policy, whatever it meant, and also the conviction of some union leaders that here was a promising means for organizing the workers in such mass production industries, largely anti-union, as steel and motors. The slogan the organizers employed, "President Roosevelt wants you to join the union," was a good slogan but poor history. Manifestations of employers' hostility to the program ranged from such childish performances as the refusal of steel executives to be introduced to William Green, President of the AFL, in the Secretary of Labor's office, to the adroit use of company unions to forestall unions recruited by "outside" agitators, to Henry Ford's employment of goons from the Detroit underworld to inaugurate through spies and brutal physical attacks a veritable reign of terror around his works.

Nor was labor without its vested interests. The AFL had been, be it recalled, established to fight units of the Knights of Labor. It never forgot that distant experience of "dual unionism." The charters it granted were guarantees against jurisdictional quarrels:

To us was given a charter of charters from the American Federation of Labor, and Gompers, McGuire, Duncan, Foster and the other men said upon the rock of tradition, autonomy, craft trades, you shall build the church of the labor movement and the Gates of Hell nor trade industrialism shall not prevail against it.

Conventions of the Federation might listen approvingly to such eloquence, but the crisis of the thirties remained. The AFL, though it made some stabs at organizing the great industries, was not succeeding. In the face of the obliteration of craft lines and the widespread employment of the relatively unskilled, the dynamism and courage of leaders like John L. Lewis of the United Mine Workers and Homer Martin, a former Baptist preacher turned auto worker, were more effective in grasping the opportunity of Section 7A. Amid personal brawls and bureaucratic protocol, Lewis and his allies in November, 1935, established the Committee for Industrial Organization. Though the Committee denied its creation was "dualism," the AFL made separation official by "suspending" the rebels. In 1938 the latter changed their name to Congress of Industrial Organizations, known also as the "CIO." Its units had won significant triumphs. In February, 1937, General Motors, beaten by the novel "sit-down strikes," recognized the United Automobile Workers and signed an agreement with them; in March of the same year the United States Steel Corporation capitulated to the Steel Workers Organizing Committee.

The course of Congressional policy contributed to these successes. Within a few months after the Supreme Court in 1935 had extinguished the NIRA experiment, Robert T. Wagner, a Democratic Senator from New York, secured the passage by Congress of the National Labor Relations Act. Customarily the bill is referred to as the Wagner Act—and fittingly, for Wagner was representing himself and his philosophy. It became law on July 5, 1935. The bill "was not a part of the President's program," wrote Roosevelt's Secretary of Labor. With the customary prelude of noble words, the Wagner Act asserted that industrial strife or unrest burdened and obstructed commerce and through a "diminution of employment and wages" served "substantially to impair and disrupt the market for goods flowing from or into the channels of commerce." The inequality in bargaining power between employers and employees aggravated "recurrent business depressions, by depressing wage scales and the purchasing power of wage earners." These evils would be obviated if the workers could join unions of their choice without discrimination and discouragement on the part of the employers, and if the employers would bargain collectively for all their workers with a union chosen by a majority of them. The act established a National Labor Relations Board (NLRB) of three members to hear complaints of unfair labor practices, to punish those guilty of them, and to conduct secret elections for the choice of a representative union. The Wagner Act did not compel either party to accept or reject collective agreements; it did not enforce an open or a closed shop; it did not interfere with the employer's right to hire and fire whom he pleased unless such acts discriminated against union activity or membership.

On April 12, 1937, the Supreme Court ruled on the constitutionality of the Wagner Act in the National Labor Relations Board *v.* Jones & Laughlin Steel Corporation. The decision written for a bare majority of 5-to-4 by Chief Justice Charles Evans Hughes found that the stoppage of the corporation's operations by industrial strife

> . . . would have a most serious effect upon interstate commerce, . . . it is idle to say that the effects would be indirect or remote. It is obvious that they would be immediate and might be catastrophic. We are asked to shut our eyes to the plainest facts of our national life and to deal with the question of direct and indirect effects in an intellectual vacuum.

Whether the act was "one-sided" was an irrelevance. "We have frequently said that the legislative authority, exerted within its proper field, need not embrace all the evils within its reach." It is impossible not to sympathize with the amazement of the four dissenters who thus saw the doctrines of the Schechter case and Carter *v.* Carter, both recently decided, evaporate before their very eyes. Unluckily for their composure, they were forming their minority opinion "in an intellectual vacuum." The utterance of the Chief Justice was more than a statement of justice; it was a strategic move in institutional life-saving, for Roosevelt had embarked upon his campaign to "pack" the Court until he got decisions less reminiscent of "horse and buggy days."

Meanwhile the Administration had been formulating other aspects of a labor policy. Roosevelt and some of his advisors brought with them to Washington in 1933 a conviction that the nation should establish a social insurance system. European nations, some of them for decades, had had such a system; a few American states were experimenting with the device and most had workingmen's compensation laws, a form of social insurance. Roosevelt, while Governor of New York, had favored a state statute for unemployment insurance. The national unemployment situation in 1933 made a study of unemployment insurance both obvious and appropriate. Should insurance cover old age and retirement as well as unemployment? Should the contributions come from the insured, the employer, or the government? Should the system accumulate an actuarial reserve sufficient to cover all payments or merely a reserve of liens upon future appropriations? Should the states or the Federal government operate the system? Where in the federal Constitution could a clause be discovered authorizing Congress to act on the premises? These were some of the questions. Fortunately, Frances Perkins had a lucky break on the score of constitutionality. Washington social gatherings have a reputation for aridity and frustration, but at one of these affairs Miss Perkins confided her misgivings to Justice Harlan Stone, who whispered back, "The taxing power of the Federal Government, my dear; the taxing power is sufficient for everything you want and need."

The Social Security System, enacted by Congress in 1935, relied predominantly upon taxes. To finance unemployment insurance, the Federal government taxed all employers in covered classes—agricultural, domestic workers, and self-employed workers were the chief exceptions—3 percent of their annual payrolls. Since a tax of this sort was deflationary and the inauguration of a new system raised other complications, the percentage was to begin at 1 percent in 1936 and reach the maximum in 1938. The bulk of these collections were to be distributed to the states within which they were made and the states made the payments to the insured in accordance with an agreed-upon "model" code. Apparently unemployment compensation would amount to half-wages for a period of twelve weeks. As the bill moved through a period of gestation, old-age insurance gained greater attention. It would remove older workers from the labor force and thus promote a different sharing of the work—a constant objective in this period. Furthermore the oldsters had become politically conscious and politically organized. Dr. Townsend, a dedicated former dentist, devised the Townsend Plan which, without costing the government anything, would have ladled out two hundred dollars of "purchasing power" per person per month; the Administration couldn't even dream so lavishly. "Townsend soldiers" were more zealous, more noisy, and in some regions more numerous than the youngsters. In California, whither sunshine drew the aged by a sort of tropism, a benevolent ex-muckraker and novelist, Upton Sinclair, led the EPIC ("End Poverty in California") movement. Little wonder Roosevelt was whipping his underlings forward in advance of the election of 1936: "We must have a program by next winter and it must be in operation before many months have passed." The Social Security Bill promised by 1948 to finance its annuities for the old by a tax of 3 percent on wages. Employers and employees each paid this percentage. The annuity was to begin at the age of sixty-five; the Social Security Administration paid the recipients without the mediation of the states.

Numerous complexities of a high order of magnitude surrounded the Social Security System: even the words were sometimes misleading. The taxes the Federal government collected could be used for any purpose; they did not finance the payments whose totals sometimes exceeded the income from taxes; appropriations by the Federal government met the insurance outgo. Those on Social Security had no firm contract with the Federal government. Probably the words of E. E. Witte, the Wisconsin professor whose research and abilities played a great part in drafting the original Social Security Act, gave the best picture of reality, "There is no guaranty against amendment or repeal. In passing this legislation the country assumes a moral obligation to make good the hopes it has aroused; in a democratic country it is inconceivable that this moral obligation to millions of citizens will not be observed." So far the historical writ has run generously. Frequent amendments have given coverage to excluded classes, have raised taxes and payments to meet changes in costs of living, and have even included payments for medical aid and care, an objective debated on and rejected in the thirties.

In May, 1937, President Roosevelt, declaring it was time "to extend the frontiers of social progress," recommended the enactment of a measure establishing a minimum wage and a maximum hour workweek in industry. "Goods produced under conditions which did not meet most rudimentary standards of decency should be regarded as contraband and ought not to be allowed to pollute the channels of interstate trade." There were some favorable auspices: in 1936 the Democratic platform had pronounced for such a law and Congress had passed the Walsh-Healey Act, establishing for concerns to which the government let contracts "prevailing minimum wages" as determined by the Secretary of Labor, the eight-hour day and the forty-hour week, and prohibiting labor by males under sixteen and females under eighteen years of age. Perhaps these signs encouraged the President to conclude, "We cannot stand still." But Congress could stall. Finally, after many vexations it enacted in June, 1938, the Fair Labor Standards Act. The bill was promises. It set a minimum wage immediately of 25 cents an hour; in seven years the legal minimum was to be 40 cents. After two years, the workweek could not exceed forty hours, except on the payment of time and a half for overtime; no producer or dealer could ship or deliver any goods made under conditions of "oppressive child labor," a phrase applied to labor by young persons under eighteen years of age; in the case of hazardous labor the permissible age was eighteen. The act did not apply to employment in agriculture, retail trade, and certain other callings. As in the case of Social Security, the fair labor standards could escalate. By 1968 the minimum wage was set at $1.60.

As we have seen, the Supreme Court had delivered in 1937 a stunning affirmation of the constitutionality of the Wagner Act. In general these later measures also won approval. As Mr. Justice Cardozo announced on one occasion, "Our concern is with power, not with wisdom." Though this might be an indirect criticism of the policies adopted, it apparently was not. Not the courts, but organized labor, emerged as the new critics of endeavors "to extend the frontiers of social progress." Both the AFL and the CIO harbored dissenters and supporters. Their twistings and turnings have a largely tactical interest; their ambivalence could not, however, blur the focus: the unions could accomplish more for their members by collective bargaining than by resort to government action. As for wages and hours, agreements between employer and employee should set these; besides, a statutory minimum wage became in practice a maximum wage. As for social security, aside from haggling over details, the AFL favored it as a means of reducing the numbers in the labor force or cushioning unemployment.

The most divisive and most vexatious measure proved to be the Wagner Act. Did its provisions and operation favor one or the other of the labor groups? Representatives of the AFL and the CIO or their constitutent unions fought savagely with one another for the designation of the chosen union. The docket of the National Labor Relations Board was clogged with these jurisdictional disputes; and nearly every agency dealing with labor, even on the merest ceremonial level, had to have representatives from the AFL and the CIO. Ill will and the classic charges of "bias, unfairness and prejudice" prevailed everywhere. The strangest alliances resulted. The more conservative elements of the AFL sounded just like John L. Lewis of the CIO as they pointed out that what the government gave it could take away. Lewis on one occasion suggested the repeal of the whole corpus of legislation here described and the return of labor policy to the economic might of organized labor. Naturally administrators, who regarded themselves as working for the interests of labor, were repelled by these exaggerations. Roosevelt, turning Shakespearian, called down "a plague on both your houses."

By the commonly used tests of membership totals, labor gained by the Wagner Act. In 1929 the number of organized workers was estimated at 3.4 million and by 1939 the estimate was over 8 million. One exceptional feature of this expansion was that it took place in a period of depression when there were still millions of unemployed. Another exceptional feature was that the unions organized the mass production industries—automobiles, steel, communications, coal mines, rubber, and garment workers. This "new unionism" deservedly attracted attention; it did not mean that the membership in the CIO ever equaled that in the AFL. Indeed, the habits of fission—Lewis called it "disaffiliation"—and fusion became so catching that withdrawals from the CIO over matters of principle or personal pique continued. In spite of the very considerable achievements of the organizational surge, the South remained relatively untouched. So did whole fields of enterprise—agriculture, office jobs, and retailing.

Agriculture in Search of an Answer

Even before measures for industrial cartelization and in behalf of labor were passed, the New Deal had turned its attention to the farm problem. Ever since World War I farmers and their associations had been demanding government aid in the solution of the farm problem, however that was defined. Sensitive to the situation, the Hoover Administration had established the Farm Board; the depression with falling agricultural prices and unpaid mortgage debts had made a mockery of its efforts. By 1932 disaffection in the great farming regions of the West was so deep that the Roosevelt campaign organizers dusted off the old hopes of an alliance between the South, which the Democratic party of course controlled, and the West, politically a more debatable region. Roosevelt's first pronouncements on farming and agriculture, while they included an emphasis upon such traditional solutions as cultivating the foreign market, and while they posed Roosevelt as understanding the desperate situation—because he, too, had lived on a farm for fifty years—sounded searching, novel, and radical. "I favor a definite policy looking to the planned use of the land." He favored an increase in prices—"purchasing power" again—in a fashion which would not stimulate "further production." Such benefits given to farmers were to be equal to those enjoyed by industrial producers under the protective tariff. When the President later submitted his bill to Congress he added, "I tell you frankly that it is a new and untrod path, but I tell you with equal frankness that an unprecedented condition calls for the trial of new means to rescue agriculture." This last assertion was accurate. Behind the details, which will follow in a moment, the President put the national government into the business of agricultural pricing or at least determining the elements of pricing. The Government's assumption of a similar role for the railroads had taken a quarter century. In the case of agriculture the motives were economic and also social: farming must be preserved for its American values.

Behind the Agricultural Adjustment Act (AAA) of May, 1933, were a multitude of advisors rarely exceeded in the New Deal days in number and diversity. On the periphery were the farm organizations and their spokesmen; these could not agree about programs but were perhaps willing to silence their differences during a period of wait-and-see. Nearer the center were the professors: M. L. Wilson at the University of Montana at Bozeman and Rexford Tugwell, from Columbia University and probably the most anti-business member of the Brain Trust. They were joined by businessmen who had become interested in the farm problem, men like George N. Peek, Bernard M. Baruch, and General Hugh Johnson. Many, though not all of these, held positions in the Department of Agriculture. The Secretary was Henry A. Wallace, an editor of an agricultural journal in Iowa and a member of a family which aided the breeding of hybrid corn and popularized its planting.

The AAA was to apply to seven basic commodities—wheat, cotton, corn, hogs, rice, tobacco, and milk and milk products. These were staples which generally had to be processed before sale, and it was feasible administratively to tax their processing to raise money for the new policy of the act. An unacknowledged reason for the selectivity of the list was the strength of the political pressures which could be exerted for the inclusion of items. The government was to enter into contract with the producers of basic commodities "for reduction in acreage or reduction in the production for market." The government was to levy on processors a tax sufficient to raise funds to pay rentals or benefits to the farmers who had voluntarily entered into these agreements. These subsidies so sought to adjust demand and supply that the farmer would receive a price that would give his commodities a purchasing power over goods he bought at the same level as in 1909–1914, when, be it remembered, the ratio was exceptionally favorable to agriculture. The parity base for tobacco, however, was timed differently.

The immediate effect of this legislation upon the course of agricultural production could not be pinpointed, for in 1934 and 1936 drought hit the agricultural West and high winds carried the valuable humus from the Dust Bowl almost literally around the world. Though literally these were dark days, they handled the agricultural "surpluses" more directly and more effectively than legislation. Production fell off, "carry-overs" melted away. Agricultural prices rose and in 1937 farm buying power equaled that of the pre-Depression years, 1924–1929. Another factor unsettling to a precise judgment was the decision of the Supreme Court in United States *v.* Butler. Early in 1936 by a vote of 6-to-3, the Justices declared the titles of the Agricultural Adjustment Act of 1933 just described unconstitutional means to an unconstitutional end. The regulation of agriculture was a power individual states must exercise; it could not be made a Federal power by purchasing farmers' compliance by a tax nominally validated on the ground of promoting the general welfare. Instead of an outburst of indignation at this decision, Henry Wallace wrote years later, "God was good to us and the farmer and the country when the Supreme Court destroyed the processing tax."

With resilience and with old arguments in new guise, the Administration first revamped the application of conservation to agriculture. The government was to make direct payments to farmers who reduced their acreage of soil-destroying crops and planted legumes, grasses, and other products which were not contributing to surpluses and lower prices. In 1938 Henry Wallace cited in behalf of a wider measure the experiences of Joseph, the insights of Confucius, and the collapse of the Farm Board. Only the last of these examples had confronted the plenty raised by the use of the internal combustion engine and the research achievements of the Department of Agriculture. The new Agricultural Adjustment Act of 1938 paid benefits to farmers who withdrew acreages from production and employed "soil-building" practices; and the act made loans to growers of corn, cotton, wheat, tobacco, and rice when the price of these staples fell below a percentage of the parity price. The government set acreage allotments for each staple, beginning with a total national allotment and continuing down through state and county allotments to those for the individual farm. If producers exceeded these limits, the government, after a referendum of producers concerned, could set marketing quotas as well. Meanwhile surpluses could be "put into" the loan and stored on the farm or elsewhere. The government was left holding the surplus. Thus the "ever-normal granary" based upon scriptural analogies was accumulated and handled. The Second Agricultural Adjustment Act ran forty-six pages in the *General Statutes of the United States.* In spite of definitions galore, there were frequent discretionary items, such as "normal supplies" or "fair" prices. Whatever the act's repercussions upon agriculture, it seemed likely that farmers would spend the winter figuring out the avenue of greatest or safest returns and that the legal professions in the farm regions would be "put back to work" if they were ever out of it. Though it may have seemed forward-looking in concept, the Second AAA continually reverted to the past for the standards of parity prices and for the sizes of "domestic allotments." Be that as it may, the "parity ratio" between prices received by farmers and prices paid increased from 64 to 93 in 1937 and the total of cash receipts from farming, including government payments, in the same period increased from $5,463,000,000 to $9 billion. In 1939 both series fell back from this peak. Whether these achievements were the reason or not, the Second AAA remained the basis of national policy during World War II and thereafter.

Public Works

Amidst all the excitement about industrial self-government and collective bargaining which accompanied the NIRA of 1933, the act's inclusion of provisions authorizing a program of public works to be financed by the Federal government tends to be ignored. Title II of the act—not voided incidentally by the Schechter decision—authorized the construction of public highways, the development of waterpower, the transmission of electric energy, the construction of public low-cost housing and slum clearance, and the establishment of subsistence homesteads. The total appropriation to carry into effect the act was $3.3 billion. The ideology of a government public works program—including in a rudimentary way the stimulation to employment and counterdepression purposes—had been stated in the internal improvements era of the early nineteenth century, but the inclusiveness of the Roosevelt policy and the extent of Federal rather than state responsibility was novel when contrasted with the prevailing ideas of a century earlier. This did not mean that the

Roosevelt program was a completely pioneering venture. Federal assistance for highways began in the Wilson years; and Herbert Hoover more
recently had embarked the Federal government upon constructing a
"high dam" in the Colorado River.

Contemporary opinion was apt to emphasize the anti-depression
posture of the Roosevelt program, as was the President himself. But meanwhile to a varied degree the relief and other appropriations, for which
the works program gave example or inspiration, began creating an
economic structure considerably different from that of pre-Roosevelt days.
The miles of improved highways constructed by grants-in-aid to the states
furnished the thoroughfares in the age of the motor car. States like New
Jersey and Pennsylvania issued or guaranteed securities for the construction of cross-state turnpikes and relied upon tolls to service the incurred
indebtedness. A nostalgic air also hovered over the long-continued effort
to provide an all-season navigation of the western waters by the construction of dams and locks around interruptions to navigation and by
containing floodwaters behind storage dams. A system of internal improvements of this sort had been completed along the Ohio in 1929 in
Hoover's day. Tows carrying bulk commodities like coal, petroleum, and
cement played a significant but minor role in the national economy.
While the government was providing competitors of the railroad with a
right of way without direct costs, it loaned the Pennsylvania Railroad the
sums to electrify its route between New York and Washington. Years later
Moley sourly observed, "It may be, however, that this was done to improve
access and egress to and from Washington for traveling bureaucrats."

More revelatory of the shift of the American economy toward urbanization was the inauguration of a program in the National Recovery Administration by which Federal policies and funds administered through
public bodies were to eliminate slums and construct "low-rent," "decent"
housing. Roosevelt would seem to have put new force behind this program
in his second inaugural. Detecting over historic time and especially during
his first administration a wide national intent to use governmental power
to establish "a new order of things," the President particularized, "I see
one-third of a nation, ill-housed, ill-clad, ill-nourished." Before the charge
ran down or was short-circuited by other legislative proposals, Congress
passed a bill providing a new authority which was to loan money—
$500 million was appropriated for three years—to local housing authori-
ties for the construction of low-rent housing. To keep the rents low
enough for those admitted to the new projects and to make the latter
self-sustaining the national government paid about a third of the rent,
the individual occupant paid a half, and the local community granted
a tax exemption.

In retrospect these steps toward innovation fell short; they proved
ineffective in eliminating slums. At least verbally the participation of the
Federal government in the electric power business was an entirely dif-

ferent matter. The expansion of these utilities under private ownership and operation had been one of the spectacular achievements after the first decade of this century. Total horsepower of all prime movers, outside the automotive field, had practically doubled between 1910 and 1920; in the meantime the portion generated in electric central stations had multiplied approximately seven times. For the kilowatts distributed from central stations steam was the customary generator and waterpower provided a little over a third. As business enterprises, electric power and light companies through holding companies merged into great organisms so intricate that even their creators could neither describe nor remember them; the regulatory agencies, usually state commissions, were just as baffled and even more helpless. This situation had long challenged Roosevelt. In April, 1933, he sent to Congress a message proposing an Authority for the Tennessee Valley, the TVA. The power potentials of the Tennessee River, rising in the mountains in the west of North Carolina and running in a great arc through Tennessee and finally northward to join the Ohio in Kentucky, had been appreciated as early as 1880, but the technology of high concrete dams and long-distance power transmission by wire were as unthought of then as the means for checking soil erosion and for impounding floodwaters. By the 1930's invention and imagination facilitated a new order of things.

More specifically the government had built during World War I at Muscle Shoals on the Tennessee a dam and plants for making nitrates, and through the twenties George Norris, a Senator from Nebraska, had prevented the government from leasing these installations to private enterprisers, including Henry Ford. All these circumstances, according to Roosevelt, led "logically to national planning for a complete river watershed." The Tennessee Valley Authority should have "the broadest duty of planning for the proper use, conservation, and development of the natural resources of the Tennessee River drainage terrain and its adjoining territory for the general social and economic welfare of the nation." This was the "spirit and vision of the pioneer." The TVA, consisting of three directors, had the power to build dams, reservoirs, transmission lines, and powerhouses along the Tennessee or its tributaries; to distribute and sell surplus electric power to states, counties, municipalities, corporations or individuals; and "to promote the wider and better use of electrical power for agricultural and domestic use," the sale and use by industry being "a secondary purpose." The Tennessee Valley Authority could or should manufacture nitrates and demonstrate their usefulness for rebuilding the soil, restore submarginal land, reforest land suitable for reforestation, and develop the Tennessee for navigation. In case anything was forgotten, a clause empowered the TVA to promote "the economic and social well-being of the people living in the river basin."

To contemporaries the TVA was the most distinctive accomplishment of the New Deal; to many it was synonymous with the New Deal. News of the dispensation spread to Europe, and Americans and Europeans followed the "herald angels" to Norris Dam and Knoxville, and wrote reports whose general tenor was "The Future is now." Once the glow had passed, disagreements came to the surface. The private power companies all over the country feared the TVA demonstration, and they adhered steadfastly to the article of the American creed which held government enterprise should not compete with the enterprise of its citizens. Some who advocated the Act were nitrate-minded; others were power-minded. The three directors of the Valley Authority had different visions or clashing temperaments and fell out with each other. Former brain-trusters cried into their beer. While Moley was hardly disconsolate over the collapse of "paternalism," Tugwell complained that compromises "ended by making the TVA little more than a public corporation for the production of hydraulic power. The wider intentions of rehabilitation were very largely lost." Yet the accomplishments were visible. Storage dams had evened out cresting flood levels; water navigation at a depth of nine feet proceeded six hundred and fifty miles upstream from the Ohio to Knoxville; electric rates, because of classifications and distributors, are a matter of controversy. The average residential rate per kilowatt hour in the mid-sixties was 0.9 cent as contrasted to the national average of 2.2 cents; the wholesale rate for industrial power might be as low as 0.2 cent per kilowatt hour for those who used over a million kilowatt hours a month. The totals of electric power had so increased and become so exigent that the TVA had turned to supplemental current generated by coal or nuclear plants.

In the first flush of his enthusiasm, Roosevelt had foreseen a series of valley authorities scattered about the nation. A precise repetition of the experiment never passed Congress. Instead the government proceeded piecemeal. Big dams were built on the Columbia, and on the St. Lawrence after a treaty with Canada and Congressional action had brought into being the St. Lawrence Seaway, and flood control dams along the Missouri tamed that river. But the reincarnation of the old dream of America as a garden, tended by farmers and villagers both, in TVA's case aided by electric power, had not achieved actuality. Instead big industries had migrated to the Tennessee Valley, drawn by cheap power, and brash commercial towns and cities had grown up to hide and cheapen the porticoes and columns of a more gracious southern age.

The Rubber Dollar

On one occasion in April, 1933, when the Secretary of the Treasury called on Roosevelt, the President, sipping breakfast coffee in his bedroom, gleefully announced he had taken the country off the gold standard. The Secretary smilingly replied, "What? Again?" This reply revealed how piecemeal, not to say obscure, was each step in the retreat to this decision. For it was a retreat—first a clutch for time to take measures to deal with domestic gold hoarding and the banking crisis; later a broadening of purpose to include an inflation of farm prices which kept going down and thus hampered the payment of agricultural debts. There was a division of opinion among the Administration's advisors over the step; more importantly there was a division of opinion in Congress, where the inflationists were clamoring for the recoinage of silver at the ratio of 16-to-1 and the printing of greenbacks. Indeed, to get the votes for the passage of the First AAA, Roosevelt had to accept the Thomas amendment, which gave the President the option of compelling the Federal Reserve or the Treasury to issue $3 billion in greenbacks made legal tender for all debts; to accept silver at a certain price in payment of intergovernmental debts; to reduce the weight of the gold or silver dollar up to 50 percent; and to restore unlimited bimetallism at a fixed ratio between the two metals. If these potential powers had all been utilized, they would have, according to one calculator, more than doubled the amount of currency in circulation. As May turned to June, the President forbade the export of gold and abrogated the gold clause in public and private contracts. Time and events moved so rapidly that the rationalizations for these changes exhibited a cultural lag. Finally, in October, Roosevelt stated some of his purposes explicitly in a fireside chat, "We shall seek to establish and maintain a dollar which will not change its purchasing and debt-paying power during the succeeding generation. . . . We are thus continuing to move toward a managed currency. This is a policy and not an expedient." Not in the chat, but in an accompanying note, the President made it clear that the policy he was following was designed to cheapen the dollar in terms of other currencies so that foreigners would increase their purchases in America and thus "our fair share of the world's trade."

When the shuffling of the President's advisors necessary for this policy was completed, the apostle of the new dispensation, Professor George Warren of Cornell, who felt the First AAA was 25 percent "hot air," was at center stage. Put more simply than was perhaps wholly fair, Warren believed a rise in the price of gold would expand its supply and sequentially the amount of money in circulation. As gold prices rose, wholesale prices of commodities would follow after. Consequently, the money managers selected target prices for cotton, corn, and wheat. Then they set the resulting price of gold from time to time at breakfast séances in Roosevelt's bedroom. The word "séance" is used advisedly, for they chose numbers at random, often because of an undefined magical quality. Morgenthau, who was in on the game, felt if people knew "I think they would be frightened." The process did not accomplish its purpose; agricultural prices did not rise to their goals. The end came in January, 1934, when Congress passed the Gold Reserve Act. The President was authorized to devalue the dollar between 50 and 60 percent of its former value. The President exercised this discretion by reducing the dollar 59.06 percent. The Secretary of the Treasury announced he would buy or sell gold at $35.00 an ounce. Granted that the President embarked upon this inflationary experiment under Congressional pressure, his messianic endorsement of the policy and the nonchalance of its administration were perilously close to frivolity. The new gold standard was not the pre-Roosevelt gold standard. Gold could be employed in foreign trade under rules laid down by the government; it was illegal for Americans to own gold coins or bullion except for a few limited purposes; decisions by the Federal Reserve had also deprived the gold reserve of its former policy-making power in banking. Meanwhile events beyond the pale of American policy initiated a great flow of gold to the United States. The rise of Hitler in Germany and the shadow of oncoming war made European wealth and capital eager for a secure sanctuary; by turning their assets into gold and transferring their gold to the United States Treasury, they found refuge. The gold stocks of the Treasury rose from 200 million ounces in 1934 to 630 million ounces by the end of 1940.

Banking

Such an unprecedented hoard of gold was bound to have a repercussion upon the banking structure. But this was not the chief reason for legislation and other action. In 1933 the banking structure had failed. The bank holiday had reduced the number of commercial banks from 17,800 to 17,300, only 12,000 of which were licensed to do business. The Federal Reserve System which had survived World War I and at least one major business downturn thereafter, had not ensured the continuance of prosperity beyond 1929, though this had been one of the objectives its administrators had shouldered, nor did it in 1932–1933 preserve the liquidity of the nation's banks, though that had been the chief purpose for enacting the Federal Reserve Act in the first place. To generate political pressure for action an available villain to point at and berate is helpful. Bankers qualified. Admittedly, men in banking's high places had through the twenties been guilty of a disproportionately high number of flatulent statements and extravagant and misleading forecasts. Anyway, on March 3, 1933, the banking structure was in ruins. Measures at immediate repair had been taken in 1933 by amendment to the Federal Reserve Act. In 1935 a more sober bit of legislation restated some of these provisions and added others.

In truth, the Administration in this area was handicapped. Tugwell was later to admit, "As a matter of fact, Wall Street . . . had together with . . . orthodox university authorities a monopoly of knowledge and competence in the field of money and banking. And they, all of them, had vested interests in the Federal Reserve System." Nor was it at all clear that the leader in the White House made good this lack of expertise. On one occasion Marriner Eccles, whom Roosevelt made chairman of the Board of Governors of the Federal Reserve System, burst into impatience at the President's inertia in banking reform and went on to add, "In judging the President's view, I do not think it would be uncharitable to use the word, 'naive.' " Nor was the prospect in Congress propitious. At one extreme sat Carter Glass, Senator from Virginia, one of the many authors of the Federal Reserve Act. Interim Secretary of the Treasury under Wilson, Glass was seventy-five years old in 1933. A bas-relief in the Federal Reserve Board Building in Washington hails him as "Defender of the Federal Reserve System." He was not likely to believe that time had made many banking instruments and ideas of Wilson's obsolete. He dominated the Senate Banking and Currency Committee and the Senate. In banking legislation, according to Eccles, "It was as though the Senate, by an unwritten amendment of the Constitution, had vested him with veto powers." At the other extreme were impatient Congressmen who could not be bothered with indirect and subtle methods, but preferred simply to inflate the currency.

One of the most important provisions of this banking legislation, opposed originally by both Glass and Roosevelt, was the requirement that all members of the Federal Reserve System have the deposits of their depositors insured by a new and separate agency, the Federal Deposit Insurance Corporation. Nonmembers could join. The result of this arrangement was to reduce drastically the number of bank failures. Small depositors, who piled up in panic "runs" on banks, were now less anxious about getting their money, and the FDIC now moved in advance to reorganize banks likely to fail. Organizational changes were designed to give the Federal Reserve Board more independence. The Secretary of the Treasury and the Comptroller were dropped as *ex-officio* members of the Reserve Board and the terms of the seven other members, now known as "Governors," were lengthened to fourteen years without reappointment. Legislation also extended in a more explicit and centralized form the control of the quantity of credit and hence of money the System could create. The newly created Federal Open Market Committee, consisting of the Governors and certain elected members, was to make all decisions to purchase or sell securities —in practice, government securities—in the market and issue directives to accomplish its decisions. Federal Reserve Banks could not otherwise "engage or decline to engage" in this operation. Be it remembered:

> . . . when the System believes that credit conditions need to be eased, it buys in the open market; when in its judgment credit should be tightened, it

sells in the open market. There is an increase or a decrease in member bank reserves which can result in an expansion or contraction of credit several times as large as the original operation.

Finally, the Board of Governors with at least four assenting "in order to prevent injurious credit expansion or contraction may . . . change the requirements as to reserves to be maintained against . . . deposits by member banks." The results of these changes would be so great that the Board exercises this power rarely. Among such occasions are appropriate adjustments to large changes in the country's stock of gold. Discount, open-market operations, changes in reserve requirements, improved and extended as above described, are general instruments of monetary management. In 1934 the Securities and Exchange Act gave the Federal Reserve Board the power to prescribe through the banks and other lenders the maximum credit, stated as a percentage, granted to customers who are buying and selling securities on margin. If the percentage of cash required for stock purchases is high vis-à-vis the percentage of credit, the Federal Reserve System could dampen security speculation, one of the boom-and-bust features of our economy.

Monetary management by the banks can set a climate for the operation of the economy. But it has limits. It could not compel bankers to lend nor individuals to borrow. Furthermore, the interest rates, "the cost of money," the Federal Reserve System sets mean more for some sorts of enterprise than for others. Certain large industries are relatively immune, for their costs, other than for money, are more determinative and they have more resources in reserve. Trade, where the cost of carrying inventories is a large item; construction, where mortgages are amortized over a long period; and institutions, like insurance companies and banks, dealing in money are more sensitive and responsive to changes in the interest rate.

Debt and Taxes

In its last two years, the Hoover Administration had run a deficit; in 1932, the deficit was roughly six times what it had been the previous year. In 1932 the total gross Federal debt was $19,487,002,000. This trend Roosevelt explicitly promised to reverse. Many of his original appointees and advisors were in favor of balancing the budget, and to that end he kept at the head of the Treasury Henry Morgenthau. Morgenthau generally prayed at the Wailing Wall of "sound" Government Finance. Gradually, step by step, through the thirties the national government retreated from its hitherto orthodox financial position. It retreated behind a smoke screen of promises or expectations of balancing the budget next year, of redefinition of what a budget was—part of the double budget was to be balanced, part was to be deficit—of homilies, "We can afford all that we need; but we cannot afford all that we want." Though taxes were raised here and there or now and then, they were generally left at the Mellon levels until 1935. Roosevelt then dropped a bomb in a request for a general revision. He proposed raising the surtax rates upon "very high incomes"—they were placed at 75 percent upon incomes in excess of $10 million—the income tax on corporations was graduated, and the excess profits tax was increased. A feature of the hearings on these and other proposals was the inability or reluctance of Secretary Morgenthau to correlate the returns from the bill with projected Federal expenditures. This would have indeed been an irrelevance, for Roosevelt's message had announced his bill was to correct the ineffectiveness of previous revenue laws in preventing "an unjust concentration of wealth and economic power. Wealth in the modern world does not come merely from individual effort but from the community." In brief, the aim was to use taxes not primarily to raise money but to accomplish various social and economic purposes. In a country where protective tariffs and taxes upon bank notes had sought the same general ends, the bill was not the novelty that enraged business asserted. The President's case would have been strengthened if he had resorted to American history for support rather than to Carnegie's rationale for private philanthropy. Though the President's purpose faded in later years, a wisp of it was still hanging about in 1940 when Congress once again passed two general revenue acts. At that time the more equal distribution of wealth and of competitive opportunities yielded to defense as the main motivation.

Meanwhile between 1933 and 1940 budgetary deficits aggregated $26.3 billion. By the latter year the Federal debt had reached the total of $42,967,531,000 or $325 per capita. On the other hand, the fiscal burden of the debt had been eased by the lower interest rate it bore and by its later due dates. In these respects the Ship of State was ready to confront the war. But the wavering of purpose, the prevalence of self and public deceit, the sudden decisions to reform society by tax bills boded ill for general agreement or stability in matters of war finance. In these respects the country was more ill-prepared than in Wilson's day. But war and the way it came sternly exacted what must be done.

A general appraisal of the New Deal and its accomplishments assumed an appropriate perspective at a later day—by the late forties or early fifties. But suddenly in the late thirties the turn of economic affairs raised questions about its short-term success. In 1937-1938 the economic indicators turned downward. Both the indices of wholesale prices and the cost of living reached their peak in the former year and

then declined. Gross national product in terms of 1929 prices fell off
$5.5 billion. There were still 10 million unemployed. "Farmers," accord-
ing to the Presidential admission in a Congressional message in late
1937, "have once more been facing acute surpluses and falling prices."
From the noisy and insistent babble of advice as to what should be
done, Roosevelt was led to conclude, "Some of these recommendations
are consistent with each other; some are at complete variance." His own
message, it must be admitted, was also equivocal. Congress was in one
place informed "that the continuance of business recovery in the United
States depends far more upon business policies than it does upon anything that may be done, or not done in Washington." Elsewhere he
added, "But obviously also, government cannot let nature take its
course without regard to consequences. If private enterprise does not
respond, government must take up the slack." The measures Roosevelt
then proposed were hardly earth-shaking; nor was the ideological shift
toward Keynesian concepts of compensatory government spending and
permanent deficits either marked or final. The domestic program of
economic and social reform still had sufficient momentum to enact, as
we have seen, the Fair Labor Standards Act of 1938.

International affairs—the rise of Hitler in Central Europe and the
advance of Japan on the Asiatic mainland—were, however, increasingly
absorbing the attention and alarm of the White House and Main Street.
In one sense this concern was a paradox. Roosevelt's first inaugural, by
implication at least, had sounded an exclusively nationalist note of
reform in our country; international affairs must not interrupt progress
toward that goal. Meanwhile in the nation a large body of opinion in
and out of Congress was conducting an autopsy to discover why the
United States had entered World War I. The answer in a simplified
form was that "profiteers," "merchants of death," and "international
bankers" had blinded the eyes of American innocence and secured
American involvement for their selfish interests. An inflamed xenophobia
inspired a series of laws designed to forestall a repetition of this cause
and effect. The German and Russian attack upon Poland in the fall of
1939; the unchecked thrust of Germany through northern and western
Europe in the spring of 1940; the German invasion of Russia in 1941;
and, finally, the Japanese destruction of the American Pacific fleet at
Pearl Harbor on December 7, 1941, compelled every American except
the doctrinaires to recast his thinking about the past and his vision of
the future.

XX

World War II
and Reconversion

As the German and Russian armies in 1939 eliminated Poland as bounded and governed since World War I, and as the Germans, turning westward in 1940 to shatter the unreal calm of the "phony war," drove the English armies from the Continent and demonstrated they could move at will by air or land through western Europe, including France, the response of the Roosevelt Administration was immediate and decisive. The United States was in mortal danger and must prepare to defend itself, and less obviously Great Britain, by the most modern military means. After a shower of preliminary appropriations and agencies, Roosevelt, on May 26, 1940, summed up in a fireside chat the pattern of things as they were to be:

We are calling upon the resources, the efficiency, and the ingenuity of the American manufacturers of war matériel of all kinds—airplanes, tanks, guns, ships, and all the hundreds of products that go into this matériel. The Government of the United States itself manufactures few of the implements of war. Private industry will continue to be the source of most of this matériel, and private industry will have to be speeded up to produce it at the rate and efficiency called for by the needs of the times.

This was a decision of great historic consequence—and an unavoidable one. Where else than in private industry were the facilities of plants and management?

The President also projected certain guidelines. The pattern of American experience seems to demonstrate that a democracy in wartime wants the reassurance that it can have guns and butter. Wilson had been moderately successful in emphasizing the necessity of choosing alternatives. At the moment Roosevelt didn't stress a forthcoming austerity. Instead he announced that an insistence upon production must not break down "any of the great social gains we have made in these past years"—specifically the shorter working day, minimum wages, social security, "assistance to agriculture," and housing. Taxes must prevent "a new group of war millionaires"; and policy must operate "so that our general cost of living can be maintained at a reasonable level." According to a subsequent press conference, the last generalization meant that a "delightful young lady," otherwise unidentified for history, might have to "forego" a new car but "not cosmetics, lipsticks, ice-cream sodas. . . ." In the same informal give-and-take, the President brushed aside the possibility of government control of railroads—"there aren't any kinks" now—and of a draft of men, women, or money, for "this isn't complete, immediate national mobilization."

The War Production Board

Whether this survey, equivalent as it was to Wilson's request for a Declaration of War against Germany in 1917, had, relative to the circumstances, as sound a grasp of the needs and demands of the war America faced or was as candid in describing the situation and forecasting future policy, was a question that had to wait upon the future for an answer. As in Wilson's time, the institutions for handling the emergency of war production were still in course of evolution. The War Industries Board had not started operating, be it recalled, until nearly eleven months after April, 1917. Roosevelt who had been an administrator in Washington during World War I must have known this: if he had forgotten, Bernard M. Baruch, the overlord of production for the earlier war, could have informed him, for Baruch was flitting in and out of the Washington shadows and was ready to share his experiences, give advice, and even intrigue about appointments. Donald Nelson later confessed, "We are too slow in taking advantage of other men's experience."

In January, 1942, five weeks after Pearl Harbor, Roosevelt regrouped his "patriotic Americans of proven merit and unquestioned ability in their special fields" into a War Production Board (WPB), centralized its powers, and appointed Donald M. Nelson as its chairman. Nelson was a Missourian. Educated as a chemical engineer, he had climbed the ladder in Sears Roebuck until he was vice-president in charge of merchandising. He was a "distribution man," who, to perform his tasks, had to know about producing the goods he purchased. Relatively speaking, he was innocent of ideology and slow to detect it in others. He was, however, certain that it was not enough to defeat America's enemies, we had to do it *within the framework of American tradition* . . . What we did was to establish a set of rules under which the game could be played the way industry said it had to play it."

Industry, since it was primarily market-minded, was predisposed to bid for orders the magnitude of which it had not seen for over a decade. Though Roosevelt's specifications of 50,000 planes and everything else in scale might be brushed aside as rhetorical flourish, the appropriation of billions of dollars was real. Still, conversion to war production had its perils. A few manufacturers, of whom Henry Ford was an example, were idealistically opposed to war work unless persuaded it was "defense"; others, mindful of the neutrality legislation of the thirties, waited for its repeal and the removal of the penalties it imposed. Conversion to war production cost money. Though the government might advance financial aid, American businessmen had enough faith and foresight to believe they would outlive the war and have to compete for peacetime markets. Would plants financed by the government and leased to war producers be the producers' after the war or would they be sold to competitors or operated by the government? These alarms were not groundless: Muscle Shoals and the TVA were there for all to see. If an enterprise financed its own expansion, how rapidly could it amortize its investment?

The Selective Service Act of September, 1940, didn't trifle with these and other hesitations. Section 8 of that act, since the unsettling prospect of private industry making profits while "our boys" fought, bled, and died under compulsion in Europe and Asia would not disappear, contained an authorization for the President to "take immediate possession" of any plant capable of producing arms and ammunition or "any necessary supplies or equipment" which refused to accept an order to undertake such production "at a reasonable price." A month later the government used the carrot instead of the stick. By an amendment to the internal revenue code it permitted enterprises to deduct from their income tax an amortization item, calculated on a five-year basis during an "emergency" period beginning in June, 1940.

Nelson frequently expressed the opinion that the task of his WPB was equivalent in difficulty to "taking the decennial census." His organization had to determine and appraise the needs of a wartime economy. The Quartermaster Corps needed supplies to clothe and feed the army; the Ordnance Department had jurisdiction over munitions, tanks, airplanes, guns, and vehicles. Since men and goods had to move across seas infested by submarines, the United States, as in World War I, had to build a breath-taking tonnage of ocean carriers. Furthermore, the civilian economy—farmers and laborers—had to be fed, housed, and enabled to move about. The United States had to perform all these services not only for itself but for Britain and Russia and even for some other nations outside the struggle. These claimants, foreign and domestic, were demanding nor did they always agree upon which of their needs were "essential" or "nonessential." In cases of emergency the army and navy, for instance, were likely to feel their needs could be met by curtailing civilian production; the government should not "pamper civilians." The Armed Services, prone to worry over disclosures violating security, were often vague about their needs. Nelson wrote, "I can truthfully say that the Armed Services never acquainted me with any of their inside plans as to their requirements." Once the needs were ascertained and a contract was signed with some firm, the War Production Board wanted to be able to "allocate" to the manufacturer the necessary tools and raw materials. In turn this primary producer would apportion supplies to subcontractors according to need.

On most counts the United States was well supplied with the basic materials—coal, petroleum, and iron ore. But iron and steel had to be fashioned into machine tools before the mass production of tanks and airplanes could get under way; the raw material of aluminum, bauxite, had to be imported, refined, and shaped before it could take form as an airplane wing. Though the country had petroleum running out of its ears, tankers had to transport it to the refining centers and markets in the Northeast; steel serviceable for the armor of tanks had to have minute amounts of a hardening ingredient. In spite of national plenty, the events of war soon shattered the illusion that a sufficient stockpile of strategic raw materials was at hand. The rapid conquest of Southeast Asia by the Japanese cut off at once shipments of raw rubber and jeopardized the plans for an army on wheels; packs of submarines in the Caribbean and off the Florida coast sank tankers so fast that supplies of petroleum products in the Northeast were critically endangered. The course of historic events seemed likely to validate the conclusion of Benjamin Franklin's old verse:

> For the want of a battle a kingdom was lost
> And all for the want of a horseshoe nail.

The government had to find avenues of escape from these shortages. In mid-1929 Congress had foresightedly passed a statute and appropriation for the purchase and stockpiling of critical materials and for the support of research to provide substitutes or the upgrading of inferior materials; the bite of conflict increased appropriations and lent urgency to the realization of the program. Even this was not sufficient.

In the field of petroleum, the Petroleum Administration for War in the Department of Commerce and the Office of Price Administration and Civilian Supply—the latter established by Congress early in 1942 and known throughout the war as the "OPA"—were both compelled to institute rationing for gasoline and fuel oil, first in the Northeast and finally on a national scale. Meanwhile the Petroleum Administration was pressing the WPB to allocate steel for two pipelines—one twenty-four inches in diameter and known as the "big inch"—to carry crude oil from the Gulf Coast producing regions to the Northeast. After the WPB cleared the way in 1942 these lines were pushed ahead, sometimes at the rate of nine miles a day, and by September, 1943, 250,000 barrels of oil a day were reaching the East. The government financed the two lines to the extent of $161.5 million. Petroleum was also an essential ingredient for the manufacture of synthetic rubber to which the United States turned as a substitute for natural rubber. American petroleum and chemical concerns had tentatively experimented with synthetic production during the thirties and had acquired patents. But an emergency crash program was a prerequisite to a pooling of patent rights and the construction of plants. Whereas when the war broke out synthetic rubber had never been manufactured anywhere on a large scale, by 1945 American producers were turning out a million long tons annually, a truly great scientific achievement. The Reconstruction Finance Corporation had met the capital outlay of $700 million. Private chemical, petroleum, and rubber companies were operating the synthetic factories for government account on a fee basis.

Ships

In the production of ships the similarities with World War I were more marked. The objective in both instances was identical. For victory, the United States had to build ships faster than the submarines could sink them. Fortunately, the nation was better prepared than in 1917. As the fleet built for that conflict became obsolete in the thirties and other shortcomings in maritime policy became apparent, Congress in 1936 had taken another try at a bill to foster and encourage the maintenance of a merchant marine as a means of national defense and a carrier of a "substantial portion of the water-borne export and import foreign commerce of the United States." To the chairmanship of the United States Maritime Commission, the agency to accomplish these aims, Roosevelt two years later appointed Vice Admiral Emery S. Land, U.S. Navy, retired. Land, who had been in the construction side of things, was a personal friend of President Roosevelt, who also wore the old school tie because of his administrative start with the navy in World War I. Land was energetic and could muster a quarterdeck brusqueness. "You know, I don't believe in the commission form of government. I think you ought to have a one-man show and shoot him at sunrise if he doesn't run it right." The emergency of preparedness and war channeled the flow of peacetime policy in a different direction.

One need was for shipyards. The United States Navy with its immense building program had preempted most of the large-scale traditional private yards, and the priority of this construction was unquestionable. The location of new yards depended upon transportation facilities to assemble supplies; the availability of labor and, even more important, of managerial ability. Although Churchill once hinted at another Hog Island with one hundred shipways, the Maritime Commission chose to establish a number of smaller yards. Those who had the contracts to build ships built the yards, but the government reimbursed them. The government then owned the facilities, which it leased to the operators. Ultimately, by 1945, the total cost of new facilities for Maritime Commission shipyards had amounted to about $600 million.

The multiplication of new yards at government expense cleared the way for outsiders, who had never built ships, to enter the field. In view of the thinness of managerial talent in the field, this could be, if safeguarded, a great advantage. Henry J. Kaiser, once the owner of a photographer's shop and later a contractor for the Hoover, Bonneville, and Grand Coulee dams, and the Bay Bridge at San Francisco, got a start in shipbuilding at yards along the West Coast. A man of energy and ideas, he was willing to take chances and do the unconventional. The building of ships was never a mass production industry, as the automobile and aircraft industries were. But the Maritime Commission, adjourning its dreams of a perfect postwar merchant marine for the United States, chose a standard-type vessel, the "Liberty Ship," which used as many flat plates as possible rather than bent ones; rather than being riveted, these flat plates were welded together, a process that saved weight and increased cargo displacement. Components from engines to rudders were standardized and subcontractors were enabled to apply machine production to them. All these materials flowed to the yards where they were put together in large sections and lifted into place by heavy booms and cranes. Since yards were specialized, they became training grounds in speed for laborers and management. Aside from "stunt ships," the time required for assembling and outfitting a "liberty ship" fell from an average of 250 days in 1941 to 41–42 days at the end of 1943. No comparable speed had been attained in World War I. Generally speaking, the building of ships had met the challenge of sinkings by 1943; in that same year the Maritime Commission shipyards built more tonnage than was under the American flag in 1939.

The Atom Bomb

At the beginning of the war, shipbuilding had a more or less usable past; the atom was largely a speculation in the mind and the imagination of men. In the western world research was the atom's natural habitat; and the danger of living where Hitler might seize, imprison, or murder them had driven scientists and thinkers to take refuge in the United States. Even before the United States entered the war, government funds via the National Defense Research Committee had begun to advise and underwrite research on the various numbered isotopes of uranium. U235 was considered the essential element "for a fission bomb of superlatively destructive power." By December, 1942, scientists had a self-sustaining nuclear reaction working at the University of Chicago; in the course of dispersed experiments they had also discovered a new element which they named plutonium. Plutonium was itself fissionable. By May, 1943, the directors of the program thought a phase had been reached when further work should be turned over to the Army Corps of Engineers. They were to build the plant for the separation of U235 and the production of plutonium. The Manhattan District, as it was called, built a huge establishment at Oak Ridge in Tennessee where it could tap the cheap power of the TVA. Another installation was erected at Hanford, Washington, on the Columbia River. Two private corporations operated the plants at Oak Ridge: the E. I. du Pont de Nemours Company operated the Hanford plant on the understanding it would receive no profits and no patent rights. It was repaid its costs and a fixed fee of one dollar. Under a contract with the University of California, the laboratory work was centralized at Los Alamos, hitherto a desert mesa in New Mexico. On July 16, 1945, the scientists exploded a successful bomb in New Mexico; on August 6, 1945, an American bomber dropped its load on Hiroshima. "Seconds later the city and most of its inhabitants ceased to exist!" Three days later a second bomb obliterated Nagasaki and raised the total death toll to 152,000. The United States thus earned the distinction of being the first and only nation to have used this invention against human beings. In monetary terms the price tag for this accomplishment was nearly $2 billion.

The spectacular explosion of the atomic bomb and the ominous value-judgments inherent in its use were not the pinnacle of success for American industrial production during World War II. The overall totals of munitions were the achievement; measured in "millions of standard 1945 munitions dollars" the monthly average output attained nearly a fifteen fold increase between the last half of 1940 and November, 1943. The total value of munitions between 1940 and August, 1945, was more than $183 billion. Of this triumphant total, aircraft accounted for about one fourth. Nelson had exulted, "Planes were flying out of Uncle Sam's star-spangled costume like a plague of moths." The building of ships constituted 22.5 percent of the total value of munitions. Together aircraft, ships, and combat and motor vehicles represented nearly three-fifths of the total. For various reasons the American industrial corporate giants played the greatest role in compiling these totals. Historically the armed services had preferred to deal with the big companies, and their abstract scheming for M-Day, plans which had never been put into action, embodied this point of view. Also, the great companies had the largest reserves of trained engineers and managers of production; like the automobile industry with its model changeovers they were used to converting wholesale and whole-hog, stripping down the plant to bare walls and fitting it with new machinery designed and built for the new processes. In 1945 the War Production Board noted that among the hundred principal organizations contributing to the armed services in expansion of facilities E. I. du Pont de Nemours & Co. led with expenditures of $915,985,000 (of which the government financed $845,570,000); General Motors, which turned out machine guns, cannon, aircraft engines, tanks, tank destroyers, shells, armored cars, was second with $911,704,000 ($809,926,000 of which was government financed). Ford—"Make the whole plane," he directed his staff—was eighth and Chrysler was ninth. Parenthetically, the War Production Board had by 1942 stopped the manufacture of cars for civilian purposes, so Roosevelt was right when he foresaw two years earlier that a "delightful young lady" would not be able to get a new car. While manufacturers were converting so successfully, their spirits, in spite of irritations, lifted. After "years in the doghouse," as the slang phrase went, they were now helping to win the war. Henry J. Kaiser personified this reversal perfectly in an address at the annual dinner of the National Association of Manufacturers in 1942, "We have fulfilled ourselves. We can dare and we can face, unafraid, *now, tonight,* whatever is to come."

The Farmers

As in World War I, agricultural production was sure to require governmental intervention. In view of Roosevelt's compulsive aversion for Herbert Hoover, it was unlikely that he would appoint a Food Administrator. Besides, by 1939 the government had already invaded the field of prices and production quotas, and, as a result of this intrusion, plus changes in agricultural technology, there was on hand a large carryover of certain commodities. Cotton on hand in 1940-1941 was twice what it had been during the previous decade; corn nearly five times; and feed grains, as a whole, nearly four times. Further increases were perhaps endangered by the outlooks policymakers and farmers had built up before the war. There was a contradiction between their inherited fear of surpluses and the new attitude when abundance became a good.

Logically, which is the way things rarely happen in the formulation of policies or in real life, agricultural planning for the war should have set goals of production for the 6 million farms enumerated in the census of 1940, or the much smaller number which produced commercially for market, and then measures to fulfill these goals should have been formulated. The War Production Board had eventually taken these two steps for industry, but there the task was easier. In agriculture the number of producing units was greater; the ideas of self-reliance and independence were more deeply rooted, although a profit-minded orientation was just as prevalent. Finally, setting goals involved questions of taste about which there is much unyielding disputation. If we are to believe roadside advertising, when Americans eat "fine foods" they desire chicken, steaks, and lobster; when they are eating for subsistence, "burgers," french fries, and catsup make the meal. If they eat by what science tells us then they surrender judgment to the dictates of the home economist, and the result is the menu of the college commons. In September, 1941, nonetheless, the Department of Agriculture issued the first set of national production goals for the coming year. These applied to some twenty crops. Some of the biggest projected increases were in peanuts and soybeans—both sources of vegetable oils; decreases were set for wheat and one variety of tobacco. The conventional peacetime means of stimulating production and apportioning commodities was the price system.

Already the interests affected had made it clear that the manipulation of the price system was not to be detached, scientific, or serene. Parity prices were the standard of desire, but most legislation had not compelled the achievement of parity prices but had stated a percentage of such prices as a purpose. Organized farmers and their spokesmen were not content with this partial loaf, nor were they convinced that Roosevelt's "hope" for a certain percentage was a firm enough commitment. In the spring and summer of 1941, before Pearl Harbor, they had succeeded in securing the passage of an act making government loans at 85 percent of parity mandatory for the five basic crops—corn, cotton, wheat, rice, and tobacco. This legislation was a partial explanation of the rise in agricultural prices. Since the general onrush of inflation reminded it disagreeably of 1915, the Administration sought some measure to stiffen control over prices. By January, 1942, the President was able to obtain from Congress the Emergency Price Control Act. Though he saluted the statute as "an important weapon in our armory," he chided the farmers for the provisions governing prices on agricultural commodities. No maximum price could be set below the "highest" of four bench marks, one of which was 110 percent of the parity prices. Roosevelt concluded, "I feel that most farmers realize that when farm prices go much above parity danger is ahead."

It was indeed! As the months passed and the Office of Price Administration set prices and introduced food rationing on many products, and the high cost of living drove discontented wage earners to ask higher wages, Roosevelt concluded that the specifications for agricultural prices must go. Empirically his campaign was successful for new provisions and a new agency, established in October, 1942, substituted different directives. Maximum agricultural prices were frozen at the level of September, 1942, and government payments already made to farmers were deducted from them. The President's argument for change had the intellectual merit of describing statistically the disruptive part agricultural prices were playing in the rising cost of living. Also, Roosevelt tried to repeat, less successfully and firmly, the formula of his first inaugural: the "threat of economic chaos" and the undefined promise to use his war powers "to avert a disaster which would interfere with the winning of the war." Actually, the Administration had adroitly brought into the conflict a new weapon. To "roll back" or to reduce food prices it adopted subsidies to producers or processers. By the summer of 1945 the government was making such payments to the tune of $1,643,400,000. By and large the farmers didn't approve of this policy. Like the industrialists, farmers looked ahead. When the markets of peace were again functioning, they wanted consumers used to paying a "natural price," not one dependent on government handouts which could be taken away or given for political considerations. "Let the consumer pay the full bill—he's making good money," expressed the farmers' attitude.

Whatever the farmers' vicissitudes, American agriculture responded magnificently to the needs of the war. It produced 50 percent more food annually than in World War I; and the index of production per capita rose from 151 in 1940 to 191 in 1945, an increase "without parallel" for agriculture. Neither a notable increase in acreage in crops nor an increase in workers accounted for this achievement. As a matter of fact, at the end of the war there were 10 percent fewer workers on the farms. The causes for success were the more lavish use of fertilizer and of farm machinery. Though the latter was rationed for an interval, farmers acquired more tractors and harvesting and haying machinery. The weather, beyond the reach of government or individual, was exceptionally favorable in 1943 and 1944; the former year attained the peak of agricultural production during the war. Meanwhile, between 1940 and 1945, the wholesale price index of all farm products nearly doubled. "As a result of war influences, farmers were in the best financial position in history at the end of World War II," concluded a student of the era.

Labor

When the Nazis overwhelmed western and northern Europe in 1940 the occasion arose for the "complete, immediate national mobilization" at which the President had hinted at the end of May. In July Roosevelt was announcing that "most right thinking persons are agreed that some form of selection by draft is as necessary and fair today as it was in 1917 and 1918." Congress in September, 1940, thereupon provided that every male citizen between twenty-one and thirty-six years of age should register and be "liable for training and service in the land or naval forces of the United States." The service period was to be for twelve months. No more than 900,000 men could be serving in the land forces at one time except in case of war. Congress in August, 1941, by a series of bills lifted most limitations imposed by this first peacetime draft in American history. The age limits were extended from eighteen to sixty-five; service was to end not later than six months after the termination of a war not yet declared. At first, the government inducted men rather slowly; but by July, 1945, the number in the armed services was 12.3 million.

The withdrawal of these individuals from civilian activity was bound to have profound effects upon manufacture and agriculture. The effects were cushioned somewhat by statutory deferments which were scrutinized continually and prayerfully by those liable to registration. The First Selective Service Act, for instance, postponed for a year the induction of students "at any college or university which grants a degree in arts or science." However helpful in preventing the colleges from losing their male students, a more useful provision for the labor force was one authorizing deferment for men "whose employment in industry, agriculture, or . . . whose activity in other endeavors is found . . . to be necessary to the maintenance of the national health, safety or interest." Most of these deferments allowed the exercise of discretion. But in 1942 the farmers' friends in Congress secured an amendment to a draft bill making mandatory the deferment of a worker "regularly engaged in an agricultural occupation or endeavor essential to the war effort."

In a paradoxical way, the failure of the Administration to solve the problem of unemployment in the thirties contributed to the nation's success in meeting the exigencies of war. The surplus of 8 million to 10 million unemployed could be and was reabsorbed into the labor force. They were not enough! The labor force recruited additional workers from boys and girls in their later teens; a second source was married women between thirty-five and fifty-four years of age, whose children were old enough to be cared for in schools; patriotism or public opinion practically lowered standards of eligible performance, which meant that many older men stayed on in the labor force. And the attractiveness of higher wage rates and urban living stimulated the migration of workers from the farms. Between April, 1940, and April, 1945, the total number in the labor force increased by 10.6 million, of which about

7.7 million was estimated as the number of additional workers drawn into the labor force by wartime circumstances.

Still, there were labor shortages. The degree of industrial skill and competence was problematical, as teenagers and older women thronged into industry. Luckily, American mass production techniques facilitated the employment of only partially skilled workers; industries of the stature of Ford provided their own in-shop training; and many youth agencies of the depression years could be bent in this direction. Often the difficulty was not labor shortage but the provision of housing for workers or of transportation to work when restrictions hedged automobile travel. Another relevant aspect of the work force was the size of union membership. Whereas in 1940 the total in the United States had been 7,282,000, by 1945 the figure stood at 12,562,100. These totals as a percentage of the civilian labor force increased from 12.7 percent to 22.4 percent. It had usually been hard to organize new recruits to industry, particularly women, but the momentum of the thirties carried over into the war years and periods of comparatively full employment and of rising prices have generally favored, nay compelled, a strong union movement.

Soon after the Japanese attacked Pearl Harbor, Roosevelt called a conference at Washington of representatives from management and from labor. The frightening drama of the moment and the President's insistence brought about a measure of agreement. The conference agreed on a no-strike and no-lockout pledge, for these would interfere with production, and recommended as a substitute for these tests of strength the peaceful arbitration of labor disputes by a National War Labor Board (NWLB), composed of representatives of labor, management, and the public. Labor and employers both wished to exclude from this board's jurisdiction the questions of union "security," such as recognition, the closed shop, the check-off of dues. President Roosevelt characteristically papered over the difficulty by insisting the agreement on the points already cited covered "of necessity all disputes that may arise between labor and management." As if the settlement of disputes were not a sufficient assignment of duties, the President under the Emergency Price Control Act of October, 1942, to which reference has already been made, ordered that increases and decreases in wage rates must be approved by the National War Labor Board.

The NWLB had an impressive, though not perfect, record of success. Without denigrating the ability or dedication of labor or employer representatives, the four public members proved to be individuals of exceptional competence and impartiality who possessed in addition the gift of persuasion. However they might differ with each other, the members of the board operated on the rule, "The majority vote of the Board represents the action of the full Board." Still, there were a few instances of noncompliance by both employers and employees. It is customary to palliate the occasional resort to strikes by calculating the ratio of days worked to days lost through strikes. In this way the parties involved emerge as pure as Ivory Soap. But rarely was quantification so misleading. When production is a process of sequential steps an interruption can cause the shortage of a strategic part. While Montgomery Ward gained the distinction of chief culprit on the management side, the United Mine Workers of America under John L. Lewis was the chief offender among unions. When the public members of the National War Labor Board accused the United Mine Workers of "cynical and repeated violations of the no-strike policy," Congress was naturally impatient. In June, 1943, it passed the War Labor Disputes Act making more specific the provision, earlier embodied in the Selective Service Act, of the President's power to seize and operate any "plant, mine or facility" if he found "an interruption of operation as a result of a strike or other labor disturbance" was unduly impeding "the war effort." The President vetoed the measure but recommended "that the Selective Service Act be amended [to] enable us to induct into military service all persons who engage in strikes or stoppages . . . in plants in the possession of the United States."

Although Congress was content for the moment to pass the War Labor Disputes Act over Roosevelt's veto, the simple idea of drafting strikers continued to gain momentum. The idea appealed to the armed services; Admiral Land, driven from pillar to post by labor turbulence in shipbuilding, was reportedly the advocate of a thorough policy: union organizers "ought to be shot at sunrise." Be it remembered he had advocated the same medicine for himself if he did not succeed on the Maritime Commission. In 1943 the contumacy of the "leaders" of the United Mine Workers shattered even Roosevelt's poise; three strikes within a short period were "intolerable." Miners had won increases in wages since 1941 of 46.9 percent. After seizing the mines and alternatively cajoling and menacing through the summer and fall, Roosevelt announced the "Government had taken steps to set up the machinery for inducting into the armed services all miners subject to the Selective Service Act who absented themselves without just cause from work in the mines under government operation." Whether the President or Lewis triumphed and, if the former, whether he did it by waving the flag over the mines or genuinely planning to draft labor, is a matter of speculation. Anyway, as Frances Perkins records, "the major task was done without resort to conscription of labor," and Roosevelt was thankful.

During the war unemployment practically disappeared. There was a moderate increase in the average length of the workweek from 38.1 hours in 1940 to 43.4 in 1945. Generally speaking, American industry responded to the demand for production by multiplying the number of shifts, sometimes "around the clock," rather than by lengthening the working day. At the same time average hourly earnings in all manufacturing rose from $0.661 to $1.023. Organized labor was dissatisfied with the latter achievement, for, according to the unions' calculations, wages did not rise as rapidly as the cost of living. President Green of the AFL protested to Roosevelt the "freezing," or "stabilization," of wages and made labor's assent contingent upon a policy of draconian price control or the limitation of profits and the elimination of "inequities." These suggestions were partially influential in shaping government tax and labor policies; in general, they give the impression of being made for the record. All in all, the AFL was as pragmatic as President Roosevelt, who once confided to Frances Perkins, "obviously we have to make shift during the war."

That's Where the Money Goes—and Comes

In July, 1940, after the collapse of western Europe before the Nazis, Congress appropriated $5 billion for the army and navy, two and a half times as much as had been appropriated in the previous fiscal year. This sum plus the authorization in March, 1941, for lend-lease—the World War II method of financing allies—signalized a scale of expenditures which the peacetime New Deal had neither dared undertake nor imagine. Over the years the dollar totals strode rapidly upwards. From July 1, 1940, to June 30, 1946, the Federal government spent $360 billion for defense and war. The expenditure of $100 billion in 1945 alone was more than ten times the highest prewar annual expenditure.

The American way of war from the Civil War on had been usually financed by a mixture of borrowing and taxes. As one evidence of the former method, the increase in the government debt had the merit of simplicity. Whereas in 1939 the total had been $40,489,532,000, it was $269,422,099,000 in 1946; the respective per capita figures were $508.48 and $1,905.42. The total of national indebtedness for the first time exceeded that of private indebtedness. For these increases and the new prominence of the debt as an item in the national economy, war was not the only explanation but it was the chief one.

The government distributed its securities through seven wartime loan campaigns and one Victory Loan. The total amount of these security sales was almost five times as much as the total cost of World War I. The government pegged the price of securities and sought to pay a low rate of interest upon them. One reason for these devices was to make the securities attractive to individual purchasers, for the consequent sterilization of their savings would reduce their power to purchase other goods and hence lessen the danger of inflation. To sell bonds to banks was more likely to lead to an increase in credit. But the Treasury did not realize its hopes. Commercial banks by 1946 had absorbed $84.4 billion of the Federal interest-bearing debt. As compared to World War I, all banks absorbed twice as great a percentage of the Federal debts. Though a democratic country could hardly compel individuals to buy bonds, it could and did take their money in the form of taxes. Taxes, in fact, bore 46 percent of the total war costs, an unsurpassed record in American history. The percentage in World War I had been 33 percent.

As far back as the financial measures of Alexander Hamilton and as continuous as the controversy over the tariff, it had been recognized that taxes were more than a mere means of raising revenue; taxes were also a way of attaining economic and social objectives. Sometimes this was a matter of design—sometimes of accident. In asking Congress for a war revenue bill in May, 1941, Roosevelt expressed his hope to the House Ways and Means Committee that they would formulate a bill which would not "make the rich richer and the poor poorer." It was comparatively easy to respond to this appeal, for the graduated federal income tax in peace and war had become the nation's chief way of raising money; its fundamental principle was "the ability to pay." Four war revenue acts from 1941 to 1944, in their timing not too precisely articulated with increasing government expenditures, consequently lowered the tax exemption to $1,000 for a married couple and raised the surtax percentage as high as 91 percent on incomes over $200,000. Normal and surtax rates on the income of corporations were raised. When Congress in World War I first enacted an excess profits tax it was resorting to a technical description of profits above a certain amount; "excess profits" out of context had the connotation of ill-gotten gains and usury, a historic concept hard to erase from the mind. The Revenue Act of 1944 levied a rate of 95 percent on excess profits—permissible deductions made this less burdensome.

By 1942 taxation policy had become openly entangled with the cost of living. As employment and disposable income in the hands of individuals and government increased, and as certain articles, because of war production, were in short supply, demand began pushing up the level of prices. The index of wholesale prices, compiled and calculated by the Bureau of Labor Statistics, rose from 78.6 in 1940 to 87.3 in 1941, and to 98 in 1942. The consumer price indexes—the cost of living—rose from 59.9 in 1940 to 69.7 in the same three-year span. The rates of the increase were less than in World War I and the Civil War; they were real, nonetheless. Though we have already anticipated the impact of these changes in our discussion of farm and wage policy, we have had to omit some general and summary conclusions. The President's seven-point program, unveiled in April, 1942, announced, "We can face the fact that there must be a drastic reduction in our standard of living." Roosevelt's main recommendations were to tax heavily while keeping personal and corporate profits at a "reasonable" level, which was defined as a low level. He also suggested "ceilings" on consumer commodities and on certain rents; stabilization of "prices received by growers for products of their lands"; rationing of "all essential commodities of which there is a scarcity," so they might be distributed "fairly" and "not merely in accordance with financial ability to pay high prices"; discouragement of "credits and installment buying"; and stabilization of "remuneration received by individuals for their work." Thus, even before the end of the road the nation became the garrison state.

To preserve discipline new agencies came into being; old ones exercised new powers, or administrators just raised their voices. The Federal Reserve Board, for instance, regulated the use of credit, including installment buying, extended to consumers. From time to time an agency or "the Great White Father," as one Price Administrator publicly called Roosevelt, shouted imperatives from the watchtower, sometimes with the assent of Congress. In July, 1942, by the Little Steel Formula, the National War Labor Board permitted a general 15 percent increase of wage rates, since the cost of living had risen by that percentage since January 1, 1941, and the purpose of the board was to preserve "peace-time standards." In April, 1945, Roosevelt signed a hold-the-line order. "We cannot tolerate further increases in prices affecting the cost of living or further increases in general wage or salary rates."

Through the tensions of these months there was a running quarrel between the President and Congress over a ceiling on salaries. In terms of yields to the Treasury this was a matter of minor detail, for it did not involve large sums or many individuals, but the quarrel was revelatory of deeply held values and aims. In April, 1942, Roosevelt stated his belief:

Discrepancies between low personal incomes and very high personal incomes should be lessened; and I therefore believe that in time of this grave national danger, when all excess income should go to win the war, no American citizen ought to have a net income, after he has paid his taxes, of more than $25,000 a year.

In view of the failure of Congress to grant this power, Roosevelt instructed the Treasury to enforce this limitation by a flat 100 percent supertax on "excessive incomes." Under pressure he later regretted he could not apply a similar limitation "to the coupon clipper." In the end Congress, through a rider to a bill, eliminated the President's power to limit salaries to $25,000. The friendly compiler of the President's speeches stigmatized the quarrel over this "comparatively mild proposal for domestic sacrifice [as] an unattractive page in the history of the home front." An examination of the whole record leaves the impression that Roosevelt was taking advantage of the emotional atmosphere of the emergency to further his ideological preference to equalize wealth. Congressional disapproval had blunted this particular weapon. Meanwhile the rise of prices slowed. The percentage of increase per year between November, 1941, and VJ Day in August, 1945, was less than half what it had been in the period of defense.

Neither history nor its trends stopped with VE or VJ Day. The war had hardly started before individuals, in and out of government, began planning what the economic structure would or should be after the war had ended. At the very moment in 1942 when H. J. Kaiser was exhorting his business colleagues to responsible leadership, he was derisively appraising the array of plans advanced by other apostles of planning. "It is a pity that there is no twentieth century Chaucer to portray adequately these modern Canterbury pilgrims . . . It is indeed a blessed thing for civilization that only a small fragment of this vast outpouring of genius will actually be tried." While Roosevelt certainly had no monopoly of planning, with him lay the power of accomplishment; he had the political skill and he had the following. Unlike Wilson, who had been repudiated in 1918 in midstream, Roosevelt had been reelected to a fourth term in 1944. In a reflective moment he had earlier analyzed for a press conference his conception of his past and of his future:

> I am inclined to think that the country ought to have it brought back to their memories . . . there was an awfully sick patient called the United States of America. It called in the "old doctor" and he gave it the remedies which cured it . . . Since then, two years ago, the patient had a very bad accident . . . and they didn't think he would live, for a while. And then he began to "come to," and he has been in charge of a partner of the old doctor. Old Doctor New Deal didn't know "nothing" about legs and arms . . . So he got his partner, who was an orthopedic surgeon, Dr. Win-the-War, to take care of this fellow who had been in this bad accident. [Dr. New Deal had a program] for the problems of 1933. Now in time, there will have to be a new program, whoever runs the government. We are not talking in terms of 1933's program. We have done nearly all of that but that doesn't avoid or make impossible or unsuccessful another program, when the time comes. When the time comes.

For him it never did. He died at Warm Springs, Georgia, on April 12, 1945.

Neither the informality of a press conference nor the playful allegory could conceal the fact, mentioned before, that Roosevelt's great virtue was concreteness. Out of the circumstances of the Depression and then of the war grew the measures he had taken. New circumstances would require new programs. Acknowledging all this, Roosevelt's summary of Dr. New Deal's remedies—thirty in number—was more an enumeration than it was an appraisal of their relative importance. Some of the items must have been prescribed by individuals standing around in the sickroom, for the doctor had neither conceived nor approved of them. Nor was the distinction between Dr. New Deal and Dr. Win-the-War as sharp as the President implied. While the objectives were substantially different, the Administration either hopefully or through compulsion insisted that the nation put all its resources at the behest of the government in order to lift the Depression or wring unconditional surrender from its foes. During all these years, whoever the doctor, the area of national action was thus enlarged and the powers of government were extended. More so in war than in peace, to be sure. But now the country was entering the peace it had gained by conquering.

As compared to the years before 1932, the country now had an agriculture where the amount the farmers could raise was limited and prices were governmentally administered, though the major share of agricultural production was outside government programs; it had "slum clearance—decent housing," but not "enough" of it; it had old age and unemployment insurance and minimum wages and maximum hours, and labor had won the right to bargain collectively; it had a public works program, to provide work, to build "thousands of permanent improvements"; it had "regional physical development, such as TVA"; it had abolished "child labor. It was not thought to be constitutional in the old days, but it turned out to be." Every catalogue of accomplishments may be as revealing in its omissions as in its inclusions. Whether or not the inflaton of the Roosevelt years was inevitable, the President did not voice reservation about the charges of Dr. New Deal and Dr. Win-the-War. Be that as it may, Miss Perkins' insight was sound when at a Cabinet meeting discussing the Republican platform of 1944 she commented, "Well, I think we should be grateful for that platform. It means that the New Deal has won forever. The country had adopted as a permanent program those items which, when we introduced them, were supposed to be radical, revolutionary, and temporary."

The Age of Anxiety

Peace, it was said, was "wonderful"; it was also troubled. As the country faced the task of "reconversion," its leaders, if historically informed, were mindful of the years after World War I and the sharp depression of 1920–1921. More speculative was the connection between that conflict and the Great Depression, but there were those to make the connection. The Depression, whatever its cause, left a sharper, more immediate anxiety as people recalled the massive dimensions of unemployment and destitution. The country did not wish to repeat the experience from which Roosevelt and World War II had rescued it. Ancillary to these two major anxieties were uncertainties over how the most recent conflict was really going to come out. Would differences in purpose and systems between the great powers, once allied, subside or become so dangerous that the new international machinery for peace keeping would be too fragile to contain them?

However remote was reassurance on all these matters, the first national task was to eliminate some of the more irritating and obvious aspects of wartime abnormality. When it was clear, for instance, the United Nations had won, it was no longer necessary to build ships or airplanes, and the American government and industry began terminating their contracts. The rationing of some items had always been somewhat marginal. A day after VJ Day gasoline became a good free from cards and coupons; jubilant drivers once again could direct filling-station attendants to "fill 'er-up" and relieve their accumulated irritations by adding, "Slop a little on the hardtop." Stoves and processed foods went off ration the same day, and by the end of the year all rationing programs for everything except sugar were things of the past. Price control was more complicated, for it was entangled with wages and the level of prices for agricultural production. The Price Control Act expired by its own statutory limitations on June 30, 1946. After some sparring between Truman and Congress, the former brought himself in October to discontinue meat prices; "the final collapse of the stabilization program had come." The OPA's power to control rents lingered until mid-1947, when it was transferred to another agency; state legislation governed rent control for a much longer period. As partial decisions arising from fatigue or preoccupation with other issues put the skids under controls, the upward course of wholesale prices resumed. They reached their postwar peak in August, 1948. The rate of increase in their index had been 16.4 percent per year between January, 1946, and the peak date. For this outcome, the monetary situation was more responsible than the absence of controls. When the Korean War, in 1950, shot the wholesale price index up again, Congress and the President agreed upon a measure authorizing price and wage control provisions—but only on a standby basis.

By and large the postwar disposition of capital goods owned by the government involved few complexities and proceeded without significant decisions. Stockpiles of metals would last or could be rotated, and superfluous ships could be kept in mothballs. According to estimates, the government also owned by 1945 from 10 to 15 percent of the nation's plant capacity. Under the terms of the acts which had provided the capital, the private enterprises which operated these plants had a chance to purchase them if they wished. Characteristically, Roosevelt had once kept his options open as to whether he favored government-owned, but not government-operated, plants, "Maybe, in other words that is a question to be taken up with the people." In the end special circumstances rather than a popular referendum imposed the details of disposal. Plants for manufacturing synthetic rubber could not be put into mothballs without marked deterioration, and "a national emergency" might require supplies. Consequently, for a few years the government made a market for the product by insisting a percentage of synthetic be used in tires. By 1948 Congress was convinced that the demand for synthetic rubber was genuine and firm—it had proved technically superior to natural rubber—and passed the Rubber Act. For the 96 percent of capacity owned by the government, the act stated, "It is further declared to be the policy of the Congress that the security interests of the United States can and will best be served by the development within the United States of a free competitive synthetic-rubber industry." The act, with certain reservations, thought it "essential" that government ownership of production facilities, and government production of synthetic rubber "along with mandatory requirements for its use, and patent pooling be terminated."

Atomic Power

Rubber policy was simplicity itself compared to a policy for the atom. At issue were the facilities constructed by the government for research and for the manufacture of the materials used in the bomb. More essential was the accumulated scientific knowledge in the heads of individuals—some connected with the government and some with learned institutions and some who were just scientists. Furthermore, the potentialities of the atom were unexplored and even unimagined. Experience with the new force was largely confined to laboratories, to medicine, and to munitions. In all such enterprises economic considerations, for instance, costs, did not operate, or at least not with any high priority. It was a question whether power generated from an atomic pile could compete commercially with power generated by the combustion of "fossil fuels," oil and coal, or from falling water. Because of the explosion of the bomb everyone had a notion of the potential peril of destruction and of pollution in the use of the atom. Sometimes it seemed as if the chief handicap to the formation of sound policy was overemphasis rather than underemphasis on the dangers of fission and, later, fusion. Senator McMahon of Connecticut, whose name was justly perpetuated by the Congressional act of 1946 for the development and control of atomic power, frequently said the bombing of Hiroshima was the greatest event in world history since the birth of Jesus Christ.

If historical analogy carried its own imperatives, logic would have suggested applying to the atom a TVA policy. Here were government facilities, built, like Muscle Shoals, almost adventitiously and now of limited use. Here were multipurpose objectives as in the Tennessee Valley. That the whole picture suggested pioneering and "our new frontier" was also to the point. From the early nineteenth century government enterprise and money had backed such projects—"internal improvements"—with uncertain prospects of profit. Perhaps the TVA experiment had lost its luster; anyway, Roosevelt was dead. Besides, policy for the atom had enough barriers to surmount without piling on any more.

Of course, the armed services were involved. The bomb was a weapon and, as we have seen, an army general headed the Manhattan Project which manufactured it. That other countries were not similarly equipped made the desire for military control all the fiercer. Besides a whole atomic armory, for instance, submarines and aircraft carriers with nuclear power, if these were feasible, promised further military advantages. The sharing of atomic secrets with allied powers and the possibility of a treaty limiting the employment of atomic weapons raised international complications. The scientific community whose knowledge and skill had invented the bomb and whose continued cooperation was essential for atomic research and technology had a faction which felt a sense of guilt for its share in Hiroshima and Nagasaki and was anxious to share effective responsibility in determining further policy. Said one of the scientists' leaders, "It is not that we will not work for the government but that we cannot work for the government. Unless research is free and outside of control, the United States will lose its superiority in scientific pursuit." Furthermore, for the moment the bomb was an American secret and a tight security might keep it so. It was questionable if it was safe to let even a Congressional committee into the mysteries.

In 1946 Congress found a solution or compromise for these and other difficulties in an Atomic Energy Commission (AEC) of five men appointed by the President with the assent of the Senate. The President was to designate the chairman of the commission. This was hardly a startling answer; commissions were an old story for the Federal government, though this one had novelty in its operative rather than its quasi-judicial functions. The act transferred to the Commission ownership of "all fissionable materials; . . . and all plants, facilities, and materials for the processing or production of fissionable materials." In practice the Atomic Energy Commission contracted with private concerns for the operation of primary productive facilities—the war precedent; through licenses, the AEC could transfer to private corporations the necessary atomic materials for the operation of a nuclear reactor which in turn generated steam and then electricity. The licensee had to observe certain safety precautions; nor could the AEC give licenses which were likely "to maintain or foster the growth of monopoly, restraint of trade, unlawful competition, or other trade position inimical to the entry of new, freely competitive enterprises." While the commission was composed of civilians, the statute provided that it have a Division of Military Applicaton, which in practice consisted entirely of officers of the armed services. The Atomic Energy Commission could and did appoint scientists to its Advisory Council and reported to a Joint Committee on Atomic Energy in Congress. President Truman appointed as the AEC's first chairman David Lilienthal, who had had vast administrative experience on the TVA.

Institutions for the control of atomic energy changed almost as rapidly as knowledge of the atom. After prolonged hearings Congress enacted in 1954 a new measure. This act put a major emphasis upon the development of atomic energy "to improve the general welfare, increase the standard of living, and strengthen free competition in private enterprise." The act loosened restrictions on research and development by other than AEC units and granted to inventors a right to patent their inventions in the area. The act also permitted the private manufacture, ownership, and operation of atomic reactors under licenses administered by the Atomic Energy Commission; the commission in granting licenses for commercial power production should give preference to high-cost power areas in the United States and to applications from public and cooperative bodies. The new orientation on the commercial use of atomic energy owed something to the explosion of a Russian bomb in 1949. Russia was obviously entitled to join the "Atomic Club," and secrets and security could not preserve the club's exclusive character. Britain also was working intensively upon a full-scale nuclear power-station, opened in 1956. At home President Eisenhower was publicizing his philosophy of "atoms for peace." In terms of industrial utilization this program meant an emphasis upon the provisions of the McMahon Act which state atomic energy should strengthen "free competition in private enterprise." Many thought this a mere platitude; Congress had considered making appropriations to the AEC for the construction and operation of atomic power plants.

Eisenhower's preferences, the act of 1954, and the pioneering impulses of certain corporations discarded the possibility of Congressional appropriations to the AEC for atomic plants. In 1954 the Duquesne Light Company of Pittsburgh made an arrangement with the Atomic Energy Commission. The company contributed $15 million to research for the reactor; built and operated the electric generating plant; paid the operating costs of the reactor; and bought steam from the AEC. Similarly the Westinghouse Company, as a contractor and builder, contributed its estimated profit to the enterprise. The installation in western Pennsylvania dedicated in 1955 was the first important commercial nuclear power plant in the United States. The trend, once under way, made spectacular advances in the sixties. In 1966 and 1967 atomic power was the favorite of electric utilities. At the end of the latter year 50 million kilowatts of power plants had been committed to nuclear units, and one electric magnate expressed the opinion, "I doubt there will ever again be any fossil-fueled plants built in New England." Even the TVA contracted for nuclear reactors to contribute to its power pool. General Electric, Westinghouse, and other corporations were building reactors and the Atomic Energy Commission was abandoning the last phase of government monopoly by selling its plants for manufacturing the atomic materials.

Labor Organizations

The atom may have been the chief anxiety of the postwar age. Remembrance of the years after World War I raised others. War production was being cut back, millions of servicemen were returning to civilian employments; the lush returns from overtime were evaporating. Perhaps the jobs themselves would also disappear. Troubled recollections of the immediate past and present were also at work. The removal of the need for sacrifice seemed to sharpen calculations as to whether past sacrifices had been equally borne. As we have seen, in the process of stabilizing prices for commodities and wages, a whipsaw effect between industrial labor and farmers had emerged. The latter, in particular, felt the government was "coddling" labor and was more quick to put ceilings on commodities than on the price of labor. The farmer toiled on in his fields hour after hour while John L. Lewis and his miners struck to receive pay for the time spent traveling between portal and coal face. No matter what the averages said, strikes interrupted production for war. Labor turbulence, as after World War I, increased with the arrival of peace. In Truman's eyes the labor situation "was assuming serious proportions" by the autumn of 1945. By May, 1946, Truman's view was an obvious understatement, for the workers on the railroads were threatening to go out. Though the employers and nearly all the unions accepted a compromise made by the President, the Locomotive Engineers and Railway Trainmen held out. Truman seized the railroads. When confrontation and threats failed to budge the leaders, Truman asked Congress for "strong emergency legislation" to permit him to draft the strikers. As he spoke, the strike collapsed. A bill embodying the President's suggestion passed the House, but Robert A. Taft, Senator from Ohio, blocked it in the Senate with the observation that Truman's request went "farther toward Hitlerism, Stalinism, totalitarianism, than I have ever seen proposed in any strike."

A strong current of popular discontent believed unions had grown too strong and arrogant through the Wagner Act, which guaranteed the right of collective bargaining through unions chosen by the workers. The act and the decisions of the National Labor Relations Board enforcing it were, it was alleged, "one-sided"; the conditions of the test of strength between employer and employee should, it was also alleged, be made "fair" and "equal." Some scholarly opinion grants the act was one-sided and was intended to be so when it passed. The act's supporters, it was said, felt the judiciary in particular had a long record of anti-union discrimination, and Congress intended to counterbalance this inferior condition by its own legislative favoritism. By 1945 a merged labor union movement with 12 million members and with the power to stop an essential service like railroading was hardly an underdog. The agitation for the repeal or amendment of the Wagner Act and the legislative history of the Taft-Hartley Act, from its passage in 1947, really contained few surprises except for those who were innocent in the ways of democratic politics. Employers, organized in the National Association of Manufacturers and the United States Chamber of Commerce, and farmers, in the American Farm Bureau Federation, favored a change; while workers, organized in labor unions, were for the *status quo*. Lobbyists swarmed; a flood of propaganda crested again and again; charges of conspiracy received the standing of facts; political aspirations clouded statesmen's pure intentions; President Truman vetoed the measure "as bad for labor, bad for management, and bad for the country"; and Congress passed the bill over his veto.

The Labor Management Relations Act of 1947 (Taft-Hartley Act) did not reject all previous legislation or experience in the area of labor-management relations. It recognized "the inequality in bargaining power between employees and employers . . . who are organized in the corporate or other forms of enterprise" and that the working of this inequality on a purely individual basis hampered the flow of interstate commerce. With greater detail and extent than hitherto, the Act did specify "unfair labor practices" on the part of labor organizations and their agents, it excluded from the contracts between employers and employees "featherbedding" or the hiring of unnecessary employees, the compulsory check-off of union dues, and the "closed" but not the "union" shop if a majority of eligible employees voted specifically for the latter. The premise behind these and other provisions was that the worker must be emancipated, to use the cliché, from the tyranny of the unions and their leaders.

The larger portion of the Taft-Hartley Act attempted to limit the resort to strikes. A labor contract between management and workers could not be terminated without sixty days' notice. During this "cooling-off" period, evidently based upon the assumption that the parties to a contract acted impetuously and in angry haste, the Federal Mediation and Conciliation Service might act to settle the quarrel. Strikes, of course, might still break out. If they affected "an entire industry or a substantial part thereof" and imperiled "national health and safety" the President of the United States was to appoint a board of inquiry to ascertain, without making recommendation, the facts in the dispute. Upon his receipt of this report the President could ask the courts to enjoin the strike or its continuance. If within sixty days no agreement had been reached in this labor quarrel, the President should reconvene the board of inquiry to bring proceedings up-to-date, the report was to be made public, and the National Labor Relations Board was to submit to the employees "the employer's last offer of settlement." If the workers accepted that final offer the injunction would be discharged. No injunction could last for longer than the eighty days necessary to cover this involved proceeding. Finally, it was unlawful for government employees to participate in any strike. An enactment in 1959 required financial reports from unions, the exclusion from union office of any person who was or had been a member of the Communist party, and other safeguards extended the protection of the individual union member.

Meanwhile the Taft-Hartley Act had let loose an uproar. Organized labor habitually referred to it as "The Slave Labor Law" and, regardless of traditions of nonpolitical affiliation, put new organizational efforts and funds behind the election of those pledged to its repeal or the defeat of those who had voted for it. Though counts of the heads which fell during the purge were favorable to repeal, the issue was too perilous for politicians to press hard. The noise and excitement subsided. Perhaps the teeth of the act didn't bite as often and as hard as the unions had feared. The President invoked the national emergency provisions of Taft-Hartley seventeen times before 1960; in nearly all cases agreements had resulted. If they could get outside the battle, unions might perhaps reflect that if they are the chosen agency of public policy they can hardly expect to escape public regulation.

Economic Advice for the President

In the last years of the war, some administrators at the working level in various departments and bureaus in Washington united their enthusiasm for a planned economy into a search for a bill which, if ultimately enacted, would apply their philosophy to the postwar economy. Most of these seekers were followers of Keynes or of his American disciples who had the country over attained appointments as economists in American institutions of higher learning, some of the highest prestige. Although individuals in the New Deal from Roosevelt down had once rejected Keynes as an intellectual leader and had expressed ignorance or bewilderment over what he meant, younger men had succeeded in understanding the terms of his theory and in drawing conclusions from his arguments.

Simply, and therefore unfairly put, Keynes believed a certain level of expenditures was a prerequisite to full employment and that if private enterprise could not meet this standard government could and should. Implicit in his theory was the idea of growth and expansion, objectives miles away from Roosevelt's early avowal that America had a closed economy and the American task was to administer what we had. The war with its deficits and its avalanche of productivity gave a demonstration of the worth of the new ideas more convincing than seminars. Theoretically and practically the need was to come to grips "with the problem of providing an economic substitute for war production."

The contributions of many administrators and some Congressmen was an employment act by which "our government assumes responsibility for the expansion of our peacetime economy so that it will be capable of assuring full employment." This purpose allayed many anxieties of the day, but the suggested means raised doubts. After a tortured legislative history, the Senate bill nearest to the Keynesian formula gave way to a House version, quite differently phrased. After a conference between Senate and House, a joint bill passed the Senate unanimously and the House decisively. The Employment Act of 1946 began with a Declaration of Policy:

It is the continuing policy and responsibility of the Federal Government to use all practicable means . . . to coordinate and utilize all its plans, functions, and resources for the purpose of creating and maintaining, in a manner calculated to foster and promote free competitive enterprise and the general welfare, conditions under which there will be afforded useful employment, for those able, willing, and seeking to work, and to promote maximum employment, production, and purchasing power.

The bill established in the Executive Office of the President a three-member Council of Economic Advisors (CEA). This Council was to analyze and interpret economic developments, appraise government programs in the light of the purpose of the act, and "formulate and recommend national economic policy to promote employment, production and purchasing power under free competitive enterprise." Thus instructed and advised, the President was to transmit to each regular session of Congress report providing a summary of the economic situation of the country and making recommendations for legislation. A joint committee of House and Senate was to study the economic report and make recommendations to Congress concerning each of the Presidential recommendations. One advantage of the proposal was its introduction of some form and system into the government's economic policy; still there remained other agencies and advisors, some of whom had considerable responsibility and independence. The Board of Governors of the Federal Reserve was one illustration; in the Cabinet the Secretaries of the Treasury and of Agriculture were also policymakers. The act explicitly recognized the role of Congress. But the Council of Economic Advisors if it attained sufficient competence and status could act as a coordinating agency. In this respect its position was somewhat similar to the Bureau of the Budget after World War I. Another analogous body, nearer in time, was the Brain Trust of the New Deal. The Employment Act of 1946 as a matter of course recognized initiative in planning as a Presidential function; it regularized the advisory function. The act followed Rooseveltian precedents further. While it did not outlaw the appointment to the Council of Economic Advisors of bureaucrats or of practical men—"good, honest, conscientious sound Americans who will not be influenced by a lot of radical people"—its specifications of the abilities requisite for appointment pointed unmistakably at academicians outside the battle and trained as professional economists. On the other hand, the act limited the scope of advising to the context of a democratic political system and of "free competitive enterprise." Finally, the CEA had no coercive power, it gave advice to which the President and Congress had to give assent preliminary to action.

Like most phrases in the act, "free competitive enterprise" required definition. Administration, rather than a glossary of current sociological and economic jargon, gave it meaning. During Truman's Administration, Leon Keyserling, though not the first Chairman of the Council, had a long term in this office and that of the vice-chairman. More relevant than Keyserling's training in economy and law, was his professionalism as a New Dealer. Tugwell had brought him to Washington where he served in the AAA, and then as legislative assistant to Senator Wagner. A colleague described Keyserling as "a man with the heart of a missionary and the ego of a politician." He was the apostle of expansion and of a long-range government policy to attain it. Sometimes he gave the impression of administering an employment act Congress hadn't passed; he certainly was impatient with some of Truman's short-range policy decisions during the Korean crisis. With the changeover to the Eisenhower Administration in 1952 there came a change in the chairmanship of the Council of Economic Advisors. Eisenhower brought to Washington Arthur F. Burns, a professional economist, a profound student of the business cycle, and at the time of his appointment Director of Research at the National Bureau of Economic Research. Burns had a patient, tolerant mind, and hoped that when facts had been ascertained in sufficient depth they would make feasible a "science of economics." He was suspicious of aggregates and large generalizations. "Subtle understanding," he had written in 1950, "of economic change comes from a knowledge of history and large affairs, not from statistics or their processing alone—to which our distressed age has turned so eagerly in its quest for certainty." Even before the passage of the Employment Act he had anticipated that for the problem of un-employment "at least in the near-time future we shall seek a solution within the framework of an individualistic capitalism."

Though Burns admitted the dominant influence of Keynes among economists, he objected to the latter's theories on several counts. What Burns' allegiances meant in terms of fiscal and monetary policies was tested by the recession of 1953–1954, the onset of which Burns early detected from the performance of the indicators. The President's Economic Report in January, 1954, saw in the end of the Korean War a chance for an "economic transition from war and inflation to peace and monetary stability." To fulfill the mandate of the Employment Act of 1946, the country must have growth and "an increase in the national output." As means of preventing a recession, the report recommended extending the coverage of unemployment insurance to about 10 million workers hitherto uncovered and increasing unemployment payments to compensate for the decline in the value of the dollar; lowering certain taxes; liberalizing financial terms of housing; and catching up on the construction of public works—"The total annual expenditure required to provide an adequate road system is apparently over a billion dollars, which compares with a current outlay of 5 million." Though the Federal Reserve determined its own monetary policy, the Council of Economic Advisors favored the lowered reserve requirements the System granted. When the country successfully skated by the depression of 1953–1954, Eisenhower reportedly commended Burns, "Arthur, you'd have made a fine chief of staff during the War."

With the changeover in administration in 1961 Kennedy was concerned by the aftermath of the recession of 1957–1958—an increase in unemployment, prices, and labor discontent. His campaign slogan, "It is time to get the country moving again," foreshadowed a more active and embracing policy in behalf of growth. His chairman of the Council of Economic Advisors was Walter W. Heller, a professor from the University of Minnesota. Heller was as self-confident about the potential power of economic science as was Arthur Burns, but Heller's was a slightly different economics. Keynesian theory had "come of age"; government action of a direct sort to move the economy "along the path of its non-inflationary potential" became axiomatic. Both Kennedy and Johnson—particularly as contrasted with Truman, who was made restless by advice from academic economists—proved apt pupils. The first two "stand out, then, as the first modern economists in the American Presidency." A speech of Kennedy at Yale "stands as the most literate and sophisticated dissertation on economics ever delivered by a President." If he lacked the fire and drama of intellectual adventure that Kennedy brought to the exposition and application of the new doctrine, Johnson possessed the knack of removing from the realm of economic discourse and policy "the deadweight of cripplingly loaded words" such as "government deficit," "balanced budget," "government spending."

Heller was as zealous as the leader of the "March of the Poor on Washington" who called for a "rededication to the Unemployment Act of 1946." Heller, however, was better informed. Though the Keynesian gospel had allegedly converted all economists, there were still differences of opinion "over the tactics and timing of fiscal and monetary moves for stabilization. We do not . . . agree on precisely when we should tighten the monetary and fiscal tourniquets in an overheating economy or loosen them in a slack one." Even in the abstract these exceptions covered a large area, and the course of contemporary events showed how difficult it was to cope with these differences. Despite all his persuasive charm, Kennedy was unable to prevail upon Congress to reduce taxes as a means of stimulating the economy; it took the memory of his martyrdom and the application of Johnson's political skill to get the policy enacted. Later Johnson found it hard to induce Congress to raise taxes to meet the expenses of the Vietnam War and to halt an unfavorable balance in foreign exchange. Politics is not as quick as thought. Perhaps this is a count against democratic government on an effective plane. Nor was a showdown President Kennedy had with the United States Steel Corporation in 1962 over its announcement of a rise in prices as necessary to meet rising costs reassuring. The proposal infuriated Kennedy, for it jeopardized his fight against inflation by defying "guide lines" for wages and prices that the Council of Economic Advisors had formulated. By public reprimand and by vague threats to use, among other things, the Sherman Anti-Trust Act and the lever of government purchases, the President forced the United States Steel Corporation to withdraw the price increase —a method and outcome which, according to an intimate advisor "was not founded on any statute or backed by any sanctions." Even when government by harassment enters by the White House door, it retains its characteristic of being a government of men and not of laws.

Be that as it may, the economy as a whole grew and yielded abundance. The economy might hesitate, as it did for moments in the administrations of Truman through Eisenhower to Kennedy. To expect the absence of all fluctuation was to expect perfection and hence be a visionary. In spite of those economic setbacks, prettily called "slumps" or "recessions," popular and some professional opinion emphasized the nation's unprecedented prosperity throughout the postwar period. Some unemployment there was—8 percent of the civilian labor force in the late forties, 5.3 percent in the late fifties—but the massive unemployment of the thirties was not repeated. Meanwhile the index of real product per man-hour for the private economy increased in constant 1958 dollars, for agriculture from 49.8 in 1947 to 155.6 in 1966. While this increase was phenomenal, putting severe strains upon the Federal policy of curtail-

A History of American Economic Life

ment by quota, the comparable figures for nonagricultural industries rose from 72.9 to 124.3. The gross national product (GNP) in constant 1958 dollars rose from 2,342,000,000 in 1950 to 3,158,000,000 in 1965. This was the "affluent society" with "built-in" correctives—for example, social insurance—against depression.

Perhaps one cautionary safeguard against self-satisfied congratulation on these mammoth accomplishments was a comparison of the per capita rate of growth of GNP with that of other periods. The average annual increments for the 1950's, 2.9 percent, were noticeably below the 4.7 percent for 1921–1929; nor were the fifties' average annual increments as high as an estimated 3.72 percent for 1879–1919. If the economy of the country was not exactly stagnant, neither was it surging upward. The rate of growth for the great industries—coal, railroads, steels, and textiles using natural fibers—which had constituted the historic base of the industrial revolutions, so many times described and variously numbered, lagged behind the growth index of manufacturing production in general. The shrinking proportions of employment in lagging enterprises was sometimes compensated for by an increase in these enterprises' productivity or by a switch to substitutes. However reassuring from the point of view of national totals, the investor or worker in a cotton factory took little comfort from the inroads of rayon, nylon, and other man-made fibers; nor in steel, did the investor or worker take comfort from the substitution of aluminum in automobile engines; nor in coal from power produced by petroleum or nuclear fuel; nor in rail transport from the growth of trucking and airplane travel.

Bigness in Business—Private and Public

The leading growth industries, those at least doubling their production between 1950 and 1960, were, in order of priority, aircraft; industrial chemicals; gas and electric utilities; natural gas and gas liquids; electrical machinery, instruments, and related products; and rubber and plastic products. Many of these categories fell into the ill-defined bag of the electronics industry; the symbol of the latter was the computer and its watchword, "automation."

These industries, though they had been transformed by new techniques and gadgets, and though airplanes were manufactured and assembled not under shelter but out-of-doors in the dry, continuous sunshine of America's Southwest, still conformed to the ideological pattern set, at least for pejorative purposes, in William Blake's verse, "dark, satanic mills." Like the old, the new industries were organized and administered not by individuals or partnerships, but by corporations. In most instances —as chemicals, electric machinery, aircraft, rubber, petroleum, and public utilities demonstrated—they were big corporations. The disadvantages, nay dangers, of this development for American politics and economics had assumed in the late nineteenth century the form of an anti-trust crusade and resulted in the Sherman Anti-Trust Act. But the trend toward bigness did not falter. Robert M. La Follette, a sincere advocate of a return to the "natural laws of competition," was prone to ask the question, "Who owns America?" The answer was "the Interests"—huge corporations united in "a consolidation of consolidations" in industry, transport, and banking. La Follette demonstrated to his own satisfaction the presence of this threat by a chart of American business giants. Though the count was amateur, the chart was inclusive and exciting. In 1932 Adolph Berle and Gardiner C. Means—both of whom subsequently became "professional" New Dealers—published *The Modern Corporation and Private Property*. Detecting a contemporary trend in "the creation of a series of huge industrial oligarchies," these academicians compiled their inventory. As of January 1, 1930, nearly every one of the two hundred largest nonbanking corporations had assets of over $100 million; fifteen had assets of over $1 billion. A. T. & T. alone controlled "more wealth than is contained within the borders of twenty-one of the states in the country." Juggling with estimates, the authors concluded that the sum of the assets of the two hundred largest corporations was 38 percent or more of the nation's total business wealth. Their conclusion—that dispersion of stock ownership gave an inner management of directors and other officers a power which could be antagonistic or indifferent to stockholders and which the stockholders were virtually unable to control—owed much to the thinking of a time as remote as that of as Samuel Slater. Conceptually, Berle and Means's conclusion was also an oversimplification. Stockholders and management had an identity of interest in that both, to paraphrase Carnegie's description of himself, were "clamorers for dividends." Be that as it may, Berle and Means inspired in part the New Deal's abrupt attack on big business in the late thirties. The momentum continued, for immediately after World War II alarmists discerned a new trend toward consolidation.

It was a safe bet for Berle and Means to assert "the end is not yet in sight." In Congressional investigations of monopoly and anti-trust there is a periodicity which should challenge the chartmakers to multiply their drawings and inferences. In 1964 a Congressional foray into these matters discovered that the five hundred largest corporations had over two-thirds of the assets of the corporations engaged in manufacturing, and that two thousand corporations, each with assets of over $10 million, accounted for 80 percent of all the resources used in manufacturing. The five largest industrial corporations had combined assets of $36 billion, which constituted 12 percent of all assets used in manufacturing. In the mid-fifties twenty-eight corporations provided approximately 10 percent of all employment in manufacturing, mining, and retail and wholesale trade. The

1964 investigation further observed, "In 1963 the revenues of General Motors were fifty times those of Nevada, eight times those of New York, and slightly less than one-fifth those of the Federal Government."

Meanwhile Congress and the courts sought to tighten the restrictions along the way against consolidation. In 1936 the Robinson-Patman Act (Patman was the persistent spokesman for small business) amended Section 2 of the Clayton Anti-Trust Act. This section had prohibited the different quotation of prices to purchasers, who were generally those engaged in distribution. The amendment forbade the various covert forms of discounts: rebates, allowances for services and advertising, and so on. Actually, closing these loopholes was less important than an amendment in 1950 to Section 7 of the Clayton Act. Originally, Section 7 had forbidden acquisitions through stock exchanges or purchases which were likely to lessen competition between the parties. The amendment of 1950 outlawed mergers through the acquisition of assets and also prohibited acquisitions "in any line of commerce in any section of the country" where their effect would be "to substantially lessen competition . . . or to tend to create a monopoly." No longer was the government confined to attacking visible and actual monopolies; it could now proceed against "incipient" monopolies. It could "nip them in the bud." Nor did the monopoly have to be nationwide; it could be regional or local.

Whether the courts facilitated or hampered the guessing game was a matter of opinion. A more vigorous enforcement of the anti-trust laws along with the habitual levying of huge payments for civil damages under the Sherman Anti-Trust Act made corporation executives chary of taking chances on any proposal on which the Department of Justice frowned. There was a new zest in anti-trust enforcement. The Anti-Trust Division had a larger staff—over two hundred lawyers—and a larger appropriation. The Report of the Attorney-General in 1964 announced the "Division's docket of cases in the Supreme Court was next to the heaviest in history," and "fines and recoveries in 1964 were the highest in history." Though there was a good deal of splitting hairs in these boasts, the anti-trust achievements of the early sixties were considerable. A perusal of cases sometimes suggests the government hunted the minnows producing candy, beer, or baby food; it also made tangential attacks on the "big ones"— Du Pont, General Motors, General Electric, Westinghouse, American Aluminum. To be the "number-one" firm in an industry seemed to invite unfavorable action—at least that was a complaint of business.

Professional economists sometimes hailed the attainment of corporate bigness as a necessary prelude to efficiency in planning and in the utilization of brains and capital. In the management and development of transportation, the national government in the post-World War II era attained a centralized role partially forecast by legislation as recent as that of the Wilson Administrations, which had begun the first important national grants-in-aid to public roads and the establishment of a Bureau of Public Roads in the Agricultural Department and had ended with the Transportation Act of 1920. This last act proposed to substitute for competition between railroads voluntary consolidations between lines under Federal permission and regulation. Though the swift advance of motor transportation compelled an enlargement of the roads program and travel by plane led to Federal intervention in the late thirties, the Eisenhower Administration was the first to accomplish innovations as wide as those of Wilson's day. The President seemed to have an ingrained preference for government invasions into the area of transportation—as long as they could be financed in orthodox fashion. Thus the first Eisenhower Administration succeeded in removing the generation-old blocks to the improvement of the St. Lawrence Seaway as long as the ships paid tolls sufficient along with the sale of electrical power to supply locks, larger canals, and deeper channels, and to meet the cost of operations. The Roosevelt and Truman Administrations had taken the first step toward the designation of a nationally aided National System of Interstate and Defense Highways (conveniently shortened to "Interstate") connecting the "principal metropolitan areas, centers, and industrial cities" of the country and aiding the states to the extent of 90 percent of the cost. Federal taxes on fuel, tires, tubes, trucks, and buses, were to go into a Federal Highway Trust Fund to assist the construction of a 41,000 mile system to be completed by the early 1970's. Eisenhower considerably increased the taxes and the appropriations.

Finally, overwhelmed by the multiplicity of the Federal agencies concerned with transportation, President Johnson prevailed upon Congress in 1966 to establish the Department of Transportation, headed by a Secretary of cabinet rank. If the note of "defense" which had characterized the highway acts was now lacking, that of "policies and programs" was now to the fore. The Department of Transportation was to seek a "coordinated transportation system, to be provided by private enterprise to the maximum extent feasible." The department did not supersede among others the Interstate Commerce Commission, the Civilian Aviation Board, or the Maritime Commission; its chief operation duties seemed by inference largely to relate to highways. Indeed, hardly had the department come into being when the Interstate Commerce Commission authorized the merger of the Pennsylvania and New York Central Railroads, rivals for over a century; and the merger of the Great Northern, the Northern Pacific, and the Chicago, Burlington and Quincy to the apparent approval of the majority of investors on Wall Street. Along the desert trail of history were strewn the skeletons of once-proud independent railroad systems, the Northern Securities case, the dreams of urban railroad imperialism, and other concepts; a "good roads movement" focused on farm roads; and the more fundamental ideals of transportation as an area of "private enterprise." If the Department of Transportation believed without modification its preliminary assertion, "The transportation system in the United States, railroads, airlines, buses, trucks, ships, barge links, automobiles, pipelines is the only one in the world operating under competitive private enterprise rather than governmental ownership," it was starting life on a shaky premise. Competition there was, but it stretched a point to label as "private" highways, canals, and airports owned and maintained by the government.

The Service Industries

Actually, the picture was quite mixed. So, it must be added, was the national economy itself. The dominant trends toward private and governmental bigness were being challenged by another significant alteration in the contours of economic life—the emergence from inferiority of the service industries: wholesale and retail trade, finance, insurance, and real estate; and "general government," which includes local governments as well as the Federal government and which provides such functional activities as highway building and education. All of the net growth of employment in the postwar period occurred in the service sector. The *increase* in employment in education alone between 1956 and 1960 was greater than the *total e*mployment in primary metal industries in either year. The service sector in the sixties accounted for more than half of the total employment in the nation and more than half of the GNP.

It still is probably straining a point to assert the United States has entered a postindustrial culture. But the shift toward service industries has brought profound changes. These industries include an exceptional proportion of women, part-time workers, and self-employed. Their workers' level of education has been higher. Workers in the government industries are less subject to cyclical unemployment. By and large, labor union organizers have always found it difficult to organize such workers. Thus, for several reasons the growth of service industries has been one factor in explaining the relative decline of union membership—which reached a peak of 26 percent of the labor force in 1953, but declined to 21 percent in 1962. For instance, workers in civil service almost universally face a statutory prohibition against participation in strikes—an old union weapon. And whereas the workers in many unionized industries do not deal directly with the public, employees in service industries confront consumers at firsthand; indeed, in supermarkets the customer does some of the work. Service firms are also smaller than those that produce commodities; as a result there has been a slight easing of the mania for incorporation. In sum, the service state has tended to become more middle-class and less proletarian. Policy, if it were popular, would respond to these circumstances.

Growing industries, whether service or not, tended to have other common characteristics. They were the outgrowth of research and development, or, in the vernacular, "R & D." At the end of the fifties total outlays for research were estimated to be $12 billion a year. Private research was concentrated in a few industrial groups: the aircraft industry alone accounted for almost a third of the total. Also, as time went by expenditures tended away from basic or "pure" research to developmental applications. No prolonged exposition is necessary to reveal the mounting importance of the government as a provider of services. The school system is predominantly that of the "public school" system from kindergarten to Ph.D. Even before World War II employment by government had mounted. In 1945 those on active duty in the armed services numbered 12,123,455; though Congress never passed a universal military service measure, it continued the draft from time to time, and throughout the fifties the numbers in the armed services on active duty fell only once below 1.5 million; in 1952 the total peaked during the Korean War at 5,764,143; in 1967 during the Vietnam war the number was 3,350,000. Since Americans fought their wars with "hardware," the military, or defense, market consumed lavishly and continuously. In the first half of the fifties, a hundred firms received two-thirds by value of all defense contracts; in the late fifties 80 percent of the aircraft industry's business was with military agencies; and throughout the decade about two-thirds of the growth in electronic sales was due to government military demand. "The most spectacular element of market growth . . . was the expansion of electricity consumption for defense purposes." It was the contemplation of these attainments which led President Eisenhower in his farewell message to the nation to warn his fellow citizens against the "military-industrial complex," lest it gain "unwarranted influence" and limit our liberties. All this was indeed a far cry from the 1890's when Henry Adams anticipated American enterprise would "break down every rival" in international competition because it was not burdened with the expense of maintaining an establishment of aristocrats, priests, and soldiers.

A Policy for American Trade, Expenditures, and Finance Overseas

Confidence like Adams' was commonplace in the expansive years at the beginning of the twentieth century, for then Americans discerned the possibility of taking over the management of the *Pax Britannica*. Within a few decades the impossibility of separating the United States from the fate of Western Europe sent millions of doughboys overseas; the resulting reversal of the American position as an exporter of goods and of capital and the wrench to adjust to this reversal during the interwar period have already been described. A statistician who has calculated the value of imports and exports and also the value of the GNP in terms of constant 1913 dollars concludes that the ratio of imports to GNP during the twenties was slightly higher, at 5.7, than in prewar years and that the ratio of exports, at 6.1, was "at approximately the same level" as before World War I. After the Great Depression the ratio of exports declined markedly, and after 1937 that of imports dropped sharply "to the lowest levels in our record." Getting to particularities, at the beginning of World War I agricultural commodities still accounted for almost half of total American exports; thereafter the percentage declined and leveled off at a little over 20 percent: as a percentage of GNP agricultural commodities were less than 1.5 percent. The impact of the Depression was so universal as to reduce percentage figures for totals and for details in nearly every instance.

During the campaign of 1932 the author of the New Deal, especially before agricultural hearers, blamed the reduced percentages on "the new economics" of his predecessor. Hoover had closed the foreign markets for American exports by condoning the adoption early in his Administration "of the highest tariff in the history of the world." This prevented "our customers" abroad from paying for our exports with shipments of their own; loaning funds to foreigners to buy from us was no substitute for this natural barter. To remedy this situation, Roosevelt advocated "a tariff policy based on reason, on the same good old-fashioned horse sense that you and I would use in our own business with our own neighbor. It is a tariff policy based in large part upon the simple principle of profitable exchange, arrived at through negotiated tariff, with benefit to each Nation." Elsewhere he suggested this process of executive action would outwit the historic method of Congressional logrolling which had shipwrecked so many tariff reform proposals. Later Henry Wallace, Secretary of Agriculture, outlined in dramatic form the dilemmas of economic isolation and economic expansion, between which *America Must Choose.* Congress in 1934 passed the Reciprocal Trade Agreements Act, which permitted the President for purposes of promoting American foreign trade to raise or lower by not more than 50 percent the duties of the tariff of 1930 by negotiated agreement with individual nations. The changes were to extend to all countries except those who were found to discriminate against American trade. The act was to expire in three years. Some fifteen agreements—the most important one was with Canada—were made in this interval. Congress then renewed the permission for this innovation.

As time went on the Roosevelt's utterances had increasingly stressed the relationship between the principle of the reciprocal trade act and the attainment of peace. Then the outbreak of World War II created new commercial relationships and also new needs for policy. As in the earlier world conflict, merchandise exports multiplied; between 1941 and 1944 they multiplied about 3 times; comparatively speaking the increase in imports from $3,222 million to $3,877 million was negligible. In 1944 the favorable balance of merchandise trade reached a peak never equaled before in American history. At the same time, of course, America was financing its own military costs abroad during war and occupation, and the Rooseveltian ingenuity in devising lend-lease instead of war debts meant the accumulation in international balances of impressive dollar totals, which were bookkeeping items rather than hard financial transactions.

As the victors foresaw the postwar difficulties of reopening the channels of international commerce and of accomplishing a rebuilding and reconstruction through international borrowing and lending, and as they also recollected the confusion and national self-interest into which these international arrangements had fallen in the 1930's they undertook to establish international agencies for these overwhelming tasks. In 1944, at the Bretton Woods Conference, those who were confident of winning the war formulated plans for an International Monetary Fund (IMF) and for the International Bank for Reconstruction and Development, more commonly known as the "World Bank." The purpose of the first institution was to assure the convertibility of foreign currencies and the stability of an international exchange rate. To this purpose the IMF was to coordinate its operations through the treasuries and central banks of the participants. It could make loans—called "drawings"—from a reserve fund it had accumulated. In fact, the International Monetary Fund resembled a central bank of last resort and a clearinghouse. The World Bank, on the other hand, was to make loans for productive purposes out of its own capital funds or the funds it raised through the sale of its own securities to private investors. Its guarantee or sponsorship would encourage this method of investment. Its loans were intended for underdeveloped countries; India, Japan, and Mexico became its chief borrowers.

While Roosevelt commended the adoption of both these proposals to Congress as one step to fulfilling the generation's "rendezvous with destiny," he was cautious enough to add, "I do not want to leave you with the impression that the Fund and the Bank are all that need to solve the economic problems which will face the United Nations when the war is over." Both these devices made a useful but hardly a major contribution to a world economy passing through chaos after World War II toward some sort of equilibrium. The postponed demand for materials and goods boosted prices in international trade, and the means and instruments for paying for commodities were either lacking entirely or in disarray. More influential toward the promotion of readjustment was the fact that the

principle of the Trade Agreements Act—it was renewed ten times—
flowered in 1947 in the General Agreement on Tariffs and Trade
(GATT), to which twenty-three nations subscribed. The number of
signatures later increased. Under the provisions of GATT nations met
at intervals at a central place for negotiating bilateral agreements for
the reduction of duties on imports. Under the most-favored-nation treatment these concessions were generalized for all members. The sixth round
of such negotiations, completed in 1967, was known as the "Kennedy
Round."

Like GATT, the offer, likewise made in 1946 by former General
George C. Marshall, the Secretary of State, was of more than transient
importance in an age of rapid change. Marshall proposed the United
States underwrite the economic development of Europe to the tune of
$17 billion in aid, if need be. Ironically, Henry Wallace characterized the
suggestion as an up-to-date prelude to American imperialism; and other
opponents feared that by increasing productivity in Europe the United
States would create new competitors for American foreign commerce.
Nonetheless, the Marshall Plan was adopted and its generosity achieved
its objectives. Expenditures for foreign aid were high in the fifties; in the
sixties, averaging a little lower, their proportion of the GNP was about
0.5 percent.

As the twentieth century went on, the old choice between protection
and free trade as a political means of managing foreign trade came to
seem rather simple and single-minded. The items once enumerated in
calculating a balance of payments—merchandise exports and imports,
tourist expenditures, investments across international boundaries, costs
of transportation, immigrant remittances, and the like—seemed trifling,
ineffective and old-fashioned. One explanation for the difference
was almost casually vouchsafed in a statute which declared nothing therein should be construed to interfere with domestic measures to aid agriculture. For agricultural commodities, whether grown in the United States
or in underdeveloped countries, were a prime factor in accounting for
exceptions to traditional policies and innovations in foreign trade policy.
American agricultural policy in the fifties had succeeded in accumulating
huge surpluses of certain products. How to work them off through foreign
trade created a quandary. In 1949 the Senate approved an International
Wheat Agreement covering the trade in wheat between four wheat-pro-
ducing nations—Australia, Canada, France, and the United States—and
thirty-seven wheat-importing countries. The agreement established maximum and minimum prices for wheat and set quotas of guaranteed sales—
those of the United States and Canada were approximately 80 percent of
the total—and of guaranteed purchases by the thirty-seven buyers, of
which those by the United Kingdom were between a third and a half. In
the fifties Congress allowed the government to sell surplus farm products

for foreign currencies, usually nonconvertible; to make shipments for emergency relief and other aid; and to buy under long-term agreements and on government credit. In 1966, for instance, Congress appropriated $190 million to buy 3 million tons of wheat for famine-stricken India. All of this happily reconciled the American need to reduce its surplus with considerations of humanity. The slogan "Food for Freedom" was supposed to bridge the breach. In the early 1960's 30 percent of the value of our total agricultural exports were made under Federally financed programs.

As an awareness sharpened of the differences between the degree of development achieved by industrial countries and nations which produced primary commodities, usually agricultural, and marketed them abroad, there were many attempts to plan or order these dual processes. Otherwise, there were gluts and scarcities, inflation and deflation, exchange difficulties—all accompaniments of market imbalances. A solution seemed to be an agreement assigning quotas of exports to producing countries and quotas of imports to consuming countries. The procedure was applied to sugar and to coffee. The intrusion of political deviations—for example, Cuba's swing toward the left—or the failure to include all interested parties, as in the case of coffee, handicapped the success of these innovations.

Nevertheless, the quota became a sort of panacea for bringing foreign commerce within the area of domestic planning. As a limited number of American oil companies secured oil concessions abroad and sought to market either the crude or refined oil in the United States, American oil companies without those advantages were outraged. After trifling with the idea of voluntary limitation, President Eisenhower through the Secretary of the Interior in 1959 clamped on mandatory controls; imports were to be 9 percent of domestic demand for petroleum products other than residual or heavy oil. The quotas were distributed among firms twice a year. In the next decade when the steel industry became alarmed at imports from abroad because wage boosts had increased American costs or strikes had created shortages to be filled, the steel producers demanded a quota on imports. So had the cotton textile industry. Informal agreements had cut down the competition from Japanese manufactures. But Dean Rusk, Secretary of State, cautioned America not to press too hard in this direction, as we had deprived Japan by war of her preferential position in the Chinese market and now we needed her as a diplomatic counterweight in the Far East.

Variations on the theme of security and power were inescapable at a time when the military-industrial complex played so dominant a role in the nation's culture and economy. The merest scrutiny of the balance of international payments showed how large and continuous were the deficit items of military expenditures abroad. Almost trivial in the twenties and thirties, deficits caused by military spending overseas were nearly $2.5 billion in 1945 and reached that level or higher in the first half of the sixties. Nor was this the total figure. To separate "relief" expenditures from "grants for military" purposes, one would seemingly have to run the figures through a centrifuge. Government enumerations, however, show military expenditures abroad were about a third of those for relief between 1945 and 1966. As early as 1958 the international payments balance of the United States began to erode. Changes became more abrupt as the Vietnam adventure became more expensive. When it came to a choice of cures, the national government preferred to impose austerity upon butter rather than guns. Singled out for more rigid control were American investments abroad, for which voluntary cooperation by business concerns—for most foreign investments overseas were "direct," as they were called—was first relied upon. In 1964, however, Congress levied a 15 percent interest equalization tax upon any stock or debt acquired by an American purchaser in a foreign corporation unless such purchaser or purchasers already owned more than 10 percent of "the total combined voting power of all classes of stock in such foreign corporation" and such corporation was in "a less developed country." That last exception excluded from the operation of the act most countries in Western Europe, the British dominions, and countries in "the Sino-Soviet block." This act with its many provisions took up nearly fifty pages in the *General Statutes of the United States.* It was reminiscent of the Acts of Trade and Navigation. Its policy was a logical development of the same aims and methods; in both instances government had taken or been granted a power to regulate the economy. The most illogical thing about this regression of policy was that it clothed its operation in the vernacular of nineteenth-century liberalism.

As this specialized outcome demonstrated, the United States, as nations go in this world, was an old country. Over historic time its people and government had passed through many phases and announced many purposes. We cannot speculate with much confidence on the ambitions and aspirations of the settlers who came on shore from the *Susan Constant* or the *Mayflower* or even of the later arrivals across the centuries. But it is sure they sought a living and the opportunity to make it from the New World they were entering. Nor could they possibly have foreseen—not even the Utopians—the material and political power which by the twentieth century they and their descendants would have amassed or created. The process had been long and it had been slow. Though there had been spurts forward of progress, not even the visionaries had been able to bring instant change. The economy, like Rome of the enduring proverb, "was not built in a day." At the moment of history known as yesterday, President Eisenhower could say, "We must have the courage to be patient." And John F. Kennedy, forty-three years old, though he felt his inaugural marked the transfer of power to a "new generation" born and "living in this century," concluded his description of his own program: "All this will not be finished in the first one hundred days. Nor will it be finished in the first one thousand days, nor in the life of this Administration, nor even perhaps in our lifetime on this planet. But let us begin."

Bibliography[*]

General Works

Although many textbooks have been written on the economic history of the United States, there is as yet no extensive or monumental treatment of the subject. During World War I the Carnegie Institution of Washington, at the instigation of Carroll D. Wright, commenced a series of *Contributions to the Economic History of the United States*. Over the decade seven *Contributions* were issued. They varied in distinction and left many areas untouched. In the thirties, Farrar and Rinehart projected in many variously titled volumes, *The Economic History of the United States*. Like its predecessor, these volumes appeared over the decades; finally under a consolidation—Holt, Rinehart, and Winston—the series lost its spirit and symmetry. The first volume, on the Colonial period, has never appeared. *The History of American Life*, 13 vols. (1927–1948), edited by A. M. Schlesinger and D. R. Fox, stresses economic as well as social and cultural factors. Its critical bibliographies are especially useful. Many aspects of economic history are peculiarly fitted for pictorial treatment; indeed, in some technical and agricultural processes, visual illustration is an absolute essential. *The Pageant of America*, 15 vols. (1925–1929) fulfills these needs.

The relation between history and geography has been traced in A. P. Brigham, *Geographic Influences in American History* (1903) and E. C. Semple, *American History and Its Geographic Conditions* (1903). Both works somewhat overstress the obvious. The best description of the geographic areas of the United States is Isaiah Bowman, *Forest Physiography* (1911), a book which transcends its title. No study of American economic-geographic conditions is complete without J. R. Smith and M. O. Phillips, *North America, Its People and the Resources, Development and Prospects of the Continent* (1942). In spite of the dangers of parceling the United States partly into geographic and partly into use areas, this is a brilliant and humane volume. C. O. Paullin, *Atlas of the Historical Geography of the United States* (1932) is the best atlas for the student of eco-

* Abbreviations: *AH, Agricultural History; AER, American Economic Review; AHR, American Historical Review; ARAHA, Annual Report of the American Historical Association; JEBH, Journal of Economic and Business History; JEH, Journal of Economic History; JPE, Journal of Political Economy; MVHR, Mississippi Valley Historical Review; QJE, Quarterly Journal of Economics.*

nomic history. United States Bureau of the Census, *Historical Statistics of the United States, Colonial Times to 1957* (1960) is indispensable.

For bibliographical assistance H. M. Larson, *Guide to Business History: Materials for the Study of American Business History* (1948) is the most useful work. It groups books and articles in categories and supplies critical estimates. The annual *Writings on American History* began to cover the bibliographical field in 1902. It listed both books and periodical articles under headings among which are social and economic history. The latest year covered by the *Writings* is 1958. With its first volume in 1911 the *American Economic Review* began the publication of excellent bibliographies, both of books and periodical articles. Occasional items in these bibliographies have reviews or critical notes. The student should not confine himself to those listed under the heading "Economic History and Geography," for the items cited under the other headings are often germane to economic history itself. With the forties, however, the entries for economic history were somewhat reduced in extensiveness. In its reviews the *Journal of Economic History,* beginning publication in 1941, redressed the balance. The excellent lists of recent publications compiled for the *Journal* by Mulford Martin do not, however, contain periodical entries.

chapter i

Founding the British Colonies

The Colonial period in the British colonies has been so extensively treated that "schools" with different emphases and topics have developed. The work of Herbert L. Osgood early in the century purposely neglected economic development in favor of a political or institutional point of view. On the other hand, C. M. Andrews, *The Colonial Period of American History,* 4 vols. (1934–1938) gives extended treatment to land systems, forms of colonization, and English mercantilist policy; and the volumes in the Schlesinger-Fox, *History of American Life,* T. J. Wertenbaker, *The First Americans, 1607–1690* (1927), and J. T. Adams, *Provincial Society, 1690–1763* (1927) are somewhat in the same tradition. In thirteen volumes an author can cover most topics, and Lawrence H. Gipson does so in his modest and magisterial *The British Empire before the American Revolution* (1936–1965). An exceedingly useful single volume is C. P. Nettels, *The Roots of American Civilization* (1938), organized on an original and stimulating basis. Insofar as the motives and practices of British colonization are at issue the old works by G. L. Beer have not outlived their usefulness. See his *The Origins of the British Colonial System, 1578–1600* (1908), *The Old Colonial System* (1912)—of which unfortunately only the volumes dealing with the period 1660–1688 were completed—and *British Colonial Policy 1754–1765* (1907), which together form a classic treatment of colonization by no means confined to Great Britain. Good treatments of that bundle of beliefs known as mercantilism are E. F. Heckscher, *Mercantilism,* 2 vols. (1935), a massive analysis of the system and a suggestive one on its downfall; E. S. Furniss, *The Position of the Laborer in a System of Nationalism* (1920) is brilliant on a phase; and Philip W. Buck, *The Politics of Nationalism* (1942) provides an interesting and conveniently short description. Louis B. Wright, *The Dream of Prosperity in Colonial America* (1965) and his *Religion and Empire, The Alliance between Piety and Commerce in English Expansion, 1558-1625* (1943) are useful reminders that things are not everything and men's concerns are not limited to those of economic historians. Somewhat more than half of Stuart W. Bruchey, *The Roots of American Economic Growth, 1607-1861, An Essay in Social Causation* (1965) is on the Colonial period. The book is an ingenious blend of bibliography and historical narrative.

When the student moves beyond the general works of Gipson; Beer, vol. one of *The Cambridge History of the British Empire* (1929); and vols. 2 and 3 of E. Lipson, *The Economic History of England* (1931-1933); for the North American experience in particular he can consult P. A. Bruce, *Economic History of Virginia in the Seventeenth Century*, 2 vols. (1895), and W. F. Craven, *Dissolution of the Virginia Company. The Failure of a Colonial Experiment* (1932). The latter's *The Southern Colonies in the Seventeenth Century, 1607-1689* (1949) is a brilliant treatment of colonial methods for the whole southern region. Richard L. Morton, *Colonial Virginia* (1960) judiciously combines political and economic factors. For New England, J. T. Adams, *The Founding of New England* (1921) disregards the old religious formulas in favor of a realistic approach. For Pennsylvania see W. I. Hull, *William Penn and the Dutch Quaker Migration to Pennsylvania* (1935). For details of companies consult W. R. Scott, *The Constitution and Finance of English, Scottish, and Irish Joint Companies to 1720*, 2 vols. (1910-1912).

Both Osgood and Andrews deal at length with the land systems of the colonies. A. C. Ford, *Colonial Precedents of Our National Land System* (1910); B. W. Bond, Jr., *The Quit Rent System in the American Colonies* (1919); and Marshall Harris, *Origin of the Land Tenure System in the United States* (1953) are excellent on all the colonies. For the northern colonies P. W. Bidwell and J. I. Falconer, *History of Agriculture in the Northern United States 1620-1860* (1925) pays attention to the land system. For New England the indispensable and most complete treatment is R. H. Akagi, *The Town Proprietors of the New England Colonies* (1924). On the southern colonies Craven's work, cited above, is the best introduction. For more details on Virginia see the work of P. A. Bruce, cited above, and for Maryland, C. P. Gould, *The Land System of Maryland, 1720-1765* (1913). For the middle colonies W. R. Shephard has written a brief introduction to the Pennsylvania system in "The Land System of Provincial Pennsylvania," in *ARAHA*, 1895, 117-125, and much more fully in his *History of Proprietary Government in Pennsylvania* (1896). Irving Mark, *Agrarian Conflicts in Colonial New York, 1711-1775* (1940) provides the background for that colony. For entails and primogeniture consult R. B. Morris, *Studies in the History of American Law* (1930).

It is unnecessary for an economic history which deals only incidentally with immigration to give a bibliography for the subject. Of the few works which have satisfactorily surmounted the special obstacles of research abroad and a knowledge of foreign languages, one of the earliest was M. L. Hansen, *The Atlantic Migration, 1607-1860* (1940). Oscar Handlin, *The Americans* (1963) treats migrants and their institutions with a touch of poetry. See also the works on indentured servants listed in the following bibliography for chapter ii. For figures of colonial population consult E. B. Greene and V. D. Harrington, *American Population before the Federal Census of 1790* (1932) and S. H. Sutherland, *Population Distribution in Colonial America* (1926). Inevitably the distribution of population leads to internal migration and the westward movement. F. J. Turner is the maker of the West in American history. Every student should read his "Significance of the Frontier in American History," the first essay in his, *The Frontier in American History* (1920). Turner has paid attention to the Colonial period in the book's next two essays, "The First Official Frontier of the Massachusetts Bay" and the more important "The Old West." For the western company promotions, C. W. Alvord has a wealth of information in his *The Mississippi Valley in British Politics*, 2 vols. (1917).

chapter ii
Subsistence, Staples, and Statutes

For the economic life of the British colonies the best general treatment is found in T. J. Wertenbaker, *The First Americans, 1607–1690* (1927), J. T. Adams, *Provincial Society, 1690–1763* (1927), and C. P. Nettels, *The Roots of American Civilization* (1938).

The colonial fur trade has not yet received complete treatment. M. G. Lawson, *Fur: A Study in English Mercantilism, 1700–1775* (1943) is the best specialized introduction. Detailed treatments of the trade in specific colonial regions are F. X. Maloney, *The Fur Trade in New England, 1620–1676* (1931); A. T. Volwiler, *George Croghan and the Westward Movement, 1741–1782* (1926); C. A. Hanna, *The Wilderness Road* (1911); and for the southern colonies, V. W. Crane, *The Southern Frontier, 1670–1732* (1928), a work which repays perusal as a whole with its picture of the influence of American economic conditions upon imperial policy.

On the timber business the only complete work is the diffuse J. E. Defebaugh, *History of the Lumber Industry of America*, 2 vols. (1906–1907). On the mast trade and naval stores production, R. G. Albion, *Forests and Sea Power* (1926) deals brilliantly with timber supplies for the royal navy, while Joseph J. Malone, *Pine Trees and Politics. The Naval Stores and Forest Policy in Colonial New England, 1691–1775* (1964) and W. G. Saltonstall, *Ports of Piscataqua* (1941) focus effectively upon forests and shipbuilding "Down East." E. L. Lord, *Industrial Experiments in the British Colonies of North America* (1898) extends the discussion of naval stores to all the colonies.

On the fisheries consult Raymond McFarland, *A History of the New England Fisheries* (1911), a factual compilation, and R. G. Lounsbury, *The British Fishery at Newfoundland, 1634–1763* (1934), a study of policy. Two government reports of value are Lorenzo Sabine, *Report on the Principal Fisheries of the American Seas*, 42nd Cong. 2nd Sess., House Misc. Doc. No. 32 (1872), a gossipy classic on the international phases, and G. B. Goode, ed., *Fisheries and Fishery Industries of the United States* (1884–1887), of which section 5, vols. 1 and 2, deals with the methods and history of the fisheries. A great deal of information on the fisheries can be obtained from the works of G. L. Beer, cited in the previous chapter, and also from W. B. Weeden, *Economic and Social History of*

New England, 1620–1789, 2 vols. (1890). Phases of the whaling industry are touched upon vividly in W. S. Tower, *History of the American Whale Fishery* (1907) and E. P. Hohman, *The American Whaleman* (1928).

Bibliographies for the study of American agriculture are provided in L. B. Schmidt, *Topical Studies and References on the Economic History of American Agriculture* (1923) and E. E. Edwards, "A Bibliography of the History of Agriculture in the United States," Dept. of Agr., *Misc. Pub.* No. 84 (1930). The best secondary introduction to agricultural history in the colonies is Lyman Carrier, *The Beginnings of Agriculture in America* (1923). This volume provides not a complete picture, but a series of invaluable notes on various features of agricultural history. In the fourth volume of L. H. Bailey, ed., *Cyclopedia of American Agriculture* (1907–1909) are two important articles, one by H. K. Holmes, "Aboriginal Agriculture—The American Indian," and the other by T. N. Carver, "Historical Sketch of American Agriculture." Three interesting sources with varied significance for American agricultural practices are Jared Eliot, *Essays upon Field Husbandry in New England and Other Papers, 1748–1762,* ed. H. J. Carman and R. G. Tugwell (1934); the anonymous *American Husbandry,* 2 vols. (1775) which has been ascribed to John Mitchell; and C. V. Woodward, *Ploughs and Politicks, Charles Read of New Jersey and His Notes on Agriculture, 1715–1774* (1941).

For northern agriculture P. W. Bidwell and J. I. Falconer, *History of Agriculture in the Northern United States, 1620–1860* (1925) is the best introduction. The narrative consists of extensive quotations connected by compositions by the authors. W. B. Weeden, cited above, gives facts on New England agriculture, as does R. R. Walcott, "Husbandry in Colonial New England," *New England Quarterly,* IX (1936), 218–252. St. John de Crèvecoeur, *Sketches of Eighteenth Century America* (1925) pictures rural life with literary charm.

L. C. Gray, *History of Agriculture in the Southern United States to 1860,* 2 vols. (1933) gives a scholarly volume to the Colonial era. See also A. H. Hirsch, "French Influence on American Agriculture in the Colonial Period with Special Reference to Southern Provinces," *AH* IV (1930), 1–9. The agricultural system of a tobacco colony is described by P. A. Bruce, cited above; T. J. Wertenbaker, *The Planters of Colonial Virginia* (1922); and A. P. Middleton, *Tobacco Coast, a Maritime History of Chesapeake Bay in the Colonial Era* (1953). Also useful are C. E. Gage, "Historical Factors Affecting American Tobacco Types and Uses and the Evolution of the American Market," *AH* XI (1937), 43–57, and V. J. Wyckoff, *Tobacco Regulation in Colonial Maryland* (1936). A. O. Craven, *Soil Exhaustion as a Factor in the Agricultural History of Virginia and Maryland, 1606–1860* (1926) is a model agricultural study. The history of other staples has been comparatively neglected.

On labor in the colonies, A. E. Smith, *Colonists in Bondage, White Servitude and Convict Labor in America, 1607–1776* (1947) is a highly readable account of the recruitment, transportation and treatment of this class of workers; R. B. Morris, *Government and Labor in Early America* (1946) deals with both free and bound labor and treats far more than migration. Detailed treatments are K. F. Geiser, *Redemptioners and Indentured Servants in the Colony and Commonwealth of Pennsylvania* (1901); C. A. Herrick, *White Servitude in Pennsylvania* (1926); Samuel McKee, *Labor in Colonial New York, 1664–1776* (1935); and L. J. Greene, *The Negro in Colonial New England, 1620–1776* (1942).

J. H. Franklin, *From Slavery to Freedom, A History of American Negroes* (1956) treats the slave trade and regional variations between colonies in the matter of slavery. Of great interest are W. E. B. DuBois, *The Suppression of the African Slave Trade to the United States of America, 1638–1870* (1896); Elizabeth Donnan, *Documents Illustrative of the Slave Trade to America* (1930–1935); and A. W. Lauber, *Indian Slavery in Colonial Times within the Present Limits of the United States* (1913). Oscar and M. F. Handlin, "Origins of the Southern Labor System," *William and Mary Quarterly,* VII (1950), 199–222 is a provocative analysis. Detailed and localized treatments are J. C. Ballagh, *White Servitude in the Colony of Virginia* (1895), and *A History of Slavery in Virginia* (1902); J. S. Bassett, *Slavery and Servitude in the Colony of North Carolina* (1896); J. R. Brackett, *The Negro in Maryland* (1889); E. McCrady, "Slavery in the Province of South Carolina, 1670–1770," *ARAHA,* 1895, 631–673; and E. I. McGormac, *White Servitude in Maryland, 1634–1820* (1904).

V. S. Clark, *History of Manufactures in the United States, 1607–1860* (1916) is the best scholarly treatment of this subject. It has a full bibliography. Hindle Brooke, *Technology in Early America: Needs and Opportunities for Study* (1966) has valuable bibliographies but trails off after 1850. The old standby, J. L. Bishop, *A History of American Manufactures from 1608 to 1860 . . . 1866,* 3 vols. (1868) has a most disorderly arrangement and should be used only as an encyclopedia with the aid of its inadequate index. R. M. Tryon, *Household Manufactures in the United States, 1840–1860* (1917) collects useful information but fails to give a clear impression, whereas W. C. Langdon, *Everyday Things in American Life, 1607–1776* (1937) is more interesting and chatty. Carl Bridenbaugh, *The Colonial Craftsman* (1950), combining personal and institutional details in a human volume, supplements his *Cities in the Wilderness* (1938). Some industries have received specialized treatment extending back into the Colonial period. The best works are B. E. Hazard, *The Organization of the Boot and Shoe Industry in Massachusetts before 1875* (1931); A. H. Cole, *The American Wool Manufacture,* 2 vols. (1926); and C. B. Kuhlmann, *The Development of the Flour-Milling Industry in the United States* (1929). Defebaugh, cited above, cannot be regarded as adequate on the lumber industry, and the same statement holds true, in spite of their multiplicity of detail, for J. B. Pearse, *A Concise History of the Iron Manufacture of the American Colonies up to the Revolution* (1876) and J. M. Swank, *History of the Manufacture of Iron in All Ages* (1892). A. C. Bining, *Pennsylvania Iron Manufacture in the Eighteenth Century* (1938) pitches everything in higgledy-piggledy but the data are there. E. N. Hartley, *Iron Works on the Saugus* (1957) is invaluable for technical details and for photographs of the restoration. An illuminating discussion of British policy toward colonial manufactures is provided by C. P. Nettels, "The Menace of Colonial Manufacturing," *New England Quarterly,* IV (1931), 230–269.

chapter iii

Trade, Traders, and the Laws

The first volume of E. R. Johnson *et al., History of Domestic and Foreign Commerce of the United States,* 2 vols. (1915) gives a brief narrative to the commerce of the American colonies and has an extensive bibliography. Nonetheless, the treatment is fragmentary and, by modern standards, limited. L. H. Gipson, *The Triumphant Empire, 1763–1766* (1961) has a vigorous account of domestic and foreign commerce.

The internal trade of the colonies still awaits adequate treatment. There is only a brief chapter in E. R. Johnson *et al.,* cited above. Seymour Dunbar, *A History of Travel in America,* 4 vols. (1915) is scatterbrained but contains useful information about early routes and has splendid illustrations. The works of Carl Bridenbaugh: *Cities in the Wilderness* (1938), *Cities in Revolt, Urban Life in America, 1743–1776* (1955), and especially *The Colonial Craftsman* (1950) give more than incidental attention to domestic commerce.

One can trace the colonial experience with money in the manuals on the history of finance: D. R. Dewey, *Financial History of the United States* (1936) and Horace White, *Money and Banking Illustrated by American History* (1902). I have found the relevant parts of W. T. Baxter, *The House of Hancock, Business in Boston, 1724–1775* (1945) give the clearest and most concrete picture of trade, money, and credit. E. J. Ferguson, "Currency Finance: An Interpretation of Colonial Monetary Practices," *William and Mary Quarterly,* Second Series, X (1953), 153–180, is a valuable corrective for the old orthodoxies. See also J. M. Sosin, "Imperial Regulation of Colonial Paper Money 1764–1773," *Pennsylvania Magazine of History and Biography,* LXXXVIII (1964), 174–198. C. P. Nettels, *The Money Supply of the American Colonies before 1720* (1934) is so brilliant one wishes it covered a longer period.

A short but excellent summary of the foreign commerce of the colonies is given by C. M. Andrews, "Colonial Commerce," *AHR,* XX (1946), 43–63, while the works of G. L. Beer, cited earlier, give a full picture of colonial commerce. These accounts might well be read in connection with the first three essays in C. M. Andrews, *The Colonial Background of the American Revolution* (1924). Richard Pares, *Yankees and Creoles. The Trade between North America and the West Indies before the American Revolution* (1956) is the best of all books on its subject and should be imitated for other interregional trades. G. M. Ostrander, "The Colonial Molasses Trade," *AH,* XXX (1956), 77–84 is convincing on this complicated business.

The Acts of Trade and Navigation and their effects have become an area for scholarly quarreling. There are good accounts in the fourth volume of C. M. Andrews, *The Colonial Period of American History* (1935–1938) and in the third volume of Ephraim Lipson, *The Economic History of England* (1931). Beer's thesis that the system was not so bad does not enjoy the repute it once did. Lawrence A. Harper, *The English Navigation Laws. A Seventeenth-Century Experiment in Social Engineering* (1939) appears to conclude the system was a "success," but his shorter "Effect of the Navigation Acts," in Richard B. Morris, ed., *The Era of the American Revolution* (1939), 3–39 assesses what the acts cost the colonies and concludes, "The colonies might have fared much worse." D. C. North, *Growth and Welfare in the American Past* (1966) disagrees with Harper's calculations. A. P. Thomas, "A Quantitive Approach to the Study of the Effects of British Imperial Policy upon Colonial Welfare, Some Preliminary Findings," *JEH,* XXV (1965), 615–638 concludes the acts were not unduly oppressive. C. P. Nettels, "British Mercantilism and the Economic Development of the Thirteen Colonies," *JEH,* XII (1952), 105–114, in taking a severer tone and using different tests, departs more widely from Beer.

The books cited in the previous chapter for various industries and staples touch upon the trade in the products with which they were concerned. For southern commerce in tobacco there are the works by P. A. Bruce, A. O. Craven, and A. P. Middleton, all cited above, and the excellent studies by C. M. Mac-Innes, *The Early English Tobacco Trade* (1926). See also Jacob M. Price, "The Rise of Glasgow in the Chesapeake Tobacco Trade, 1707–1775," *William and Mary Quarterly,* Third Series, XI (1954), 163–199 and J. H. Soltow, "Scottish Traders in Virginia, 1750–1775," *Economic History Review,* XII (1959), 83–98. These studies are given personal life in L. B. Wright, ed., *Letters of Robert Carter, 1720–1727. The Commercial Interests of a Virginia Gentleman* (1940). On Maryland's trade consult C. P. Gould, *Money and Transportation in Maryland, 1720–1765* (1915) and M. C. Morriss, *Colonial Trade of Maryland, 1689–1715* (1913).

On merchants, their activities and their social setting, F. S. Tolles, *Meeting House and Counting House, the Quaker Merchants of Colonial Philadelphia, 1682–1763* (1948) is brief but suggestive; and A. L. Jensen, *The Maritime Commerce of Colonial Philadelphia* (1963) stresses economic and political methods. V. D. Harrington, *The New York Merchant on the Eve of the Revolution* (1935) is one of the best local studies. On North Carolina, consult C. C. Crittenden, *The Commerce of North Carolina, 1763–1789* (1936) and for South Carolina, Leila Sellers, *Charleston Business on the Eve of the American Revolution* (1933). Stuart W. Bruchey, *Robert Oliver, Merchant of Baltimore, 1783–1819* (1956) is fuller on a later period but has a useful summary of Baltimore's commercial position at an earlier time. The work of Bernard Bailyn is at last closing the New England gap and more. See his *The New England Merchants in the Seventeenth Century* (1955) and his "Communications and Trade: The Atlantic in the Seventeenth Century," *JEH* (1953), 378–387. On the New England merchants J. B. Hedges, *The Browns of Providence Plantations* (1952) and W. T. Baxter, *The House of Hancock, Business in Boston, 1724–1775* (1945) are the most important studies of individual enterprises. For other ports consult B. M. Bigelow, "Aaron Lopez: Colonial Merchant of Newport," *New England Quarterly,* IV (1931), 757–776; J. D. Phillips, *Salem in the Eighteenth Century* (1937); and M. E. Martin, *Merchants and Trade of the Connecticut River Valley, 1790–1820* (1939).

A history of shipbuilding in the colonies would fill a grave deficiency. Bernard Bailyn and Lotte Bailyn, *Massachusetts Shipping, 1697–1714* (1959) shows, given the documents, what can be done by a prose narrative and computerized statistics. Ralph Davis, *The Rise of the English Shipping Industry in the Seventeenth and Eighteenth Century* (1962) reveals the role of America's opposite number. Henry Hall, "Report on the Ship-Building Industry of the United States," *Tenth Census, 1880,* VIII (1884) is inadequate on the early period. Of particular interest for the landlubber are John Robinson and G. F. Dow, *The Sailing Ships of New England, 1607–1907,* Marine Research Society, Second Series (1934), profusely illustrated, and E. P. Morris, *The Fore-and-Aft Rig in America, A Sketch* (1927).

chapter iv
A New Start: Agricultural Expansion and Agricultural Methods

In *The History of American Life*, this period is treated by J. A. Krout and D. R. Fox, *The Completion of Independence, 1790–1830* (1944), and C. R. Fish, *The Rise of the Common Man, 1830–1850* (1927). D. C. North, *The Economic Growth of the United States, 1790–1860* (1961) has chapters on regional growth which skillfully interrelate the many factors involved. In the *Economic History of the United States,* Paul W. Gates has written *The Farmer's Age. Agriculture, 1815–1860* (1960).

There is no account of the fur trade that is wholly satisfactory. H. M. Chittenden, *The American Fur Trade of the Far West*, 3 vols. (1902) is a classic, but like many classics is too discursive. Bernard De Voto, *Across the Wide Missouri* (1947) does not go much beyond Chittenden, but has marvelous illustrations. Katherine Coman, *Economic Beginnings of the Far West*, 2 vols. (1912) remains the best treatment. See also John E. Sunder, *The Fur Trade of the Upper Missouri, 1840–1963* (1965). G. L. Nute, "The Papers of the American Fur Company: A Brief Estimate of Their Significance," *AHR*, XXXII (1927), 519–538 is a very stimulating monograph. For the trade in the nearer West see W. E. Stevens, *The Northwest Fur Trade, 1763–1800* (1928) and A. P. Whitaker, *The Spanish-American Frontier, 1783–1795* (1927), the latter brilliantly written. I. A. Johnson, "The Michigan Fur Trade," *Michigan Historical Publications,* Fifth Series, Pt. 1 (1919) and F. J. Turner, *The Character and Influence of the Indian Trade in Wisconsin* (1891) are local treatments. K. W. Porter, *John Jacob Astor, Business Man*, 2 vols. (1931) gives adequate treatment to this big businessman of the fur trade.

On the lumber industry, J. E. Defebaugh, *History of the Lumber Industry of America*, 2 vols. (1906–1907) is useful for the eastern United States, but unfortunately does not touch the western industry. W. F. Fox, "A History of the Lumber Industry in the State of New York," Dept. of Agr., Bur. of Forestry, *Bull.* No. 34 (1902); A. G. Hempstead, *The Penobscot Boom and the Development of the West Branch of the Penobscot River for Log Driving* (1931); and particularly R. G. Wood, *A History of Lumbering in Maine, 1820–1861* (1933) are valuable for methods and industrial organization. A vivid and charming picture of the Maine industry is provided by J. S. Springer, *Forest Life and Forest Trees* (1851). Isaac Stephenson, *Recollections of a Long Life, 1829–1915* (1915) connects eastern and western lumbering in an interesting personal narrative. Frederick Merk, *Economic History of Wisconsin during the Civil War Decade* (1916) and A. M. Larson, *History of the White Pine Industry in Minnesota* (1949) are the best works on western lumbering. The folklore of the lumberman, in so far as it is printed, can be found in James Stevens, *Paul Bunyan* (1925). Jenks Cameron, *The Development of Governmental Forest Control in the United States* (1928) writes vigorously of government policy and popular attitudes during this neglected period.

On public land policy Thomas Donaldson, *The Public Domain, Its History with Statistics* (1884) is a government report to which most secondary works owe their material. In the latter category, B. H. Hibbard, *A History of the Public Land Policies* (1924) is a largely factual chronicle and R. M. Robbins, *Our Landed Heritage: The Public Domain, 1776–1936* (1942) is an interpretation mixing economic, political, social, and legal ingredients. The phases of the public land system have been fortunate in the treatment they have received: J. F. Jameson, *The American Revolution Considered as a Social Movement* (1926)—to which F. B. Tolles, "The American Revolution Considered as a Social Movement: a Re-evaluation," *AHR*, LX (1954), 1–12 states some reservations—and T. P. Abernethy, *Western Lands and the American Revolution* (1937); P. J. Treat, *The National Land System, 1785–1820* (1910); R. G. Wellington, *The Political and Sectional Influence of the Public Lands, 1828–1842* (1914); G. M. Stephenson, *The Political History of the Public Lands from 1840–1862* (1917); H. S. Zahler, *Eastern Workingmen and National Land Policy, 1829-1862* (1941). A compact introduction to many of the large-scale speculations and purchases in this period is Shaw Livermore, *Early American Land Companies, Their Influence on Corporate Development* (1939). For details on specific undertakings consult for the Ohio Company and Scioto Associates the introduction to A. B. Hurlburt, *The Records of the Original Proceedings of the Ohio Company,* I (1912) and J. S. Davis, "William Duer: Entrepreneur," in vol. 1 of his *Essays in the Earlier History of American Corporations,* 2 vols. (1917); on the Yazoo speculations, see C. H. Haskins, "The Yazoo Land Companies," *Papers of the American Historical Association,* V, 395–437; on Symmes, the introduction in B. W. Bond, Jr., *The Correspondence of John Cleves Symmes, Founder of the Miami Purchase* (1926); on western New York, E. P. Oberholtzer, *Robert Morris, Patriot and Financier* (1903); H. I. Cowan, *Charles Williamson, Genesee Promoter* (1941); and P. D. Evans's excellent, "The Holland Land Company," *Buffalo Historical Society Publications,* XXVIII (1924); on the Western Reserve, P. P. Cherry, *The Western Reserve and Early Ohio* (1921).

A beginning has been made on the study, expensive both in time and in money, of land disposal and holdings in particular areas. On the unique New York situation, D. W. Ellis, *Landlords and Farmers in the Hudson Mohawk Region, 1790–1850* (1946) is the standard treatment. On the anti-rent wars Henry Christman, *Tin Horns and Calico* (1945) is colorful and oblivious to the value of orderly development. N. A. McNall, *The First Half-Century of Wadsworth Tenancy* (1945) is a short case-study. For individual states, consult R. L. Lokken, *Iowa Public Land Disposal* (1942) and P. W. Gates, "The Disposal of the Public Domain in Illinois, 1848–1856," *JEBH* (1930), III, 216–240 and his *Frontier Landlords and Pioneer Tenants* (1945). He has dealt with this theme in a large setting in "Land Policy and Tenancy in the Prairie States," *JEH*, I (1941), 60–82 and "Recent Land Policies of the Federal Government," *Supplementary Report of the Land Planning Committee to the National Resources Board,* VII, 60–85.

It is unnecessary to give a complete bibliography for the westward movement. Turner has three stimulating essays—"The Middle West," "The Ohio Valley in American History," and "Significance of the Mississippi Valley in American History"—in his *The Frontier in American History* (1920). Of the many texts on the westward movement, R. E. Riegel, *America Moves West* (1947) and R. A. Billington and J. B. Hedges, *Westward Expansion* (1949) have extensive bibliographies. In view of the importance of agriculture in the United States it is at once astonishing and depressing that it has received so little attention from the general historian and even from the specialist. The bibliographies of L. B. Schmidt and E. E. Edwards, cited in chapter ii, continue to be useful. P. W. Bidwell and J. L. Falconer, *History of Agriculture in the Northern United States, 1620–1860* (1925) gives the most extended treatment. The period between 1800 and 1840 is the best-handled. The volume has an extensive bibliography. *Agriculture of the United States in 1860, Compiled from the Original Returns of the Eighth Census* (1864) pictures progress to that date and has short sketches of worth on the history of agricultural machinery, the beef industry, and wheat cultivation. C. L. Flint, "Progress in Agriculture," in *Eighty Years' Progress* (1861) is an old work which contains some useful information, in spite of the narrative's gross disproportion. As for the costs of farming, a beginning has been made in C. H. Danhof, "Farm-Making Costs and the 'Safety Valve,' 1850–1860," *JPE*, XLIX, 317–359 and "The Fencing Problem in the Eighteen Fifties," *AH*, XVIII (1944), 168–186.

The best description of the physiographic regions in the West is given in the works of Bowman and J. R. Smith, cited among the general works. A. B. Hulburt, *Soil: Its Influence on American History* (1930) ought to be three times as long to be useful. The agricultural conquest of the West is best traced by state and sectional histories. Of state histories notable examples for Illinois are S. J. Buck, *Illinois in 1828* (1917), T. C. Pease, *The Frontier State, 1818–1848* (1922), A. C. Cole, *The Era of the Civil War, 1848–1870* (1919), and W. V. Pooley, *The Settlement of Illinois, 1830–1850* (1908); and for Wisconsin B. H. Hibbard, *The History of Agriculture in Dane County* (1904), J. G. Thompson, *The Rise and Decline of the Wheat-Growing Industry in Wisconsin* (1909), and Frederick Merk, cited above. Allan G. Boque, *From Prairie to Corn Belt. Farming on the Illinois and Iowa Prairies in the Nineteenth Century* (1963), is an exceptional combination of scholarship, balance, and wit. On particular crops or on animal husbandry consult R. A. Clemen, *The American Livestock and Meat Industry* (1923); C. T. Leavitt, "Transportation and the Livestock Industry of the Middle West to 1860," *AH*, VIII (1934), 20–33; J. W. Thompson, "A History of Livestock Raising in the United States, 1607–1860," Dept. of Agr., *Agricultural History Series*, No. 5 (1942); C. B. Kuhlmann, *The Development of the Flour-Milling Industry in the United States* (1929). A difference of scholarly opinion has converged on whether the South was a market for the wheat, corn, and livestock of the Northwest. The arguments of two of the contestants, Albert Fishlow and Robert W. Fogel, are represented in R. L. Andreano, ed., *New Views on American Economic Development* (1965), pp. 187–224. More recently J. G. Clark, *The Grain Trade in the Old Northwest* (1966) calmly sheds additional light on the subject.

The agricultural revolution in this country can be traced with some difficulty through the pages of Bidwell and Falconer, cited above. N. S. B. Gras, *A History of Agriculture in Europe and America* (1923) is a provocative book, but its treatment of American agriculture is brief. The English background is interestingly described in R. E. Prothero, *English Farming, Past and Present* (1912). T. H. Marshall, "Jethro Tull and the 'New Husbandry' of the Eighteenth Century," *Economic History Review*, II (1929), 41–60 takes a more hostile view of

Tull's contributions, as does E. P. Prentice, *American Dairy Cattle: Their Past and Future* (1942) of Bakewell's. Since R. C. Loehr, "The Influence of English Agriculture on American Agriculture, 1775–1825," *AH*, XI (1937), 3–15 is brief, the student must turn to individual farmers or reformers. Aside from sketches in the *Dictionary of American Biography*, see A. O. Craven, *Edmund Ruffin, Southerner* (1932); P. L. Haworth, *George Washington, Country Gentleman* (1925); H. A. Kellar, ed., *Solon Robinson, Pioneer and Agriculturist. Selected Writings*, 2 vols. (1936–1937); H. J. Carman, ed., *Jesse Buel: Agricultural Reformer* (1947); and E. D. Ross, "Horace Greeley and the Beginnings of the New Agriculture," *AH*, VII (1933), 3–17. From L. H. Bailey, *Cyclopedia of American Agriculture*, 4 vols. (1907–1909) some idea can be gained of the institutions for spreading and developing scientific agriculture; consult the articles on agricultural education, agricultural societies, and periodicals. A. C. True, "A History of Agricultural Experimentation and Research in the United States, 1607–1925," Dept. of Agr., *Misc. Pub.* No. 251 (1937) does little more than make lists. W. C. Neely, *The Agricultural Fair* (1935) and A. L. Demaree, *The American Agricultural Press, 1819–1860* (1941) are highly useful.

Sectional treatments of the agricultural transformation are rare. P. W. Bidwell, "Rural Economy in New England at the Beginning of the Nineteenth Century," *Transactions of the Connecticut Academy of Arts and Sciences*, XX, 241–399 gives information not included in the larger cooperative work. R. J. Purcell, *Connecticut in Transition, 1775–1818* (1918); U. P. Hedrick, *A History of Agriculture in the State of New York* (1933); and C. R. Woodward, *The Development of Agriculture in New Jersey, 1640–1880* (1927) are informative. A. O. Craven, *Soil Exhaustion as a Factor in the Agricultural History of Virginia and Maryland, 1606-1860* (1926), a book far transcending its title, and H. F. Wilson, *The Hill Country of Northern New England* (1936) deserve imitation. For cattle, C. T. Leavitt, "Attempts to Improve Cattle Breeds in the United States, 1790–1860," *AH*, VII (1933), 51–67 and G. F. Lemmer, "The Spread of Improved Cattle through the Eastern United States to 1850," *AH*, XXI (1947), 79–83 are excellent. See also Prentice, cited above, and J. W. Thompson, "A History of Livestock Raising in the United States, 1607–1860," Dept. of Agr., *Agricultural History Series* No. 5 (1942). Edward Wiest, *The Butter Industry in the United States* (1916) has a brief background for dairying. The sheep industry has been adequately treated by L. G. Connor, "A Brief History of the Sheep Industry in the United States," *ARAHA*, 1918, I, 89–107 and C. W. Wright, *Wool-Growing and the Tariff* (1910). In this connection and others see A. H. Cole, "Agricultural Crazes, A Neglected Chapter in American Economic History," *AER*, XVI (1926), 622–639. Matters of plant improvement are generally neglected. C. R. Ball, "The History of American Wheat Improvement," *AH*, IV (1930), 48–71 is sketchy for this period. On soil fertility, A. P. Usher "Soil Fertility, Soil Exhaustion, and Their Historical Significance," *QJE*, XXXVII (1923), 385–411 and A. F. Gustafson and others, *Conservation in the United States* (1949) are admirable summaries of modern thinking. For historic conceptions and methods consult Angus McDonald, "Early American Soil Conservationists," Dept. of Agr., *Misc. Pub.* No. 449 (1941). The Harvard Press has reissued Edmund Ruffin, *An Essay on Calcareous Manures* (1961) with an enlightening introduction by J. C. Sitterman. On machinery there is a popular account in the second volume of *A Popular*

History of American Invention, ed. Waldemar Kaempffert, 2 vols. (1924). An able and judicious narrative of the invention of the reaper is given by M. F. Miller, "The Evolution of Reaping Machines," Dept. of Agr., Off. of Exp. Sta., *Bull.* No. 103 (1902). W. T. Hutchinson, *Cyrus Hall McCormick* (1930, 1935) brings scholarship and new research to two volumes which are a landmark in business biography.

chapter v

Southern Agriculture

The most magisterial treatment of the economics of southern agriculture is L. C. Gray, *History of Agriculture in the Southern United States to 1860,* 2 vols. (1933). On the history of particular crops there are J. C. Robert, *The Tobacco Kingdom: Plantation, Market, and Factory in Virginia and North Carolina, 1800–1860* (1938); and for rice, the excellent introduction in J. H. Easterly, *The South Carolina Rice Plantation as Revealed in the Papers of Robert F. W. Allston* (1945) and A. V. House, "The Management of a Rice Plantation in Georgia, 1834–1861," *AH,* XIII, 206–217. On cotton M. B. Hammond, *The Cotton Industry. An Essay in American Economic History* (1897) still remains the standard. On the cotton gin, consult Constance McL. Green, *Eli Whitney and the Birth of American Technology* (1956) and Jeanette Mirsky and Allan Nevins, *The World of Eli Whitney* (1952).

Scholars naturally prefer to combine treatments of slavery with those of southern society. The standard treatments used to be U. B. Phillips, *American Negro Slavery* (1918) and *Life and Labor in the Old South* (1929). Unhappily, Phillips has become a whipping boy for revisionists; he has been dismissed as an "apologist" for slavery and perhaps for being quaint. K. M. Stampp, *The Peculiar Institution, Slavery in the Ante-Bellum South* (1956) acknowledges Phillips' contribution while differing from his assumptions. A refined approval of Phillips' work are the comments of E. D. Genovese, D. M. Potter, K. M. Stamp and E. M. Elkins in "Race and Class in Southern History," *AH,* XLI (1957), 359–372. A. H. Conrad and J. R. Meyer, "The Economics of Slavery in the Ante-Bellum South," *JPE,* LXVI (1958), 95–130 is an important article which implies a contempt for other than economic standards of judgment. Eugene D. Genovese, *The Political Economy of Slavery* (1961) assails Conrad and Meyer and gets back to Phillips. With one puff Robert E. Russel, "The General Effects of Slavery upon Southern Economic Progress," *Journal of Southern History,* IV (1938), 34–54 blows out a dozen myths. A. H. Conrad and others celebrated the tenth anniversary of the original paper by Conrad and Meyer in "Slavery as an Obstacle to Economic Growth in the United States: A Panel Discussion," *JEH,* XXVII (1967), 518–560.

Amidst a great deal of controversy, salutary detailed studies are filling in the picture of an economic and social order. S. H. Clark, *The Tennessee Yeoman, 1840–1860* (1942) and Herbert Weaver, *Mississippi Farmers, 1850–1860* (1945) demonstrate the plantation was spectacular and the farm the norm. C. S. Sydnor, *Slavery in Mississippi* (1935) has a different spotlight than the Weavers. It also contributes to the discussion of the "profitability" of slavery. J. H. Moore, *Agriculture in Ante-Bellum Mississippi* (1958) goes beyond both. T. P. Govan, "Was Plantation Slavery Profitable?" *Journal of Southern History*, VIII (1942), 513–535 corrects Sydnor's errors. Shorter but equally important are F. L. and H. C. Owsley, "The Economic Basis of Society in the Late Ante-Bellum South," *Journal of Southern History*, VI (1940), 24–45 and P. H. Buck, "The Poor Whites of the Ante-bellum South," *AHR*, XXXI (1925), 41–53.

On the slave trade consult W. E. B. Du Bois, *The Suppression of the African Slave Trade to the United States of America, 1638–1870* (1896); Frederic Bancroft, *Slave-Trading in the Old South* (1931); and W. H. Stephenson, *Isaac Franklin, Slave-Trader and Planter of the Old South* (1958).

National Bureau of Economic Research, *Trends in the American Economy in the Nineteenth Century, Studies in Income and Wealth*, XXIV (1960), 225–315; and P. A. David, "The Growth of Real Product in the United States before 1840, New Evidence, Controlled Conjectures," *JEH*, VII (1967), 151–195; and G. R. Taylor, "American Economic Growth before 1840: An Exploratory Essay," *JEH*, XXIV (1964), 427–444 all measure agricultural growth and arrive at somewhat different conclusions.

chapter vi

Internal Improvements and Domestic Commerce

The bibliography of domestic trade and transportation is unusually complete for an economic subject, and most American historians have treated the subject extensively in their general works. The best secondary account is G. R. Taylor, *The Transportation Revolution, 1815–1860*, vol. 4 in the *Economic History of the United States* (1951). The volumes in the Carnegie Series by E. R. Johnson *et al.*, *History of Domestic and Foreign Commerce of the United States* (1915) and B. H. Meyer, C. F. Macgill, *et al.*, *History of Transportation in the United States before 1860* (1917) are both unsatisfactory, but for different reasons. More contemporary than these works are the reports of travelers, of which Michel Chavalier's *Society, Manners, and Politics in the United States* (1839) is an informative example. Fortunately, one of the few extensive surveys of the field of domestic commerce ever made was in 1851–1852, and the results are published in I. D. Andrews, *Report on the Trade and Commerce of the British North American Colonies and upon the Trade of the Great Lakes and Rivers*, 32nd Cong. 1st Sess., Ex. Doc. No. 136 (1853), which has extremely valuable appendices. John G. Clark, *The Grain Trade in the Old Northwest* (1966) is unsurpassed as a study of trade in wheat, flour, and corn. W. F. Switzler, *Report on the Internal Commerce of the United States*, 50th Cong. 1st Sess., House Ex. Doc. No. 6, Pt. 2 (1888) completes the picture for the internal river basins. Of the many regional studies of transportation, primarily railroad strategy, the most useful are U. B. Phillips, *A History of Transportation in the Eastern Cotton Belt to 1860* (1908); W. J. Lane, *From Indian Trail to Iron Horse, Travel and Transportation in New Jersey, 1620–1860* (1939); H. P. Baker, *Formation of the New England Railroad Systems* (1937); E. C. Kirkland, *Men,*

Cities and Transportation. A Study in New England History, 1820–1900, 2 vols. (1948); Stephen Salsbury, *The State, the Investor, and the Railroad. The Boston and Albany, 1825–1867* (1967); J. W. Livingood, *The Philadelphia-Baltimore Trade Rivalry, 1780–1860* (1947); W. W. Belcher, *The Economic Rivalry between St. Louis and Chicago, 1850–1880* (1947); and Merl E. Reed, *New Orleans and the Railroads: The Struggle for Commercial Empire, 1850–1860* (1966).

Though A. B. Hulbert has made a study of separate turnpikes, the early history of highways and highway transportation is in desperate need of scholarly attention. The turnpikes have been covered systematically in J. A. Durrenburger, *Turnpikes, a Study of the Toll Road Movement in the Middle Atlantic States and Maryland* (1931) and P. E. Taylor, "The Turnpike Era in New England," Unpublished MS. Thesis, Yale University (1934). F. J. Wood, *Turnpikes of New England* (1919) summarizes the history of individual projects. P. D. Jordan, *The National Road* (1948) is the best on that enterprise.

For the invention of the steamboat, J. T. Flexner, *Steamboats Come True* (1944) is a good summary. Admirable works on individual inventors are: H. W. Dickenson, *Robert Fulton: Engineer and Artist* (1913); Greville and Dorothy Bathe, *Oliver Evans* (1935); and Thomas Boyd, *Poor John Fitch: Inventor of the Steamboat* (1935). The history of commerce on the eastern waters is almost untouched. M. E. Martin, *Merchants and Trade of the Connecticut River Valley, 1750–1820* (1939) is an exception. The coasting trade is also comparatively untreated, but see R. G. Albion, *The Rise of New York Port, 1815–1860* (1939); J. G. B. Hutchins, *The American Maritime Industries* (1941); Kirkland, cited above; and W. J. Lane, *Commodore Vanderbilt: An Epic of the Steam Age* (1942) for a beginning. J. H. Morrison, *History of American Steam Navigation* (1903) remains more useful than its successors. On the Mississippi the definitive account is L. C. Hunter, *Steamboats on the Western Rivers: An Economic and Technological History* (1949). This should be supplemented by L. D. Baldwin, *The Keelboat Age on Western Waters* (1941) and W. J. Petersen, *Steamboating on the Upper Mississippi* (1937). For the Great Lakes, Harlan Hatcher, *Lake Erie* (1945) in the American Lake Series has the most material on navigation.

Contemporary accounts of internal improvements are the Report of Albert Gallatin on Roads and Canals in the *American State Papers*, Miscellaneous, I, 724–921; S. H. Mitchell, *Mitchell's Compendium of the Internal Improvements of the United States* (1835); and H. S. Tanner, *A Description of the Canals and Railroads of the United States* (1840). Undoubtedly the best summary of the canal era and the philosophy behind it is Carter Goodrich *et al., Canals and Economic Development* (1961). It has not superseded all the articles published elsewhere by its contributors. Of these the more important are Carter Goodrich, "The Virginia System of Mixed Enterprise, A Study of State Planning of Internal Improvements," *Political Science Quarterly*, LXIV (1949), 355–387; Julius Rubin, "Canal or Railroad? Imitation and Innovation in the Response to the Erie Canal," *Transactions of the American Philosophical Society*, New Series, LI, No. 7 (1961), 5–106; and H. J. Cranmer, "Canal Improvement, 1815–1860," *Trends in the American Economy in the Nineteenth Century*, National Bureau of Economic Research, *Studies in Income and Wealth*, XXIV (1960), 547–570. See J. B. Rae, "Federal Land Grants in Aid of Canals," *JEH*, IV (1944), 167–177, and for a somewhat wider bearing, Albert Fishlow, cited below.

On the individual canals, the classic for the Erie, N. E. Whitford, *History of the Canal System of the State of New York*, 2 vols. (1906) remains useful. Nathan Miller, *The Enterprise of a Free People. Aspects of Economic Development in New York during the Canal Period, 1792–1838* (1962) is a sophisticated modern treatment. See also D. M. Ellis, "Rivalry between the New York Central and the Erie Canal," *New York History*, XXIX, 268–300. On other canals the best narratives are A. L. Bishop, "The State Works of Pennsylvania," *Transactions of the Connecticut Academy of Arts and Sciences*, XIII (1908); G. W. Ward, *The Early Development of the Chesapeake and Ohio Canal Project* (1899); E. L. Bogart, *Internal Improvements and State Debt in Ohio* (1924); W. F. Dunaway, *History of the James River and Kanawha Company* (1922); E. J. Benton, *The Wabash Trade Route in the Development of the Old Northwest* (1903); J. W. Putnam, *The Illinois and Michigan Canal* (1918); C. L. Jones, *The Economic History of the Anthracite Tide-Water Canals* (1908); Christopher Roberts, *The Middlesex Canal, 1793–1860* (1938); and W. S. Sanderlin, *The Great National Project: A History of the Chesapeake and Ohio Canal* (1946). The financing of internal improvements is, of course, discussed in the above works. More specialized treatment is provided in the extremely valuable contemporary account, Alexander Trotter, *Observations upon the Financial Position . . . of Such of the States . . . as Have Contracted Public Debts* (1839) and in the monographs of L. H. Jenks, *The Migration of British Capital to 1875* (1927); R. C. McGrane, *Foreign Bondholders and American State Debts* (1935); G. S. Callender, *English Capital and American Resources*, Unpublished MS. Thesis, Harvard College; B. W. Ratchford, *American State Debts* (1941); and R. W. Hidy, *The House of Baring in American Trade and Finance* (1949).

The best introduction to railroad planning and railroad hunger is Carter Goodrich, *Government Promotion of American Canals and Railroads, 1800–1890* (1960). To Rubin and Hartz's works, previously cited, add Milton Heath, *Constructive Liberalism. The Role of the State in Economic Development in Georgia to 1860* (1950) and Forrest Hill, *Roads, Rails, and Waterways. The Army Engineers in Early Transportation* (1957).

The appraisal of the railroad as an economic force and more particularly as "dispensable" or "indispensable" is the work of R. W. Fogel, *Railroads and Economic Growth: Essays in Econometric History* (1964) and Albert Fishlow, *American Railroads and the Transformation of the Ante-Bellum Economy* (1965), which the author correctly says "more closely resembles an abridged economic history of the period than a conventional chronicle of an industry." Fishlow refuses to throw the baby out with the bath water. P. H. Cootner, "The Role of the Railroads," *JEH*, XXIII (1963), 477–521 is another modest dissertation; but that beneath each dissent lies a deeper dissent is revealed by Matthew Simon and Harry N. Scheiber, "Discussion," *JEH*, XXIII (1963), 522–528.

On technical details consult David Stevenson, *Sketch of Civil Engineering of North America* (1859) and *A Popular History of American Invention*, ed. Waldemar Kaempffert, 2 vols. (1924), occasionally inaccurate. The text of W. H. Brown, *History of the First Locomotives in America* (1877) is accompanied with interesting silhouettes or sketches of early engines; J. E. Watkins, "The Development of the American Rail and Track," *Report of the U.S. National Museum* (1889), 651–708 has valuable illustrations; and Angus Sinclair, *Development of the Locomotive Engine* (1907) is a useful summary. A. D. Turnbull, *John Stevens: An American Record* (1928) is the life of a pioneer transportation-inventor. Studies of local roads are included in the regional studies earlier cited and in Milton Reizenstein, *The Economic History of the Baltimore and Ohio Railroad, 1827–1853* (1897); F. W. Stevens, *The Beginnings of the New York Central Railroad* (1906); Edward Hungerford, *The Story of the Baltimore and Ohio Railroad, 1827–1927* 2 vols. (1928); S. M. Derrick, *Centennial History of South Carolina Railroad* (1930); and H. G. Brownson, *History of the Illinois Central Railroad to 1870* (1915). L. H. Haney, *A Congressional History of Railways in the United States to 1850* (1908) and Frederick Merk, "Eastern Antecedents of the Grangers," *AH* (1949), XXIII, 1–8 contribute details to railroad and state relationships; see also the works earlier cited in connection with internal improvements.

chapter vii
Foreign Commerce

Douglass C. North, *The Economic Growth of the United States, 1790–1860* (1961) has written the essential book integrating the history of foreign trade and commerce with the domestic life of the nation. It is prudent to read also his "The United States Balance of Payments, 1790–1860," in the National Bureau's *Trends in the American Economy in the Nineteenth Century* (1960), along with Eric Lampard's commentary. The vital statistics for American commerce can be obtained from *American State Papers* (1832–1839) and after 1822 from the valuable annual *Report of the Secretary of the Treasury on Commerce and Navigation.* Figures for the earlier period are provided by Timothy Pitkin, *A Statistical View of the Commerce of the United States of America* (1816, 1835) and Adam Seybert, *Statistical Annals* (1818).

The struggle against the commercial and navigation systems of Europe is best prefaced by R. L. Schuyler, *The Fall of the Old Colonial System, A Study in British Free Trade* (1945). K. E. Knorr, *British Colonial Theories, 1570–1850* (1944) covers a wider chronological sweep. The best overall picture of the American attack upon the British and other systems is in J. G. B. Hutchins, *The American Maritime Industries and Public Policy, 1789–1914* (1941), a volume which is at the same time the most notable history of American shipbuilding and operation. This should be supplemented for the critical earlier period by V. G. Setser, *The Commercial Reciprocity Policy of the United States, 1774–1829* (1937). This has the virtue of not focusing on the British. Admirable studies dealing with phases of the issue are S. F. Bemis, *Jay's Treaty: A Study in Commerce and Diplomacy* (1924); F. L. Benns, *The American Struggle for the British West India Carrying-Trade, 1815–1830* (1923); W. F. Galpin, *The Grain Supply of England during the Napoleonic Period* (1925); L. W. Maxwell, *Discriminating Duties and the American Merchant Marine* (1926); and C. S. Graham, *Sea Power and British North America, 1783–1820. A Study in British Colonial Policy* (1941). On the tariff F. W. Taussig, *The Tariff History of the United States* (1914) describes duties and their impact but neglects concepts. Joseph Dorfman in the second volume of *The Economic Mind in American Civilization, 1606–1865* (1946) dissects the theorizers on both sides of the issue.

On the new trades the best summary for the Orient is Tyler Dennett, *Americans in Eastern Asia* (1922). K. S. Latourette, "The History of Early Relations between the United States and China, 1784–1844," *Transactions of the Connecticut Academy of Arts and Sciences*, XXI (1917) is admirable. K. W. Porter, *The Jacksons and the Lees: Two Generations of Massachusetts Merchants, 1765–1844*. 2 vols. (1937) has a capital account of the trade with India in his introduction. Adele Ogden, *The California Sea Otter Trade: 1784–1848* (1941) and H. W. Bradley, *The American Frontier in Hawaii* (1924) work in details of the Pacific nexus; and J. D. Phillips, *Salem and the Indies* (1947) is highly readable. For the South American trades, A. P. Whitaker, *The United States and the Independence of Latin America, 1800–1830* (1941) includes among other matters an admirable account. There is an excellent chapter in Harry Bernstein, *Origins of Inter-American Interest, 1700–1812* (1945). See also D. B. Goebel, "British Trade to the Spanish Colonies, 1796–1823," *AHR*, XLIII (1937), 288–320 and "British-American Rivalry in Chilean Trade, 1817–1820," *JEH*, II (1942), 190–202. J. F. Rippy, *Rivalry of the United States and Great Britain over Latin America, 1808–1830* (1929), pays attention to commercial considerations.

There are some histories of commodity trades: M. B. Hammond, *The Cotton Industry* (1897) and Sister M. A. Hess, *American Tobacco and Central European Policy, Early Nineteenth Century* (1948), the latter a pioneering study. This approach should be explored for other commodities. Bingham Duncan does so in "Diplomatic Support of the American Rice Trade, 1835–1845," *AH*, XXIII (1949), 92–96. On the trade of particular districts, S. E. Morison, *The Maritime History of Massachusetts, 1783–1860* (1921) and R. G. Albion, *The Rise of New York Port, 1815–1860* (1939) are unusual because of their wide scholarship and literary charm. See also R. R. Russel, *Economic Aspects of Southern Sectionalism, 1840–1861* (1924) and F. R. Rutter, *South American Trade of Baltimore* (1897) for the South; and W. H. Rowe, *The Maritime History of Maine* (1948) and W. G. Saltonstall, *Ports of the Piscataqua* (1941) for New England.

On the organization of foreign commerce, N. S. Buck, *The Development of the Organization of Anglo-American Trade, 1800–1850* (1925) is the nearest to a complete treatment. Cleona Lewis, *America's Stake in International Investments* (1938) is too brief on this period. L. H. Jenks, *The Migration of British Capital to 1875* (1927), written with insight and literary distinction, is essential. R. C. McGrane, *Foreign Bondholders and American State Debts* (1935) does justice to an unpleasant episode. Inevitably R. W. Hidy, *The House of Baring in American Trade and Finance* (1949), a perceptive study, ties together many threads. On the organization of a particular trade, H. D. Woodman, *King Cotton and His Retainers* (1968), is superb.

J. G. B. Hutchins, *The American Maritime Industries*, cited earlier, supersedes previous general histories of the merchant marine. See also R. G. Albion, *Square-Riggers on Schedule* (1938). Probably the best introductions to naval architecture for the layman are H. I. Chapelle, *The History of American Sailing*

Ships (1935) and A. K. Laing, *Clipper Ship Men* (1944), intended as a boy's book but thus comprehensible to the adult landlubber. A. H. Clark, *The Clipper Ship Era, 1843–1869* (1910) is a classic, and C. C. Cutler, *Greyhounds of the Sea: The Story of the American Clipper Ship* (1930) is beautifully illustrated and concludes with exceedingly valuable tables of voyages, records, and ships. Information and illustrations concerning individual vessels have also been collected in several volumes by F. C. Matthews on American clipper and commercial sailing-craft. For steamships consult D. B. Tyler, *Steam Conquers the Atlantic* (1939). Varied estimates on subsidies are in Royal Meeker, *History of Shipping Subsidies* (1905) and M. M. McKee, *The Ship Subsidy Question in United States Policies* (1922).

chapter viii
State and Nation in Banking and Finance

Paul Studenski and H. E. Krooss, *Financial History of the United States* (1963) covers this wide field excellently and incorporates modern thinking without evangelism. Supplementary studies on phases are Sidney Ratner, *American Taxation: Its History as a Social Force in a Democracy* (1942) and B. U. Ratchford, *American State Debts* (1941), an admirable treatment. On the finances of the Revolution and after there is a good discussion in R. A. East, *Business Enterprise in the American Revolutionary Era* (1938). See also Allan Nevins, *The American States during and after the Revolution* (1924) and C. L. Ver Steeg, *Robert Morris, Revolutionary Financier* (1954), which shows that what came afterwards had precedent. On price fixing Anne Bezanson, "Inflation and Controls, Pennsylvania, 1774–1779," *JEH*, VIII, Supplement (1948), 1–20 is illuminating.

Any discussion of banking of interest to others than technicians of the subject should consider the ideas and social conceptions conditioning the banking system. Three volumes which accomplish this objective are H. E. Miller, *Banking Theory in the United States before 1860* (1927); Fritz Redlich, *The Molding of American Banking: Men and Ideas, 1781–1840* (1947), more successful in describing the impact of ideas upon banking devices; and Bray Hammond, *Banks and Politics in America from the Revolution to the Civil War* (1957), a felicitous merger of wit, common sense, and perception.

The best introduction to the problems and institutions of the Federal government is in the *Papers of Alexander Hamilton*, "On Public Credit" and a "National Bank," ed., W. C. Syrett, VI, VII (1962, 1963). J. T. Holdsworth and D. W. Dewey, *The First and Second Banks of the United States* (1910) still contains the most usable account of the First Bank. J. O. Wettereau, "The Branches of the First Bank of the United States," *Tasks of Economic History* (1942), 66–100 whets the appetite for more. The best account of the bank is W. B. Smith, *The Economic Aspects of the Second Bank of the United States* (1953). It is compelled to stray into the field of political action. On this wider theme Arthur M. Schlesinger, Jr., *The Age of Jackson* (1945) is more concerned with the ideological tone of the Jackson Administration than the accomplishments of the Bank; T. P. Govan,

Nicholas Biddle, Nationalist and Public Banker, 1786–1844 (1959) is prone to use rosy words about commonplace actions. Redlich, already cited, lauds Biddle more persuasively. Joseph Dorfman, *The Economic Mind in American Civilization, 1606–1865* (1946) has a perspicacious chapter on Jacksonianism in his second volume; Marvin Myers, *The Jacksonian Persuasion, Politics, and Belief* (1957) shows that demagogues are real. For the establishment of the BUS see K. L. Brown, "Stephen Girard, Promoter of the Second Bank of the United States," *JEH*, II (1942), 125–148. On the subtreasury consult E. R. Taus, *Central Banking Functions of the United States Treasury, 1789–1941* (1943) and David Kinley, *The Independent Treasury of the United States and Its Relations to the Banks of the Country* (1910).

For state banking Bray Hammond, already cited, has the key. For particular jurisdictions or kinds of banks, consult Oscar and M. F. Handlin, *Commonwealth, A Study of the Rôle of Government in the American Economy: Massachusetts* (1947); Louis Hartz, *Economic Policy and Democratic Thought in Pennsylvania, 1776–1860* (1948); R. C. McGrane, *Foreign Bondholders and American State Debts* (1935); R. E. Chaddock, *The Safety Fund Banking System in New York, 1829–1866* (1910); and on the Suffolk system W. S. Lake, "The End of the Suffolk System," *JEH*, VII (1947), 183–207.

Of the works on individual banks, N. S. B. Gras, *The Massachusetts First National Bank of Boston, 1784–1934* (1937); F. C. James, *The Growth of Chicago Banks*, 2 vols. (1938); and Allan Nevins, *History of the Bank of New York and Trust Company, 1784–1934* (1934) are useful. H. M. Larson, *Jay Cooke, Private Banker* (1936) has a chapter on private banks in this period. See also, A. J. Schwartz, "The Beginning of Competitive Banking in Philadelphia, 1782–1809," *JPE*, LV (1947), 417–431. On the centralization of banking in private practice, M. G. Myers, *The New York Money Market: Origins and Development* (1931) covers the national scene. See also, J. E. Hedges, *Commercial Banking and the Stock Market before 1863* (1938).

chapter ix

The Phases of Industrial Production

The best complete volume on manufacturing still remains V. S. Clark, *History of Manufactures in the United States, 1607–1860*, 3 vols. (1929). H. J. Habakkuk, *American and British Technology in the Nineteenth Century* (1962), written to support a thesis, contains a mass of material of general applicability. R. M. Tryon, *Household Manufactures in the United States, 1640–1860* (1917) is an indispensable narrative, cutting across specific industries for a general picture of a phase of production. T. S. Ashton, *The Industrial Revolution, 1760–1830* (1948) is a handy and enlightening volume on the English background. Hamilton's "Report on Manufactures" and supporting documents can best be consulted in Vol. 10 of H. C. Syrett, ed., *The Papers of Alexander Hamilton* (1966), or in A. H. Cole, ed., *Industrial and Commercial Correspondence of Alexander Hamilton Anticipating His Report on Manufactures* (1928). A. P. Usher, *A History of Mechanical Inventions* (1954) and Siegfried Giedion,

Mechanization Takes Command (1948) are quite different but valuable general introductions to the matter of technology.

The subject of mechanization, along with others, arises in the histories of individual industries. The best of these in my estimation are A. H. Cole, *The American Wool Manufacture,* 2 vols. (1926); C. F. Ware, *The Early New England Cotton Manufacture: A Study in Industrial Beginnings* (1931); Peter Temin, *Iron and Steel in Nineteenth Century America. An Economic Enquiry* (1964); F. J. Deyrup, *Arms Makers of the Connecticut Valley. A Regional Study of the Economic Development of the Small Arms Industry, 1798–1870* (1948); Nathan Rosenberg, "Technological Change in the Machine Tool Industry, 1840–1910," *JEH,* XXIII (1963), 414–446; J. T. Lincoln, "The Beginnings of the Machine Age in New England: David Wilkinson," *New England Quarterly,* VI (1933), 716–732; and E. H. Knowlton, *Pepperell's Progress; History of a Cotton Textile Company, 1844–1945* (1948). While Peter Temin, cited above, takes issue with him, L. C. Hunter, "Influence of the Market upon Technique in the Iron Industry of Western Pennsylvania up to 1860," *JEBH,* I (1929), 241–281 has not been superseded.

On the factors in industrial advance the bibliographies for the earlier chapters on trade and transportation give some idea about markets and references for their study. Of the specialized works L. E. Atherton, *The Pioneer Merchant in Mid-America* (1939) is in a class by itself. R. R. Russel, *Economic Aspects of Southern Sectionalism, 1840–1861* (1923) interweaves southern markets with other themes. Biographies of individual inventors as industrialists are not numerous, but Eli Whitney has stirred much attention among historians. Jeanette Mirsky and Allan Nevins, *The World of Eli Whitney* (1952) says the most that can be said for Whitney; C. M. Green, *Eli Whitney and the Birth of American Technology* (1956) takes a more middle ground; R. S. Woodbury, "The Legend of Eli Whitney and Interchangeable Parts," *Technology and Culture,* I (1960), 235–255 is described by its title.

On the methods by which capital was accumulated and managed, Lance Davis, "Sources of Industrial Finance: The American Textile Industry, A Case Study," *Explorations in Entrepreneurial History,* IX (1957), 189–203 and his "The New England Textile Mills and the Capital Markets: A Study of Industrial Borrowing, 1840–1860," *JEH* (1960), 1–30 emphasize the contributions of banking loans. The corporation has accumulated a more extensive literature. J. S. Davis, *Essays in the Early History of American Corporation: Eighteenth Century Business Corporations in the United States,* 2 vols. (1917) is the definitive account for the period before 1800. It contains an excellent account of the SUM. Statistical and descriptive material for the nineteenth century are provided by G. H. Evans, Jr., *Business Incorporations in the United States, 1800–1943* (1948). Consult also W. C. Kessler, "Incorporation in New England: A Statistical Study, 1800–1875," *JEH,* VIII (1948), 43–63 and his "A Statistical Study of the New York General Incorporation Act of 1811," *JPE,* XLVIII (1940), 877–882; William Miller, "A Note on the History of Business Corporations in Pennsylvania, 1800–1860," *QJE,* LV (1940), 150–160; and Lance Davis, "Stock Ownership in the Early New England Textile Industry," *Business History Review,* XXXII (1958), 204–222. For the conceptual backgrounds Louis Hartz, *Economic Policy and Democratic Thought: Pennsylvania* (1948) and Oscar and M. F. Handlin, *Common-*

wealth: A Study of the Rôle of Government in the American Economy: Massachusetts (1947) are essential. See also the Handlins' "Origins of the American Business Corporation," *JEH*, V (1945), 1–23.

The social and intellectual setting for the industrial growth in this era is described in C. L. Sanford, "The Intellectual Origins and New-Worldliness of American Industry," *JEH*, XVIII (1958), 1–16; J. E. Sawyer, "The Social Basis of the American System of Manufacturing," *JEH*, XIV (1954), 361–379; and Samuel Rezneck, "The Rise and Early Development of Industrial Consciousness in the United States, 1760–1830," *JEBH*, IV (1932), 784–811. Leo Marx, *The Machine in the Garden. Technology and the Pastoral Ideal in America* (1964) is exceptionally perceptive.

chapter x

The Labor Market, Labor Conditions, Grievances

No treatment of labor during the period is possible without reference to the ten volumes in *A Documentary History of American Industrial Society* (1910–1911). Edited by J. R. Commons and others, this work contains valuable documents and introductions. H. J. Habakkuk, *American and British Technology in the Nineteenth Century: The Search for Labour-Saving Inventions* (1962) necessarily says a great deal about the American labor market.

There are a great number of histories of labor and of organized labor, many of which are characterized by partisanship and doctrinaire views. On the whole, the best single treatment remains the first volume in J. R. Commons *et al., History of Labour in the United States* (1918), which pays more attention to the philosophy and organization of the labor movement than the conditions under which the laborer worked. P. S. Foner, *History of the Labor Movement in the United States* (1947) has the same interests but is more opinionated. An overall picture of working conditions is provided by Norman Ware, *The Industrial Worker, 1840–1860* (1942), a brilliant work, and by vol. 2 of Jürgen Kuczynski, *A Short History of Labour Conditions under Industrial Capitalism* (1943). The data on wages and hours in this chapter were derived from Kuczynski's volume, A. H. Hansen, "Factors Affecting the Trend of Real Wages," *AER*, XV (1925), 27–42; *Report of the Committee on Finance (Senate) on Wholesale Prices, Wages, and Transportation* (Aldrich Report), 52nd Cong. 2nd Sess., Sen. Rep. No. 1394; and "History of Wages in the United States from Colonial Times to 1928," *Bulletin of the United States Bureau of Labor Statistics*, No. 604. R. C. Layer, *Earnings of Cotton-Mill Operatives, 1825–1914* (1955) is based upon exceptional material. E. W. Martin, *The Standard of Living in 1860. American Consumption Levels on the Eve of the Civil War* (1942) blends description and statistics in an exceptionally interesting manner. The impact of depression upon labor is described in part in Samuel Rezneck, "Depression of 1819–22," *AHR*, XXXIX (1933), 28–47 and "Social History of an American Depression, 1837–43," *AHR*, XL (1935), 662–687; and G. W. Van Vleck, *The Panic of 1857, An Analytical Study* (1943).

Women and child workers have received excellent treatment in Edith

Abbott, *Women in Industry, with an Appendix on Child Labor before 1870* (1910); H. L. Sumner, *History of Women in Industry in the United States*, 61st Cong. 2nd Sess., Sen. Doc. No. 645, IX (1911); and J. B. Andrews and W. D. P. Bliss, *History of Women in Trade Unions*, 61st Cong. 2nd Sess., Sen. Doc. No. 645, X (1911). The Lowell system has fascinated investigators, not always free from prepossessions. C. F. Ware, *The Early New England Cotton Manufacture; A Study in Industrial Beginnings* (1931) and C. L. Sanford, "The Intellectual Origins and New-Worldliness of American Industry," *JEH*, XVIII (1958), 1–16 are both dependable and illuminating. Hannah Josephson, *The Golden Threads, New England's Mill Girls and Magnates* (1949) is more tightly schematic.

The last chapter in H. W. Farnam, *Chapters in the History of Social Legislation in the United States to 1860* (1938) is a good introduction to the labor legislation of this period. More details are provided in J. K. Towles, *Factory Legislation of Rhode Island* (1908); C. E. Persons, "Early History of Factory Legislation in Massachusetts," in *Labor Laws and Their Enforcement*, ed., S. M. Kingsbury (1911); A. M. Edwards, *The Labor Legislation of Connecticut* (1907); F. R. Fairchild, *The Factory Legislation of the State of New York* (1905); and J. L. Barnard, *Factory Legislation in Pennsylvania: Its History and Administration* (1907). For children consult F. L. Otey, *The Beginnings of Child Labor Legislation in Certain States: A Comparative Study*, 61st Cong. 3rd Sess., Sen. Doc. No. 645, VI (1910). For differing interpretations of Commonwealth *v.* Hunt, see L. W. Levy, *The Law of the Commonwealth and Chief Justice Shaw* (1957) and Walter Millis, "Commonwealth *v.* Hunt," *Columbia Law Review*, XXXII (1932), 1128–1169. The utopian and community efforts of the era have an extended bibliography. An excellent introduction is A. F. Tyler, *Freedom's Ferment* (1944).

A small library has accumulated about the measurement of the performance of the economy. One collection on this subject is R. L. Andreano, ed., *New Views of American Economic Development* (1965) which includes pertinent articles by the editor and G. R. Taylor, Robert Gallman, and Raymond Goldsmith. Other collections are National Bureau of Economic Research, *Trends in the American Economy in the Nineteenth Century* (1960) and their *Output, Employment and Productivity in the United States after 1800* (1966). All these essays should be supplemented by the papers by Rostow, Kuznets, and North in W. W. Rostow, ed., *The Economics of Take-off into Sustained Growth* (1963).

chapter xi
The Railroad Business

Customary themes, such as apparent alterations in the political climate and the occurrence of wars, have led historians to overestimate the advantages of dividing the last hundred years into periods ending or beginning with 1900. If only the census dates would oblige, a better case could be made for dividing our economic history at 1915. General accounts touching on economic affairs for the era from 1860 to 1915 are available in the volumes of the *History of American Life:* Allan Nevins, *The Emergence of Modern America, 1865–1878*

(1927); A. M. Schlesinger, *The Rise of the City, 1878–1898* (1933); I. M. Tarbell, *The Nationalization of Business, 1878–1898* (1936), really written by other hands; and H. U. Faulkner, *The Quest for Social Justice, 1898–1914* (1931). In the series of the *Economic History of the United States* the relevant volumes are F. A. Shannon, *The Farmer's Last Frontier (Agriculture), 1860–1897* (1945); E. C. Kirkland, *Industry Comes of Age. Business, Labor, and Public Policy, 1860–1897* (1961); and H. U. Faulkner, *The Decline of Laissez Faire, 1897–1917* (1951). Two works cover the effects of the Civil War: Ralph Andreano, ed., *The Economic Impact of the American Civil War* (1962) and D. T. Gilchrist and W. D. Lewis, eds., *Economic Change in the Civil War Era* (1965). Both books are collections of scholarly articles: the second covers a period longer than that of the conflict. E. D. Fite, *Social and Industrial Conditions in the North during the Civil War* (1910) shows how far enthusiasm can prevent accurate appraisals.

On population and migration, H. S. Shryock, Jr., *Population Mobility within the United States* (1964) pays limited attention to the late nineteenth century. An encyclopedic account is Simon Kuznets and Dorothy Thomas, *Population Redistribution and Economic Growth, United States, 1870–1950*, 3 vols. (1957); the essays in vols. 2 and 3 are of most interest to the nonspecialist. It is impossible here to give a bibliography for politicoeconomic thought and action. The classic account is the third volume of Joseph Dorfman, *The Economic Mind in American Civilization* (1949). Dorfman has the rare talent of giving the devil his due. Sidney Fine, *Laissez Faire and the General-Welfare State. A Study of Conflict in American Thought, 1865–1901* (1956) lets the reader know he is on the side of the angels; R. G. McCloskey, *American Conservatism in the Age of Enterprise. A Study of William G. Sumner, Stephen J. Field, and Andrew Carnegie* (1951) is out to trample on villains. E. S. Redford and C. B. Hagan, *American Government and the Economy* (1965) is stronger on administration than thought.

The history of American transportation in the modern period has to be pieced together from various sources. Contemporaneous information is provided by H. V. Poor, *Poor's Manual of the Railroads of the United States* (1868); *The Commercial and Financial Chronicle* (1871–); and the Interstate Commerce Commission, *Annual Report on the Statistics of Railways in the United States* (1889–) and its *Annual Report* (1887–). *The Final Report of the Industrial Commission* (1902) is an admirable summary in cross-section for transportation at the turn of the century. It should be supplemented by vols. 4 and 9 of the same report, which contain the evidence and summaries of the evidence, excellently classified. Additional government documents of fundamental importance for railroad history are the *Report of the Select Committee on Transportation Routes to the Seaboard* (Windom Report), 43rd Cong. 1st Sess., Sen. Rep. No. 307, Pts. 1–2 (1874); *Report of the Senate Select Committee on Interstate Commerce* (Cullom Report), 49th Cong. 1st Sess., Sen. Rep. No. 46, Pts. 1–2 (1886); and *Hepburn Committee, Proceedings of the Select Committee on Railroads, New York Assembly*, 5 vols. (1879).

For more detail and contemporary flavor on internal commerce the student should consult the *Reports on Internal Commerce* issued for about a decade after 1876 by the Bureau of Statistics, Treasury Department. Especially valuable in this series are the reports for 1876, 44th Cong. 2nd Sess., House Ex. Doc. No. 46, Pt. 2 (1877); and for 1887, 50th Cong. 1st Sess., House Ex. Doc. No. 6, Pt. 2 (1888).

Of the regional histories of transportation E. C. Kirkland, *Men, Cities and Transportation. A Study in New England History,* 2 vols. (1948) remains the most full for the period to 1900. E. E. Riegel, *The Story of the Western Railroads* (1926) is highly useful. In the following state histories there is considerable attention to transportation: Frederick Merk, *Economic History of Wisconsin during the Civil War Decade* (1916); A. C. Cole, *The Era of the Civil War, 1848–1870* (1919); W. W. Folwell, *A History of Minnesota,* 5 vols. (1921–1930); and H. H. Bancroft, *History of California,* 7 vols. (1890).

For individual roads Stuart Dagget, *Railroad Reorganization* (1908) has admirable short chapters. The number of competent railroad histories is rapidly increasing. For railroads east of the Mississippi consult H. D. Dozier, *A History of the Atlantic Coast Line Railroad* (1920); J. I. Bogen, *The Anthracite Railroads* (1927); S. M. Derrick, *Centennial History of South Carolina Railroad* (1930); Edward Hungerford, *The Story of the Baltimore and Ohio Railroad, 1827–1927,* 2 vols. (1928) and his *Men and Iron; the History of the New York Central* (1938); and E. H. Mott, *Between the Ocean and the Lakes, the Story of Erie* (1901); and G. H. Burgess and M. C. Kennedy, *Centennial History of the Pennsylvania Railroad Company* (1949). In general such of these as are "official" histories are less valuable for the recent period. *High Finance in the Sixties,* ed. F. C. Hicks (1929) includes the classic account of Erie railroad activities by C. F. Adams, Jr., with much other interesting material. Adams' chapters can be found also in his *Chapters of Erie and Other Essays* (1886), written in collaboration with his brother Henry Adams. On the trans-Mississippi West R. R. Russel, *Improvement of Communication with the Pacific Coast as an Issue in American Politics, 1783–1864* (1948) supersedes most earlier work except G. L. Albright, *Official Explorations for Pacific Railroads, 1853–1855* (1921). Of the many histories of the Union Pacific the best, though somewhat opinionated, is R. W. Fogel, *The Union Pacific Railroad: A Case in Premature Enterprise* (1960). On the other roads consult Stuart Daggett, *Chapters on the History of the Southern Pacific* (1922); G. D. Bradley, *The Story of the Santa Fé* (1920); A. M. Borak, "The Chicago, Milwaukee, and St. Paul Railroad," *JEBH,* III (1930), 81–117; J. B. Hedges, *Henry Villard and the Railways of the Northwest* (1930); H. O. Brayer, *William Blackmore, Early Financing of the Denver & Rio Grande Railway and Ancillary Land Companies, 1871–1878* (1949); and R. C. Overton, *Burlington Route, a History of the Burlington Lines* (1965), a model business-history. Julius Grodinsky, *Transcontinental Railroad Strategy, 1869–1893* (1962) is highly illuminating.

Most of the usable biographies deal with the western railroad magnates, though W. J. Lane, *Commodore Vanderbilt, An Epic of the Steam Age* (1942) is a brilliant exception. *The Memoirs of Henry Villard,* 2 vols. (1904) are brief on his railroad experience. J. G. Pyle, *The Life of James J. Hill,* 2 vols. (1917) and George Kennan, *E. H. Harriman,* 2 vols. (1922) have the characteristics of "authorized" biographies, and H. J. Eckenrode and P. W. Edmunds, *E. H. Harriman: The Little Giant of Wall Street* (1933) does not make good the deficiency. E. P. Oberholtzer, *Jay Cooke, Financier of the Civil War,* 2 vols. (1907) combines truth and discretion with unusual success, while H. M. Larson, *Jay Cooke, Private Banker* (1936) adds new material. H. G. Pearson, *An American Railroad Builder, John Murray Forbes* (1911) is excellent. No one should neglect Oscar Lewis, *The Big Four: The Story of Huntington, Stanford, Hopkins, and Crocker* and of the Building of the Central Pacific (1938), vividly written. E. C. Kirkland, *Charles Francis Adams, Jr., 1835–1915. The Patrician at Bay* (1965) traces the career of a versatile man who happened to be President of the Union Pacific. H. G. Prout, *A Life of George Westinghouse* (1921) gives an explanation of this inventor's contributions to railroad building. T. C. Cochran, *Railroad Leaders, 1845–1890* (1953), and A. M. Johnson and B. E. Supple, *Boston Capitalists and Western Railroads* (1967) have a wider bearing than most citations.

On special phases of railroad history there are for finance two excellent histories, W. Z. Ripley, *Railroads: Finance and Organization* (1915) and F. A. Cleveland and F. W. Powell, *Railroad Promotion and Capitalization in the United States* (1909), which has an excellent bibliography useful for the whole of railroad history. C. S. Longstroth has written on the early pools in *Railway Co-operation in the United States,* Publications of the University of Pennsylvania, Series in Political Economy and Public Law, No. 15 (1899). Julius Grodinsky, *The Iowa Pool. A Study in Railroad Competition, 1870–84* (1950) needs considerably more background for understanding. For the course of consolidation consult the Interstate Commerce Commission, *Intercorporate Relationships of Railways in the United States as of June 30, 1906,* Special Report No. 1 (1908), some of which information is repeated in a later report by the same body, 60th Cong. 1st Sess., Sen. Doc. No. 278.

Matters of finance and consolidation raised issues of government relationships. Though somewhat outdated, L. H. Haney, *A Congressional History of Railways in the United States, 1850–1887* (1910) gives a reliable background. It is a pity that the Federal Coordinator of Transportation, *Public Aids to Transportation, Aids to Railroads and Related Subjects* (1938) and Board of Investigation and Research, *Report on Public Aids to Transportation* (1945) are not just a little more useful. There is a need for studies of aid policies in individual states, something on the order of Hartz, Heath, and Handlin for the earlier period. J. W. Million, *State Aid to Railways in Missouri* (1896) is useful; and F. B. Simkins and W. H. Woody, *South Carolina during Reconstruction* (1932) hint what could be done for the South. H. H. Pierce, *Railroads of New York, A Study of Government Aid, 1826–1875* (1953) is a masterly analysis of local aid in an important state. B. U. Ratchford, *American State Debts* (1941) gives data which can be sorted to secure railroad investments. On the land policy J. B. Sanborn, *Congressional Grants of Land in Aid of Railways* (1899) is the old standard. Those who enjoy quarreling, academic variety, should read R. S. Henry, "The Railroad Land Grant Legend in American History Texts," *MVHR,* XXXII (1945), 171–191 and the symposium in that volume, 556–576. Of the histories on how railroads used their land, P. W. Gates, *The Illinois Central Railroad and Its Colonization Work* (1934) and R. C. Overton, *Burlington West: A Colonization History of the Burlington Railroad* (1941) are outstanding. See also J. B. Hedges, "The Colonization Work of the Northern Pacific Railroad," *MVHR,* XIII, 183–203 and R. S. Hunt, *Law and Locomotion. The Impact of the Railroad on Wisconsin Law in the Nineteenth Century* (1958).

On national regulation consult Kirkland, cited above, for the New England experiment and S. J. Buck, *The Granger Movement* (1903) for the West. Lee Benson, *Merchants, Farmers, & Railroads; Railroad Regulation and New York Politics, 1850–1887* (1955) enlarges the understanding of eastern influences behind legislation. On national legislation W. Z. Ripley, *Railroads: Rates and Regulation* (1912) is a good summary, though it swallows the progressive attitudes almost without question. Gabriel Kolko, *Railroads and Regulation, 1877–1916* (1965) shows some railroad officials wanted regulation. J. M. Blum's essay in vol. 5 of E. E. Morison, ed., *The Letters of Theodore Roosevelt* (1952) is the authoritative treatment of the Hepburn Act.

A compact history of waterways in this period is still to be written. Various census monographs provide material not always of the desired sort: T. C. Purdy, "Report on Steam Navigation in the United States," *Tenth Census, 1880,* IV (1883); *Report on Transportation Business in the United States at the Eleventh Census: 1890,* Pt. 2 (1894); *Transportation by Water, 1906* (1908); and *Transportation by Water, 1916* (1920). Other government publications are *Inland Water Transportation in the United States,* Dept. of Commerce, Bur. of Foreign and Domestic Commerce, Misc. Series No. 119 (1923); *Final Report of the National Waterways Commission,* 62nd Cong. 2nd Sess., Sen Doc. No. 469 (1912); and *Report of the Committee on the Merchant Marine and Fisheries on Steamship Agreements and Affiliations in the American Foreign and Domestic Trade,* 63rd Cong. 2nd Sess., House Doc. No. 805 (1914). On canals the references cited in chapter vii are useful; on the Mississippi L. C. Hunter, *Steamboats on the Western Rivers* (1949) and M. L. Hartsough, *From Canoe to Steel Barge on the Upper Mississippi* (1934); on the Great Lakes, Knut Gjerst, *Norwegian Sailors on the Great Lakes* (1928), covering far more than its title, and the volumes in the American Lakes Series, particularly Harlan Hatcher, *Lake Erie* (1945). On the coasting trade, J. G. B. Hutchins, *The American Maritime Industries and Public Policy, 1789–1914* (1941) covers both coasts. E. C. Kirkland, cited above, deals with the New England coasting trade before 1900.

Upon the electric railroad George Hilton and J. F. Drie, *The Electric Interurban Railways in America* (1960) is divided almost equally between an encyclopedia, with small maps, of individual interurbans and a descriptive introduction on historical development. For the breakdown and decline consult *Proceedings of the Federal Electric Railway Commission,* 3 vols. (1920), with a poor index. This material is elaborately analyzed by D. F. Wilcox, *Analysis of the Electric Railway Problem Prepared for the Federal Electric Railway Commission* (1921). E. S. Mason, *The Street Railway in Massachusetts* (1932) is a model state history. On the good-roads movement the appendix in C. L. Dearing, *American Highway Policy* (1941) furnishes a good introduction. See also W. E. Fuller, "Good Roads and Rural Free Delivery of Mail," *MVHR,* XL (1955), 67–83.

chapter xii
The New Industrial State

A complete bibliography of manufacturing development in the United States after the Civil War would be one of modern American history. The effect of the Civil War upon this industrialization is a matter of dispute. Articles of varied points of view have been collected in E. D. Andreano, ed., *The Business Impact of the American Civil War* (1962). D. T. Gilchrist and

W. D. Lewis, *Economic Change in the Civil War Era* (1965) has articles bearing on the facets of economic development, but seems to bury a definite answer to the problem. The most detailed single volume for the longer period is V. S. Clark, *History of Manufactures in the United States, 1860–1914* (1928), organized on a different scheme from its predecessors. Technical changes are best followed in *A Popular History of American Invention,* ed. Waldemar Kaempffert, 2 vols. (1924). Chronological cross-sections of industrial development are best provided by *Report on the Manufactures of the United States at the Tenth Census,* II (1883); by the *Report of the Industrial Commission,* whose vols. 1, 7, 13, and 14 deal with manufacturing and business; and Bureau of the Census, *Census of Manufactures, 1914,* I, II (1918). Edwin Frickey, *Production in the United States, 1860–1914* (1947); W. H. Shaw, *Value of Commodity Output since 1869* (1947); and Solomon Fabricant, *The Output of Manufacturing Industries, 1899–1937* (1940) measure America's industrial achievement.

The material on specific industries is abundant, particularly for those which have been in the public eye. On natural resources B. H. Hibbard, *A History of Public Land Policies* (1924) provides details for government policy, and the *Report of the National Conservation Commission* (1909) adds a summary of development to prophecies of the future. On particular industries consult for the timber industry the admirable monograph by John Ise, *The United States Forest Policy* (1920). On the minerals the standard works are Harold Barger and S. H. Schurr, *The Mining Industries* (1944); A. B. Parsons, ed., *Seventy-Five Years of Progress in the Mineral Industry, 1871–1946* (1948); and more in detail for coal, H. N. Eavenson, *The First Century and a Quarter of American Coal Industry* (1942). On iron F. P. Wirth, *The Discovery and Exploitation of the Minnesota Iron Lands* (1937) and on oil John Ise, *The United States Oil Policy* (1926) are fundamental.

The history of the automobile has inspired popular and colorful authors to write books about it. J. B. Rae, *The American Automobile. A Brief History* (1965), is neither shallow nor uninteresting. His *American Automobile Manufacturing. The First Forty Years* (1959) is longer and moves with less vigor. Fact and legend have clung to Henry Ford, partly because his own published ramblings have contributed to the blurred image. Allan Nevins and F. E. Hill, *Ford,* 3 vols. (1954–1963) is based on the Ford archives. If in spots it seems too understanding, an effective antidote is K. T. Seward, *The Legend of Henry Ford* (1948).

Scholars are in the course of providing a history of the electrical industry. The best introduction to electricity is H. C. Passer, *The Electrical Manufacturers, 1865–1900; A Study in Competition, Entrepreneurship, Technical Change and Economic Growth* (1953). On further details consult the excellent R. L. Thompson, *Wiring a Continent: The History of the Telegraph Industry in the United States, 1832–1866* (1947); Matthew Josephson, *Edison* (1959); H. G. Prout, *The Life of George Westinghouse* (1921), describing the contribution of Edison's great rival; A. A. Bright, Jr., *The Electric-Lamp Industry* (1949); and W. R. Mac-Laurin, *Invention and Innovation in the Radio Industry* (1949).

Of the many volumes on the oil industry, P. H. Giddens, *The Birth of the Oil Industry* (1938) and his informing pictorial history, *Early Days of Oil* (1948) are on the pioneering period. H. F. Williamson and A. R. Daum, *The American Petroleum Industry,* 2 vols. (1959, 1963) gives the most complete industrial picture. Allan Nevins, *Study in Power: John D. Rockefeller, Industrialist and Philanthropist,* 2 vols. (1953) and R. W. and M. W. Hidy, *History of Standard Oil (New Jersey)* (1955) complement each other. V. S. Clark, cited above, treats the oil industry on the technical side. Peter Temin, *Iron and Steel in Nineteenth Century America. An Economic Inquiry* (1964) integrates technical change, which it describes admirably, with other factors.

The manuals can provide details on science, technology, and education; an introduction which puts these diverse elements into order is provided by K. A. Birr, "Science in American Industry," in D. D. Van Tassel and M. G. Hall, eds., *Science and Society in the United States* (1966). W. Paul Strassmann, *Risk and Technological Innovation. American Manufacturing Methods during the Nineteenth Century* (1959) has conclusions somewhat less shattering and excellent chapters on individual industries. Though the title of H. G. J. Aitken, *Taylorism at Watertown Arsenal. Scientific Management in Action, 1908–1915* (1960) sounds limited, the book is not. F. B. Copley, *Frederick W. Taylor,* 2 vols. (1923) is an extravagant but essential biography. F. W. Taylor, *The Principles of Scientific Management* (1911) repays perusal. See also *Scientific Managament since Taylor,* ed. E. E. Hunt (1924). W. L. Thorp, *The Integration of Industrial Operation,* Census Monographs III (1924) gives insight on the scale of industry.

For industrial regionalization the works on special industries are useful. An excellent introduction is provided by the essay of R. A. Easterlin in the third volume of Simon Kuznets and Dorothy S. Thomas, eds., *Population Redistribution and Economic Growth, United States, 1870–1950,* 3 vols. (1957–1960). Consult also F. B. Garver, F. M. Boddy, and A. J. Nixon, *The Location of Manufactures in the United States, 1899–1929* (1933) and G. E. McLaughlin, *Growth of American Manufacturing Areas: A Comparative Analysis with Special Emphasis on Trends in the Pittsburgh District* (1938). The self-consciousness of the South finds excellent expression in H. W. Odum, *Southern Regions of the United States* (1936) and R. B. Vance, *Human Geography of the South* (1932). Consult also the excellent monographs of Broadus Mitchell, *The Rise of Cotton Mills in the South* (1921) and Broadus and G. S. Mitchell, *The Industrial Revolution in the South* (1930).

chapter xiii

Big Business and Popular Response

There is a large library on the business developments and organization of the period. The recurrent interest in big business has meant that much of this literature is topical and ephemeral. To this generalization H. R. Seager and C. A. Gulick, Jr., *Trust and Corporations Problems* (1929), with its excellent summaries of individual industries, and M. W. Watkins, *Industrial Combinations and Public Policy* (1927), an admirable interpretation, are exceptions. A. D. Chandler, Jr., *Strategy and Structure. Chapters in the History of the Industrial Enterprise* (1962) thoughtfully portrays the predestination leading to a decentralized business structure in big enterprises. The titans who accomplished this and other transformations are dealt with in spirited fashion in Matthew Josephson, *The Robber Barons* (1934). C. M. Destler, "Entrepreneurial Leadership among the 'Robber Barons': A Trial Balance," *JEH*, VI, Supplement (1946), 28–49 takes an acid view, while William Miller, "American Historians and the Business Elite," *JEH*, IX (1949), 184–208 combats myths. On institutions G. H. Evans, Jr., *Business Incorporations in the United States, 1800–1943* (1948); G. H. Stigler, *Five Lectures on Economic Problems* (1950); and M. A. Adelman, "The Measurement of Industrial Combination," *The Review of Economics and Statistics*, XXXIII (1951), 269–296 are indispensable.

On competition and consolidation in individual industries some of the works cited in the previous chapter make contributions. For anthracite consult Eliot Jones, *The Anthracite Coal Combination in the United States* (1914); J. I. Bogen, *The Anthracite Railroads* (1927); M. W. Schlegel, *Ruler of the Reading: The Life of Franklin B. Gowen, 1836–1889* (1947); and C. K. Yearley, Jr., *Enterprise and Anthracite. Economics and Democracy in Schuylkill County, 1820–1875* (1961). Bituminous is well summarized in *What the Coal Commission ·Found* (1925). For the automobile industry the books of J. B. Rae, cited in a previous chapter, are the best, as is that of H. C. Passer on the electrical manufacturers; J. W. Stehman, *The Financial History of the American Telephone and Telegraph Company* (1925); and N. R. Danielian, *A. T. & T., The Story of Industrial Conquest* (1939) are good on phases.

For the oil industry as a whole, Williamson and A. R. Daum, *The American Petroleum Industry*, previously cited, justly lead the parade of two-volume works. R. E. and M. W. Hidy, *Pioneering in Big Business* (1955) covers the Standard Oil enterprises within the Grasian framework until 1911. Allan Nevins, *Study in Power: John D. Rockefeller, Industrialist and Philanthropist*, 2 vols. (1953) is the best biography. The student will find J. T. Flynn, *God's Gold* (1932) briefer but not as authoritative, and will wish to examine I. M. Tarbell, *The History of the Standard Oil Company*, 2 vols. (1904) for its historic importance. J. D. Rockefeller, *Random Reminiscences of Men and Events* (1909) condenses many events but, told in his own words, they remain interesting.

For iron and steel consult H. R. Mussey, *Combination in the Mining Industry: A Study in Concentration in Lake Superior Iron Ore Production* (1905) and Abraham Berglund, *The United States Steel Corporation* (1907). Peter Temin, cited above, emphasizes the "economies of scale" and their impact on the steel industry. J. H. Bridge, *The Inside Story of the Carnegie Steel Company* (1903), highly partisan, "exposes" Carnegie; B. J. Hendrick, *The Life of Andrew Carnegie*, 2 vols. (1932) has a pietistic tone.

The best account of investment banking is chapter 21 in Fritz Redlich, *The Molding of American Banking. Men and Ideas, Part II, 1840–1900* (1951). Informative biographical approaches are H. M. Larson, *Jay Cooke, Private Banker* (1936), treating the times as well as the man; E. P. Hoyt, Jr., *The House of Morgan* (1966) and F. L. Allen, *The Great Pierpont Morgan* (1949), a readable and benign interpretation. See also Cyrus Adler, *Jacob H. Schiff. His Life and Letters*, 2 vols. (1928); Robert McElroy, *Levi Parsons Morton* (1930); and sketches in the *Dictionary of American Biography*. *The Report of the Committee to Investigate the Concentration of Control of Money and Credit* [Pujo Committee], 62nd Cong. 3rd Sess., House Rep. No. 1593 (1913) is a historic document, unbalanced but indispensable. The work of Wall Street has yet to receive competent historical attention, but a glimpse of its activities is afforded by Henry Clews, *Fifty Years in Wall Street* (1908) and T. W. Lawson, *Frenzied Finance*

(1905), an extravagant exposé. Two valuable critiques of Wall Street are L. D. Brandeis, *Other People's Money and How the Bankers Use It* (1914) and W. Z. Ripley, *Main Street and Wall Street* (1927).

Joseph Dorfman's third volume, *The Economic Mind in American Civilization, 1865–1918* (1949) summarizes briefly the thought on monopoly and competition. The legislative background of the Sherman Anti-Trust Act, as well as the agitational background, is covered by H. B. Thorelli, *The Federal Antitrust Policy. Origination of an American Tradition* (1954). This is a curious volume. Encyclopedic in detail and erudition, it unhesitatingly accepts the assumptions of Americans who were anti-business. W. H. Taft, *The Anti-Trust Act and the Supreme Court* (1914), an early interpretation of the act's meaning, gains importance because of its author. Walter Hamilton and Irene Till, *Antitrust in Action,* Temporary National Economic Council (TNEC), Monograph 16 (1940) and Milton Handler, *A Study of the Construction and Enforcement of the Federal Antitrust Laws,* TNEC, Monograph 38 (1941) have views common when F.D.R. attacked the trusts. Handler's is the more useful book. J. W. Jenks and W. E. Clark, *The Trust Problem* (1917) was written in a time when the dust of enactment and earlier enforcement had begun to settle. The history of taxation as an economic instrument remains to be written. Sidney Ratner, *American Taxation. Its History as a Social Force in a Democracy* (1945) is opinionated and not selective enough. Elmer Ellis, "Public Opinion and the Income Tax," *MVHR,* XXVII (1940), 225–242 shows what can be done.

The Progressive movement has produced more books on political theory than on its own history. G. E. Mowry, *The Progressive Movement, 1900–1920. Recent Ideas and New Literature* (1958) puts both theory and history in fair focus. Scholars frequently write that H. F. Pringle, *Theodore Roosevelt* (1931) no longer holds water, but they can't avoid using it. Of the wealth of new publication on Roosevelt and economic policy the most objective and sophisticated are J. M. Blum, *The Republican Roosevelt* (1954), an essay; G. E. Mowry, *The Era of Theodore Roosevelt, 1900–1912* (1958); R. W. Wiebe, *Businessmen and Reform: A Study of the Progressive Movement (1961);* and Gabriel Kolko, *The Triumph of Conservatism. A Reinterpretation of American History, 1900–1916* (1963).

Woodrow Wilson's ideas on business regulation are best summarized in his *The New Freedom* (1913). William Diamond, *The Economic Thought of Woodrow Wilson* (1943) has a brief systematic treatment of the Wilsonian philosophy and L. D. Brandeis, *The Curse of Bigness* (1935), a collection of papers, summarizes the beliefs of a man who greatly influenced the President. A. S. Link is at work on an authoritative life of the President. Vol. 2 in Link's, *Wilson: The New Freedom* (1956) explores the business legislation of the first Wilson Administration.

chapter xiv
The Money Question

Many of the general works cited in chapter viii continue their treatment into the post-Civil War period. A. D. Noyes, *Forty Years of American*

Finance: A Short History of the Government and People of the United States since the Civil War, 1865–1907 (1909) and *The War Period of American Finance, 1908–1925* (1926) take a spirited overall view, though a journalistic impatience with unsound money mars the treatment. F. C. James, *The Growth of Chicago Banks,* 2 vols. (1938) has some excellent chapters on the national scene. Milton Friedman and A. J. Schwartz, *A Monetary History of the United States, 1867–1960* (1963) covers a larger area than its title suggests. It focuses upon the stock of money and conjectures in an original way about the effect upon the economy and politics of changes in monetary supply.

For the period of Civil War and Reconstruction the standard treatment on the greenbacks was for years W. C. Mitchell, *A History of the Greenbacks with Special Reference to the Economic Consequences of Their Use, 1862–65* (1903); D. C. Barrett, *The Greenbacks and Resumption of Specie Payments, 1862–1879* (1931) is an inferior duplicate and extension. One of the most trenchant refutations of the Mitchell thesis is Bray Hammond, "The North's Empty Purse," *AHR,* LXVII (1961), 1–18. Between two longer statements of the new viewpoint, Irwin Unger, *The Greenback Era. A Social and Political History of American Finance, 1865–1879* (1964) and R. P. Sharkey, *Money, Class and Party. An Economic Study of Civil War and Reconstruction* (1959) there is much agreement, but the former strikes me as the more historical and subtle. For the movement as thought or philosophy consult the third volume of Joseph Dorfman, *The Economic Mind in American Civilization* (1949) and the four essays in C. M. Destler, *American Radicalism, 1865–1901* (1946). On other phases A. M. Davis, *The Origin of the National Banking System* (1910) and H. M. Larson, *Jay Cooke, Private Banker* (1936) provide needed details.

The silver movement was in large measure a Populist movement. Allan Weinstein, "Was there a 'Crime of 1873'?" *Journal of American History,* LIV (1967), 307–326, corrects a legend. J. D. Hicks, *The Populist Revolt* (1931) is the standard work on its subject. Destler, already cited, adds details. W. H. Harvey, *Coin's Financial School,* ed., Richard Hofstadter (1963) is a classic landmark of propaganda. For the difficulties of the Cleveland Administration with bimetallism, J. A. Barnes, *John C. Carlisle, Financial Statesman* (1931) is the most illuminating and extensive account.

On the banking system after the Civil War, consult for the national banks O. M. W. Sprague, *History of Crises under the National Banking System* (1910). C. C. Barnett, *State Banks and Trust Companies since the Passage of the National-Bank Act* (1911) deals with these newcomers, and J. M. Chapman, *Concentration of Banking* (1934) just touches the issue for this period. Centralization in practice is described in M. G. Myers, *The New York Money Market, Origins and Development* (1931); and through the Treasury in David Kinley, *The Independent Treasury System of the United States and Its Relations to the Banks of the Country* (1911); and E. R. Taus, *Central Banking Functions of the United States Treasury, 1789–1941* (1943). The latter's claims for her institution in this period are sweeping.

Most literature on the origins of the Federal Reserve System reads as if the participants were trying to establish who wrote the Ten Commandments. This applies to Carter Glass, *An Adventure in Constructive Finance* (1927); H. P. Willis, *The Federal Reserve System* (1923); P. M. Warburg, *The Federal Reserve*

System: Its Origin and Growth (1930), which contains documentary material; and J. L. Laughlin, *The Federal Reserve Act: Its Origin and Problems* (1933), largely reminiscent. A. S. Link, *Wilson. The New Freedom,* II (1956) sorts out the various interests and personalities in a convincing fashion, while Gabriel Kolko, *The Triumph of Conservatism. A Reinterpretation of American History, 1900–1916* (1963) builds a case of Byzantine complexity implicating the big business community. On the structure of the Federal Reserve System, E. W. Kemmerer, *The ABC of the Federal Reserve System, Its Purpose and Function* (1947) is a useful view of a maturer system.

chapter xv

The Farmer in the Machine Age

Since no complete history of American agriculture for the period since 1860 exists comparable to those of Bakewell, Falconer, Gates, and Grey for the pre-Civil War period, a good place to begin is the excellent bibliographical guide of E. E. Edwards, "A Bibliography of the History of Agriculture in the United States," Dept. of Agr., *Misc. Pub.* No. 84 (1930). While scholars are battling Edwards' categories, the general reader may peruse studies somewhat detailed on eras and areas, but which give a readable insight into a larger picture. Of these I have found that Paul Gates, *Agriculture and the Civil War* (1965); G. C. Fite, *The Farmers' Frontier, 1865–1900* (1966); Allan G. Bogue, *From Prairie to Corn Belt. Farming in Illinois and Iowa Prairies in the Nineteenth Century* (1963); and Fred Shannon, *The Farmers' Last Frontier, Agriculture, 1860–1890* (1945) give a sense of farming as a way of life, though sometimes Shannon leaves the impression it was unlikely any farmer could survive the end of the nineteenth century. More official and formal is the mountain of information accumulated in the publications of the Department of Agriculture. Of these the annual *Yearbook* is the best.

Monographs have dealt with particular features of agriculture or with agricultural regions. Of the former group these are valuable: R. A. Clemen, *The American Livestock and Meat Industry* (1923); Meyer Jacobstein, *The Tobacco Industry in the United States* (1907); N. M. Tilley, *The Bright-Tobacco Industry, 1869–1929* (1948); M. B. Hammond, *The Cotton Culture and the Cotton Trade* (1897); L. G. Connor, "A Brief History of the Sheep Industry in the United States," *ARAHA,* 1918, I, 89–197; C. W. Towne and E. N. Wentworth, *Shepherd's Empire* (1946); Winifred Kupper, *The Golden Hoof* (1945); H. J. Webber and L. D. Batchelor, *The Citrus Industry,* I (1948); Edward Wiest, *The Butter Industry in the United States* (1916). R. B. Vance, *Human Factors in Cotton Culture* (1929) is a vivid human work. The perennial fascination of the cattle kingdom finds embodiment in E. E. Dale, *The Range Cattle Industry* (1930); E. S. Osgood, *The Day of the Cattleman* (1929); Louis Pelzer, *The Cattleman's Frontier* (1936); R. G. Cleland, *The Cattle on a Thousand Hills; Southern California, 1850–1870* (1941); and countless articles.

Among the regional studies there are J. W. Hopkins, *Economic History of the Production of Beef Cattle in Iowa* (1928); Staff of Iowa State College and

Iowa Agricultural Experiment Station, *A Century of Farming in Iowa, 1846–1946* (1946); E. Van D. Robinson, *Early Economic Conditions and the Development of Agriculture in Minnesota* (1915); M. E. Jarchow, *The Earth Brought Forth; A History of Minnesota Agriculture to 1885* (1949); J. K. Howard, *Montana, High, Wide, and Handsome* (1944); and R. B. Vance, *Human Geography of the South: A Study in Regional Resources and Human Adequacy* (1932); and the numerous works on Wisconsin which might well be imitated by other states —Joseph Schafer, *A History of Agriculture in Wisconsin* (1922); B. H. Hibbard, *The History of Agriculture in Dane County* (1904); J. G. Thompson, *The Rise and Decline of the Wheat Growing Industry in Wisconsin* (1909). State histories, particularly those cited in chapter xi for Wisconsin, Illinois, and Minnesota, have value. Unique among regional studies are the fascinatingly written, W. P. Webb, *The Great Plains* (1931); J. C. Malin, *Winter Wheat in the Golden Belt of Kansas* (1944), so good it discourages textbook writers; E. M. Dick, *Vanguards of the Frontier* (1941) and *The Sod-House Frontier, 1854–1890* (1937); and L. J. Arrington, *Great Basin Kingdom: An Economic History of the Latter-Day Saints, 1830–1900* (1958). B. I. Wiley, "Salient Changes in Southern Agriculture since the Civil War," *AH*, XIII (1939), 64–76 and J. D. Hicks, "The Western Middle West, 1900–1914," *AH*, XX (1946), 65–77 are stimulating summaries. See also R. H. Taylor, "The Sale and Application of Commercial Fertilizers in the South Atlantic States to 1900," *AH*, XXI (1947), 46–52.

The geographical and climatological bases of agriculture can be traced in J. R. Smith and N. O. Phillips, *North America* (1942). Only a few sections of the beautiful *Atlas of American Agriculture* published by the United States Department of Agriculture have so far appeared. In the *Agriculture Yearbook* of 1921 O. E. Baker has an exceedingly valuable and interesting "A Graphic Summary of American Agriculture" with maps.

On the public land system, B. H. Hibbard, *A History of the Public Land Policies* (1924) furnishes many details. More lively is R. M. Robbins, *Our Landed Heritage, The Public Domain, 1776–1936* (1942). Thomas Donaldson, *The Public Domain*, 47th Cong. 2nd Sess., House Misc. Doc. 45 (Ser. No. 2158) remains the mine from which most studies are dug. Examinations and appraisals of land administration and practice of policy are in P. W. Gates, "The Homestead Law in an Incongruous Land System," *AHR*, XLI (1936), 652–681, his "Recent Land Policies of the Federal Government" in *Supplementary Report of the Land Planning Committee to the National Resources Board*, VII, 60–85, and his *Fifty Million Acres* (1954); F. A. Shannon, "A Post Mortem on the Labor-Safety-Valve Theory," *AH*, XIX (1945), 31–38; S. A. Moss, "Land Policy and Stock Raising in the Western United States," *AH*, XVII (1943), 14–30; Thomas Le Duc, "Public Policy, Private Investment, and Land Use in American Agriculture, 1625–1875," *AH*, XXXVII (1963), 3–9; the relevant chapters for a Wisconsin county in Merle Curti, *The Making of an American Community* (1959); and H. H. Dunham, *Government Handout. A Study in the Administration of the Public Lands, 1875–1891* (1941). A. E. Sheldon, *Land Systems and Land Policies in Nebraska* (1936) should stimulate other state studies.

The special phases of land policy—reclamation, irrigation—have excited much enthusiastic and some bitter writing. Of the early work, Elwood Mead, *Irrigation Institutions* (1903) is a scholarly treatment. R. P. Teale, *The Eco-*

nomics of Land Reclamation in the United States (1927) is the best modern account. *The U.S. Reclamation Service: Its History, Activities and Organization,* Service Monographs of the United States Government, No. 2 (1919) and J. W. Haw and F. E. Schmidt, *Report on Federal Reclamation to the Secretary of the Interior* (1935) are excellent summaries. Here, too, detailed work is hitting home. See J. T. Ganoe, "The Desert Land Act in Operation," *AH,* XI (1937), 142–157, "The Desert Land Act since 1891," *AH,* XI, 266–277 and "Beginnings of Irrigation in the United States," *MVHR,* XXV (1938), 59–78. The adjustments in law and techniques compelled by dry areas are described in M. W. M. Hargreaves, *Dry Farming in the Northern Great Plains, 1900–1925* (1957).

On tenancy in general see the articles in the *Agricultural Yearbook* of 1923; the one by L. C. Gray, "The Trend in Farm Ownership," *Annals of the American Academy of Political and Social Science* (March, 1929); *Farm Tenancy, Report of the President's Committee, Prepared under the Auspices of the National Resources Committee* (1937); the excellent analysis by E. A. Goldenweiser and L. E. Truesdell, *Farm Tenancy in the United States,* Census Monographs, IV (1924); and by J. D. Black and R. H. Allen, "The Growth of Farm Tenancy in the United States," *QJE,* LI (1937), 393–425. Shu-Ching Lee, "The Theory of the Agricultural Ladder," *AH,* XXI (1947), 53–61 is stimulating. L. F. Cox, "Tenancy in the United States, 1865–1900," *AH,* XVIII (1944), 97–105 doubts the agricultural ladder existed. For the plantation and tenancy consult Vance and Hammond, cited above; and C. O. Brannen, "Relation of Land Tenure to Plantation Organization," Dept. of Agr., *Bull.* No. 1269; *Plantation Farming in the United States,* Census Bulletin (1916); B. I. Wiley, *Southern Negroes, 1861–1865* (1938); V. L. Wharton, *The Negro in Mississippi, 1865–1890* (1947); R. P. Brooks, *The Agrarian Revolution in Georgia, 1865–1912* (1914); and Oscar Zeichner, "The Transition from Slave to Free Agricultural Labor in the Southern States," *AH,* XIII (1939), 22–32.

The classics on agricultural labor are P. F. Brissenden, *The I.W.W.* (1919) and Carleton Parker, *The Casual Laborer and Other Essays* (1920). But a student will find L. F. Cox, "The American Agricultural Wage Earner, 1865–1900," *AH,* XXII (1948), 95–114 indispensable and P. S. Taylor, "The American Hired Man: His Rise and Decline," *Land Policy Review,* VI (No. 1), 3–17 interesting. "Labor Unionism in American Agriculture," Dept. of Labor, *Bull.* No. 836 (1945) is brief on this period.

The references on agricultural invention in chapter v are still useful. H. W. Quaintance, *The Influence of Farm Machinery on Production and Labor* (1904) is a standard account. Leo Rogin, *The Introduction of Farm Machinery in Its Relation to the Productivity of Labor in the Agriculture of the United States during the Nineteenth Century* (1931) deals in detail with the plow and with wheat production. On cotton consult G. C. Fite, "Recent Progress in the Mechanization of Cotton Production," *AH,* XXIV (1950), 19–28. For the period since 1900 see the suggestive article of O. E. Baker, "Changes in Production and Consumption of Our Farm Products and the Trend in Population," *Annals of the American Academy of Political and Social Science* (March, 1929).

Governmental participation in agricultural development is described by W. L. Wanlass, *The United States Department of Agriculture, A Study in*

Administration (1926) and by the shorter studies of A. C. True, a member of the Department of Agriculture in the *Yearbooks* of 1897 and 1899. The same author in collaboration with V. S. Clark wrote *The Agricultural Experiment Stations in the United States* (1900). The various bureaus of the Department have received monographic treatment in the following Service Monographs of the United States Government: Milton Conover, *The Office of Experiment Stations* (1924); F. W. Powell, *The Bureau of Animal Industry* (1927); G. A. Weber, *The Bureau of Chemistry and Soils* (1928); Jenks Cameron, *The Bureau of Dairy Industry* (1929); and G. A. Weber, *The Plant Quarantine and Control Administration* (1930). See also E. D. Ross, "The United States Department of Agriculture during the Commissionership," *AH*, XX (1946), 129–143 and C. R. Woodward, "Woodrow Wilson's Agricultural Philosophy," *AH*, XIV (1940), 129–142.

Agricultural education has been treated in A. C. True, "A History of Agricultural Extension Work in the United States, 1785–1923," Dept. of Agr., *Misc. Pub.* No. 15 (1928). E. D. Ross, *Democracy's College: The Land Grant Movement in the Formative Stage* (1942), is outstanding. It would be quite impossible to cite histories of all individual educational institutions giving agricultural instruction, but E. D. Ross, *A History of Iowa State College of Agriculture and Mechanic Arts* (1942) and Merle Curti and Vernon Carstensen, *The University of Wisconsin, A History, 1848–1925,* 2 vols. (1949) are models.

A history of agricultural science in modern times remains to be written. A. C. True, *A History of Agricultural Experimentation in the United States, 1607–1925* (1937) becomes more and more of a catalogue as it reaches modern times, and T. S. Harding, *Two Blades of Grass: A History of Scientific Development in the U.S. Department of Agriculture* (1947) succeeds in being popular rather than in solving the genuine problems of dealing with scientific agriculture. At the other extreme is the staccato of Paul De Kruif, *Hunger Fighters* (1928). A series of articles, particularly in *Agricultural History*, points a middle way, though not always competently realized: B. T. Galloway, "Plant Pathology; A Review of the Development of the Science in the United States," *AH*, II (1928), 49–60; A. G. McCall, "The Development of Soil Science," *AH*, V (1931), 43–56; K. A. Ryerson, "History and Significance of the Foreign Plant Introduction Work of the United States Department of Agriculture," *AH*, VII (1933), 110–281; C. R. Ball, "The History of American Wheat Improvement," *AH*, IV (1930), 48–71; and G. F. Johnson, "The Early History of Copper Fungicides," *AH*, IX (1935), 67–79. For the battle with insect pests consult L. O. Howard, *A History of Applied Entomology,* Smithsonian Miscellaneous Collections, LXXXIV (1930) and his highly personalized *Fighting the Insects* (1933). For plant introduction see D. G. Fairchild, *The World Was My Garden; Travels of a Plant Explorer* (1938).

The grievances of the farmer against the distributive and credit systems are described in the works on farm movements. S. J. Buck, *The Granger Movement* (1913) deserves its position as the standard treatise on the subject. J. D. Hicks, *The Populist Revolt* (1931) continues the narrative to a later date. Theodore Saloutos and J. D. Hicks, *Agricultural Discontent in the Middle West, 1900–1939* (1951) avoids propaganda and sentimentalism. For special articles consult R. H. Bahmer, "The American Society of Equity," *AH*, XIV

(1940), 33–63 and W. P. Tucker, "Populism Up-to-Date: The Story of the Farmers' Union," *AH*, XXI (1947), 198–208. Of the many books on the vexed subject of the Non-Partisan League, R. L. Morlan, *Political Prairie Fire* (1955) is the best work.

On agricultural marketing there is an extensive bibliography, most of it describing practices current at the time of writing. Of such works, "American Produce Exchange Markets," *Annals of the American Academy of Political and Social Science*, XXXVIII, No. 2 (1911) and vol. 6 of the *Report of the Industrial Commission* on the "Distribution of Farm Products" (1901), and H. C. Emery, *Speculation on the Stock and Produce Exchanges of the United States* (1896) are valuable. For an important modern feature consult the too-brief A. H. Putnam, "Futures Trading with Particular Reference to Agricultural Commodities," *AH*, VII (1933), 68–80. For the wheat trade there are H. M. Larson, *The Wheat Market and the Farmer in Minnesota, 1858–1900* (1926), an admirable pioneer work; C. H. Taylor, *History of the Board of Trade of the City of Chicago*, 3 vols. (1917); the exhaustive *Report of the Federal Trade Commission on the Grain Trade*, 7 vols. (1920–1926), of which vols. 1–3 are particularly valuable; Federal Trade Commission, *Methods and Operations of Grain Exporters*, 2 vols. (1922–1923); and G. A. Lee, "The Historical Significance of the Chicago Grain Elevator System," *AH*, XI (1937), 16–32. For cotton the best approach is the *Report of the Commissioner of Corporations on Cotton Exchanges*, 60th Cong. 1st Sess., House Doc. 912, 2 Pts. (1908). W. H. Hubbard, *Cotton and the Cotton Market* (1927) is a clear description. Morton Rothstein, "The International Market for Agricultural Commodities," in D. T. Gilchrist and W. D. Lewis, eds., *Economic Change in the Civil War Era* (1965), pp. 62–72 is indispensable.

The history of cooperative movements can be traced in Buck, Fossum, and Larson, all cited above. An excellent capsule introduction is R. H. Elsworth and Grace Wanstall, "Farmers' Marketing and Purchasing Cooperatives, 1863–1939," Farm Credit Admin., Cooperative Research and Service Division, *Misc. Rep.* No. 40 (1941). Consult also Albert Shaw, *Cooperation in the Northwest* (1888); A. G. Warner, *Three Phases of Coöperation in the West* (1887); A. H. Hirsch, "Efforts of the Grange in the Middle West to Control the Price of Farm Machinery, 1870–1880," *MVHR*, XV (1929), 473–496; O. N. Refsell, "The Farmers' Elevator Movement," *JPE*, XXII (1914), 872–895, 969–991; W. Gee and E. A. Terry, *The Cotton Coöperatives in the Southeast* (1933); and E. G. Nourse, *Fifty Years of Farmers' Elevators in Iowa*, Bulletin of the Agricultural Experiment Station, Iowa State College of Agriculture and Mechanics Arts, No. 211 (1923). O. M. Kile, *The Farm Bureau Movement* (1921) and R. H. Elsworth, "Agricultural Coöperative Associations: Marketing and Purchasing, 1925," Dept. of Agr., *Technical Bull.* No. 40 give later developments. For government assistance to the marketing process see J. C. Malin, "The Background of the First Bills to Establish a Bureau of Markets, 1911–1912," *AH*, VI (1932), 107–129. On farm credit the best summaries are in E. S. Sparks, *History and Theory of Agricultural Credit in the United States* (1932) and J. B. Norman, *Farm Credits in the United States and Canada* (1924). Allan G. Bogue, *Money at Interest. The Farm Mortgage on the Middle Border* (1955) realistically takes some of the fire out of the shibboleth.

The measurement of agricultural production and of many other features of farming is accomplished in Harold Barger and Hans H. Landsberg, *American Agriculture, 1899–1939* (1942); in Robert Gallman, "Commodity Output, 1839–1879," and M. W. Towne and W. D. Rasmussen, "Farm Gross Product and Gross Investment in the Nineteenth Century," both in National Bureau of Economic Research, *Trends in the American Economy in the Nineteenth Century, Studies in Income and Wealth,* XXIV (1960); and William N. Parker and J. L. V. Klein, "Productivity Growth in Grain Production in the United States, 1840–1860 and 1900–1910," in National Bureau of Economic Research, *Studies in Income and Wealth,* XXX (1966).

chapter xvi

The Wage Earner Under Competition and Monopoly

The literature dealing with labor and its conditions is probably more controversial than that in any other field of modern economic history, with the possible exception of the relations between government and industry. In both cases the reason is the same. Such writing tends to be either an attack upon or a defense of the capitalist system. Curiously the field of labor history, as far as writing and research are concerned, has been for years in the doldrums.

Unfortunately, the ten volumes of the monumental *A Documentary History of American Industrial Society* (1910–1911) stop at 1880. For this deficiency there is partial compensation in the increasing amount of government publications. In 1890 the publication of the *Bulletin of the Bureau of Labor* commenced. The early numbers of this bulletin were monographs on various features of labor history. Later it became the *Bulletin of the United States Bureau of Labor Statistics,* cited in this chapter simply as *Bulletin.* In accordance with its change of title more attention was given to statistical data, but other subjects, such as labor legislation and court decisions, are included. The *Bulletin* is a mine of information on wages, hours, prices, union standards, and industrial accidents. The *Monthly Labor Review,* a government publication, contains shorter articles than the *Bulletin.* In addition there are the *Reports of the Commissioner of Labor* until 1913, which generally are of a monographic nature. The bureaus in the Department of Labor, such as that for women and children, have important publications.

There have been surveys of the whole labor movement at intervals. The *Report of the Industrial Commission* (1901) devotes vols. 7 and 14 to "Labor, Manufactures and General Business"; vol. 12 to "Capital and Labor Employed in the Mining Industry"; and vol. 17 to "Labor Organizations." Later comes the *Report of the Commission on Industrial Relations,* 64th Cong. 1st Sess., Sen. Doc. No. 415, 11 vols. (1916). The valuable material in this survey is practically inaccessible because of the poor index. In 1916 the Rand School undertook the publication of *The American Labor Year Book.* Unfortunately, this useful work has not appeared every year. Finally, the student is fortunate in the two-volume continuations of Commons's earlier work, *History of Labour in the United States, 1896–1932* (1935). These new volumes no longer confine themselves to the labor-union movement. D. D. Lescohier writes on working conditions and Elizabeth Brandeis on labor legislation in the third volume, while Selig Perlman and Philip Taft devote the fourth volume to labor movements. Of the shorter treatments Jürgen Kuczynski, *A Short History of Labour Conditions under Industrial Capitalism,* II (1943) and P. S. Foner, *History of the Labor Movement in the United States* (1947) are useful. On labor personnel Stanley Lebergott, *Manpower in Economic Growth, the American Record since 1800* (1964) is a persuasive demonstration of the "new economic history" while J. D. Durand, *The Labor Force in the United States, 1890–1960* (1948) focuses more on the later period.

The *Report of the Immigration Commission* (1911) contains the most material on this subject. This report in 41 volumes is abstracted in two volumes, 61st Cong. 3rd Sess., Sen. Doc. No. 747 (1911). Sixteen of the *Report*'s volumes deal with immigrants in industry. Unfortunately, the usefulness of the work is jeopardized by errors of interpretation which have been pointed out with considerable intensity by I. A. Hourwich, *Immigration and Labor* (1912). There are works on particular races, of which R. F. Foerster, *The Italian Emigration of Our Times* (1919) is important for its subject and its value. Harry Jerome, *Migration and Business Cycles* (1926) is a statistical treatment with graphs of an important phenomenon. For migrations, international and domestic, the best work is Simon Kuznets and D. S. Thomas, *Population Redistribution and Economic Growth. United States, 1870–1950,* 3 vols. (1957–1964). C. H. Wesley, *Negro Labor in the United States, 1850–1925* (1927) and C. G. Woodson, *A Century of Negro Migration* (1918) treat this important racial migration. Other data have been published by the Department of Labor.

In view of the attention which it has aroused, the labor of women and children has received little excellent historical treatment. Most of the historical works in the nineteen volumes of the *Report on the Conditions of Women and Child Wage Earners in the United States,* 61st Cong. 2nd Sess., Sen. Rep. No. 645 (1910–1913) are best on the earlier period. In this series H. L. Sumner, *History of Women in Industry in the United States* is an exception. The whole *Report* is conveniently summarized in *Bulletin,* No. 175 (1916). Exceedingly interesting figures and interpretations are given in J. A. Hill, *Women in Gainful Occupations,* Census Monographs, IX (1929).

D. D. Lescohier's treatment in the third volume of the *History of Labour in the United States, 1896–1932* (1935) and Kuczynski, cited above, have done a great deal to dissipate the obscurity hiding the history of labor conditions. Perhaps because it is the greatest puzzle, the course of wages has received extended treatment. "History of Wages in the United States from Colonial Times to 1928," *Bulletin,* No. 604 provides raw material without interpretation or standards of judgment. It is generally admitted that the data in the earlier "Aldrich Report," *Wholesale Prices, Wages, and Transportation,* 52nd Cong. 2nd Sess., Sen. Rep. No. 1394, 4 vols. (1893) are not typical enough for generalization. For the general trend the best approaches are A. H. Hansen, "Factors Affecting the Trend of Real Wages," *AER,* XV (1925), 27–42 and P. H. Douglas, *Real Wages in the United States, 1890–1926* (1930), a masterpiece of statistical erudition and exposition. Edith Abbott, "The Wages of Unskilled

Labor in the United States, 1850–1900," *JPE*, XIII (1905), 321–367; Whitney Coombs, *The Wages of Unskilled Labor in Manufacturing Industries in the United States, 1890–1924* (1926); and P. F. Brissenden, *Earnings of Factory Workers, 1899 to 1927, Census Monographs*, X (1929) deal with more limited areas.

For the effects of industrial changes upon industrial education consult P. H. Douglas, *American Apprenticeship and Industrial Education* (1921); and W. E. Weyl and A. M. Sakolski, "Conditions of Entrance to the Principal Trades," *Bulletin*, No. 67, 681–780. The subject of industrial hygiene and fatigue has not yet been reduced to a scientific basis. Josephine Goldmark, *Fatigue and Efficiency* (1912) was a pioneer work. P. S. Florence, *Economics of Fatigue and Unrest* (1924) is an interesting work. In 1908 F. L. Hoffman summarized "Industrial Accidents," *Bulletin*, No. 78, 417–465, and frequent issues of the *Bulletin* have since dealt with that subject. M. C. Cahill, *Shorter Hours, A Study of the Movement since the Civil War* (1932) is less a scientific analysis of hours worked than of the agitation and methods by which reduction was accomplished.

Mention has already been made of J. R. Commons, *et al., History of Labour in the United States*, 2 vols. (1918) and D. D. Lescohier, *et al., History of Labour in the United States, 1896–1932* (1935) as good summaries of the labor movement. Lloyd Ulman, *The Rise of the National Trade Union. The. Development and Significance of Its Structure, Governing Institutions, and Economic Policies* (1955) and Philip Taft, *The A. F. of L. in the Time of Gompers* (1957) are splendid exceptions to the dearth of recent writing in labor history. Jonathan Grossman, *William Sylvis, Pioneer of American Labor: A Study of the Labor Movement during the Civil War* (1945); N. J. Ware, *The Labor Movement in the United States, 1860–1895* (1929), a superior treatment of the Knights of Labor; and L. L. Lorwin, *The American Federation of Labor: History, Policies, and Prospects* (1933) are all important. Since the A. F. of L. was so much the reflection of Samuel Gompers, L. S. Reed, *The Labor Philosophy of Samuel Gompers* (1930) and R. H. Harvey, *Samuel Gompers, Champion of the Toiling Masses* (1935), both excellent books, have bearing at this point. Herbert Harris, *American Labor* (1939) is excellent for its narrative of significant unions. On "left-wing" unionism there is the brief account by Louis Levine, "The Development of Syndicalism in America," *Political Science Quarterly*, XXVIII (1913), 451–479 and P. F. Brissenden's longer able account, *The I.W.W.: A Study of American Syndicalism* (1919). Of biographies of labor leaders, J. R. Buchanan, *The Story of a Labor Agitator* (1903) gives a drama of the days of the Knights of Labor; T. V. Powderly, *Thirty Years of Labor, 1859–1889* (1889) and, even more revealing, his *The Path I Trod* (1940) are excellent. Samuel Gompers, *Seventy Years of Life and Labor*, 2 vols. (1925) is interesting on the personal side but tells little new about the labor movement. Leo Wolman, *The Growth of American Trade Unions, 1880–1923* (1924) contains exceedingly valuable tables at the end of the text. The industrial conflict, made more effective by organization, has its dark implications explored in the scholarly Samuel Yellen, *American Labor Struggles* (1936). Of the specific instances described by R. V. Bruce, *1877: Year of Violence* (1959); Wayne Broehl, *The Molly Maguires* (1964); Henry David, *The History of the Haymarket*

Affair. A Study in the American Social Revolutionary and Labor Movements (1936); and Almont Lindsey, *The Pullman Strike* (1942), Bruce is too popular, while the latter three are scholarly.

The histories of separate industries cited in chapter xii often deal fully with their peculiar labor problems. Books from the purely labor side are less frequent. On textiles, in addition to Cole and Copeland, cited above, the *Report on the Strike of Textile Workers in Lawrence, Mass., in 1912* by the Bureau of Labor, 62nd Cong. 2nd Sess., Sen. Doc. No. 870 (1912) shows conditions of life and labor in a textile center of the North, while H. L. Herring, *Welfare Work in Mill Villages: The Story of Extra-Mill Activities in North Carolina* (1929) treats a controversial subject interestingly and judiciously. R. W. Dunn and Jack Hardy, *Labor and Textiles* (1931) is a leftwing approach. For the shoe industry D. D. Lescohier, *The Knights of St. Crispen, 1867–1874* (1910) deals excellently with the early period; A. E. Galster, *The Labor Movement in the Shoe Industry* (1924) places its emphasis on the later period.

Coal has received a great deal of attention. Andrew Roy, *A History of the Coal Miners of the United States* (1907) deals with episodes and personalities of the early period; and J. W. Coleman, *The Molly Maguire Riots, Industrial Conflict in the Pennsylvania Coal Region* (1930) and M. W. Schlegel, *Ruler of the Reading: The Life of Franklin B. Gowen* (1947) treat judiciously this *cause célèbre*. A. E. Suffern, *The Coal Miner's Struggle for Industrial Status* (1926) traces the growth of instruments for industrial government. The strike of 1902 is described by "Report of the Anthracite Coal Commission," *Bulletin*, No. 46 (1903) and by Elsie Gluck, *John Mitchell, Miner* (1929). Of the *Report of the United States Coal Commission*, 5 vols. (1925) the first three volumes give an exceedingly valuable picture of the whole of the miners' life. This work is summarized in *What the Coal Commission Found* (1925) by the members of the staff of the Commission. Carter Goodrich, *The Miner's Freedom* (1925) is more interpretive. Anna Rochester, *Labor and Coal* (1931) treats the industry from the radical viewpoint. On nonunion fields Winthrop Lane, *Civil War in West Virginia* (1921) pictures the drama, and A. F. Hinrichs, *The United Mine Workers of America and the Non-Union Coal Fields* (1923) applies cold analysis.

Conditions in the iron and steel industry have always aroused attention. Grossman, cited above, deals with a pioneer. H. E. Hoagland, "The Rise of the Iron Moulders' International Union," *AER*, III (1913), 296–313 is particularly interesting on early cooperative enterprises; C. D. Wright, "The Amalgamated Association of Iron and Steel Workers," *QJE*, VII (1893), 400–432; and J. A. Fitch, *The Steel Workers* (1910) treat the early movement. In 1911 the Bureau of Labor received a mandate to investigate the conditions in the industry. Its *Report on Conditions of Employment in the Iron and Steel Industry in the United States*, 62nd Cong. 1st Sess., Sen. Doc. No. 110, 4 vols. (1913) is authoritative. The strike of 1892 led to the Congressional reports—52nd Cong. 2nd Sess., Sen. Rep. No. 1280 and 52nd Cong. 2nd Sess., House Rep. No. 2447 —both of which are illuminating on the use of detectives. C. A. Gulick, Jr., *Labor Policy of the United States Steel Corporation* (1924) treats the situation with excellent detachment.

On other industries, Louis Levine, *The Women's Garment Workers* (1924) is a model of union history; R. W. Dunn, *Labor and Automobiles* (1929); Grace Hutchins, *Labor and Silk* (1929); and Charlotte Todes, *Labor and Lumber* (1931) are valuable in spite of a pronounced "class-conscious" point of view. Samples of employers' associations are described sympathetically in C. E. Bonnett, *History of Employers' Associations in the United States* (1956). A. G. Taylor, *Labor Policies of the National Association of Manufacturers* (1928) is a valuable scholarly treatment.

Labor and the law is a province by itself. The movement for labor legislation in this country, its course and accomplishment, still awaits treatment. The legislation in various states has been treated monographically: A. M. Edwards, *The Labor Legislation of Connecticut* (1907); F. R. Fairchild, *The Factory Legislation of the State of New York* (1905); A. S. Field, *The Child Labor Policy of New Jersey* (1909); J. L. Barnard, *Factory Legislation in Pennsylvania* (1907); J. K. Towles, *Factory Legislation of Rhode Island* (1908); C. E. Persons et al., *Labor Laws and Their Enforcement with Special Reference to Massachusetts* (1911). E. F. Baker, *Protective Labor Legislation with Special Reference to Women in the State of New York* (1925); C. M. Beyer, "History of Labor Legislation for Women in Three States," Dept. of Labor, Women's Bureau, *Bull.* No. 66 (1920); and E. R. Beckner, *A History of Labor Legislation in Illinois* (1929) are all excellent for their portrayal of the causes and forces working in behalf of such legislation.

On the law governing labor activities, E. E. Witte, *The Government in Labor Disputes* (1932) and C. O. Gregory, *Labor and the Law* (1946) are the best summaries. A. T. Mason, *Organized Labor and the Law* (1925) and Edward Berman, *Labor and the Sherman Act* (1930) are also valuable. The United States Strike Commission, *Report on the Chicago Strike of June-July, 1894* (1895) gives the background for a great injunction case. But everyone should read the lucid volume by Felix Frankfurter and Nathan Greene, *The Labor Injunction* (1930). G. G. Groat, *Attitude of American Courts on Labor Cases* (1911) is admirable. It should be supplemented by *The Dissenting Opinions of Mr. Justice Holmes* (1929) and *The Social and Economic views of Mr. Justice Brandeis* (1930), both edited by Alfred Lief. Also of interest on the same subjects are Edward Berman, *Labor Disputes and the President of the United States* (1924) and M. R. Carroll, *Labor and Politics: The Attitude of the American Federation of Labor toward Legislation and Politics* (1923). A. R. Ellingwood and Whitney Coombs, *The Government and Labor* (1926) is a collection of statutes and cases. The student can keep abreast of this field through the *Bulletin* and the *American Labor Legislation Review*, which began publication in 1911.

chapter xvii

An International Economic Order

Naturally, this bibliography is not even partially complete on the subjects of foreign trade and investment, both aspects of world history. Adequate treatments of the role of the United States in world affairs generally did not appear until the 1920's. The Council on Foreign Relations undertook in 1928 the publication, unfortunately now abandoned, of an excellent yearly volume, *Survey of American Foreign Relations*, really a collection of monographs on specialized subjects. The Foreign Policy Association has issued varied publications which manage to treat passing events with impartiality and to apply past history to an understanding of the present. In 1922 the quarterly *Foreign Affairs* began the publication of articles important for their points of view if not for their disclosures.

The government documents dealing with foreign commerce are too numerous to be enumerated. The Departments of Agriculture, State, Commerce and Labor, and of Commerce have all had bureaus concerned with foreign trade. The Department of State issued an annual *Commercial Relations* from 1855 to 1902; the State Department began in 1880 the publication of *Monthly Consular and Trade Reports* and in 1898 *Advance Sheets of Consular Reports*. The Treasury published a *Monthly Summary of Commerce and Finance* from 1866 to 1903. When the Department of Commerce and Labor was established it took over the *Commercial Relations, Monthly Consular and Trade Reports, Daily Consular and Trade Reports*, the successor to the *Advance Sheets of Consular Reports*, and the *Monthly Summary of Commerce and Finance*. The first was discontinued in 1912 and the second in 1910. The Department of Commerce also issues publications dealing with features of foreign trade under the titles of *Special Agents Series, Miscellaneous Series, Special Consular Reports, Trade Information Bulletin*, and *Trade Promotion Series*. It also issues the annual *Foreign Commerce and Navigation of the United States*, which was published until 1903 by the Treasury. An understanding of these publications and of the work of the government in behalf of foreign commerce is best derived from L. F. Schmeckebier and G. A. Weber, *The Bureau of Foreign and Domestic Commerce: Its History, Activities, and Organization* (1924).

There are few secondary works on all phases of America's overseas outthrusts. In the matter of shipping J. G. B. Hutchins, *The American Maritime Industries and Public Policy, 1789–1914* (1941) is indispensable on both subject-matter headings. Robert Lipsey, *Price and Quantity Trends in the Foreign Trade of the United States* (1963) has both the statistics and the explanations for them. Most historical work on foreign investments has seemingly not outgrown Cleona Lewis, *America's Stake in International Investments* (1938).

When matters of tariffs are involved the best book on the United States remains F. W. Taussig, *The Tariff History of the United States* (1914), which gives details and effects of legislation and is itself an unwitting period-piece of inference and argument. On the details of reciprocity the United States Tariff Commission, *Reciprocity and Commercial Treaties* (1919) is a genuinely brilliant performance. On American colonialism the Philippines have occasioned the most writing. The best approaches to the islands' economic relations with the United States are J. E. Reyes, *Legislative History of America's Economic Policy toward the Philippines* (1923) and W. C. Forbes, *The Philippine Islands*, 2 vols. (1928), a voluminous and judicious narrative by an admirer of the American achievement. The contrasting appraisal of their economic advantages is illustrated by R. S. Tucker, "A Balance Sheet of the Philippines," *Harvard Business Review*, VIII, 10–23, and in the report of C. A. Thompson, *Condi-*

tions in the Philippine Islands, 69th Cong. 2nd Sess., Sen. Doc. No. 180 (1926). "Philippine Independence" *F.P.A. Information Service,* VI, Nos. 3–4, contains an excellent summary of economic development.

Export of agricultural products has received treatment in William Trimble, "Historical Aspects of the Surplus Food Production of the United States, 1862–1902," *ARAHA* (1918), I, 222–239, and in E. G. Nourse, *American Agriculture and the European Market* (1924), the best summary of this commerce. Douglass C. North, *Growth and Welfare in the American Past* (1966) has a stimulating chapter of hypotheses about American agriculture and foreign trade. As for the results of industrialism, in addition to Lipsey, cited above, consult Harold Williamson and A. R. Daum, *The American Petroleum Industry,* I (1959), the best of the books on this theme; and Pt. 1 of the *Report of the Federal Trade Commission on the Meat Packing Industry* (1918–1920); and for tobacco Pt. 1 of *Report of the Commissioner of Corporations on the Tobacco Industry* (1909) and J. W. Jenkins, *James B. Duke, Master Builder* (1927).

The concerns of this chapter can be covered from the point of view of geographical or national areas as well as that of commodities. Unhappily, the number and caliber of the works describing American economic relations with the nations and regions of the world is not proportioned to their relative commercial importance. As a sample of the better volumes, consult S. A. Southard, *American Industry in Europe* (1931) for the complete picture of a novel movement; for Canada H. L. Keeneyside, *Canada and the United States* (1952) is an excellent but summary approach.

American commercial relations with the Orient are excellently handled in the article "The New Pacific," *Survey of American Foreign Relations for 1930,* 1–342; and in A. W. Griswold, *The Far Eastern Policy of the United States* (1938). Tyler Dennett, *Americans in Eastern Asia* (1922) deals with the period before the twentieth century. The campaign to increase investments in China and in Manchuria is described sympathetically by Herbert Croly, *Willard Straight* (1924) and with a more pro-Japanese point of view in P. H. Clyde, *International Rivalries in Manchuria, 1689–1922* (1928). F. V. Field, *American Participation in the China Consortiums* (1931) is a lucid account of an extremely complicated subject.

For Latin American economic relations the best brief treatment is J. F. Rippy, *Latin America and the Industrial Age* (1944); and for the strategic Caribbean area the best introductions are the excellent section on "The Caribbean," *Survey of American Foreign Relations for 1929,* 1–329, and D. G. Munro, *The United States and the Caribbean Area* (1934). For details on a specific case-history and for controversy see F. U. Adams, *Conquest of the Tropics* (1913), a syrupy panegyric, for which C. D. Kepner and J. H. Soothill, *The Banana Empire, A Case Study of Economic Imperialism* (1935) and C. D. Kepner, *Social Aspects of the Banana Industry* (1936) are acrid antidotes. The two best works on the United States and Mexico are Ernest Gruening, *Mexico and Its Heritage* (1928) and J. F. Rippy, *The United States and Mexico* (1926). See also the convenient narrative on "Mexico and the United States," *Survey of American Foreign Relations for 1931,* 1–315. F. W. Powell, *The Railroads of Mexico* (1921) and Edgar Turlington, *Mexico and Her Foreign Creditors* (1930) are both useful. Harold Williamson *et al., The American Petroleum*

Industry, II (1963) and G. S. Gibbs and E. H. Knowlton, *History of Standard Oil Company (New Jersey), The Resurgent Years, 1911–1925* (1956) dispel sensationalism about petroleum imperialism in Mexico.

The comparative availability of valid statistics and the interest in the use of them for present policy has led economic historians to measure in a lavish way the economic growth of the United States since the Civil War. Though they all do not use the same tests, there is considerable duplication in their efforts; refinements of measurement are always possible. Of the volumes available, I have found most useful Arthur F. Burns, *Production Trends in the United States since 1870* (1934); Simon Kuznets, *National Product since 1869* (1946) and *National Income, A Summary of Findings* (1946); J. W. Kendrick, *Productivity Trends in the United States* (1961), which has an interesting analysis of the ideology and operational factors involved; and two volumes by the National Bureau of Economic Research in their series on *Studies in Income and Wealth*, XXIV (1960), XXX (1966).

chapter xviii
War and Normalcy

The economic history of World War I has stimulated less research and writing than World War II. The best introduction to World War I is J. M. Clark, *The Costs of the World War to the American People* (1931). This is an ingenious volume and one free from dogma. A projected series dealing in detail with aspects of the war has produced works of very uneven worth. W. D. Hines, *War History of American Railroads* (1928) is marred by a defensively apologetic tone; G. B. Clarkson, *Industrial America in the World War: The Strategy behind the Line, 1917–1918* (1923) may seem overenthusiastic if it were not for the fact that enthusiasm was a feature of the time. B. H. Hibbard, *Effects of the Great War upon Agriculture in the United States and Great Britain* (1919) has the merit of contemporaneity and that is all. E. M. Hurley, *The Bridge to France* (1927) is administrative name-dropping.

The best approach to the Food Administration is in Herbert Hoover, *The Memoirs of Herbert Hoover. Years of Adventure, 1874–1920* (1951). W. C. Mullendorf, *History of the United States Food Administration, 1917–1919* (1941) is pedestrian and complete. The financial history of these years is covered fairly in Paul Studenski and H. E. Krooss, *Financial History of the United States* (1963). W. G. McAdoo, *Crowded Years. The Reminiscences of William G. McAdoo* (1931) discovers very few reasons for second thoughts. Stanley Lebergott, *Manpower in Economic Growth. The American Record since 1800* (1964) deals precisely with the conditions of labor, while Philip Taft, *The A. F. of L. in the Time of Gompers* (1937) is the best approach to labor policy.

On the postwar years until the great depression of 1929 the report by the Committee on Recent Economic Changes of the President's Conference on Unemployment, *Recent Economic Changes in the United States*, 2 vols. (1929) collects a series of essays by specialists. On agriculture G. C. Fite, *George N. Peck and the Fight for Farm Parity* (1954) and Theodore Saloutos and J. D.

Hicks, *Agricultural Discontent in the Middle West, 1900–1939* (1951) give a judicious picture. For industrial policy, Louis Galambos, *Competition & Co-operation: The Emergence of a National Trade Association* (1966) makes a specific instance serve a larger purpose. For labor consult the volumes by Taft and Lebergott cited above. On the great steel strike of 1919, David Brody, *Labor in Crisis: The Steel Strike of 1919* (1965) has the advantage of perspective over contemporary investigations. On the policies of the Federal Reserve the best introduction is L. V. Chandler, *Benjamin Strong, Central Banker* (1955). E. R. Wicker, *Federal Reserve Monetary Policy, 1917–1933* (1966) corrects or accepts Chandler and provides additional information. See also Milton Friedman and A. J. Schwartz, *A Monetary History of the United States, 1867–1960* (1963). There are useful summaries of the foreign debt and trade situation in Council of Foreign Relations, *Survey of American Foreign Relations, 1928* (1928), 149–227, 333–487, and in the 1930 *Survey* (1930), 429–473.

chapter xix
The New Deal

It is probably more rewarding to learn about the New Deal from the words of its participants than to learn about it from its opponents, contemporary analysts, and, with a few exceptions, from secondary works by other outsiders. Luckily, the New Dealers were an articulate and scribbling lot. If they didn't tell all the first time, they hazarded a second go. The classic and essential source is of course *The Public Papers and Addresses of Franklin Delano Roosevelt* (1938–1950). The collection is in thirteen volumes; the arrangements of documents and the provision of introductions and notes was usually done by "my old friend," Samuel I. Rosenman. Each volume has an index; and the notes, which are summaries, frequently give references to statutes and court decisions. All this amplitude and convenience cannot conceal the high artfulness of the total presentation.

Frances Perkins, *The Roosevelt I Knew* (1946), while admitting "all doubts have been resolved in his favor," kept her head, retained the capacity to make distinctions, and wrote an extraordinarily perceptive volume. In comparison Francis Biddle, *In Brief Authority* (1962) was only for a moment near the center of power, but the detached observation of a Philadelphia aristocrat is worth a volume of adulation. In my estimation Raymond Moley's, *The First New Deal* (1968) is more informative and judicious than his earlier *After Seven Years* (1939). R. G. Tugwell's second try, a series of essays in *The Western Political Quarterly*, I (1948), 131–153, 373–385; II (1949), 545–580; III (1950), 390–427; IV (1951), 295–312, 469–486; V (1952), 84–93, 274–289, 483–503; VI (1953), 320–341, in spite of a somewhat pompous effort to relate the author to the whole historic course of socioeconomic thought, is valuable for its inadvertent admissions and obiter dicta. Donald R. Richberg, *My Hero: The Indiscreet Memoirs of an Uneventful but Unheroic Life* (1954) had the saving and agreeable advantage of a sense of irony about himself and others. J. M. Blum, *From the Morgenthau Diaries, Years of Crisis, 1926–1938* (1959) is really a skillfully arranged documentary.

F. B. Freidel, *The New Deal in Historical Perspective* (1959) is a highly useful annotated bibliography. F. B. Freidel, *Franklin D. Rosevelt,* 3 vols. (1952–1956) gets his man to the White House. Of R. G. Tugwell's, *The Democratic Roosevelt. A Biography of Franklin D. Roosevelt* (1957) one is tempted in partial paraphrase to say "Franklin, with all thy faults we love thee still." Bernard Bellush, *Franklin D. Roosevelt as Governor of New York* (1955) is an enthusiastic picture of Roosevelt's accomplishment. F. L. Allen, *The Big Change: America Transforms Itself, 1900–1950* (1952); W. L. Leuchtenberg, *Franklin D. Roosevelt and the New Deal, 1932–1940* (1963); and A. M. Schlesinger, Jr., *The Age of Roosevelt,* 3 vols. (1959–1960) are all quite different books but all have been much acclaimed. From the point of view of economic development, the best detailed account is Broadus Mitchell, *Depression Decade from New Era through New Deal, 1929–1941* (1947). Since the author's philosophy is that of a conventional liberal socialist, the volume expresses a certain impatience with the Roosevelt Administration; it is not, however, doctrinaire. H. V. Hudson, *Slump and Recovery, 1929–1937. A Survey of World Economic Affairs* (1938) has the advantage of a transatlantic disengagement. It is particularly good on the role of the inflationists.

The concept of industrial self-government and the NRA is a tangle, so that an approach via individual industrial codes is most revealing. The best key is E. M. Hawley, *The New Deal and the Problem of Monopoly: A Study in Economic Ambivalence* (1966), an admirable account of the NRA and the struggle to find a substitute policy. Highly useful in this connection are Louis Galambos, *Competition & Cooperation. The Emergence of a National Trade Association* (1966) for the cotton industry, and Sidney Fine, *The Automobile under the Blue Eagle. Labor, Management and the Automobile Manufacturing Code* (1963). The latter has a detached account of labor; more colorful on this score but not more authoritative are Allan. Nevins and Frank E. Hill, *Ford: Decline and Rebirth, 1933–1962* (1962). R. H. Baker, "The National Bituminous Coal Commission. Administration of the Bituminous Coal Act, 1937–1941," *The Johns Hopkins University Studies in Historical and Political Science,* Fifty-ninth Series, No. 3 (1941) deals with one of NRA's descendants.

On labor during the New Deal, the best approaches are the topical essays collected in Milton Derber and Edwin Young, eds., *Labor and the New Deal* (1957). Philip Taft, *The A. F. of L. from the Death of Gompers to the Merger* (1959) is an inside view of union labor during this period. On social security, E. E. Witte, *The Development of the Social Security Act* (1962) and Witte's papers collected by R. J. Lampman, *Social Security Perspectives* (1962) give a clear authoritative account. Indispensable on another phase of labor policy is Irving Bernstein, *The New Deal Collective Bargaining Policy* (1950). The material on agriculture is as overwhelming as an avalanche. A good guide, with bibliography, is G. C. Fite, *American Agriculture and Farm Policy since 1900* (1964). Theodore Saloutos and John D. Hicks, *Agricultural Discontent in the Middle West, 1900–1939* (1951) puts both farm organizations and farm policy in perspective.

On fiscal and monetary policy, Paul Studenski and Herman E. Krooss, *Financial History of the United States* (1963) is exceptionally evenhanded. E. A. Goldenweiser, *American Monetary Policy* (1951) skillfully blends history, a description of techniques, and the details of policies, real and proposed. It is the best single approach for the ordinary reader. Milton Friedman and A. J. Schwartz, *A Monetary History of the United States, 1867–1960* (1963), while lucid in exposition, is more for the specialist. Their *The Great Contraction* (1965) is a chapter from their *Monetary History*. Marriner S. Eccles, *Beckoning Frontiers. Public and Personal Recollections* (1951) is one of those told-to books but adds the flavor of personality to an institutional subject. R. C. and Gladys C. Blakey, "The Revenue Act of 1935," *AER*, XXV (1935), 673–690, and "The Two Federal Reserve Acts of 1940," *AER*, XXX (1940), 724–735 seek to give perspective to a fleeting moment.

chapter xx
World War II and Reconversion

Of the sources mentioned in the bibliography for the preceding chapter, the thirteen volumes of *The Public Papers and Addresses of Franklin Delano Roosevelt* continue to be useful. Most volumes of biographies of New Dealers either end at the war years or concentrate on the military and international preoccupations of their leader and his times. Resort must be had to the official histories of agencies. Generally, these volumes are written under common handicaps; the necessity to treat every decision and to mention every name and the superabundance of documentation which makes these goals attainable. The most useful volumes are James W. Fesler *et al.*, *Industrial Mobilization for War. History of the War Production Board and Predecessor Agencies, 1940–1945* (1947); Harvey C. Mansfield and associates, *A Short History of OPA* (1947); *The Termination Report: National War Labor Board,* I (1949). Standing outside the official umbrellas of the agencies are David Novick *et al.*, *Wartime Production Controls* (1949) and Frederick C. Lane, *Ships for Victory. A History of Shipbuilding under the U.S. Maritime Commission in World War II* (1951). The last is exceptionally well organized and interesting.

Donald M. Nelson, *Arsenal of Democracy. The Story of American War Production* (1946) reveals the chairman of the WPB was no innocent in Washington. A curious volume, half starry-eyed and half-irritated, Bruce Catton, *The Warlords of Washington* (1948) stuns the reader with the intricacy of Washington intrigue. On the atom bomb, James P. Baxter, III, *Scientists Against Time* (1946) has two brief chapters. Much has come out since then. The magisterial account up to the explosion of the bomb is R. G. Hewlett and Oscar E. Anderson, Jr., *The New World, 1939* (1946). Leslie R. Groves, *Now It Can Be Told. The Story of Manhattan Project* (1962) is by a military participant. On war finance, Paul Studenski and Herman E. Krooss, *Financial History of the United States* (1963); Milton Friedman and A. J. Schwartz, *A Monetary History of the United States, 1867–1960* (1963); and E. A. Goldenweiser, *American Monetary Policy* (1951) continue to be useful. On labor, Philip Taft, *The A. F. of L. from the Death of Gompers to the Merger* (1959) makes humdrum policies sound that way; Arthur Goldberg, *AFL-CIO, Labor*

United (1956) is by a judicious participant. See also Bruno Stein, "Labor's Role in Government Agencies during World War II," *JEH,* XVII (1957), 389–408.

Where contemporary history or current events begin is always a matter of dispute. Perhaps a workable dividing line is with the post-World War II era. One of the first tasks is to get the chronology straightened out. Harold G. Vatter, *The U.S. Economy in the 1950's* (1963) does that and more. It assembles a great deal of hard-to-find material, taps unusual periodicals, and provides frequent theoretical analyses which the reader can accept or reject as he thinks best. Harry Truman, *Memoirs,* 2 vols. (1955, 1956) and Dwight D. Eisenhower, *The White House Years,* 2 vols. (1963, 1965) don't demonstrate much except that dullness knows no party lines. On one, though probably minor phase of reconversion, see G. T. White, "Financing Industrial Expansion for War: The Origin of the Defense Plant Corporation Leases," *JEH,* XIX (1959), 156–183; Harry A. Millis and Emily C. Brown, *From the Wagner Act to Taft Hartley. A Study of National Labor Policy and Labor Relations* (1950) is exceptionally fair; R. H. Lee, *Truman and Taft-Hartley, A Question of Mandate* (1966) has primarily a political slant. Richard S. Kirkendall, *Social Scientists and Farm Politics in the Age of Roosevelt* (1966) is stimulating particularly on the Board of Agricultural Economics, but most of the book is background for reconversion. A. J. Mutosow, *Farm Policies and Politics in the Truman Years* (1967) demonstrates the possibility of motion about a fixed point. So does the largely personal and garrulous account of Eisenhower's Secretary of Agriculture, Ezra T. Benson, *Cross Fire. The Eight Years with Eisenhower* (1962). On the peacetime employment of the atom, Morgan Thomas, *Atomic Energy and Congress* (1956) is primarily a political narrative; Lewis L. Strauss, *Men and Decisions* (1962) has a convincing section. The beginning of the President's Council of Economic Advisors is the theme of S. K. Bailey, *Congress Makes a Law. The Story Behind the Employment Act of 1946* (1950); E. S. Flash, Jr., *Economic Advice and Presidential Leadership, The Council of Economic Advisors* (1965) continues the story. Flash is the more dispassionate but both volumes are distracted by what-might-have-beens. The CEA's first chairman, E. G. Nourse, in *Economics in the Public Service. Administrative Aspects of the Employment Act* (1953) has not written the last word but gives an excellent analysis of this strategic measure. Arthur F. Burns, *The Frontiers of Economic Knowledge* (1954) contains chapters which make his general economic philosophy explicit. Walter W. Heller, *New Dimensions of Political Economy* (1966) makes everything seem too easy.

A library is always being written and published on chronological cross sections of the contemporary economic structure. It is pointless to cite them all. Vatter, cited above, is useful. So is Victor R. Fuchs, "Some Implications of the Growing Importance of the Service Industries," National Bureau of Economic Research, *Forty-fifth Annual Report* (June, 1965), 5–16; R. E. Lipsey, *Price and Quantity Trends in the Foreign Trade of the United States* (1963) is the essential foundation in this area.

Index